AN INTRODUCTION TO
ANCIENT EGYPT

AN INTRODUCTION TO
ANCIENT EGYPT

FARRAR STRAUS GIROUX
NEW YORK
In Association with
BRITISH MUSEUM PUBLICATIONS LIMITED, LONDON

© 1979, The Trustees of the British Museum
ISBN 0 374 83343 5 (*cased*)
ISBN 0 374 84339 2 (*paper*)
Published in association with British Museum Publications Ltd
by Farrar Straus Giroux
19 Union Square West
New York 10003

First published in 1964 as *A General Introductory
Guide to the Egyptian Collections in the British Museum*
Reprinted 1971 and 1975.
Revised and reset with additional illustrations, 1979

Designed by Patrick Yapp

Set in Photina 10 on 12 point
Printed in Great Britain
at the University Press, Oxford
by Eric Buckley
Printer to the University

CONTENTS

LIST OF COLOUR PLATES

NOTE: *The page numbers given are those opposite the colour plates, or, in the case of a double-page spread, those either side of the plate.*

LIST OF BLACK AND WHITE ILLUSTRATIONS

PREFACE

The text of this volume is based closely on that of *A General Introductory Guide to the Egyptian Collections in the British Museum*, first published in 1964. In its title the 1964 *Guide* followed the example of earlier publications of 1909 and 1930, but its content written by I. E. S. Edwards, A. F. Shore and T. G. H. James, was planned along somewhat different lines. Its aim was to provide an outline of the physical, historical, and cultural background of the collection; it was not intended to be a comprehensive catalogue of the sixty-five thousand objects in the Department of Egyptian Antiquities. In the present revision it has been decided to modify the title, emphasizing thereby that the book is an *Introduction* to the culture of ancient Egypt, not a *Guide* in the strictest sense.

In preparing this new edition, the framework of the old *Guide* has been preserved, but the opportunity has been taken to bring the text up to date in the light of recent discoveries, and to introduce many new illustrations. As in the old *Guide* royal names have, in accordance with current practice, been given mostly in the forms in which they were preserved in the Classical histories. Likewise, spellings of place-names, with very few exceptions, follow the style found on the maps of the Survey of Egypt. The dates used in this revision show many small variations from those adopted in 1964. For all periods down to the end of the New Kingdom, the chronology set out in the third edition of the *Cambridge Ancient History*, vols. I and II (Cambridge, 1970–75), has been adopted. For the subsequent, very controversial, period down to the Twenty-sixth Dynasty (when relatively precise dating can be achieved), the system proposed by K. A. Kitchen in his *Third Intermediate Period in Egypt* (Aris and Phillips, Warminster, 1973) is followed.

The revisions of the text have been carried out by members of the staff of the Department, Miss Carol Andrews, Dr M. L. Bierbrier, Mr W. V. Davies, Miss Alexandrina Logan-Smith and Dr A. J. Spencer. Miss Logan-Smith has acted also as general editor of the whole.

T. G. H. JAMES
Keeper,
Department of Egyptian Antiquities,
The British Museum

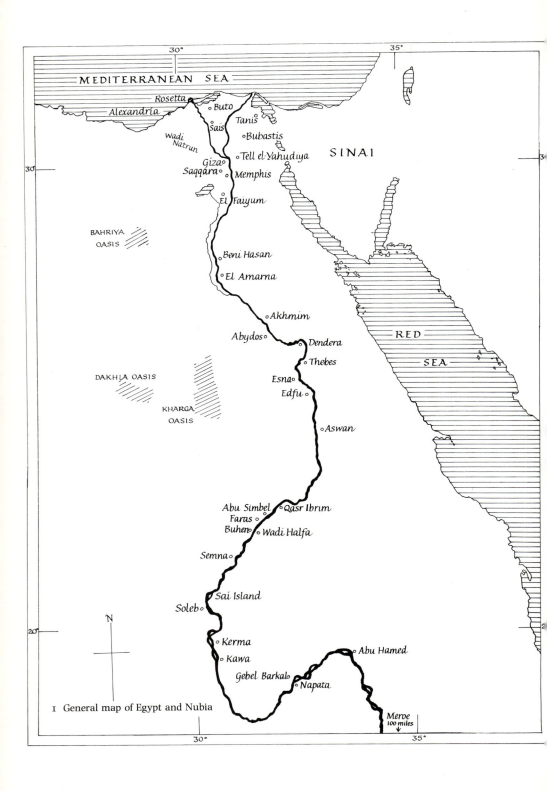

MEDITERRANEAN SEA

Rosetta
Alexandria
○ *Buto*
Sais
Tanis
○ *Bubastis*
Wadi Natrun
○ *Tell el-Yahudiya*
SINAI
Giza
Saqqara
○ *Memphis*
○ *El Faiyum*
BAHRIYA OASIS
○ *Beni Hasan*
○ *El Amarna*
○ *Akhmim*
Abydos
○ *Dendera*
○ *Thebes*
DAKHLA OASIS
Esna ○
Edfu ○
RED
KHARGA OASIS
○ *Aswan*
SEA
Abu Simbel ○ *Qasr Ibrim*
Faras ○
Buhen ○ *Wadi Halfa*
Semna ○
Sai Island
Soleb ○
○ *Kerma*
○ *Abu Hamed*
○ *Kawa*
Gebel Barkal ○
○ *Napata*

N

Meroe
100 miles

1 General map of Egypt and Nubia

CHAPTER ONE

THE LAND OF EGYPT
AND ITS NATURAL RESOURCES

The land

Egypt has been called the gift of the Nile, and it is true that without the Nile Egypt as a fertile, well-populated country would not exist. In ancient times the country stretched from the Mediterranean Sea in the north to the First Cataract at Aswan in the south, a distance of about 750 miles by river. Today the southern boundary lies only a few miles north of Wadi Halfa in the Sudan, but the effective land of Egypt is still that area to the north of Aswan. After passing through the formidable granite barrier of the First Cataract the Nile follows a course northwards through a sandstone belt that stretches almost as far as Edfu. Thereafter the valley is composed of limestone deposits which continue as far north as Cairo. A short distance to the north of Cairo the river divides and forms the Delta, which is a region about 14,500 square miles in area, composed of alluvial deposits. Today the Nile flows through the Delta in two principal channels, of which the eastern enters the Mediterranean at Damietta and the western at Rosetta. In antiquity there were three principal channels known in the Pharaonic Period as 'the water of Pre', 'the water of Ptah', and 'the water of Amun', and in classical times as the Pelusiac, the Sebennytic, and the Canopic branches. The other branches mentioned by classical writers such as Herodotus were not principal channels, but subsidiary branches from the Sebennytic (the Mendesian and Saitic or Tanite) or artificially cut (the Bolbitine and Bucolic).

The land of Egypt is principally the valley of the Nile and, more precisely, that part of the valley that is cultivated. In antiquity the cultivated area was determined by the height to which the Nile rose in its annual inundation. The flood-waters (p. 21) not only watered the fields; they also brought with them a deposit of rich alluvium which renewed the fertility of the land with almost unfailing regularity. This black deposit provided a contrast between the inhabited land of Egypt and the uninhabited tawny-coloured desert which was so striking that it caused the ancient Egyptians to name their land Kemet 'The Black' (⌂𝕂⊛). The desert lands were known as Deshret 'The Red' (⬚🠟⊛). The modern name Egypt is derived from the Greek *Aigyptos* which probably represents ⬚⬚⬚⬚⊛ *ḥwt-kʒ-Ptḥ* 'Hikuptah', one of the ancient names of Memphis, the capital of the country during the Old Kingdom.

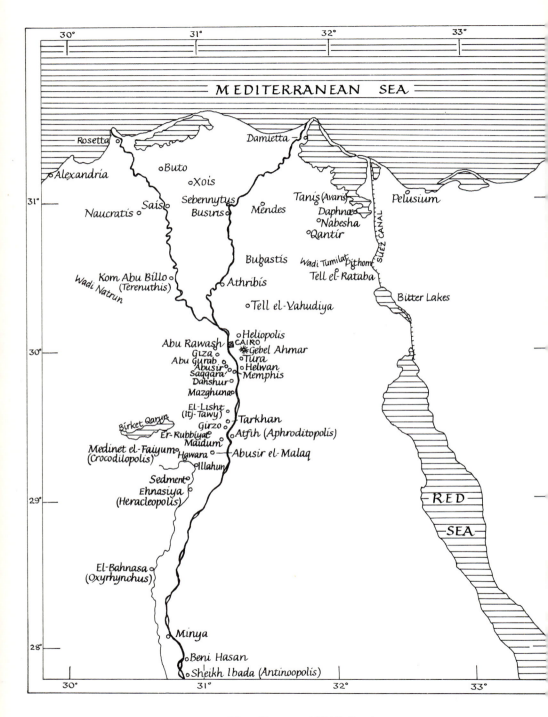

MEDITERRANEAN SEA

Rosetta
Damietta
Alexandria
Buto
Xois
Pelusium
Tanis (Avaris)
Sebennytus
Naucratis
Sais
Mendes
Daphnæ
Busiris
Nabesha
Qantir
Bubastis
Wadi Tumilat
Pithom
Kom Abu Billo
(Terenuthis)
Tell el-Rataba
Wadi Natrun
Athribis
Bitter Lakes
Tell el-Yahudiya
Heliopolis
Abu Rawash
CAIRO
Gebel Ahmar
Giza
Tura
Abu Gurab
Helwan
Abusir
Memphis
Saqqara
Dahshur
Mazghuna
El-Lisht
(Itj-Tawy)
Tarkhan
Birket Qarun
Girzo
Er-Rubbiyat
Atfih (Aphroditopolis)
Maidum
Medinet el-Faiyum
Hawara
Abusir el-Malaq
(Crocodilopolis)
Illahun
Sedment
Ehnasiya
(Heracleopolis)
RED
SEA
El-Bahnasa
(Oxyrhynchus)
Minya
Beni Hasan
Sheikh Ibada (Antinoopolis)

SUEZ CANAL

2 Map of Lower and Middle Egypt

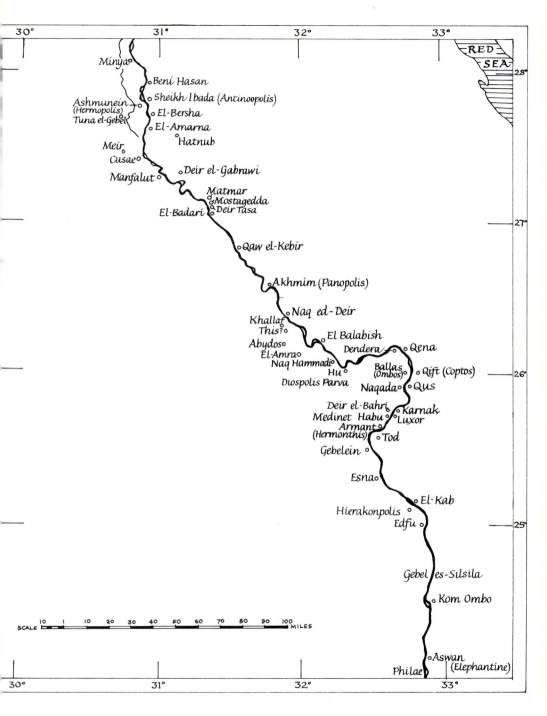

3 Map of Upper Egypt from Beni Hasan to Aswan

The administrative organization of the country was confined to the same habitable, cultivated land, the valley proper with such oases as were easily reached from the valley. From early times the land was divided into two principal regions, today called Upper and Lower Egypt. Upper Egypt, known in pharaonic times as Shemau, was divided into twenty-two administrative areas which are called nomes, the Greek term for these districts. The ancient name for a nome was 𓈖𓉻𓏏, more simply, 𓈇 (*spʒt*). The first nome was that of Elephantine (modern Aswan), just north of the First Cataract and the twenty-second was that of Aphroditopolis (modern Atfih) to the south of Cairo. The frontier between Upper and Lower Egypt has never been precisely determined. The twenty-first nome comprised the region known as the Faiyum, a natural depression lying a few miles from the Nile Valley to the west of Aphroditopolis and watered by an offshoot of the Nile called the Bahr Yusuf. The Faiyum, which today has an area of about 850 square miles, was first exploited by the kings of the Middle Kingdom who established their capital not far from its entrance at Itj-towy near the modern El-Lisht. In the north of the Faiyum is a lake, the Birket Qarun, which has always been a haunt of wild fowl and a centre for hunting.

In the Western Desert there are several oases which may be considered as having been part of Egypt in ancient times although they were always regarded more as frontier regions, to be exploited, than as integral parts of the country itself. Such administration as they had was based on the seventh Upper Egyptian nome, the capital city of which was Diospolis Parva (modern Hu). Chief among these oases was El-Kharga, known in antiquity as the Southern Oasis. It lies eighty miles to the west of the Nile Valley, and a further forty miles to the west is El-Dakhla, a smaller oasis. North of Kharga on the latitude of El-Hiba and seventy miles west of the Nile is El-Bahriya, the Northern Oasis.

Lower Egypt, known in ancient times as To-mehu ('The Northern Land'), was, like Upper Egypt, divided into nomes. This part of the land of Egypt consisted chiefly of the Delta, which in early antiquity was very largely still an undeveloped region of marshland and scrub. Its organization into nomes was, therefore, a process that suffered modification from time to time as the country was opened up and developed. Ultimately the number of nomes was twenty, of which the first was the nome of Memphis.

In antiquity the desert-lands that bordered the cultivated Nile Valley, while coming under the control of the government of Egypt, were not considered, it would seem, as integral parts of the country itself. The Libyan desert on the west of the Nile Valley is a desolate area of sand dunes and rocky wastes (Plate I).

Apart from the large oases of El-Kharga, El-Dakhla, and El-Bahriya and a few smaller oases which were sporadically occupied and cultivated and used as places of banishment for political and other prisoners, this desert had little to attract the ancient Egyptian. It was, however, crossed by a network of ancient tracks that linked the Nile Valley with the Sudan and the cultivated coastal strips and oases of Libya. The Eastern or Arabian Desert, on the contrary, was much exploited in antiquity. Different in character from the Libyan desert, it is largely a mountainous, rocky region, the source of many minerals and hard stones which were used in great quantities by ancient craftsmen. It is, however, without oases, and wells are few and widely separated.

Inasmuch as these desert-lands were not parts of Egypt proper, they were treated in the same way as the peninsula of Sinai and the land of Nubia: they were areas to be exploited, but not incorporated into the administrative organization of the land of Egypt. The nome-structure was reserved, therefore, for the cultivated lands of the valley together with the Delta.

The Nile and the inundation

The Nile, which both made possible and maintained life in Egypt, was also the principal highway of the land. Until the early New Kingdom (c. 1600 BC) the Egyptians lacked wheeled conveyances and the horse. Travel on land was carried out either on foot or by donkey. The river offered the obvious means for travel and traffic by boat was considerable from an early date. As no point in the valley was more than a few miles from the river, it became a highway that could take the traveller, the trader, or the royal official anywhere in the realm. During the period of the annual inundation when most of the cultivated area was covered by water this usefulness of the Nile could further be exploited. Flat-bottomed barges could convey heavy cargoes such as building-stones and monumental sculptures directly from the quarries, situated in the cliffs bordering the flooded valley, to their destinations in temples and cemeteries, which were situated just beyond the limits of the flood-waters.

Travel on the Nile was facilitated by the direction of the prevailing wind which, with almost unceasing regularity, blows from the north. A boat travelling south, therefore, against the flow of the stream, could use sails; one travelling north could proceed with the current. In times of calm or when the wind and the current were adverse, oars were used. The river was used for travel to such an extent that the regular words for 'go north' and 'go south' were determined in the hieroglyphic script by boats: 'go north' or perhaps more strictly 'go downstream' has a boat with no sail (⛵): 'go south' or 'go upstream' has a boat with

a sail (⛵) e.g. 35292 (fig. 4). Egyptians thought of travel in terms of movement on the Nile and they had difficulty in describing properly direction outside Egypt. There is a famous sentence in the Tombos stele of Tuthmosis I in which the Euphrates, a river that flows from north to south, is called 'that reversed water that goes downstream [i.e. the Egyptian word which equally means 'go north' in terms of the Nile] in going upstream [i.e. 'going south']'.

4 Wooden model boa

The Nile, which for its last 900 miles runs through the land of Egypt, has its origins in the heart of Africa. Of the two principal streams which unite at Khartum, the longer, the White Nile, derives its main flow from the waters of Lake Victoria. Other contributory sources are Lake Edward and Lake Albert.

About 600 miles south of Khartum lies Lake No, where the main stream is joined by another tributary, the Bahr el-Ghazal (Gazelle River), flowing in from the west. A further tributary, the Bahr el-Zaraf (Giraffe River), joins the main stream, from the east, about 60 miles north of Lake No, and between this point and Khartum the river is enlarged by the water of the Sobat, which also flows from the east. The total length of the tributaries, which make up the White Nile as far as Khartum, is about 1,560 miles. At Khartum, the modern capital of the Republic of the Sudan, the White Nile is joined by the second principal stream, the Blue Nile, which rises in Lake Tana in Ethiopia and is about 1,000 miles long. From Khartum to the sea the united streams, which form the river known as the Nile, follow a course about 1,913 miles long and are joined by one tributary only, the Atbara, which also rises in the Ethiopian highlands. Between Khartum and Aswan the Nile in six places runs through regions where the flow of the stream is broken up by the exceptionally rocky nature of its bed. These six stretches of the river are known as the cataracts and they are all to a greater or lesser extent difficult for navigation.

The special characteristic of the Nile, which has made it so important for Egypt, is its annual inundation, caused ultimately by rains which fall in Central Africa, and melting snow and rains in the Ethiopian highlands. By the end of May in Egypt, the river was at its lowest level. During the month of June the Nile, between Cairo and Aswan, began to rise, and a quantity of 'green water' appeared at this time. The cause of the colour is said to be myriads of minute organisms which subsequently putrefy and disappear. During August the river rose rapidly and its waters assumed a red muddy colour, which was due to the presence of the rich red earth brought into the Nile by the Blue Nile and the Atbara. The rising of the waters continued until the middle of September, after which they remained stationary for two or three weeks. In October a further slight rise occurred, and then they began to fall; the fall continued gradually until, in the May following, they were at their lowest level once more. The order of the rising of the various tributaries in the south, swollen by spring rains, is as follows: the Sobat rises about 15 April, the Gazelle and Giraffe rivers about 15 May, the Blue Nile at the end of May, and the Atbara a little later. The united waters of these streams reached Egypt about the end of August and caused the inundation to reach its highest point. Vast quantities of rich earth were brought down by the floods of the Blue Nile and Atbara and much of this matter was deposited in a thin layer over the land which was flooded.

Until recent years when the flow of the river has been controlled, even during the inundation season, by the Sudd el-'Ali dam at Aswan and by barrages at Esna, Nag Hammadi, Asyut, and to the north of Cairo, the average rise during the inundation period seems to have been approximately the same as it was in antiquity. Ancient records, both those preserved in classical authors and the visible evidence of ancient Nilometers, show that a flood of 6 metres was perilously low and that one of 9 metres was so high as to cause much damage: a flood of 7–8 metres was ideal for every purpose. In effect this meant that the whole valley of the Nile was flooded up to the edge of the rising ground of the desert. Towns and villages and the dykes that carried paths as well as serving as water barriers, remained above the water-level except in years of very heavy floods. When the waters fell back within the banks of the river in the autumn the land was covered with a deposit of the soil brought down in the flood-waters; it was this regular addition to the land that made the country so exceptionally fertile.

The ancient Egyptians understood fully to what extent their life and prosperity depended on the unfailing regularity of the inundation. The occasional phenomenon of an insufficient rise and the consequent shortage of food were enough to remind them that they could not expect a good flood as inevitable. They never, therefore, regarded the river and its gifts with com-placency. The Nile was known in antiquity by the name *iteru*, usually translated as 'river'; the inundation was called Hapy and was worshipped as a god. The religious and secular litera-ture from very early times is full of references to the desirability of high inundations and the misery attendant on the failure of the flood. Nomarchs regularly boasted that they were able, through their providence, to feed the people of their nomes even in years when the Nile ran low. Hapy was, therefore, constantly the subject of the prayers of the Egyptians. He was represented as a bearded god with a cluster of water-plants on his head: he was shown with pendent female breasts indicative of his fertility and sometimes pouring water in libation. In mythology it was held that the inundation originated in underground caverns situated in the region of the First Cataract to the south of Aswan. The gods of this region, Khnum, Anukis, and Satis, possessed especial importance inasmuch as they could interfere with the inundation. An inscription carved during the Ptolemaic Period on the island of Siheil records a famine which supposedly took place throughout Egypt during the reign of a king identified by some historians as Djoser of the Third Dynasty (c. 2660 BC). In a dream Khnum announced to the king that the failure of the inundation was due to the neglect of the gods of the cataract region. The king by a decree re-established the territories and offerings of the gods, ensuring thereby that the flood should rise unfailingly thereafter to the required height.

Agriculture

In ancient times the economy of Egypt was based primarily on agriculture. It has been said that the lot of the Egyptian farmer

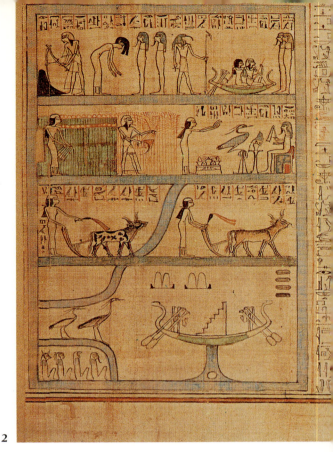

Plate 2
Agricultural scenes
from the *Book of
the Dead* of the
priestess Anhai

Plate 3
Theban tomb
painting showing
the checking of a
boundary stone

Plate 4
Fowling scene from
a Theban tomb

2

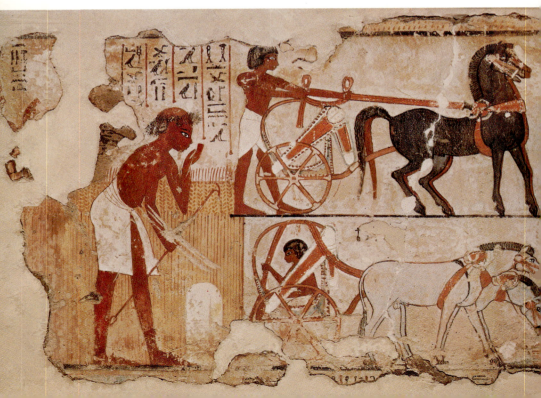

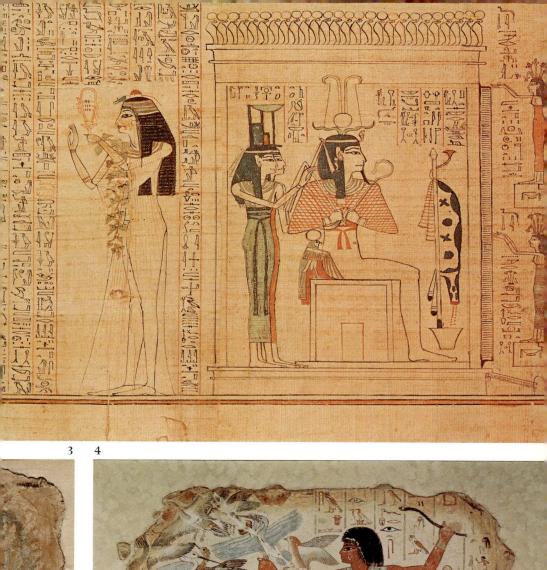

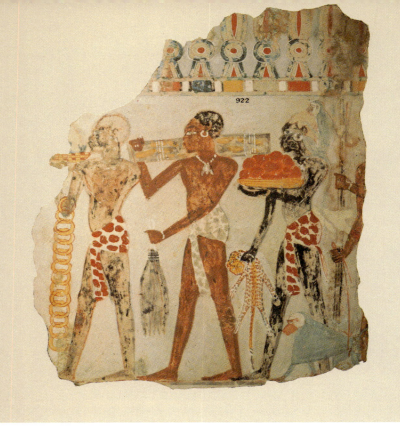

. was far happier than that of his contemporaries in other countries. Yet ancient texts from Egypt contain many jibes aimed at the life of the peasant in the field; but these jibes are probably not to be accepted literally because they were written by scribes who had a professional bias against manual labour. There is plenty of evidence that the Egyptian farmer worked hard, but it is also certain that, except in years when the inundation was inadequate, his toil was readily rewarded by good results and not nullified by unpredictable natural calamities. This happy state of affairs was due in the first place to the behaviour of the Nile, and secondly to the regular pattern of the climate of the country. Sunny, cloudless skies are common throughout the year; rainfall in Upper Egypt is negligible; at Cairo it rarely exceeds 5 cms a year and in the Delta it is rarely more than 20 cms. Such rain as does fall comes during the winter months. During the summer months the whole of Egypt is hot and dry; in the winter for the most part the weather remains dry and can be still very hot, especially in Upper Egypt. The prevailing wind throughout the country blows from the north (p. 21), but in Lower Egypt there is rather more variation than in Upper Egypt due to the nearness of the Mediterranean Sea.

The conditions of climate and the phenomenon of the inundation simplified the task of the Egyptian farmer but did not release him from the essential processes of ploughing, sowing, and reaping. Many of the tools used by the ancient farmer are exhibited in the Fourth Egyptian Room together with wooden models from tombs of the Old Kingdom–Middle Kingdom illustrating certain of the activities on the land (p. 207). The agricultural year began when the inundation subsided, leaving the earth soaked and overlaid with a thin layer of silt. The first tasks were the rehabilitation of the land and the planting of the crops before the ground dried out and became hard. Rehabilitation of the land included the clearing out of irrigation canals and ditches, the re-establishment of landmarks and the re-surveying of fields. The urgency of this work demanded special efforts, organized centrally no doubt, in each nome, with labour being conscripted as required. The recurrent character of these duties, and the constant endeavour to avoid being conscripted for them, led those who could afford to pay to appoint deputies who would perform the duties on their behalf. So fundamental for the continuance of Egyptian life were these duties that it was thought that they would be needed in the after-life. Consequently, from the early Middle Kingdom a man of means provided in his tomb a *shabti* (p. 169) who would carry out such duties on his behalf in the after-life. The earliest version of the *shabti*-formula (by which the figure is invoked to perform these duties) occurs on the outer wooden coffin of Gua (30839): 'If this Gua is assigned to royal field-works to the . . .(?) of the department, to re-establish(?) the dykes, to turn over the new fields of the reigning king, "Behold me", thou shalt say to any messenger who shall come concerning this Gua in his round. "Take up your mattocks, your hoes, your yokes and your baskets in your hands, as any man does for his master".'

The rehabilitation of the land was followed by the planting of the crops. There is some indication that canals and ditches were used to carry water from the Nile to fields after the inundation had ended, but in general crops were allowed to grow and ripen without further watering, as was the case in modern Egypt before the introduction of perennial irrigation. The harvesting of the various crops took place in the spring and was in a normal year completed by May. Land could then lie fallow for two months before the inundation again covered the fields. Gardens which were situated around villages, farms, and the country-houses of the rich had to be watered regularly both because they were usually laid out on high ground not reached by the flood and because of the type of crop grown. Such gardens remained in cultivation throughout the year and they were irrigated principally from canals from which water was raised by means of the *shaduf*, a well-sweep with a counterpoise. This primitive machine, which is still much used in Upper Egypt today, was adequate for light irrigation but not suitable for general field-irrigation. Marginal land which was not reached by the waters of the inundation was also irrigated in this way and could be used for summer cultivation. The crops raised on such land were, however, insignificant compared with the produce of the inundated area.

The principal crops sown after the inundation were corn and flax. Of corn emmer was the chief crop, followed by barley, which was designated either 'Upper Egyptian' or 'Lower Egyptian', and wheat. The last was grown only in small quantities until the Ptolemaic Period when it became the principal crop. Barley, in addition to its primary use for bread (ancient examples of which are on display) was largely employed in the manufacture of beer, the chief drink of the ancient Egyptians. Beer was made by fermenting barley-bread; the process of straining the mash made from this bread into the beer-vat is represented in a number of wooden models from tombs of the Old Kingdom–Middle Kingdom (e.g. 55728 from Sedment and 45196 from Asyut, fig. 5). The scenes and groups in which are depicted the preparation of bread together with the processes of grinding the corn, kneading the dough, and baking (e.g. 40915) are concerned, no doubt, as much with beer-

Wooden model of
a brewer

manufacture as with the making of food. The cultivation of
emmer, barley and flax dates back at least to Neolithic times.
During the historic period flax was a crop of great importance,
as is shown by the frequent representations of the flax-harvest
in tomb-scenes. It was used chiefly for the manufacture of linen,
which was the only fabric available to the ancient Egyptians
apart from woollen materials of which there is little evidence
until Hellenistic times. Ancient examples of linen garments in
the collection are on display.

The methods used for ploughing, sowing, and harvesting the
cereal crops and flax are well known. The tombs of all historic
periods contain scenes which illustrate these activities. Plate 2
reproduces part of a vignette from the papyrus containing the
Book of the Dead of Anhai, a priestess of Amun during the
Twentieth Dynasty (10472). In the vignette Anhai is shown

engaged in agricultural activities in the Egyptian equivalent of the Elysian Fields. The second register shows her ploughing with a team of two cows. The usual plough consisted of a share which was sometimes shod with bronze (as in the case of the exhibited example, 50705), fastened to a pole to which the team was harnessed. The handle was formed either by a backward continuation of the share, if there were no separate pole, or by an attachment to the pole. Tomb-scenes show that the activity of ploughing was carried on concurrently with sowing; sometimes the sower is shown casting the seed before the plough, in which case the plough served as a harrow; sometimes the seed is cast behind the plough into the furrow and then trodden in by flocks of sheep and goats that are driven over the furrows (as can be seen in one scene from the tomb of Ur-ir-en-Ptah, 718). Ground which was particularly hard was broken up by hoes of the kind seen in the top register of Plate 2. Three wooden groups are exhibited showing teams ploughing (51090, 51091, and 52947); another (63837), which includes a figure of a man using a hoe to dig earth for bricks, illustrates the use of this tool. There are also a single figure of a man wielding a hoe (45195) and several actual examples of hoes on exhibition (e.g. 22863).

The grain crops were cut with wooden sickles set with flint teeth (e.g. 52861) and only the tops of the stems bearing the ears were cut. These tops were collected in large panniers or sacks and carried away on donkey-back to the granary. The standing straw was, no doubt, pulled up afterwards and used for many purposes, such as bedding, thatching, brick-making, and sometimes in mummification. Flax was harvested by being pulled in bundles straight from the ground. The roots and tops were trimmed off and the bundles bound up and taken away. The middle register in the vignette from the papyrus of Anhai (Plate 2) shows on the left the harvest of flax (which is coloured green on the original) and of emmer (which is red).

The harvesting of emmer and barley was followed by threshing, winnowing, and storing of the grain. A reproduction of the harvest scenes from the tomb of Menna, exhibited in the corridor of the Third Egyptian Room, illustrates all these activities. Threshing was performed by cattle which were driven round the threshing floor while men forked away the spent ears. Wooden winnowing 'fans' (e.g. 18206) were used to toss the mixed grain and chaff into the air and the wind carried away the chaff. The clean grain was finally stored in granaries. Of the wooden tomb-models of granaries exhibited, one (2463) shows the owner of the farm seated on a platform above the store-chamber while a woman grinds corn in the court below; another (21804) has the names of the different grains written above the chambers of the granary; a third from a tomb at Beni Hasan (41573) contains some ancient grain.

The inevitable sequel to the harvest was the payment of taxes. Although the whole land of Egypt was in theory the property of the king, a kind of private ownership of land undoubtedly existed as early as the Old Kingdom. The practice of making grants to temples, nobles, and private persons (for mortuary estates) led to a position in which land was held as if by right, to be sold, bought, rented, and, consequently, to be worked privately and to be assessed officially for taxes. The details of the organization of tax-collection are not known. It is probable that the nome authority organized collection within each nome and that the great temples had their own private systems for the collection of taxes from the vast temple estates. While the crops were still standing the tax assessors visited the fields and took measurements, using the rope stretching methods illustrated in the Fourth Egyptian Room. On the basis of such measurements the tax assessment was made. Part of a scene of such an assessment (37982, Plate 3) comes from a Theban tomb of the Eighteenth Dynasty (probably that of Nebamun) and it includes a figure of a senior assessor who bends over a limestone stela marking the corner of a cornfield. He checks that the limits of the property are correctly defined before the assessment-survey begins. The text above his head gives the oath he swears: 'As the Great God who is in the heaven endures, the stela is correct, its (. . .?) stands up.' The title of the man who was originally represented walking behind him (only traces now remain) is also preserved; he is called 'Controller of the measuring of the granary'.

Two other important products of agriculture in ancient Egypt were oil and wine. Oil is frequently mentioned as an alternative to grain as a standard material for barter and its uses otherwise were many in cooking, lighting, cosmetics, ointments, and embalming. Many different kinds of oil are mentioned in texts but few are identified with certainty. Olives were not successfully grown in Egypt until the Ptolemaic Period; however, in earlier times olive-oil was imported. The fruit of the moringa tree was the only satisfactory alternative source of oil in quantity; other plants indigenous to the country which could produce suitable oil were the lettuce, the castor-oil plant, flax (for linseed oil), the *balanos* tree, the radish, saffron, and sesame.

Wine was produced from grapes and from dates, grape wine being the more highly regarded in antiquity. The best wine came from the Delta and from the oases of Kharga and Dakhla where viticulture was practised on a large scale. Vines were also cultivated to a lesser extent in small estates and gardens, and scenes of the vintage are common in tombs of the New Kingdom: the harvesting of grapes, their treading in large vats, and the storing of the juice in pottery jars. After fermentation the wine was sealed in jars and the jars marked with the place and year of vintage.

The culture of vines, as has already been mentioned, was practised in the gardens of estates in the New Kingdom. Most of the other vegetables and fruits grown in ancient Egypt were likewise cultivated in gardens where special arrangements were made for continuous irrigation. A garden was usually close to the farm or villa on ground raised above the level of the inundation, it had a pool to act as a reservoir, usually shaded by trees (as in the case of the garden shown in wall-painting 37983) and was intersected by ditches. These ditches and pools were filled by means of *shadufs* with water from canals leading from the Nile, and the irrigation of the gardens was effected either by directing water straight from a ditch on to a plot, or by means of water pots filled at the pool. Common garden-crops were beans, lentils, lettuce, onions, leeks, melons and other gourds, fruit (e.g. dates, figs, pomegranates), and flowers (much used for garlands at religious and secular festivals). A subsidiary product of Egyptian horticulture was honey, which was much prized as a sweetening agent.

Cattle- and poultry-breeding, the origins of which can be traced back to predynastic times (see, for example, the group of cows from El-Amra, 35506), were already highly developed in the Old Kingdom. Animals and birds were extensively reared not only for food but also for ritual purposes. The daily sacrifices at the temples and the provision of meat offerings in funerary services made great demands on the stock available and necessitated a high degree of skill in breeding and rearing. Oxen and sheep, much used as sacrifices, were the principal animals bred; goats, pigs, and donkeys were also kept for more general utilitarian purposes. In the Old Kingdom many desert animals like the antelope and oryx were captured and fattened, but it is not clear whether the Egyptians were successful in breeding them in captivity. There was usually sufficient rough grazing on the edge of the desert to raise herds of small cattle locally in Upper Egypt, but herds of cows were mostly pastured in the Delta.

Cattle were branded for identification purposes; a brand in the shape of horns (∪) is exhibited with other agricultural tools in the Fourth Egyptian Room (58817). His cattle were the pride of the farmer; thus many tombs contain scenes in which the deceased owner is shown viewing his herd or inspecting it at the time of census when taxes were assessed. Tomb painting 37976 is part of such a scene of cattle-inspection; it came from a Theban tomb of the Eighteenth Dynasty which was made for an official, a scribe and counter of grain, probably called Nebamun.

Another fragment from the same tomb (37978) bears part of a companion scene in which geese and other fowl are brought before the deceased owner. Geese were domesticated in remote antiquity and bred for the table and for ritual sacrifice. Other fowl are often shown in captivity, sometimes being forcibly fed. Wild fowl were captured in clap-nets in organized operations in the marshes and reared in the fowl-houses of estates and temples.

The marshes, which figure so largely in tomb scenes as the haunts of wild fowl and the places for hunting expeditions, were located in the Delta, round the lake in the Faiyum and in those depressions in the Nile Valley near the desert edge in which the flood-waters were trapped after the inundation. Organized hunting expeditions visited these marshes to catch birds and fish as a regular business. Private parties also went hunting in the marshes, women accompanying the men in their light boats. Fowling as a sport was practised with the throw-stick, cats being used to flush the birds. Wall painting 37977 (also from the tomb of Nebamun(?), Plate 4) illustrates such a fowling party and actual throw-sticks are exhibited in the Fourth Egyptian Room. With the throw-sticks are exhibited other instruments used in fishing and hunting—harpoons, a net (36886), bows and arrows, and an unusual bow-case with painted scenes of the chase on its sides (20648).

The resources of the land of Egypt

An account has been given of the agricultural riches of the land of Egypt; not only was the country exceptionally fertile for the raising of crops but it was also rich in its animal and bird life. Furthermore, the Nile teemed with fish and, although fish were held to be abhorrent to the gods, fishing was much practised both as an industry and as a sport. Dried fish, in particular, were used as food by ordinary people and many tombs contain scenes of fishing with nets together with the gutting and drying of the catch. A bowl of dried fish (36191) is shown in the Fourth Egyptian Room with other examples of food and fruits found mostly in Theban tombs of the New Kingdom.

Raw materials closely connected with the Nile, which will be dealt with more fully elsewhere, were papyrus (p. 92) and river-mud (pp. 206 ff.). The papyrus was a particularly useful plant of which scarcely any part was wasted. The flowers were used for decorative purposes, the stems, when complete, were employed as a primitive building material, and when separated into rind and pith were turned respectively into a fibre used for boxes, mats, ropes, and cord, and into a smooth, supple, thin writing material of great durability. Black Nile-mud was used for bricks and for pottery. Another type of mud, practically free from organic matter, found in certain valleys to the east of the Nile in Middle and Upper Egypt was also used in antiquity for producing a light grey-coloured ware with a greenish tinge.

For most domestic building and for many more formal structures sun-baked bricks were used, brick being the cheapest and easiest material to obtain and very easy to use (p. 206). The desire to construct buildings of greater size with the added advantages of imperviousness to water and durability led to the development of stone-construction at an early date in the historic period (p. 191). The Egyptian stone-mason was particularly fortunate in the materials available to him in the Nile Valley itself, or, more properly, in the cliffs and hills that edged the valley. From Cairo to Edfu the cliffs are mostly limestone; the quality varies considerably from place to place with the best stone being found not far to the south of Cairo at Tura and in parts of the Theban necropolis. South of Edfu the stone is mostly sandstone, the material that was used for most of the great temples from the Eighteenth Dynasty onwards. Finally, at Aswan in the region of the First Cataract there are great deposits of granite, both red and black.

Other stones used to a certain extent as building material were to be found in the immediate neighbourhood of the Nile Valley; chief among these were alabaster, the principal quarry of which was at Hatnub near El-Amarna in Middle Egypt; basalt, which is found in a number of places throughout the land and which was worked mostly in the Faiyum in the Old Kingdom, and quartzite, a very hard compact species of sandstone, most conveniently quarried in the Gebel Ahmar, to the north-east of Cairo.

Long before the time when the Egyptians first began to use stone for building they had worked it in small quantities to produce vases (p. 188). These vases were the great glory of Egyptian art in the Late Predynastic Period and during the Early Dynastic Period. Stones of all kinds were used and the Eastern Desert was scoured for its wealth of hard volcanic rocks. The stones mostly employed, in addition to those already mentioned as building materials, were breccia, diorite, dolerite, dolomite, various porphyritic rocks, schist, and serpentine. In the Eastern Desert also were found many semi-precious stones which were used to make jewellery; of these the most common were agate, amethyst, carnelian, chalcedony, felspar, garnet, jasper (red, yellow, and green), onyx, rock crystal, and turquoise. The precious stones such as emerald and beryl that existed in the Eastern Desert were not exploited until much later in the Graeco-Roman Period.

Two stones which played a great part in Egyptian economy throughout history, but which lacked the dignity of the great building stones, the beauty of the hard volcanic stones, and the charm of the semi-precious stones, were steatite and flint. The former, being soft and easy to work, was used for a variety of small objects; in particular the vast majority of Egyptian scarabs are made of steatite. As early as Badarian times the Egyptian learned how to glaze beads made of steatite (for glazing, see p. 213). This stone also is found in the Eastern Desert. Flint, on the other hand, is found freely throughout the valley of the Nile as nodules in the limestone or exposed on the surface where the surrounding limestone has been weathered away. From the very earliest times flint was used for tools and weapons, and even after the discovery of copper it continued in use for certain purposes: it seems to have acquired a ritual significance during the historic period for the knives used to slaughter and dismember sacrificial animals were usually made of flint. An admirable example of the 'ripple flaking' achieved during the manufacture of a flint blade is seen in the Pitt-Rivers knife (p. 40, fig. 9).

The wealth of stones found in Egypt satisfied most domestic needs and little had to be imported from abroad. Expeditions into the Nubian Desert for diorite and amethyst and to Sinai for turquoise were scarcely more than extensions of the exploration of the Eastern Desert. The only regular import of stone from elsewhere was that of lapis lazuli which probably came from Afghanistan via the Near Eastern trade routes: it was much used for jewellery and small figures and sometimes as an inlay. Obsidian, which was also used occasionally from predynastic times onwards for small objects like arrow-heads and amulets, and later for scarabs and small statuary, probably came from the coast of Ethiopia and may possibly have formed part of the trade with Punt (p. 36).

At an early period the Egyptians learned how to work metals and by the beginning of the Dynastic Age they had developed the techniques of mining and refining and were already seeking outside Egypt itself for additional sources of supply. The most important metal found in Egypt was gold; not only was it used lavishly in the arts and crafts of the country, but it became a powerful diplomatic weapon in the New Kingdom. The principal gold-bearing region was the Eastern Desert, and traces of ancient workings can be found in many places between the Nile and the Red Sea (p. 219); but much gold was obtained from Nubia where it was acquired by trading, as tribute, or from direct working by Egyptians when the country formed part of the Egyptian Empire. Gold came also as tribute from Asia, but probably in small quantities only. The wall paintings from the tomb of Sobkhotpe illustrate the manner in which gold arrived in Egypt from these places: two fragments show negroes bearing piles of gold ingots and gold rings (921 and 922, see Plate 5)—the unworked raw material; on a third fragment Asiatics are represented bearing articles of tribute, many of which are elaborately wrought vessels made of gold (37991). Silver, on the other hand, was not available in Egypt in a condition in which it could easily be mined and refined. In early times it was clearly rarer than gold and it was not until the Late New Kingdom that objects of silver equalled in number and value those of gold in important burials. Most of the silver probably had to be imported from Asia. Electrum, as used in Egypt, was probably always a natural alloy of silver and gold, the 'whiteness' of it depending on the proportions of the two metals. It was obtained from workings in the Eastern Desert.

The most common 'industrial' metal used in Egypt was copper, which was used in alloy with arsenic and, from the Middle Kingdom, with tin. Until recently it was thought that much of the copper used in ancient times was mined and smelted in Sinai. There is, however, very little evidence from antiquity to support this theory: it is certain, on the other hand, that copper was obtained from the Eastern Desert. Some copper also was imported, for the most part from Cyprus. In all probability arsenic and tin had to be imported from Asia. In consequence the general use of arsenical copper and bronze (the alloy of copper and tin) in Egypt developed later than elsewhere in the ancient Near East. In spite of their ability to master the most intractable materials and to develop advanced technical skills, the ancient Egyptians remained surprisingly backward in their use of metals (p. 218 ff.). Iron ores of various kinds exist in many parts of the Eastern Desert, but there is no evidence that they were mined and smelted until the Late Period, and not in any quantity until the Roman Period.

While Egypt was rich in stones of all kinds and in metals and other mineral resources, it was poor in timber. No large trees suitable for producing planks of good size grew in Egypt and there were very few small trees indigenous to the country which were of any use in carpentry or joinery. The acacia, sycomore-fig, dom-palm, and tamarisk were used to some extent in joinery and in small-scale carpentry and as the frameworks of boats; the date-palm was of no use in carpentry, but its trunk could be employed either whole or halved as roofing. From the earliest historic period and possibly even in the Late Predynastic Period, timber suitable for large-scale carpentry and for boat building was imported from the Levant. The most common source for this imported timber was the hinterland of the Syrian coast, the famous cedar wood of the mountains of Lebanon.

From the enumeration of materials available to the ancient Egyptians it will appear that in many respects the Nile Valley with its flanking deserts was able to satisfy most of the requirements of the Egyptian craftsmen. In addition to the general categories already dealt with, the raw materials for glaze and glass (the Sixth Room), for paints (e.g. 5547) and cosmetics (the Fourth Room), and for most of the preparations used in mummification were readily available in Egypt proper in antiquity. The needs of a civilized society were not, however, fully satisfied by the produce of the homeland, and trade-routes were developed to countries far afield. Western Asia could be approached by land and by sea, but the sea-route to the Syrian coast was most favoured from early times. Ships could carry large cargoes and they could move more quickly and reach any part of Egypt along the Nile. The port which handled most trade with Egypt was Byblos and the great sea-going ships used on the run to Byblos and elsewhere were called Byblos-ships. From Asia Minor came wood and wine, olive oil and metals, especially tin in later times. In the Mediterranean, sea-trade was also developed with Cyprus and, from the New Kingdom, with Crete, the Greek islands, and Greece. Sinai was reached by land via the isthmus of Suez. Land travel was laborious and dangerous, expeditions suffering much from shortage of water and attacks from desert tribes. Donkeys and asses were the only transport- and pack-animals available until the Eighteenth Dynasty. The route to Sinai was first opened up in the Early Dynastic Period and the chief prize there was, apparently, turquoise. Figure 6 (691) shows a fragment of a scene from Sinai in which Sanakhte, first king of the Third

6 Sanakhte smiting his enemies

Dynasty, smites the desert-dwellers: on the right of the fragment the word for 'turquoise' occurs, 🦉 🛏 ⌒ ...

Many 'exotic' commodities were obtained from a region called Punt, the location of which has never been precisely established. It may have been part of the Somaliland coast. The first records of expeditions to Punt are preserved from the Fifth Dynasty. It is not known how often subsequent expeditions were sent but they were certainly dispatched from time to time until the reign of Ramesses III. Punt, also called 'God's Land', was the land of romance from which all kinds of strange, delightful things came —incense, gold, sandal-wood, ebony, giraffes, baboons, ivory, leopard-skins. The trade was carried on in sea-going ships from harbours on the Red Sea coast. The main route from the Nile Valley to the Red Sea coast passed through the Eastern Desert along the Wadi Hammamat, leaving the valley opposite Coptos and reaching the sea in the neighbourhood of old Quseir.

Trade with Nubia and countries to the south was conducted chiefly by land. Nubia was, for long periods, subjected to direct control by Egypt and was exploited accordingly. From the Middle Kingdom the principal commodity sought there was gold, but other materials were also obtained, such as diorite and amethyst. Through Nubia, too, came many of the products of equatorial Africa, some of which have already been mentioned as coming from Punt. The cast of the scene from the temple of Ramesses II at Beit el-Wali in Nubia, which is exhibited on the south wall of the Third Egyptian Room, shows clearly what the Egyptians were accustomed to get from Africa. The files of tribute-bearers bring leopard-skins, giraffe-tails, giraffes, monkeys, leopards, cattle, antelopes, gazelles, lions, ebony, ivory, ostrich-feathers and eggs, fans, bows, shields made of fine hides, and gold. African trade came into Egypt either through Aswan, where it was sub-jected to careful control, or by way of the line of oases running in a south-westerly direction from Kharga to Darfur in the Sudan. By this latter route some illicit trade was carried on. The only beast of burden available was the donkey; a pottery camel-figure found in the predynastic settlement at Abusir el-Melek is unique. Camel-figures otherwise do not occur until the Roman Period: a toy camel of this period is exhibited in the Fourth Egyptian Room (26664).

CHAPTER TWO

AN OUTLINE OF ANCIENT EGYPTIAN HISTORY

The terms used to describe the various periods of Egyptian history need some explanation. The first truly historical period is that which begins with the invention of writing and it is generally known as the Dynastic Period. It is a period extending from about 3100 BC to 332 BC and it derives its name from the thirty-one dynasties into which the successive kings of Egypt were divided in a scheme preserved in the work of Manetho, a priestly historian who lived during the reigns of the first two Ptolemies. The Dynastic Period is further divided into a number of relatively distinct shorter periods: the Early Dynastic Period (First and Second Dynasties, c. 3100–2686 BC), also known as the Archaic or Thinite Period, the Old Kingdom (Third to Sixth Dynasties, c. 2686–2181 BC), the First Intermediate Period (Seventh to Tenth Dynasties, c. 2181–2050 BC), the Middle Kingdom (Eleventh and Twelfth Dynasties, c. 2050–1750 BC), the Second Intermediate Period (Thirteenth to Seventeenth Dynasties, c. 1750–1567 BC; this period includes the Hyksos Period), the New Kingdom (Eighteenth to Twentieth Dynasties, c. 1567–1085 BC), the Late New Kingdom (Twenty-first to Twenty-fourth Dynasties, c. 1085–715 BC), the Late Period (a general term covering the whole period from the Twenty-third Dynasty to the Ptolemaic Period; it includes the Saite Period—the Twenty-sixth Dynasty). The Dynastic Period was followed by the Ptolemaic Period (332–30 BC) during which time Egypt was ruled by kings of Greek descent, and by the Roman Period (after 30 BC), when the country became a province of the Roman Empire.

The unlettered cultures which flourished in Egypt before the beginning of the Dynastic Period and which exhibit some of the characteristics which mark the earliest phases of Egyptian culture in the Dynastic Period are known as predynastic. The various stages of the predynastic cultures are discussed below. Such traces of human life as are found in the Nile Valley dating from before the Predynastic Period are usually described in the terms used for European Prehistory—Palaeolithic, Mesolithic and Neolithic.

The Prehistoric Period

The earliest remains of man's occupation of the Nile Valley and its neighbouring deserts are large, roughly shaped flint tools and

smaller flint scrapers, some of which are exhibited in the Sixth
Egyptian Room. These primitive tools, made by the Palaeolithic
inhabitants of Egypt, have been found principally on the desert
hills and terraces bordering the Nile Valley in Upper Egypt. At
this period North Africa was inhabitable throughout and Palaeolithic man ranged over the whole area, living the life of a nomad
and hunter. The traces left by him in Egypt are no different from
those left elsewhere in North Africa. In late Palaeolithic times the
climate of the region changed markedly and pastures turned
from grass to desert. Man withdrew from his old hunting-grounds
to the neighbourhood of the Nile where traces of more settled
occupation have been found in the shape of domestic refuse heaps
near the sites of dried-up lakes and swamps. The use of flint was
much developed by this time and smaller, finer tools for
specialized purposes have been found, including arrow-heads
and serrated blades which have been described as sickle-blades.

The possession of sickles presupposes the growing of cereal-
crops, but there is no direct evidence in support of the view that
such crops were cultivated in Egypt in late Palaeolithic times.
The first positive evidence of such cultivation comes with the
first remains of settlements in the Neolithic period. Occupation-
sites of this period have been discovered on the western edge of
the Delta, in the Faiyum, and in Middle Egypt. The inhabitants of
these sites clearly lived a settled agricultural life growing crops
of cereals and flax, making linen and baskets, crude pottery,
and a wide variety of stone and flint tools. Objects from a particularly fruitful site on the northern edge of the Faiyum form the
Museum's most important group of Egyptian Neolithic material:
among these objects are a wooden sickle with flint blades still
set in position (58701, fig. 7) and a finely woven fibre basket
(58696).

The predynastic cultures

Little was known about the very early inhabitants of Egypt until
the end of the nineteenth century when discoveries of predynastic cemeteries were made in Upper Egypt by Petrie and
other excavators. The earliest discoveries were made at Naqada
and consequently the principal predynastic cultures are
distinguished as Naqada I (early) and Naqada II (late). The
policy of naming the predynastic cultures after the sites of the
first discoveries was continued in subsequent excavations, giving
rise to the names Amratian (from the village of el-Amra),
Gerzean (from el-Girza), and Semainean (from Semaina in
Upper Egypt). These names are, however, best discarded, since

7 Wooden sickle with
flint blades

they are merely duplicate terms for different stages of the Naqada I and Naqada II cultures. Amratian is essentially the same as Naqada I, Gerzean as Naqada II, and Semainean has been found to fall entirely in the early part of the First Dynasty. The earliest known predynastic culture, which was not discovered until the 1920s, is known by the separate name of Badarian, from the village of el-Badari. Guy Brunton, the excavator of this site, also proposed the existence of the Tasian culture (after Deir Tasa), which he believed to pre-date the Badarian period, but the evidence of the excavations suggests that Tasian is not to be regarded as independent but only as a phase of the Badarian culture. From graves of the Badarian Period the earliest copper objects found in Egypt have been recovered. Some small rings or beads are exhibited in the Sixth Egyptian Room. The use of copper was, however, still in its infancy and efficient smelting of ore had probably not yet begun. The pottery of the Badarian Period is particularly fine. Many different shapes were made and there developed a type of red-polished ware with blackened top which was to become very common in later periods. Much of the pottery is extremely thin and often decorated with delicate combed lines. Similarly, the uses of other materials like flint, ivory, bone, and stone were developed: a primitive form of glazing steatite beads was invented: for the first time the human figure was modelled (e.g. 59679, fig. 8). Among stone objects palettes of slate for grinding eye-paint are first found commonly in Badarian graves; stone vases may also have been first manufactured in the Badarian Period. It was in fact a period of great technical advance.

Terracotta figure of a Badarian woman

The Naqada I period, which succeeded the Badarian, is characterized by distinctive styles of pottery, including polished red ware, highly burnished, often with black, carbonized rims, or with white-painted incised decorations. This decoration may be in imitation of wickerwork or it may consist of simple scenes of animals and of hunting. Stone vessels are not common; those that have been found are mostly of basalt with decorative lug-handles and small conical bases. Slate palettes of simple shapes are commonly found in the graves of the period and disk-shaped mace-heads of granite and other hard stones may testify to the development of warlike tendencies although there is some reason to believe that these objects may have had a ritual purpose only. The large numbers of finely-cut flint arrow-heads, on the other hand, were no doubt used equally for fighting and for hunting. Flint was still the material mostly used for tools and weapons.

The bodies found in graves in the early predynastic cemeteries of Upper Egypt show that the typical Egyptian of the time was slimly built with long delicate features. From the rather crude figures in clay and ivory found in their tombs it appears that the men of this Upper Egyptian race wore beards and long penis-sheaths, features which connect them ethnically with the Libyans.

Remains of the more advanced Naqada II culture occur at many sites throughout Egypt, often at places which have also yielded the earlier Naqada I artifacts, showing a continuity of occupation through these two consecutive phases of pre-dynastic culture. The Naqada II period was a time of considerable progress, as shown by the fine flint tools, copper implements, beads of hard stone, and of crude glazed composition which have been found in graves of that age. The graves themselves show improvement of design over the earlier simple pits, with reed matting and wood used to protect the burial. Slate palettes in animal form with eyes made of circular shell-beads are found in most graves, together with a distinctive style of buff pottery with decoration in purple paint. Hard stone was used for the manufacture of vases, which became more numerous than previously, and for pear-shaped mace-heads which superseded the disk-form of the Naqada I period. The occasional use of non-Egyptian materials like lapis lazuli shows that there was some trade contact at this early date between Egypt and Asia.

The progress achieved at this time led to further advances by the latter part of the Naqada II period, such as the introduction of brick-lined graves and refinements in the manufacture of implements, an excellent example of which is the Pitt-Rivers flint knife with an ivory handle, upon which are carved figures of animals in low relief (68512, fig. 9).

Nothing certain is known about the political organization in Upper and Lower Egypt during the Early Predynastic Period. It is generally thought that there existed two loose confederations made up of communities which corresponded to some extent with the later nomes. The political centres seem to have been Naqada (Nubt) in the south with Seth as the chief deity and Behdet in the north with the falcon-god Horus as chief deity.

In the Late Predynastic Period (i.e. the latter part of the Naqada II culture) the two confederations postulated above became more clearly defined and their leaders were already identified by their distinctive crowns which formed an important

9 Flint knife with a carved ivory handle

10 Slate palette decorated with the scene of a hunt

part of royal symbolism in historic times. The 'king' of Lower Egypt wore the red crown ( ) and the 'king' of Upper Egypt wore the white crown ( ). Two new capital cities were now established at Buto in the Delta and at Hierakonpolis in Upper Egypt. The period seems to have been one of continuous struggle and some of the individual events are known from the elaborately carved slate palettes which have been preserved. The Hunters' Palette and the Battlefield Palette exhibited in the Sixth Egyptian Room are two such monuments. The former (20790, fig. 10) shows the hunting of two lions and other wild animals; the scene contains possibly symbolic references to the national struggle. The latter (20791) on one side shows a lion, probably representing a king, seizing his enemies. The final conquest of the north by the south which led to the unification of the two kingdoms of Upper and Lower Egypt was effected by a king known to history as Menes. No contemporary monument bears a royal name that can with certainty be read as Menes, but he is generally identified with the king Narmer who is shown wearing both the red and the white crowns on a great palette now in Cairo. With the unification of the kingdoms begins the historic period in Egypt.

Early Dynastic Period (c.3100–2686 BC)

After the unification of the country a considerable administrative reorganization was effected. One of the few positive acts of this reorganization of which we know anything was the establishment of a new administrative capital at Memphis which lay at the junction of Upper and Lower Egypt. Tradition credits the legendary Menes with its foundation. Little is known about the history of Egypt during the first two dynasties. A Fifth Dynasty annalistic inscription, parts of which are preserved in Cairo (the Cairo Annals), Palermo (the Palermo Stone), and London

(University College), contains entries which are laconic and serve principally the purpose of identifying a year by some outstanding event. Most of these events are religious in character, such as the setting up of cult-statues, but occasionally an entry is more informative. Thus, one year of Djer, the third king of the First Dynasty, is designated by the phrase 'smiting of Sinai (?)', from which it may be reasonably deduced that punitive expeditions were sent beyond the limits of Egypt very soon after the establishment of the united kingdom. Similar grains of information can be gleaned from the texts found on the wooden and ivory labels used to identify the contents of boxes deposited in early tombs. One ivory label in the British Museum collection (55586, fig. 11) comes from Abydos and shows Den, the fifth king of the First Dynasty, braining a kneeling, bearded enemy;

the text of the scene reads 'the first time of smiting the East'. It has been thought that the event so commemorated was an early expedition into Sinai. Other tablets bear scenes of a religious and ritual character (e.g. 32650), and meagre though the evidence is, it does enable some evaluation to be made of the extraordinary advances in civilization made during this early period. Two cemeteries containing many important tombs of the Early Dynastic Period have been found at Abydos and Saqqara. There has recently been a great deal of dispute as to which of these two cemeteries contains the royal tombs of the period, but, when all the evidence is considered, there can hardly be any doubt that Abydos was the royal cemetery, and that the Saqqara tombs belonged to high officials. The tombs at both places have yielded many small objects which reveal the technical skill and artistic achievement of the Egyptians at the beginning of the historic period. In these tombs are found architectural elements in stone—the earliest in Egypt—and roofing timbers of such a size that the wood must have been imported from the coastal forests of western Asia. Small objects of materials not native to Egypt, such as lapis lazuli and ebony (?), further testify to the existence of trade connexions with Asia and tropical Africa.

11 Den striking an Asiatic chieftain

Unfortunately, the material remains of the two earliest dynasties do no more than provide tantalizing hints of what was happening politically in the country. It seems probable that the unification of Upper and Lower Egypt was a solution imposed by the successful conquerors from the south and that the tendency towards the dissolution of the union became stronger as the central authority weakened. This tendency was ever present in ancient Egypt and was due principally to the difficulty of ruling a country seven hundred miles long with only the Nile as the means of communication. Apparently some relaxation of the central authority occurred towards the end of the First Dynasty and from a period of political dissolution emerged the Second Dynasty, the first king of which was either Raneb or Hotepsekhemwy. The name of the latter, meaning 'the Two Powers are appeased', possibly preserves the memory of such an upheaval and the re-establishment of the single authority. The establishment and maintenance of the unity of the country had in these early times become a prime political aim and its significance for the kings of the earliest dynasties is evident in the entries that occur on the Palermo Stone to mark the beginning of each reign: 'Unification of Upper and Lower Egypt, Encircling of the Wall'. The wall here is the great white wall of the new capital Memphis and the reference is to one of the ceremonies of the coronation-festival. In the Sixth Egyptian Room is a small figure of a king dressed in the cloak characteristic of these ceremonies (37996). The statuette is of ivory and was excavated by Petrie at Abydos (fig. 54). It represents a king of the First or Second Dynasty, but there is no inscription to identify him precisely.

The largest object in the collection of the Museum from the Second Dynasty is a grey granite stela bearing the name of Peribsen, the sixth king of the dynasty (35597). The name is contained in a rectangular frame, known as a *serekh*, the lower part of which represents the façade of some great building, possibly a palace. This frame is surmounted by a figure of the Seth-animal, instead of the Horus-falcon which had been regularly used in this position by all kings from the beginning of the First Dynasty. In this substitution it is possible to detect some internal political change which prompted Peribsen to transfer the royal allegiance from Horus, traditionally the deity and ancestor of the king of unified Egypt, to Seth, his divine rival. The next king, who ascended to the throne with the name Khasekhem, 'the Power has appeared', reverted to the practice of writing the Horus-falcon over his name, but he later seems to have reconciled the theological dispute. He then changed his name to Khasekhemwy ('the two Powers have appeared'), written beneath both the Horus-falcon and the Seth-animal. At the same time he added to his name the phrase, 'the two Lords are content in him', which can only refer to the rival gods. The real reasons for these internal movements remain, unfortunately, obscure, but they may ultimately have led to the change which resulted in the establishment of the Third Dynasty.

The Old Kingdom (c.2686–2181 BC)

The Early Dynastic Period, in spite of the paucity of its material remains, was undoubtedly a great formative time in which the bases of Egyptian civilization were firmly established. By the end of the Second Dynasty artistic conventions had been evolved, hieroglyphic writing had advanced so far that it quickly became a flexible vehicle for the transmission of continuous narrative; techniques in craft and industries were highly developed. Egypt was in fact ready for an efflorescence of civilized activity which was to be marked by a sophistication strongly in contrast with the stiff archaic culture of the preceding period. The king whose reign ushered in this new epoch was Djoser and the chief agent in the transformation was Imhotep, the royal architect whose fame in later times was so great that he was ultimately venerated as a god and equated by the Greeks with Asklepios, their own god of healing (p. 133). The most striking monument of Djoser and Imhotep, and that which now characterizes the inauguration of the new epoch, was the Step Pyramid at Saqqara, with its great enclosure containing many buildings connected with the ritual ceremonies performed by the king. The complex, built of limestone, was faced with the fine white stone of Tura. Although stone had been used for some architectural features in tombs of earlier times, no building had previously been wholly constructed of stone; never before had such skill and mastery over material been shown. The architectural conception as a whole is, however, the outstanding feature of the monument which has, ever since its construction, remained a positive reminder that in Djoser's reign Egyptian civilization came of age. That the ancient Egyptians themselves thought so is shown not only by the evidence of later inscriptions scribbled on parts of the Step Pyramid buildings by visitors, and by the undoubted antiquarian interest taken in the pyramid in the Saite Period, but also by the fact that Djoser's reign is specially emphasized in the Turin King List of the Nineteenth Dynasty, by the unusual use of red ink. There is some doubt as to whether he was the first or second king of the Third Dynasty. His rival for this position is Sanakhte, a shadowy king of whom few monuments are known. Both Djoser and Sanakhte sent expeditions to Sinai in search of turquoise and possibly copper, and in the course of their expeditions the local Bedouin were subdued. Records were left in Sinai by both kings, and part of a relief of Sanakhte is now in the British Museum (691, fig. 6). It is also possible that during Djoser's reign the southern boundary of the kingdom was fixed at the First Cataract.

The expansion of power during the Fourth Dynasty is more adequately documented by the monuments and written records preserved from that time. During this dynasty pyramid-building reached its zenith. The culmination of the development may be seen in the Great Pyramid of Cheops, the second king of the dynasty. This structure, which dominates the desert plateau at Giza somewhat to the north of Memphis, on the west of the Nile, remains one of the most remarkable buildings ever erected by man. It is not, however, generally realized that in ground plan it is only a little larger than the northern pyramid built at Dahshur by Sneferu, the first king of the dynasty. Excavations have revealed the extent to which Egypt was highly organized from the early Fourth Dynasty with all departments of life and administration controlled from the royal residence at Memphis, where the king, the 'good god', was supreme. The king's pyramid was surrounded by the mastaba-tombs (p. 178) of the members of his family and of the great nobles who served him at court and at the provincial nome centres. From the inscriptions in the tombs of the nobles it is clear that the king was the focus of existence; to him all honour and duty were owed and from him all favours issued. The titles held by the nobles give some indication of the highly organized nature of administration. The false door stela of Kanefer, a son of Sneferu, now exhibited in the Egyptian Sculpture Gallery (1324) contains an enumeration of his titles which amount to 47, covering all departments of administration—priestly, civil, judicial, military, financial, and personal to the sovereign. Undoubtedly the holding of many of the titles was nominal but they presuppose that actual administrative functions were highly organized on well-defined departmental lines. The efficiency of administrative organization at this time is in nothing better exemplified than in the construction of the pyramids. The contention that these vast structures were built by slave labour is now generally discounted in favour of the view that the bulk of the building was carried out during the season of inundation when agricultural workers could not cultivate their fields. Only during this season was sufficient labour available. Furthermore when the Nile was in flood it was relatively easy to transport the quarried stone from the hills on the east of the Nile to the desert-plateau where the pyramids were erected. It is estimated that the Great Pyramid when complete contained about 2,300,000 blocks of stone of an average weight of $2\frac{1}{2}$ tons, the movement of which from quarry to site alone must have needed an organization of labour vast in extent. Cheops' successor, after the short intermediate reign of Radedef, was Chephren, who also built his pyramid at Giza; it is a little smaller than the Great Pyramid but from its situation on slightly higher ground it appears to be larger. Chephren also was probably the king whose likeness was preserved for posterity in the features of the great Sphinx which lies close to the Valley Temple of Chephren's pyramid. This great human-headed lion, carved out of a single knoll of rock, possibly represents the king as the sun-god, protecting the royal cemetery. Formidable though these building achievements of Sneferu, Cheops, and Chephren were, they undoubtedly put an excessively heavy strain on the economy of the country, for no attempt was ever made again to equal them. The pyramid of Mycerinus, a later king of the Fourth Dynasty, which completes the trio of large pyramids at Giza, is very much smaller in size, while Shepseskaf, the next king, built himself a large stone mastaba-tomb at Saqqara.

The history of the Fourth Dynasty is largely an account of its monuments, for very little is known about the activities of its kings in other respects. Inscriptions in Sinai and in the diorite quarries in Nubia show that expeditions were sent to obtain materials from these places and that these expeditions were commonly escorted by military contingents. From the Palermo Stone it is known that Sneferu sent a large punitive expedition into Nubia and another against the Libyans. Recent discoveries show that a copper-smelting factory was operating at the northern end of the Second Cataract during the Fourth Dynasty. The recording of the arrival of a number of sea-going ships laden with timber in Sneferu's reign further suggests the continuance of trade with western Asia through Byblos. During the Fifth Dynasty the sending of expeditions to Nubia, Sinai, and Libya is more fully recorded. There is also one mention of an expedition during the reign of Isesi, the eighth king of the dynasty, to the region of Punt. Knowledge of these enterprises comes largely from the biographical inscriptions set up in their tombs by the important nobles who acted as expedition commanders. One of the most interesting is that of Ptahshepses exhibited in the Egyptian Sculpture Gallery (682). Ptahshepses was born during the reign of Mycerinus, married a daughter of Shepseskaf, and continued in life and office at least until the reign of Nyuserre, the sixth king of the Fifth Dynasty. The increasing freedom of the nobles who were able thus not only to set up inscriptions celebrating their own personal achievements but even to marry members of the royal family is one indication of the relaxation of the strong personal authority that had characterized the rule of the Fourth Dynasty kings.

The concept of kingship also underwent modification during the Fifth Dynasty, partly because of the increased allegiance to the cult of the sun-god Re, worshipped at Heliopolis, partly owing to the growing influence of the myths of the Osiris legend (pp. 147 ff.). According to a story which was popular during the Middle Kingdom, the first three kings of the dynasty (Userkaf, Sahure, and Neferirkare) were the children of the wife of a priest of Re, the god Re himself being their father. From the early Fifth Dynasty every king called himself 'son of Re', a title which had been used previously only by a few fourth-dynasty kings. In honour of Re and in commemoration of the relationship between Re and the king, at least six of the Fifth Dynasty monarchs built elaborate sun-temples at Abu Gurab, some miles to the south of Giza. In addition to sun-temples they also built pyramids, some at Abu Sir and others at Saqqara, but these pyramids were very much smaller than the great structures of the early Fourth Dynasty. Nevertheless, they were greatly enhanced by extremely fine painted decorations in relief, and by the variety of architectural detail executed in fine hard stone as well as limestone, in the pyramid-temples and the ancillary buildings. A tall granite palm-tree column with a capital carved in the form of palm fronds bound together from the pyramid-temple of Unas, the last king of the dynasty, stands in the Sculpture Gallery (1385). The maintenance of the services connected with the cults of the successive dead kings was arranged by the establishment of foundations supported by grants of land freed from burdensome taxes and levies. In the Fifth Dynasty foundations of this kind were also set up for the maintenance of the sun-temples. Some of the documents relating to the temple of Neferirkare, compiled in the reign of a successor Djedkare Isesi, the eighth king of the dynasty, are preserved in the British Museum (10735). They form part of the earliest group of inscribed papyri yet discovered in Egypt (fig. 32).

An innovation of great importance was introduced into the pyramid of Unas: the walls of the vestibule and burial chamber were covered with religious texts concerned with the fortunes of the king after his death. These texts are now called the *Pyramid Texts*; they occur also in pyramids of the Sixth Dynasty (p. 178). The tombs of the nobles, which during the Fourth Dynasty were of modest size and were grouped closely around the royal pyramid, were, during the Fifth Dynasty, constructed on a far more ambitious scale and were less closely associated with the pyramid of the king. This development, which indicates a further diminution of the dependence of the noble on his monarch, was carried a stage further during the Sixth Dynasty when it became customary for the great noble to be buried in his nome, the local seat of his power, far away from the royal residence and the royal cemetery. The administration of affairs throughout Egypt became, during this dynasty, much decentralized and consequently the local officials became more important and more independent. This relaxation of central authority was to end in its complete dissolution, followed by a period of anarchy which is known as the First Intermediate Period. For the greater part of the Sixth Dynasty, however, the kings were sufficiently strong to maintain the unity of Egypt and to prosecute vigorous policies inside the country and abroad.

For this dynasty more than for any of the earlier dynasties the inscriptions from the tombs of high officials provide much information about the activities of the kings. From such sources the expanding nature of Egyptian foreign policy emerges. Under the kings Pepi I, Merenre, and Pepi II expeditions were sent deep into Nubia and Libya, into western Asia and Sinai, and to Punt. The descriptions of some of these expeditions show that the intention was frequently far more punitive than it had been in earlier times and that foreigners were recruited to supplement the slender domestic forces of the Egyptian army.

It was during the long reign of Pepi II, who is thought to have reigned about ninety-four years, that the central administration ultimately collapsed. The events which brought about the dissolution of central control are not known. Decentralization of administration and the consequent increase in power of provincial governors, especially in the case of the Governor of Upper Egypt, undoubtedly contributed to the process. In addition, the aged Pepi II in his last years could hardly have prosecuted the vigorous policies that had characterized the early part of his long reign. In ancient Egypt the relaxation of strong central government was almost always followed by political fragmentation of the country. Such appears to have happened either in the last years of or soon after the end of the reign of Pepi II, and brought about the downfall of the Old Kingdom.

The First Intermediate Period (c.2181–2050 BC)

The Sixth Dynasty, after the death of Pepi II, is credited with two or three shadowy rulers by the king lists. The time of political anarchy which followed the collapse of the central authority at the end of the Sixth Dynasty is known as the First Intermediate Period. The internal chaos in the country seems to have been intensified by the activities of groups of Bedouin who reached the Delta at about the same time. Very little is known about Egypt during this period, which lasted approximately one hundred and thirty years. Manetho's Seventh Dynasty may have been little more than a coalition of nobles centred on Memphis who tried to hold together the crumbling central authority. His Eighth Dynasty has a little more historical substance; its kings exercised some control from Memphis as far south at least as Coptos, where inscriptions bearing some of their names have been found. Otherwise Egypt was ruled locally by the nomarchs who, in the conditions of the time, became virtually regional princes. Inscriptions set up in their tombs reveal the extent to which these nomarchs were obliged to administer their territories as independent units, often engaging in petty warfare with their neighbours. The inevitable outcome of this inter-nome rivalry was the emergence of certain strong nomes with which weaker nomes became at first allied in confederacy and later bound in political dependence. The first nome to take a lead in this manner was the twentieth nome of Upper Egypt, the capital city of which was Heracleopolis. The rise of Heracleopolis (about 2160 BC) coincided with the decline of the Eighth Dynasty, and Achthoes the nomarch of Heracleopolis, to whom must be assigned the credit for establishing the new dynasty, claimed the kingdom of Egypt, assuming the throne-name of Meryibre. He pursued an active and (if the tradition preserved in Manetho is to be believed) ruthless policy of reducing Middle Egypt to his control, but he does not appear to have had any success in winning over the most southerly nomes of the country or the Delta. The Ninth and Tenth Dynasties were composed of nineteen kings ruling from Heracleopolis, several of whom bore the name Achthoes. While they never succeeded in gaining control of the whole of Egypt, they undoubtedly established a strong, stabilizing régime in the northern part of the country. In the Delta Asiatic influence was largely eradicated and trade with western Asia by the sea-route re-established, as is demonstrated by the use of Lebanese cedar wood for the large painted coffins which are so characteristic of the Heracleopolitan culture. Memphis again became the administrative capital of the northern part of Egypt and the kings were buried in the old royal cemetery at Saqqara. One of the kings named Achthoes, who had the prenomen Nebkaure, is chiefly famous as the king to whom a disgruntled Egyptian made a series of complaints in one of the most popular of Egyptian stories (p. 101).

Meanwhile, in southern Egypt a struggle for power had developed between changing confederacies of nomes among which those of Edfu (the second) and of Thebes (the fourth) were predominant. Thebes was a town that had only recently achieved prominence in its nome at the expense of Hermonthis, the old nome-capital. It was ruled by a family of nomarchs,

mostly called Inyotef, who followed a lively policy of aggrandize-
ment in southern Egypt. At first their efforts were principally
directed at securing hegemony in the south, but when this had
been achieved a clash with Heracleopolitan power in the north
was inevitable. The struggle between north and south acquired
a new significance when one of the Theban Inyotefs challenged
the position of his Heracleopolitan contemporary by assuming
the title 'King of Upper and Lower Egypt'. This 'king' Inyotef
Sehertowy ruled a 'kingdom' which remained the small
southern confederacy of nomes; but to future generations of
Egyptians he was regarded as the founder of the reunified
country and the first king of the Eleventh Dynasty. His successor
Inyotef Wahankh succeeded in extending his dominions as far
north as Aphroditopolis. The fine limestone stela of Tjetji
(614, fig. 12) records the limits of the kingdom at Elephantine
and This. Tjetji was a high official who held office under
Wahankh and his successor Inyotef Nakhtnebtepnefer. The
struggle between Thebes and Heracleopolis was resolved in the
reign of the next Theban king, Nebhepetre Mentuhotpe II, who
finally succeeded in reducing the northern power. After reuniting
the whole of Egypt under one authority he took the Horus-name
of Smatowy, 'He-who-unites-the-Two-Lands'. From this reunification (about 2050 BC) dates the beginning of the period now
called the Middle Kingdom.

The Middle Kingdom (c.2050–c.1786 BC)

The stages by which Nebhepetre Mentuhotpe completed the
reunification of Egypt are not known. What can be discovered
from contemporary inscriptions is that he pursued a very
energetic policy of consolidation and rehabilitation. The re-
establishment of a single administration for the whole country
was followed by campaigns in the north against the Libyans and
the Bedouin and in the south against the Nubians. The mines
and quarries were reopened and trade routes re-established. At
the end of his long reign of about fifty years Mentuhotpe II
could claim to his credit the formation of the Egyptian state
which achieved such great success politically and artistically
during the Middle Kingdom. His own tomb was constructed
according to a highly original plan in a bay in the cliffs at
Deir el-Bahri on the west bank of the Nile at Thebes. The reliefs
which decorated the associated temple were carved in a most
accomplished manner, far removed from that of the dispro-
portionate, awkward work of the First Intermediate Period,
and resuming much of what was best in late Old Kingdom
Memphite art. Fragments of these reliefs can be seen in the
Egyptian Sculpture Gallery.

12 Limestone stela of
Tjetji

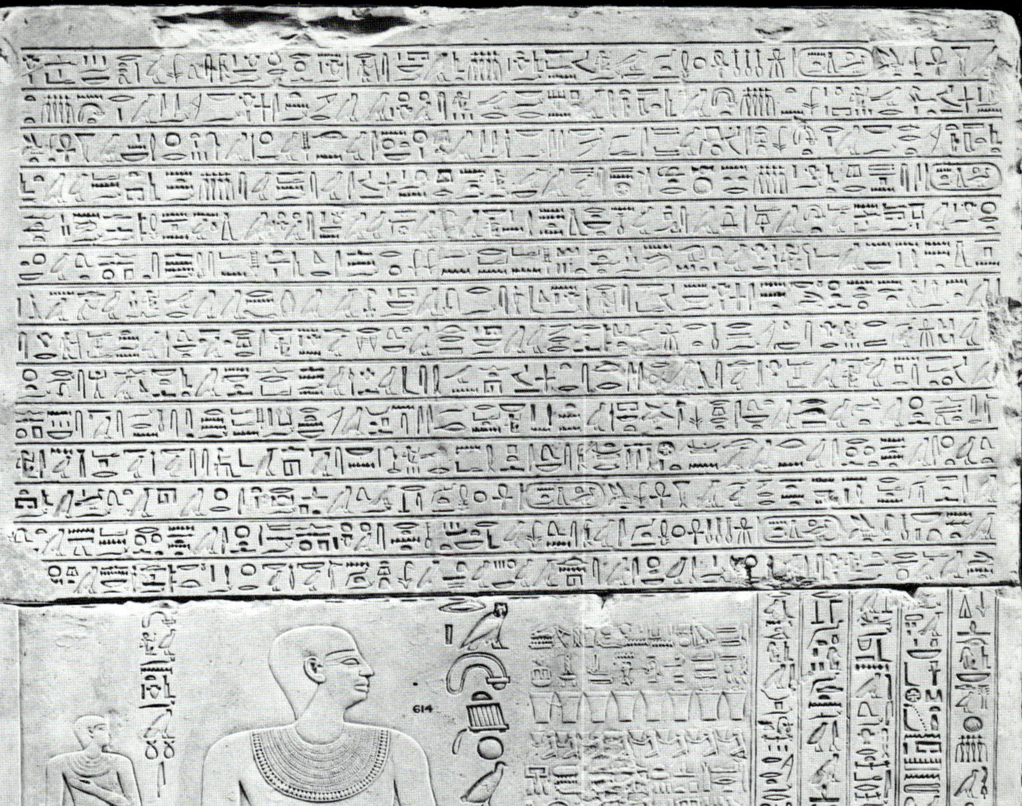
614

Among the activities which regularly indicated the revival of Egypt after a period of decline was the reinstitution of expeditions to Punt. The first expedition of the Middle Kingdom took place in the reign of Sankhkare Mentuhotpe III, the son and successor of Mentuhotpe II. It is recorded in an inscription carved in the Wadi Hammamat through which ran the road from the coast of the Red Sea to Coptos—the road along which the Punt expeditions travelled. Another inscription in the same place helps to make clear how the Eleventh Dynasty ended and the manner in which the ruling family was replaced by that of the Twelfth Dynasty. This second inscription records an expedition to the Wadi Hammamat in the reign of Nebtowyre Mentuhotpe IV, the last king of the Eleventh Dynasty. It was led by a vizier called Ammenemes and was remarkable for the occurrence of several incidents which were interpreted as significant omens. In about 1991 BC the government of Egypt was taken over by a certain Ammenemes who as king is now known as Ammenemes I. It is highly probable that he is to be identified with the Ammenemes of the Wadi Hammamat inscription and it is generally thought that he assumed control as king either when the government under Nebtowyre broke down, or on the death of that king.

Under the kings of the Twelfth Dynasty (c. 1991–1786 BC), of whom Ammenemes I was the first, Egypt once more became a highly organized, well-administered country with vigorously prosecuted policies in respect of Nubia, Libya, and western Asia. To ensure the strength and continuity of government it became the practice from the very beginning of the dynasty for the ruling king to accept, as a co-regent for the last years of his reign, his eldest son and intended successor. The wisdom of this arrangement was demonstrated at the end of the reign of Ammenemes I when that king was assassinated and his son, Sesostris I, was able to take over control immediately although he was on campaign in the Western Desert. An important move, designed to ensure a proper control over the whole country, was the transference of the seat of administration from Thebes in the south to a place at the entrance to the Faiyum in the north near the junction of Upper and Lower Egypt. This new capital was named Itj-towy, 'Seizer of the Two Lands', and in its neighbourhood the kings of the Twelfth Dynasty built their principal residences. They were subsequently buried in pyramids built at Itj-towy, at Dahshur (in part of the Old Kingdom royal necropolis), at Illahun, and at Hawara some miles to the south of Itj-towy.

One of the principal reasons for the political disintegration of Egypt during the First Intermediate Period was the increasing power and independence of the nomarchs. During the Twelfth

Dynasty steps were taken to ensure that their power was limited. From the inscriptions found in tombs of the nomarchs in Beni Hasan and elsewhere it emerges that Ammenemes II (1929–1895 BC) re-established nome-boundaries in some cases and that he, in other respects, reorganized the administration of the whole country so as to ensure greater central control and to curb the excessive power of the nomarchs. By the end of the dynasty the influence of these noble princes was completely broken and no longer are their tombs found in the provincial cemeteries. It has been suggested that the king responsible for this development was Sesostris III (1878–1843 BC), who may even have abolished the office of nomarch. Three statues of this king are shown in the Egyptian Sculpture Gallery (684, 685, 686; fig. 70).

In foreign affairs Egypt was particularly active during the Twelfth Dynasty, the pattern of activity being established by Ammenemes I. To keep out from the Delta the continuous waves of infiltrating Asiatics from the east, Ammenemes I constructed a fortification known as the Walls of the Prince. Very little is known of the actual warfare in western Asia during the dynasty apart from a foray by the General Nesymont in the joint reign of Ammenemes I and Sesostris I and an expedition by Sesostris III; it seems probable that the visibly active policy of the Egyptian kings was in itself sufficient to keep the migrant tribes of the area away from the borders of Egypt. The discovery of Egyptian objects of Twelfth Dynasty date in Syria and Palestine reveals, however, that there was considerable contact between Egypt and those countries, not least through the ancient port of Byblos. Two of the most interesting objects of the period in the British Museum were acquired in Beirut and probably came from Byblos: first is the diorite sphinx (58892) of Ammenemes IV (1798–1790 BC), exhibited in the Fifth Egyptian Room. The face of this sphinx was reworked in later times. The second is the gold plaque of the same king, exhibited in the Sixth Egyptian Room (59194, fig. 13). Throughout the Twelfth Dynasty Nubia presented a

13 Gold plaque of Ammenemes IV

great problem to the Egyptian kings. For many reasons it was found necessary to extend Egyptian control over the lands to the south of the First Cataract. Apart from the need to secure the southern boundaries of the kingdom, it was essential to ensure safe access to the mineral-bearing areas in Nubia and to establish the trade routes farther south into the heart of Africa. Under Ammenemes I Lower Nubia was annexed, and a fortress was established at the northern end of the Second Cataract at Buhen under his successor Sesostris I. Later in the Dynasty, most probably during the reign of Sesostris III, a series of fortresses was constructed in the districts of the First and Second Cataracts. The warlike temperament of the local tribes, particularly of those now called the C-group and Kerma peoples, forced the Egyptian kings to take vigorous precautions to prevent any sudden revolt against the occupying forces and to foil any attempts at infiltration over the southern boundary of Egypt established by Sesostris III at the southern entry to the Second Cataract, and protected by the fortresses of Semna and Kumma. To this end strict provisions were made regulating the movement of the native peoples living in the area of Egyptian influence and check-points were set up to regulate trade and immigration. The extent of effective Egyptian penetration southwards at this period has never been determined with certainty, although evidence of penetration south of the Second Cataract has been found in the form of various isolated inscriptions. Undoubtedly by the middle of the Twelfth Dynasty a large and permanent native settlement had been established at Kerma at the southern end of the Third Cataract, giving its name to the culture found there. The threat of aggression from Kush, the Egyptian name for this Nubian kingdom, is reflected in a group of despatches (a copy of which was deposited in Thebes), sent out from the fortress of Semna, and recording the movements of Nubians in that region. These documents, written early in the reign of Ammenemes III, admirably illustrate the well-organized administration developed by the Egyptians in Nubia (10752).

Much of the activity undertaken by the kings of the Twelfth Dynasty outside the narrow limits of the valley of the Nile was stimulated by the demands of the arts and crafts which flourished so vigorously during this time. As in the Old Kingdom, expeditions were regularly sent to exploit the quarries and mines in the Eastern Desert, Lower Nubia, and Sinai. Sea-borne expeditions visited Punt to obtain the exotic products of equatorial Africa, and Syria to obtain wood; it is possible that regular trade was established with Crete. Knowledge of the activities of Egyptian kings in foreign lands is preserved often only in the memorials set up in distant places by the officials concerned.

Ammenemes IV, who succeeded Ammenemes III, maintained the stability of the state and even prosecuted policies abroad in the tradition of his predecessors. He did not, however, equal them in energy, perhaps because he was already an old man when he was made co-regent with his father. The dynasty ended with Sobkneferu, his sister, of whom little is known.

Second Intermediate Period (c.1786–1567 BC)

The period between the end of the Twelfth Dynasty and the beginning of the Eighteenth Dynasty is generally called the Second Intermediate Period. Of the five dynasties allotted to this time by the late historian Manetho, three are native Egyptian and two are probably to be assigned to Hyksos rulers. The historical sequence of events has not yet been satisfactorily established and it appears that a certain amount of overlapping took place not only between the native and foreign dynasties but also within the limits of the individual dynasties. In brief the sequence seems to have been as follows: the centralized government of the whole country continued to function during the Thirteenth Dynasty until the increasing weakness of the central control gave opportunities to Asiatic settlers in the Delta to establish a separate kingdom in the north. These Asiatics are known as the Hyksos, a name derived from the Egyptian words *ḥekau-khasut*, 'princes of foreign countries'; they do not appear to have been an invading race but settlers who took advantage of chaotic conditions to seize power in the Delta, later extending their control farther south.

Manetho assigns sixty kings to the Thirteenth Dynasty and indeed the names of a large number of kings possibly belonging to the dynasty have been preserved on monuments and small objects. It is clear that the breakdown of central authority after the end of the Twelfth Dynasty was a gradual process and that the pattern of government was maintained both in the south and the north for many years. The credit for this state of affairs seems to rest more on the able viziers and other administrative officers of the time than on the kings who succeeded each other in rapid succession. The capital of the country remained in the north, friendly relations were maintained with Byblos and western Asia, and control was still exercised in Nubia. Some temple building was undertaken and there is much evidence of other activity within Egypt, indicative of a relatively settled political condition. Furthermore, artistic traditions were to a great extent maintained and the lamentable decline in style and technique so noticeable in the art of the First Intermediate Period was avoided. The statuette of Meryankhre Mentuhotpe in the Fifth Egyptian Room (65429, fig. 14) illustrates this maintenance of standards.

4 Schist statuette of Meryankhre Mentuhotpe

Nevertheless, the unstable position of the kings of the period, the precise reasons for which cannot now be determined, eventually led to such a weakening in government that Lower Egypt became progressively detached from the rule of the Thirteenth Dynasty kings. Of the Fourteenth Dynasty little is known except that it consisted of a large number of rulers (seventy-six according to Manetho) who seem to have controlled part of the western Delta from the town of Xois, capital of the sixth Lower Egyptian nome. It is possible that this region began to secede soon after the end of the Twelfth Dynasty and that the Thirteenth and Fourteenth Dynasties were largely contemporaneous.

No precise details are known of the rise to power of the Hyksos rulers in the eastern Delta. It is generally thought that Asiatic settlers, powerful locally, succeeded in about 1720 BC in establishing some sort of régime with its capital at Avaris and with Seth as its god. The line of rulers, forming the Fifteenth Dynasty, assumed control in about 1670 BC. The names of the minor Hyksos royalties of the Sixteenth Dynasty who apparently ruled concurrently with the Hyksos kings are preserved, for the most part, on scarabs. The Hyksos kings, on the other hand, can be identified as six in number, some of whom were rulers of great vigour and achievement. Their influence extended throughout Egypt although they did not apparently rule directly in the Theban area. Scarabs bearing their names have been found at Kerma in the Sudan and in Palestine. Antiquities found in Crete and western Asia testify to the widespread nature of their contacts. The granite lion (987), exhibited in the Fifth Egyptian Room, bears the name of Khyan, the third of the Hyksos kings; it was found in Baghdad. The tradition that the Hyksos were merciless tyrants who imposed a harsh rule on a resisting native population seems to have been deliberately fostered as early as the Eighteenth Dynasty, although indirect evidence from the period of their rule and from the early Eighteenth Dynasty itself in no way supports this tradition. On the contrary, the Hyksos seem in many ways to have ruled in the manner of native rulers, taking Egyptian names and fostering Egyptian culture. The great Rhind Mathematical Papyrus, part of which is exhibited in the Third Egyptian Room (10058, Plate 9), was written in the reign of Auserre Apophis I. This ruler, who occupied the throne for over forty years, apparently maintained good relations with Upper Egypt until comparatively late in his reign when a clash with a rising dynasty of Theban princes became inevitable.

One of the most interesting objects surviving from the Hyksos Period in the British Museum is the ivory figure of the forepart of a sphinx clutching an Egyptian by the ears (54678). The sphinx is thought to represent one of the Hyksos kings and the piece may have been made at the time when the Hyksos were establishing their suzerainty over Egypt. It was found in a tomb in a cemetery at Abydos containing some graves belonging to the Pan-grave people. These Pan-grave people were of Nubian stock who came to Egypt apparently to serve as professional soldiers. For some time during the Second Intermediate Period they preserved their native customs; their graves give evidence of a way of life different from that of the contemporary Egyptians (e.g. the black incised jar from Mostagedda, 63038). In later times they were more completely assimilated into Egyptian life, abandoning their old burial habits.

The movement which ended in the liberation of Egypt from the Hyksos domination began in Thebes. About 1650 BC the Thirteenth Dynasty was succeeded by a new family of rulers, known as the Seventeenth Dynasty. The members of this line, who affected the royal titles and attempted to preserve the culture and tradition of the Middle Kingdom, are divided into two groups. The earlier group consists of rulers who were seemingly content to confine their power to a small group of nomes in Upper Egypt. They probably acknowledged the suzerainty of the Hyksos and made no effort to improve their position politically.

A coffin in the Second Egyptian Room, made of wood overlaid with gold leaf, belonged probably to Nubkheperre Inyotef, the first king of the second group of Seventeenth Dynasty kings (6652). The kings of this second group asserted their claim to the throne of the whole of Egypt by prosecuting a policy which ultimately led to a violent clash with the Hyksos rulers. The struggle reached a peak under Kamose who not only penetrated Nubia at least as far as the Second Cataract, but also succeeded in carrying the war to the gates of Avaris itself. In the Fourth Egyptian Room there is an axe-head inscribed with Kamose's name (36772). The final defeat of the Hyksos and their expulsion from Egypt took place about 1567 BC under Kamose's successor, Amosis, the founder of the Eighteenth Dynasty.

New Kingdom (1567–1085 BC)

The character of the Eighteenth Dynasty as a whole was established by the policies of the early kings of the dynasty. These policies were in turn determined largely by the necessities of the situation that faced Amosis I when he became king of a united Upper and Lower Egypt after the capture of Avaris. The immediate steps that needed to be taken were the securing of the fortresses in the north, on the east and west of the Delta, the re-establishment of the central administration of the land of

Egypt, the consolidation of Egyptian control in Nubia and the reopening of trade routes to Africa and Asia. As at the beginning of the Middle Kingdom, a great upsurge of enthusiasm and activity followed the reunification of Egypt after the expulsion of the Hyksos. Amosis I followed up his successes in the Delta by besieging and reducing, after a three years' siege, the Hyksos stronghold of Sharuhen in southern Palestine. This new positive policy of aggression in Asia itself was followed by Amosis' immediate successors, especially Tuthmosis I, who penetrated as far as the Euphrates, defeating the strong kingdom of Mitanni and setting up a stela on the eastern bank of that river. The activities of the early kings of the Eighteenth Dynasty, were, however, devoted far more to the conquest of Nubia and the extension of Egyptian power southwards up the Nile. Amosis succeeded in recovering the country as far south as the Second Cataract, but further operations were hampered by subversive movements in Lower Nubia which had to be quelled. To promote Egyptian policy in Nubia, Amosis instituted the high office of viceroy, an office which remained of great importance throughout the New Kingdom. Amenophis I and Tuthmosis I extended the southern boundary well beyond the Third Cataract and continued the work of Amosis in rehabilitating the series of fortresses built during the Middle Kingdom. Similarly, these early Eighteenth Dynasty kings took firm steps to reconstitute the boundaries of Egypt on the west of the Delta, campaigning vigorously and successfully against the Libyans. Within Egypt itself the re-establishment of the united kingdom was marked by a great revival in temple building, especially at Karnak, and in a renaissance in art which derived its inspiration largely from the best work of the Middle Kingdom. Tuthmosis I was the first king to build his tomb in the Valley of the Kings. This valley on the west bank of the Nile at Thebes was chosen because of its remoteness and relative inaccessibility, and throughout the New Kingdom it was used as the burial place for the kings of Egypt.

Tuthmosis II, who succeeded Tuthmosis I in about 1512 BC, suffered apparently from poor health and was unable to continue the policies of his predecessors with equal vigour. He died at a comparatively young age, leaving as his heir and successor the boy Tuthmosis III. In view of the youth of the new king, his stepmother Hatshepsut assumed the position of regent and for a short time discharged this function with appropriate discretion. In the second year of the new reign, however, Hatshepsut either of her own volition, or at the instigation of a group of powerful officials, asserted her personal claim to the throne, secured her own coronation and successfully supplanted the young king,

5 Statuette in black
granite of the
steward Senenmut

ruling with apparently complete control over the whole of
Egypt for about twenty years. Tuthmosis III was not deposed
but was deprived of all effective power. Positive evidence of what
happened during this time is lacking, but there is no reason to
suppose that there was any deliberate lull in Egypt's aggressive
foreign policy. The outstanding monument of the reign is the
funerary temple of the queen at Deir el-Bahri which was built
under the direction of her favoured steward Senenmut. Some of
the scenes on the walls of this temple show an important trading
expedition sent to the region of Punt. A granite statue (174)
shows Senenmut nursing Neferure, the daughter of Hatshepsut,
for whom he served as tutor (fig. 15).

In about 1482 BC Tuthmosis III succeeded in re-establishing
himself as sole ruler, in the twenty-first year of his nominal reign.
It is not certain whether his triumph followed the ousting of
Hatshepsut or the death of that queen. The new régime was not
at first openly hostile to the achievements and memory of its
predecessor. Only towards the end of the reign of Tuthmosis III
was positive hostility expressed in a campaign of destruction
and mutilation designed to efface the memory of Hatshepsut.
Her name was hammered out on monuments and buildings
throughout the land. About the same time as the rehabilitation
of Tuthmosis III a great revolt of subject princes occurred in
Syria which resulted in the withdrawal of Egyptian garrisons to
southern Palestine. It may in fact have been the revolt that
enabled the king to recover his throne. He acted at once with
great vigour and in 1481 BC inflicted a severe defeat on the
rebelling princes at Megiddo. He did not, however, rest merely
at re-establishing the *status quo* (from the Egyptian standpoint)
in western Asia; in a series of well-planned, brilliantly executed
campaigns he followed up his initial success by extending the
limits of Egyptian control far to the east, across the Euphrates
and to the north, to the boundaries of the Hittite Empire. Control
over the conquered territories was exercised by local princes
who could be trusted, their fidelity in most cases being stimulated
by the presence of Egyptian envoys. In a similarly energetic
manner he extended the southern limits of the Egyptian Empire
beyond the Fourth Cataract in the Sudan, founding the
important trading and garrison town of Napata in the region of
that cataract. A positive and beneficial result of all this activity
was a marked increase in Egypt's contacts with distant countries
and a consequent development in trade and the exchanging of
embassies. The prosperity of the country, combined with the
stimulation received from foreign contacts, led to a dramatic
increase in artistic activity in Egypt. New temples were built,
great additions made to the existing national shrines; sculpture

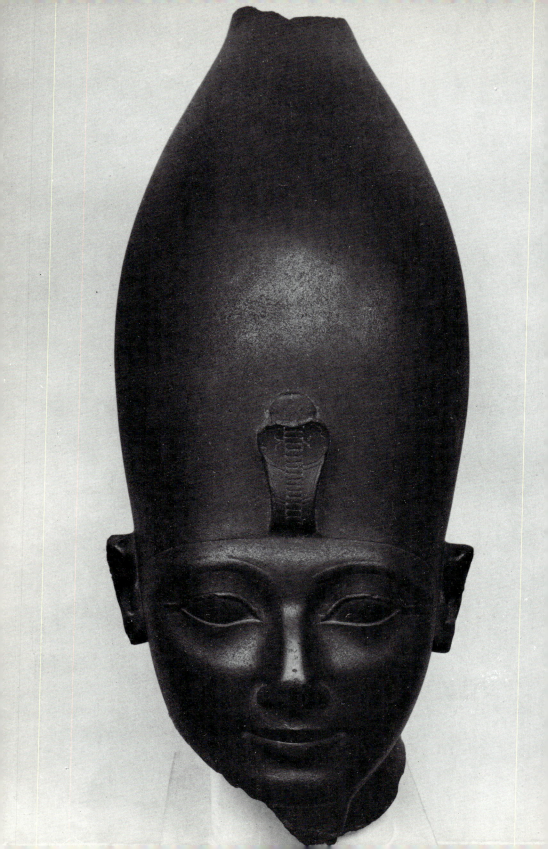

and painting flourished and the minor arts profited from the
wealth of precious materials now available. Figure 16 shows
a life-size head in schist of a king who has been identified as
Tuthmosis III (986). The identification is, however, not certain.

The active policies of Tuthmosis III were continued by his
successors Amenophis II and Tuthmosis IV. The former, who was
unusually tall and strong for an Egyptian king, penetrated farther
south in the Sudan than any of his predecessors, but apparently
retained the effective boundary of the Egyptian empire at Napata.
He and Tuthmosis IV maintained Egyptian prestige in Asia, the
latter considerably strengthening the position by securing a
marriage with a daughter of the King of Mitanni, the powerful
buffer-state lying between the empires of Egypt and of the
Hittites. A fine bronze kneeling figure of Tuthmosis IV, presenting bowls of ointment to a god, is exhibited in the Fifth Egyptian
Room (64564); the granite model sacred bark of Mutemuia, his
Mitannian wife, is in the Egyptian Sculpture Gallery (43).

Amenophis III, the son and successor of Tuthmosis IV, became
king of Egypt when her fortunes had reached their zenith
(fig. 17). Abroad her empire was secure, its limits established at

Karoy in the Sudan and at Naharin in western Asia, as Amenophis III proclaimed in the text placed on one of a series of large scarabs which were issued by him to commemorate important happenings of his reign (examples of all the known commemorative scarabs are shown in the Sixth Egyptian Room). At home the country was settled and prosperous. No special effort was required of the new king to maintain the situation apart from a single punitive expedition to the Sudan in his fifth year, and possibly a few tours of western Asia in the early years of the reign. Foreign policy was otherwise restricted in the Sudan to the fostering of Egyptian ways and civilization accompanied by the extensive building of temples in some of which the king himself was worshipped as a god; in Asia to the development of friendly relations with the rulers of the subject principalities of the empire and of the countries bordering the empire. Some of the diplomatic correspondence from this reign and from that of Akhenaten written in Akkadian, the lingua franca of the period, was discovered at El-Amarna and part is preserved in the Department of Western Asiatic Antiquities of the Museum. Relations with several of the foreign kings were cemented by marriages between Amenophis III and daughters of the kings. The arrival in Egypt in year 10 of one of these princesses, Gilukhepa, daughter of King Shuttarna of Mitanni, was celebrated on one of the great commemorative scarabs.

Within Egypt prosperity and the attendant settled conditions enabled Amenophis III to devote himself to extensive building operations and to the fostering of the arts. Great temples were constructed, among which the temple of Luxor dedicated to Amen-Re, the god of the empire, was the most unusual in design and the most beautiful in appearance. Of several representations of the king in the British Museum, one of the most interesting is that on a small stela found at El-Amarna where the king is shown seated with his principal wife Tiy, a woman of non-royal birth whose strong personality left a considerable mark on the reign (57399, fig. 18). In this representation, which may have been carved after the death of the king, Amenophis III is shown as an old, obese man, slumping in his chair, an uncharacteristic pose for Egyptian kings and unlike the formal, conventional representations of the king found, for example, in the two colossal seated statues in the Egyptian Sculpture Gallery (4 and 5). It is a representation made when Egyptian art had developed strikingly realistic tendencies after the introduction of the worship of the Aten (p. 137). There is evidence that shows that the cult of the sun-disk already flourished during the reign of Tuthmosis IV (e.g. the scarab 65800 exhibited in the Sixth Egyptian Room which bears a text mentioning the Aten) and

3 Sandstone stela of
Amenophis III and
Queen Tiy

during the reign of Amenophis III it gained steadily in importance until it was formally adopted by his son. The precise order of
events at the end of the reign of Amenophis III is uncertain; it is
possible that for the last years of his reign he associated his son
with himself on the throne and that this son, first as Amenophis IV
and then as Akhenaten, took control of government. However,
it is also possible that Akhenaten only came to the throne on his
father's death. At first the centre of government remained at
Thebes but the devotion of the young king to the cult of the
Aten (for whom he constructed a temple at Karnak) brought
him into conflict with the priesthood of Amun and its adherents.
This conflict was resolved early in his reign by the proscription
of the worship of Amun and other state gods and by the moving
of the capital from Thebes to a site in Middle Egypt which was
then named Akhetaten, 'the Horizon of the Aten' (now called
El-Amarna). Here, with the support of his wife Nefertiti and of
a party of faithful courtiers, he was able to devote himself to
the promotion of the new religion (pp. 137–8). In the realm
of foreign affairs Akhenaten did little to preserve the empire as
he received it from his predecessors. His inactivity and lack of
interest provided the opportunity for subversive movements

among the dependent princes and for successful incursions into friendly territories by hostile states. Many of the Amarna letters contain urgent appeals for assistance from loyal but hard-pressed vassal princes and provide a vivid picture of the gradual loss of Egyptian influence in Syria in the face of the growing power of the Hittites.

19 Fragment of a relief showing the head of Akhenaten

On his sculpture and reliefs Akhenaten is depicted as a person of unusual physical appearance; he is shown with an enlarged head, pronounced stoop, and heavy hips. It is not certain how much this appearance was due to his own physical peculiarities or to the artistic style of the period (fig. 19). He found little general support for his régime and towards the end of his reign of seventeen years suffered many set-backs which obliged him to modify his policies. Apart from the troubles in the empire his position was weakened by hostile movements within Egypt which eventually necessitated a *rapprochement* with the priesthood of Amun, though possibly not in his own lifetime. The agreement between the factions of Aten and Amun appears to have begun under Smenkhkare. He reigned as co-regent with Akhenaten for about two years and survived him by only a few months, being succeeded by Tutankhamun. In the reign of the last the return to the worship of Amun as the principal state god, and the abandonment of Akhetaten in favour of Thebes were finally accomplished. One of his chief advisers was General Horemheb who had a splendid tomb constructed for himself in the necropolis of Saqqara, panels from which can be found in the Museum's collection (550, 551, and 552, fig. 20).

Inscribed panel
from the tomb of
Horemheb

Tutankhamun died while still a youth and he was succeeded for a short time by Ay, an elderly noble, who possibly reinforced his claim to the throne by marrying the widow of Tutankhamun, Ankhesenamun. With his reign it may be said that the interlude of the Amarna period came to an end. It is possible that Ay was made king by Horemheb to act as a transitional monarch until he himself was ready to take over the royal power. When Ay died in about 1348 BC Horemheb became king and a new era of positive government began for Egypt. His active policies were aimed at securing the internal stability of Egypt and her prestige abroad as they had existed before Akhenaten. Under the Nineteenth Dynasty the Amarna period was formally forgotten, the memory of Akhenaten eradicated from the records of the land, and his name hacked out of texts wherever it occurred; the town of Akhetaten and many buildings associated with Akhenaten were dismantled. Horemheb was credited with a reign that followed immediately that of Amenophis III.

The reign of Horemheb (who did not belong to the royal family of the Eighteenth Dynasty) served as a transition between the Eighteenth Dynasty and the Nineteenth Dynasty which was founded by Ramesses I in about 1320 BC. Ramesses I had clearly been groomed for the throne by Horemheb, who had made him his vizier in Lower Egypt. The family of Ramesses sprang from the Delta and one of the notable changes made later in the new dynasty was the moving of the royal residence from Thebes (which still remained the administrative capital) to Piramesse in the eastern Delta, a town occupying the site of Avaris, the ancient stronghold of the Hyksos. Ramesses I, who reigned for a short time only, and his son Sethos I continued the work of Horemheb in restoring the damaged pride of Egypt's temples and gods and in reasserting the authority of Egypt in Nubia and western Asia. Much work was done at Karnak in the national shrine of Amun, but the outstanding achievement in the field of temple-building was the new Osiris temple built by Sethos I at Abydos. In foreign affairs Sethos engaged in settling an insurrection in Nubia, in repulsing the Libyans from the western Delta and, principally, in pushing the limits of the Egyptian empire in Asia to the Orontes. The Hittites had by now become a major threat to the Egyptian Empire in Asia, and Sethos, after inflicting a defeat on them beyond the Orontes, eventually withdrew south of Qadesh.

Ramesses II, who succeeded his father in 1304 BC, after a period of association with him as co-regent, was eager to reopen the struggle. A preliminary campaign in his fourth year was followed in the subsequent year by a great attack which culminated in a battle at Qadesh on the Orontes. The Hittite and

Egyptian records give divergent accounts of the outcome of this struggle, and it is probable that neither side could properly claim a victory. Ramesses, however, made out that a great triumph had been achieved through his own valour, and the battle was celebrated in a bombastic composition which was inscribed on the walls of a number of temples in Egypt and Nubia. Parts of two copies on papyrus are preserved in the British Museum and pages from both are exhibited in the Third Egyptian Room (10181 and 10683). In the years following the battle constant vigilance and frequent punitive expeditions were needed to preserve the security of the Asiatic Empire. Ultimately, in his twenty-first year, Ramesses II concluded a treaty with Khattushilish, king of the Hittites, the effect of which was subsequently cemented by a marriage between Ramesses and a daughter of Khattushilish. For the remainder of his long reign of sixty-seven years peace prevailed in the Egyptian Asiatic Empire.

The early years of Ramesses II's reign were in general devoted to settling external troubles. A campaign in Nubia was celebrated in reliefs carved on the walls of a rock-cut temple at Beit el-Wali; the large painted casts on the walls of the Third Egyptian Room reproduce the scenes. Early in the reign too there was a clash with sea-raiders known as the Sherden—a warning of much greater troubles that were to assail Egypt in future generations. Apart from the threat of trouble from the west of the Delta, which was countered by the construction of a series of fortified outposts, the greater part of Ramesses' reign was relatively free from warfare. The vigorous activity of the early years was consolidated by strong administration and firm diplomacy in Nubia and Asia and the king was enabled to devote his energies to building and to the development of his royal reputation as Egypt's greatest king. The tone of his work was set by the inscription which he set up in the Osiris temple of Sethos at Abydos which he completed. In this text he revealed himself as a ruler with a firm belief in his own ability to achieve great things; and in his reign he succeeded in fostering his reputation to such an extent that even in the Classical Period he was regarded as the great Egyptian king *par excellence*. This reputation was perpetuated largely by means of the great buildings erected throughout Egypt during his reign. One of his most remarkable monuments is the rock-temple of Abu Simbel in Nubia with its four immense seated figures of the king. In all the great centres in Egypt he built new temples or added considerably to existing buildings. Statues, large and small, glorified his person (e.g. 19, Plate 7) and many representations of earlier kings were usurped for Ramesses by the substitution of his names for theirs (e.g. 61).

Merneptah, one of Ramesses II's many sons, became king at an advanced age and was almost immediately faced with a crisis which had been developing for some years. Ethnic movements in northern Asia Minor and the Aegean resulted in attempts by migrant tribes to gain a foothold in the Delta. Ramesses II had repulsed such an attempt by the Sherden. Other tribes had been successful in establishing themselves to the west of the Delta. Forts erected by Ramesses II were not adequate to deal with more than local forays and in Merneptah's fifth year a considerable incursion was made into the Delta. A pitched battle was fought at Pi-yer, an unidentified place in the western Delta, Merneptah securing a decisive victory, which for some time relieved Egypt of pressure from Libya.

The later history of the Nineteenth Dynasty is hard to establish; even the sequence of the kings is uncertain. The historical summary in the Great Harris Papyrus (see below) declares that the country fell into decline and that for a time a Syrian named Arsu took control of Egypt. He is generally identified with the Chancellor Bay, an influential courtier at the end of the dynasty. The state of anarchy in this period has probably been exaggerated in order to extol a new-comer, called Sethnakhte, who established a new ruling line known as the Twentieth Dynasty. After a short reign he was succeeded by Ramesses III, the last great king of the New Kingdom, in whose reign Egypt both experienced a revival of glory and prosperity and suffered attacks which presaged her downfall as an imperial power. Three great campaigns were conducted by Ramesses III to repulse attacks made or threatened against the Delta. Two in years 5 and 11 were against the Libyans in coalition with various so-called Peoples of the Sea, among whom the Meshwesh were most prominent. In year 8 a serious attack came from the east, by land and sea, the invading forces again being composed of Peoples of the Sea (but not the Sherden, by then mercenaries in the Egyptian army). Ramesses III succeeded in gaining brilliant victories in all these crises and preserved the land of Egypt itself from invasion. Thereafter, Ramesses III undertook no further large-scale military operations, a few modest forays against insurgent tribes in southern Palestine being the extent of his activities abroad. With Egypt at peace for the greater part of his reign Ramesses III was able to foster trade and engage in extensive building works. The principal monument of his reign is his great mortuary temple at Medinet Habu (Plate 15), which became the administrative centre of the Theban necropolis during the late Twentieth Dynasty. Some idea of the prosperity of the land can be gained from the great lists of donations to temples recorded in the papyrus known as the Great Harris, now preserved in the

British Museum (fig. 34). This document, part of which is shown in the Third Egyptian Room, was prepared under Ramesses IV (fig. 21) to glorify the memory of his father. There is reason, however, to doubt that all was as well as it was painted in the Egypt of Ramesses III. Other documents record a strike of workers in the royal necropolis and a harim conspiracy directed at the life of the king himself towards the end of his reign. These subversive movements probably indicated a deterioration in

21 Kneeling figure of Ramesses IV

prosperity and political stability which became more marked in the subsequent reigns. From the death of Ramesses III in about 1166 BC until the end of the Twentieth Dynasty about 1085 BC eight kings, all called Ramesses, occupied the throne. In this period Egypt finally lost the remnants of her Asiatic Empire and suffered serious economic consequences thereby. Towards the end of the dynasty it was discovered that the royal tombs at Thebes were suffering wholesale plundering. Many of the documents dealing with the investigation of the thefts and the legal action taken subsequently have been preserved and some are in the British Museum, such as the Abbott Papyrus (10221) and Papyrus 10053 which are exhibited in the Third Egyptian Room (p. 120 ff.).

During the last years of the reign of Ramesses XI power in Egypt was virtually divided between the High Priest of Amun at Thebes, named Herihor, who styled himself king at Thebes, and Smendes who governed Lower Egypt from Tanis. The king himself apparently withdrew to his Delta residence, and while recognized as monarch, he exercised no real authority. This division of the country, in which both parts existed apparently on amicable terms, continued for many generations.

Late Dynastic Period (1085–332 BC)

After the death of Ramesses XI the royal attributes were assumed by Smendes, who, relying probably on a connexion with the old ruling house, established a new dynasty, called the Twenty-first by Manetho, with its capital at Tanis in the Delta. Simultaneously the line of the High Priests of Amun, possibly descended from Herihor, assumed control in the south at Thebes. The members of the priestly dynasty did not claim for themselves the title of king of Upper and Lower Egypt and only rarely did they place their names in cartouches. Their efforts were aimed at developing the state of Amun in coexistence with the secular authority ruling from Tanis, and it seems that both sides were careful not to encroach on each other's prerogatives. One great task undertaken by the High Priests was the salvage of the old royal burials at Thebes, the plundering of which had caused such a scandal in the late Twentieth Dynasty. Those mummies which remained undamaged were in many instances rewrapped and they, together with such of their funerary equipment as had survived, were transferred to the tomb of Queen Inhapy at Deir el-Bahri and to the tomb of King Amenophis II in the Valley of the Kings. Here they remained, together with the burials of the High Priests of the Twenty-first Dynasty and their families, until the late nineteenth century. From these hiding-places came the *Book of the Dead* of Pinudjem, High Priest of Amun

under King Siamun, now in the British Museum (the Campbell Papyrus, 10793), the wooden *shabti*-board of Neskhons, the wife of Pinudjem (16672), exhibited in the Third Egyptian Room and the *Book of the Dead* of Herihor and Nodjmet (10541, fig. 22). The régime of the Tanite kings seems to have been without distinction and it was superseded apparently without any strife by that of the kings of the Twenty-second Dynasty, in about 945 BC.

During the Twentieth Dynasty colonies of Libyan (or Meshwesh) mercenaries had been established on Egyptian territory mostly in the Delta. Sheshonq I, the first king of the Twenty-second Dynasty, came from a Libyan military family in Bubastis and had previously served as a general under the last ruler of the Twenty-first Dynasty. He secured the allegiance of the High Priests of Amun by breaking the tradition of hereditary appointment that had lasted throughout the Twenty-first Dynasty, appointing his own son to the office. It is also known, from the Old Testament (1 Kings xiv. 25–26), that Sheshonq conducted at least one military campaign into Palestine in the course of which he carried off the treasures of the temple in Jerusalem; but it is not clear whether this campaign was prompted by simple aggressive intentions, or was launched in support of Jeroboam, pretender to the throne of Judah in the reign of Rehoboam (2 Chron. xii. 2–9). The scanty records of

22 Vignette from the *Book of the Dead* of Queen Nodjmet and Herihor

events which have been preserved from the Twenty-second Dynasty indicate that Egypt was in a very unsettled state. In spite of the move by Sheshonq I to attach Thebes more closely to the northern monarchy, the forces of separation in Thebes were continually exerted, especially when the High Priest of Amun, usually the son of the reigning king, did not have his residence at Thebes. During the reign of Osorkon II (c. 874–850 BC) one High Priest called Harsiese even assumed a royal titulary, but he was eventually replaced by the king's son. Part of a granite relief from Bubastis, exhibited in the Egyptian Sculpture Gallery, shows Osorkon II with his wife Karoma (1077, fig. 23). The state of the land during the dynasty may be deduced from the long inscription of the High Priest Osorkon, son of Takelothis II, in the temple of Karnak. From this text it is clear that there were many subversive groups active in different parts of the country and, in spite of the fairly close relations between Thebes and the king at this time, it was not easy to maintain peace throughout the land. In the succeeding reign of Sheshonq III (c. 825–773 BC) further troubles led to changes in the High Priesthood at Thebes and also to the establishment in the Delta of a parallel ruling line, the Twenty-third Dynasty, by a certain Petubastis, in about 818 BC. The lack of a strong central authority in Egypt always resulted in antiquity in the disintegration of the state into smaller units. Good relations between the kings of the Twenty-first and early Twenty-second Dynasties, ruling in the north, and the High priests of Amun, ruling at Thebes, went some way to keeping unity in the land; but when, from about 818 BC, even the outward forms of accord were absent, there was nothing to prevent the natural dichotomous tendency from developing. During the last reigns of the Twenty-second Dynasty and those of the concurrent Twenty-third Dynasty, further fragmentation took place and the process was halted only by the arrival in Egypt of a conqueror from the south.

For many years the town of Napata in the neighbourhood of the Fourth Cataract in the Sudan, after the withdrawal northwards of the Egyptians, had been ruled by a native Sudanese dynasty which preserved many Egyptian customs including the worship of the god Amun. The Napatan prince Kashta occupied the whole of Lower Nubia, but it was left to his successor Piankhi to make a decisive intervention in Egyptian affairs. His most determined opponent was Tefnakhte of Sais, a Delta ruler who seems to have attained considerable power in Lower Egypt, occupied Memphis, and was in the process of extending his influence southward. In about 727 BC Piankhi undertook a major campaign into Egypt to check his rival's advance. He took

and his wife Karoma   Ashurbanipal, whose forces occupied Memphis and may have

76 AN INTRODUCTION TO ANCIENT EGYPT

what is written by Greek historians, but it seems that he devoted himself mostly to domestic affairs and to the promotion of good relations with Egypt's neighbours. During his reign the Divine Adoratrice of Amun at Thebes was Ankhnesneferibre, whose great sarcophagus is exhibited in the Egyptian Sculpture Gallery (32, fig. 25). Amosis died in 526 BC, thereby just escaping the doom which had threatened Egypt for many years since the rise of Persian power in the east. In 525 his successor Psammetichus III was defeated at Pelusium, Memphis was besieged and captured, and the whole of Egypt fell to Cambyses, who became the first king of the Twenty-seventh Dynasty.

Under the Persian kings of the Twenty-seventh Dynasty Egypt was reorganized as a satrapy of the Persian Empire. Greek tradition tells of the terrible sufferings of the land during this time, but contemporary evidence from Egypt does not confirm the tradition. Both Cambyses and his successor Darius I seem to have introduced administrative changes which greatly benefited the land; laws were codified; great public works undertaken, such as the completion of the canal begun in the reign of Necho II, connecting the Nile with the Red Sea; even new temples were built and old ones restored. In the years after the defeat of the Persians by the Greeks at Marathon (490 BC) an attempt was made in the Delta to throw off the foreign yoke. Xerxes, who succeeded Darius I in 486 BC, stamped out this revolt and is credited with having imposed a more severe administration on Egypt in consequence. Contemporary evidence of events in Egypt during the fifth century is very scanty and knowledge of what was happening there is derived principally from Greek writers. In 465 BC the accession of Artaxerxes I following the death of Xerxes was the signal for a new rising in the Delta, led by Inarus, a local prince, who was probably a descendant of the Saite royal family. At first the Egyptians had considerable success and gained control of most of the Delta. Unexpected help then arrived in the form of a considerable fleet sent by Athens in 459 BC, with which the Egyptians succeeded in capturing most of Memphis; but not the inner fortress to which the Persians had fled. For some time Inarus and the Athenians maintained their hold on Lower Egypt but ultimately they were unable to resist a well-planned counter-attack of the Persians under Megabyxus. In 454 BC the end came; Inarus was taken as a captive to Persia and slain, while the Athenians were almost wiped out. Resistance to the Persians continued in the north-western corner of the Delta under Amyrtaeus, a local prince, but no account of his activities has been preserved. His rebellion was soon crushed. The Egyptian tradition, as recounted by Manetho, ends the Twenty-seventh Dynasty with the death of

25 Figure of Ankhnesneferibre on the lid of her sarcophagus (see also fig. 59)

Darius II in 405 BC although documents dated to the early years of his successor Artaxerxes II are known from Elephantine.

The subsequent Twenty-eighth Dynasty is given only one king, named Amyrtaeus, possibly a descendant of the insurgent Amyrtaeus; of his reign little is known. He succeeded in expelling the Persians from Egypt and had secured control of Elephantine by his fifth year (400 BC). With his death came a change in the ruling house, the kings of the new Twenty-ninth Dynasty springing from Mendes in the Delta. The history of this dynasty and of that of its successor is, in so far as it is known, a long struggle to maintain the independence of Egypt against repeated attempts by the Persians to re-annex it as a satrapy. In their struggle the Egyptians relied heavily on Greek help. Nepherites I (398–393 BC), the first king of the Twenty-ninth Dynasty, contracted an alliance with Sparta which never in fact proved of much benefit; Achoris, a later king of the dynasty, engaged the services of Chabrias, a mercenary Athenian captain, who was, however, recalled to Athens on the complaint of Pharnabazus, the Persian satrap. In 373 BC a great attack was launched by Pharnabazus against Nectanebo I, then king of Egypt, the first ruler of the Thirtieth Dynasty which originated from Sebennytus in the Delta. The attack was, however, defeated by unexpected resistance and the arrival of the inundation. Further attacks were for the time averted by a revolt of satraps within the Persian Empire. Teos, the successor of Nectanebo I, felt himself strong enough in 360 BC to launch an attack on his own account against the Persians in Phoenicia. He enlisted the aid of the Spartans and Athenians but the expedition ended in a fiasco which resulted in Teos being supplanted by Nectanebo II, a young relative. Nectanebo II, like Nectanebo I before him, was a considerable builder and patron of the arts. His great granite sarcophagus is exhibited in the Egyptian Sculpture Gallery (10). The Persian king was now Artaxerxes Ochus and he determined to win back Egypt to the Persian Empire. After preliminary skirmishes the final assault was launched in 343 BC, and ended with the flight of Nectanebo II to Nubia. Once more Egypt became a satrapy of the Persian Empire and so she remained until 332 BC, the Persian kings being designated by some ancient writers as the Thirty-first Dynasty. Finally in 332 BC the Persian rule in Egypt was ended by the arrival of Alexander the Great who, although also a foreigner, was apparently welcomed as a deliverer. Alexander stayed for only a short time in Egypt but endeavoured to make himself acceptable to the native population by performing the necessary sacrifices to the gods of Memphis and by visiting the temple of Amun at Siwa. He was formally installed as Pharaoh and he reorganized the administration of the country. Before leaving Egypt to continue his campaign against the Persians he founded the city of Alexandria.

Ptolemaic Period (332–30 BC)

After its conquest by Alexander the Great, Egypt was organized as a province of the new Macedonian Empire. In 323 BC Alexander died suddenly and shortly afterwards Ptolemy Lagus was sent to Egypt as satrap by Philip Arrhidaeus. In the dissolution of the Macedonian Empire which occurred in the following years Ptolemy became more and more the master of an increasingly independent Egypt, but it was not until 305 BC that he finally became king of Egypt, taking the additional name of Soter ('Saviour') and establishing the so-called Ptolemaic Dynasty. Under the Ptolemies Egypt flourished and Egyptian civilization assumed a new appearance. In administration the country was organized on Greek lines with Greek becoming the official language; in art, new ideas were introduced from the Greek world, profoundly affecting the age-old traditions and conventions of Egyptian art (fig. 26); in military affairs the army

26 Schist head of a king

was fully reorganized on Macedonian lines and turned into an efficient fighting machine. In religious matters, however, the Ptolemies were careful not to offend the scruples of the native population and although many strange gods were introduced into Egypt during this time, both Greek and Asiatic, the principal deities of the Egyptian pantheon were sedulously cultivated. Some of the greatest temples were constructed during the Ptolemaic Period. In the reliefs in these temples the Ptolemies are regularly shown as kings in the ancient Egyptian manner and there is good reason to believe that they did in fact endeavour to behave as such; they adopted Egyptian royal titles and their names were written in cartouches. Their outlook, however, was very different and they paid particular attention to developing commerce; new ports were built and contacts with Asia and the classical lands developed. They were also enthusiastic patrons of learning and one of their finest memorials was the great library of Alexandria founded by Ptolemy I. Another enlightened ruler was Ptolemy V Epiphanes, who was an especial benefactor of the native temples; in his honour was passed the decree inscribed on the Rosetta Stone (24, fig. 28 and p. 82 f.). The rule of the Ptolemies did not, unfortunately, remain enlightened and energetic. By the early first century BC such empire as had been acquired in Asia was lost and internal control began to slacken. Dynastic squabbles increased the instability of the régime and the interest taken in Egyptian affairs by the Romans did not help to stabilize the situation. Under Ptolemy XII Auletes (80–51 BC), Roman intervention became actual and thereafter the Egyptian king was little more than a dependant on Rome. In 30 BC the Ptolemaic Dynasty ended with the death of Cleopatra VII and of Caesarion, and Egypt became formally a Roman province.

CHAPTER THREE

LANGUAGE, DECIPHERMENT AND WRITING MATERIALS

The ancient Egyptian language bears affinities to both the Semitic and the Hamitic groups of languages: at least 300 Semitic and 100 Hamitic words have been identified and, in addition, a number of words found in Egyptian seem to be shared by both groups. The following are some examples:

Egyptian	Semitic	Hamitic
m(w)t 'die'	mwth (Hebrew)	emmet (Berber)
nfr 'good'		nefir (Bedja)
djbꜥ 'finger'	isbaꜥ (Arabic)	giba (Bedja)
šms 'follow'		šimiš (Bedja)
gm 'find'		egmi (Touareg)
qfn 'bake'		ekref (Berber)
ḥsb 'count'	ḥasaba (Arabic)	

In order to account for these foreign elements the suggestion has been made that the language, as it is known to us, evolved independently after a fusion of races had taken place. Certainly the similarities appear to be too numerous to be explained as an outcome of commercial or other intercourse of infrequent or ephemeral kind. However, there is also reason to believe that ideas reached Egypt in very early times through occasional contacts with the inhabitants of other countries, even as far away as Mesopotamia, though by what channel is unknown. A number of inventions including the cylinder seal, stone mace-head of pear-shape and some distinctive artistic motifs, and architectural designs in brick, all of which were employed by Sumerians in Mesopotamia, were suddenly adopted in Egypt at the end of the period which preceded the foundation of the First Dynasty under Menes. Since no corresponding trace of Egyptian influence can be observed in the Sumerian products of the time (the so-called Jemdet Nasr and First Early Dynastic Period) it may be inferred that the movement was not in both directions. Egypt's debt to Sumer, however, does not seem to have been confined to the knowledge of a few artifacts and artistic conventions; certain words in the Egyptian language, particularly agricultural terms and the names of certain cereals, resemble very closely the corresponding terms in Sumerian and are almost certainly derived from the latter. Unquestionably the most important of Sumer's contributions must be counted the imparting of the principles of writing. It is true that the Sumerian syllabic signs expressed both consonants and vowels, whereas only the consonants were indicated in Egyptian hieroglyphs, but the basic method of using a sign to express not only the actual object which it represented but also other words or even parts of words having a like sound (the rebus principle) is common to both scripts. Furthermore, both scripts added sense-signs—the so-called determinatives—to words in order to indicate in a general way their meaning. The differences are of a kind which would be expected to occur in systems which developed independently; thus the determinative in Egyptian was placed at the end of a word while in Sumerian it was prefixed. The Egyptians alone employed signs representing single consonants (alphabetic signs) and, whereas in Sumer picture writing soon developed into the cuneiform script, the Egyptians retained the hieroglyphic script for nearly 3,500 years, from about 3100 BC until the end of the fourth century AD, the last known hiero-glyphic inscription, on the Island of Philae, being dated to AD 394. The latest hieroglyphic inscription in this collection is dated to AD 296 in the reign of Diocletian (1696).

At about the turn of the third century AD the Egyptians began to write their language in a script composed of the Greek alphabet, to which were added seven characters derived ultim-ately from hieroglyphs. In this form the language came to be known as Coptic (fig. 27), a word which is no doubt a corruption of the Greek word *Aiguptios*. Knowledge of how to read and to write the hieroglyphic script was lost probably soon after it had been superseded and no key to its meaning was discovered until 1799 when some French soldiers in Napoleon's army working under an officer named Bouchard found the Rosetta Stone (fig. 28) while digging the foundations of an addition to a fort,

27 Coptic ostracon recording the receipt of money (*below*)

28 The Rosetta Stone (*opposite*)

later called Fort Julien, near the town of Rashid (Rosetta) on the western arm of the Nile near the sea. The stone was ceded to the British under Article XVI of the Treaty of Alexandria in 1801. It reached this country in February 1802.

The immediate importance of the Rosetta Stone, as its discoverers realized, lay in the fact that the old Egyptian hieroglyphic text was accompanied by a Greek translation which could be read. A third inscription on the stone was written in demotic, a cursive script developed late in Egyptian history and used, almost exclusively, for secular documents: the language of the demotic version was Egyptian. Thus the stone displayed three scripts but only two languages, Egyptian and Greek.

For twenty years after the stone had reached this country attempts were made by European scholars to decipher the hieroglyphic and demotic texts. A Swedish diplomat named J. D. Åkerblad (1763–1819) was probably the first to achieve any substantial success when in 1802 he identified, by comparison with the Greek text, several proper names, e.g. Ptolemy, given in the demotic version; he also recognized, through knowing their Coptic equivalents, the words for 'Greeks' and 'temples' and the pronouns 'him' and 'his'. Dr. Thomas Young (1773–1829), the well-known physicist, was responsible in 1819 for the next important advance; among his contributions perhaps the most valuable was his demonstration of the correctness of a guess by the Abbé J. J. Barthélemy and C. J. de Guignes (1721–1800) that the groups of hieroglyphs written within oval rings (the so-called cartouches) on the Egyptian monuments gave the names of kings, and he was able to show that the name of Ptolemy, likewise within a cartouche, occurred several times on the Rosetta Stone. He also succeeded in equating eighty-six groups of signs in the demotic version with Greek words, but the phonetic values which he gave to these demotic groups were mostly incorrect.

Young's achievement, considerable though it must be reckoned, cannot be compared with that of Jean François Champollion (1790–1832), who must be regarded as the real decipherer of the Egyptian hieroglyphic script. What had been for Young probably little more than a pastime was for Champollion a burning passion. Moreover, with his greater familiarity with languages, Champollion was better equipped than Young.

Champollion's triumph may be said to have begun in 1822 when he was able to reaffirm Young's reading of the cartouches of the Rosetta Stone containing the name of Ptolemy, and also to substantiate Young's deduction that the name of Cleopatra occurred in a cartouche on a fallen obelisk found at Philae by W. J. Bankes in 1815 and transported in 1819, together with its base-block, to his park at Kingston Lacy, Dorset. The base-block bore a Greek inscription which mentioned both Ptolemy (Ptolemaios) and Cleopatra and since the hieroglyphs in one of the cartouches on the obelisk agreed with the supposed writing of the name Ptolemy on the Rosetta Stone it was conceivable that the other cartouches concealed the name of Cleopatra. Three of the signs in the cartouches were identical with the signs read P, O, and L in the cartouche of Ptolemy and their sequence was correct; only the T was different; but Champollion was not perplexed by this discrepancy because both he and Young had recognized that different signs could have the same values by the principle of homophony.

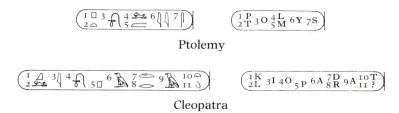

Ptolemy

Cleopatra

Champollion announced his discovery in September 1822 in a communication to the Académie des Inscriptions entitled *Lettre à Monsieur Dacier relative à l'alphabet des hiéroglyphes phonétiques.* Apart from Ptolemy and Cleopatra he was able to give the hieroglyphic writings and transcriptions of the names of more than seventy rulers of Egypt from Alexander the Great (332–323 BC) to Antoninus Pius (138–161 AD). No further demonstration of the predominantly phonetic nature of the hieroglyphic script, as used in Hellenistic and Roman times, was necessary, but it still remained to be proved that the character of the script was the same in pharaonic times. Almost immediately after the publication of his initial discoveries Champollion was able to decipher the cartouches of Ramesses and Tuthmosis, and by so doing to show that the principles underlying Egyptian hieroglyphs of the earlier period were not different from those which prevailed towards the end of their long history. Eighteen months later he published a book entitled *Précis du système hiéroglyphique* in which he gave, largely correctly, interpretations of not only a long list of royal names but also of words and phrases and even complete sentences. Before his death at the age of 42 on 4 March 1832, Champollion had made further substantial contributions to Egyptology including many additions to his repertoire of signs and words.

In order to appreciate the difficulties which confronted Champollion and the early decipherers it is necessary to bear in mind that the hieroglyphic script consists not of a short alphabet of the kind used by the Phoenicians and the Greeks in later times but of a very large number of signs. Approximately 700 different signs are now known and they can be divided into two main classes: (*a*) ideograms (from the Greek *idea* 'form' and *gramma* 'written character') or sense signs, and (*b*) phonograms (from the Greek *phone* 'sound' and *gramma* 'written character') or sound-signs. An ideogram indicates the meaning of a word pictorially without showing how it is to be read; thus the ideogram 𓇳 representing the sun may signify the sun itself or almost any word associated in meaning with the sun and its characteristics, e.g. light, brightness, day, to rise, to shine, etc. Similarly the ideogram 𓊛 may signify several kinds of boat, ship, or vessel and also the verbs expressing sailing. Phonograms indicate the consonantal spelling of words, but not the vowels. They are of three kinds: (1) alphabetic signs representing a single consonant, e.g. 𓂋 (the mouth) *r*, 𓂧 (the hand) *d*, 𓋴 (a piece of cloth) *s*; (2) biliteral signs representing two consonants, e.g. 𓉐 (a house) *pr*, 𓎟 (a basket) *nb*, 𓃹 (hare) *wn*; (3) triliteral signs representing three consonants, e.g. 𓊵 (a loaf on a mat) *ḥtp*, 𓄤 (heart and windpipe) *nfr*.

The Alphabet

Sign	*Transcription*	*Sound-value*
𓄿	(vulture) *ꜣ*	Glottal stop (as in 'bottle' when pronounced by a Cockney)
𓇋	(flowering reed) *ꞽ*	I
𓇌	(two flowering reeds) *y*	Y
𓏭	(oblique strokes) *y*	Y
𓂝	(forearm and hand) *ꜥ*	Ayin of the Semitic languages
𓅱	(quail chick) *w*	W
𓏲	(cursive development of 𓅱) *w*	W
𓃀	(foot) *b*	B
𓊪	(stool) *p*	P
𓆑	(horned viper) *f*	F
𓅓	(owl) *m*	M
𓈖	(water) *n*	N
𓂋	(mouth) *r*	R
𓉔	(reed shelter) *h*	H
𓎛	(wick of twisted flax) *ḥ*	slightly guttural *h*
𓐍	(placenta?) *ḫ*	CH (as in loch)
𓄡	(animal's belly) *ẖ*	slightly softer than *ḫ*

Sign	*Transcription*	*Sound-value*
𓊃	(door bolt) *s*	S
𓋴	(folded cloth) *s*	S
𓈙	(pool) *š*	SH
𓈎	(hill) *ḳ*	Q
𓎡	(basket with handle) *k*	K
𓎼	(jar-stand) *g*	G (as in goat)
𓏏	(loaf) *t*	T
𓍿	(tethering rope) *ṯ*	Tj
𓂧	(hand) *d*	D
𓆓	(snake) *ḏ*	Dj

All these letters are consonants, even though the weak 𓄿, 𓇋, and 𓅱 at the end of a syllable were probably assimilated to a preceding a, i, and u. Vowels were not written by the ancient Egyptians; it is therefore difficult, and often impossible, to ascertain the pronunciation of words, but it may be sometimes deduced from the Coptic derivatives. As a mere aid to pronunciation Egyptologists insert a short *e* between consonants, e.g. *ḥetep* 'rest', *per* 'house', using *a* for *ꜣ* and *ꜥ*, and *u* for *w*.

When writing a word the Egyptian scribe could, in most cases, adopt one of several different methods. He could write simply the ideogram, accompanied as a rule by a vertical stroke, e.g. 𓉐𓏤 (*per*) 'house', 𓇳𓏤 (*rꜥ*) 'sun'. More frequently, however, he would use phonograms followed by an ideogram which would convey the general meaning of the word (the ideogram in this position being called a determinative by modern grammarians), e.g. 𓂧𓊪𓏏𓊛 (*depet*) 'boat', 𓅱𓃀𓈖𓇳 (*weben*) 'rise', 'shine'. When a suitable biliteral or triliteral phonogram existed he would generally use it and frequently he would add some alphabetic signs, even if they were already included in the phonogram, e.g. 𓊵𓏏𓊪 (*ḥetep*) 'rest', which consists of the triliteral phonogram 𓊵 (*ḥtp*) plus *t* and *p*; 𓌻𓅓𓂋𓉴 (*mer*) 'pyramid' is composed of the biliteral sign 𓌻 (*mr*) plus *m* and *r* followed by a picture of a pyramid used as a determinative. So cumbrous and illogical does this multiplicity of signs seem that it is hard to understand the process of thought by which it was evolved, and even more difficult to imagine why it should have continued with so little development over so long a period of time.

To discover the significance of a hieroglyphic sign, and even to be able to read a royal name, though vital as preliminaries to further progress, would have been but barren achievements if it had not been possible also to translate the texts in which they occurred. That the decipherment of the script and the translation of words were able to proceed side by side and to assist each other was due, in the main, to the good fortune which allowed Coptic to survive until the sixteenth century as the language of the Christian population of Egypt. Even at the present day it is still read, though not understood, in the Coptic churches. Its vocabulary consists of Egyptian words supplemented by a considerable number of words borrowed directly from Greek. The following are examples of some Egyptian words and their Coptic equivalents:

⌒	(rȝ) mouth	ро	(ro)
(pt) heaven		пе	(pe)
(kmt) Egypt		кнмє	(keme)
(bin) bad		ḃⲱⲱⲛ	(boon)

Champollion realized the importance of Coptic and, at an early age, acquired a mastery of it. As a result, he was able to translate words in the Greek version of the Rosetta Stone into Coptic and, when he had discovered the principles of the hieroglyphic script, to search in the appropriate places in the hieroglyphic version for words which corresponded in spelling with those of his Coptic translations. His task was made more difficult because the hieroglyphic text was written, in accordance with the regular practice, without any division between the words. As the number of signs deciphered increased he was able to apply the same method in reverse and to translate into Coptic characters words which he could read in hieroglyphic texts and thus obtain the meaning. This method had, however, its limitations both because the Egyptian words which had been preserved in Coptic were few in comparison with the immense hieroglyphic vocabulary and because many words in Coptic had developed so far from their forms in earlier times as to be difficult to recognize as derivatives. When Coptic could offer no assistance in interpreting a word it was necessary to resort either to deduction, chiefly based on several occurrences of the same word in different contexts, or Hebrew in which were preserved many words from the common Semitic stock which had become incorporated into the Egyptian language. By these means scholars have succeeded in determining the reading of nearly all the hieroglyphic signs and the meaning of a very high proportion of the vocabulary.

In addition to hieroglyphic, Egyptians employed two other scripts, both of which were descendants of the hieroglyphic script, one directly and the other indirectly. The names given to these scripts are hieratic (from the Greek *hieratikos* 'priestly') and demotic (Greek *demotikos* 'popular'), sometimes called enchorial (Greek *enkhorios* 'native'), which has already been mentioned in connexion with the Rosetta Stone. They were thus named because in Greek times hieratic was used only for religious texts (although in earlier times it was also used for literary, business, and other secular documents), whereas demotic was reserved exclusively for secular purposes. In contrast with the hieroglyphic script, which could be written in either direction, hieratic and demotic were always written from right to left. They were usually written in ink on papyrus (fig. 29), potsherds, or flakes of limestone (fig. 30); only rarely and at a late date were they carved on stone (fig. 31).

Hieratic, in its earliest form, differs from hieroglyphic to no greater extent than would naturally happen as a result of using a rush pen instead of a pointed tool; the angular signs are more rounded and are drawn with less detail. Sporadic examples on stone dating from the First to the Third Dynasties are known, but the earliest considerable body of hieratic texts is a group of late Fifth Dynasty papyri from Abu Sir (fig. 32). By the Eleventh Dynasty it had developed into a much more distinctive and cursive script; in certain cases, two or more signs were joined to form a ligature. Texts were usually written in vertical columns, as often in hieroglyphic inscriptions, the signs being arranged so that when two or more stood side by side in a column they would

29 Hieratic letter of the Eleventh Dynasty (*left*)

30 Hieratic ostracon recording arrears of water for necropolis workers (*right*)

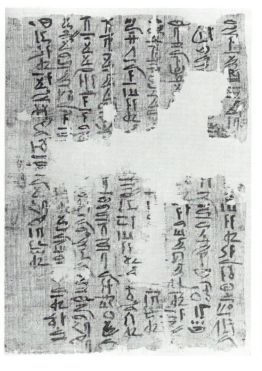

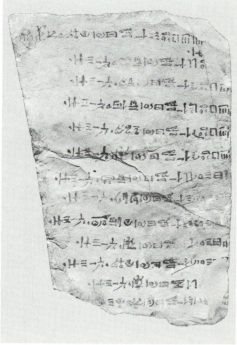

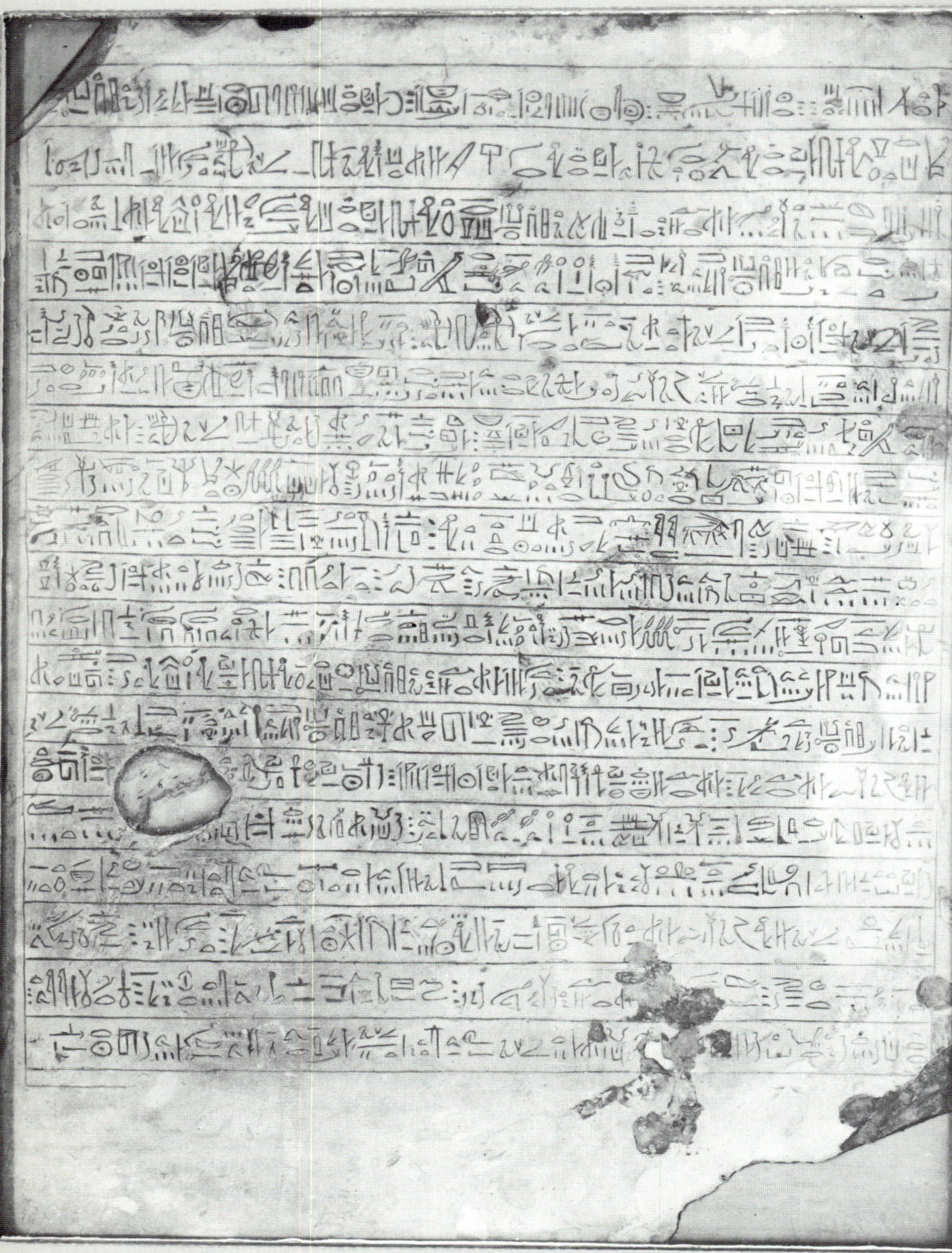

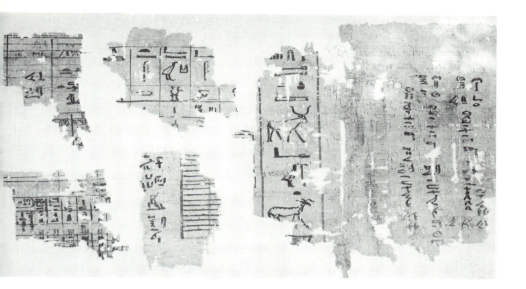

31 Twenty-first Dynasty hieratic copy of the decree establishing the *ka*-chapel of Amenhotpe, son of Hapu (*opposite*)

32 Old Kingdom temple accounts written in hieratic (*above*)

be read from right to left (fig. 32). In the Twelfth Dynasty this method was gradually discontinued and, instead, the Egyptian scribes began to write their texts in horizontal lines, a practice which not only was continued to the end of Egypt's history but also influenced the development of the script by allowing the writer to adopt a more cursive hand than would have been possible if he had been writing in vertical columns. This natural tendency was further aided by the avoidance of signs representing elaborate hieroglyphs, or by the substitution for such a sign of an oblique stroke, and by the introduction of some new signs, though these innovations were few in number. By the Eighteenth Dynasty a clear distinction existed between the well-formed hieratic used for literary purposes and the more cursive hieratic employed for business documents. So quickly did the divergence progress that long before the end of the New Kingdom the two scripts might not have been thought to be derived from a common ancestor. Moreover, two even more cursive scripts, namely demotic and the so-called abnormal hieratic, developed out of the business hieratic of the late New Kingdom. Not more than about forty-five documents written in abnormal hieratic have been identified (of which one long text is in this Museum, 10798). One of the earliest, dealing with the sale of a collection of *shabtis* (10800), dates probably to the Twenty-second Dynasty and so clearly belongs to the formative period of the script. In its fully developed form abnormal hieratic does not occur until the reign of Piankhi (Twenty-fifth Dynasty); the latest document dates to the first half of the reign of Amosis II (Twenty-sixth Dynasty).

Demotic documents (fig. 33), which are numbered in hundreds, extend over a period of a thousand years from the twenty-first year of Psammetichus I (Twenty-sixth Dynasty) to the middle of the fifth century AD. From the evidence available at present it seems that demotic originated in Lower Egypt, spread southwards in Saite times and quickly superseded abnormal hieratic, itself a product of Upper Egypt. Examples of hieratic and demotic dating from many different periods are shown in the Third and Fourth Egyptian Rooms.

Of the various materials, apart from stone, on which the ancient Egyptians wrote their documents, the most important was certainly papyrus. The derivation of the Greek word *papyros*, first found in the writings of the philosopher and natural historian Theophrastus (fourth–third centuries BC), is unknown. It is, however, most probably a word representing *pa-per-aa* 'that of a king', so called because in Greek times the production of papyrus may have been a royal monopoly. It is used with reference both to the plant *Cyperus papyrus* (which in ancient times grew in abundance in the marshes and pools of Egypt, but it is not now found in the Nile Valley north of Khartum) and to the writing material made from the stems of the plant. Satisfactory results have been obtained in practical experiments in manufacturing the writing material in this Museum by the following method: The long stems were first cut into pieces, each about 30 cms in length. After peeling off the rind, the pith was cut lengthwise into fairly thin slices which were placed side by side. A second layer of slices was then laid above the first and at right-angles to it. The two layers were then either pressed or beaten until they became welded together. No adhesive of any kind was used apart from the natural starch in the juice which was discharged from the slices during pressing or beating. When this method was used on mature stems a tendency to blotchiness, which had occurred with young stems, was absent and a smooth white surface was produced. Probably even greater smoothness could have been achieved by burnishing the papyrus with a stone or wooden polisher when it was thoroughly dry. The finished sheet possessed an upper surface with horizontal fibres (known as 'recto') and an under surface with vertical fibres ('verso').

Papyrus was made in sheets which never exceeded about 48 cms in height and about 43 cms in width. Several of the sheets might be joined by pasting the edges together so that the fibres ran in the same direction in all the sheets, and the long strip thus produced would be rolled with the horizontal fibres on the inside, until it was required for use. Specimens of both the widest and the longest papyri at present known are exhibited in the Third Egyptian Room. The widest, a Book of the Dead, named after its

33 Upper part of a demotic document dated 270 BC

34 The Great Harris Papyrus

donor the Greenfield Papyrus (10554), measures 49·5 cms in width; the longest, the so-called Great Harris Papyrus (9999, fig. 34), is 41 metres in length. As an invention papyrus seems to be as old as the hieroglyphic script, for an uninscribed roll was identified in the mastaba of a First Dynasty noble named Hemaka at Saqqara. The earliest written examples are the fragmentary temple account books of the late Fifth Dynasty from Abu Sir, most of which are now in this collection (10735, fig. 32).

As a rule, a scribe, holding the roll in his left hand, wrote first on the side which had horizontal fibres, the 'recto'. When writing in vertical columns he began at the outer end of the roll and added column on to column, unrolling the papyrus as he progressed, until he had either reached the inner end or completed what he had to write. A different method was necessary when writing in horizontal lines; the scribe would write a top line of whatever length he wished and then write successive lines of the same length until he had reached the bottom of the page, when he would unroll more of the papyrus and write a further 'page' in the same way but not necessarily of the same width. Blank spaces between the pages varied from document to document but they were generally not less than about 1·5 cms or more than about 2·5 cms. The action of 'writing' with a rush pen resembled painting, the hand being held away from the written surface and not resting upon it. There was, therefore, no danger of smudging what had been written.

35   Hieratic ostracon with an excerpt from an inquiry into the ownership of a tomb

Other materials used by scribes were flakes of white limestone and potsherds (both of which are called ostraca by Egyptologists) and wooden boards, frequently overlaid with gesso. In contrast with papyri, documents written on these materials were generally of an ephemeral character, e.g. school exercises, drafts of contracts, deeds and letters, records of attendance at work, inventories, magical texts, oracles (fig. 35), etc.; these materials were also used for plans and sketches (41228, 8506–8, and 5601). The wooden boards covered with gesso painted white were probably used in schools for hieratic texts intended as models for students to copy; each board has a small hole bored in it, probably to hold a leather thong on which it could be suspended from a peg when not in use. The text on a board could be washed off, and, if necessary, the board could be repainted or resurfaced with gesso and used many times for different texts. A selection of the Museum's collection of more than 8,000 ostraca and of writing boards is exhibited in the Fourth Egyptian Room. Dressed leather and vellum were sometimes used for documents of a kind more often written on papyrus, e.g. a series of additions of fractions written on leather which a scribe probably used as a mathematical table (10250, c. 1700 BC) and the Book of the Dead of the late Eighteenth Dynasty scribe Nakht (10471 and 10473) written partly on vellum and partly on papyrus. Ivory, clay, and linen were also used and, at least in late times, even bronze, as is shown by two Ptolemaic-Roman tablets inscribed in demotic and hieroglyphs (57371 and 57372).

The trade-mark of the Egyptian scribe was his palette. As a rule it was made of a rectangular piece of wood, from 20–43 cms long, from 5–8 cms in width, and about 1·5 cms in thickness. At one end were two, and sometimes several, cavities for holding black, red, and other inks in the form of solid cakes. Black ink was made of carbon and red ink consisted of finely ground red ochre: both were mixed with a weak solution of gum so that they congealed when they dried. In order to dissolve the ink again it was only necessary for the scribe to dip his brush in water and rub it on the surface of the cake, as would be done with modern water-colour paint. The brush itself was made of the stem of a rush, *Juncus maritimus*, which was shortened to about 15–25 cms in length, the tip being first cut on a slant and then chewed by the scribe to break up the fibres. Brushes were kept in a slot carved out of the middle of the palette (fig. 36). In the later examples the slot is sometimes partly covered by a sliding lid. Pens made of a reed, *Phragmites*

36   Wooden scribal palettes

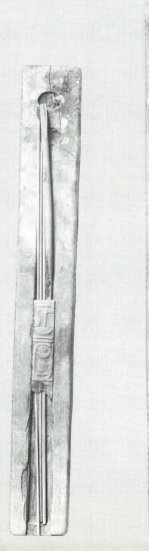

communis, cut to a point and split in two at the tip were first used by Greeks residing in Egypt in the third century BC. A series of palettes ranging in date from the Sixth Dynasty to the New Kingdom is exhibited in the Fourth Egyptian Room. Many of the examples show hieratic inscriptions in ink, some of which appear to be notes scribbled by the scribe, e.g. measurements and records of sacks delivered (5524), names (12783), accounts (5518), etc. The hieroglyphic inscriptions are generally invocations to Thoth, the god of writing, and in consequence they may indicate that the palettes were part of their owners' funerary equipment.

Proficiency in the art of writing was not easily acquired. Pupils in the scribal schools were first set to copy excerpts from well-known literary works, one of the most common apparently being the so-called *Book of Kemit* (e.g. ostracon 5640), a didactic composition which is devoted partly to enunciating moral principles and partly to extolling the profession of the scribe. Ostraca inscribed with excerpts from this book invariably date from the New Kingdom: they are, however, written in a large hand and the text is arranged in vertical columns so that they resemble the hieratic documents of the Middle Kingdom. These anomalies are probably to be explained as evidence that pupils were taught to write in the bold script of the Middle Kingdom before they developed their own style of handwriting. As their skill advanced the pupils copied not only the classics of Egyptian literature but also model letters, mathematical exercises and lists of technical words, place-names, etc. (e.g. the Hood Papyrus, 10202, and a leather strip, 10379). Their copies were often imperfect but the fact that so much has been preserved of what the ancient Egyptians regarded as their most important literary and educational productions is due mainly to their schoolboys.

Scribes enjoyed certain privileges, including relief from taxation. Their profession was frequently contrasted favourably with other occupations in compositions which pupils in schools were set to copy (e.g. Anastasi Papyrus II–V, 10243, 10246, 10249, and 10244; Papyrus Sallier I, 10185 and Papyrus Lansing, 9994). Nowhere, however, is their profession more highly evaluated than in the Chester Beatty Papyrus IV (10684):

As for those learned scribes from the time of the successors of the gods, (even) those who foretold the future, it has come to pass that their names endure forever, although they themselves are gone, having completed their lifespan and all their kindred are forgotten.

They did not make for themselves pyramids of copper or stelae of iron. They could not leave children as heirs to pronounce their names; they made as heirs for themselves the writings and books of instruction which they had compiled.[1]

[1] For the whole text, see Gardiner (1935), 38–9.

CHAPTER FOUR

EGYPTIAN LITERARY AND OTHER WRITINGS

Egyptian writings are generally classified both according to their subject-matter and according to the phase of the language to which they belong. Three main phases are distinguishable to which grammarians have given the following names: Old Egyptian (First–Eighth Dynasties, *c.* 3100–2160 BC), Middle Egyptian (Ninth–Mid-Eighteenth Dynasties, *c.* 2160–1380 BC) and Late Egyptian (Mid-Eighteenth–Twenty-fourth Dynasties, *c.* 1380–715 BC). It was the second of these phases, Middle Egyptian, which the Egyptians themselves regarded as the classical phase, the writings of which served as models in schools in later times; it was also Middle Egyptian which the scribes of the Twenty-fifth and Twenty-sixth Dynasties (*c.* 747–525 BC) adopted in their literary compositions. Late Egyptian became common in documents of the Amarna Period, apparently owing to a deliberate attempt by Akhenaten to break away from the traditional literary style in order to bring the written language into line with the vernacular. Unlike his artistic innovations it survived the collapse of his revolution and continued in use for many generations thereafter; indeed some of the best-known literary works in Late Egyptian date from the Nineteenth and Twentieth Dynasties.

Even without taking historical records into account (see Chapter 2) the variety of subject displayed in Egyptian literature is surprisingly wide. Among the different branches, most of which are represented in the Museum's collection, the following are perhaps the most interesting:

Wisdom literature

The texts in this category deal chiefly with practical wisdom. As their Egyptian title 'Instructions' would suggest, they are didactic works composed of maxims and precepts. One of the earliest examples is the *Instruction of Ptahhotep*, a vizier of the Fifth-dynasty king Djedkare Isesi (*c.* 2380 BC), who complains to the king that he has grown old and wishes to make way for his son. The king tells him to instruct his son in behaviour appropriate in a high official for 'there is no one born wise'. The instruction begins with these words: 'Do not be arrogant because you are learned; do not be over-confident because you are well-informed. Consult the ignorant man as well as the wise one.' More than forty maxims follow and the discourse ends with the assurance that if the young man reaches his father's position sound in body and the king is contented with his work then he shall enjoy a long life. One of the earliest known copies of these instructions is contained in papyrus 10371, written about 2000 BC.[1]

An indication of the popularity of another didactic work, *The Instruction of Ammenemes I*, is the fact that part of it is preserved in no fewer than four papyri (of which one is Papyrus Sallier I, 10185, verso 8), a leather roll, now in the Louvre, three wooden tablets and about fifty ostraca (e.g. 5623, 5638). One papyrus only (Papyrus Sallier II, 10182) contains the entire work, but it is far from accurate. All these texts date from the New Kingdom. In content this composition differs from the other wisdom literature in so far as it is more biographical. Like the earlier *Instruction to Merikare*, which is preserved on an Eighteenth Dynasty papyrus at Leningrad, it consists of advice given by a king to his son and heir. In the case of Ammenemes I, the first king of the Twelfth Dynasty, the alleged reason for issuing the 'Instruction' was an attempt on his life which may have been caused by a harim conspiracy. Apart from describing the attack and giving his son advice, the aged king narrates some of his achievements and confirms that he has chosen as his successor his son Sesostris I who had already been co-regent for ten years.[2] Some authorities, who believe that the assassination took place, regard this 'Instruction' as a work composed after the event, the author being a scribe named Achthoes of Sebennytus about whom another papyrus in the collection (Papyrus Chester Beatty IV, 10684) says: 'It was he who made a book as the (?) Instruction of King Sehetepibre' (i.e. Ammenemes I). This same Achthoes, the son of Duauf, was certainly the author of a well-known 'Book of Instruction' (also part of Papyrus Sallier II, 10182, and Papyrus Anastasi VII, 10222; extracts are given in Papyrus Chester Beatty XIX, 10699 and on an ostracon 29550). In the introduction he states that he composed it for his son Pepi 'as he sailed south to the Residence, to place him in the school for scribes, among the children of magistrates, the foremost of the Residence'. Commonly known as the *Satire of the Trades*, this work glorifies the profession of the scribe by enumerating the hardships associated with other occupations. Its main theme is expressed in the words 'See, there is no occupation free from directors except for that of the scribe: he is his own director'.[3]

Because they contain many ideas which are also expressed in the Old Testament Book of Proverbs, the thirty chapters of the *Teaching of Amenemope, son of Kanakht* (10474, fig. 37),[4] have attracted much attention both from Egyptologists and from

[1] Translations of the whole text: Erman (1927), 54–66; Pritchard (1955), 412–14; Simpson (1972), 159–76; Lichtheim (1973), 61–83. Papyri 10371, 10435, and 10509.

[2] Translations: Erman (1927), 72–4; Pritchard (1955), 418–19; Simpson (1972), 193–7 Lichtheim (1973), 135–9.

[3] Translations: Erman (1927), 67–72; Pritchard (1955), 432–4; Lichtheim (1973), 184–92.

[4] Translations: Pritchard (1955), 421–5; Simpson (1972 241–65.

37 Part of a papyrus containing *The Teaching of Amenemope, son of Kanakht*

Biblical scholars. An almost verbal parallel occurs, for example, in the opening lines of the first chapter: 'Give your ears, listen to the words which are spoken, give your mind to interpreting them. It is profitable to put them in your heart' (cf. Proverbs xxii. 17). Although some authorities have suggested that it was Amenemope who made use of an earlier Hebrew compilation of proverbs, most critics have argued that the loan was in the other direction. The text, which is completely preserved in the papyrus, was probably copied in the Twenty-first Dynasty (*c.* 1000 BC), but the composition is believed to be from a work which is considerably older.

Only two books of instruction which were actually composed in the New Kingdom have yet to come to light. The more famous, known as the *Maxims of Ani,* is preserved on a papyrus (Papyrus Boulaq IV) in the Cairo Museum, but two extracts are included in the Chester Beatty Papyrus V (10685). The author of the second book, the fullest version of which is found on an ostracon in this collection (41541) bore the name Amennakht. Both these authors were sacerdotal scribes, Ani in the funerary temple of Queen Nefertari and Amennakht in the so-called 'House of Life'—an institution associated with several temples in Egypt where religious and secular works were composed and copied. In this respect, at least, the books differed from the older wisdom literature, some of which was produced by kings and the rest by officials in the royal circle.[1]

Translations of the *Maxims of Ani:* Erman (1927), 234–42; Pritchard (1955), 20–1; French translation only of the *Instructions of Amennakht: Rd'E* 10 (1955), 61–72.

A book of instruction contained in a demotic papyrus (10508, fig. 38), dating to the late Ptolemaic Period, *c.* 100 BC, is named after its writer *The Instructions of Onkhsheshonqy.* In the Introduction Onkhsheshonqy son of Tchainefer relates how he was imprisoned for complicity in a plot against Pharaoh and wrote

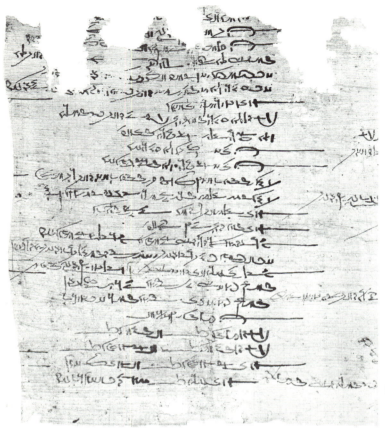

38 Part of a papyrus
containing *The
Instructions of
Onkhsheshonqy*

39 Part of the *Story of
the Eloquent Peasant*

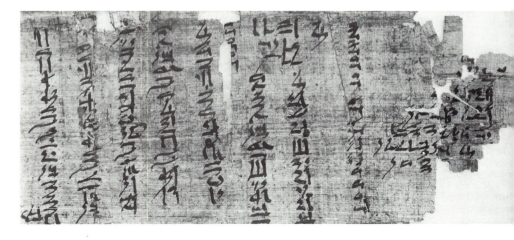

the instructions for his son from prison. The insistence on practical instruction is close to that embodied in the *Maxims of Ani*: 'Do not long for your home when you are at work', 'Do not drink at a merchant's house, he will charge you for it' and 'Do not acquire wealth until you have a strong-room'; the high moral tone of Amenemope is lacking. There is a likelihood that Onkhsheshonqy's collection of proverbs was first compiled only a few centuries before their commital to papyrus: there does not seem to be a Middle Kingdom original at their root.[1]

The *Story of the Eloquent Peasant* (partly preserved in the Butler Papyrus of the Twelfth Dynasty, 10274, fig. 39), although generally classed as a narrative, may also be regarded as a treatise on equity with a narrative background.[2] In the course of a journey to Egypt to sell the products of his plot of land, a peasant of Wadi Natrun, by a trick, is robbed of his asses by an Egyptian landowner. Having failed to persuade the landowner to return the asses, he goes to the high steward, who tries to help him by bringing an action against the landowner before the local magistrates but is unsuccessful. The peasant again appeals to the high steward to use his influence on his behalf. So greatly is the high steward impressed by the peasant's eloquence that he goes to tell the king about it. The king instructs the high steward to provide the peasant with food and to detain him so that he may go on speaking, and tells the high steward to write down what he says. Nine petitions were then recorded on papyrus and sent to the king who, when he had read them, was so impressed that he ordered the high steward to give judgement himself in favour of the peasant and to reward him with not only the restoration of his own asses and their loads, but also the possessions of the unjust landowner. Another Twelfth Dynasty papyrus (10754) preserves fragments of a somewhat similar work containing the moral sayings of a scribe named Sisobk, who was imprisoned but eventually released upon a petition of a dancer.

Meditations and pessimistic literature

The years of political unrest and social and economic instability which followed the Old Kingdom (pp. 48 ff.) furnished the setting for a class of literature which was invariably pessimistic and sometimes prophetic in character. At least one of the works in this category, the *Admonitions of Ipuwer*,[3] which is preserved on a papyrus dating from the New Kingdom in the Leiden Museum, may well have been composed before the end of this troubled period. Another work, which seems to be of the same date, is a remarkable *Dialogue of a Pessimist with his Soul*[4] (Berlin Museum, 3024) in which a man contemplates suicide

Translation: Glanville (1955).

Translations: Erman (1927), 116–31; Pritchard (1955), 407–0; Simpson (1972), 31–49; Lichtheim (1973), 169–84.

Translations: Gardiner (1909); Erman (1927), 92–108; Simpson (1972), 210–9; Lichtheim (1973), 149–63.

Translations: Erman (1927), 86–92; Pritchard (1955), 405–7; Goedicke (1970), 211–17; Simpson (1972), 201–9; Lichtheim (1973), 163–9.

but is dissuaded by his soul. As a piece of literature it belongs to the same *genre* as the Book of Job, but it is far inferior in spiritual content.

With its setting in the court of Sneferu, the first king of the Fourth Dynasty, the *Prophecy of the Great Lector Priest Neferty* (completely preserved only in Leningrad Papyrus 1116B, but an excerpt is inscribed on a writing-board of the Eighteenth Dynasty in this collection, 5647, verso) presents a dismal account of conditions in the future from which the country would ultimately be saved by the advent of a king from the south named Ameny who would build the 'Walls of the Prince' in the eastern Delta and thereby prevent the incursions of marauding bands of Asiatics.[1] Since Ameny is almost certainly to be identified with Ammenemes I, the first king of the Twelfth Dynasty, it may be conjectured that the 'prophecy' was composed during his reign to bolster his claim to the throne. The wickedness of men and the corruption of society are the main theme of another well-known pessimistic work attributed to a priest of Heliopolis, Khakheperreseneb, found on an Eighteenth Dynasty writing-board (5645 and fig. 40). It is clear from the name of the writer, which embodies the prenomen of Sesostris II, that these *Meditations of Khakheperreseneb*[2] cannot date from earlier than the second half of the Twelfth Dynasty but there can be little doubt that the conditions to which they refer were those which prevailed in the First Intermediate Period. Pessimism of a different kind is reflected in the so-called *Song of the Harper* (Papyrus Harris 500, 10060): the transitoriness of life and scepticism

40 Eighteenth Dynasty writing board containing the *Meditations of Khakheperreseneb*

[1] Translations: Erman (1927), 110–15; Pritchard (1955), 444–6; Simpson (1972), 234–40; Lichtheim (1973), 139–45.

[2] Translations: Gardiner (1909), 95–112; Erman (1927), 108–10; Simpson (1972), 230–3; Lichtheim (1973), 145–9.

concerning the next life are the subjects with which it deals: 'Those who built chapels, their places are no more . . . their walls are destroyed . . . as though they had never been'—and it recommends a hedonistic attitude towards the present life:

Be glad therefore; forgetfulness is profitable to you.

Follow your desire as long as you live. Put myrrh on your head, clothe yourself in fine linen. . . .

Do things (while) you are on earth. Do not be upset until that day of lamentation comes to you. . . .

Make holiday and do not weary of it. See, no-one is allowed to take his goods with him and no-one who has gone comes back again.[1]

The preface to this song states that it was inscribed in front of the figure of a harpist in the tomb of one of the kings called Inyotef—very probably one of the Inyotefs of the Eleventh Dynasty—but the extant copies all date from the New Kingdom.

A similar theme is expressed in an inscription on a stela of Late Ptolemaic date (147) in which a deceased woman named Taimuthes addresses her husband from her tomb. She says:

O my brother, my kinsman, my friend, the Greatest of the Master-Craftsmen (i.e. High Priest of Ptah), cease not to drink, to eat, to get drunk and to make love. Make holiday, pursue your desire day and night. Do not allow anxiety in your heart. How many are our years upon earth? As for the West [the land of the dead] it is a land of sleep and darkness, a burdensome place for those who dwell in it. The glorious ones sleep in their god-like forms; they cannot awake to see their brothers; they cannot look upon their fathers and mothers; they lack wives and children. . . . Would that I had flowing water (to drink). . . . Would that my face were turned towards the north wind on the river bank. . . .

Poetry, lyrics, and hymns

Vowels not being represented in writing it is impossible to discover any strict metre in Egyptian poetical compositions. What can be detected is a strophic arrangement generally consisting of three or four lines, each strophe often beginning with the same word. Parallelism of construction and of meaning, alliteration, and even word-play were also devices employed in poetry but so far no trace of rhyme has been found. The excerpt from the *Song of the Harper* already quoted demonstrates both that a standard comparable with the level of some of the poetical passages in the Old Testament was sometimes attained, and also that strict metre was not a necessary element in the structure of Egyptian lyrics. In every probability each line consisted of a certain number of accented syllables separated by a number of unaccented, or only weakly accented, syllables as in Coptic poetry of Christian times.

Translations:
man (1927), 132–4;
itchard (1955), 467;
mpson (1972), 306–7;
chtheim (1973),
4–7.

Music and singing were regular concomitants of daily occupations and religious festivals in Egypt. Workers in the fields sang
simple folk songs as they laboured, guests at dinner-parties were
entertained by songs and dances while they ate and drank, and
the gods were worshipped by laudatory hymns often sung to the
accompaniment of the harp. No recognizable musical notation
seems to have been devised so that the tunes played are lost, but
the words of many songs and hymns have been preserved. A song,
which accompanies a threshing scene in the beautifully
decorated tomb of an Eighteenth Dynasty nobleman named
Pahery at El-Kab, is put in the mouth of a herdsman as he drives
the oxen pulling the threshing sledge:

> Thresh for yourselves, thresh for yourselves, you oxen.
> Thresh for yourselves, thresh for yourselves.
> Straw for (you) to eat, corn for your masters.
> Let not your hearts grow weary; there is refreshment (?).

A painting from the tomb of a Theban nobleman named
Nebamun (37984, Plate 9), who lived in the middle of the
Eighteenth Dynasty, reproduces a banqueting scene in which
the guests are entertained by dancers, a woman playing two
reed-pipes and three singers who also beat time by clapping
their hands. Part of their song, written in the spaces between
the musicians and the dancers, reads as follows:

> [Flowers of sweet] scents which Ptah sends and Geb makes to grow.
> His beauty is in every body.
> Ptah has done this with his own hands to gladden (?) his heart.
> The pools are filled anew with water.
> The earth is flooded with his love.

Love songs no doubt originated as simple spontaneous
utterances, but by the time they were committed to writing in
the Nineteenth Dynasty they had become rather artificial and
studied; they had ceased to be intimate exchanges and had
developed into songs sung at banquets. Among three cycles of
such songs in the Papyrus Harris 500 (10060) is one in which
a maiden describes the flowers in her garden, the names of which
bring to her mind some fresh thought about her lover:

> There are *saamu*-flowers in it before which we are glorified. I am
> your foremost sister. I am yours as is the acre of land which I made to
> flourish with flowers and all manner of sweet-scented herbs. Pleasant
> is the channel in it which you dug with your own hand for our refresh-
> ment in the north wind, a beautiful place for walking hand in hand. My
> body is satisfied and my heart rejoicing at our going together. Hearing
> your voice is pomegranate wine: I live when I hear it. If ever I see you
> it is better for me than eating and drinking.

In the first cycle of songs in this papyrus, containing many references to the Memphite region, a young man outlines the way in which he will trick his love into visiting him:

I shall lie down inside and feign sickness.
My neighbours shall come in to see me
and my girl will come and put the physicians to shame
For she knows my disease.[1]

The Chester Beatty Papyrus I, which is not in the collection, has a cycle of seven songs each with its own title. In the first song the lover describes his mistress as

One alone, a mistress without equal, more beautiful than mortal man . . . her excellence shines bright, her skin gleams, her eyes are beautiful when she gazes, sweet her lips when she speaks. . . . She steals my heart in her embrace. She turns the head of every man, captivating him at sight.[2]

A papyrus of the Second Intermediate Period, or slightly later, now in the Moscow Museum, preserves a group of hymns which date back to the Old Kingdom. By the time when the papyrus was written, the hymns had been adapted to the cult of the crocodile-god Sobk (to whom a hymn on a Twelfth Dynasty papyrus from the Ramesseum, 10759, is also dedicated), but originally they were intended for the veneration of the royal crowns and the king himself. They depend mainly on parallelism for their effect and are rather monotonous, but they show that even in the third millennium BC the Egyptians had gained some appreciation of literary form. Far better, both in imagery and in their use of metaphor, are some hymns to King Sesostris III of the Twelfth Dynasty (c. 1878–1843 BC):

How great is the lord for his city: he is a refuge which rescues one in fear from his enemy.
How great is the lord for his city: he is a cool and refreshing shade in summertime.
How great is the lord for his city: he is a warm dry corner in wintertime.
How great is the lord for his city: he is a mountain which shuts out the storm when heaven rages.[3]

[1] Translations: Simpson (1972), 297–306, 308–15.
[2] Translation: Simpson (1972), 315–25.
[3] Translations: Simpson (1972), 279–84; Lichtheim (1973), 198–201.

Several Pharaohs of the New Kingdom from Tuthmosis II onwards were the subjects of *Victory Hymns*, generally inscribed on stelae which were set up in their temples. Tuthmosis III's victory hymn, carved on a stela from Karnak now in the Cairo Museum, is partly written in prose, but the middle portion is clearly poetical and is divided into ten stanzas, each beginning with the words 'I have come'. The speaker is none less than the god Amun himself.

I have come
That I may grant to you to trample on the chiefs of Phoenicia,
That I may strew them beneath your feet throughout their lands;
That I may cause them to see your majesty as Lord of Rays
  When you shine in their faces in my image.
I have come
That I may grant to you to trample on those who are in Asia
  And smite the heads of the Asiatics of Syria;
That I may cause them to see your majesty equipped with your panoply,
  When you take up the weapons of war in the chariot.[1]

Ramesses II in his hymn on a stela at the temple of Abu Simbel adopted a less repetitive mode of presentation and also employed a much more graphic style as the following excerpt will show:

. . . A jackal swift of foot seeking his attacker, traversing the circuit of the earth in a moment of time . . . who puts to flight the Asiatics, fighting upon the battlefield. They break their bows and are given over to the fire. His might has power over them, as when a flame seizes hold of scrubland, and a storm-wind is behind it; like a fierce flame when it has tasted the heat of the blaze and all within it scream as they are destroyed. King of Upper and Lower Egypt, Ramesses.

Ruler mighty in destroying those who know not his name; like a hurricane howling loudly (?) over the ocean and its waves are like mountains and none can approach it; but all that are in it are sunk in the Underworld. King of Upper and Lower Egypt, Ramesses.

The bold images of this piece are not typical of Ramesside style. A more representative example of court poetry of the period is the Battle of Qadesh poem which Ramesses had recorded on the walls of many of his temples. Part of this poem is contained in two papyri, Chester Beatty III (10683) and Sallier III (10181). In the latter:

His majesty appeared like Montu. He put on his panoply of war, he donned his armour. He was like Baal in his might . . . Their hearts become faint in their bodies; their arms grow weak and they cannot shoot their arrows. (His majesty) plunged them into the water as crocodiles plunge.

The Nile and many of the gods were worshipped in hymns which often display deep religious feeling. *The Hymn to the Nile* (Papyrus Sallier II, Papyrus Anastasi VII, and Papyrus Chester Beatty V, 10182, 10222, and 10685) is thought to have been composed in the Middle Kingdom but the earliest extant copies, all very corrupt, date from the Nineteenth Dynasty (*c.* 1250 BC).

Hail O Nile, who issues forth from the earth, who comes to give life to
  the people of Egypt. Secret of movement, a darkness in daylight.
Praised by his followers whose fields you water.
Created by Re to give life to all who thirst.

[1] Translation: Simpson (1972), 285–8.

Who lets the desert drink with streams descending from heaven.
Beloved of the earth-god, controller of the corn-god, who causes the
    workshops of Ptah to flourish.
Lord of fish who causes the water-fowl to sail upstream . . .
Who makes barley and creates wheat so that temples celebrate . . .
When the Nile overflows, offerings are made to you, cattle are slaughtered
    for you, a great oblation is made to you, birds are fattened for you,
    desert lions are trapped for you that your goodness be repaid.[1]

Hymns to the sun-god date back to the royal Pyramid Texts of
the Fifth and Sixth Dynasties. By the time of the Eighteenth
Dynasty they were often inscribed on the walls of private tombs
and on the funerary stelae of private persons. At that time also
they began to represent the sun-god, Amen-Re, as the universal
creator, a conception which is well exemplified in a sun-hymn
carved on a stela of two architects named Suty and Hor, who
lived in the reign of Amenophis III (826, fig. 52).

> Creator are you, fashioner of your own limbs;
> One who brings into being, himself unborn;
> Unique in his qualities, traversing eternity
> Upon roads with millions under his guidance.

In this same hymn the unique position of the sun-god and his
authority over all lands and peoples is unequivocally stated:

> Sole lord taking captive all lands every day,
> As one beholding those that walk therein.

Only a few years after this text had been carved, Amenophis III's
son, Akhenaten, composed his famous *Hymn to Aten*, the sun's
disk, which has often been compared with Psalm 104 and which
is the first truly monotheistic composition in the literature of the
world. Its key-note is the all-embracing love of Aten for the works
which he has created:

> . . . At dawn when you rise in the horizon, when you shine as the
> Aten by day, you dispel darkness and give forth your rays. The Two
> Lands are in festival, they wake up and stand on their feet for you have
> raised them up. They cleanse their bodies and put on their clothes, their
> arms are raised in praise at your appearance. The whole land performs
> its work. All beasts are content with their pasturage. Trees and plants
> grow green. The birds fly from their nests, their wings (stretched) in
> praise of your spirit. All small beasts skip upon their feet, all that fly
> and alight live because you have arisen. Boats sail north and south like-
> wise; all roads open at your appearance. The fish in the river leap before
> you; your rays are in the depths of the ocean.
> Creator of the foetus in women, maker of seed in men, who creates
> life in the son in the womb of his mother, soothing him that he may not
> weep; nurse in the womb who gives breath that all may live whom he
> has made. . . .

[1] Translation:
Lichtheim (1973),
204-10.

How countless are your works! But they are concealed from sight. O unique god like whom there is no other. You created the earth according to your desire when you were alone: all men, all creatures great and small which are upon earth going on their feet and that which is aloft flying upon wings; the foreign lands too, Syria, Nubia and Egypt herself. You set each man in his place and provide their requirements; everyone has his sustenance and his lifespan is reckoned. Their tongues are distinguished in speech and their natures likewise. Their complexions are different. You have distinguished foreign peoples. . . .[1]

The hymn ends with lines in which Akhenaten expresses his belief that he alone on earth has true knowledge of the Aten and his intentions towards mankind. It was probably part of the ritual performed by Akhenaten in the temple of Aten at Amarna. Clear evidence that hymns were sung in temple services is afforded by a papyrus (Chester Beatty IX, recto, 10689) which includes hymns to be sung by the whole congregation.

In addition to hymns glorifying the principal deities, Egyptian religious literature includes a few examples of poetical compositions of a very different kind. They are more intimate and in many respects they resemble the penitential psalms of the Old Testament. Some are written on papyrus, e.g. a prayer to Amun by a poor litigant in court (Papyrus Anastasi II, 10243, recto viii. 5–ix. 1), but the majority are carved on the stelae of humble workmen of the Nineteenth Dynasty, who dwelt at Deir el-Medina and whose lives were spent carving and painting the tombs of the kings and nobles at Thebes. A member of that community named Neferabu, who had been stricken with blindness for swearing falsely by the god Ptah, has left the following message to posterity on his stela (589):

I am a man who swore falsely by Ptah, Lord of Truth; and he caused
    me to see darkness in daylight.
I shall proclaim his power to the one who does not know him, and the
    one who does,
To the small and the great.
Beware of Ptah, Lord of Truth!
He will not overlook the deed of any man.
Beware of uttering the name of Ptah falsely;
Lo, he who utters it falsely,
He is cast down.
He caused me to be as the dogs of the streets,
When I was in his hand;
He caused men and gods to take note of me,
I, a man who had done an abomination against his lord.
Just was Ptah, Lord of Truth, towards me
When he punished me.
Pardon me; look upon me that you may pardon me.

[1] Translations: Pritchard (1955), 370–1; Simpson (1972) 289–95.

Magic

Magic in its various forms enters into a very large body of Egyptian literature. Besides such Books of Magic as the *Harris Magical Papyrus* (10042) and the *Salt Magical Papyrus* (10051), which include hymns as well as incantations, there are many collections of spells against diseases and other misfortunes (e.g. Chester Beatty Papyrus VII, 10687). Every day of the year was believed to possess some magical significance, which rendered it good, bad, or partly good and partly bad, and *Calendars of Lucky and Unlucky Days* (e.g. Sallier IV, 10184 recto) were compiled for purposes of reference. One papyrus (Chester Beatty III, 10683) gives a list of dreams and their interpretations, each dream beginning with the words 'If a man see himself in a dream'; then follows a short description of the dream, a bald statement that it is good or bad, and finally its interpretation:

If a man sees himself in a dream

  eating donkey flesh, good, it means his promotion;

  seating himself upon a tree, good, it means the destruction of all his ills;

  looking into a deep well, bad, it means being put in prison;

  eating an egg, bad, it means the seizure of his possessions beyond repair.

Problems of many kinds might be solved by consulting an oracle. The highest offices in the land, even the kingship, were occasionally filled by oracular revelation. Disputes which arose over matters of property could be settled by reference to an oracle: ostracon 5624 (fig. 35) for instance, describes how the deified king Amenophis I decided the ownership of a tomb in favour of a workman in the Theban necropolis named Amenemope; another ostracon (5625) mentions a dispute concerning the occupation of a house at Thebes which the same deity was asked to settle. A Twentieth Dynasty papyrus (10335) narrates the oracular proceedings which led to the identification of a thief who had stolen five garments from a certain Amenemwiya, a keeper of a store-house. At one period in the end of the New Kingdom children wore long cylindrical amulets often of metal (a Middle Kingdom example is in the Sixth Egyptian Room) containing narrow rolls of papyrus inscribed with long oracular texts promising divine protection against all kinds of misadventures. The following quotation from a papyrus of this kind (10083) gives the declarations attributed to three deities:

We shall keep her safe from Sakhmet and her son.

We shall keep her safe from the collapse of a wall and from the fall of a thunderbolt.

We shall keep her safe from leprosy, from blindness . . . throughout her whole lifetime.

The pharaonic tradition of magic continued well after Egypt was absorbed into the Roman Empire: Papyrus Anastasi 1072 (10070) contains a collection of magical spells and recipes written in demotic with glosses in Greek, dated to the third century AD.

Egyptian stories

These often included a description of some incident involving magic, none more entertainingly than the *Story of Cheops and the Magicians* recounted in the Westcar Papyrus[1] a document in Berlin which dates from Hyksos times. After listening to some stories of wonders performed by magicians in the days of his predecessors, Cheops sent for a magician named Dedi, who succeeded in joining the severed heads of a goose, a duck, and an ox, so that the birds were again able to cackle and quack and the ox to low. The story continues with an account of the miraculous birth of triplets sired by the sun god himself upon the wife of one of his priests. Dedi forecasts that these three children will grow up to become the first kings of a new dynasty. The papyrus breaks off just when it seems that the children's where-abouts are about to be betrayed to Cheops. In spite of the king's Herod-like intentions we must assume that he was thwarted for the first three kings of the succeeding Fifth Dynasty bore the same names as the three children.

At least in some details, the adventures of Sindbad and the *Story of the Shipwrecked Sailor*[2] (written on a Middle Kingdom papyrus in Leningrad) have something in common. The sole survivor of the wreck, the sailor was cast up on an enchanted island where he was befriended and encouraged by a serpent of fabulous appearance: 'He was thirty cubits long, and his beard was more than two cubits long. His body was plated with gold, his eyebrows were of real lapis lazuli.' Eventually, as the serpent had foretold, he was rescued by another ship and taken safely back to Egypt.

In the *Story of the Two Brothers* (D'Orbiney Papyrus, 10183), elements which in origin belonged to folk-tale and mythology have been woven into a continuous narrative.[3] It begins with an account of life on a farm in which Bata helps his elder brother, Inpu, i.e. Anubis, in his agricultural work. Inpu's wife, however, makes amorous overtures to Bata and, having failed to achieve her aim, falsely alleges to Inpu that Bata has ill-treated her after she refused his advances. Inpu then lies in wait behind the door of the byre ready to kill his brother when he returns with his cattle at sunset; as the first cow enters her stall she warns Bata of his danger and he flees, pursued by his brother armed with a spear. The sun-god intervenes, creating a stretch

[1] Translations: Erman (1927), 36–47; Simpson (1972), 15–30 Lichtheim (1973), 215–22.

[2] Translations: Erman (1927), 29–35; Simpson (1972), 50–6; Lichtheim (1973), 211–15.

[3] Translations: Erman (1927), 150–61; Pritchard (1955), 23–5; Simpson (1972), 92–107.

of water full of crocodiles between the brothers. Bata, thus protected, as a sign of good faith mutilates himself and is able to convince his brother of his innocence. Inpu returns to his house, slays his wife, and throws her to the dogs.

Bata tells his brother that he will go to the Valley of the Cedar and will place his heart on top of the flower of the cedar. Having reached the valley and having built a castle for himself, Bata takes to himself a wife, who 'was more beautiful than any woman in all the world', specially created by the gods to relieve his loneliness. Eventually a lock of her hair is carried by the sea to the Pharaoh and its perfume induces him to send soldiers to carry her off. Having reached his court she persuades the king to have the flower on the cedar containing Bata's heart cut down. The heart of Bata falls with the flower and he himself dies.

Inpu learns of Bata's death by a previously arranged magic sign and immediately sets forth to the Valley of the Cedar where, after a long search, he finds his brother's heart in the form of a fruit and brings him back to life. Bata, revivified, takes on the form of a bull and carries Inpu home to Egypt on his back. Inpu becomes Pharaoh's favourite; Bata reveals himself to his one-time wife who persuades the king against his will to slaughter the bull, but two drops of his blood fall to the ground outside the palace and grow into two persea trees in which Bata continues to live. Again he reveals himself to his wife and again she attempts to be rid of him by inducing the king to cut down the trees so that they can be made into furniture. While the carpenters are fashioning the furniture the woman comes to see them and swallows a splinter which has flown into her mouth. As a result she becomes pregnant and gives birth to a child who is none other than Bata. When he grows up the king makes him crown prince and at length he succeeds to the throne of Egypt. His one-time wife is denounced and put to death (presumably) and his faithful elder brother Inpu is made his heir.

The Blinding of Truth by Falsehood (Chester Beatty II, 10682) belongs to the same class of allegorical literature as the *Story of the Two Brothers* and is also of Ramesside date. Unfortunately the beginning of the papyrus is missing, but the plot may be deduced from what follows.[1] A knife which Falsehood had entrusted to his brother, Truth, had somehow been lost or damaged. When Truth offered to replace it, Falsehood claimed it was impossible because of its size and value. Acting on Falsehood's demand the tribunal of the gods condemned Truth to be blinded and to become Falsehood's door-keeper. After some further adventures Truth begat a son who, when he grew up, determined to avenge his father. Having picked a quarrel with

Translations:
ardiner (1935), 4–6;
mpson (1972),
7–32.

Falsehood over the possession of an ox, the boy took him to the divine tribunal and by a trick obtained the verdict. As a punishment Falsehood was beaten and blinded and made to serve as Truth's door-keeper.

A simple but touching narrative of Ramesside date, which is preserved in the Harris Papyrus 500 (10060), is the *Story of the Foredoomed Prince*.[1] When the goddesses of fate, called the Seven Hathors, came to visit the prince on the day of his birth they decreed that he should die by a crocodile, a snake, or a dog. His father, the king, in order to protect him from exposure to these hazards, built a castle for the prince and kept him within its walls. At length the boy persuaded his father to let him have a dog as a pet and subsequently to leave the castle and go to Syria, accompanied by his dog. When he arrived there he found the young nobles competing for the beautiful daughter of the local chief, her father having promised her hand in marriage to the youth who would first succeed in climbing to her window, seventy cubits above the ground. The prince joined in the contest and won, the daughter becoming his devoted wife. By her watchfulness he was saved from an attack by a snake. The end of the papyrus is very damaged but it seems that when his own dog threatened him the prince sought refuge in the sea where a crocodile caught him. The papyrus breaks off just after the crocodile offers escape if the prince will kill an enemy for him. It has been supposed, however, that the story had a happy ending.

Another story written on the same papyrus (10060) is an historical romance known as the *Capture of Joppa*. Its beginning is missing, but it clearly refers to the Palestinian campaign of Tuthmosis III.[2] Having failed to take Joppa by direct assault, his general Djehuty achieved victory by a stratagem involving the introduction into the city of two hundred soldiers hidden in baskets pretending to have been captured by Joppa's prince.

The *Story of King Apophis and Seqenenre* (Sallier I, 10185) has sometimes been regarded as an historical romance.[3] The Hyksos king Apophis sent a messenger to Seqenenre (*c.* 1600 BC) complaining that the hippopotami in the hippopotamus pool at Thebes were disturbing his sleep. Since the residence of Apophis lay at Avaris in the Delta, more than five hundred miles distant from Thebes, the complaint was clearly without substance. In every probability, as Sir Gaston Maspero observed (*Les Contes populaires de l'Égypte ancienne*, 4th ed., pp. xxvi-xxvii), the story was 'simply the local variant of a theme popular throughout the entire East. The kings of those times were wont to send one another problems to be solved on all sorts of matters, the condition being that they should pay one another a kind of

[1] Translations: Erman (1927), 161-5; Simpson (1972), 85-91.

[2] Translations: Erman (1927), 167-9; Pritchard (1955), 22-3 Simpson (1972), 81-4

[3] Translations: Erman (1927), 165-7; Pritchard (1955), 231-2; Simpson (1972 77-80.

Demotic papyrus containing the story of Setne-Khaemwese and the prince of Nubia

tribute or fine according as they should answer well or ill to the questions put to them.' Unfortunately the young scribe Pentawer, who copied this story in the time of King Merneptah (*c.* 1236–1223 BC) never completed his work and Seqenenre's answer is not recorded. It used to be assumed that Amen-Re came to the assistance of the Egyptian king and the story ended with the outwitting of Apophis and Sutekh his god. However, the mummy of Seqenenre (probably the hero of the story) preserved in the Cairo Museum bears such frightful wounds that he must have fallen in battle, and there are indications that he did not die victorious. Nevertheless it was one of his sons who finally drove the Hyksos from Egypt (p. 57).

Four great demotic historical romances have survived from the Late Period, two from the Petubastis cycle and two from the Setne-Khaemwese cycle (fig. 41). The first of the stories concerning king Petubastis has been called the *High Emprise for the Cuirass* and is contained in the Papyrus Krall dated to the end of the second century AD.[1] It purports to be a history of events written down during the reign of a king Petubastis, possibly based on the Twenty-third Dynasty king of that name. Petubastis reigns at Tanis in the Delta but has powerful equals in Inaros, ruler of Heliopolis, and another Delta king called apparently Wer-tep-Amen-Niwt. Inaros has a cuirass which on his death is seized by Wer-tep-Amen-Niwt. Petubastis tries to console Inaros' son Pamay by ordering a great funeral for his father but

Translation: spero (1915), 7–42.

Pamay still demands the return of the cuirass which Wer-tep-Amen-Niwt refuses to do even when summoned before Petubastis. War threatens: Wer-tep-Amen-Niwt calls up his forces and Pamay and the Great Chief of the East, Pakell, call up theirs. After Pamay with his advance guard are caught by Wer-tep-Amen-Niwt, only the arrival of reinforcements saves him from defeat; then Petubastis arrives and a fight between picked champions of the two armies is arranged. It turns into a full-scale battle with Montubaal, another son of Inaros, spreading such slaughter that Petubastis is forced to ask him to stop in return for the cuirass. However, when they find Pamay he is about to kill Wer-tep-Amen-Niwt and then Petubastis has to intervene to prevent his own son Ankhhor being slain. Meanwhile Minirmy seizes the cuirass by force and returns it to Heliopolis; Petubastis is commanded to write down the history of the events.

The second story of the Petubastis cycle is on a papyrus in Strasbourg which dates to the first half of the first century AD.[1] It has been entitled the *High Emprise for the Throne* and is basically the same story as that involving the cuirass except that the object of contention is now the throne of Amun and the events clearly take place some years after those just described. The throne, held by the High Priest of Amun, on his death is seized by Petubastis' son Ankhhor. In reprisal Amun's sacred bark is carried off by the High Priest's son. Neither will return the stolen objects so armies are drawn up but the High Priest's son captures Ankhhor, Petubastis' son, and the royal champion Wer-tep-Amen-Niwt and keeps them in the stolen bark. Amun himself is continually participating to give advice in person. Meanwhile Minirmy, son of Inaros, does combat with one of the priests which lasts for days without result, then royal reinforcements arrive. Presumably Petubastis won eventually and the throne stayed with his son. Scraps of other stories from the cycle are also in existence.

The Adventure of Setne-Khaemwese and the Mummies is contained in two fragmentary papyri in Cairo dated to the Ptolemaic period.[2] The hero Setne is based on prince Khaemwese, a historical son of Ramesses II who had a reputation as a wise man and scholar. By the time the cycle was composed Setne has become a magician. The story takes place at Memphis where the real Khaemwese must have spent much of his life as High Priest of Ptah. Setne is tempted by the dead magician Naneferkaptah to steal from his tomb the Book of Thoth which gives its possessor the power to charm heaven and earth, night, the mountains and water; to understand the language of birds and reptiles, to see to the depths of the sea, and, greatest spell of all, to resurrect the

[1] Translation: Maspe(1915), 243-62.

[2] Translations: Masp(1915), 115-44;
Griffith (1900), 16-4(

dead from the tomb. After a search in the Memphite necropolis Setne finds and enters Naneferkaptah's tomb where he meets the dead magician, his wife Ihwery and son Merib. Ihwery recounts her marriage with her brother, his recovery of the Book of Thoth from Coptos, the subsequent drowning of her son and herself and their burial at Coptos. Naneferkaptah himself was drowned shortly afterwards but managed to keep the Book of Thoth with him so although buried at Memphis was able to use its powers to keep the ghosts of his wife and son with him. Setne plays him at *senet* for the book and is losing badly until his brother uses amulets to rescue him and the book. Against Pharaoh's advice Setne refuses to return it to Naneferkaptah so the succubus Tabubu seduces him into transferring all his property to her and even agreeing to the slaying of his own children and then vanishes. On awaking Setne returns the book to Naneferkaptah who asks that the bodies of his wife and son be reburied with him at Memphis. Their bodies, hidden at Coptos, are found with magic aid and then taken to Memphis for reburial with Naneferkaptah.

The True Story of Setne-Khaemwese and his Son Si-Wsir is contained in papyrus 10822 which has on its reverse a land register written in Greek dating to the first century AD.[1] In this story Setne's wife Mekhweskhet is childless but after incubation in the Temple of Ptah receives advice and accordingly after following it becomes pregnant. The child, called Si-Wsir after a dream of his father's, is a prodigy. One day he and Setne witness the funeral of a rich man and a beggar but when Setne expresses the wish that his burial may be as sumptuous as the rich man's, Si-Wsir wishes him the beggar's funeral. Setne is distraught until his son takes him by magic to see the treatment of rich and poor in the Other World. There a splendidly-clad man is revealed as the beggar; the rich man is in hell with a door pivot in his eye.

A new episode begins with the arrival of a man termed the Prince of Nubia bringing a sealed letter which must be read unopened or Egypt must admit Nubia's supremacy. Setne becomes ill with worry because he cannot do the feat but Si-Wsir succeeds. The letter is about a man called Hor who is encouraged by the King of Nubia to use magic to transport Pharaoh to Nubia for a beating. An Egyptian also called Hor uses the Book of Thoth to protect Pharaoh on subsequent occasions then reverses the process so that the Nubian king is carried to Egypt three times and beaten. The Nubian Hor enlists his mother's aid before going to Egypt to seek out his namesake. The two compete at magic, the Nubian is beaten and about to be killed when his mother intervenes. The two promise never to return and are allowed to go. Si-Wsir then unmasks the

Translations: Maspero (1915), 144–70; riffith (1900), 42–66.

messenger as the Nubian Hor and reveals himself as the Egyptian Hor reincarnated. The Prince of Nubia is consumed by fire and Si-Wsir vanishes. Setne is desolate but then his wife conceives another son. . . .

Travel

This is represented by the *Story of Sinuhe* and the *Adventures of Wenamun*. In all, five papyri and more than twenty ostraca (e.g. 5629) inscribed with excerpts from Sinuhe's narrative are known; so large a number of copies would not have been preserved if the tale had not been exceptionally popular.[1] The story begins with a reference to the death of Ammenemes I, the first king of the Twelfth Dynasty (*c.* 1991–1962 BC). Sinuhe, when he heard the news, was returning with the king's co-regent, Sesostris I, from a military expedition against the Libyans. For reasons which are nowhere fully explained, but were somehow connected with a conversation which he overheard between the king's sons, Sinuhe felt that his life was in danger and decided to flee from Egypt. Since Ammenemes I, the dead king, may well have died as the result of a conspiracy Sinuhe could have been implicated either as an enemy of the new king or as his ally. A graphic account is given of his flight to Palestine, where eventually Amunenshi, king of the Upper Retjenu, befriended him, gave him his eldest daughter in marriage and made him head of a tribe and commander of his army. The royal favours led to jealousy and a local warrior challenged him to a duel which Sinuhe describes in a lively passage. After many years during which he accumulated great wealth, Sinuhe, being advanced in age, felt the urge to return to the land of his birth. Sesostris I, who had heard of Sinuhe's successes, invited him back and promised him a lavish burial when his days were over. The story ends with a description of his ceremonial return to Egypt and his regal reception.

The *Adventures of Wenamun* may represent the actual report of an ill-fated journey from Thebes to Byblos:[2] if so it would explain why no copies of the text have come to light to supplement an incomplete papyrus in Moscow. Wenamun was an emissary sent by Herihor to the Lebanon in order to obtain cedarwood needed for the state-barge of Amun at Thebes. After being robbed of his money, Wenamun suffered misfortunes and indignities in the ports of Palestine and Syria, but eventually the prince of Byblos allowed him to leave for Egypt in one of his own ships. His troubles were, however, not at an end, for when the narrative breaks off Wenamun had been cast by a storm on the shores of Cyprus and is pleading for his life and the lives of the crew of the prince of Byblos.

[1] Translations: Erman (1927), 14–29; Pritchard (1955), 18–22; Simpson (1972) 57–74; Lichtheim (1973), 222–35.

[2] Translations: Erman (1927), 174–85; Pritchard (1955), 25–9; Simpson (1972), 142–55; Goedicke (1975), 149–58.

In a somewhat different category from the two works previously mentioned must be placed a famous satirical letter of the Nineteenth Dynasty (Papyrus Anastasi I, 10247). The letter was written by a scribe named Hori, who held a position in the royal stables, to another scribe and army commander named Amenemope.[1] In an earlier letter Amenemope had claimed the title of Maher, a word of uncertain derivation which was apparently applied to someone who had travelled in Palestine and Syria. Hori replies by naming many localities which he believes Amenemope has not seen and by describing some of the hazards of a Maher's life. A long cross-examination follows on various towns, mountains, streams, roads, beginning with Byblos and ending in the Delta. Earlier in the letter Hori had propounded a number of mathematical problems which he claimed Amenemope would not be able to solve. Teachers at scribal schools often chose excerpts from this letter (e.g. ostracon 50724) for their students to copy, probably because it gave them practice in spelling foreign words and place-names.

Letters

In his letter, Hori jeers at Amenemope for having written an unintelligible letter, a taunt which could not fail to provoke resentment, for Egyptian scribes were carefully trained at school in the technique of letter-writing. No doubt much of their time, not only at school but also after completing their training, was thus occupied, if the number of letters preserved may be regarded as indicative. Many of those which have survived were certainly models, intended for instruction, but actual communications are also numerous. The oldest letter known, written on papyrus, dates from the Sixth Dynasty (c. 2250 BC) and is now in the Cairo Museum. It contains a protest by a military commander, whose troops are working in the Tura quarries, because six days were required for providing his men with new clothing when one day should have been sufficient. Several Middle Kingdom letters have survived: one Eleventh Dynasty example (10549, fig. 29), also from an army commander, whose name was Nehsi, complains that a female member of his household named Senet is short of provisions although he had sent grain to a certain Kay, her father; the commander believes that it is Kay's wife, whose character is like that of his stepmother, who is trying to starve the girl. A papyrus found at the Ramesseum in Thebes (10752) gives copies of a series of letters received from an official stationed in the Second Cataract fortress of Semna in the reign of Ammenemes III of the Twelfth Dynasty (c. 1842–1797 BC); they deal with the movements of the Nubians and their visits to the fortress to sell their wares. Of the numerous letters which

Translations: Erman
(1927), 214–34;
Pitchard (1955),
475–9.

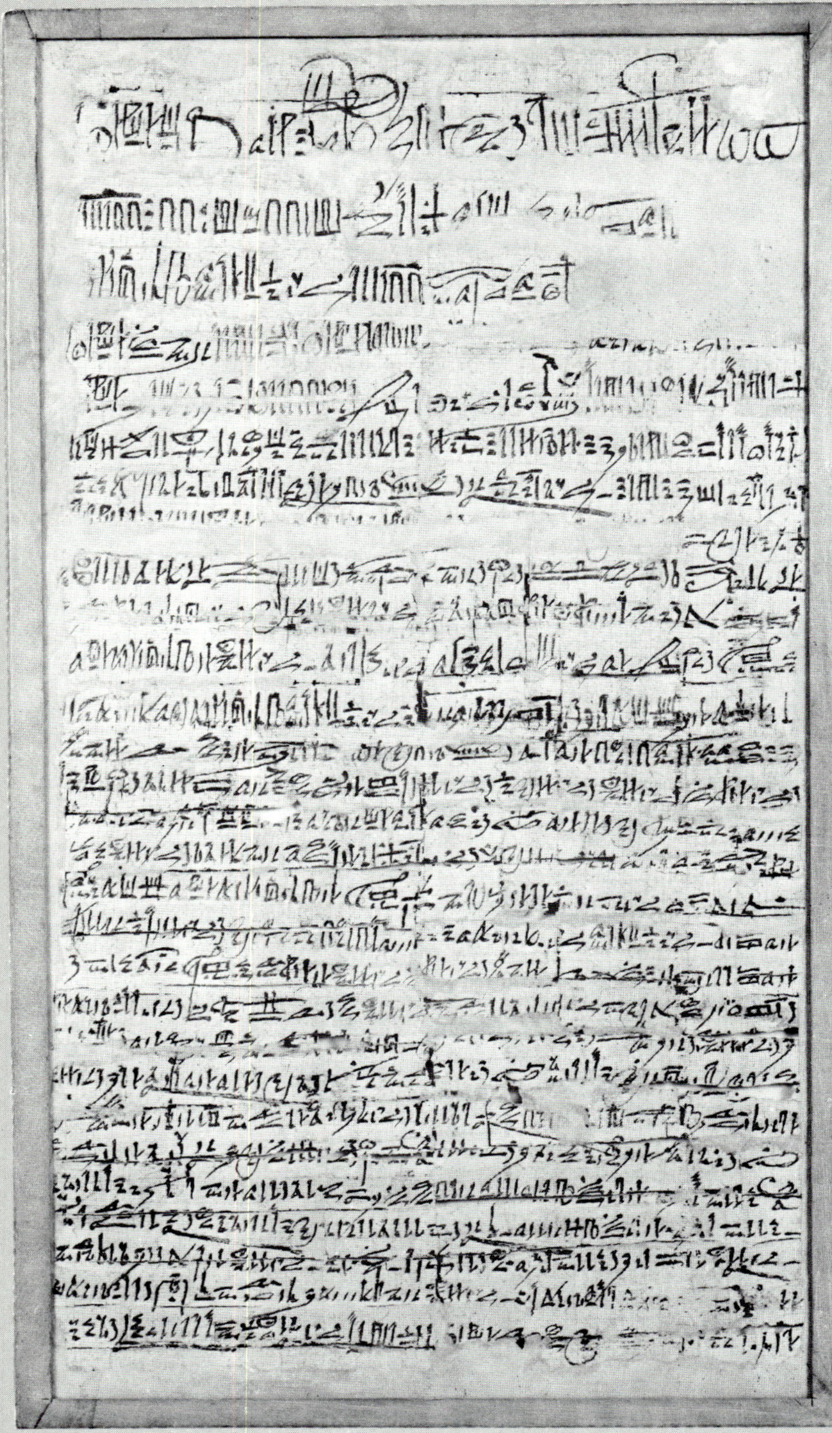

date from the New Kingdom, some of the most interesting are those which have come from Deir el-Medina, the Theban village occupied by the artists and craftsmen who constructed the Ramesside royal tombs (e.g. nos. 10100, 10284, 10300, 10326, 10375, 10412, 10417, 10430, 10433). These letters occasionally mention incidents in the lives of members of this community which can be confirmed from other documents. A letter addressed to Paankh, son of the priest-king Herihor, is written in the fluent hand of one of the best-known scribes in the community, Butehamun (10375, fig. 42).

Letters were sometimes written to friends and relations who had died. As a rule they were written on bowls containing food-offerings so that they would be seen by the intended recipients when they visited their tombs to partake of the offerings. Such letters were not prompted by a desire to remain in communication with a dead friend; their purpose was to seek the aid of the deceased person in some way, generally to bring to an end some undesirable interference in the affairs of the writer or his household. A dead friend might, for instance, be asked to prosecute a troublesome departed spirit before the divine tribunal in the Next World. Extant examples of such letters, which are not numerous, date from the Sixth to the Nineteenth Dynasties (c. 2345–c. 1200 BC).

Undoubtedly stemming from these letters to the dead are documents in the demotic script written to various deities imploring their aid, often in situations for which there can be no legal redress. In one such papyrus (10845) dated to the first century BC, Pasherdjehuty and Naneferher, the children of their father's first marriage, complain that as soon as their mother died they were cast out by their father who took another wife. Their prayer is addressed to the Ibis, the Hawk and the Baboon, three gods of the Memphite necropolis. A typical pastoral letter written in Coptic by a bishop to his congregation is recorded on ostracon 32782 (fig. 43).

Letter addressed to the General Paankh by the scribe Butehamun (*opposite*)

Coptic ostracon recording a letter from a bishop to his congregation (*right*)

Business and legal records

These frequently shed most valuable light on the economic and social conditions of their times. In many cases these texts, especially those on ostraca, deal with trifling transactions and matters which were purely ephemeral: lists of objects given in exchange for a bed (5636 and 5644) or for a bull (5649), quantities of water conveyed by various water-carriers (5638), objects lent by one woman to another (29560), etc. One ostracon (5634) dated to the fortieth year of the reign of Ramesses II (c. 1264 BC) contains a register of the names of some workmen engaged on the royal tomb, each name being followed by a note of the days on which the man was absent from work and the reason for his absence; among the reasons given are sickness, caring for another workman who was sick (and mentioned as 'sick' in his own record), brewing beer and domestic hindrances. From this document it is apparent that every tenth day was a rest day. Legal documents deal with a wide range of subjects, from private contracts and trials for petty larceny to state trials for participation in conspiracies against the king or acts of robbery committed in the royal tombs at Thebes. The writer of an ostracon (5631) which dates from the Nineteenth–Twentieth Dynasties (c. 1200 BC) mentions that he had been condemned to a term of forced labour for embezzlement, but his father had appealed to the king and had obtained his release. Papyrus Salt 124 (10055) describes a series of charges laid before the Vizier (who was also the Chief Justice) by a certain Amennakht against a chief foreman of the workmen in the royal tomb named Peneb (the owner of stelae 272–3). Among the charges are accusations of having stolen objects from the tomb of King Sethos II (c. 1216–1210 BC), allegations of offences against the wives of fellow workmen, and other irregularities which included abuse of privilege. The papyrus does not unfortunately record the outcome of Amennakht's complaint, and the fate of Peneb remains unknown. More informative are some papyri which deal with judicial inquiries conducted at Thebes in the sixteenth and seventeenth years of Ramesses IX (c. 1142–1123 BC) and the nineteenth and twentieth years of Ramesses XI (c. 1114–1085 BC) into robberies which had occurred in the Theban necropolis. Seven of the twelve known papyri in the group are in the collection of the Museum (10052, 10053, 10054, 10068, 10221, 10383, and 10403). From one of these documents, the Abbott Papyrus (10221), it is clear that both the mayor of the city of Thebes, Paser, and the mayor of Western Thebes, Paweraa, had reported that several tombs, among them those of kings and queens, had been violated and their contents plundered. Investigation carried out in the necropolis during the inquiry

Plate 7
Upper part of a colossus of Ramesses II

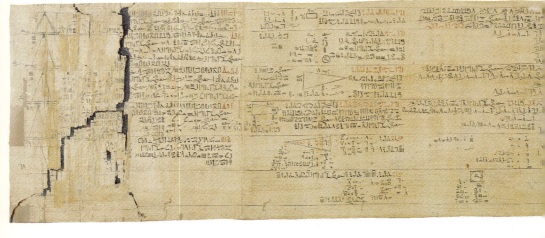

8

9

10

Plate 8

Part of the Rhind
Mathematical
Papyrus

Plate 9

Banqueting scene
from a Theban
tomb

Plate 10

Lid of the coffin of
Hornedjitef

showed that the charges made by Paser were greatly exaggerated and it is hard to believe that, in making his report, he was not trying to discredit his colleague on the west bank. Nevertheless serious robberies had been committed, including the plundering of the tomb of King Sobkemsaf (c. 1650 BC) and his wife Nubkhaas, and the tomb of Isis, wife of King Ramesses III (c. 1198–1166 BC), from whose temple at Medinet Habu a gilded portable shrine had also been stolen. In the main the papyri are devoted to recording the evidence given by the accused, some of whom were acquitted, and lists of the objects found in the possession of the guilty parties.

Very many of the demotic papyri which have survived are concerned with business transactions and throw much light on social life in Egypt during the last three centuries BC. One of the longest known demotic papyri (10026, fig. 44), contains the cession of certain property at Thebes by the woman Nes-Khons to her eldest son Pana with four witness copies. The date is December 265 BC. Although there is a good deal of variation in detail in such cessions and their accompanying bills of sale (in this case not present because the cession is really a will) the general contents are stable. A bill of sale usually runs:

(1) date (sometimes with the names of eponymous priests and priestesses);

(2) names of the contracting parties in the form X says to Y;

(3) the payment involved: 'You have made me content with the price of my (e.g. house)' then details of the property;

(4) a clause of surrender: 'I give to you my (e.g. house)';

(5) a possession clause: 'Yours is my (e.g. house)';

(6) receipt of payment: 'I have received the price of my (e.g. house) from your hand';

(7) a clause excluding the former owner from further rights: 'I have no claim against you in its name';

(8) security from others' claims: 'No man has legal rights against you in my name, in anyone's name from this day forth';

(9) a deed clause: 'Yours are its deeds and records';

(10) an oath to carry out the promises;

(11) closing formula: 'There are no legal claims against you' or the confirmation of the transaction by a third party, usually a relative of the first party;

(12) the scribe's signature.

The deed of cession has many identical clauses but instead of clause (3) there is a clause of surrender: 'I renounce all claim on your (e.g. house)'; there is no clause (6) and after clause (10)

Plate 11
Queen Ahmes-Nefertari

is a closing pledge: 'I have made the deed of cession for you in the matter of my (e.g. house)'. The witnesses of the transaction, usually 16 in number, sign their names and filiation on the verso of the papyrus. Sometimes, as in this case, up to four of the witnesses were required to copy out the document in their own hand on the recto.

44 Demotic papyrus containing details of a cession of property by the woman Nes-Khons

Scientific literature

Egyptian writings of a scientific nature are limited to the fields of mathematics, astronomy, and medicine. At what date the study of mathematics began is not known, but it was certainly long before the earliest extant mathematical documents were written. These documents are not sets of rules but lists of problems and their solutions. The Rhind Mathematical Papyrus (10057 and 10058, Plate 8) begins with a long table of the division of 2 by odd numbers from 3 to 101 and continues with eighty-four problems of an arithmetical kind which include mensuration, the calculation of areas, and the measurement of angles of slopes. The following are examples of these problems:

(*a*) Divide 2 by 97.

(*b*) A circular container of 9 cubits in its height and 6 in its breadth. What is the amount that will go into it in corn?

(*c*) Method of reckoning a circular piece of land of diameter 9 *khet*. What is its area in land?

(*d*) A pyramid 140 (units) in length of side, and 5 palms and a finger in its slope. What is the vertical height thereof?

Three lines of partly mutilated text, which serve as a preface, state that the papyrus was copied from 'a writing of antiquity' by a scribe named Ahmose who lived in the time of the Hyksos king Auserre Apophis (*c.* 1575 BC). To about the same date may be ascribed a list in duplicate of twenty-six sums in the addition of fractions written on a strip of leather (10250). In every probability this list was intended as a kind of ready-reckoner.

The Egyptians adopted a decimal notation, the highest unit employed being 1,000,000. Addition and subtraction of whole numbers presented no difficulties. Multiplication, except for the most simple cases in which a number had either to be doubled or to be multiplied by ten, involved a somewhat laborious process of doubling and adding. Thus in order to multiply 77 by 7 they wrote out the following table:

$$1 \times 77 = 77$$
$$2 \times 77 = 154$$
$$4 \times 77 = 308$$

The multipliers 1, 2, and 4 were first added together, giving a total of 7, and then the corresponding products (i.e. 77, 154, and 308), thereby obtaining 539 as the quotient. Division was achieved by reversing the process:

$$1 \times 7 = 7$$
$$2 \times 7 = 14$$
$$4 \times 7 = 28$$
$$8 \times 7 = 56$$

In this case they added the products, the sum of which amounts to 77 (i.e. $7+14+56$), then by adding the corresponding multipliers (i.e. 1, 2, and 8) they obtained the desired result of 11.

Apart from $\frac{2}{3}$ and (rarely) $\frac{3}{4}$ no fractions were written with numerators higher than unity. Thus, instead of writing $\frac{2}{11}$ the Egyptians wrote $\frac{1}{6}+\frac{1}{66}$. No doubt tables of the kind shown on the strip of leather (10250) and in the first section of the Rhind Mathematical Papyrus were kept at hand to save the necessity of working out complex fractions. Multiplication and division of fractions were achieved by the same process as was employed in multiplying and dividing whole numbers.

Two measures of capacity were, at least from the Middle Kingdom onwards, normally in use: the *heqat*-measure, approximately a bushel, and the *hin*-measure, about $\frac{1}{2}$ litre. The *heqat* was divided in fractional parts $\frac{1}{2}$, $\frac{1}{4}$, $\frac{1}{8}$, $\frac{1}{16}$, $\frac{1}{32}$, and $\frac{1}{64}$, and 16 *heqat* might be expressed as a sack (*khar*). Other liquid measures are known, but their sizes have not been determined.

Linear measurement was usually expressed in terms of cubits. Two cubits of different length were in use: the royal cubit (52·3 cms), which was employed as a measurement in building, being equal to 7 palms (of the hand) or 28 fingers, and the short cubit (about 45 cms) being equal to 6 palms or 24 fingers. For long measurements another unit, the 'river-measure' corresponding with the Greek *schoinos* (roughly 10·5 km or 20,000 cubits) was used.

Area and weight were likewise measured in specialized units and fractions of units, the most common being the *setjat* (100 cubits squared, roughly $\frac{2}{3}$ acre) and the *deben* (about 91 grammes).

Time was measured in terms of years and subdivisions of a year, each year consisting of 12 months of 30 days (i.e. three 10-day weeks), to which were added 5 intercalary days giving a total of 365 days. For purposes of dating, the year was divided into three seasons, each of 4 months: 'inundation', 'winter', and 'summer'. The day was further divided into 24 hours, 12 hours of day and 12 hours of night; the length of the hour varied according to the season. Both water-clocks and shadow-clocks (933 and 938) were used to measure hours; a different calibration for each month was sometimes marked on the water-clocks (*clepsydrae*) in order to allow for the varying length of the day (fig. 45).

45 Fragment of a water-clock dated to the reign of Alexander the Great

Astronomical observation

A systematic kind of astronomical observation certainly began in very early times. The most ancient astronomical texts at present known are found on the lids of wooden coffins dating from the Ninth Dynasty (c. 2150 BC). These texts, the so-called 'diagonal calendars' or 'diagonal star clocks', give the names of the decans (stars which rose at ten-day intervals at the same time as the sun), of which there were thirty-six. The purpose of these charts was to enable the deceased to tell the time of the night or the date in the calendar. Star charts of essentially the same kind, but more elaborate, were reproduced in the New Kingdom on the ceiling of the tomb of Senenmut, Queen Hatshepsut's architect, and on the ceiling of the cenotaph of Sethos I at Abydos. In the tombs of Ramesses IV, VII, and IX, a figure of a seated man is shown together with a net of stars. The accompanying inscriptions, which relate to the first and the sixteenth day of each month, give the position occupied by a star at each of the twelve hours of the night in relation to the seated figure: 'over the left ear', 'over the right ear', etc. The signs of the zodiac were not introduced into Egyptian astronomy until Ptolemaic and Roman times, when they were sometimes represented on the ceilings of temples and the lids of coffins (6705 and 6678; Plate 10). Although there is no evidence that the Egyptian civil calendar possessed an astronomical basis, proof is available that a careful check was kept on the occurrence of at least one sidereal event in relation to the civil calendar. This event was the annual rising of the dog-star, Sirius, at the same time as the sun (i.e. heliacally), approximately on 19 July of the Julian calendar. Since the civil calendar of 365 days made no allowance for leap years it gained one day in every four years on the astronomical calendar (which was used for agriculture and for determining the dates of religious festivals), with the result that the two calendars became progressively out of step until at the end of 120 years the civil year would be a month ahead of the astronomical year. Eventually at the end of 1,460 years the two calendars would again coincide, but only for four days. Censorinus mentions that a heliacal rising of Sirius on the first day of the civil year occurred in AD 139, from which it has been calculated that a similar coincidence must have occurred in the pharaonic period in 1321–1317 BC and 2781–2773 BC. By a fortunate chance three texts have been preserved which record the date, in the civil year, on which Sirius rose heliacally: (a) 11th month, day 28, of an unspecified year of Tuthmosis III; (b) 11th month, day 9, of the ninth year of Amenophis I, and (c) 7th month, day 25, of the seventh year of Sesostris III. Translated into terms of the Julian calendar these three dates become approximately 1469, 1537, and 1872 BC.

Invaluable as these three dates are for pin-pointing the reigns in question, little progress in reconstructing Egyptian chronology could have been made without help from other sources. The

documents which afford the greatest information are the fragmentary Royal Annals (the so-called Palermo Stone and its
congeners in Cairo and University College London) which, however, record with many lacunae only kings and the principal
event in each year of their reigns down to the Fifth Dynasty; the
mutilated Royal Canon of the Turin Museum, compiled in the
Nineteenth Dynasty, which gives the names of the kings in
chronological order, the length of their reigns, and the total
number of years occupied by each dynasty; the History of
Manetho (written in Greek in the third century BC and preserved
only incompletely in the works of other writers) which follows
the same pattern as the Royal Canon of Turin; and lastly the
innumerable inscriptions and papyri dated to such and such
a year of a named king. In spite of many gaps and, especially in
Manetho, copyists' errors, these four sources provide an
immense amount of information about the length of individual
reigns and the duration of many dynasties. Second to them only
in importance are the lists of kings arranged in chronological
order found in the temples of Abydos and Karnak, and in a tomb
at Saqqara. Though far from complete, these lists (one of which
was found in the temple of Ramesses II at Abydos and is now in
this Museum, 117) contain many names which are missing
from the documents previously mentioned, but they lack details
of the length of reigns and corruptions sometimes occur. By far
the most complete and the best preserved is the famous list of
king Sethos I which still stands in his temple at Abydos.

Medical works

These are relatively numerous. In this Museum there are eight
examples: three, dating from the Twelfth Dynasty, were found
in the Ramesseum (10756–8) and are among the earliest
medical papyri known; 10758 is actually written in cursive
hieroglyphs rather than hieratic, which indicates that it was
composed much earlier. It deals with stiffness in the limbs;
10757 contains spells and prescriptions for pregnant women
and newly-born children. The London Medical Papyrus (10059)
dating from the late Eighteenth Dynasty contains sixty-three
recipes but just over a third are medical, the remainder being
purely magical. One spell claims to have been found at night
in the sanctuary of the Temple of Isis at Coptos by a lector-
priest: 'The earth was in darkness but the moon shone on this
papyrus scroll on every side and it was brought as a marvel to
the majesty of king Khufu'. The Chester Beatty Medical Papyrus VI
(10686, fig. 46) and three further papyri of lesser importance,
Chester Beatty X dealing with aphrodisiacs, XV and XVIII
(10690, 10695 and 10698), date to the Nineteenth Dynasty.

6 The Chester Beatty Medical Papyrus VI

Since many ailments were thought to be caused by evil demons, magic was considered the most effective method of treatment; spells suitable for use in such cases were therefore interspersed with prescriptions of drugs and were intended to be recited while the drugs were being administered. Alternative prescriptions are often given for a disease, so that if one remedy failed to effect the cure another remedy could be tried. The ingredients of the prescriptions were generally the fat or blood of animals, plants and vegetables, honey, and all the common liquids. Ointments were generally mixed with honey or animal fat including goose-grease. Surgery was practised by the Egyptians, but mainly in cases of injury. A papyrus in the possession of the New York Academy of Medicine, known as the Edwin Smith Papyrus, lists the appropriate surgical treatment for wounds of the head and thorax. The Ebers Papyrus in Leipzig and a Twelfth-dynasty papyrus from Illahun in the Petrie collection also contain information about surgical treatment, the former in connexion with boils and cysts and the latter with reference to gynaeco-logical conditions.

CHAPTER FIVE

RELIGIOUS BELIEFS

General considerations and origins

An account will be given in the next chapter of the funerary beliefs and customs of the Ancient Egyptians. Here it is only necessary to say that the interest shown by the Egyptians in their fate after death and the elaborate preparations made by them for their burial arose in part from their passionate interest in life itself. The vast majority of religious texts which have survived are mainly funerary in intent, but they provide valuable information about the general religious beliefs of the Egyptians, or at least of certain classes of Egyptians. The complexity of these beliefs and the great number of their gods suggest that Egyptian thinking in religious matters was haphazard and confused. Much of the apparent confusion is, however, understandable when it is realized that by the time of the Late New Kingdom, two thousand years of development had taken place; simple, primitive beliefs had been turned into complicated theological systems. Much of this development resulted from the additions contributed by successive generations to what they had inherited; much of the confusion sprang from the unwillingness of the Egyptians to discard outmoded or contradictory beliefs; much of the proliferation of gods was prompted by political reasons.

Written texts from which substantial information about religious beliefs can be extracted do not occur before the Fifth Dynasty (the *Pyramid Texts*, p. 171), but their subject-matter is to a large extent derived from earlier compositions, some elements undoubtedly dating from very primitive times. Useful evidence from the Predynastic Period is largely confined to what may be deduced from burial customs, but some additional information on the nature of the gods at this early time can be extracted from the decoration of painted vases and from the objects placed in tombs. Many predynastic burials contain small female figurines of pottery, ivory, and other materials, and it is thought that these may represent a primitive fertility- or mother-goddess. Buff-coloured Late Predynastic pottery with painted designs also carry representations of a large female figure which has similarly been identified as a fertility-goddess. Examples of female figurines (fig. 47) and of the painted pottery can be seen in the Sixth Egyptian Room and of the former also in the Fifth Egyptian Room. Many of the small animal figures found in predynastic burials may in the same manner represent

47 Ivory figure of a Badarian woman

gods, and the early slate palettes in the forms of animals, birds, fishes, and other creatures may also possess religious or amuletic properties connected with primitive deities associated with these creatures. It is possible, for example, that in the small hippopotamus-figures and palettes in the form of hippopotami, examples of which can be seen in the Sixth Egyptian Room, the later hippopotamus-goddess Thoeris may be distinguished, but it is impossible to be certain that such an identification is correct. Further, the correspondence in form between predynastic animal-shaped objects and theriomorphic deities of the historic period may not indicate any certain continuity of cults between the two periods. That continuity in the case of some cults did take place, however, is shown by the appearance on predynastic objects of distinctive cult-signs which were used during the historic period. The slate palette 35501 (fig. 48) bears in low relief a sign which has been identified as a rudimentary form of the cult-object of Min, a god whose antiquity is otherwise attested by large primitive stone figures found at Coptos, the cult-centre. This sign and others of a similar kind are also found, shown mounted on poles, in the painted scenes on buff-coloured pots of the Late Predynastic Period. These signs are thought to be the crests or banners of the predynastic nomes or their equivalents. Their presence, so represented, on pots, further confirms the great antiquity of some of the later cults of Egypt. Apart from the Min-sign, the distinctive crossed arrows of the goddess Neith have been identified. Standards of a more elaborate type, similar to those used in the writing of nome-signs in later times, are found on a few of the proto-dynastic slate palettes, and further testify to the antiquity of some deities. The Hunters' Palette (20790, fig. 10) carries three representations of standards, two with falcons and feathers and one consisting of what has been described as an elaborately decorated spear. These signs are similar to those which are later used to write 'west' and 'east' in hieroglyphs, and it is probable that they here stand for the district standards of western and eastern regions, possibly of the Delta. Falcon-deities in later times had cult-centres in the western Delta. The decorated spear likewise was probably a district cult-sign. The inference to be drawn from these and other representations is that in predynastic Egypt each district had its own deity or cult-object. Of the nature of the individual cults nothing is known, but it may be assumed that they consisted mostly of simple primitive beliefs of local importance. Their significance increased or diminished, however, according to the political fortunes of the districts and this phenomenon was to become a special characteristic of the religious history of Egypt in later times.

8 Schist palette with the emblem of Min

With the unification of Egypt and the beginning of the Historic or Dynastic Period, the gods of the small districts of the land encountered a crisis from which some emerged as national gods, while others remained only locally worshipped. The order of events leading up to the unification is not fully known; neither are the political groupings in the final conflict known. It is possible that the Upper Egyptian and Lower Egyptian coalitions of states both revered the falcon Horus as their principal god. There is some evidence to suggest that Horus was originally a Lower Egyptian god, but it seems certain that he eventually became the great state god of a unified Egypt from his position as the principal deity worshipped by the conquerors from Hierakonpolis who ultimately subdued Lower Egypt and founded Memphis. Among the Upper Egyptian local gods who profited from this victory were Seth of Ombos and Thoth of Hermopolis. Of these two, the former developed an essentially malevolent character, being later regarded as the arch-enemy of Horus; the latter was held to be the scribe of the gods. At the same time other gods achieved prominence, for political reasons principally, and among those who retained their importance throughout the Dynastic Period were Ptah and Re. Ptah was the local god of Memphis, while Re, the sun-god, was worshipped at Heliopolis, a short distance to the north of Memphis. This process by which local deities were elevated to become national gods was repeated from time to time throughout Egyptian history. Thus, during the First Intermediate Period the ascendancy of Heracleopolis brought with it the temporary elevation of Arsaphes, the ram-headed deity of that city. At about the same time the Theban god Month became the principal deity of the southern confederacy of nomes which ultimately won control of the whole of Egypt. After this triumph, for reasons that are not fully understood, Amun, an obscure god, became in the Middle Kingdom the great state god. His claim to this position was reinforced at the beginning of the New Kingdom inasmuch as he was the principal god of the Theban kings who had driven out the Hyksos, and with his enhanced status he became the god of the Egyptian empire. Neith, the goddess of Sais, whose cult-sign, the crossed arrows, is found on predynastic objects, achieved special prominence during the Twenty-sixth Dynasty, the kings of which came from Sais.

To a great extent the fortunes of any local cult in Egypt depended on political developments, but the elevation of particular deities rarely affected the local status of the majority of gods. Over the years most of these local deities were assimilated into the Egyptian pantheon, fulfilled their minor roles in the general myths, and contributed their particular elements to the

49 Bronze figure of an Apis bull dedicated by Peteesi

amalgam of religious beliefs. As a result, the gods who played some part in the daily religious life of the Egyptians were very varied in character and infinitely various in form. In many of the important religious centres for political reasons the principal god was associated with two other local deities to form a divine family, known as a triad. At Memphis Ptah had Sakhmet as his consort and Nefertum as his son; at Thebes the triad consisted of Amun, Mut, and Khons; at Elephantine it consisted of Khnum, Anukis, and Satis. Numerically the Egyptian pantheon was immense. In early times most gods were worshipped in the forms of animals and inanimate objects (p. 129). At some point, probably early in the historic period, the idea of anthropomorphism had gained currency and the gods were represented with at least human bodies. The theriomorphic conception still persisted, however, to a limited extent, and many gods were shown with human bodies and animal or other shaped heads. In official religion, as opposed to private and personal religion, this unusual mixture of anthropomorphism and theriomorphism seems to have had no more than a representational significance. It is probable, however, that locally the old cults retained a close attachment to the original forms of the gods; but this allegiance to gods in animal and other forms does not become strikingly apparent until the Late Period when the cults of gods in animal forms were widely revived. Most of the figures of gods in animal forms date from this time (fig. 49) and the large Late Period animal-cemeteries in the cult-centres testify to the popularity of this type of worship (p. 161). Figures of gods, in animal, human, and mixed form are exhibited in the Fifth Egyptian Room and brief descriptions of the principal gods are given below (pp. 149 ff.).

Private religion

Any discussion of religion in ancient Egypt is complicated by the necessity to distinguish between official religion and private religion, and one of the principal problems is to determine whether the Egyptians recognized the existence of divinity as an abstract element or considered it only as an aspect common to a vast number of particular deities. Most of the religious texts are concerned with official religion or with the various funerary cults, and while much is known about what the Egyptian (especially in the highest ranks of society) thought in connexion with his fate after death, little is known about the way in which religion affected him while he was alive. The complicated theologies developed at places like Heliopolis and Hermopolis (pp. 146 f.), and which undoubtedly existed in a lesser degree at most of the cult-centres, were the fabrications of priests, kept exclusive, and made unapproachable for ordinary folk. High theology at Heliopolis and Thebes affected the conception of the kingship, but the subtle myths of creation and of the behaviour of the gods (pp. 147 f.) could have had little appeal to most people. Some knowledge of the great gods inevitably percolated down to the lower classes, but the evidence provided by the occasional prayers of simple workmen which have been pre-served shows that this knowledge was superficial and usually confined to a few simple ideas about the basic characteristics of the god invoked (p. 108). This state of affairs is hardly surprising when it is realized that the great temples were not built for public worship but for the regular private practice of the cults by the priests, with only occasional public festivals. In these festivals the people participated more probably for the splendour of the pageantry and the concomitant 'fun of the fair' than for reasons of piety. Some idea of the excitement generated on the occasion of a great festival is conveyed by the account given by Ikhernofret, the chief treasurer of Sesostris III, who was sent to Abydos to conduct the festival of the 'Going-forth of Wepwawet'; the events of the festival included a ceremonial procession to the legendary tomb of Osiris and a dramatic re-enactment of the revenging of Osiris' death by Wepwawet. The well-preserved texts in the Temple of Horus at Edfu provide abundant informa-tion about the private and public festivals celebrated at Edfu throughout the year, and again it is clear that participation by the people took place only in those festivals which involved processions, such as that of the sacred marriage of Horus of Edfu with Hathor of Dendera. The so-called Ramesseum Dramatic Papyrus (10610) preserves part of the ritual drama enacted by priests representing characters in the Osiris legend at the time of the enthronement of King Sesostris I of the Twelfth Dynasty.

It is unlikely that Egyptian religion, as represented by the great cults, was ever a vital influence on the religious beliefs of the ordinary people. The presence of the great temples no doubt inspired feelings of awe and mystery; in addition they engendered subsidiary cults of great popular appeal, often attached to architectural features of the buildings. At Memphis, for example, there was the cult of Horus 'on the corner of the southern door'. In Thebes many of the royal mortuary temples developed in time secondary cults more acceptable to the humble people. Popular cults also evolved out of the posthumous reputations of famous men. The worship of Imhotep in the Late Period arose from his long-established reputation as a physician and a sage. In the Theban necropolis the craftsmen who worked on the tombs especially revered the memory of Amenophis I and his mother Ahmes-Nefertari, who were held to be the patron deities of the necropolis (Plate 11). Other gods who achieved considerable popular followings in the New Kingdom and later were foreign deities introduced into Egypt by soldiers returning from the Asiatic wars, by foreign prisoners, and by foreign craftsmen. These gods no doubt appealed to the humble Egyptian because they were in no way connected with the overpowering state-cults, from full participation in which he was prevented by social considerations. Deities like Anat, Astarte, and Qadesh were worshipped in a private manner from Tanis in the north to Thebes in the south (fig. 50); particular allegiance to such cults existed in those quarters of Memphis inhabited largely by foreigners and also in the community of workmen, already mentioned, who lived in the Theban necropolis and worked on the royal tombs. Many of these workmen were of foreign origin or in contact with foreigners. From their village at Deir el-Medina has come much material providing valuable information about private religion during the New Kingdom. One interesting fact which has emerged from discoveries at Deir el-Medina is that ancestor-cults flourished in the Theban area (and possibly elsewhere) at this period. Formalized busts were kept in niches in the houses and were undoubtedly the object of worship. Examples of such busts are exhibited in the Fifth Egyptian Room (270, 49735, 61083).

Apart from the formal attachment to specific cults, the ordinary Egyptian's religion seems to have consisted largely of magical

practices and the invocation of those deities who might protect him from the dangers of daily life. One of the most popular deities in this respect was Bes, a dwarf with leonine features, who not only brought happiness to the home, but also protected it in general ways. His image was represented on beds, head-rests, mirror-handles, and other domestic articles. Amulets for the living, carved from hippopotamus ivory, often bear figures of a creature like Bes (p. 160 and fig. 51); their purpose was to keep away snakes and other harmful creatures, some of which were, to judge from the forms carved on the amulets, the imaginary inhabitants of the desert. In the Theban area during the New Kingdom the goddess Meresger provided protection against

o Stela depicting the goddess Qadesh standing on a lion (*opposite*)

51 Amuletic wand in ivory (*above*)

serpents, and another deity whose figure was worn as an amulet against snakes and scorpions was Shed (65842). In later times Shed became identified with a form of Horus-the-Child, represented standing on crocodiles and holding in his hands snakes, scorpions, and gazelles (thought to possess a special malevolence). Small stelae, called Cippi of Horus, incorporate the god so represented (sometimes also with a head of Bes above the figure of Horus) and often bear magical texts; examples are shown in the Fifth Egyptian Room. The Middle Kingdom ivory wand-amulets mentioned above also carry representations of Thoeris, a goddess shown as a pregnant female hippopotamus, standing on its hind legs. This deity was at all periods much revered at all levels of society as the protectress of women in child-birth. Objects often designated as 'toys' may well in many instances have been used for ritual rather than for purely recreational purposes: the so-called 'dolls', small figures in wood and clay, some merely flat ovoid boards with painted faces and rows of beads to indicate hair (e.g. 22613), others three-dimensional in representation (55595). Toys as such were of course made and used. Two fine examples, executed in wood, are on display in the Fourth Egyptian Room, one a cat with a moveable jaw (13671) the other a horse mounted on four wheels (26687).

The belief in the efficacy of magic to achieve desired ends was not limited to the more humble classes of Egyptians. The consulting of lists of lucky and unlucky days, the use of amuletic texts for the protection of the individual against dangers in particular circumstances and the existence of papyri bearing magical compositions for various purposes (p. 109), all testify to the devotion of all Egyptians to magical practices.

Between the simple religious beliefs of humble Egyptians and the elaborate theological formulations of the great state-cults lay a further stratum of religious thinking which may occasionally be distinguished through rare personal utterances found in tomb-inscriptions and through the literary compositions which are usually termed pessimistic and wisdom texts (pp. 97–103). In such compositions may be discerned the most profound religious thinking manifested in ancient Egypt. In the Old Kingdom a trace of such independent thinking appears in the texts in tombs of certain high officials of the Sixth Dynasty, particularly at Saqqara. Ideas of responsibility and retribution occur for the first time when the authority of the Egyptian king was experiencing its first serious challenge. In many Old Kingdom texts the Great God occurs as a divine being invoked for funerary benefits. Whether this Great God is to be identified with one particular member of the Egyptian pantheon has never been established—he may have been the deceased king; but the very existence of an unnamed deity reveals that the Egyptians could think about divinity perhaps without investing it with concrete form. During the First Intermediate Period this new attitude to religious matters developed in the painful circumstances that accompanied the dissolution of the central control. It was in this period that the first semi-philosophical texts were composed, and it is in these texts that moral and religious problems are first probed, even if only in a simple manner. God is here often considered as an abstract idea and not always in terms of named deities. The most unusual of these texts is the *Dialogue of a Pessimist with his Soul* (p. 101). During the New Kingdom the effect of this intellectual approach to religious and moral questions, which previously had been exercised largely in a personal manner, impinged to a small extent on religion within the framework of the great state-cults. In funerary religion it can be distinguished in the terms of the Negative Confession in Chapter cxxv of the *Book of the Dead* (p. 156). Organized state theology, however, gave few opportunities for the development of this type of religion, and the vehicle for its expression remained literary compositions. The *Teaching of Amenemope* (p. 98), for example, contains collections of didactic utterances after the manner of the biblical *Book of Proverbs*. Other Egyptian texts contain passages for which striking parallels can be found in the Bible, and outstanding among them is the hymn composed, perhaps by Akhenaten himself, in honour of the Aten, which in many particulars resembles Psalm 104 (p. 107). The acceptance of the cult of the Aten by Akhenaten during the Eighteenth Dynasty was in some respects a triumph for the strain of personal religion which subsisted behind the façade of the state religion. Most people who were sufficiently religious to seek spiritual satisfaction apart from the doctrinal and mythological complexities of the official system were in no position to do more than express their thoughts in semi-religious literary compositions or by introducing individual elements into conventional religious compositions. The inscription of Hor and Suty (p. 107), two architects at the court of Amenophis III, contains, besides a conventional prayer to the sun-god Re, a finely expressed prayer to the Aten (826, fig. 52). Such individual expressions are rare in Egyptian monumental texts, although some prayers to Amun reveal unusual personal piety; but this prayer of Hor and Suty shows that during the reign of Amenophis III even high officials were prepared to depart far from the conventional in their public religious pronouncements. Such behaviour on the part of private people probably incurred no disapproval, but the sponsoring of such ideas by the king himself was a different matter. The allegiance of Amenophis IV (who later changed his name to Akhenaten) to the cult of the Aten ran contrary to all that was expected of the king of Egypt. As a result the clash between himself and the entrenched priesthoods of the state-cults, particularly that of Amen-Re, was exceptionally bitter. The cult of the Aten could easily be tolerated as a subsidiary to the principal cults of the land, but as the chosen cult of the king himself it necessarily had to be resisted (p. 62). The nature of the cult was basically monotheistic; it was not anthropomorphic, its manifestation being the sun's disk, the giver of light, heat, life, and all that prospered the earth and its creatures. In sculptural representations the Aten is shown as the sun's disk with rays ending in hands holding the sign for 'life'. In the cult special emphasis was placed on Maat, the concept of 'truth and order', which always played an important role in Egyptian religion (see p. 140).

The new faith was free from involved theology and complicated mythology, but it lacked moral content and seems to
have been considered a personal religion for Akhenaten and
his family. Services to the Aten were conducted in open temples
far different from the gloomy sanctuaries of the old state gods.
In spite of the inherent potentiality of Atenism to become a
universal creed, there is no evidence that it was ever held to be
accessible to non-Egyptians.

52 Stela of the
architects Hor and
Suty

Official religion

Throughout the history of ancient Egypt divine cults were maintained in the principal towns of the land. Many of these cults were of great antiquity, but they remained local; others attained national importance for political reasons (p. 130). In every important sanctuary, however, a daily ritual was carried out which, already by the Old Kingdom, had achieved a remarkable standardization throughout the country. This ritual formed the basis of the official religion. In origin it was developed from the procedure of worship in the sanctuary of Re at Heliopolis; in its practice in provincial temples the local deities were identified with Re. The reason for this uniformity was not only the great influence of the Heliopolitan cult, but also the fact that the king, in all temples regarded as the high-priest, was the son of Re. Furthermore, the widespread adoption of the cult of Osiris towards the end of the Old Kingdom helped to standardize forms of worship. The relationship of the king with the god was equated with that of Horus with Osiris; in the practice of the cult the god therefore became Osiris, and the king, as principal officiant, was Horus. From the Middle Kingdom onwards the two strains of Heliopolitan sun-worship and Osirianism became inextricably woven together in the daily ritual, and the utterances used at every stage in the ceremonies reveal this theological tangle.

The organization of the temple ritual was designed to enhance the relationship between the king and the god, and was therefore an intensely personal form of worship at the highest level. Ordinary Egyptians may be said to have participated in it only in so far as their destiny was closely linked with that of the king and because his well-being was ultimately their own well-being. Ideally the king himself performed the daily ritual to the god, but for practical reasons he was rarely in a position to do so. His place therefore was regularly taken by a priestly deputy. In temple reliefs, however, it is always the king who is shown performing the services to the god. It is probable that the king himself endeavoured to fulfil his ritual duty in the greatest temples on the principal feast-days. The first act in the ceremonies was the procession at dawn to the temple and the ritual purification and dressing of the king in the House of the Morning. Every temple had such a building adjoining it and in it the king was sprinkled with water from the sacred pool by priests in the guise either of Horus and Thoth or of Horus and Seth; he was then purified with natron, dressed in the appropriate garments and handed the necessary ritual implements, after which he was ready to perform the service of the god. The form of this service was the same whether performed by the king or his deputy. The first act of the officiant within the temple was to kindle a fire and to charge a censer with charcoal and incense. The shrine containing the cult-statue of the god was then approached, the seals of the doors broken and the doors opened. After offering incense to the god the officiant made obeisance, recited a hymn, presented honey or a figure of the goddess Maat, and burnt more incense before the god. The offering of the figure of Maat was a highly significant part of the ritual, since Maat represented the divinely-appointed ordered state of the land, which had to be preserved for the well-being of the gods. Practically all the activities of the Egyptian state religion, including the building of the temples themselves, was devoted to the maintenance of Maat, so that the gods might be contented and Egypt would benefit as a consequence.

The next stage in the daily ritual consisted of the removal of the figure of the god from its shrine, stripping it of its garments and adornments of the preceding day, a general purification, and clothing it once more. The figure was then replaced in its shrine, ready to receive the ritual feast which followed. Before the shrine stood an offering-table on which the various courses of the feast were placed and consecrated. In turn each was offered to the deity symbolically, and at the end, after a final purification with incense, the doors of the shrine were closed and sealed. The final act of the officiant in the daily ritual service was the purification of the room containing the shrine and the careful sweeping away of all footprints. A shrine for a cult-image, exhibited in the Egyptian Sculpture Gallery (1134; fig. 53), comes from the island of Philae and may have contained a figure of the goddess Isis. In the Sixth Egyptian Room is a case containing bronze objects used in ritual ceremonies; among them are two censers (58543 and 41606), a sceptre of the type used in the presentation of the repast to the god (22842), libation vessels (e.g. 36318), and other vessels for sacred liquids; particularly fine are three great situlae of the Late Period (38212, 38213, 38214) used probably for offerings of milk. In the same case are shown bronze terminals of standards carried in religious processions (54010, 64545).

The daily service was the principal act of worship in the temple and in it the public had no part. Access to the inner parts of the temple was denied everyone except the priesthood attached to the temple and the king or his representative. Limited access to the front court seems to have been permitted and, from the Middle Kingdom, favoured persons were allowed to place votive statues there. Many of the private statues exhibited in the Fifth Egyptian Room belong to this category. Otherwise public participation in the rites of temple worship was limited to attendance at the great festivals, some of which have been

53 Monolithic shrine from Philae

already mentioned (p. 132). Every sanctuary had its calendar of festival days on which the important events of the myth of the local deity were commemorated publicly. In small religious centres these festivals were held as local celebrations, but the festivals of the national gods became great occasions for public demonstrations of enthusiasm. Many of the festivals coincided with important seasonal events and were closely associated with agriculture, such as the Festival of the Coming-forth of Min at harvest time and the Festival of Sokaris, celebrated at Memphis towards the end of the inundation season. Other festivals occurred when visits were made by one god to another in a neighbouring sanctuary; of these the greatest was the Festival of Opet, held in Thebes in the second month of the inundation season. At this time the god Amun journeyed from Karnak to Luxor to celebrate his union with the divine mother (Mut) in the Luxor temple. The procession by boat on the Nile with the bark of Amun accompanied by the barks of Mut and the divine child Khons was an occasion for great excitement. At such times Amun was accustomed to make oracular pronouncements, and, during the New Kingdom at least, the king always endeavoured to attend in person. Of less political importance, but of great popular appeal, was the Festival of the Valley in the second month of the summer season, when Amun left Karnak and crossed the Nile to visit the temples on the west bank. The necropolis workmen possessed special privileges to take part in the procession on this occasion.

From the point of view of the kingship the most important festival was the *Sed*, at which the union of Egypt under one crown was re-enacted and the authority of the king renewed. Normally the *Sed*-festival took place after the king had ruled thirty years, and thereafter it was repeated at three-yearly intervals. There are, however, instances of its being held earlier than the thirtieth year, perhaps on the thirtieth anniversary of the king's becoming crown prince. It was always held at Memphis and to it came all the gods of the land to pay homage to the king. A small ivory royal figure exhibited in the Sixth Egyptian Room (37996, fig. 54) is of early dynastic date and represents a king wearing the characteristic short cloak associated with the *Sed*-festival ceremonies. Among the various acts performed in the course of the festival were the double coronation of the king as ruler of Upper Egypt and of Lower Egypt, a ritual dance and the running of four courses by the king, and the conducting of the king in a litter to visit the chapels of Horus and Seth who presented him with four arrows to be discharged against his enemies at the four cardinal points of the compass.

54 Ivory figure of a king

The priesthoods in the temples throughout Egypt were organized in regular classes; each temple had its corporation of priests consisting of 'prophets' (ḥmw-nṯr, literally 'servants of the god') and 'ordinary' or 'weeb-priests' (wꜥbw, literally 'pure ones'). Theoretically the king was high-priest in every temple, but in fact the duties were carried out by the 'first prophet'. Until the New Kingdom in most temples, and for much longer in small temples, the senior priestly offices were occupied by high civil officials; in the Middle Kingdom, for example, the nomarch was regularly high-priest in the sanctuary of the principal nome-god. The weeb-priests were organized into four groups, often called phyles, and each group served in the temple for one month at a time. The phyle on duty was responsible for the day-to-day running of the temple; its members received payment in kind, partly from temple revenues and partly from the daily offerings to the gods. The daily ritual of the god was performed by the high-priest or his deputy. Priests were not exempt from state services, taxes, and other national obligations, but from time to time the priesthoods of specific temples were granted privileges of immunity for special reasons, as in the case of the priests and other staff of the great temple of Osiris at Abydos by Sethos I. By receiving special immunity and by the influx of vast wealth, certain priesthoods developed great power during the New Kingdom. The outstanding example of this development was the priesthood of Amun at Thebes. Its overt power in the Eighteenth and Nineteenth Dynasties was considerable, but this power became proportionately even greater during the Twenty-first Dynasty when it was able to establish a virtually independent priestly state within the kingdom of Egypt (p. 69).

The actual temple buildings at the various sanctuaries throughout Egypt were regarded as the dwellings of the gods and the places in which the king could communicate with the gods. It is probable that the foundation of all important new temples was carried out by the king in person. The foundation ceremonies began with the surveying of the site, and by fixing the four corners by means of astral observation directed on the circumpolar stars. The king himself made and laid the four corner-bricks and helped to prepare the first foundations. Sets of model tools, amulets, and other objects were deposited in pits at various points around the temple walls. Many of the model tools exhibited in the Fourth Egyptian Room came from such foundation-deposits. When the temple building was completed, purified and consecrated, the king handed it over to its god.

As a rule the Egyptian temple was set in a sacred enclosure surrounded by mud-brick walls. From the exterior, the walls of the temple proper have something of the appearance of a fortress, since that is exactly what the Egyptians considered the temple to be—a fortress defending Egypt against all forms of evil. Entrance to the temple itself was gained through two pylons, beyond which lay an open court. This court sometimes had colonnades along the sides and an altar in the middle (Plate 15). Next, along the temple-axis, came the hypostyle, a pillared hall often surrounded by small rooms devoted to the storage of temple equipment and to the performance of subsidiary rites. Finally, there was the sanctuary, a dark room containing the cult-figure of the god placed in a shrine. Outside the walls of the temple, but within the sacred compound, were the domestic buildings of the priestly staff, the workshops, storerooms, and other ancillary structures. Great temples, like the cathedrals of Europe, were not built quickly; the building was continued by successive kings and plans were frequently modified. The most remarkable example of this constant growth is the great temple of Amen-Re at Karnak which, with its subsidiary temples, buildings, and lakes, occupies an enclosure, each side of which is about one-third of a mile in length. Such buildings were far more than religious centres; the great mortuary temple of Ramesses III at Medinet Habu became in the Late New Kingdom the administrative centre of the whole Theban Necropolis (p. 67). The temples were also great landowners, and the administration of their estates and revenues demanded large non-priestly staffs. It is probable that a new temple at the time of its foundation was presented with an endowment of land with the income from which its upkeep could be financed. Originally, as all land in Egypt was strictly the property of the king, the possession of land-endowments depended on the favour of the king (p. 29). In time, however, property-holding, whether on the part of temples or private persons, came to be regarded more and more as a right and less as a privilege; in consequence large estates were built up, especially by temples. Records show that temples in Lower Egypt might hold land in Upper Egypt and vice versa. From time to time, as different cults achieved prominence, different temples were favoured with endowments; land thus endowed was no doubt frequently reclaimed by the crown if circumstances required it. Nevertheless, vast areas of Egypt were by the New Kingdom held as temple domains, and the evidence offered by the Great Harris Papyrus (9999, fig. 34) suggests that Ramesses III was in his life able to donate about one-tenth of the cultivable area of Egypt to temples. With land went people and small industries, and from the labour of the former and the products of the latter the temples derived their principal wealth. Large temples were sometimes also granted the revenues of mines and other undertakings normally regarded as royal monopolies. They received income in the form of personal tithes and voluntary donations by private persons.

Myths and legends

About every Egyptian god many stories were told, but the stories varied from period to period and from place to place. As a result, the mythology of Egyptian religion is very complicated. Nevertheless, certain traditions remained generally constant throughout history and may be considered the basic myths of the religious system. Such were the principal creation myths, the legend of the struggles of Horus and Seth, and the Osiris cycle.

The origin of the world and the nature of the gods who took part in its creation were subjects of constant interest to the Egyptians. Three distinct cosmogonies were formulated in the earliest times based on the traditions of Heliopolis, Hermopolis, and Memphis. In later periods the Heliopolitan system was generally accepted, elements of the other systems being incorporated. According to the Heliopolitan tradition the world began as a watery chaos called Nun, from which the sun-god Atum (later to be identified with Re) emerged on a mound. By his own power he engendered the twin deities Shu (air) and Tefnut (moisture), who in turn bore Geb (earth) and Nut (sky). Geb and Nut finally produced Osiris, Isis, Seth, and Nephthys. The nine gods so created formed the divine ennead (i.e. company of nine) which in later texts was often regarded as a single divine entity. From this system derived the commonly accepted conception of the universe represented as a figure of the air-god Shu standing and supporting with his hands the out-stretched body of the sky-goddess Nut, with Geb the earth-god lying at his feet. The second cosmogonical tradition was developed at Hermopolis, the capital of the fifteenth nome of Upper Egypt, apparently during a time of reaction against the religious hegemony of Heliopolis. According to this tradition, also, chaos existed at the beginning, before the world was created. This chaos possessed four characteristics identified with eight deities who were grouped in pairs: Nun and Naunet, god and goddess of primordial water, Heh and Hehet, god and goddess of infinite space, Kek and Keket, god and goddess of darkness, and Amun and Amunet, god and goddess of invisibility. These deities were not so much the gods of the earth at the time of creation as the personifications of the characteristic elements of chaos out of which earth emerged. They formed what is called the Hermopolitan ogdoad (company of eight). Out of chaos so conceived arose the primeval mound at Hermopolis and on the mound was deposited an egg from which emerged the sun-god. He then proceeded to organize the world. The Hermopolitan idea of chaos was of something more active than the chaos of the Heliopolitan system; but after the ultimate triumph of the latter system, a subtle modification (no doubt introduced largely for political reasons) made Nun the father and creator of Atum. The third cosmogonical system was developed at Memphis, when it became the capital city of the kings of Egypt. Ptah, the principal god of Memphis, had to be shown to be the great creator-god, and a new legend about creation was coined. Nevertheless, an attempt was made so to organize the new cosmogony that a direct breach with the priests of Heliopolis might be avoided. Ptah was the great creator-god, but eight other gods were held to be contained within him. Of these eight, some were members of the Heliopolitan ennead, and others of the Hermopolitan ogdoad; Atum, for example, held a special position; Nun and Naunet were included; also Tatjenen, a Memphite god personifying the earth emerging from chaos, and four other deities whose names are not certain, but who were probably Horus, Thoth, Nefertum, and a serpent-god. Atum was held to represent the active faculties of Ptah by which creation was achieved, these faculties being intelligence, which was identified with the heart and personified as Horus, and will, which was identified with the tongue and personified as Thoth. Ptah conceived the world intellectually before creating it 'by his own word'. The whole Memphite system was in fact intellectually based, and remained throughout Egyptian history a system particularly attractive to religious theorists. A treatise embodying the essence of the Memphite theology is preserved on a slab of basalt now exhibited in the Egyptian Sculpture Gallery (498). It was composed at an early date, and committed to stone during the Twenty-fifth Dynasty by the order of king Shabaka. Unfortunately this stone —the so-called 'Shabaka Stone'—was subsequently used as a nether mill-stone, and much of the text has been lost. The document known as the Bremner-Rhind Papyrus (10188) includes, among other religious texts, two monologues of the sun-god describing how he created all things.

Many distinct traditions contributed to make the legend of the struggle between Horus and Seth not only one of the most important but also one of the most confused episodes in Egyptian mythology. The original tale of the struggle between the two gods became unusually complicated when Osirianism was incorporated into the main stream of Heliopolitan theology. Horus then as the son of Osiris achieved a new significance. In origin, however, the tradition seems to be based on a simple story of antagonism between two divine persons. The Heliopolitan Horus, on the one hand, was the warrior-god, the king-god, and at the same time a god of heaven; his eyes were originally

identified with the sun and the moon. A modification brought
about undoubtedly by the Heliopolitan identification of Re as
the sun-god led to the solar eye being attributed to Re, while
Horus was assigned the lunar eye. Seth, on the other hand, was
a god of the desert and of malevolent design; he snatched away
the eye of Horus which was retrieved only after a violent
struggle. This eye, known as *udjat*, according to some versions
was cast away by Seth before it could be retrieved, and it was
found by Thoth lying in pieces. Thoth restored it whole and
from this act it perhaps received its name *udjat*, which can mean
'that which is sound'. An important act in the drama of this
struggle is the trial that took place to decide between the rival
claims of Horus and Seth. There seems little doubt that the basic
issue to be decided was one of sovereignty, at first, who should
receive the crowns of Upper and Lower Egypt, subsequently,
who should succeed Osiris as king. The final justification of
Horus in his claim is the classic prototype of the judgement of
the deceased before Osiris in the after-life (p. 156). In a literary
composition of the New Kingdom, the *Contendings of Horus and
Seth*, the struggle is given as being over the solar eye of Re,
and the trial, involving a series of contests between Horus and
Seth, is carried out before the tribunal of the gods. Another
version of the struggle is preserved in the inscriptions in the
Ptolemaic temple of Horus at Edfu. Here Horus is represented as
the warrior-protector of Re in a series of campaigns against
Seth.

The cycle of legends concerning Osiris belonged originally to
a very different tradition from that which gave rise to the
creation myths already described. It is thought that the simple
story of Osiris may have been based on actual historical events
that took place at an early period in the Delta. Its appeal was
more immediate than that of the cosmogonical theologies of
Heliopolis and elsewhere, hence its remarkable success after its
introduction into the corpus of royal religious traditions in the
course of the Old Kingdom. The story never occurs in a consecutive form in Egyptian texts, but the host of references to component incidents in these texts confirms the general sequence
of events given in the account related by the Greek author
Plutarch. Osiris, according to the legend, was a just and beneficent king ruling over Egypt from the Delta. His reign was
brought to an end by Seth, his brother, who, for reasons of
jealousy, slew him. Plutarch relates that Seth prepared a fine
chest and invited Osiris to a feast attended by a group of conspirators bent on killing him. The chest was offered to the guest
who fitted it and the conspirators all tried it in turn, with no
success. Osiris' turn came and as soon as he lay inside, the lid

was fastened and the chest thrown into the Nile. Earlier allusions to this occasion suggest that Seth killed Osiris by drowning. The body of Osiris was then recovered by Isis, his wife, perhaps from Byblos, but Seth succeeded in stealing it and dividing it into fourteen (or sixteen, according to other versions) pieces which were scattered throughout Egypt. Isis with the help of her sister Nephthys sought the pieces and found them all with the exception (according to Plutarch, but not to most ancient sources) of his phallus. His body was reconstituted by the magic of Isis, who then succeeded in conceiving and bearing a child called Horus. She brought him up in secret in the Delta, and when he was old enough he took up the struggle with Seth, determined to avenge the death of his father. After many contests Horus prevailed and defeated Seth. In certain details the Osiris story owed much to other myths, especially that of the struggle between Horus and Seth. It exhibits that genius possessed by the Egyptians for adapting and harmonizing different traditions and systems without actually discarding anything. Texts of all periods contain references to Horus, Seth, and Osiris which show that the Egyptians were capable of regarding the various mythological threads either as individual stories or as parts of complicated traditions. The widespread success of the cult of Osiris was undoubtedly due to the realistic elements in the tale of his sufferings and to the hope offered by the belief in his resurrection after death. At first the king alone was identified with Osiris on his death, but from the Late Old Kingdom the possibility of enjoying a similar posthumous fate was extended to all classes of Egyptians. Osiris was further venerated as the personification of the Nile in inundation and as the god of vegetation, but it is unlikely that in his earliest form he was so regarded.

LIST OF PRINCIPAL GODS

AMEN: *see* Amun.

AMON: *see* Amun.

AMUN (AMEN, AMON), 𓇋𓏠: the great god of Thebes of uncertain origin; represented as a man, sometimes ithyphallic; identified with Re as Amen-Re; sacred animals, the ram and the goose.

ANAT, 𓏠𓏜: goddess of Syrian origin, with warlike character; represented as a woman holding a shield and an axe.

ANHUR: *see* Onuris.

ANPU: *see* Anubis.

ANQET: *see* Anukis.

ANUBIS (ANPU), 𓇋𓈖𓊪: the jackal-god, patron of embalmers; the great necropolis-god.

ANUKIS (ANQET), 𓏠𓈖𓈎: goddess of the cataract-region at Aswan; wife of Khnum; represented as a woman with a high feather head-dress.

ARSAPHES (HERISHEF), 𓁷𓏤: ram-headed god from Heracleopolis.

ASAR: *see* Osiris.

ASTARTE, 𓍿𓇋𓂋𓏏: goddess of Syrian origin; introduced into Egypt during the Eighteenth Dynasty.

ATEN, 𓇋𓏏𓈖: god of the sun-disk, worshipped as the great creator-god by Akhenaten.

ATUM (TUM), 𓏏𓇋: the original sun-god of Heliopolis, later identified with Re; represented as a man.

BAST: *see* Bastet.

BASTET (BAST), 𓎶: cat-goddess whose cult-centre was at Bubastis in the Delta; in the Late Period regarded as a beneficent deity.

BES, 𓃀𓋴: dwarf-deity with leonine features; a domestic god, protector against snakes and various terrors; helper of women in child-birth.

BUTO: *see* Edjo.

EDJO (WADJET, BUTO), 𓇋𓏏: the cobra-goddess of Buto in the Delta; tutelary deity of Lower Egypt, appearing on the royal diadem, protecting the king.

ERNUTET: *see* Renenutet.

GEB, 🦆: the earth-god; husband of Nut; member of the ennead of Heliopolis; represented as a man.

HAPY, 𓎛: god of the Nile in inundation; represented as a man with full, heavy breasts, a clump of papyrus on his head, and bearing heavily laden offering-tables.

HAROERIS, 𓅃: a form of Horus, the 'Elder Horus'; identified with the falcon-god and particularly the patron of the king.

HARPOCRATES (HOR-PA-KHRED), 𓅃: Horus-the-Child, a late form of Horus in his aspect of being son of Isis and Osiris; represented as a naked child wearing the lock of youth and holding one finger to his mouth.

HARSIESIS, 𓅃: a form of Horus, specifically designated 'son of Isis'.

HATHOR, 𓉡: goddess of many functions and attributes; represented often as a cow or a cow-headed woman, or as a woman with horned head-dress; the suckler of the king; the 'Golden One'; cult-centres at Memphis, Cusae, Gebelein, Dendera; the patron deity of the mining-region of Sinai; identified by the Greeks with Aphrodite.

HAT-MEHIT, 𓆛: fish-goddess of Mendes in the Delta; sometimes represented as a woman with a fish on her head.

HEQET, 𓆏: frog-goddess of Antinoopolis where she was associated with Khnum; a helper of women in child-birth.

HERISHEF: *see* Arsaphes.

HOR-PA-KHRED: *see* Harpocrates.

HORUS, 𓅃: the falcon-deity, originally the sky-god, identified with the king during his lifetime; also regarded as the son of Osiris and Isis, for the former of whom he became the avenger; cult-centres in many places, e.g. Behdet in the Delta, Hierakonpolis and Edfu in Upper Egypt. *See also*, Haroeris, Harpocrates, Harsiesis, Re-Harakhty.

IMHOTEP (IMOUTHES), 𓇋: the deified chief minister of Djoser and architect of the Step Pyramid; in the Late Period venerated as the god of learning and medicine; represented as a seated man holding an open papyrus; equated by the Greeks with Asklepios.

IMOUTHES: *see* Imhotep.

ISIS, 𓊨: the divine mother, wife of Osiris and mother of Horus; one of the four 'protector'-goddesses, guarding coffins and Canopic jars; sister of Nephthys with whom she acted as a divine mourner for the dead; in the Late Period Philae was her principal cult-centre.

KHEPRI, 🪲: the scarab-beetle god, identified with Re as a creator-god; often represented as a beetle within the sun-disk.

KHNUM, 🐏: ram-headed god of Elephantine, god of the Cataract-region; thought to have moulded man on a potter's wheel.

KHONS, ☾: the moon-god, represented as a man; with Amun and Mut as father and mother, forming the Theban triad.

MAAT, 🪶: goddess of truth, right, and orderly conduct; represented as a woman with an ostrich-feather on her head.

MIN, ⚊: the primeval god of Coptos; later revered as a god of fertility, and closely associated with Amun; represented as an ithyphallic human statue, holding a flagellum.

MONTH (MUNT), 🦅: originally the local deity of Hermonthis, just south of Thebes; later the war-god of the Egyptian king; represented as falcon-headed.

MUNT: see Month.

MUT, 🦅: the divine wife of Amun; cult-centre at Asheru, south of the main temple of Amen-Re at Karnak; originally a vulture-goddess, later represented usually as a woman.

NEBET-HET: see Nephthys.

NEFERTUM, 🪷: the god of the lotus, and hence of unguents; worshipped at Memphis as the son of Ptah and Sakhmet; represented as a man with a lotus-flower head-dress.

NEHEB-KAU, 🐍: a serpent deity of the underworld, sometimes represented with a man's body and holding the eye of Horus.

NEITH (NET), 🛡: goddess of Sais; represented as a woman wearing the red crown; her emblem, a shield with crossed arrows; one of the four 'protector'-goddesses who guarded coffins and Canopic jars; identified by the Greeks with Athena.

NEKHBET, 🦅: vulture-goddess of Nekheb (modern El-Kab); tutelary deity of Upper Egypt, sometimes appearing on the royal diadem beside the cobra (Edjo).

NEPHTHYS (NEBET-HET), 🏠: sister of Isis; one of the four 'protector'-goddesses, who guarded coffins and Canopic jars; with Isis acted as mourner for Osiris and hence for other dead people; represented as a woman.

NET: see Neith.

NU: see Nun.

NUN (NU), ᵒᵒᵒ⌐: god of the primeval chaos.

NUT, ᵒ⌐: the sky-goddess, wife of Geb, the earth-god; represented as a woman, her naked body curved to form the arch of heaven.

ONNOPHRIS: *see* Unnefer.

ONURIS (ANHUR), ⌐: god of This in Upper Egypt; the divine huntsman; represented as a man.

OSIRIS (ASAR), ⌐: the god of the underworld, identified as the dead king; also a god of the inundation and vegetation; represented as a mummified king; principal cult-centre, Abydos.

PTAH, ⌐: creator-god of Memphis, represented as a man, mummiform, possibly originally as a statue; the patron god of craftsmen; equated by the Greeks with Hephaestus.

PTAH-SEKER-OSIRIS, ⌐: a composite deity, incorporating the principal gods of creation, death, and after-life; represented like Osiris as a mummified king.

QADESH, ⌐: goddess of Syrian origin, often represented as a woman standing on a lion's back.

RA: *see* Re.

RE (RA), ⌐ʘ: the sun-god of Heliopolis; head of the great ennead, supreme judge; often linked with other gods aspiring to universality, e.g. Amen-Re, Sobk-Re; represented as falcon-headed; *see also* Re-Harakhty.

RE-HARAKHTY, ⌐: a god in the form of a falcon, embodying the characteristics of Re and Horus (here called 'Horus of the Horizon').

RENENUTET (ERNUTET, THERMUTHIS), ⌐: goddess of harvest and fertility; represented as a snake or a snake-headed woman.

RESHEF (RESHPU), ⌐: god of war and thunder, of Syrian origin.

RESHPU: *see* Reshef.

SAKHMET, ⌐: a lion-headed goddess worshipped in the area of Memphis; wife of Ptah; regarded as the bringer of destruction to the enemies of Re.

SARAPIS: a god introduced into Egypt in the Ptolemaic Period having the characteristics of Egyptian (Osiris) and Greek (Zeus) gods; represented as a bearded man wearing the modius head-dress; the Egyptian writing of the name (⌐, i.e. Osiris-Apis) may not signify the true origin of this god.

SATET: *see* Satis.

SATIS (SATET), 𓏤𓂝: goddess of the Island of Siheil in the Cataract-region; represented as a woman wearing the white crown with antelope horns; the daughter of Khnum and Anukis.

SEBEK: *see* Sobk.

SEKER: *see* Sokaris.

SELKIS (SELKIT, SERQET), 𓋹𓂝: a scorpion-goddess, identified with the scorching heat of the sun; one of the four 'protector'-goddesses, guarding coffins and Canopic jars; shown sometimes as a woman with a scorpion on her head.

SELKIT: *see* Selkis.

SEPDET: *see* Sothis.

SERQET: *see* Selkis.

SESHAT, 𓏲𓂝: the goddess of writing; the divine keeper of royal annals; represented as a woman.

SET: *see* Seth.

SETH (SET, SUTEKH), 𓃩: the god of storms and violence; identified with many animals, including the pig, ass, okapi, and hippopotamus; represented as an animal of unidentified type; brother of Osiris and his murderer; the rival of Horus; equated by the Greeks with Typhon.

SHU, 𓆄𓀭: the god of air; with Tefnut, forming the first pair of gods in the Heliopolitan ennead; shown often as a man separating Nut (sky) from Geb (earth).

SOBK (SEBEK, SUCHOS), 𓆌𓆏: the crocodile-god, worshipped throughout Egypt, but especially in the Faiyum, and at Gebelein and Kom Ombo in Upper Egypt.

SOKAR: *see* Sokaris.

SOKARIS (SOKAR, SEKER), 𓅨: a falcon-headed god of the necropolis; cult-centre in Memphis.

SOPDU, 𓊗𓅆: the ancient falcon-god of Saft el-Henna in the Delta; a warrior-god, protector of the eastern frontier; represented often as an Asiatic warrior.

SOTHIS (SEPDET), 𓊗𓇼: the dog-star Sirius, deified as a goddess; shown as a woman with a star on her head.

SUCHOS: *see* Sobk.

SUTEKH: *see* Seth.

TATJENEN, 𓏏𓈖𓈖: the primeval earth-god of Memphis; later identified with Ptah.

TAURT: *see* Thoeris.

TAWERET: *see* Thoeris.

TEFNUT, ⊙: the goddess of moisture; with Shu forming the first pair of the Heliopolitan ennead.

THERMUTHIS: *see* Renenutet.

THOERIS (TAURT, TAWERET), ⊙: the hippopotamus-goddess; a beneficent deity, the patron of woman in child-birth.

THOTH, ⊙: the ibis-headed god of Hermopolis; the scribe of the gods and the inventor of writing; the ape as well as the ibis being sacred to him.

TUM: *see* Atum.

UNNEFER (WENEN-NEFER, ONNOPHRIS), ⊙: a name meaning 'he who is continually happy', given to Osiris after his resurrection.

UPUAUT: *see* Wepwawet.

WADJET: *see* Edjo.

WENEN-NEFER: *see* Unnefer.

WEPWAWET (UPUAUT), ⊙: the jackal-god of Asyut in Middle Egypt; a god of the necropolis and an avenger of Osiris.

CHAPTER SIX

FUNERARY BELIEFS AND CUSTOMS

Most of the objects preserved from the ancient civilization of Egypt come from temples and tombs and this fact necessarily leads to the supposition that the Egyptians were a particularly religious people obsessed with death and burial. If more were generally known of the daily life of the Egyptians and of the purely secular side of their life, their interest in the gods and the after-life would seem less of an obsession. One fact that would emerge clearly is that the apparently overwhelming pre-occupation with death springs essentially from the Egyptian's devotion to life and the good things available to him in the beneficent land of Egypt. In general it was thought that the best existence a man could expect in the after-life was one that contained all that was most desired in the life on earth. The ideas of what a man might have to encounter in his progress to achieve this idyllic reconstruction of his life in Egypt varied from period to period according to the current dominant religious beliefs, but the end was apparently always the same, whether declared explicitly or hoped for implicitly. The hope was present undoubtedly in the earliest simple burials in which modest offerings and equipment were included; as time advanced this hope was established more firmly and the funerary arrangements were elaborated to provide fully for the expected state of bliss.

The tangle of confused and contradictory ideas which form the main body of Egyptian funerary beliefs was the result of thousands of years of development in which new conceptions were continually being incorporated without ousting those with which they were not in harmony. Consequently it is not possible to give accounts of most of the important elements in funerary thought which will apply to all places and all classes of society. In death, as in life, the Egyptian expected to belong to an hierarchic society in which the best was reserved for the king and the nobles and it is from their graves that most of the information about Egyptian burial customs comes. The resulting account is therefore necessarily one-sided; yet it may be said that at every level the Egyptian's aspiration for his existence after death was that it should consist of the best available to him in his life on earth. In order that he might fully participate in his appointed life hereafter it was necessary that his name should continue to exist, that his body should remain intact and that he should be regularly supplied with necessary food and drink. In the periods of high civilization these ends were achieved by the provision of a tomb containing the incorruptible mummy and inscribed with texts incorporating the owner's name and with scenes that would secure for him by magical means food and drink and other desirable things when the services of the appointed tomb-servants ceased to be carried out.

The early history of the ideas underlying these funerary beliefs is unknown; the first truly informative funerary texts occur in the Old Kingdom and it is clear that many centuries of slow development lie behind the formulations they embody. One concept which in origin applied only to the king but which later was extended to all classes was that of the possession of a spiritual entity called the *Ka*. It is not possible to give a wholly consistent account of the *Ka* because it was an elusive conception capable of various interpretations at different periods. To a certain extent it corresponds with the 'self' of a man. It was born with a man and formed an integral part of his being and was yet in some respects regarded as distinct from him, certainly from his bodily 'self'. It was for his *Ka* that a man provided all the paraphernalia of funerary equipment, food and drink in his tomb, and the tomb itself was known as the 'house of the *Ka*'. Another spiritual entity which can be identified approximately with what is now called the 'soul' was the *Ba* or *Bai*. The *Ba* was thought to leave the body at the moment of death and it was generally represented as a human-headed bird (Plate 14). It was more generally the concrete manifestation of the innate ability possessed by a man's soul to assume different forms both in life and in death; this ability was particularly important when the man was dead for it was necessary for the soul to leave the tomb during the daytime to revisit the outer world where it could transform itself into whatever form might be useful to accomplish its purpose. At night the *Ba* returned to the tomb and the body which was its proper home.

The beliefs of the Egyptians about the after-life were greatly developed when the solar religion of the Old Kingdom, which was principally royal in application, was superseded by the cult of Osiris, which envisaged a posthumous existence which could be enjoyed by men of all ranks. Osiris, the dead king and king of the dead, offered hope of survival in the after-life and the dead person was in fact identified with Osiris. In order to achieve this identification and to secure the Osirian resurrection the deceased needed to be tested and declared 'true of voice' a process carried out in the presence of forty-two assessor-gods. The judgement scene from the *Book of the Dead* prepared for the scribe Ani is a typical example (Plate 13). In the Hall of Judgement Ani, with his wife Tutu, stands by the scales on which his heart (for the Egyptians, the seat of intelligence) is being weighed against a feather representing Truth. The scales are watched by Anubis, the jackal-god of the necropolis, and a record is being kept by Thoth, the ibis-headed god. The deceased denies a specific sin to each assessor, the sins being related to behaviour in life and revealing the general moral attitude of the ancient Egyptians. This 'Negative Confession' completed, the deceased is declared 'true of voice' and led into the presence of Osiris.

Mummification

The preservation of the body, held to be so important for the well-being of a dead man in his after-life, became one of the principal aims of Egyptian funerary practices at a very early period. In the Predynastic Period bodies were buried for the most part in simple shallow graves and covered sometimes with a skin or a mat of woven work. The hot dry sand acted as a powerful desiccating agent and the body was naturally preserved as is shown by the example in the reconstructed predynastic burial in the Second Egyptian Room (32751). The appearance of the body after this drying process is that of a skeleton covered with skin; some hair remains on the head. Towards the end of the Predynastic Period burials became more elaborate and a kind of chamber was prepared for the body. No longer did the corpse come into contact with the hot desiccating sand and the natural process of putrefaction took place: a measure intended to afford greater protection had in fact the opposite effect. It seems possible that this change in the fate of the corpse was soon appreciated and attempts were made to secure artificially the effect formerly achieved naturally by the contact of the body with sand. Evidence is very scanty for the first three dynasties; but the discovery of bodies whose individual limbs were wrapped tightly with linen bandages suggests that at first it was thought that by keeping the body carefully covered decomposition could be prevented. The contrary, however, would have been the case and it is not until the Fourth Dynasty that good evidence exists to show that the Egyptians realized that one necessary step towards preventing decomposition was the removal of the internal organs. The tomb of Hetepheres, mother of the king Cheops, contained a partitioned calcite chest with bandaged packages of viscera still soaking in a dilute solution of natron. During the Old and Middle Kingdoms no fixed method of preparing the corpse was practised and very few bodies from these periods which can properly be called mummies have survived. In some cases the viscera have been removed, in others the brain; sometimes the body has been dehydrated; sometimes the appearance of a well-preserved corpse has been effected by the use of large quantities of linen wrappings and masks fashioned in the image of the deceased. By the New Kingdom, however, the basic requirements needed to obtain adequate preservation were fully understood. Even so, the results achieved fell far short of good preservation. The process was basically one of dehydration of the body after the removal of the brain and viscera. The name 'mummy' comes from an Arabic word (of Persian origin) meaning 'a body preserved by bitumen', the word for 'bitumen' in Arabic being *mumiya*; but bitumen was not in fact normally used in the embalming process. Late documents from Egypt (e.g. the demotic papyrus 10077, fig. 33) and the works of Greek writers, particularly Herodotus, provide most of the written evidence about mummification. The period spent on preparing the body for burial between death and interment was seventy days, about one-half of this time being devoted to the drying of the body. Immediately after death the corpse was handed over to the embalmers whose first task was to remove those parts which would putrefy most quickly, namely the viscera and the brain. The former were removed through an incision made in the left side of the abdomen and the latter through the nose by puncturing the ethmoid bone. The heart, however, as the seat of understanding, was regularly left in the body. It used to be thought that the principal stage in mummification was a long period of soaking in a bath containing a solution of natron, a naturally occurring compound of sodium carbonate and sodium bicarbonate. Recent investigations have shown, however, that it is far more probable that dry natron was used, the effect of which was to dehydrate the body efficiently, to dissolve body fats, and to leave the skin supple but not tender. The internal organs were treated with natron separately. All the materials used in this process were carefully preserved and buried in the vicinity of the tomb, if not in the tomb itself, for it was important that the essential juices extracted should not be divorced completely from the body. Finally the body-cavity was sometimes packed with linen and the abdominal incision sewn up and covered with a plate of leather or other material bearing a representation of the eye of Horus, a powerful protective amulet. The eye sockets likewise were plugged with wads of linen or inset with artificial eyes. After the body had been treated with ointments, spices, and resins it was wrapped in a series of bandages, part of the intention of which was to restore to the body some of the bulk and form which it had lost during the dehydrating process. The relative failure of mummification to retain the form and appearance of the body in life was evidently a matter of great concern to the Ancient Egyptians and many different methods were practised from time to time to improve the results obtained. Most elaborate measures were taken during the Twenty-first Dynasty when the skill of the embalmers reached its highest peak of achievement. The bodies of important people were subjected after dehydration to a packing of the limbs with materials such as linen, fats, and even mud so that the limbs might be restored to their forms before dehydration. In the same period the internal organs were replaced in the abdominal cavity (see below). Everything in fact was done to restore the body to its form during life. These elaborate measures were continued for only a short period and in subsequent times the treatment of the corpse became progressively more simple, the skill of the embalmers being exercised increasingly on bandaging. A good example of a well-bandaged mummy is that of Pasheryenhor (6666) exhibited in the First Egyptian Room (fig. 55); it dates to the period between the Twenty-second and Twenty-sixth Dynasties. In the Roman Period the outer wrappings were frequently arranged in intricate patterns of cross-strapping (13595).

In order to protect further the mummified, carefully wrapped body, amulets of various kinds were placed on the body and within the wrappings. Perhaps the most important was the heart scarab which was placed on the breast. It carried on its undersurface a short exhortation to the heart not to act as a hostile witness against the deceased when it was in the balance in the Judgement Hall of Osiris. A group of heart scarabs is exhibited together with other amulets in wall-cases 96 and 97 in the Third Egyptian Room; the most interesting and one of the earliest is that of King Sobkemsaf of the early Seventeenth Dynasty (7876). Ordinary small scarabs were also used for amuletic purposes on mummies of the New Kingdom and later. The legends engraved on such scarabs (many examples of which are shown in the Sixth Egyptian Room) consist mostly of divine symbols and short amuletic texts. Other amulets commonly found on mummies are the Eye of Horus, the djed-pillar, the girdle of Isis, and the uadj-sceptre; also small figures of deities were regularly used for amuletic purposes. Of special interest is the set of composition amulets from a mummy of the Twenty-sixth Dynasty, found at Nabesha in the Delta, which is exhibited, according to the arrangement on the body itself, in wall-case 96 (20577). Amulets of this type became common during the New Kingdom and even more numerous in the Late New Kingdom and Late Period. Two special categories of amuletic objects found with mummies are ivory wands and hypocephali. The former are found in graves of the Middle Kingdom and appear to have been used in life as well as in death (p. 135). They are regularly made of hippopotamus ivory and are engraved with the creatures

55 Mummy of
Pasheryenhor

they were intended to combat as well as those gods particularly associated with the home, Bes and Thoeris (fig. 51). Hypocephali are found in burials of the Saite Period and later; they are usually made of linen stiffened with plaster, although a few examples are made of other materials such as bronze (37330). They are found beneath the heads of mummies and are decorated with vignettes depicting various universal deities and with extracts from Chapter CLXII of the *Book of the Dead* designed to bring warmth to the body.

In the account of mummification given above it was stressed that one of the essential preliminaries to successful mummification was the removal of the internal organs. Equally important for the continued well-being of the deceased in his after-life was the careful preservation of these organs, and from the Old Kingdom onwards until the Ptolemaic Period it was customary to place the embalmed viscera in four jars which are now called Canopic jars. The name Canopic is strictly speaking incorrect; it was used by early scholars who saw in these jars with human-headed stoppers confirmation of the story related by classical writers of Canopus, the pilot of Menelaus, who was buried at Canopus in Egypt and was worshipped locally in the form of a jar with a human head and a swollen body. The earliest Canopic jar in the collection was made for a man called Wahka who lived in the late Eleventh Dynasty (58780) and the earliest complete set belonged to Gua, an official of the early Twelfth Dynasty (30838). Gua's jars are of alabaster with human-headed stoppers of painted wood, the set being contained in a wooden Canopic chest. The viscera placed in the four jars were protected by four minor deities, the sons of Horus, named Duamutef (the stomach), Qebhsenuef (the intestines), Hapy (the lungs), and Imsety (the liver), and the jars themselves were identified with the four protective female deities Neith, Selkis, Nephthys, and Isis. Until the end of the Eighteenth Dynasty the jar-stoppers were in the form of human heads; thereafter each jar had a stopper carved in the form of the head of its appropriate protective genius: for Duamutef a jackal head, for Qebhsenuef a falcon head, for Hapy an ape head, and for Imsety a human head. During the Twenty-first Dynasty, when it was usual to replace them inside the body-cavity, the viscera were made up into four packages, each one accompanied by a wax figure of the corresponding son of Horus. Yet the practice of including a set of Canopic jars in the full equipment of a tomb was so established that jars were supplied simply to fulfil the formal need. A fine set of this kind is shown in fig. 56; it was made for Neskhons, the wife of Pinudjem, High Priest of Amun at Thebes (59197–200). Dummy solid jars were also used during the Ptolemaic Period

Canopic jars of
Neskhons

when the process of mummification was carried out in a very
perfunctory manner, the viscera often being left in the body.
A representative series of Canopic jars and chests is exhibited
in the First Egyptian Room.

A development of the Egyptians' identification of certain of
their gods with particular animals was the practice of animal
mummification. In general the mass mummification and burial
of sacred animals was a phenomenon of the Ptolemaic and
Roman Periods. The animal-cemeteries were situated in the
neighbourhood of the appropriate cult-centres. Thus Bubastis,
the centre of worship of the cat-goddess Bastet, has large cat
cemeteries, while Hermopolis in Middle Egypt has large ibis
cemeteries, the local god being the ibis-headed Thoth. The actual
mummification of animals and birds was very crude and the body
was often skeletal before being bandaged; but the bandaging was
carried out with great skill and every effort made to produce
a wrapped mummy convincing in appearance. Although most
animal mummies are late in date the practice of venerating
particular animals in this manner existed in earlier periods,
particularly the sacred bulls of Memphis, Heliopolis, and
Hermonthis. The Apis bulls of Memphis were buried in a vast
catacomb in the Saqqara necropolis known as the Serapeum.
The mummification of these animals, only one of which existed
at any one time, was performed thoroughly; a full embalming
process was employed, and the large alabaster tables used for
the preparation of the body have recently been found in the
neighbourhood of the temple of Ptah at Memphis. The bull-
mummies were finally buried in huge stone sarcophagi.
Examples of animal mummies and coffins are exhibited in the
First Egyptian Room.

Coffins

Coffins were in general not used in the burials of the Pre-dynastic Period; in the earliest times the body was placed in a shallow grave and covered sometimes with skins or matting to protect it from the sand and other filling piled directly above it. In later predynastic times wood-revetted or bricked chambers with roofs were made to receive the body which was then placed in the grave wrapped as formerly or in a wicker basket. A few burials have been found in which primitive coffins of wood, clay or pottery were used but they are exceptional and it was not until the Early Dynastic Period that a coffin became a regular part of the funerary equipment. No actual examples of coffins made for kings or important nobles have survived from this period; men of humbler position were buried in coffins constructed of reeds (fig. 57), or were laid in simple trays or wooden chests, the last occasionally with panelled sides reproducing the form of the early great mastaba-tombs (p. 175). Typical coffins of wood and reeds, dating from the First Dynasty, are exhibited in the Second Egyptian Room.

During the Old Kingdom a type of coffin was developed which was used until late in the Middle Kingdom. The form was a simple rectangular chest made from large planks of imported wood, mostly cedar. The coffin of Nebhotep (46629) of Sixth-dynasty date, illustrates the form and also the way in which such coffins were constructed out of unevenly shaped planks. It also exhibits on one side the two eyes of Horus which were regularly

57 First Dynasty burial in a reed coffin

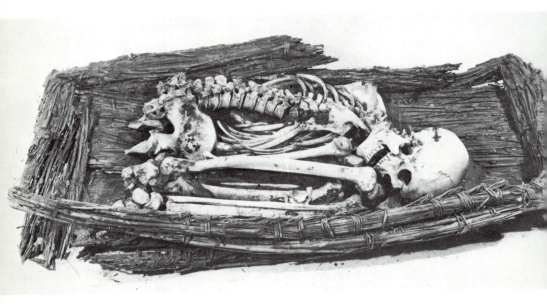

placed at one end both to act as amuletic protection of the body within and also possibly to enable the dead man to look out. This coffin has no decoration apart from simple bands of texts; in some other coffins the sides bear painted representations of doors beneath the double Horus-eyes and of palace-façade decoration. This latter type of decoration is found commonly on the great stone sarcophagi placed in the tombs of kings and high officials during the Old Kingdom to receive the inner wooden coffins. During the First Intermediate Period burials became less elaborate and tombs were rarely decorated; more attention was paid to the coffin, the ultimate receptacle of the corpse. Inner and outer wooden coffins of the chest type were frequently used, usually decorated on the insides with texts and representations which largely fulfilled the purpose of the mural scenes and inscriptions in Old Kingdom tombs. Coffins of this kind were most common during the Eleventh Dynasty and they were also used in the burials of provincial nobles and high officials during the Twelfth Dynasty. The most important part of the decoration consisted of excerpts from the *Coffin Texts*, a body of funerary texts, which derived from the old royal *Pyramid Texts* (p. 171) of the Fifth and Sixth Dynasties. The adaptation of the *Pyramid Texts* for use by non-royal persons was one result of the democratization of Egyptian life which followed the breakdown of the exclusive royal power at the end of the Old Kingdom. The purpose of these texts was to ensure the well-being of the deceased by magical means. Figure 58 shows the inside end of the inner coffin of Gua (30840), a high official whose tomb was found at El-Bersha in Middle Egypt; it bears a substantial extract from the *Coffin Texts* and part of the so-called 'frieze of objects' commonly included in the decoration of these great wooden coffins. This frieze usually contains representations of objects some of which were amuletic and some useful in a more practical way. The floors of this inner coffin and of the outer coffin of the same man (30839) are inscribed with texts from the *Book of the Two Ways* accompanied by a plan by which the deceased could find his way in the underworld. These coffins of Gua, and others of similar type, are exhibited in the Second Egyptian Room.

Stone coffins were rarely used except in royal burials during the Middle Kingdom when they were usually simple coffers with flat lids. Occasionally, as in the case of those made for the princesses buried at Deir el-Bahri, the sides were decorated with scenes of daily life and offering-texts.

A change in the manner of preparing the mummified body for burial during the Twelfth Dynasty prompted a modification in coffin design. It became customary to cover the head of the corpse

with a mask made usually of layers of linen and gesso, moulded to the form of the face, the latter being sometimes gilded. A good example of a Middle Kingdom mask of this kind on exhibition belonged to an unidentified lady of high rank, probably a princess (29770). The characteristic mummy of the period with heavy bandaging and mask became the basic form on which coffins were modelled thereafter. In so preparing the body and burying it in a coffin shaped like a mummy, the Egyptians reinforced the identification of the deceased with the god Osiris who was

58 Texts and painted decoration on the inner coffin of Gua

regularly shown as a mummified king. The decoration of the earliest anthropoid mummiform coffins, which were heavily built of wood, was designed to achieve the same effect; the surfaces were commonly painted with a feather design, thought to represent the wings of the goddess Isis, protecting the body of Osiris. Feather decoration of this kind is usually called *rishi*— the Arabic word for 'feather'. One of the Museum's coffins of this type has the decoration gilded, the colour of the gold being an unusually light lime-colour (6652). This coffin was made for a king Inyotef (possibly Nubkheperre) of the Seventeenth Dynasty.

In the New Kingdom coffins were normally made of wood or cartonnage (moulded linen and plaster) and were mummiform. Stone sarcophagi on the other hand were not common except in royal burials. During the Eighteenth Dynasty the kings were buried in simple but finely inscribed stone sarcophagi which contained inner and outer mummiform coffins of gold and gilded wood. In the Nineteenth Dynasty the royal stone sarcophagus was no longer rectangular, but mummiform and inscribed with funerary texts and representations. Parts of the lid of the great alabaster sarcophagus of Sethos I are in the Museum, though not exhibited; the fine coffer of this sarcophagus is preserved in the Sir John Soane Museum in Lincoln's Inn Fields. Of rare stone sarcophagi made for non-royal persons, a good example is that of the Viceroy of Kush, Merymose, who served under Amenophis III, which is exhibited in the Central Saloon of the Egyptian Sculpture Gallery (1001). It is mummiform and made of black granite finely carved with texts and divine representations. Fragments of an outer mummiform sarcophagus for the same man are also preserved in the Museum. The decoration of non-royal wooden and cartonnage coffins was mostly simple in the Eighteenth Dynasty, texts being inscribed in yellow paint on a ground of black paint. Towards the end of the dynasty and during the Nineteenth Dynasty coffin-equipment was often more elaborate, like that of the lady Henutmehit. Three separate units are preserved, each heavily decorated and gilded; first a cartonnage mummy-cover with figures of gods in open-work, backed by purple linen; next an inner coffin with finely modelled face and heavy wig; finally, an outer coffin, similarly decorated (48001, 48001A; Plate 12).

In the later New Kingdom inner and outer anthropoid mummiform coffins were heavily decorated within and without with religious scenes and amuletic symbols. A series of these coffins is shown in the Second Egyptian Room. The base colour regularly used is yellow and the decorations are painted in bright colours, some of the individual elements being first modelled in relief in gesso. Among the common scenes and symbols found on the outside are the winged sun-disk, the winged scarab-beetle, representations of the deceased adoring various gods, figures of gods and goddesses, often winged and shown in protective attitudes, the sun-god passing through the divisions of the underworld in his bark, the funeral procession, the judgement-scene in the underworld, the resurrection of Osiris, and various demons of the underworld. On the insides, the regular scenes include the goddess Nut, the *djed*-pillar, the deified Amenophis I, the human-headed *Ba*-bird, the adoration of the sun-god and other deities, underworld demons, and sacred symbols. In the period following the Twenty-first Dynasty the decline in the craft of mummification was accompanied by a deterioration in the design and decoration of coffins. One development, which can be traced to the practice of placing moulded mummy covers over the corpse as early as the Eighteenth Dynasty, was the close-fitting cartonnage case shaped to the form of the mummified body. These cases were decorated with scenes similar to those found in the inner coffins of the preceding period, but they did not in general take the place of the inner coffin. Burials of rich and influential people were still provided with at least two wooden coffins, sometimes with three; the outer coffins were increasingly ponderous and crude in design and were decorated with scenes and texts executed in indifferent style. Stone mummiform coffins also became fashionable again, sometimes being used instead of the outer wooden coffin. Wooden coffins of the Late Period are exhibited in the First Egyptian Room and stone coffins in the Egyptian Sculpture Gallery. Also in the Sculpture Gallery can be seen examples of the great stone sarcophagi which contained the nests of coffins in the burials of kings and very important nobles in the Late Period. Of special interest are those of the princess Ankhnesneferibre of the Twenty-sixth Dynasty and the king Nectanebo of the Thirtieth Dynasty. The former (32) is a rectangular chest finely inscribed with texts from the *Book of the Dead* and with low-relief representations of Ankhnesneferibre (on the lid), the goddess Nut (on the reverse side of the lid, fig. 59; not now visible), and the goddess Hathor (on the bottom of the coffer). The coffin of Nectanebo (10) is rounded at one end and is inscribed with scenes and texts from the *Book of what is in the Underworld*.

In the Ptolemaic Period the tradition of the Late Period was continued. Outermost coffins were frequently made in the form of a chest with vaulted lid and four corner posts in a type developed towards the end of the Late Period. The mummy itself was often covered with an openwork cartonnage case and all

59 The goddess Nut carved on the schist sarcophagus of Princess Ankhnesneferibre (see also fig. 25)

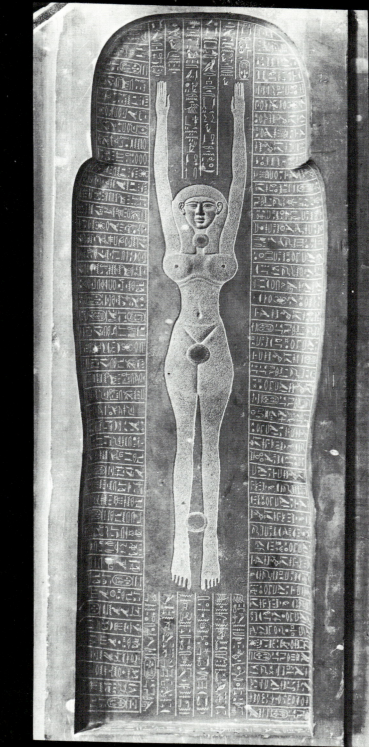

elements of the equipment were inscribed with religious texts. The First Egyptian Room contains many examples of coffins of the Ptolemaic Period and also of the subsequent Roman Period (p. 243).

Shabtis and other funerary equipment

From the earliest times the tombs of the Egyptians were provided with an equipment designed to satisfy the needs of the deceased in his after-life. At first this equipment consisted principally of objects that might be used by the deceased in the way in which they were used in the daily life of the time. In simple graves there were pottery vessels and baskets containing food and drink, simple tools, and other utensils. In the tombs of kings and nobles from the time of the early dynasties there were placed, in addition, articles of furniture, chests of clothing, jewellery, and other objects of value. Many of the objects exhibited in the various rooms of the Egyptian Department in the British Museum came from tombs and formed originally parts of individual tomb-equipments. Most of the vessels of pottery, composition, stone, and metal may so be classified and also most of the 'objects of daily life' exhibited in the Fourth Egyptian Room. These objects, however, were actually used in the daily life of the times when they were placed in tombs and are not to be regarded solely as funerary equipment. This term is applied here to those objects the purpose of which was more closely connected with the fate of the deceased in the after-life, and which had no part in daily life. Some of the objects of this kind found in close association with the mummy, such as amulets, have already been mentioned (p. 159); others are shabti-figures, Ptah-Seker-Osiris figures, papyri with religious texts, and magical bricks. Model utensils and tools and the wooden models of scenes were made specially for burials, but represent actual objects used in daily life, or activities carried on in daily life.

Shabti-figures are exhibited in the Third Egyptian Room. The name shabti is of uncertain meaning. The same figures were called shawabtis in the New Kingdom and ushabtis in the Late Period; hence it would appear that the Egyptians themselves were in doubt about the original meaning. The Ancient Egyptians believed that in the underworld, as in Egypt itself, there would be a regular need for work on the land such as was required after the annual inundation of Egypt by the Nile (pp. 24 f.). Each year the rehabilitation of the land, involving the re-establishment of property boundaries, the rebuilding of dykes and cutting of canals, followed the subsiding of the flood waters, and these tasks were accomplished by the conscription of

Plate 12
Inner coffin of
Henutmehit (*opposite*)

Plate 13
Weighing the heart
from the *Book of the
Dead* of the scribe
Ani (*overleaf*)

Plate 14
Vignette from the
Book of the Dead of
the scribe Ani
showing the Ba (soul)
hovering over the
mummy

labour. It was possible, however, for a man of means to avoid this *corvée* by supplying a deputy, and the intention of the *shabti*-figure was to act as the deceased's deputy for such tasks in the underworld. The coffin of Gua mentioned above (p. 163) carries an early version of the magical text used to secure this substitution; in the New Kingdom the text (incorporated as Chapter VI of the *Book of the Dead*) usually ran as follows: 'N. says "O shabti! If N. is detailed for any tasks to be done there (in the underworld), as a man is bound, namely to cultivate the fields, to flood the banks (of the fields—i.e. to water them) and to carry away sand to the east and to the west, then say thou, 'Here am I'."' The earliest *shabti*-figures were made of wood or wax in the form of a mummy and simply inscribed with the name of the deceased owner; they were sometimes placed in small coffins. In the New Kingdom more care was used in making the figures, which were usually carved in stone and inscribed with the *shabti*-text. The form remained that of a mummy, for it represented the deceased as Osiris. At this time *shabtis* were first made with tools in their hands—baskets, mattocks, hoes. Some *shabtis* are finely carved, especially those made for kings, such as that of Amenophis II (35365; fig. 60). In the Eighteenth Dynasty glazed composition was first used in their manufacture and thereafter it was the material most commonly employed, almost to the exclusion of other materials. The design of *shabtis* deteriorated throughout the Late New Kingdom and Late Period until the Twenty-sixth Dynasty when very finely modelled pieces were again made. The practice of providing *shabtis* in burials seems to have died out at the end of the Dynastic Period. A rare, apparent *shabti*-figure of the Roman Period, in polychrome glazed composition, is that of a sailor named Soter (30769). The *shabti*-figures of members of the Napatan royal family of Twenty-fifth Dynasty date and later represent an interesting development of Egyptian culture in Nubia where, in the Late Period, the ruling family was devoted to the worship of Amun and followed Egyptian funerary practice (p. 73). In the Middle Kingdom *shabtis* were provided singly in burials, sometimes in small coffins, and were thus true deputies. In later times, however, large numbers were buried, especially in royal tombs. Some New Kingdom *shabtis*, buried singly in coffins (e.g. 53892), may have had some other function. In the Late New Kingdom it became customary to provide one *shabti* for each day of the year with 'overseer' figures added to control the gangs into which the 'worker'-*shabtis* were organized. These overseers are represented usually not as mummies; they wear skirts and carry whips of office. The large numbers of *shabtis* were accommodated in special *shabti*-boxes, examples of which are exhibited with

Plate 15
Part of the temple
built by
Ramesses III at
Medinet Habu

the *shabtis* in the Third Egyptian Room. The burial of the lady Neskhons contained two boards bearing decrees concerning her *shabti*-figures. One of these boards is in the Museum (16672); the text shows that Neskhons paid for the *shabtis*, but it is not clear whether she bought them as slaves or made the payment to reimburse them for their work.

An object characteristic of burials of the Late Period is the Ptah-Seker-Osiris figure representing a triune deity embodying some of the characteristics of Ptah, the god of creation, Seker (or Sokaris) the god of the necropolis, and Osiris, the god of the underworld. The earliest figures belonging to this category, coming from Nineteenth Dynasty burials, represent Osiris alone, shown as a mummiform king standing on a pedestal. In some cases the figure is hollow and was intended to hold a copy of the *Book of the Dead* inscribed for the deceased owner. Such a figure was that made for the priestess of Amen-Re, Anhai, who lived in the Twentieth Dynasty (20868); the fine papyrus contained in the figure is now exhibited in the Third Egyptian Room (10472). The papyrus of Hunefer (9901) was also found in a Ptah-Seker-Osiris figure (9861). In the Late Period the figures have the triple divine association with Ptah, Sokaris, and Osiris, and it often happens that the bases of the figures contain small papyrus rolls in substitution for the larger rolls and also small portions of the bodies of the deceased. The figure made for Nesuy (9737) exhibited with that of Anhai in the Third Egyptian Room has a small figure of the god Sokaris, represented as a mummified falcon, placed on the pedestal which is made in the form of a coffin. This base no doubt represented the coffin in miniature and the fragment of body placed within represented the whole body of the deceased.

The placing with a burial of papyri inscribed with specialized funerary texts was a custom which developed in the Eighteenth Dynasty and became common thereafter. The idea of furnishing a burial with funerary texts was, however, very much older. In the Old Kingdom the tombs of private persons contained many texts, mostly consisting of short, set formulae, designed to ensure the continuation of offerings for the deceased in the future. Royal pyramids of the same period (p. 178) contained large extracts from the body of texts known as the *Pyramid Texts*. In the Middle Kingdom the great wooden coffins of private persons were inscribed with *Coffin Texts* (p. 163), which were the literary and religious descendants of the *Pyramid Texts*. A papyrus preserved in the British Museum (10676) written in a Middle Kingdom hieratic, close in character to the script used on the coffins, contains many sections of the *Coffin Texts* and it is possible that it was originally used in a Middle Kingdom burial

Shabti-figure of
Amenophis II

in the way in which the later copies of the *Book of the Dead* were used. Part of this papyrus is exhibited with examples of the *Book of the Dead* in the north-eastern division of the Third Egyptian Room. The *Book of the Dead* is the name now given to a collection of religious and magical texts known to the Egyptians as the *Chapters of Coming-forth by Day*. This extended composition was the descendant of the *Pyramid Texts* and *Coffin Texts* and its principal aims were to secure for the deceased a satisfactory after-life and to give him the power to leave his tomb when necessary. No copy contains the text of the whole work, each owner clearly having obtained for himself those sections which he particularly needed or as much as he could afford. In many cases the copies were prepared especially for individual customers; other copies were written as 'stock' examples with blank spaces in which the names of the purchasers could be inserted. The finest copies are beautifully illustrated with coloured vignettes, examples in the collection being those made for Ani (10470), Hunefer (9901), and Anhai (10472; Plate 2). In the Late New Kingdom and Late Period, the vignettes were commonly done as brush and black-ink drawings. The best examples of this type are contained in the Papyrus of Nesitanebtashru (10554), a daughter of Pinudjem I, High-priest of Amun, and Neskhons. Good illustration is not, however, always accompanied by good text; the text of the Papyrus of Ani is full of errors; on the other hand the Papyrus of Nu (10477) has an excellent text accompanied by relatively simple vignettes. Of the many sections making up the whole work the one that is found in most copies is Chapter cxxv, which deals with the judgement of the deceased before Osiris; this chapter is often accompanied by a vignette showing the weighing of the heart before the 42 assessor-gods (pp. 156 f. and Plate 13). In the Saite Period the text of the *Book of the Dead* underwent a considerable revision, new sections being added, old sections discarded, and others reworded. The new version, used thereafter, is now called the Saite recension; a good example is the Papyrus of Ankhwahibre (10558) of the Ptolemaic Period. From the Late New Kingdom other religious works were sometimes placed with burials. Of these the most common was the *Book of what is in the Underworld*, a composition which in the early dynasties of the New Kingdom was inscribed on the walls of the royal tombs. It deals primarily with the progress of the sun-god in his bark through the underworld by night—a progress with which the fate of the deceased could be identified, a journey from death to resurrection through the divisions of the underworld in the course of which the deceased experienced regeneration. The Papyri of Henttowy (10018) and

Ankhefenkhons (9980) contain versions of this work. Among other compositions found in funerary papyri of the Late Period and concerned with the fate of the deceased person are the *Book of Traversing Eternity* (see, e.g. Papyrus 10091) and the *Book of Breathings*, a copy of which is contained in the Papyrus of Kerasher (9995) which is illustrated with vignettes appropriate to the *Book of the Dead*. Some late funerary papyri contain very little text, but a wealth of illustrations, the vignettes being taken from the repertoire of all the contemporary funerary texts. Examples of such papyri, which are purely magical in intention, are those of Pashebutenmut (10007) and of Pedikhons (10004) exhibited with the other funerary texts in the Third Egyptian Room.

The vignettes of the funerary texts of the New Kingdom and later are filled with strange deities, the significance of many of whom remains unestablished. In the tombs of kings of the Eighteenth and Nineteenth Dynasties wooden figures resembling some of these deities have been found. A collection of such figures is exhibited in the north-west section of the Third Egyptian Room. They are all bird- or animal-headed and come from royal tombs in the Valley of the Kings at Thebes.

In the same section of the Third Egyptian Room is a group of objects found in the burial of a lector-priest named Idy who lived during the Sixth Dynasty. It consists of stone vessels and a large number of copper model tools and utensils including a small altar fully equipped with miniature vessels (fig. 61). The practice of

Model copper objects and altar from the tomb of a priest, Idy

placing model or miniature objects in tombs was prompted by a magical intention similar to that underlying the representation of objects on the walls of tombs. The models and the representations served in place of actual, usable objects. The original reason for employing models was economy, but it seems that in later periods models were sometimes used in preference to actual objects because they could be made specifically for funerary purposes and be more elaborate than the real objects. The gilded wooden ointment and incense model containers inscribed with the name of Ramesses II, exhibited in the Fourth Egyptian Room, seem to be models of this kind. The wooden false vessels for ointments painted to simulate different hard stones and glass, which are shown in the Third Egyptian Room, may also have been used in preference to actual glass and stone vessels and not because they were cheaper to produce. Many of the model tools in the Fourth Egyptian Room were likewise made as parts of funerary equipment. Specially interesting are the miniature hoes and baskets which were intended for the use of the deceased or his *shabti* in carrying out work on the land in the after-life (e.g. those of Heqreshu, 32693).

In tombs of the late Old Kingdom to Middle Kingdom were placed wooden models representing many kinds of domestic, agricultural, and other activities. They were substitutes for the scenes, painted or carved on the walls of earlier tombs, showing similar activities, and, like these scenes, they were intended to serve as magical substitutes for the existence the deceased hoped to enjoy in the after-life. Among the examples exhibited in the Fourth Egyptian Room are models of butchery (41576, 58083), brewing (55728, 36423, fig. 5), baking (45197, 40915), ploughing (51090, 52947), and brick-making (63837, fig. 80); also miniature granaries (2463, 21804) and boats. Of the last the majority are model cargo-boats or travel-boats; but two (9524, 9525, Plate 17) are funerary boats with mummies on deck intended probably to represent the journey of pilgrimage to Abydos, which was commonly regarded as desirable from the Middle Kingdom onwards. The burials of humble people in the Middle Kingdom were not equipped with sets of models, but frequently they contained pottery model houses, in the forecourts of which were representative offerings, the whole being intended to provide sustenance and homes for the *Kas* of the deceased owners. These pottery houses are usually called soul-houses, and examples are exhibited with the wooden models.

A further form of amuletic protection provided for burials of the New Kingdom comprised a set of four magical bricks placed in niches in the four walls of the burial chamber. These bricks were by prescription made of unbaked mud and each carried an amulet, the northern a mummiform figure of wood, the southern a reed fitted with a wick, representing a torch, the eastern a figure of a jackal made of unbaked clay, and the western a *djed*-pillar of blue composition. The bricks were inscribed with short individual texts which formed part of Chapter CLI of the *Book of the Dead*, and their intention was to prevent the approach of the enemies of the deceased from the four cardinal points.

Tombs and tomb-stelae

The graves of the Predynastic Period have already been mentioned (p. 157). In general they were simple oval or rect-angular pits, mostly shallow, sometimes brick-lined or revetted with wood, but commonly without structural features of individual distinction. The more elaborate, carefully con-structed graves had wooden roofs, above which were piled rough mounds of sand and rubble. Burials at that time, and throughout Egyptian history, were made on the desert-edge, beyond the cultivation, where they in no way diminished the area of cultivable land available and were above the level of the flood-waters of the Nile. The simple burial in the desert-sand consisting of a shallow pit and mound continued to be the normal type of grave for people of humble situation during the Early Dynastic Period. Tombs of kings and important officials and nobles, on the other hand, were from the beginning of the First Dynasty elaborate structures.

In the First and Second Dynasties the great tombs of nobles consisted of subterranean burial chambers with large mud-brick superstructures. At first the superstructures were sur-rounded on all sides with deep recesses in imitation probably of the façades of palaces and other great secular buildings of the period. Later the recesses were reduced in number to two, placed at the north and south ends of the eastern side. These recesses served as false doors, the larger southern one as a chapel for the practice of the funerary cult. The subterranean parts of these tombs contained many store-chambers for the less-important funerary goods. The superstructure was rectangular, low in proportion to its length and with a convex roof; the sides were painted with coloured patterns which represented, probably, the woven mat-hangings of secular buildings. In many cases subsidiary burials were placed around the principal tomb which suggests that, at the beginning of the Early Dynastic Period, the primitive custom of burying the great man's relatives with him at the time of his death was retained. The subsidiary burials were similarly provided with small superstructures with two false door recesses. Tombs with low rectangular superstructures are usually called mastabas, this name having been used by the native workmen of early excavators, who saw a similarity between the superstructures and the benches (mastabas) found outside native houses. The stelae with which some of the earliest tombs were supplied were simple stone memorials bearing, in the case of a royal burial, the name of the king (e.g. 35597 that of Peribsen of the Second Dynasty, fig. 62), and, in the case of a private person, his name and title. Not until the end of the First Dynasty were the first truly funerary stelae produced, that is stelae carved with scenes and texts directly connected with the securing of posthumous benefits for the deceased. From the first, the scene on funerary stelae took the form which persisted throughout the Old Kingdom on the panel incorporated in the large false door stelae. It consisted of a representation of the deceased seated at an offering table piled with sliced loaves of bread and of simple texts enumerating various food and drink offerings and the titles and name of the deceased. The early funerary stela was placed apparently in the southern niche on the eastern side of the mastaba.

In these early mastabas stone was used only to a limited extent for lining burial chambers, for the lintels and jambs of doorways and for the portcullises which sealed the entrance passages. In general stone was introduced to give greater security to the most important part of the tomb, the burial chamber. Most of the changes in design and technique in the development of tomb-architecture in the early period were the result of attempts to make the burial more secure from tomb robbers. The most remarkable development, however, was the construction of the Step Pyramid at Saqqara for Djoser, the first king of the Third Dynasty. The whole complex of funerary buildings connected with this pyramid was within a great enclosure wall and was built of stone. The pyramid itself has six steps and rises to a height of about 60 metres; it is not square in plan, being approximately 125 metres from east to west and 110 metres from north to south. Beneath the pyramid are the burial chamber and a network of passages and small chambers used for storing the funerary equipment and for the burials of members of the royal family. At the south end of the enclosure is a great mastaba beneath which is a duplicate set of chambers reproducing those immediately connected with the burial chamber beneath the pyramid. The walls of some of the rooms under the mastaba and pyramid are decorated with blue glazed composition tiles, arranged to represent primitive hangings of matting, and fine low reliefs showing Djoser performing various religious ceremonies. On the north side of the Step Pyramid is a mortuary temple and a small chamber containing the statue of the dead king. The former was intended for the practice of the funerary

62 Stela of Peribsen

cult of the king and the latter as a substitute for the body of the king for the reception of offerings. The chamber containing a statue of the deceased became a regular feature of Old Kingdom burials and it is now usually called the *serdab* (the Arabic word for 'cellar'). The Step Pyramid enclosure contained also a number of buildings planned for the celebration of the dead king's jubilee ceremonies in his after-life; the purpose of other buildings in the enclosure is unknown. The whole complex was intended to provide for the dead king a setting in which he could fulfil his function as a monarch after death and it is probable that it contained in its plan most of the features characteristic of the royal palace at Memphis.

The step pyramid form was used by the later kings of the Third Dynasty, but it was then superseded by the true pyramid which was thereafter used by kings throughout the Old Kingdom and during the Middle Kingdom. The change in design was probably due to a change in religious beliefs. The Great Pyramid at Giza, built for Cheops, the second king of the Fourth Dynasty, may be taken as characteristic of the type. It is built mostly of local limestone and was originally faced with fine limestone from the quarries of Tura on the east bank of the Nile. Its four sides were almost identical in length, having been originally about 230 metres long: its height when complete was about 146 metres. From fig. 63 it can be seen that two changes of plan

Section of the Great Pyramid at Giza

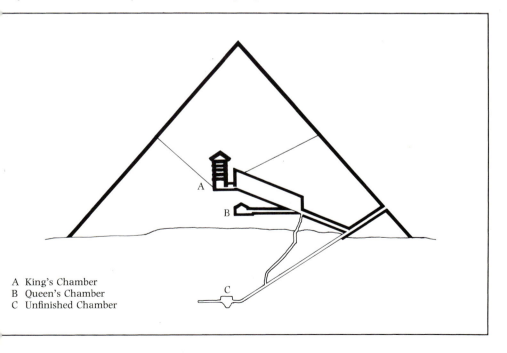

A King's Chamber
B Queen's Chamber
C Unfinished Chamber

were made in deciding the position of the burial chamber. At first a subterranean chamber was excavated at the end of a long descending corridor. Before it was completed it was abandoned and a second chamber prepared within the masonry of the pyramid; this chamber has erroneously been called the Queen's Chamber. For some reason it was later decided to prepare another room for the royal burial and the so-called King's Chamber was constructed above the Queen's Chamber. It was approached by a lofty gallery of majestic proportions. The King's Chamber is built of granite and its roof is relieved of the weight of the pyramid-mass above by five cell-like relieving chambers. A large granite sarcophagus for the royal body (contained, no doubt, in a wooden inner coffin) is still in the chamber. No royal mummies of the Old Kingdom have been found intact; it used to be thought that the wooden coffin and human remains found in the pyramid of Mycerinus, also at Giza, belonged to the original burial. The coffin, preserved in the reserve collections in the British Museum (6647), is now recognized as a replacement coffin provided probably in the Saite Period when the interest in their past led the Egyptians to investigate the monuments of their ancestors. Moreover, scientific tests have shown that the human remains are of relatively modern date, being probably those of an Arab intruder during the Middle Ages.

On the east side of the Great Pyramid is the mortuary temple, in which the funerary cult of the dead king was practised, and from it a stone causeway leads to the edge of the desert to the so-called Valley Temple in which the final rites were performed on the body of the king before it was taken to the pyramid. The Valley Temple of the Great Pyramid is unexcavated as it lies beneath a modern village. The walls of the two temples and the causeway were probably decorated with painted reliefs; the pyramid itself was uninscribed within and without.

During the Fourth Dynasty very large pyramids were built for three kings, Sneferu, Cheops, and Chephren. Thereafter far smaller pyramids were constructed, no doubt because the effort and resources needed for them constituted less of a drain on the economy of the country. Basically, however, the plan of a royal pyramid-complex remained the same, consisting of the pyramid, mortuary temple, causeway, and valley temple. The pyramids of Unas, the last king of the Fifth Dynasty, and of the kings and the last queens of the Sixth Dynasty were distinguished by having the burial chambers and ancillary rooms decorated with funerary texts, known as *Pyramid Texts* (p. 171).

Private burials during the Old Kingdom continued to be made in mastaba-type tombs wherever the nature of the site available permitted; elsewhere rock-cut tombs were prepared. The plan of

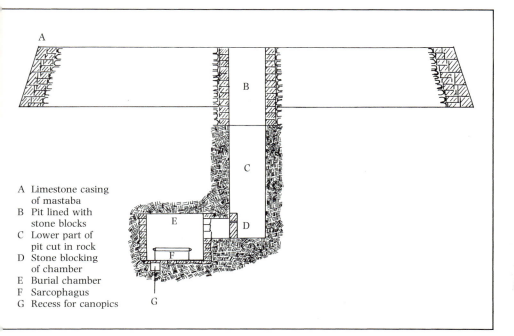

A Limestone casing
  of mastaba
B Pit lined with
  stone blocks
C Lower part of
  pit cut in rock
D Stone blocking
  of chamber
E Burial chamber
F Sarcophagus
G Recess for canopics

64 Section of a
   mastaba

the mastaba-type tomb remained in essence what it had been in
the Early Dynastic Period, consisting of a subterranean burial-
chamber and a rectangular superstructure with a chapel for the
performing of the funerary cult (fig. 64). Many changes and
developments, however, took place during the course of the
Old Kingdom, the principal being the use of stone in the construction of the superstructure, the increase in size of the chapel,
and the placing of the burial-chamber at the bottom of a deep
shaft. In the early Old Kingdom the superstructures were
commonly built of solid masonry and rubble with the chapel
added either as a separate small structure or as a chamber partly
built outside the main mass of the superstructure and partly
penetrating it. At Giza the mastabas of the nobles, who served
under Cheops, were grouped in regular lines around his pyramid.
At Saqqara and elsewhere this regularity was not so strictly
observed although it remained customary for great officials to
have their tombs in the neighbourhood of the pyramid of the
king whom they had served. This change in custom resulted
partly, no doubt, from the weakening of the great authority of
the kings. A further indication of the diminution of dependence
on the part of the nobles can be seen in the mastabas of the Fifth
and Sixth Dynasties when compared with those of the Fourth
Dynasty. As mentioned above, the chapels of the early Old
Kingdom mastabas were small chambers; they were equipped

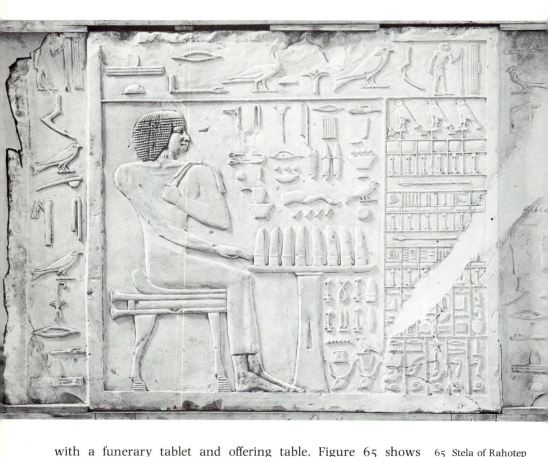

with a funerary tablet and offering table. Figure 65 shows a typical Fourth Dynasty funerary stela (1242) which comes from the mastaba of Rahotep at Maidum. The mastaba-chapels of the early Old Kingdom at Maidum sometimes are decorated with a few scenes of daily life. Later in the Old Kingdom the chapel developed into a series of rooms which eventually filled the whole of the superstructure of the mastaba. One room was reserved for use as the mortuary chapel and it held the offering table and texts intimately connected with the cult of the deceased. These texts usually included an offering list containing sometimes as many as a hundred items, which was intended to act as a magical substitute for the proper provision of actual offerings; it was accompanied by scenes of the deceased receiving offerings and of the preparation and bringing of offerings. Most important, however, was the false door or stela through which the dead man was believed to gain access to the earthly world from the tomb; it incorporated the old funerary tablet and texts consisting of the titles and dignities of the deceased and prayers

65 Stela of Rahotep

to the funerary deities for the continuation of offerings. Adjacent to the mortuary chapel was the *serdab*, the room containing the statue of the deceased. It was generally a sealed room with a squint through which the statue could see and also receive (if only symbolically) the offerings placed in the chapel or represented on its walls. The other rooms in the superstructure of a large mastaba were used partly as stores for funerary equipment, but principally for the representation of scenes showing the deceased owner watching and participating in activities common in his life on earth which he hoped to continue enjoying in the after-life. In the Egyptian Sculpture Gallery, at the south end, are many good examples of Old Kingdom false doors and most of the scenes of one small mastaba chapel (718). The last was made for a high official, called Urirenptah, at Saqqara. It consisted of one room only which held false doors for the deceased and his wife and scenes of daily life. The false door devoted to Urirenptah incorporates a long offering-list; the scenes include sowing and reaping, representations of ships, offering bearers, butchers, musicians at the funerary feast, and the preparation of the deceased's bed.

During the Late Old Kingdom it became customary for high local officials, the nomarchs, to be buried in their provincial localities and not in the neighbourhood of the royal pyramid. In many places the land on the west bank of the Nile was not suitable for cemeteries of the kind found in the Memphite area and a new type of tomb was evolved which made use of the cliffs which were near the Nile in Upper Egypt. In such rock-cut tombs no superstructure was built, but the chapel and other rooms which in mastabas were included in the superstructure were excavated in the cliff-face. A shaft or descending passage led from one of these rooms to the burial chamber. In the case of very important people the tombs were often provided with terrace platforms, sometimes incorporating elaborate architectural features, and formal façades. The approach to a tomb of this kind might be by a causeway from the cultivated land or by a flight of steps. The types of scene and inscription found in these tombs are similar to those in contemporary mastaba-tombs in the Memphite necropolis. Frequently, however, inasmuch as the provincial noble felt himself more independent than the noble at court, he showed this independence by including in his tomb a fulsome account of his career and personal achievements.

During the First Intermediate Period and Middle Kingdom the rock-cut tomb remained the common type in Upper Egypt. In some cases, as at Beni Hasan and Qaw, very elaborate tombs were cut deep into the cliffs and, at Qaw, they were provided with unusually grand ancillary buildings, including valley temples after the manner of pyramid-complexes. In the neighbourhood of the royal pyramids at El-Lisht, Illahun, and Dahshur, court officials were buried in mastabas, continuing the burial traditions of the Old Kingdom in the Memphite necropolis. The decoration of these tombs was in general similar to that found in tombs of the Late Old Kingdom. Many rock-cut tombs have no wall decorations, sometimes because the condition of the rock was too poor to receive them, sometimes possibly for reasons of economy. In such cases it was common for the burial to be provided with models representing some of the activities usually shown in the painted or relief-decorations (p. 174). The use of models subsequently was extended even to burials provided with good mural decorations. Poor rock which was not suitable for carving was often plastered and painted; where the rock was very bad the chambers of a tomb were sometimes lined with fine limestone slabs which could be carved. After the end of the Old Kingdom the false-door stela became less common and new smaller types of stela were evolved, the texts and representations of which incorporated the essential elements of the Old Kingdom stelae in the offering scene, the dignities and titles of the deceased, and formulae for securing offerings for the deceased. In addition it was not uncommon for the stela to include an account of the deceased's career. A fine example is the stela of Tjetji (614, fig. 12), a high official who served under the kings of the Early Eleventh Dynasty, exhibited in the Sculpture Gallery. Many smaller funerary stelae of Middle Kingdom nobles and officials are also exhibited in the same gallery; among them are some from Abydos where, at this period, it was common for a man of position to set up a cenotaph, associating himself in death thereby with Osiris, the god of the underworld, whose chief cult-centre was Abydos.

A dramatic change in the form of the royal tomb came with the construction at Deir el-Bahri on the west bank of the Nile at Thebes of the mortuary-complex of Nebhepetre Mentuhotpe II, the great king of the Eleventh Dynasty who reunited Upper and Lower Egypt after the divisions of the First Intermediate Period (p. 50). In plan this structure was original: the mortuary temple was built on a raised terrace and embodied a podium bearing a small pyramid or, possibly, a square mastaba, and surrounded by colonnades. At the end of a long corridor lay the tomb proper beneath the cliffs; under the pyramid was a cenotaph approached by a long tunnel from the forecourt. The temple was connected with the valley temple by a very long open causeway. This type of structure was never repeated although a similar complex was probably planned for Mentuhotpe III. During the Twelfth

Dynasty the kings established their capital in the north and returned to the pyramid type of burial characteristic of the Memphite necropolis. The pyramids of this time were, however, far inferior in size and construction to those of the great period of the Fourth Dynasty. In some cases the cores were brick-built. The associated temples and other buildings were likewise less grand. Great care was taken, however, over the construction of the internal chambers in these pyramids, the work being executed with extreme accuracy in the hardest materials. In certain cases the arrangement of the passages was deliberately complicated, with corridors on different levels, accessible only through concealed entrances. The purpose of these measures was to protect the burial from plunderers, but in no case were they wholly successful.

Royal burials during the Second Intermediate Period continued to be made in pyramids; the few surviving examples in the Memphite region show a continuation of the style of construction of the Twelfth Dynasty. In Thebes no actual royal pyramids have survived, but traces found by excavation reveal that they were very modest structures of mud-brick. The prominence which a pyramid gave to a burial no doubt greatly attracted the attentions of tomb robbers and it is surprising that the form remained in fashion for so long. It was ultimately abandoned in Egypt for royal burials early in the Eighteenth Dynasty. From the reign of Tuthmosis I, throughout the New Kingdom, kings were buried in rock-cut tombs in the so-called Valley of the Kings, a remote valley lying in the hills on the west bank of the Nile at Thebes. These tombs consisted of a series of corridors and rooms, extending many hundreds of feet into the rock (fig. 66). The farthest room was usually the burial chamber,

66 Plan of the tomb of Seti I

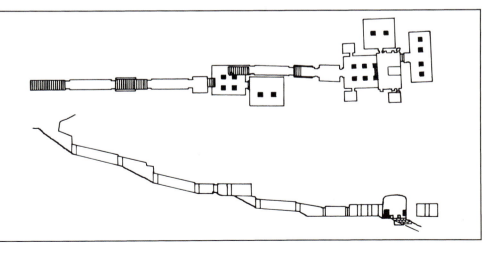

the others being reserved for the storage of equipment and for the performance of funerary ceremonies. The walls were covered with mythological texts and representations designed to facilitate the progress of the deceased king to his ultimate goal in the after-life (p. 172). Royal mortuary temples and valley temples were now no longer built in close connexion with the tombs; each king constructed a single mortuary temple on the edge of the cultivation on the west bank of the Nile, some distance from the Valley of the Kings. A different plan was adopted for the tomb and temples constructed for Queen Hatshepsut. For her, a valley temple was constructed on the edge of the cultivation and connected by a long causeway with a mortuary temple of very unusual design constructed in a bay in the cliffs at Deir el-Bahri, close to the mortuary temple built for Mentuhotpe II. This temple consisted of a series of open terraces with colonnades and the royal tomb was situated in the cliff behind (p. 59).

New Kingdom private tombs of officials and nobles, of which the best examples are in the Theban necropolis, are, for the most part, more simple than the tombs of people of similar station of the Old and Middle Kingdoms. The basic plan consisted of a transverse entrance chamber and a short corridor which led to the chapel (fig. 67). The burial-chamber was reached by a shaft

67 Plan of a New Kingdom private tomb

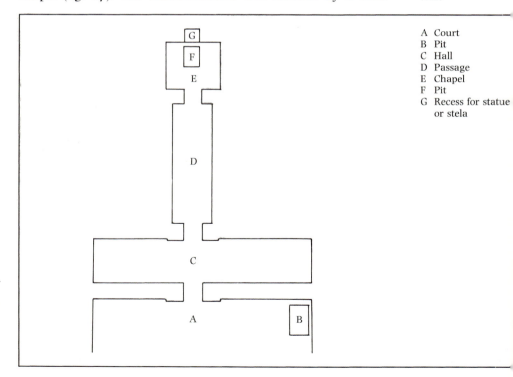

A Court
B Pit
C Hall
D Passage
E Chapel
F Pit
G Recess for statue or stela

or a descending passage from inside or outside the upper rooms. Most Theban tombs are rock-cut, but some have constructed façades and exterior courts. The special interest of these tombs lies in the painted and relief decoration found on the walls of the chapels and transverse chambers. These decorations contain some of the most lively representations of Egyptian daily activities. Parts of painted scenes from Theban tombs are exhibited in the Third Egyptian Room (p. 205 and Plates 3–5, 9). The principal stela in a typical Theban tomb was found at the end of the chapel (occasionally at one end of the transverse chamber) with an offering table in front. No longer was the stela used to present the biography of the deceased; information on his life and career were now incorporated in the texts included on the walls of the tomb. Lesser officials and members of the families of great men associated themselves with the principal burials by placing stelae in the forecourts of the great tombs, or by carving them on any available space in the neighbourhood. Such stelae bear texts devoted to securing funerary benefits for their owners, with appropriate prayers to the funerary deities. Similar small stelae are found with burials of men of modest station elsewhere in Egypt and many examples can be seen in the Egyptian Sculpture Gallery. This custom persisted until the Roman Period.

Few royal burials of the Late New Kingdom and Late Period have been discovered and the royal necropolises of the various dynasties in most cases remain to be identified. At Tanis in the Delta some tombs of kings of the Twenty-first and Twenty-second Dynasties have been found, consisting of stone chambers built just below ground level, with modest superstructures above. They were sited within the temple enclosure in the city. The Ethiopian kings of the Twenty-fifth Dynasty were buried in their southern capital, Napata, where they constructed at El-Kurru and Nuri small pyramids of which the angles of the faces were far less acute than those of the traditional Egyptian pyramid. One or more subterranean chambers were provided for the burial and in some cases the walls of one of these chambers were inscribed with the Negative Confession from Chapter cxxv of the *Book of the Dead* (p. 157).

The most remarkable private tombs of the Late Period are those constructed in the Theban necropolis for people like Mentuemhat, a fourth prophet of Amun (1643), and Pedamenope, also a high priestly official. These tombs are vast subterranean complexes of rooms, the walls of which are covered with religious texts derived from the sacred books formerly reserved for royalty. The tomb of Mentuemhat also has finely carved and painted reliefs inspired by Old and Middle Kingdom prototypes. Elaborate mud-brick chapels with pylons were constructed for these burials. In the Memphite necropolis the important tombs of the Late Period consisted of chambers inscribed with versions of the *Pyramid Texts*, placed at the bottom of exceptionally deep shafts.

It would appear that after the end of the New Kingdom, the varied fortunes suffered by Egypt affected not only the political stability of the country but also the regular evolution of funerary architecture. In consequence large cemeteries of great tombs were not developed and uniformity in tomb-design, so characteristic of the great necropolises of earlier periods, was not maintained. The exhaustion of land suitable for burials in the neighbourhood of the principal cities contributed to this development and late tombs are often found fitted among earlier tombs wherever space was available. By the Ptolemaic Period the custom of having elaborate tombs had largely been abandoned, except no doubt in the case of royal persons and the very highest officials; but of such tombs few are known. Burials of this period, both of simple people and of minor officials, were often made within the superstructures of earlier tombs especially in places where old cemeteries were silted up with sand and with the decayed brickwork of ancient superstructures. Coffins were placed simply in brick compartments or straight into shallow graves; funerary equipment was scanty and unelaborate. The depressed status of the Egyptian in this late period is suitably reflected in the humble nature of his burial.

CHAPTER SEVEN

ARTS AND CRAFTS

The burial customs of the Egyptians described in the previous chapter and the climatic and topographical features described in the first chapter account for the vast number of objects of funerary purpose or daily use which have survived from Egypt. Most of this material comes from Middle and Upper Egypt. The Delta, with a higher water-table and more Mediterranean-like climate, its settlements lying in less close proximity to the desert edge, has proved hitherto less rewarding in finds of material remains. Only a few town sites have been scientifically excavated and these too have as a rule yielded little reward.

The exploitation of the full richness of the country's natural resources is reflected in the wide range of techniques and manufactures practised by the Egyptian craftsman. Illustrative material will be found in the Upper Egyptian Rooms. In the Fourth Egyptian Room are examples of stone vases, wooden models, furniture and receptacles, metal tools and weapons, weights and measures, toys, musical instruments, toilet objects, household utensils in faience and metal, and woven fabrics and basketry. The Fifth Egyptian Room contains small sculpture in stone, wood and metal, terracotta and ivory; it includes some of the finest achievements of the Egyptians in this field of art. Jewellery, bronze, faience, and glass objects, and pottery are displayed in the Sixth Egyptian Room. Taken in conjunction with the scenes of craftsmen at work in the tombs, these remains provide a body of evidence for the arts and crafts, skills and manufactures, unrivalled in the ancient world from the point of view of quantity, state of preservation, diversity of material, and quality of production.

Most of the techniques employed by the Egyptian craftsman are already in evidence in the earliest settlements which can be traced back to predynastic times. It is not possible to do more than guess at the process of accident or experiment which resulted in the discovery of the means of exploiting the various resources of Egypt. With the unification of Egypt greater skills were developed in the use of materials long familiar, owing to the increased availability of metal for tools. By the Old Kingdom Egypt had already reached a standard of material culture which was not fundamentally altered until the Roman Period.

Stoneworking

Of all the crafts in which Egyptians showed early mastery, stoneworking is perhaps the most characteristic of the ancient

civilization, and certainly it was the craft in which it achieved
some of its finest and most memorable work. The great natural
wealth of Egypt in diverse ornamental stone, which lay close at
hand on the desert edge or in the great ranges of the eastern
hills, was exploited in the Predynastic Period for the making of
stone vessels (fig. 68). The earliest of them are usually of basalt,
of simple design with broad flat rims and flat spreading bases of
the type illustrated by 64354. Vessels of this kind were found in
a disturbed context at the site of El-Badari and may be contemporaneous with the earliest of the predynastic cultures.
Certainly by the time of the Naqada I Period stone vessels were
made in great quantity, the usual forms being slightly curved
in a barrel- or heart-shape with two lug handles for suspension.
Egyptian alabaster (calcite), basalt, breccia, granite, and
porphyritic rock were all worked in the earlier Predynastic
Period as well as the softer limestone. In the later Predynastic
Period, in addition to these stones, schist, serpentine, and
steatite were also used.

Great numbers of stone vessels have been recovered from royal
and private tombs of the Early Dynastic Period and of the Third
and Fourth Dynasties. The hoard of vessels from the subterranean
galleries of the Step Pyramid of Djoser is numbered, for instance,
in thousands. This was the period of highest artistic achieve-

68 Stone vessels dating
from the Pre-
dynastic period to
the Eighteenth
Dynasty

ment, a variety of stones being chosen and a wide range of
shapes fashioned. The complete mastery of the material is well
demonstrated by the manner in which the craftsmen could shape
and fashion hard stone as if it were clay. A fine example of this
plastic quality is a red breccia vase (35306) in the form of a sitting
dove or pigeon, measuring from beak to tail 19 cm. The body
has been hollowed out to form an effective receptable, the opening being a hole with narrow rim placed on the top of the back
of the bird, the diameter of which is just over 2·5 cm. On the side
of the bird, where the wings would come, are two pierced lug
handles for suspension by cords. The head and neck are finely
modelled, with eyes made by smooth bored holes, one of which
still retains its original inlay of blue.

Representations in tomb scenes of the vessels being made as
well as examination of finished and unfinished examples show
that the hollowing out was done, once the outside had been
roughly fashioned, by drilling the stone. The drill, rotated by
a bow, was fitted with a tubular bit made probably of copper,
its action assisted by the use of an abrasive powder, perhaps
finely ground quartz. The cylindrical core left by the drill was
broken away by driving wedges into the drill-cut. The central
hole was then enlarged by means of a drill, rotated by a wooden
crank handle weighted on each side, fitted with crescent-shaped
bits of flint or other hard stone, of varying sizes and shapes. The
process was continued until the required size of hole was
achieved; the manner in which the drill was used for the under-
cutting of the shoulders is not known. The final stage of the
work was the careful shaping of the inside of the vessel and
the polishing of the surface with stone burnishers.

Stone vessels continued to be made throughout the Dynastic
Period, but from the Old Kingdom onwards there was considerably less use of the harder stones, alabaster being by far the most
common material. Vessels are often inscribed with short vertical
columns of hieroglyphs enclosed within a rectangular frame,
giving the names of kings with conventional epithets; of more
interest than usual is the text on the alabaster vase 57322 which
is inscribed on one side with the name of Djedkare-Isesi
(c. 2390 BC) and on the other with the information that the vase
contained ointment for one of the king's ladies.

In the Middle Kingdom the majority of vessels were small and
were used for containing cosmetic preparations. Particularly
attractive are small vases of pale blue anhydrite, a stone which
was used only in the Twelfth Dynasty. With the New Kingdom
several new shapes were introduced, the more common being
provided with one or two loop handles, often in the form of the
head and neck of an animal or a bird. Another popular form was

an amphora with ribbed handles, the base of which fitted into a stone stand. Examples of finely polished hard stones have survived; 24432 is a ribbed loop-handled vase with a diorite lid, 4734 is a diorite amphora with ribbed handles, one of which is partly restored. Stone anthropoid vessels, probably intended for magical purposes, are also found (30459, 29907). Fine vessels continued to be made in the Late Dynastic and Ptolemaic Periods, in the latter usually imitating classical forms. An interesting example from the point of view of technique is an alabaster hydria, of the Ptolemaic Period, which was made in four separate parts originally cemented together (35295).

With the exception of the small cosmetic jars, the majority of surviving stone vases were doubtlessly intended for funerary use only, providing a more durable and permanent receptacle for food and drink among the tomb equipment than the everyday clay pots. A wide variety of special types of stone vessel, however, was used for measuring liquids. Each variety had its special name, and in addition to being containers for beer, wine, milk, oil, and honey, some types were also used to measure solids like grain and incense. 4659 is an alabaster jar with lid of New Kingdom date, of the type called by the Egyptians *hin*; the inscription states that its capacity is $8\frac{1}{6}$ *hin*. Actual measuring gives as its equivalent about $8\frac{1}{2}$ pints, the *hin* corresponding approximately to a fraction over a pint. From the New Kingdom large high-sided bowls of stone filled with water were also used to measure time: two fragments of such clepsydrae or water-clocks in the collection date from the end of the Dynastic Period. No. 933 is a basalt fragment inscribed on the outside with texts relating to Alexander the Great; on the inside of the vessel the twelve hours of the night are marked by vertical lines of small holes, a different line being used for each month. The vessel was filled with water which drained away through a small hole in the base (fig. 45). No. 938 is another basalt fragment inscribed on the outside with a scene of Philip Arrhidaeus before the god Min.

The skill in stoneworking acquired from the manufacture of stone vessels was first applied to architecture at the beginning of the First Dynasty. The more plentiful supply of copper and the making of copper tools (see below pp. 222 f.) enabled the stone to be quarried from the rock bed and huge slabs to be dressed. This new development was first employed for monuments of a funerary nature, both royal and private, to make pavements, stairways, doorways, and portcullises and to line a room with a course of masonry (p. 176). The first building completely of stone was the funerary complex of Djoser at Saqqara (the Step Pyramid) which was constructed throughout of small blocks of fine limestone (p. 44); the style of architecture clearly imitates the early reed and wood constructions of the preceding ages, a feature which remains a dominant motif for the columns and capitals in Egypt throughout its ancient history and provides one of the most pleasing aspects of its architecture.

From the time of the Step Pyramid, increasing use was made of stone to build the superstructures of the funerary monuments of both royal and private persons, the primary reason for its adoption as a building material being its durability and its protective possibilities for monuments which in Egyptian belief were to last for ever. Ordinary houses, palaces, and until the New Kingdom probably also the great majority of local cult temples, were still constructed of sun-dried mud-brick, except for those parts which practical experience had shown required some stronger, more durable, and more impervious material like thresholds, lintels, door-posts, bases for columns of wood, and slabs for the wash-room (p. 32). For these local limestone was easily available.

The three main building stones were limestone, sandstone, and granite. Core masonry of Old Kingdom constructions at Giza and Saqqara was of the local surface rock taken from the vicinity of the building site. For the outer casing, great quantities of a good quality limestone free of nummulites were transported across the river from the vast quarries in the Moqqatam hills to the south-east of Cairo, in the region of Tura and Masara. The stone was soft, easily quarried with the copper tools available, but hardened on exposure to the air. It was capable of receiving and retaining the most sensitive and delicate work of the sculptor's chisel. It was removed economically, a block being isolated on four sides by means of trenches cut into the rock and detached from its bed by the making of slot holes at the base into which were inserted wooden wedges. These were wetted; as they swelled, so the block split away horizontally. The good strata of the rock were followed by tunnelling, a hollow space being first driven along the whole length of the layer to be worked between the roof of the tunnel and the top of the first blocks to be detached, to enable a mason's gang simultaneously to cut vertically downwards behind and around the block, and so gradually lower the floor of the quarry. The quarrymen used chisels of stone and metal, which were struck with wooden mallets (fig. 69), and stone hammers or pointed stone mauls, apparently not fitted with hafts. This fine limestone from Tura was highly prized throughout the Dynastic Period and the great man-made caves, with pillars of the living rock left to prevent a collapse of the roof, were already a familiar tourist sight in Greek and Roman times (Herodotus ii. 124; Strabo 17, i. 34).

Stonemason's mallet

Though there is little good quality limestone in the Theban area, the remains of Middle Kingdom constructions there show that limestone continued to be the chief building stone. Sandstone was also used to a limited extent. The capillary attraction of water up through the lower courses of limestone masonry and the subsequent crystallization of salt on the surface, as well as ancient and modern re-use of the blocks and the burning of the stone to make lime for fertilizer, account for the almost total disappearance of Middle Kingdom temples.

Limestone continued to be chiefly employed in the early part of the Eighteenth Dynasty, but in the reign of Tuthmosis III increasing use was made of sandstone which became henceforth the building stone of the great temples of Upper Egypt (p. 32). The change was due to the closeness of good quality sandstone to the river on both sides at Gebel es-Silsila, which could easily be transported to Thebes, to satisfy the great demand for stone which the lavish building programmes of the New Kingdom pharaohs required. The method of quarrying was the same as that for limestone, the blocks being extracted by both open and underground quarrying. Its use enabled a greater span of architrave to be achieved. The surface, however, rarely allowed the same fineness of relief as limestone to which there was a partial return in the reign of Sethos I (p. 65).

Granite, both the pink and the black varieties, was regularly used throughout the Dynastic Period for greater strength and greater effect, a preference being shown for the coarser-grained stone. The manner in which limestone was painted to imitate granite is itself proof of its desirability in Egyptian eyes. Doorways, columns, whole shrines, and burial chambers were constructed of the stone. It came from the region of the First Cataract by Aswan. In the first instance use was probably made of detached boulders, but as early as the Old Kingdom the stone was already being quarried from the rock-bed for columns and casing stones. To reach a block of the suitable strength and quality, the top stratum of rock was broken away by first heating and then rapidly cooling it with water. A block of the required size was then detached by pounding a trench with balls of dolerite and splitting it from the rock bed by means of wedges, the slots being made by a stone or metal tool worked in conjunction with an abrasive powder.

Other stones used to a limited extent in building were alabaster, quartzite, and basalt, usually in connexion with the most important rooms. The resources lay for the most part close to water transport, though the most highly prized alabaster came from Hatnub, some 15 miles into the desert south-east of El-Amarna. When the stone had been extracted, it was lashed to sledges which were dragged, usually by teams of men but also by oxen. Water or other liquid was poured on the ground to ease the passage of the sledge. Wheeled transport does not seem to have been used to shift loads in the Dynastic Period, though a wheel used to push forward a scaling ladder is shown in a relief in the Fifth Dynasty tomb of Kaemheset at Saqqara. The difficulties of overland transport of the stone explain the large numbers of men recorded on the rocks in the Wadi Hammamat by the quarrying expeditions; these expeditions to the desert quarries were major operations conducted at irregular intervals according to the need of the moment and the taste of the individual pharaoh. They were maintained by the king and in the New Kingdom comprised prisoners of war as well as levies of Egyptians. They normally took place during the period from December to April when men could best be spared from the land and be put to hauling the quarried blocks (p. 45).

The blocks were taken by the most practical route to the nearest point on the river; from there they were transported by water on barges as close as possible to the building site. Sites were levelled, the floor beaten down and the lines of the walls and doorways marked out by use of a surveyor's cord. Rough architectural plans of buildings on both papyrus and ostraca have survived; one ostracon in the collection (41228) from Deir el-Bahri, of New Kingdom date, gives the plan of a small peripteral chapel, 27 cubits square (i.e. a little over 14 metres square). No true foundations were laid, the lines of the walls being marked at the most by shallow trenches. Much of Egyptian masonry is no more than a core of rubble enclosed by ashlars of dressed stone. To raise the blocks in the course of construction, no pulley seems to have been used before the Roman Period; the blocks were manhandled into position by means of wooden baulks, rockers, and ramps of earth and brick. To assist in the final placement, a thin layer of gypsum plaster was spread over the joints to act as a lubricant rather than as a binding material.

The method of decorating the stonework with carvings in relief is shown by the large number of models and trial pieces and also by the unfinished state of surviving monuments. After the final dressing of the blocks (or in the case of rock-cut tombs the preparation of the rock face) the surface was divided up into squares by a series of horizontal and vertical lines which might be incised on the stone or made by stretching at regular intervals across the walls a string dipped in red ochre. Over this grid the design was roughly sketched out, usually in red but sometimes in black paint, the draughtsman working from a drawing on a small scale similarly divided.

In some cases the image was merely engraved on the stone with incised lines. In the other cases the outline was first isolated by a furrow cut around it, the background was lowered to the required depth and the details of the figures modelled. The delicate shallow raised relief, for which the Tura limestone provided an ideal vehicle, shows Egyptian art at its best. This type of work had, however, the disadvantage that it could be easily damaged or usurped and doubtlessly this consideration, as well as the saving in time and labour, gave rise to the less decorative deep-sunk relief, in which the design and modelling were cut below the level of the surface.

The representation of the human figure in the reliefs followed strict conventions. The figures are invariably shown with the head in profile but the eye as if from the front; the shoulders are represented frontally, chest in three-quarter view and legs in profile. Feet and hands may be represented without distinction between left and right. The oddity of the anatomy is lessened by the fluency and firmness of the Egyptian line and by the strict canon of proportion maintained, admirably illustrated by a drawing-board with a seated figure of Tuthmosis III over a grid (New Kingdom from Thebes, 5601).

At the same time as the Egyptians were applying the newly gained skill in quarrying and dressing stone blocks to masonry and relief, they began also to fashion stone sculpture in the round, not only in soft stone but also in the hard or ornamental stones highly prized for their ability to receive and retain a high polish. Only a little, and that usually on a small scale, has survived from before the Third Dynasty; from then onwards the increasing adoption of stone for the construction of royal and private tombs, of mortuary and later cult temples, is reflected in the number of surviving stone statues which formed part of their embellishment. In the Old Kingdom the mortuary and valley temples attached to the pyramids were adorned with numerous statues of gods and of the king for whom each complex was intended. These representations of the kings, which by the Fifth Dynasty had already reached the proportions of the monumental and colossal, are generally held to be among the finest achievements of Egyptian art.

In Old Kingdom statuary the king was invariably represented standing with the left foot advanced or seated on a cubic block representing throne or chair. The statues were frontally posed and there is no suggestion of movement or action. Statues were provided with a back pillar reaching from the base up to the level of the shoulder, neck or head. It is uncertain whether this pillar, which is a constant element in Egyptian statues, was deliberately incorporated into work for technical reasons—as

70 Sesostris III

a safeguard against the splintering of the stone—or whether it had some symbolic purpose. The body of the figure was summarily executed, according to a fixed canon of proportion similar to that used in relief and in painting. The effect was to emphasize the head and it was to the modelling of this part of the statue that the greatest skill and art were devoted. The features were idealized to convey the essential god-head of the king. Not until the Middle Kingdom, with the statues of Sesostris III (684–686; fig. 70), was there a suggestion in the lines of the features and in the heavy frowning expression of the human qualities of the king.

Royal statuary of the New Kingdom, usually of monumental proportions in hard stone from the time of Amenophis III, displays a conventional idealized look without conveying the same sense of divinity as the best of the Old Kingdom royal sculpture. The style is well represented in the collection with the statues and heads of Amenophis III which have come from his mortuary temple, now destroyed, behind the Colossi of Memnon in Western Thebes. The two seated statues in black granite at the southern end of the Egyptian Sculpture Gallery (4; fig. 71, and 5) are typical of figures found in New Kingdom temples. The large limestone head (3) is noteworthy for the scale and care of its construction. The dramatic change which marks Amarna sculpture is foreshadowed by the unusual treatment of the same king in the nearby statues (6; fig. 72, and 7). The Nineteenth Dynasty is represented by a number of statues of Ramesses II, the largest of which (19; Plate 7), so typical of the monumental scale of the work of the reign, has been made from a piece of granite containing a geological flaw; the present sharp contrast between the upper and lower part of the head may originally have been concealed by painting. On a different scale is the attractive figure of the king as a young man (67).

In the fashioning of a statue, the design was first marked out in red ochre on a block roughly of the size and shape required. The next stage of the work was the rough blocking out of the stone without distinguishing face, arms, or legs. This process and the modelling of the features were carried out with the use of guide lines in subsequent stages. The working of soft stone was comparatively easy with the available copper (and later bronze) chisels; in the case of hard stone the modelling was done by pounding away with a ball of dolerite, and by rubbing with stones of various sizes held in the hand with the aid of an abrasive powder (probably quartz sand). Sawing, using at first only copper blades fixed in a wooden handle, made use of an abrasive. The stone was drilled and bored in the method long employed in the working of stone vessels (p. 189).

71 Amenophis III
72 Amenophis III (*inse*

The final stages of the work, done by eye alone, consisted of modelling the features with patient light bruising and burnishing. In the completed statue all traces of the working were removed by the final polishing. The inscription would be added, and even in the case of statues with a high and pleasing polish, paint would be applied in flat washes of colour in order to make the statue as lifelike a replica of the owner as possible.

The earliest private sculpture in this Museum goes back to the Third Dynasty, the style and skill of which are illustrated by the red granite seated figure of the ship-builder Bedjmes, depicted

73 Bedjmes, a ship-builder

holding an adze over his shoulder (171; fig. 73). Private statuary
was intended for the tomb and its main development follows
closely the conventions set by royal sculpture. It was static,
frontally posed, the features idealized without, however, carrying
the authority of the divine kingship. Its quality depends largely
upon the care with which the details have been indicated and
the time which has been spent in the process of rubbing.

Common in the mastabas of the Fourth Dynasty is the painted
limestone statue of a man and his wife, represented in the
collection by the statue of Katep and Hetepheres (1181; fig. 74).

76 Meri, a steward

The large painted limestone statue of Nenkheftka (1239; fig. 75) is typical of the succeeding dynasty. The two seated statues of the steward Meri of the Eleventh Dynasty (37895 and 37896; fig. 76) indicate by the quality of their work the return to the strong centralized government and politically stable conditions after the First Intermediate Period. In the Twelfth Dynasty it was possible apparently for private persons to place statues of themselves in temples; new forms were introduced which reduced the time spent over the modelling of the body, like the standing or seated figures wearing long tight-fitting cloaks reaching from the neck to the ankles; block statues were also introduced in which the person is represented squatting, only the head, feet and arms protruding from the entire block. One of the earliest of this style is the statue of Sihathor, treasurer of the king in the reign of Ammenemes II, which still rests in its original niche

75 Nenkheftka
    (*opposite*)

(569, 570; fig. 77). The type continued to the end of the Ptolemaic
Period.

77 Stela and block
statue of Sihathor

The seated limestone statuette of Tetisheri, grandmother of
Amosis the founder of the Eighteenth Dynasty, one of a pair
dedicated by a member of her household at Thebes, marks the
return of good workmanship after the Second Intermediate
Period (22558). The complete mastery of technique in the working of hard stones is exemplified in the statues of high officials
of the Eighteenth Dynasty. Many of these statues are con-

3 Statue of a nobleman and his wife

ventional in form, but some, like the striking figure of Senenmut, holding the princess Neferure (174; fig. 15), are very imaginative in conception. During the New Kingdom, beginning just before the Amarna Period, great attention was paid to the elaborate representation of daily costume and wigs. This development is well exemplified in the collection by a statue of an unknown man and his wife (36; fig. 78). Considerable art was required to render these repetitive details without giving the impression of complete lifelessness.

The last period of great sculpture begins with the Twenty-fifth Dynasty, when in addition to close copying of Old and Middle Kingdom examples, a class of more realistic, more mature likenesses is met with, of which the crystalline limestone head of an old man (37883; fig. 79) is an outstanding example. In this period there is a noticeable increase in the use of the harder stones, particularly schist and basalt, and until the end of the Ptolemaic Period they continue to be carved by the Egyptian sculptors with their traditional skill.

79 Head of an old ma[n]

Painting

The earliest form of painting in Egypt is the decoration on pottery from the periods Naqada I and Naqada II (pp. 208 ff.; fig. 81). In the Dynastic Period paint was freely used on papyrus, plaster, pottery, stone, and wood. It is perhaps surprising that little use was made of linen as a painting ground; it is not until the Roman Period that linen shrouds were painted with representations of the deceased and with scenes and objects of significance in the funerary ritual. Among the rare exceptions are the small cloths of linen, dating from the New Kingdom, painted with scenes of funerary significance, originally placed over the breasts of wooden anthropomorphic coffins at Thebes (43215–16).

The pigments used in the preparation of paint were either naturally occurring minerals or artificially prepared mineral substances; carbon in the form of soot, lamp-black, or powdered charcoal was used for black; azurite and, from the Middle Kingdom, a frit (a crystalline compound of silica, copper, and calcium) for blue; powdered malachite (a copper ore) for green; oxide of iron for pink; red ochre, and, from the Roman Period, red lead for red, and yellow ochre for yellow. The pigment was finely ground on stone palettes and mixed with water. Glue, gum, or egg was added as an adhesive.

The paint was applied by means of brushes of many different kinds. The largest were generally made of sticks of fibrous wood, one end of which had been soaked in water and frayed out, and were used when large surfaces were to be covered. Details, outlines, and work of a delicate kind were executed with finer brushes made of a single stem of rush with a frayed end, and identical with the type of brush used by the scribe (pp. 94 f.).

Painted scenes are found in tombs in place of carved relief, at first probably for reasons of economy. At Thebes the quality of the limestone of the necropolis area is poor and for that reason, with some notable exceptions, the majority of the tombs contain painted scenes of the type illustrated by the fragments in the Third Egyptian Room. A smooth ground for painting was prepared by covering the rough-dressed walls of the corridors and chambers of the tombs with a layer of mud plaster to fill up the irregularities of the surface. Over this a coat of lime plaster was superimposed. The surface was then divided into squares by means of strings dipped in red ochre paint, as in the case of the preparation of a wall for relief (p. 193). The design was roughly sketched out over this grid. The same conventions in delineating the human figure were observed; in the representation of a banquet scene from a Theban tomb (37984, Plate 9) the drawing of two of the woman-musicians full-faced and the bodies of the dancers in profile is exceptional. The method of rendering landscape, without perspective, giving as it were a bird's eye-view, is admirably illustrated by the representation of an ornamental fish-pond in the garden of the scribe Nebamun, around which a variety of trees has been planted (37983). Colour was applied flatly but some attempt was made from the Eighteenth Dynasty to render shading. It appears on the soles of the feet and on the toes of the women musicians in 37984. The long flowing garments are shown as transparent, the limbs first being painted in red or yellow and a thin streaky wash of white applied over them. Considerable skill with the brush is shown in the rendering of detail, particularly in the case of birds and animals, as in the body of the hare (37980), the fur of a cat, and details of butterflies and birds (37977), or in the markings of the geese (37978). By artistic convention the skin of men is represented as red-brown, while that of women is generally yellow. For the most part colour is rendered naturalistically, particularly in the cases of animals, birds, fish, and plants.

When the painting was completed, the paint was usually protected by a thin layer of varnish, originally colourless, the exact composition of which is uncertain.

Brickmaking

Though stone was employed from the Early Dynastic Period for funerary monuments of both royal and private persons and later also for the cult-temples or 'houses of the gods', the palaces of kings and houses of ordinary people were built of sun-dried Nile mud-brick. Brickmaking required less skilled craftsmen than the quarrying of stone: the bricks were easier to transport and handle in bulk than stone and the raw material lay plentifully at hand. Practical experience no doubt proved the suitability of such buildings as living quarters. Brick provided houses of sufficient durability, dramatic and sudden storms, which might leave a trail of damage, being very infrequent. Such buildings could also be easily adapted, enlarged or divided up to suit the changing needs of families.

The method of brick-making is illustrated by a wooden tomb model of Middle Kingdom date from Beni Hasan (63837; fig. 80). The mud used was the alluvial deposits of the Nile after the inundation. When a deposit of the right consistency had been selected near the building site, the mud would be carried in buckets or jars to the brickyard. Here it would be mixed with water, drawn from a convenient pool, the work being done with the foot or with the hoe. It was the usual practice to knead in at the same time some chopped straw or other vegetable matter. This improved the binding quality of the mud and also at the same time by chemical action increased the strength and plasticity of the mud.

The mud was then ready for shaping into bricks: it was carried in baskets or jars to the brickmaker who—as the Egyptians termed it—struck the bricks. He used a hollow wooden rectangular mould, the exact size of the intended brick, and held it by its handle flat on the level area of ground chosen to mould the bricks. After sprinkling the bottom and sides with a little chopped straw, he filled the mould with handfuls of the treated mud, pressing it down firmly. When the mould was full, it was

Wooden model of
brickmakers

removed, leaving behind the moist brick; another would be
struck by its side until the whole area was covered with a regular
series of bricks. Here they would be left for two or three days
until the fierce heat of the sun had thoroughly dried them out.
They would then be carried in slings from a yoke (5413, from
Thebes, New Kingdom, 35928–29) which was normally
balanced on one shoulder only. Bricks might be stamped while
still moist with a wooden die inscribed usually with the name
of a king (6012, Tuthmosis III; 6016, Amenophis III) but also
with the name of the building for which they were to be used.
Bricks stamped with the names of private persons (13176, of
the Steward of Amun, Djehutymes) fall into a different category,
since they were used for decorative purposes in private tombs.

    Although the technique of preparing baked bricks was known
from early times, the Egyptians only employed such bricks in
places where they had a particular advantage, such as in floors
or underground structures exposed to damp. The earliest known

use of baked brick in this way dates to the Middle Kingdom (c. 1900 BC) and further instances occur in later periods. Baked bricks were more generally used in the Roman Period.

The actual size of bricks varies according to their use and their date. The bricks of the Early Dynastic Period are all small; then comes an increase in size until the Middle Kingdom, followed by a fluctuation until the Twenty-sixth Dynasty, after which there is a decrease until modern times. From the Old Kingdom to the Ptolemaic Period, two distinct groups of bricks were in use: a small type suitable for house building or for private tombs, commonly measuring $30 \times 15 \times 8$ cm, and a larger type used for official buildings, such as temples and palaces, measuring from 35 to 45 cm in length.

Ceramic

The river clay was also the material for the manufacture of a wide range of domestic implements, the most common of which were household pots. The earliest pots date back to the Badarian Period (p. 39): they are of simple shape, mostly in the form of open bowls without true brims or handles. The walls of the pots are thin; the regularity and evenness of the shape are note-worthy, the more so since they were built up by hand without the use of a wheel. Before firing the pots were polished with a quartz pebble to give the characteristic burnished red look. For variety, pots were blackened around the rim—or completely —probably simply by placing them in the smoke of a charcoal fire. Also characteristic of the period is a ripple-line decoration produced by the running of a comb-like instrument over the wet clay (59667, from El-Badari).

The pottery of the succeeding predynastic cultures is essentially the same ware, though in both shape and size there is consider-able development. Brims are found and two, sometimes three, lug-handles for suspending the vessel. The most noticeable innovation is the introduction of incised, painted, and occasion-ally modelled decoration. In the Amratian Period (Naqada I) incised representations of animals are found, like the hippo-potamus (30965), the lion (49019), and the snake (30970). Five clay hippopotami decorate the rim of a shallow bowl from Matmar (63408). A lizard crawling upwards is modelled on the outside of another black and red pot of unknown provenance (53885).

The earliest painted designs are geometric patterns in white or cream coloured paint on the polished red clay. Pictorial scenes with animals, plants, or figure subjects are less common. The out-line is usually filled in with cross-hatching. The ability of the Egyptian draughtsman to capture with an economy of line the

I Painted pottery
vessel

essential outline of an animal is well shown in the figure of
a hippopotamus drawn in white on a red pot (53882).

In the Gerzean Period (Naqada II) the typical decoration is
dark red or purple on buff-colour or pinkish-red, the colour of the
pot being due to the use of clay deposits in the wadis of the
eastern desert around Qena, still the centre of a thriving pottery
industry. Geometrical designs continue to predominate but they
are more varied and the outline patterns are blocked in. Particularly characteristic are bulbous pots, often standing over 60
cms high, with pictorial representations in a haphazard arrangement, the interpretation of which is, and is likely to remain,
a matter of some uncertainty (fig. 81). They commonly show a
semicircular design with a fringe usually thought to be ships
with a bank of oars: at the prow there is often a plant design
variously identified as the *aloe* or the Abyssinian banana tree.
The boat is provided with a central cabin or shrine equipped with
a standard bearing a design which sometimes, but not invariably,
can be identified with the later nome-standards. By the side of
the cabin there is often a female figure in a characteristic pose
with both arms above her head. Wavy lines represent water and
long-legged birds appear, of the type called *niw* in later Egyptian

texts and usually identified with the flamingo or ostrich. Other pots of this period show spiral decoration perhaps in imitation of stoneware (30908). A more unusual scene is shown on a terracotta rectangular open box from El-Amra (32639; fig. 82). On the long sides are representations of long-horned deer, horizontal lines, and S-shaped patterns. On the short sides there are, at one end, the usual type of boat, at the other, four fish nibbling at a ball of food.

With the end of the Predynastic Period, the native decorated ware of Egypt disappears: even the black-on-red pots which had persisted throughout the predynastic cultures seem no longer to have been made in Egypt proper, though their use continued in Nubia and their type reappears in the burials of Nubians in Egypt in the Second Intermediate Period (pan-graves). Large numbers of foreign painted pots have been found in Egypt, reflecting the busy flow of trade in the third and second millennia BC. They are found from the end of the Predynastic Period, throughout the Old and Middle Kingdoms with the apparent exception of the Second and Third Dynasties. Foreign models also supplied the prototypes for the more elaborate forms, like the spouted ewer from El-Badari (58032, Fourth Dynasty). During the Twelfth Dynasty and Second Intermediate Period are found pots and sherds of Minoan, Cypriot, and Syrian origin; among the pots more widely distributed in Egypt and Nubia are the small jugs, ordinarily black, with incised designs filled in with white pigment ('Tell el-Yahudiya' ware).

The native pottery of the dynastic period is utilitarian. The more common shapes are bulbous; true brims, handles, and spouts are lacking (except in imported ware) until the end of the Eighteenth Dynasty. The base of the pot might be flat, or pointed to stand upright in the ground, or rounded to be placed on a light wooden stand (2470, 2471, New Kingdom, c. 1400 BC) or round clay pottery rings. Occasionally ink hieratic inscriptions on the pots give an indication of the use to which they were put. The larger storage jars with pointed bases were for wine or beer; the small bulbous types were used for grain, fruits of various kinds, for meat, oil, honey, and cooking fat. Open-bowl types were probably mainly cooking vessels or crucibles: flat saucer-like types were used for serving food.

It is not until the middle of the Eighteenth Dynasty that the native ware of Egypt is again painted. The most striking examples come from El-Amarna. The jars are painted in light blue on a buff-coloured background with details picked out in red and black. The designs are most commonly floral patterns of petals and leaves in horizontal bands imitating the garlands shown in the painted tomb scenes to have decorated vessels at banquets (37984, 37985, New Kingdom from Thebes, c. 1400 BC). Two large vases with splayed bases and pottery caps of this type (59774–5) have hieratic inscriptions in ink describing the contents as wine from a Delta vineyard. Relief also reappears, like Hathor-heads (58460).

With the end of the Eighteenth Dynasty the native pottery types of Egypt revert to the drab and utilitarian. Not until Roman times did decorated pottery reappear; particularly noteworthy are the thin open beakers from Meroitic cemeteries, with painted designs of birds, animals, flowers, etc. (fig. 99), derived from pharaonic and Hellenistic art. The type is well represented in the collection from finds made at Faras in Lower Nubia. The tradition of painted ware continues into the confused period following the collapse of the Meroitic Kingdom, among the people known as the X-group, either the Blemmyes or the Nobatai of classical texts; typical examples of this last manifestation of the dynastic art may be seen in the material from Qasr Ibrim.

Terracotta

Although clay was widely employed for bricks, pottery and household utensils, there was relatively little use of the material for figurines. From the Predynastic Period come a number of crude steatopygous female figurines, with beak-like faces, prominent breasts, and thick legs usually in a kneeling position with arms raised. A more unusual figure is that of a woman from El-Badari (59679; fig. 8), more naturally modelled, in a standing pose with arms crossed: and at El-Amra there was found among the grave equipment an unusual model of four oxen (35506). After the Predynastic Period it is probably true to say that the Egyptians showed little predilection for the use of clay for plastic forms; the most common types, apart from figures of animals in the Old and Middle Kingdoms, are crude female figures of bound figures of captives (56912–13), the most likely purpose of which was for use in magical practices designed to secure fertility, safe child delivery, and power over personal enemies or malignant forces. An exception to the general rule is the series of anthropomorphic pots in burnished red clay, often in the form of a woman with a child on her back (24652, 54694). They date from the second half of the Eighteenth Dynasty.

It is not until the Late Period that terracotta becomes typical, as a result of the increasing influence of the Greek and later Hellenistic world upon the daily life of Egypt. A large number of terracotta heads of persons of many different races, dating perhaps from the seventh century BC, has been recovered from Memphis, and in the Ptolemaic and Roman Periods the use of terracotta becomes widespread.

The majority of figurines, which served as votive offerings or household images, are representations of healing and saviour gods. From the Roman Period also dates the widespread use of clay lamps. Some, like a lamp with two wickholders on a stand in the form of the god Bes from the Faiyum (15485), have some pretence to individuality, but the majority belong to the familiar types current throughout the Mediterranean world. The usual shape of the lamp is lentoid made in two pieces from moulds and frequently stamped on the base with the potter's mark, a letter, or simple geometric design. They are provided with a central opening for filling with oil and a nozzle with a hole for a wick of twisted flax or papyrus. A common type has modelled on its upper surface a representation of a frog, the body sometimes pricked with a stylus (38453). They belong perhaps for the most part to the third and fourth centuries AD. More uncommon are lamps in the form of a human face with oil-hole at the top of the forehead and burner at the base of the neck (15478), or a lamp with loop handle decorated with a frog and mythological animals (20785). Use of clay lamps continued late into the Coptic Period.

Faience and glazed stones

Faience, or more properly glazed composition, is more typical of dynastic Egypt for plastic art than terracotta. It appears as early as the Predynastic Period. Glazed objects from this early time are mostly beads; as well as the composition material, solid quartz or steatite is used as a core. Glazed solid quartz was in use until the end of the Middle Kingdom, mostly for beads, small amulets, and pendants, only a few larger objects being known. The hardness of quartz and the difficulty of shaping it probably prevented its greater employment; steatite, being a soft stone, was particularly suitable for carving into small objects like amulets and small figures of gods, and it proved an ideal base for glazing. It does not disintegrate under heat. Glazed steatite objects are found throughout the Dynastic Period and it is by far the most common material for scarabs.

Faience consists of a core made of small grains of quartz sand or quartz pebbles or rock crystal ground into a fine powder. In this dry form the body material was light and friable but had no coherence and it is uncertain by what means it was bound together for shaping. Of the suggestions which have been made, the most likely is the small addition of a weak solution of natron or salt which when heated would combine chemically with the quartz to produce a coherent but friable mass, which could be worked with the fingers. For small objects the material was shaped in open red pottery moulds, large numbers of which have been discovered from the New Kingdom. The popularity of this composition material for small objects of personal ornament (beads, pendants, rings), for funerary equipment (amulets, shabti-figures, pectorals), or house decoration (tiles, inlays of floral patterns) was due to the ability to mass-produce them in moulds from cheap materials.

The normal glaze used by the Ancient Egyptians is similar in composition to ancient glass and was made by heating together sand (silica with lime impurities) and natron or plant ash; it is therefore an alkali glaze and would not adhere to ordinary pottery. The introduction of a lead compound into glaze seems to occur first in the Late Dynastic Period. It did not replace the alkali glazes and was applied to the normal composition core. The glazing of pottery, made possible by the lead glazes, is not found before Roman times.

The precise method of glazing is uncertain, but the probability is that the glaze was applied as a viscous fluid coating the object. Glaze and body material were then fused together by heating, giving the manufactured object its strength and coherence.

The most common colour of the glaze is blue, green, or greenish-blue. The colour is due to the addition of a copper compound. A particularly vivid blue is characteristic of the New Kingdom, typical examples of which are a plaque with a figure of the royal scribe and treasurer, Amenemope, before Osiris (6133) and a bowl with a design of lotus and papyrus (4790; fig. 83); it is the common colour of the shabti-figures of

83 Blue faience bowl

the Twentieth and Twenty-first Dynasties (p. 169). From about the middle of the Eighteenth Dynasty white, yellow, and red become common; polychrome faience work seems to have reached its highest stage of development and is well exemplified in objects from El-Amarna. A fine example of the variety of colours of faience at this time is the floral collar with inlaid lotus-flower terminals (59334). The component elements are yellow mandrake fruits, green palm leaves, and lotus petals, white with purple tips, separated by small coloured disks. Among the more attractive combinations of colours is purple on a white background found on a type of *shabti*-figure (8964, 34013) and on a kohl-pot inscribed with the cartouche of Tutankhamun and his queen Ankhesenamun (2573). An example of faience work, unusual for its design, execution, and colouring, which shows the art of the New Kingdom at its best, is a small vessel for perfume found at Sesebi, in Upper Nubia, glazed white with an applied decoration in blue and black (64041; fig. 84); around the shoulder runs a frieze of lotus petals alternately indicated in blue and black. Below each of the two handles hangs a blue lotus flower flanked by two buds. Around the base is a design of an open lotus flower, its petals blue and black. Fine work in faience continues in the Ramesside Period, as is shown by the faience bowl (4796) inscribed with the name and titles of Ramesses II.

Characteristic of the Thirtieth Dynasty is the combination of dark blue on light blue; it is found on *shabti*-figures (35225) and on small objects of daily use like the dish with three compartments for ointment, with its lid, in the shape of a lotus capital (63980).

These small objects of daily use in faience demonstrate more clearly than any other class of antiquities from Egypt the taste and artistic genius of its ancient people. Inspired largely in their choice of decoration by the natural flora and fauna of the Nile Valley, and brilliantly coloured in monochrome or polychrome as a result of the alkaline glaze, they make an immediate appeal to the modern eye.

The achievements of the faience workers are best exemplified in the glazed composition tiles and inlays which decorated houses or palaces and in the drinking cups modelled in low relief, in imitation of engraved metal work. The earliest examples of tiles date back to the Early Dynastic Period; large numbers of them, measuring about 6 × 4 cms, and blue or green in colour, were used in the underground passages of the Step Pyramid of Djoser (Third Dynasty) to form a panelling imitating hangings of reed mat (2438–40). From houses and palaces of El-Amarna come numerous polychrome tiles with floral patterns, the more common being small plaques of white chrysanthemums with yellow centres. Similar tiles are found in Ramesside palaces at Qantir and Tell el-Yahudiya in the Delta and at Medinet Habu at Thebes. Particularly remarkable for the skill with which the different coloured glazes were fused to the composition core are tiles used to decorate the throne-dais from these palaces bearing representations of foreigners with the detail of their gaily patterned dress carefully executed. The larger tiles seem to have been modelled by hand, the composition material being made into a coarse paste, moulded, and dried by exposure to heat before the glazes were applied.

Faience cups become common from the Eighteenth Dynasty. The usual form which the cup takes is a lotus flower on a thin

4 Faience vessel

stem (24680, 26226, 26227) or a pomegranate fruit (21918, 59398). From the later Dynastic Period comes a series of vessels elaborately modelled in low relief: 65553 is a fragment from the base of a dish with a head of Bes on one side, and on the other a frieze of desert animals, a gazelle, an antelope, a lioness, an ostrich, an ibex, a camel, and another antelope. Animals, birds, and fishes occur on the interior of another dish (57385). The tradition continued into the Roman Period though the fine thin walls of the dynastic work and thin evenly applied glaze are replaced by a coarser ware and glassier glaze. No. 62639, with its figures of birds, animals, baskets of fruit, and petals, probably carved, is an example of Roman work at its best. Other techniques of decoration popular in the Roman Period are incised patterns on the core material before glazing (29352) or the application of strips of the body material of lighter colour to the vase to suggest a pattern of laurel leaves (58430).

Glass

Though the ancient glaze is itself glass, and glass may be said therefore to have been known to the Egyptians at an early date, it was not until the Eighteenth Dynasty that the material was used independently, with the sporadic exception of some small beads and amulets. The technique which was applied to the making of glass vessels was a natural development of the technique of glazing, the composition core being replaced by one of sandy clay which was removed on the completion of the manufacture. In view, however, of the date of its first appearance in Egypt, some hundreds of years after the production of faience vessels and figures, it is possible that the introduction of the manufacture of glass vessels in Egypt was a consequence of the contact with Syrian cities following the military conquests of the early Eighteenth Dynasty.

The ancient glass was formed by strongly heating quartz sand and natron in clay crucibles with a small admixture of colouring material, normally a copper compound, perhaps malachite to produce both green and blue glass, though an analysis shows also the use of cobalt which would have been imported. Heating would be continued until the ingredients fused into a molten mass. The exact point at which to stop the heating was probably known by experience, but tongs may have been used to remove small quantities for testing. As the mass cooled, it might be poured into moulds, rolled out into thin rods or canes about 3 mm in diameter, or the crucible broken away and the mass left to be used as required. Examples of the raw glass, recovered from glass factories, may be seen exhibited in the Sixth Egyptian Room.

In the manufacture of a glass vessel, the first stage was to fashion on the end of a metal rod a core of sandy clay to the shape of the interior of the intended vessel. The core was then dipped in a crucible of molten glass and perhaps spun a few times, acquiring thereby a coat of irregular thickness with spherical air bubbles. While the glass was still hot, the glass-maker might add with a pair of tongs a mass of molten glass and shape it into a splayed foot, pinch out the lip, and add a bent glass rod for a handle. When the vessel had cooled, the outer surface might be polished. The core was then scraped out.

The earliest dated glass vessels of this type bear the cartouche of Tuthmosis III; they are represented in the collection by a small vessel, blue in imitation of turquoise, on which the pre-nomen and floral pattern have been painted (47620, Plate 16). A dark blue, imitating lapis lazuli, is common, and yellow imitating gold, white imitating silver. Transparent glass is not found.

Glass of different colours was also partially fused together to produce a conglomerate, as in the dish 27727, but the most striking decoration is found in vases of polychrome ware. The sandy core was first dipped in a molten glass of dark colour, then, while the mass was still hot and the coating semi-viscous, thin rods of manufactured glass of different colours were wound around the object. The cold rods softened on contact with the still hot mass of the base and fused into the surface in horizontal bands of colour. By drawing a sharp metal instrument upwards and downwards over the surface, the glass-worker was able to tease the bands into a series of loops or chevrons. The remarkable skill with which this technique could be applied is illustrated by the reassembled polychrome vessel in the shape of a fish, from El-Amarna (55193).

The limitations of the technique, a certain intractability in the material, and the brittleness of the finished product prevented the same general range of employment of glass as of faience. For the most part objects made of glass are seldom more than 10 or 15 cms in height. It was used chiefly for the manufacture of eye-paint pots in the shape of a palm-column (2589, 64334, 64335) or perfume jars with lids (24391). An unusual example of a cosmetic container in glass is the dish in the form of a shell (65774). Glass was often used for inlay, like the profile faces of royal persons (16375, 54264, 64121). Glass figurines are rare; the damaged, but finely modelled, head of a king from a sphinx (16374) was first modelled and cast solid; the details of the head-dress and face were incised after moulding.

Glass, for reasons perhaps not merely connected with taste, does not seem to have been made in Egypt in the Late Dynastic Period. No glass, for instance, was found in the royal tombs of the

Twenty-first and Twenty-second Dynasties at Tanis. It does not reappear until the Ptolemaic Period. A firmly dated Ptolemaic example is a plaque of opaque glass, originally red in colour, but now mostly green, which formed part of a foundation deposit, inscribed in black on one side with the names of Ptolemy IV Philopator (221–205 BC) and his queen in Greek; on the other side the same text is repeated in the hieroglyphic script (65844).

Towards the end of the Ptolemaic Period, sometime in the first century BC, the technique of blowing glass was developed, and during the Roman Period Egypt was, with Syria, one of the main centres of glass-working. By the end of the third century AD, to judge from the number of fragments of glass vessels found at town sites, glass was generally used to provide rich and poor alike with vessels for the table or containers for a woman's toilet preparations. Opaque glass was still common in the Roman Period, like the cobalt blue cup 64188, but the majority of vessels were of clear glass, the shapes for the most part following the models of the potters. The ribbed examples 59835 and 64189 may have been the result of blowing glass into moulds. The clear glass of the ancient period has acquired in the course of time an iridescent colour, due to the flaking of the glass into layers which refract the light like a prism (59833, 59838).

Metal-working

Associated with the ancient fundamental rocks of the Eastern Desert are deposits of gold, silver, copper, lead, iron, and zinc. Of these neither zinc nor iron was mined in pharaonic Egypt. Zinc and brass (an alloy of copper and zinc) were unknown in the ancient world before the classical period. Iron objects found in archaeological excavations are few in number from dynastic Egypt, and analysis has shown that the earliest examples are of meteoric origin. In this connexion it should be noted that the piece of iron found by J. R. Hill (2433) in the course of excavations conducted by Colonel Vyse at the Great Pyramid in 1837 is almost certainly intrusive, in spite of the precise statement of the finder regarding the circumstances of the discovery. The scarcity of iron may be judged from the paucity and size of the iron objects found in the tomb of Tutankhamun in comparison with the number and weight of gold objects. Though there is an increase in the use of iron in Egypt from the Twenty-sixth Dynasty onwards, it is not until the Ptolemaic Period that iron tools are at all usual; in the Roman Period household implements of iron, like knives and flesh hooks, become common.

Lead, gold, silver, and copper were all known to the Egyptians from predynastic times. The process of extracting lead by roasting the ores was a simple one and was early mastered. Ores are reported from a number of areas, mostly near the Red Sea coast. The chief ore found in Egypt is galena, the sulphide of lead, which was used in the manufacture of *kohl*, the ancient eye-paint, from predynastic times. The raw material was finely ground on palettes which were among the most common items of grave equipment in the predynastic tombs. The palettes of the Badarian Period were flat and rectangular in shape with a notch in the side; in the subsequent predynastic cultures they were frequently made of green schist and shaped in the likeness of birds, animals, and fish. They reached the height of their development with the series of large ceremonial palettes from royal tombs finely carved on both sides with scenes commemorating political or religious events.

We hear almost nothing in Egyptian records of mining activities for lead. It was used in the main for small objects of daily use, or ornaments like sinkers for fishing nets, rings, etc. A siphon, strainer, and small cup, found together at El-Amarna, are of lead (55147-9). Like all metal in Egypt it could be used as a medium of exchange and valuation; from a problem in the Rhind Mathematical Papyrus (*c.* 1650 BC, p. 122) we learn that it had half the value of silver and a quarter that of gold.

The galena deposits of Egypt, unlike those at Laurion worked by the ancient Athenians, are not rich in silver content. Until the Middle Kingdom silver was of more value than gold, and analysis of objects of the Old and New Kingdoms shows that the ancient silver of Egypt is a natural alloy of gold with silver in a sufficiently high percentage to impart a white colour. The depreciation in the value of silver in relation to gold was no doubt due to its importation during the Middle and New Kingdoms from Asiatic sources by way of both trade and tribute. Imports must have been on a considerable scale, for in spite of the quantity of gold which came to Egypt from Nubia in the New Kingdom the ratio of gold to silver was constant at 2:1.

The gold-bearing region of the Eastern Desert extends, broadly speaking, from a short distance to the north of the modern road from Qena to Quseir, southwards into the modern Sudan. The main areas of exploitation are to be found in three concentrations which have their natural outlet on to the Nile Valley at Qena or Qift, and at El-Kab or Edfu, and at the mouth of the Wadi Allaqi, where in the Middle Kingdom the Egyptians built the forts of Kuban and Ikkur.

Gold occurs both in the alluvium of the wadi-beds and in the veins or dikes of white quartz which are present in the igneous rocks of the great central range of hills between the Nile and the Red Sea, running parallel to the river. Recovery of the gold from the alluvium was a simple matter, given a body of unskilled labour and water with which to wash the auriferous gravel. By running water down a sloping surface over the gravel, the lighter material was carried off and the heavier gold was left behind as fine particles or occasionally as small nuggets. In the case of the quartz veins, exploitation necessitated considerable organization, involving the use of skilled miners or quarrymen, to extract the rock and a large body of labour to crush the matrix with heavy stone mortars (rotary grinders were not known in ancient Egypt). The gold was then extracted by washing the finely ground quartz in the same way as the alluvial deposits.

The thoroughness with which the ancients prospected for gold, removing the alluvial gravel and following the gold-bearing quartz veins, has often been remarked upon. There are no centres of modern exploitation which do not have some indication of ancient working: deep galleries, open cuts, numerous stone ore-crushers, troughs, washing tables, and stone huts. It is, however, not always possible to say whether these workings are of pharaonic, Ptolemaic, Roman, or Moslem date.

The Egyptians themselves left few written records which bear directly upon the nature of their expeditions or upon the organization of the mines. There is nothing at the ancient sites in the nature of the official commemorative stelae and rock tablets which are found at the quarries of ornamental stone. The absence of official inscriptions may in part be explained by the nature of the rock—usually granite—in which the quartz veins occur; it does not lend itself to carving. The passage of workmen to and fro from the sites is attested by occasional *graffiti* in the sandstone area. Certainly at some periods there seem to have been permanent settlements in the desert, banishment to which was one of the punishments inflicted upon criminals by the courts, as we learn from the accounts of the investigations into the activities of the tomb robbers in the Twenty-first Dynasty (pp. 120 f.). The gold itself reached Egypt either in the form of dust tied in linen bags, or small fragments of metal fused into small ingots or rings (see the painted scene of Nubians bringing gold tribute from a Theban tomb, about 1400 BC, no. 921).

Copper does not occur in its metallic state in Egypt; it was extracted from ores as early as the Badarian Period, being used for small implements like needles and borers. A number of areas show traces of ancient mining and smelting both in the Eastern Desert and also in Sinai, at the Wadi Maghara and Serabit el-Khadim. The ore was smelted close to the site at which it was mined or it was dragged on sledges to the nearest point at which sufficient supplies of fuel could be obtained. The crushed ore was mixed with charcoal on the ground or in a hollow pit; practical experience no doubt taught the value of siting the fire in the best position to take full advantage of air currents. Representations of metal-working in scenes from the tombs show the metal being placed in an open clay crucible on a charcoal fire the temperature of which was raised by using blow-pipes. Some time, early in the New Kingdom, a form of bellows was introduced; a pair of inflated skins was worked by foot and a current of air directed on the embers by means of clay nozzles. Primitive though the method was, it was sufficient to obtain the required temperatures for casting metal, but the amount of ore normally worked upon at any one time must have been small and the metal produced contained considerable impurities, the heating and reheating of it being the only method of refining.

The addition of a small proportion of tin to copper produces bronze, and results in a lower melting-point, an increased hardness, and a greater ease in casting. The date of the introduction of bronze into Egypt is uncertain. The alloy does not seem, on present evidence, to have been known in Egypt before the Middle Kingdom, but from that time onwards it was regularly used for tools and weapons until it was replaced by iron. Tin does not occur in Egypt and it is not known whether the bronze used was originally all imported in a manufactured state or whether the alloying was done in Egyptian workshops. It may perhaps be significant that among the many names known in the hieroglyphic texts for minerals, there is none which can be certainly identified as the word for tin. Before the introduction of tin, Egyptian copper was hardened by the addition of arsenic. It is not yet known how or whence the arsenic was obtained, though a foreign source seems likely. Arsenical copper was employed from the Early Dynastic Period right up to and including the Middle Kingdom, after which it was largely supplanted by bronze.

In the workshop the crude metal was weighed before issue to the metal-worker. Scenes of metal-working regularly include a representation of the weighing of metal in a balance, which is otherwise depicted only in vignettes of the weighing of the heart in the judgement scene from the *Book of the Dead* (Plate 13). The Egyptian balance in its simplest form consisted of a wooden beam suspended from its centre point by a cord held in the hand and drilled at the ends to take a single cord and hook for pans, in one of which the weights were placed and in the other the metal. From at least the Fifth Dynasty the beam was supported by an upright standard. A plummet line was hung parallel to the upright so that the weigher could check the accuracy of the balance by comparing the plummet with a rectangular board attached at right angles to the balance arm. In the course of time improvements in design were made ensuring greater precision, though the basic principle of weighing remained unaltered throughout the Dynastic Period. From the Middle Kingdom the pans were suspended by four cords (38241, bronze pan, Ptolemaic Period; 57369, pair of silver pans, Ptolemaic Period, with a hieroglyphic inscription referring to the goddess Hathor, from a balance used perhaps in the rites of her temple at Dendera). By the New Kingdom two further refinements increased the accuracy of the balance. The rectangular board was replaced by a pointed metal tongue. Tubular beams, terminated with flanges in lotus or papyrus form, were introduced so that the strings of the pans came out together from inside the beam and diverged from the lowest point of the edge of the flange. This is the design of the elaborate standard balances illustrated in vignettes in the *Book of the Dead* of the New Kingdom. Representations of the Roman Period (e.g. 9995, sheet 4, Papyrus of Kerasher) suggest that the balance had disappeared from daily use and that the draughtsman was reproducing a thing of which he had no direct knowledge.

Large numbers of weights have survived from Egypt. They are, for the most part, made from the harder stones and are simple in shape, the duck, lentoid, and animal forms familiar in Western Asia being rare. The great majority of weights are unmarked. Actual weighing shows that there were a number of different standards in use. Weights marked with the unit and standard to which they belonged (or with their equivalent value in another standard) are uncommon. No. 38546, a felspar weight of 1,021 grammes from Gebelein, inscribed with the figure 5 and the name of Amenophis I, belongs to the ancient gold standard, indicated by the writing of the hieroglyphic ideogram for 'gold' (*nub*). It is the most commonly named of all the standards. In texts of the New Kingdom the weight of metal is usually expressed in a number of *deben* which consisted of 10 *kite*, approximately 140 grains or 91 grammes.

The dynamic development of the material culture of Egypt, which coincided with the unification of the country, must be largely attributed to the more plentiful supply of copper and to its use in making tools. Flat objects, like chisels, knives, axe-heads, and adzes, were cast in open pottery moulds, the final shaping of the tool and the hardening of its cutting edge being done by hammering. Since, in the early period, the Egyptians did not possess tongs suitable for holding hot metal, this hammering was done cold.

Metal tools or models of tools are not uncommon from funerary equipment or foundation deposits (p. 143). Because of the value of all metal, care was taken to weigh tools before they

85 Copper tools

were issued to workmen and again when they were returned to store, to ensure that there had been no pilfering of the metal. Theft of metal tools figures large in the surviving records of trials. Of particular interest, both for their rarity and for their firm dates, are the tools marked with royal names, two chisels (66208–9) and an adze-head (66207) with the name of Userkaf (fig. 85), an adze-blade of the Hyksos king, Auserre Apophis (66206), an axe-head tied with its original leather thongs to a wooden handle inscribed with the name of Tuthmosis III (36770), an axe-head of Amenophis II (37447), and another inscribed 'King of Upper and Lower Egypt, Usermare-setepenre, beloved of Horus Lord of Tanis' (66211), probably Sheshonq III.

The personal weapons of the Egyptian soldiers comprised daggers, swords, spears, and axes. Daggers were short with rounded cheek pieces of bone or ivory. The sword was little more than a long dagger for thrusting and slashing in close-in fighting; the short, straight, two-edged blade had grooves, which might take the form of lotus stems and birds (27382, 32211, Eighteenth Dynasty). A curved scimitar-like sword with handle fashioned in one piece (called in Egyptian texts *khepesh*) was introduced on the pattern of Western Asiatic models during the

Second Intermediate Period (27490, from Tell el-Rataba, Eighteenth Dynasty). The spear had a pointed metal blade and metal butt riveted to a wooden shaft. The main weapon of the Egyptian infantryman was the battle-axe. In the Old and Middle Kingdoms rounded and semicircular forms, designed for slashing and cutting, predominated, the most popular of these being the type with three rear tangs forming open scallops in the blade. A particularly fine scalloped axe in the collection consists of a bronze blade riveted to a hollow silver tube which was originally fitted on a wooden haft (36776, Middle Kingdom, fig. 86). An identical battle-axe hafted in precisely this manner is shown in the hand of one of the body-guards of a Twelfth Dynasty nomarch (1147, fig. 87). In the Second Intermediate Period, a new form of battle-axe was evolved, suited for piercing rather than slashing, with a narrow, elongated blade and concave sides. The elaborate axe-heads with open fretted designs which appear from the beginning of the Middle Kingdom were more often ceremonial rather than functional. The designs most favoured were details of the hunt, or fighting animals, like the two bulls with their horns engaged (36764). No. 36766, from the early Eighteenth Dynasty, gives one of the earliest representations on Egyptian objects of a man riding bareback on a horse. These axe-heads were fitted to wooden hafts and secured by leather thongs in the manner well illustrated by 65663. Until the New Kingdom, the Egyptian soldier seems to have had no defensive armour except for his shield of tough leather stretched over a wooden brace (49245, Middle Kingdom) to which it was attached without an additional frame. Defensive mail coats made by riveting small bronze plates to leather jerkins were also adopted during this period; helmets first appear on battle scenes with representations of foreign mercenary elements in the Ramesside Period. From the Roman Period comes a suit of armour in crocodile skin in three pieces, one for the breast, one for the shoulder, and one for neck and head (5473, from Manfalut).

Copper, and later bronze, provided material for a wide range of domestic utensils in addition to tools and weapons. Household vessels, cauldrons, ewers, basins, ladles of metal formed, with textiles, part of a householder's negotiable property which could be used for barter. Among articles of the toilet, circular flat disks were used for mirrors from the beginning of the Dynastic Period, the polished metal giving a good reflecting surface (22830). The surface of the mirrors was not decorated before the Twenty-first Dynasty, when scenes of ritual significance were sometimes incised upon them. The mirrors were fitted to metal, wooden, faience, or ivory handles, mostly shaped like a papyrus column,

86 Bronze axe with silver handle

37 Procession of armed attendants

a club, or a Hathor head. Two protecting falcons also appeared on the cross-pieces. Glass mirrors did not occur before the Roman Period.

Pins, tweezers (for the extraction of thorns as well as the removal of hair), and razors are also common. The last in the New Kingdom consisted of a small flat piece of metal, shaped not unlike a miniature axe with sharp edge, which was fixed in a curved wooden handle and rotated by the fingers. These objects of daily use are for the most part simple in design; among the more unusual examples is the handle of a toilet implement in the form of a man on horseback (36314).

The use of metal for figure subjects is comparatively rare before the Late Dynastic Period. The Palermo Stone records the making of a copper statue of Khasekhemwy of the Second Dynasty; a remarkable copper statue of Pepi I in Cairo of the Sixth Dynasty is, however, the earliest surviving example of metal sculpture. The precious nature of all metal in Egypt no doubt accounts for the rarity of early pieces, since much of the metal would eventually have been melted down and re-used. On the other hand, the wealth of Egypt from the New Kingdom onwards, when the empire was at its height, may explain the apparent increase in the number of metal statues of kings and gods from the Eighteenth Dynasty. The kneeling figure of a king making an offering (64564), inscribed on the girdle with the prenomen of Tuthmosis IV without cartouche, is the earliest in the series of the inscribed statues of kings. The outline of the eyes and eyebrows is inlaid with silver: small pieces of alabaster painted black to indicate the iris and eyeball are inserted in the eye sockets.

Of statues of private individuals, the standing figure of a priestly official under Psammetichus I, Khonsirdais (14466; fig. 88), 34 cms high, is exceptionally fine in its detail. Khonsirdais is shown standing with left foot forward clad in a long pleated garment over which is the priestly 'leopard skin' passing over the left and under the right shoulder. Originally he held in his hands a figure of a god which was cast separately and secured to the group by a metal tenon. On the right shoulder is incised a figure of Osiris; the front of the skirt has an incised scene of the dead man before Osiris.

The majority of bronzes reproduce figures of gods, sacred animals, and emblems, and date for the most part from the Saite and Ptolemaic Periods. The method of casting was that of the lost-wax technique (cire-perdue). Small objects were normally cast solid; a model of the object was first fashioned in beeswax and coated with clay. When this was heated the clay hardened and the wax melted and ran out through holes left in the clay. When the clay mould had hardened, the metal was introduced through the holes. After the metal had cooled, the mould was broken away.

In the interests of economy, larger statues were shaped in quartz sand which was then thinly coated with beeswax. A clay mould was made in the same manner as if the object were to be solid cast. On heating, the core hardened and the metal was introduced to replace the thin coating of beeswax—now melted—which lay between the mould and the inner core of sand. It is not known how this inner core was held rigid during the process. When the metal had cooled the clay was broken away and the object was given final touches with the chisel.

Gold and silver were also cast to make small statues in the same manner as copper and bronze. The two metals are first found early in the Gerzean Period (Naqada II), mostly in the form of solid beads. The ability to work large masses of the material is shown by the gold coffin of Tutankhamun in Cairo which weighs more than 300 lb. Gold was the first objective of the ancient and modern tomb plunderer; bowls, figure sculpture, and solid gold funerary masks are uncommon and most surviving examples of the goldsmith's craft are items of personal jewellery which was worn by both sexes. Notable examples of this work in the collection are the pair of gold bracelets with inlay of semi-precious stones made for Nemareth, son of Sheshonq I (14594–5), an open-work plaque with a representation of Ammenemes IV offering unguent to the god Atum (59194; fig. 13) and two gold spacer beads with three recumbent cats inscribed on the back with the name Nubkheperre Inyotef and his queen Sobkemsaf (57699–700). Three strands of a necklace passed through it,

88 Khonsirdais, a priestly official

probably of gold beads and semi-precious stones; the most important of the stones used in jewellery are agate, amethyst (particularly in vogue in the Middle Kingdom), beryl, carnelian, crystal, felspar, garnet, haematite, jasper (green, red, and yellow), lapis lazuli, and turquoise. Drilling the beads by means of a multiple bow-drill is shown in the fragment of tomb painting in the Third Egyptian Room (920, Eighteenth Dynasty). Other items of gold jewellery were diadems for the hair or wig, finger rings, girdles, and anklets. Ear-rings were introduced from Western Asia during the New Kingdom.

When the gold was not cast solid, it was beaten on a flat stone with another stone in the craftsman's hand into a sheet of even thickness. The design was executed with a hand punch on the back (repoussé work) and with a chasing tool on the front. Gold wire was made from the sheet by cutting narrow strips off the edge or, for a more continuous thread, by cutting the sheet in the form of a spiral. By the Middle Kingdom the art of attaching grains of the metal to a gold surface for decoration was mastered (granulation). A type of jewellery particularly characteristic of Egypt is an open-work pectoral, in which the design was executed on the back frame in fine chased repoussé work: on the front were a series of gold cells (cloisons) which were filled with coloured inlay of semi-precious stones or glass held in position generally by a bed of cement but in the best work also by the walls of the cells. Heat was not used in the case of glass inlay as is the practice in true cloisonné enamel work.

Gold in sheet form was used to decorate wooden furniture: thick sheet gold (i.e. foil) was hammered directly on to the wood and fixed by small gold rivets. Thinner sheets were attached by an adhesive, probably glue, on a prepared base of plaster. The finest sheet (gold leaf) was freely used to gild statues, mummy masks, coffins, and other items of funerary equipment. It was applied over a layer of plaster, but the nature of the adhesive used by the Egyptian craftsman has not been identified by analysis.

Woodworking

Wooden objects are found from the Predynastic Period but fine woodwork was not possible before the Early Dynastic Period when copper tools became available. Examples of the carpenter's tools (fig. 89), mostly found together in a woven basket in a Theban tomb of New Kingdom date, are exhibited in the Fourth Egyptian Room. For the preliminary shaping of a length of wood or log, use was made of axes, to trim and split the timber, and of saws, which occur from the Early Dynastic Period. The saw used by the Egyptians was of the pull variety, that is to say the cutting

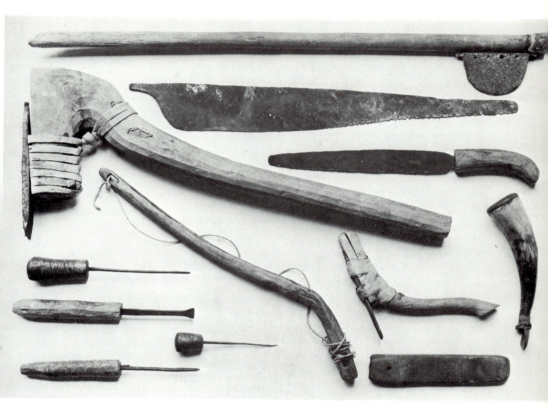

39 Carpenter's tools

edge of the teeth was set towards the handle and the saw-cut made on the pull of the saw, and not on the push. The most efficient method of using this type of saw was to cut vertically down from the top with the tip of the saw pointing upwards. Small pieces of wood, easy to work, were held upright by hand, but heavier timber was tied to a pole fixed firmly to the ground. The lashing was kept tight by a stick weighted with a heavy stone acting as a tourniquet. The saw could then be operated with two hands from a standing position. A small wedge was inserted in the saw-cut to prevent binding; as the carpenter cut down the piece it was necessary for him from time to time to relash it higher up the vertical post. For shaping, planing, and smoothing the wood, adzes of different sizes were used. Joints were cut by chisels, with different sizes and shapes to the cutting edge. They were struck by wooden mallets. Hammers of modern form, with metal heads, were not used. Holes were bored by bradawls of metal with wooden handles or drilled by means of a bow-drill. The metal bit of the drill was held upright, its top turning in half a dom-palm nut held in the hollow of the hand. Rapid sawing with the bow rotated the bit. An important item in the equipment was an oil flask and honing-stone. The plane was unknown in ancient Egypt, the work of smoothing being done by adzes and by rubbing the object with sandstone rubbers. There is no firm evidence for the use of the lathe for turning before the Roman Period. The rounded terminals and legs of furniture, for instance, were fashioned by hand and eye: square, level, and plumb-rule could be used to check.

With the help of these tools, the woodworker was capable of extremely fine joinery which made possible the construction of strong wooden boxes, coffins, and furniture. Wood was carefully cut into lengths and firmly joined by dovetailing and cramps; corners were fitted by different kinds of mitre joints and separate pieces by mortice and tenon joints and sometimes lashed together with leather thongs. Dowels of wood were used in the construction of coffins; small wood or ivory dowels or pins of copper or gold fixed inlay work of faience and ivory. Glue was probably used to secure inlay as early as the Early Dynastic Period but it was not widely used otherwise before the New Kingdom. A piece of six-ply wood from a coffin discovered in the Step Pyramid of Djoser, the separate layers of different woods secured by pins, shows the rapid development of the craft of woodworking. Veneer is found in furniture of the Eighteenth Dynasty.

The general nature of the Egyptian box or chest did not greatly vary over the centuries. Typical examples from the New Kingdom are an ebony box inlaid with tinted and untinted ivory and plaques of faience (5897), a shallow painted wooden casket from Akhmim (21818), and a chest of sycomore wood (5907) which belonged to the ship's captain, Denegro. The designs on boxes are usually drawn from hieroglyphic signs of amuletic significance or from conventional floral motifs and block patterns. The covers of these examples are detachable. Hinged lids also occur in the Eighteenth Dynasty. Metal locks and keys were unknown before the Roman Period. Examples are found of coffin lids being permanently sealed by an elaborate device of tumblers. Boxes were sometimes constructed to enable the cover to be secured, thus preventing the contents from spilling out if they were knocked or dropped, but the only means of safeguard against pilfering was to secure the lid to the box by lashing around the projecting knobs on the lid and the side of the box which could then be sealed with a lump of mud bearing a seal impression.

Though wooden furniture is represented in tomb scenes from the Old Kingdom, actual surviving examples before the New Kingdom are not very common. Egyptian houses were probably always sparsely furnished, use being made of low divans of mudbrick covered by cushions. The normal items of furniture were chairs, stools, tables, and jar-stands. Some of the light open wicker-work examples of stools (2476) and of jar stands (2470, 2471) clearly derive in design from reed and rush constructions of the Predynastic Period. Other stools are three-legged (2481, a type used by craftsmen at their work) or four-legged (2472). Particularly popular in the New Kingdom was a type of folding stool (29284), consisting of two pairs of crossed uprights pivoted about half-way down, with carved duck-head terminals inlaid with ivory and ebony. The seat was of leather, stretched across two curved wooden cross-pieces. Chairs are usually low, with seats of plaited cord mesh, generally no more than 20–25 cms from the ground. The legs are carved usually in the form of a lion's paw or, less commonly after the New Kingdom, a bull's hoof; backs are high and straight, often decorated with open-work designs of amuletic signs and figures of Bes; in 2480 the back panel has small insets of ivory in the design of four lotus stems and flowers. No. 2479 is a higher chair, with straight, uncarved legs, and sloping back. No. 2469 is a low table supported on three splayed legs. On the flat surface is painted a representation of the goddess Renenutet in snake form before an offering table; an inscription contains the conventional formula of the funerary offering for a certain Paperpa, from whose tomb the table doubtlessly comes.

An Egyptian would also possess a wooden bed-frame provided with a footboard. The finely carved fragments from a bed (21574) overlaid with decoration in silver and gold come perhaps from a royal tomb at Thebes. In place of pillows, which would have been too uncomfortable for the hot nights of Egypt, the bed would be provided with a head-rest, the greater number of which are of wood. The rest consisted of a carefully carved, fitted, crescent-shaped piece for the back of the head, supported on a wooden pedestal; more elaborate forms are also found, like that shaped in the likeness of a crouching hare (20753). Head-rests may be carved with the name and title of the owner, perhaps also with a prayer for a good night's rest, and in examples made for funerary rather than everyday use, with Chapters from the *Book of the Dead* on the base of the pedestal (35804).

The technical skill of the Egyptian woodworker is best seen in boat-building and chariot-making; in both cases the ability of these objects, built up of small pieces, to withstand the stresses and strains in their use depended upon knowledge of the natural quality of different woods, and the strength and accuracy of the joinery which gave them their strength and rigidity. The earliest boats were made of papyrus or reed, and the characteristic high prow of the typical Egyptian boat is a legacy of this early material. Already by the Early Dynastic Period local wood was used for constructing river craft. The smallness of the planks which could be obtained from timber from local sources resulted in the development of a technique described by Herodotus ii. 96 and depicted in a number of tomb scenes. The shell of the boat was built up by joining small pieces of wood; there was no keel and no ribs. Sea-going vessels were constructed of larger imported planks along the same lines as river craft, with the exception that greater rigidity and strength was given to the frame by trussing the boat at the prow and the stem and running between them a hogging truss which passed over wooden crutches.

The chariot is believed to have been introduced by the Hyksos invaders; it was used in the struggle between them and the Theban kings of the Seventeenth Dynasty. It was employed in the New Kingdom in warfare, in hunting, inspection of estates, and for official appearances. It consisted of a light wooden frame with open back, set forward of a short axle fitted to two wheels of four or six spokes. A pole projected from the centre of the axle beneath the carriage, terminating in a yoke to which a pair of small-framed horses were harnessed by leather accoutrements. Particularly remarkable is the skill with which the wheels were joined together from separate segments and bound with leather tires. To bend the wood, a piece was tied to a forked post stuck in the ground, welted, and bent with the help of a lever.

The carving of solid woods into statues, models, and household equipment was also practised with high skill throughout the ancient period. It is clear that in many cases the provision of statues of offering bearers and of models in the period from the end of the Old Kingdom to the Middle Kingdom was a substitute for carved stone relief and stone statues. If such figures charm, it is rather in the state of their preservation, particularly of their colour, and the interest of the subject-matter rather than in their skill of carving. The statues of the tomb owner were, however, also often of wood—such indeed form a large proportion of surviving wooden statues—and the choice of material was not necessarily dictated by reasons of economy. Wood statues were provided, for instance, for royalty from the First Dynasty and persisted to the New Kingdom. Three of these large over-life-size figures, all of New Kingdom date, from the royal tombs of the Valley of the Kings at Thebes (854, 882–3) are in the collection.

The statues of private persons, broadly speaking, follow in their pose and style the conventions of stone sculpture. They are usually carved in one piece, except for the arms which are fitted on by mortice and tenon joints. Some of the best examples of this class of work are: the statue of Meryrehashtef as a young man

90 Figure of
Meryrehashtef

(55722, fig. 90), one of a group of statues from his tomb at Sedment of Sixth-dynasty date, in which the arms are carved in one piece with the body; the small but attractive standing figure of Netjernakhte from his tomb at Beni Hasan, Twelfth Dynasty (65440); and the standing figure of an official elaborately draped from the time immediately following the Amarna Period (2320). No. 47568 is a finely carved bust of what must have been a large statue, from a tomb at Akhmim of the Sixth Dynasty.

In these statue-figures the woodworker was limited by the religious conventions of the patron; greater freedom of style is to be found in the small objects of wood. Particularly attractive is the series of cosmetic jars and containers from the New Kingdom carved in various forms, a running jackal with a shell in his mouth (38187), a negro girl carrying a small chest on her head (32767), a swimming girl (38186), a cucumber (5980), or a bouquet of lotus flowers and buds, some of the latter in tinted ivory (5965, from Memphis). The figure of a young girl playing a harp (48658) is also a good example of the less formal style of Egyptian art.

Ivory-work

Ivory from the tusks both of the hippopotamus and of the elephant was used, like wood, for a variety of small objects as well as for inlay, either in its natural state or stained pink. The use of ivory had a certain magical significance; it was employed, for instance, for the making of flat curved wands (often referred to as knives) on which were incised with a fine line the figures of various demons and deities (p. 135; fig. 51). Finely carved objects include handles for knives and wands, toilet spoons, button seals, and gaming pieces. The ivory pieces are mostly small, but larger objects were also built up, for instance the head-rest of Gua (30727, Twelfth Dynasty) with the support in the form of the girdle of Isis.

Fine carving goes back to the Badarian Period; a particularly skilful example from that time is an unguent pot (63057) from Mostagedda in the form of a hippopotamus.

Figurines in ivory date back to the Predynastic Period; they are mostly in the form of naked women (p. 128; fig. 47). An exceptionally fine early ivory is that of a standing figure of a king (37996; fig. 54), found in a temple at Abydos, probably of the First Dynasty, clothed in a garment usually associated with the *sed*-festival, the detail of the quilted pattern of the cloak being carefully done (p. 142).

Weaving

Weaving was one of the earliest crafts to be developed; fragments of woven textiles date back to the earliest of the predynastic cultures and already show advanced skill. The small fragment of woven linen from the Faiyum (58761) is of two-ply thread, lightly spun, with 8–10 warp threads and 10–12 weft threads per centimetre. It dates from before 3100 BC, perhaps even 4000 BC. Textiles of the Early Dynastic Period were woven with 64 threads to a centimetre in the warp and 48 in the weft (modern cambric of a fine quality contains about 56 threads to the centimetre). Throughout their history the Egyptians had a high reputation as skilled weavers; a particularly fine cloth is frequently mentioned in the Old Testament as byssus.

The woven cloth of Egypt was almost invariably of linen. Until the Middle Kingdom there was no breed of sheep which produced wool; a small piece of woven woollen material (55137) was found at El-Amarna, but the scarcity of wool from the Dynastic Period suggests that there may have been a certain religious taboo against its use for garments. Silk was not introduced until the Ptolemaic Period: cotton fragments from Nubian sites have been found dating to the Roman Period, but in Egypt itself woven cotton does not occur before Coptic times.

Flax, the source of linen thread, is frequently shown in agricultural scenes in tomb reliefs and paintings. It was pulled up by the roots (not cut with the sickle like cereal crops), and taken to a man who removed the boles by pulling the flax through a wooden combing implement. The stalks were then trussed together for transporting.

The preparation of the thread was begun by soaking the stalks for a number of days in water to soften them (retting) and to begin the separation of the fibrous matter (i.e. the tow) from the woody tissues. The operation was completed by beating the soaked matter on a block of stone with a wooden mallet, after which the fibres were removed with a sharp-toothed comb (hackling).

When the fibres were dry, they were drawn out length-wise and loosely twisted into roves following the natural direction of the twist of the drying fibres to the left. The work was done by women who rolled the fibres on the upper part of their thigh, squatting on the ground with their right knee tucked under the body. It was at this stage of the work that the thread began to be formed and to acquire the strength and elasticity needed for woven fabrics, the individual fibres being pressed together and adhering by virtue of the irregularities on the surface. When sufficient quantity had been obtained, the roves were loosely wound on scraps of pottery or on pottery reels into balls. They were placed in pots to prevent them rolling away and spun by hand on a spindle, a slender stick tapering at one end and weighted towards the top with a whorl, generally of wood or stone but sometimes of pottery. The typical Middle Kingdom whorl was flat and cylindrical (35928), that of the New Kingdom was domed (6477). The shaft of the spindle did not greatly vary. It had a spiral groove at the top to receive the thread. Later this was replaced by a metal hook (38147).

Until the New Kingdom spinning seems to have been the work of women. Thenceforth it was done by both men and women. The simplest method of spinning was for the woman to stand and guide the single roves from the pot through her fingers on to the spindle which she rotated by raising one knee and rolling it on her thigh. The distaff, a stick to hold the prepared fibres from which the thread was spun, did not come into general use in Egypt until the Roman Period. A quicker method of spinning was to draw the rove out of the pot, pass it over a forked stick, and attach it to the spindle which was rotated between the palms of the two hands. The finest quality thread was produced by a third method, in which the action of the spindle helped in drawing and attenuating the thread. The rove was drawn through the fingers of the left hand, attached to the spindle which was rotated by a flick of the fingers, and allowed to drop and swing, the weight of the whorl helping to maintain the spin.

The earliest looms in Egypt were horizontal. The warp was stretched between two wooden beams attached at the corners to four short pegs which were driven into the ground. The warp might be set up directly on the beams of the loom or might be wound over three pegs set in a wall and transferred to the loom. The threads of the warp were then divided into two; the odd-number threads were lashed to a wooden stick (heddle rod) and raised to make a space through which the weft thread passed, either as a ball or wound on a stick spool. The space for the return of the weft thread was made by turning on edge a flat piece of wood passing through the weft (sled-rod).

By the New Kingdom, probably as one of the innovations of technique introduced during the Hyksos Period, the horizontal loom was replaced by a vertical loom in which the warp was stretched between two beams fastened to an upright wooden frame. In contrast with work on the horizontal loom, representations show that the loom was operated by men, sitting or squatting at the base of the frame. The method of making the passage for the weft threads was unaltered.

Most woven material from the Dynastic Period consists of linen wrappings and bandages from mummies; lengths of cloth were also commonly included in the burial equipment, usually inscribed in ink in hieratic with the name of the owner, the date at which it was taken into use, or the quality of the cloth. The size of these sheets may be considerable; no. 37105 measures

4·57 × 1·83 ms. and is marked 'Cloth of the singer of the god's wife, king's wife and king's mother, Aahmes Nefertari (may she live) Sitdjehuty'. The cloth was intended to serve the dead person for everyday purposes.

Actual garments from the Dynastic Period are rare. Until the New Kingdom the regular dress was white and the garments were draped and pleated, not tailored. Representations of coloured or patterned textiles are rare, and usually they are worn by foreigners. Fragments of patterned textiles do not survive from before the New Kingdom; their introduction at this time may be due to the vertical loom. Most of the patterned textiles which have survived date from the fourth century AD and in style and choice of pattern and decoration owe little to pharaonic Egypt (see pp. 255 ff.). The main fabric is usually plain linen cloth; where the decoration was to be applied, warp and weft were not interwoven but placed side by side; the pattern was then woven on one, two, three, or more threads which formed the warp, while the weft consisted of the coloured and more bulky material, usually wool. This was afterwards beaten down with large wooden weaver's combs to hide the warps (20747, 35926).

Mat-making and basketry, crafts closely allied to textile weaving, were also fully developed in the Predynastic Period. The fragment of woven reed matting (59700) comes from Badari; boat-shaped baskets of grass stems, possibly for sowing grain, like no. 58696, are characteristic of the predynastic Faiyum.

Mats were woven on horizontal looms of rush, reed, and the coarse grasses of Egypt. The patterns of the mat weaves are reproduced in early architecture (see p. 191) and remain one of the dominant artistic motifs of the Dynastic Period.

Baskets were made by coiling a fibrous core spirally into the shape required; the principal material employed was palm leaf with the split rib of the branches for foundation. Baskets were the most common form of household container after clay pots and might serve a number of purposes analogous to wooden boxes. No. 2566, of palm leaf, originally contained a linen tunic, no. 6026 a set of carpenter's tools, and no. 6027 model bronze tools with the name of Tuthmosis III. Receptacles were also made of cane and papyrus (but not plaited); 2561 contained a wig (2560). An unusual example of cane and reed construction is the model table with offerings (5340, Eighteenth Dynasty).

Reed, flax, and halfa-grass were also employed for ropes from predynastic times. In the Dynastic Period palm fibre was generally employed, but the large thick cables required in the hauling of stone were of papyrus. The process of making these papyrus ropes is illustrated in the copy (lower register, right) of a painted scene from the tomb of Khaemwese at Thebes of New Kingdom date. Three men are at work; two stand twisting together two separate strands. The third is seated holding a spike between the strands. There are four finished ropes coiled above the figures, a bundle of papyrus stems, and a group of six tools: two spikes, two twisting tools, a mallet, and a knife.

CHAPTER EIGHT

ROMAN AND CHRISTIAN EGYPT AND THE KINGDOM OF MEROE

The defeat of the Egyptian navy at the battle of Actium in 30 BC, the ensuing death of Antony and suicide of Cleopatra VII, mark the beginning of a new and distinct period in the history of Egypt. The country and the people were drawn more firmly than ever into the world of the eastern Mediterranean. The effect of the Roman occupation is readily apparent in the material remains of Egypt reflecting the daily life of the inhabitants. Certain aspects of the change have already been noted in the previous pages: the widespread use of terracotta for clay lamps (p. 212), of glass for household purposes (p. 216), and of iron for domestic implements (p. 218); the adoption of the reed pen (p. 94), of metal keys and locks (p. 230), and of the lathe in carpentry (p. 230). Even in matters of dress and jewellery the fashions in Egypt differ little from the general pattern of the eastern Mediterranean.

In theory the Roman emperors were the legitimate heirs of the pharaohs, possessed of full traditional titles and absolute powers; on the carved reliefs of the Upper Egyptian temples most of the emperors until the middle of the third century are found depicted in accordance with the ancient iconography, their names written within cartouches in the hieroglyphic signs. In practice the country was incorporated as a province of the empire and was administered by a prefect formally appointed by the emperor from the equestrian order. It remained part of the Roman, and later Byzantine, Empire until the Moslem invasion of AD 641.

Towards Egypt the early emperors maintained an attitude of suspicion which explains the unique character of the province in the Roman world. Behind this attitude lay the memory of the havoc caused by the intervention of Cleopatra upon the lives of Julius Caesar and Antony. Moreover the agricultural wealth of Egypt and the strength of its natural frontiers were factors very much present in the minds of the early emperors, who, in their determination that the country should not become a base for treason, forbade access to it by high officials without permission.

The last two centuries of Ptolemaic rule had been marked by dynastic feuds and a general weakening of authority. Considerable disorders had occurred, particularly in Upper Egypt. Something of the general condition of Egypt may be gathered from Strabo's account of his journey through the country soon after the Roman occupation (*Geographica*, Book 17). Heliopolis is described as entirely deserted, Abydos as only a small settlement, and Thebes as a collection of villages: the last was destroyed by Ptolemy IX Soter II after an abortive revolt in 88 BC. The Romans had little difficulty in quickly bringing order to the whole of Egypt as far as Aswan, the traditional southern frontier.

There can be no doubt that the general security, peace, and ordered government which the Roman administration established brought prosperity, at least for the first two centuries. Improvements were effected in agriculture, and it was probably during the Roman Period that the *saqia*, or waterwheel driven by an ox, and the *norag*, a wheeled sledge drawn over the threshing-floor to extract the grain from the ears, were introduced.

The bulk of the population consisted of the Egyptian-speaking element whose way of life can have been hardly affected by the change of rule, except in so far as the Roman administration was more efficient in the collection of taxes. Receipts for these taxes written in the demotic script on limestone flakes or pottery sherds form the greater proportion of the large numbers of ostraca in the native language found from the Roman Period. The ancient religion still enjoyed a measure of official patronage, particularly in Upper Egypt where the great series of temples, at Dendera, Esna, Kom Ombo, and Philae were completed or further embellished during the first two centuries AD. Like the work of the Ptolemaic Period, the construction during the Roman Period scarcely differs in its architecture from the tradition of the Upper Egyptian temples of the New Kingdom, except for the introduction of new types of capitals, the inclusion of underground chambers, and the erection of *mammisi* ('birthplace'), small temples in the style of the old peripteral shrines in which the ritual of the birth of the infant god was performed. In these temples the daily ceremonies were still performed and the great feasts celebrated. The continued vigour of the native culture is shown by the fact that the majority of our existing copies of demotic literary works were made in the first two centuries AD; most categories of the ancient literature are represented, and some of the wisdom literature and stories, in particular, compare favourably with any earlier compositions of their kind.

A smaller proportion but still numerous element of the population were the descendants of the Greek, Macedonian, and other racially mixed but hellenized immigrants who had been attracted to Egypt, mainly as soldiers, administrators, traders, and bankers, following the invasion of Alexander the Great and the founding of the Macedonian dynasty of the Ptolemies. Some had been established in Egypt for nearly three hundred years

Plate 16
Vase decorated with the prenomen of Tuthmosis III

Plate 17
Wooden model funerary boat

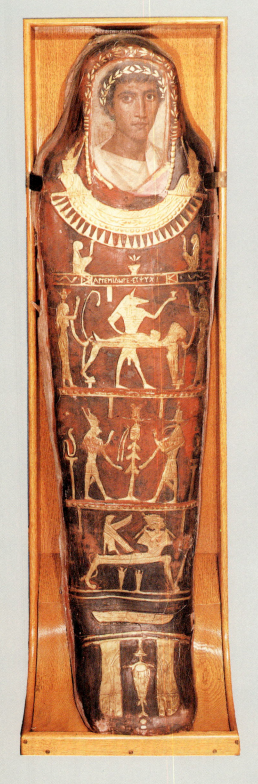

and they thought of Egypt as their homeland. They had settled not only in the Greek foundations of the Ptolemies but also throughout the Nile Valley in the old nome-capitals. Their numbers received a fresh influx of strength from the settlement, particularly in the Faiyum, of disbanded veterans of the legions. This cosmopolitan group was distinguishable from the old indigenous population by their mode of speech and education. They spoke and wrote in Greek and were educated in the normal Hellenistic pattern on the classical authors, particularly Homer, and retained, so far as they were allowed to do so, the social and political institutions of the Greek *polis*. Their loyalty to the Greek tradition and belief in their intellectual superiority ensured the survival of Hellenistic culture. Under the Roman administration they enjoyed a privileged position and it is to them that we owe the preservation of the many papyri of Greek literary works and artistic productions in the purely Hellenistic style.

The chief centre of the Hellenistic culture remained Alexandria. The city was deprived by the Romans of certain of the privileges which it had enjoyed under the Ptolemies, and throughout the first century its relations with the emperors were embittered. Disturbed though its civil life was, it continued to enjoy great prosperity from its port and to maintain its reputation as a centre of learning. It is unfortunate that relatively little of its ancient splendour has been recovered; the remains are for the most part below the present water-table and it is difficult to say to what extent the city retained its Hellenistic traditions in art and sculpture.

The point of greatest contact between the Hellenistic element of the Egyptian people and the old indigenous population was in the sphere of popular religion and funerary practices. The immigrants adopted Egyptian theophorous names and honoured, in particular, deities, like Harpocrates and Isis, who were considered as healers and saviours. In popular religion the Egyptian deities were assimilated to Hellenistic ones and representations occur in which Hellenistic dress is added to the traditional Egyptian iconography or Egyptian symbols to traditional Greek forms: Haroeris appears as a falcon-headed man dressed in the armour of a Roman legionary (fig. 91), sometimes seated on a horse spearing a crocodile; Hathor as a standing female figure with a cow's head wearing a long cloak; Anubis as a standing figure with a jackal-head and the accoutrements of Hermes; Isis in the guise of Demeter or Aphrodite. In Alexandria Egyptian deities were incorporated into Greek mystery religions and these had a wide vogue in Mediterranean countries. Particularly popular outside Egypt, but less so in the country itself, was Sarapis, whose cult was introduced by Ptolemy I Soter to form a common

Plate 18
Mummy case of Artemidorus with painted portrait (*left*)

Plate 19
Painted portrait of a woman (*right*)

bond between his Greek and Egyptian subjects. Possibly the god was a hellenized form of Osorapis, the mummified bull whose cult at Memphis was well established before the Ptolemaic Period. Sarapis was given human form, his head similar to the Hellenistic concept of Zeus. By the Roman Period he was associated with Isis and Horus.

In funerary customs the Hellenistic element outside Alexandria adopted, as all foreign elements in Egypt hitherto had done, the

91 Figure of Haroeris in the dress of a Roman legionary

practice of mummification. Though the actual process of mummification was more often than not inadequately carried out, the decoration of mummies during the Roman Period was more elaborate than at any other time. The nature of the decoration shows that the dead man believed that as a result of the elaborate ritual which accompanied the actual embalming process he would experience the miraculous benefits which Osiris had enjoyed. Scenes from the myth of Osiris and from the various ceremonies conducted for him by Anubis are found painted on the linen shrouds enclosing the mummy or are depicted on the coffin itself (e.g. 21810, Plate 18).

It is clear from earlier practices, like the provision of linen cartonnage and gold masks (p. 165) and the emphasis of the funerary statues upon the features as compared with the treatment of the rest of the body that the survival of the individual personality was closely associated in ancient belief with the preservation of the individual features of the face. In the Dynastic Period neither the masks nor the statue-heads are true portraits of the individual but are idealized. With the Roman Period a new departure is seen in the provision of plaster-heads and painted portraits in a naturalistic style: in view of the date of their first appearance it is probable that the realistic element, which had always been a prominent feature of Roman sculpture, derives from Roman influence. The greater proportion of the painted portraits has been recovered from Hawara and Er-Rubbiyat in the Faiyum, and for that reason they are often referred to as 'Faiyumic portraits'. Examples have, however, been found in a number of sites from Saqqara in the north to Aswan. The earliest examples date from the first half of the first century AD, the majority fall within the second and third centuries, and perhaps about a quarter of the number belong to the fourth century, about which time the practice of mummification was gradually abandoned in favour of simple interment of the dead in their everyday costume.

The early portraits are painted on thin panels of cypress, usually about 43 cms high and 23 cms wide, and no more than 1·6 mm thick, roughly trimmed to a point or arch at the top; they were placed over the face of the mummy and secured in position by the bandages (29772, Plate 19). In later examples thicker panels are more usual, generally rectangular in shape and on average about 30 cms high and 20–23 cms wide. A smaller number of portraits painted on the linen shroud have survived, the majority representing young children (68509, Plate 20).

Some of the portraits, particularly during the fourth century, were executed in tempera. The pigments, most of which were well known in the Dynastic Period (see pp. 204 ff.), were mixed in water with the addition of an adhesive material, probably egg-white or gum, and applied with a brush, sometimes directly on the canvas, sometimes on a prepared ground of gypsum plaster or whiting (chalk).

Water-colours being easily damaged and the pigment affected by moisture or the action of the air, the medium chosen for the majority of the portraits was beeswax, to which the appropriate pigment was added in a coarsely ground state. It produced a more robust portrait with a luminosity and enrichment of colour reminiscent of modern oil-painting. The technique of painting in wax was already widely practised in the Hellenistic world, but it had not previously been employed in Egypt. The manner of painting is described by Pliny the Elder in his *Natural History*, xxxv. 31, 39, 41, where he uses the term 'encaustic'. So far as the mummy portraits are concerned, there seems to be no question of fusing cold wax on to the surface of the panel by the application of artificial heat; in the warm climate of Egypt it was possible to apply the wax in more or less liquid form by means of a brush, provided the work was quickly executed. The usual practice followed by the painter seems to have been first to out-line the head and the features in black or occasionally red wash upon a prepared white background or directly upon the wood. He then filled in the background in grey, running his brush freely round the outline sketch and covering the remainder of the background with long, full, horizontal or slanting strokes. The drapery and hair were painted in the same way. In some cases the flesh received similar treatment, but usually the wax was applied more thickly. There is still considerable doubt concerning the manner in which this effect was achieved. The coloured wax may have been poured and modelled on the panel from the bowl of a warmed ladle or worked in a creamy state with a hard blunt point, perhaps a brush stiffened by constant use. Another possibility is that the wax was simply applied with a brush repeatedly over the same area.

In the earlier examples, the impressionistic handling of the paint and the suggestion of movement in the pose derive from the tradition of classical portrait painting of which the mummy panels are almost our only surviving examples. The subjects are drawn usually with the face turned slightly to the left or right but sometimes frontally. They are never in profile. Head, shoulders, and the upper part of the breast are usually shown; examples executed directly on the canvas of the shroud might be full length. Gradations of the individual colour, the use of shading and of highlights, give the portraits a strikingly modern appear-ance; at close quarters the work looks casual; particularly noticeable are the heavy line of the eyebrows, the white streak down the nose, the thick red smear of the lips separated by a black line and the heavy shading under the chin. But from a distance of one or two metres these prominent features merge and blend with the background.

This tradition was still observed in the third century, but by the fourth there had emerged a different style in which there was a more formal geometrically balanced arrangement of the features and hair. The figures are almost invariably full-faced. The drawing is less assured, particularly around the mouth with its pursed underlip.

Both men and women are shown wearing the ordinary costume of daily life current throughout the Hellenistic world, consisting of a loose sack-like tunic, usually of linen but later also of wool, passing over both shoulders, with an opening for the neck and two projecting sleeves. The normal colour of the costume was white for men, and usually red, but also blue, green, and white, for women. It was decorated with two vertical bands (clavi) which in the eastern Mediterranean had no significance of rank. In the fourth century a coloured border appeared around the neckline of the tunic worn by women. One or two of these garments were worn. In portraits of the first and second centuries AD it was customary for men and women to be depicted with a loose garment of the same colour over the tunic, draped over either shoulder or wrapped around both. Women are almost always shown with necklaces and ear-rings derived from models current in the Hellenistic world. The arrangement of the hair and beards of the men and the coiffure of the women follow closely the fashions set by the imperial family at Rome, and provide one of the clearest indications of the date of individual portraits.

Portraits painted on the canvas shroud of a mummy can only have been painted after death, and probably the portraits on thick panels of the later series were for funerary use only. The degree of individual characterization of the best of the early first-century portraits suggests that they may have been studies from life, intended in the first instance to be hung in the lifetime of the owner in the living-room of his home. It is, however, noticeable that in nearly every case the subject is portrayed in the prime of youth and beauty, features at rest with a look of calm and serene repose. The probability is that at least from the second century most portraits were painted after death, the painter reducing the wide range of subjects to a small number of well-defined types.

The plaster portrait head-pieces are found from the beginning of the Roman Period until the middle of the third century. The majority come from Middle Egypt; they were used concurrently with the painted panels. In the earliest type the head-piece was made hollow to fit over the skull which lay level with the body and it might be secured by cords passed through holes in the base. Gradually the head-piece was raised at an angle to the neck, to give the appearance of a man lying on a high pillow. The eyes were in the first place painted but from the second century translucent glass was commonly employed.

92 Painted plaster mask

The emergence of the portrait masks is foreshadowed by the superimposing of naturalistic details on masks more or less in the Egyptian style, particularly in the treatment of the hair. The gold mask attached to the mummy of a young boy from Hawara (22108) is fashioned in the conventional way but an alien element is introduced in the realistic arrangement of the curly hair. In the fine mask of a woman, probably from Meir (26799), the hair falls in two ringlets on either side of the neck, possibly representing a more naturalistic treatment of the ancient wig associated with goddesses.

The representations of the head-pieces, like the panel portraits, follow the convention of the fashions set by the imperial family. Generally speaking, however, the modeller of the masks did not succeed in conveying the individual likeness of a person to the same degree as the portrait painter. A notable exception, which must be one of the earliest of the realistic masks, is the head-piece of a man found at Hu (Diospolis Parva) in Upper Egypt (30845; fig. 92).

The graves of the mummies fitted with plaster head-pieces or painted portraits were seldom marked with commemorative stelae recording the names of the deceased. Private funerary stelae, however, continued to be used in the Roman Period; some are carved in a purely Egyptian style with representations of gods, below which there is a short conventional text in the hieroglyphic or demotic script: others, like a stone stela with a Greek epitaph in elegiac verse mourning the untimely death of the child Politta at the age of five, set between two columns supporting a gabled pediment (1206), are in the subject matter of their texts and form of their decoration derived from Greek tradition. From the early Roman Period onwards, the two styles were intermingled; in the stela (59870; fig. 93), of a type found in great numbers at Kom Abu Billo (Terenuthis), the deceased is represented clothed in Greek style reclining on a cushioned couch with right arm outstretched, holding in the hand a libation cup. The attitude of the figure goes back in origin to the Athenian grave reliefs. The stela is given a mixed architectural setting with gabled pediment of the kind seen on Greek stelae set on two columns with lotus-form capitals peculiar to Egypt.

93 Funerary stela

In the background is the representation of the Anubis-animal. Similar stelae are found with the deceased standing, arms extended at right angles from the body and bent upwards at the elbow in the *orans* position.

In the fourth century AD, to judge from excavations at Akhmim and Antinoopolis, there was a radical change in the burial customs of the country. The dead person was buried in the worn-out garments of daily life consisting of one or two tunics and outer cloak of the type depicted in the mummy portraits and sometimes with cap, socks, leather belt, and sandals. Below the neck there might be a small crescent-shaped pillow of stuffed cut-leather (26565). Hangings were sometimes wrapped around the body as a grave cloth. The depth at which the bodies were buried varied, some being just below the surface, others over 3 metres. The body might rest on a wooden board or be placed in direct contact with the sand. Only occasionally was there any form of prepared substructure, or the marking of the grave by memorial stones. Though in some cases there was a perfunctory attempt to embalm by the use of bitumen, generally speaking the preservation of the body was due to natural desiccation owing to the circumstances of the burial.

With the final abandonment of the painted wooden coffins, of the painted burial cloths, of the plaster head-pieces, and the mummy portraits, the last lingering traces of the dynastic civilization disappear. It is difficult not to connect the change in the mode of burial with a fundamental change in belief. There is no indication in the burials of what may have taken the place of the ancient belief in the kingdom of Osiris and the efficacy of mummification. Perhaps the change was accelerated by the widespread adoption of Christianity throughout Egypt.

The history of the spread of Christianity in Egypt cannot be traced in detail in either the archaeological remains or the literary evidence. According to a tradition which goes back to the fourth century AD the church at Alexandria was founded by the evangelist Mark. No trace of this primitive church has survived; in all probability it was completely destroyed during the great pogroms against the Jews of Alexandria towards the end of the first century. Christians do not emerge as an effective, developed society, playing an important part in the intellectual life of the city, until the foundation in about AD 180 of the catechetical school by Pantaenus. The Alexandrine church was essentially Greek rather than Egyptian: its language was Greek, its leading figures were steeped in the tradition of Hellenistic thought and scholarship.

The diffusion of Christianity from Alexandria to the rest of Egypt seems to have been slow. Even among the many private letters in Greek found in Egypt there are only a few which can be assigned with certainty to a date before the end of the third century. Little progress was made, so far as we can judge, among the Egyptian-speaking element of the population. There are, for instance, few native Egyptians among the martyrs of the persecutions of the second century. The first patriarch at Alexandria who is said to have been concerned to convert the native Egyptians is Dionysius (247–264 AD).

In contrast with the apparent initial slow progress of conversion of the Egyptians, from the middle of the third century sudden and dramatic headway was made, which the persecution associated with the name of Diocletian failed to arrest. The persecution seems to have fallen particularly heavily in Egypt and it is from the date of Diocletian's accession in AD 284 that the Coptic church still reckons its years.

As a result of the need to provide the new converts with translations of the scriptures, the ancient native tongue of Egypt received fresh stimulus. Already by the end of the first century AD attempts had been made to write the Egyptian language in Greek letters supplemented by a fairly large number of demotic signs. The purpose seems to have been to render more accurately the correct pronunciation of spells and in particular the names of demons and magical words of power, since the texts are magical in content and largely unintelligible. The collection of spells written in a fine demotic hand probably of the third century AD, which goes by the name of the London and Leiden Magical Papyrus (British Museum 10070 and Leiden I. 383) contains about 640 words with transcriptions in Greek characters over the native script (fig. 94).

94 London magical papyrus

Though the original impetus to write Egyptian in Greek letters was not of Christian origin, the sudden emergence of Coptic (p. 88) and its standardization as a literary language, with a distinct grammer and regular orthography, was due to the need to supply translations of the scriptures in the vernacular. Its earliest use in this connexion is for glosses in Coptic of Greek words in a text of Isaiah and of a Greek–Coptic vocabulary of Hosea and Amos, both of the third century AD. The earliest surviving copies of books of the Old and New Testament date from the first half of the fourth century. Translations into Coptic from lost Greek originals of the Gnostics, found at Nag Hammadi (Chenoboskion), and of the Manichaeans in the Faiyum, both dating from the fourth century, show the establishment of heretical sects among the native-speaking Egyptians contemporaneously with the spread of orthodox Christianity.

The rapid adoption of Christianity by the Egyptian-speaking element of the population manifests itself in the remarkably quick hold which monasticism gained in Egypt. According to tradition the first hermit was Paul, who took to the desert at the time of the Decian persecution of AD 251. To escape the persecutions may have been the primary reason for the beginning of the monastic movement but undoubtedly a factor which must also be taken into account is the state of the Egyptian economy in the third century. In common with the rest of the Roman Empire, Egypt suffered from a general depression brought about by over-taxation and the consequent abandonment of the cultivation of marginal land. Conditions were aggravated in Egypt by the invasion of an army of seventy thousand sent by Zenobia, queen of Palmyra, in AD 268. At the same time the southern frontier, which had been undisturbed since the time of Augustus, was threatened by the Blemmyes, a tribe now in occupation of Lower Nubia. The word used of the solitary—anchorite—is also found in early pre-Christian papyri to describe one who withdrew his labour. A third factor which probably encouraged the movement to the desert was the climate and geography of Egypt: there was no lack of unoccupied desert to withdraw to and the warmth of the climate made it possible to live outside the villages without undue hardship.

The life of the solitary remained the ideal of Egyptian monasticism. The hermit was ideally pictured as one who went out to the desert to guard the valley settlement from the incursions of the demons who inhabited the wastes in a physical form. Food and drink were supplied to him miraculously by a palm which furnished twelve clusters of dates a year, one for each month, and by a spring yielding a cupful of water a day. His spiritual food was brought down by supernatural means from heaven itself and at the moment of his death he was visited by a fellow monk, who gave him spiritual comfort for his last and terrible journey and carried out the service of burying him.

Such was the ideal which is conveyed to us in simple narratives of the early hermits preserved in Coptic literature. In practice the rigorous life of the solitary was followed by few: a communal way of life with a set rule developed. The true founder of monasticism was Antony. According to the traditional life, Antony was born about AD 251. He came of a moderately wealthy Egyptian family and neither spoke nor read Greek. His retirement to the desert was said to be the result of hearing the passage in the gospel of Matthew read in church which relates how Jesus told the young man to sell all and follow him. The fame of his life attracted disciples and these he organized into a loose community in which each member had his own cell (*laura*), often some miles distant one from another; here each monk followed his own way of life, but the community met on Saturdays and Sundays for the celebration of the Eucharist. The lauriate system of Antony was that adopted in and around the Wadi Natrun on the western side of the Delta. Lying as it does close to the Mediterranean littoral, it was much frequented by those who came to Egypt to see the ascetics. An early collection of simple tales connected with the monks of these settlements known as the *Apophthegmata Patrum* was current in Greek, Syriac, and Coptic.

The model or pattern for western monasticism was, however, the more rigid rule of Pachomius, which according to tradition he received from the hands of an angel, a scene depicted in western medieval manuscripts. In the Pachomian system there was a relaxation of the rule of solitude and an insistence upon organized work. The monks were organized into houses according to trades, sleeping three to a cell and eating in a common refectory attached to each house.

During the fourth and fifth centuries numerous monasteries were established in the Nile Valley and in the Delta. Except for tax receipts, there is a marked decrease in the first century AD in the number of legal and business documents in the Egyptian language: it now reappears in the Coptic form, vast quantities of Coptic ostraca and papyri being recovered from monastic sites relating to the secular and religious activities of the monasteries and their relations with the surrounding laity. A selection of such ostraca is exhibited in the Fourth Egyptian Room (fig. 27).

The monks of Egypt were particularly loyal, at times fanatically so, to the patriarchs at Alexandria. The solid support which they gave to the patriarchs accounts to a large extent for the prestige and power of the Alexandrine Church at the oecumenical councils called to define dogma and suppress heresy. It also enabled the patriarchs to act contrary to the policies of emperors, by then ruling from Byzantium; in the course of the fourth century the church of Egypt developed strong nationalist feeling and this, as much as the doctrinal point at issue, led to the condemnation of the Egyptian Church at the fourth council of Chalcedon in AD 451 for its adherence to monophysite doctrine that in the person of Christ there was only one nature.

The bulk of the carved stonework from the monasteries dates from the fifth to the ninth centuries AD and consists of tombstones and decorated architectural fragments, few of which have been found still standing in position. Much of the material has no known provenance and there are many problems in connexion with its dating. The work is executed in limestone and sandstone, the tradition of work in hard stone having died during the third century. With the exception of a form of cross, derived from the *ankh*, the hieroglyphic sign for 'life' (fig. 95), there is almost no

95 Memorial stone for Pleinos

trace of the art of the Pharaonic Period. The style and subject matter of its decorative work can be traced back to the sculptured fragments found at Oxyrhynchus and Ahnas (Ehnasiya), which date from the beginning of the fourth century. The term Coptic is by general consent applied to this work, though for the most part it does not seem to have come from Christian buildings and may be considered as the last manifestation of Hellenistic work.

The carved relief of the architectural fragments of this early Coptic sculpture is drawn from familiar Hellenistic decoration, consisting for the most part of plant ornamentation and geometric designs seen at its best in friezes with acanthus and vine-leaf scrolls inhabited by birds and animals.

Particularly common at Ahnas are the friezes, niches, and other architectural elements with figure subjects in high relief, cut so deeply that at times they are almost detached from the plain background. In contrast with the general Hellenistic style,

Fragment of a niche with the head of a woman

the proportions of the figures show the clumsiness commonly associated with Coptic art, particularly in the small heads, conventional treatment of the hair, and the large eyes: the movements are angular and the forms sharply outlined. The subjects of the representations are drawn from the familiar repertoire of late pagan and classical mythology: Aphrodite, Herakles, Leda, Erotes, Nereids often riding on dolphins, Nymphs and other semi-divine powers, and personifications of the Earth, of the Nile, of Plenty (Euhemera), and of Good Fortune (Tyche). The style is illustrated by a female head of unknown provenance (36143; fig. 96) which formed the top of a niche.

When the Christian communities built monasteries and churches, they used the current decorative style incorporating the repertoire of motifs with which they were familiar. They were influenced in the course of time by the art of other Christian communities of the eastern Mediterranean. In general there was a tendency for the ornamentation to become more abstract, less naturalistic and less deeply cut. The decorative pattern of the friezes was simplified and monotonously repeated. The deep-cut relief characteristic of the Ahnas style disappeared, and figure subjects became uncommon except on tombstones. Free-standing sculpture is unknown.

Large numbers of Coptic tombstones, most of them dating from the seventh and eighth centuries, have been recovered. Neither in their inscription nor in their relief do they owe anything to the funerary stelae of dynastic Egypt, but clearly evolve from the style of the mixed Romano-Egyptian stelae of the third and fourth centuries (p. 246). The inscriptions carved upon them usually give the name and status of the deceased introduced by one of the common Christian funerary formulae, sometimes invoking the intercession of local saints (676). Only a few, and these of late date, contain more poetic compositions with reflections on death. If the date of the death is recorded, it is usually only by the year of an indiction, the cycle of fifteen years which was introduced at the time of Diocletian for administrative reasons (1328, 1801). Some stelae contain no more than the text; others are carved in flat relief, the common themes being the representation of the deceased standing with his hands raised in the *orans* position (1523), birds (618), foliate borders, crosses with and without an encircling wreath (1520), and the façade of a building rendered in an increasingly less naturalistic style (1328, 1801). In the late period the memorial stones are usually small with rounded tops or large slabs, rectangular in form or carved at the top with a gabled pediment. In the earlier period, up to the sixth century, there was more diversity of type: the upper part of a stela from El-Badari (1811), carved in the form of an *ankh*-cross, the loop filled with a chubby-faced mask and surrounded with a gaily painted decoration of vine stems and grapes, is of a type which seems to have been confined to Middle Egypt. The niche with a carved figure of a young boy (1795; fig. 97), which comes from a Christian necropolis at Oxyrhynchus, belongs to a type which, judging from the objects held in the hand of examples from Antinoopolis, was originally pagan, then adapted for Christian burials. Also from Oxyrhynchus comes a standing figure which presumably once stood in a similar niche (1841).

Some of the original impact of the Coptic sculpture is lost by the disappearance in most cases of all traces of its original colour which would have concealed the general lack of modelling and the absence of fine detail in the carving. The use of colour was an

97 Niche with figure of a young boy

essential part of the decorative nature of Coptic art in general and may best be judged from the textiles which have survived in quantity from the fourth century onwards, mainly in the cemeteries of Antinoopolis and Akhmim. The art of fine weaving goes back to Egypt to the Predynastic Period (see pp. 234 ff.), though relatively little has survived apart from plain linen weaves. The appearance of the textiles now in the fourth century AD is due to the change in burial customs described on p. 248.

Broadly speaking, the style of textiles follows the same lines as the stonework. The earliest of the larger tapestries show in their choice of subject, in their treatment of the figures, and in the naturalistic shades of colour, characteristics of late Hellenistic work. They are well illustrated in the two fragments of a large loop tapestry in wool on linen from Akhmim (20717; Plate 21) with a representation of two Erotes in a boat surrounded by a guilloche border at the corners of which are well-modelled masks within small roundels.

The evolution of the more specifically Coptic style is shown by the large tapestry in coloured wools and undyed thread on linen approximately 1·50 m. wide and 1·80 m. high with two lateral and one broad medial vertical bands, the intervening space being occupied by two large standing figures set against an open background studded with decorative rosettes (43049; fig. 98).

98 Tapestry with divine figures

The lateral bands show dancing male and female figures against a background of vine tendrils within a border of heart-shape pattern. The medial band has a formalized floral border and dancing figures with shields and flying cloaks enclosed within a scroll pattern. The large standing female figure, on the right of the tapestry, is wearing a long green skirt and blue-spotted red cloak. She draws a bow with her right hand and a quiver with three arrows is slung on her back. The male figure on the left wears a pointed cap of western Asiatic origin which is a mark of divine or heroic stature and is dressed in a short green kilt and red cloak fastened over his left shoulder. The female figure with bow and arrow is probably to be identified as Artemis, and the male figure with one of the heroes famed as hunters with whom she is associated in late classical myth, perhaps Actaeon, Orion, or Meleager. The treatment of the figures, with the stressed whites of the eye, heavy eyebrows, stylized treatment of the hair, and even rendering of the colour, marks the transition to the Coptic Period.

The bulk of the surviving textiles of the fourth to the sixth century consists of costume ornaments, with tapestry woven designs usually of dyed wools with linen threads for small details. Surviving examples show that there were different methods of arranging the ornamentation on the tunic, which in its essential form differed little from the costume depicted on the mummy portraits of the first four centuries AD. In its simplest form the tunic contained only two vertical bands running over the shoulders down to the hem and one or two bands ornamented in similar style around the cuffs (18198). A continuous broad horizontal band might run around the neck opening (21789). In more elaborate decorated costumes woven panels or roundels were added, usually on the shoulders or near the bottom corners at the front and back. In later tunics the bands are regularly shortened to about waist-level and terminated in a roundel or pendent ornament. Roundels are far more common than the square panels. The large oblong cloths (for example 21795) were probably used as an outer garment loosely draped over the shoulders like a cloak in the manner indicated in the mummy portraits. They were used also as covering at night and were faced with long loops for extra warmth.

The earliest of the costume ornaments are of intricate geometric patterns woven in purple wool and undyed linen thread (21516). They are characteristic of the fourth century. Purple was the standard colour used in the monochrome work. The designs for both monochrome and polychrome work were drawn from the repertoire of late Hellenistic art: fish, animals of the chase, particularly the desert hare and lions (21790),

Plate 20
Portrait painted on a linen shroud

baskets of petals and fruits (17172), trees, the most common of which was the vine-stem growing out of a vase or basket. Figure subjects are common, sometimes apparently drawn from popular stories of the classical heroes, identification of which is uncertain in the absence of detail; the figure of a nude man and woman set apparently in a meadow or garden (21791) may perhaps represent Herakles and one of the classical heroines with whom he was associated. The mythical creatures of classical invention also appear, like the half-human half-horse centaur or half-horse half-fish hippocampus. The scenes are often animated, leaping boy warriors with flying cloaks, dancing figures, with their heads tossed back, and mounted hunters (21802). Several elements, not necessarily harmonious, were combined in one piece, the central design enclosed by a surrounding border of intertwining stems, forming scrolls for further subjects (17172). Vertical bands were given a continuous decoration of figure or animal subjects within a border of interlaced pattern, particularly male or female dancers, shepherds holding a staff or a lion by the tail, and hunted animals (18198).

The earliest indication of polychrome tapestry for costume ornament is the addition of small detail usually in red (17171, 21791, 21795). The widespread use of polychrome weaving for this purpose probably dates from the sixth century. The range of subject and decoration remains similar to the monochrome patterns which are still found, but the treatment of the human figure shows a more specifically Coptic style. There is a tendency for schematic forms, large heads squashed down on the shoulders, the eyes large with prominent whites, the hair treated in stylized curls or stretched like a sponge across the top of the head. Hands and the lower part of the legs receive sketchy treatment. A characteristic example is the small square panel depicting a leaping warrior within a rectangular frame of coloured heart-shape petals (17176).

Christian subjects are rare before the seventh century and not common until the eighth. The figures are commonly woven on a red background, in a highly stylized but decorative form, which give the impression of having been built up from rectangular segments. The most common themes are haloed figures of saints, either standing or on horseback (18233). Scenes drawn from biblical stories, their subject not always readily apparent, also occur (18221).

The sequence of the textiles from the Egyptian burial grounds continues until the twelfth century, by which time the Christian church of Egypt had become a minority element in the population, not immune from persecution; the language itself was falling into obsolescence; by the eleventh century its literature lost its force and Arabic–Coptic grammars and vocabularies were first compiled. From the thirteenth century service books were regularly provided with Arabic translations, and by the sixteenth Coptic had probably ceased to be a spoken language even in the villages of Upper Egypt, its use being confined entirely to the recitation of the liturgy, for which purpose it is still read.

Similarly, after the ninth century, the art of the Copts is increasingly influenced by the Islamic world, until in much of its decoration only the presence of a cross or inscription in Coptic betrays its Christian purpose. Christian antiquities of this late period, which include remarkable examples of wood carving from the ancient churches of Cairo, are preserved in the collections of the Department of Medieval and Later Antiquities.

South of Egypt proper lay the independent kingdom of Meroe which had come into existence after the Twenty-fifth Dynasty in the seventh century BC. The kings of the Twenty-sixth Dynasty, the Persian emperors and the Ptolemies had not succeeded in bringing Nubia under their control; the Romans challenged the power of Meroe by a punitive expedition in 23 BC under Petronius, Governor of Egypt, who captured Qasr Ibrim and succeeded in sacking the capital, Napata, itself (p. 71). Though the treaty following this victory gave the Romans access to that stretch of Lower Nubia between Aswan and Hierosykaminos (the Dodekaschoinos), the power of Meroe over the rest of Lower Nubia was by no means broken. Roman influence remained only in the northern part, reflected in the completion or construction of a number of temples. The Meroites successfully petitioned for the return of Qasr Ibrim, a fortress valued not only for its strategic position but also, apparently, for religious reasons.

Knowledge of the expedition itself is derived from the detailed descriptions made by the classical historians Strabo, Pliny and Dio Cassius. At least one further expedition, recorded both by Pliny and by Seneca, took place between 61 and 67 AD. From this time onwards there was a gradual deterioration of Meroitic power in the south, evident in the less elaborate preparations for burial and in fewer imported goods. The chronology for this period is uncertain, the next firm date occurring only in a demotic graffito at Philae, which records that in AD 253 envoys were sent from Meroe with gifts for the temple, reflecting a special reverence for Isis among the Meroites. The decision made by the Emperor Diocletian in AD 296 to withdraw all his troops and to set the southern frontier of Egypt at Philae undoubtedly hastened the economic decline of Meroitic Nubia, and by the middle of the fourth century AD the Meroitic kingdom was at an end. An inscription of King Aezanes of Axum in

Ethiopia (AD 325–375) reveals that when he marched through the Butana, another nomadic group, the 'Noba', were already in possession of Meroe.

Such interventions in Meroitic history reflect the continuing influence of the Mediterranean powers. The forms and decoration of Meroitic pottery are particularly illuminating, for they illustrate vividly the combination of Mediterranean and African traditions. The British Museum possesses several fine specimens of Meroitic painted wares (e.g. 51615; fig. 99). The ancient religion and art forms of dynastic Egypt survived at Meroe until the fourth century AD and, although the Napatan royal cemeteries were abandoned in favour of burial at Meroe, the tradition of pyramid tombs continued (719; fig. 100). Fine metalwork was produced, examples of which may be seen among the bronze objects on exhibition (63585; fig. 101). The Meroitic kingdom evolved its own alphabetic script, which has been preserved for the most part in dedicatory inscriptions on stone libation bowls and similar objects. The inscription carved on a rectangular stela (1650) with the names of Queen Amanirenas and Akinidad and found at Meroe is one of the surviving texts of a more historical interest.

Following the disintegration of the Meroitic kingdom, Nubia was overrun by various nomadic tribes. By the fifth century AD

99 Meroitic pottery
vessel

100 Carved relief from
a pyramid chapel
at Meroe

three distinct kingdoms, Nobatia, Makuria, and Alwa, had been   101 Bronze aegis
formed. Christianity penetrated slowly into Nubia from Egypt,
and finally in the middle of the sixth century AD the area was
formally converted by emissaries sent from Constantinople. In
spite of the Arab conquest of Egypt in 641, a Christian kingdom
continued to survive in Nubia until probably the early fifteenth
century but eventually succumbed to internal divisions,
renewed nomadic and Egyptian pressure, and declining trade.
Objects in the collection from Christian Nubia include a fine red
sandstone frieze (606) and a red sandstone capital (1636) from
the seventh-century cathedral at Faras, which was later to be
rebuilt and decorated with magnificent frescoes. Other artifacts
from the Christian period at Qasr Ibrim are part of the collections
in the Department of Medieval and Later Antiquities.

LIST OF THE PRINCIPAL KINGS OF EGYPT

(Overlapping dates usually indicate coregencies. All dates given are approximate.)

FIRST DYNASTY

c. 3100–2890 BC

Narmer (Menes)
Aha
Djer
Djet (Uadji)
Den (Udimu)
Anedjib
Semerkhet
Qaa

SECOND DYNASTY

c. 2890–2686 BC

Hotepsekhemwy
Raneb
Nynetjer
Peribsen
Khasekhem (Khasekhemwy)

THIRD DYNASTY

c. 2686–2613 BC

Sanakhte
Djoser
Sekhemkhet
Khaba
Huni

FOURTH DYNASTY

c. 2613–2494 BC

Sneferu
Cheops (Khufu)
Redjedef
Chephren (Khafre)
Mycerinus (Menkaure)
Shepseskaf

FIFTH DYNASTY

c. 2494–2345 BC

Userkaf
Sahure
Neferirkare Kakai
Shepseskare Isi
Neferefre
Nyuserre
Menkauhor Akauhor
Djedkare Isesi
Unas

SIXTH DYNASTY

c. 2345–2181 BC

Teti
Userkare
Meryre (Pepi I)
Merenre
Neferkare (Pepi II)

SEVENTH DYNASTY

c. 2181–2173 BC

EIGHTH DYNASTY

c. 2173–2160 BC

NINTH DYNASTY

c. 2160–2130 BC

Meryibre Achthoes I (Khety I)
Nebkaure Achthoes II

TENTH DYNASTY

c. 2130–2140 BC

Wahkare Achthoes III
Merykare

ELEVENTH DYNASTY

c. 2133–1991 BC

Tepya Mentuhotpe I
Sehertowy Inyotef I
Wahankh Inyotef II
Nakhtnebtepnefer Inyotef III
Nebhepetre Mentuhotpe II
Sankhkare Mentuhotpe III
Nebtowyre Mentuhotpe IV

TWELFTH DYNASTY

c. 1991–1786 BC

Sehetepibre Ammenemes I
1991–1962 BC
Kheperkare Sesostris I
1971–1928 BC
Nubkaure Ammenemes II
1929–1895 BC
Khakheperre Sesostris II
1897–1878 BC
Khakaure Sesostris III
1878–1843 BC

Nymare Ammenemes III
1842–1797 BC
Makherure Ammenemes IV
1798–1790 BC
Sobkkare Sobkneferu
1789–1786 BC

THIRTEENTH DYNASTY
c. 1786–c. 1633 BC

Sekhemre Sewadjtowy
  Sobkhotpe III
Khasekhemre Neferhotep
Meryankhre Mentuhotpe

FOURTEENTH DYNASTY
c. 1786–c. 1603 BC

FIFTEENTH DYNASTY
(Hyksos)
c. 1674–1567 BC

Mayebre Sheshi
Meruserre Yakubher
Seuserenre Khyan
Auserre Apophis I
Aqenenre Apophis II

SIXTEENTH DYNASTY
c. 1684–c. 1567 BC

SEVENTEENTH DYNASTY
c. 1650–1567 BC

Nubkheperre Inyotef VII
Senakhtenre Tao I, 'the
  Elder'
Seqenenre Tao II, 'the
  Brave'
Wadjkheperre Kamose

EIGHTEENTH DYNASTY
c. 1567–1320 BC

Nebpehtyre Amosis I
  (Ahmose)
1570–1546 BC
Djeserkare Amenophis I
  (Amenhotpe I)
1546–1526 BC
Akheperkare Tuthmosis I
1525–c. 1512 BC
Akheperenre Tuthmosis II
c. 1512–1504 BC
Makare Hatshepsut
1503–1482 BC

Menkheperre Tuthmosis III
1504–1450 BC
Akheprure Amenophis II
1450–1425 BC
Menkheprure Tuthmosis IV
1425–1417 BC
Nebmare Amenophis III
1417–1379 BC
Neferkheprure Amenophis IV
  (Akhenaten)
1379–1362 BC
Ankhkheprure Smenkhkare
1364–1361 BC
Nebkheprure Tutankhamun
1361–1352 BC
Kheperkheprure Ay
1352–1348 BC
Djeserkheprure Horemheb
1348–1320 BC

NINETEENTH DYNASTY
c. 1320–1200 BC

Menpehtyre Ramesses I
1320–1318 BC
Menmare Sethos I
1318–1304 BC
Usermare Ramesses II
1304–1237 BC
Baenre Merneptah
1236–1223 BC
Menmire Amenmesses
1222–1217 BC
Userkheprure Sethos II
1216–1210 BC

TWENTIETH DYNASTY
c. 1200–1085 BC

Userkhaure Sethnakhte
1200–1198 BC
Usermare-Meryamun,
  Ramesses III
1198–1166 BC
Hiqmare Ramesses IV
1166–1160 BC
Usermare Ramesses V
1160–1156 BC
Nebmare Ramesses VI
1156–1148 BC
Usermare Ramesses VII
1148–1141 BC
Usermare Ramesses VIII
1147–1140 BC
Neferkare Ramesses IX
1140–1123 BC

Khepermare Ramesses X
1123–1114 BC
Menmare Ramesses XI
1114–1085 BC

TWENTY-FIRST DYNASTY

c. 1085–945 BC

At Tanis
Hedjkheperre Nesbanebded
  (Smendes)
Akheperre Psusennes I
Amenemope
Siamun
Psusennes II

At Thebes (*High Priests*)
Herihor (temp. Ramesses XI)
Paiankh
Pinudjem I
Masaherta
Menkheperre
Pinudjem II

TWENTY-SECOND DYNASTY

(Libyan or Bubastite)
c. 945–715 BC

Hedjkheperre Sheshonq I
c. 945–924 BC
Osorkon I
c. 924–889 BC
Takelothis I
c. 889–874 BC
Usermare Osorkon II
c. 874–850 BC
Takelothis II
c. 850–825 BC
Sheshonq III
c. 825–773 BC
Pami
c. 773–767 BC
Sheshonq V
c. 767–730 BC
Osorkon IV
c. 730–715 BC

TWENTY-THIRD DYNASTY

c. 818–715 BC

Pedubastis I
c. 818–793 BC
Osorkon III
c. 777–749 BC

TWENTY-FOURTH DYNASTY

c. 727–715 BC

Tefnakhte
Bakenrenef (Bocchoris)

TWENTY-FIFTH DYNASTY

(Nubian or Kushite)
c. 747–656 BC

Piankhi (Piye)
c. 747–716 BC
Neferkare Shabaka
c. 716–702 BC
Djedkaure Shebitku
c. 702–690 BC
Khunefertemre Taharqa
690–664 BC
Bakare Tanutamun
664–656 BC

TWENTY-SIXTH DYNASTY

(Saite)
664–525 BC

Wahibre Psammetichus I
664–610 BC
Wehemibre Necho II
610–595 BC
Neferibre Psammetichus II
595–589 BC
Haibre Wahibre (Apries)
589–570 BC
Khnemibre Amosis II
  (Amasis)
570–526 BC
Ankhkaenre
  Psammetichus III
526–525 BC

TWENTY-SEVENTH DYNASTY

(Persian)
525–404 BC

Cambyses
525–522 BC
Darius I
522–486 BC
Xerxes
486–465 BC
Artaxerxes I
465–424 BC

Darius II
424–405 BC
Artaxerxes II
405–359 BC

TWENTY-EIGHTH DYNASTY
404–399 BC

Amyrtaeus
404–399 BC

TWENTY-NINTH DYNASTY
399–380 BC

Nepherites I
399–393 BC
Khnemmare Achoris (Hagor)
393–380 BC

THIRTIETH DYNASTY
380–343 BC

Kheperkare Nectanebo I
380–362 BC
Teos
362–360 BC
Snedjemibre Nectanebo II
360–343 BC

PERSIAN KINGS
343–332 BC

Artaxerxes III Ochus
343–338 BC
Arses
338–336 BC
Darius III
336–332 BC

MACEDONIAN KINGS
332–305 BC

Alexander the Great
332–323 BC
Philip Arrhidaeus
323–317 BC
Alexander IV
317–305 BC

THE PTOLEMIES
305–30 BC

Ptolemy I Soter I
305–282 BC
Ptolemy II Philadelphus
284–246 BC
Ptolemy III Euergetes I
246–222 BC
Ptolemy IV Philopator
222–205 BC
Ptolemy V Epiphanes
205–180 BC
Ptolemy VI Philometor
180–145 BC
Ptolemy VII Neos Philopator
145 BC
Ptolemy VIII Euergetes II
170–116 BC
Ptolemy IX Soter II
 (Lathyros)
116–107 BC
Ptolemy X Alexander I
107–88 BC
Ptolemy IX Soter II
 (restored)
88–80 BC
Ptolemy XI Alexander II
80 BC
Ptolemy XII Neos Dionysos
 (Auletes)
80–51 BC
Cleopatra VII Philopator
51–30 BC

NAMES OF THE PRINCIPAL KINGS OF EGYPT

(*including the Roman Emperors*)

During the Early Dynastic Period, the chief name (Horus-name) of the king was written in a rectangular frame called a *serekh*. The bottom part of the frame contained a design of panelling, and the whole was surmounted by a figure of a falcon–the god Horus. In the case of Peribsen of the Second Dynasty, the Seth-animal replaced the falcon, while the *serekh* of Khasekhemwy was surmounted by both falcon and Seth-animal. A second name sometimes accompanied the Horus-name, or was used independently; it was introduced by one or both of the two titles 'King of Upper and Lower Egypt' and 'The Two Ladies'.

FIRST DYNASTY

Narmer   Aha   Djer   Djet   Den

Anedjib   Semerkhet   Qaa

SECOND DYNASTY

Hotepsekhemwy   Nynetjer   Peribsen   Khasekhemwy

THIRD DYNASTY

Sanakhte   Djoser   Sekhemkhet   Khaba

From the Old Kingdom the Egyptian king normally possessed five names: the Horus-name, the 'Two Ladies'-name, the Golden Horus-name (of uncertain origin), the prenomen (preceded by the title 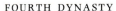, translated usually 'King of Upper and Lower Egypt') and the nomen (preceded by the title 𓅭𓇳 'Son of Re'). The nomen was first used by kings of the Fifth Dynasty who were specially devoted to the worship of Re. Prenomens and nomens were regularly enclosed within ovals called cartouches, which depict loops of rope with tied ends. By having his name so enclosed, the king possibly wished to convey pictorially that he was ruler of all 'that which is encircled by the sun'. From the late Eighteenth Dynasty onwards additional epithets were regularly introduced into the cartouches. In times when the claim to the throne of all Egypt was disputed kings sometimes avoided the 𓇓𓏏 -title and used 𓊹𓄤 , 'the good god'. The names within cartouches are those by which a king is normally identified.

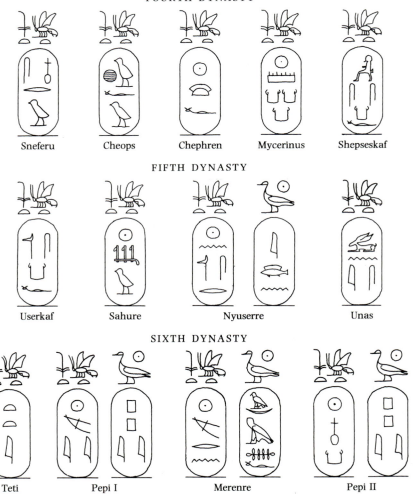

FOURTH DYNASTY

Sneferu   Cheops   Chephren   Mycerinus   Shepseskaf

FIFTH DYNASTY

Userkaf   Sahure   Nyuserre   Unas

SIXTH DYNASTY

Teti   Pepi I   Merenre   Pepi II

ELEVENTH DYNASTY

Inyotef   Mentuhotpe II   Mentuhotpe III   Mentuhotpe IV

TWELFTH DYNASTY

Ammenemes I   Sesostris I   Ammenemes II

Sesostris II   Sesostris III   Ammenemes III   Ammenemes IV

THIRTEENTH DYNASTY

FIFTEENTH DYNASTY
(Hyksos)

Sobkhotpe III   Neferhotep I   Khyan   Apophis I

SEVENTEENTH DYNASTY

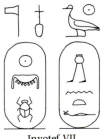

Inyotef VII

Seqenenre II

Kamose

EIGHTEENTH DYNASTY

Amosis I

Amenophis I

Tuthmosis I

Tuthmosis II

Hatshepsut

Tuthmosis III

Amenophis II

Tuthmosis IV

Amenophis III

Akhenaten

Tutankhamun

Horemheb

NINETEENTH DYNASTY

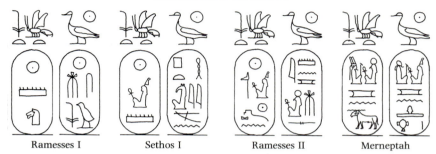

Ramesses I Sethos I Ramesses II Merneptah

TWENTIETH DYNASTY

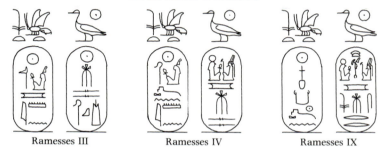

Ramesses III Ramesses IV Ramesses IX

TWENTY-FIRST DYNASTY   TWENTY-SECOND DYNASTY

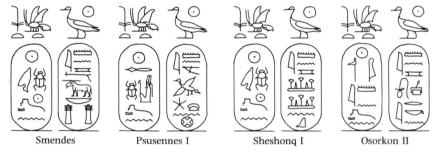

Smendes Psusennes I Sheshonq I Osorkon II

TWENTY-FIFTH DYNASTY

Piankhi Shabaka Taharqa

TWENTY-SIXTH DYNASTY

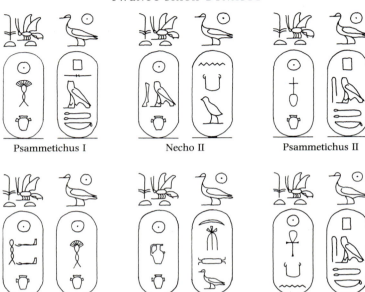

Psammetichus I   Necho II   Psammetichus II

Apries   Amosis II   Psammetichus III

TWENTY-SEVENTH DYNASTY

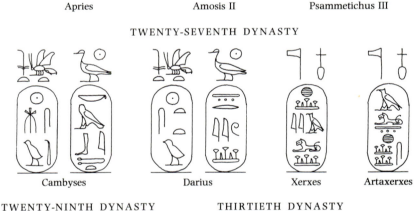

Cambyses   Darius   Xerxes   Artaxerxes

TWENTY-NINTH DYNASTY   THIRTIETH DYNASTY

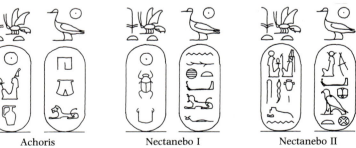

Achoris   Nectanebo I   Nectanebo II

MACEDONIAN KINGS

Alexander the Great   Philip Arrhidaeus

PTOLEMAIC DYNASTY

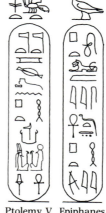

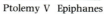

Ptolemy I   Soter I   Ptolemy II Philadelphus   Ptolemy V Epiphanes   Cleopatra VII

ROMAN EMPERORS

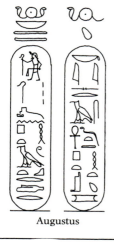

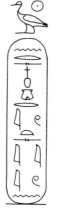

Augustus   Tiberius   Trajan   Diocletian

BIBLIOGRAPHY

CHAPTER TWO

E. Bevan. *A History of Egypt under the Ptolemaic Dynasty.* London, 1927.
The Cambridge Ancient History. Vols. I and II. 3rd ed. Cambridge, 1970–5.
Sir A. H. Gardiner. *Egypt of the Pharaohs.* Oxford, 1961.

CHAPTER FOUR

Erman (1927): A. Erman. *The Literature of the Ancient Egyptians.* London, 1927.
Gardiner (1909): A. H. Gardiner. *The Admonitions of an Egyptian Sage.* Leipzig, 1909.
Gardiner (1935): A. H. Gardiner. *Hieratic Papyri in the British Museum.* Third Series. London, 1935.
Glanville (1955): S. R. K. Glanville. *Catalogue of Demotic Papyri in the British Museum.* Vol. II. London, 1955.
Goedicke (1970): H. Goedicke. *The Report about the Dispute of a man with his Ba.* Baltimore, 1970.
Goedicke (1975): H. Goedicke. *The Report of Wenamun.* Baltimore, 1975.
Griffith (1900): F. Ll. Griffith. *Stories of the High Priests of Memphis.* Oxford, 1900.
Lichtheim (1973): M. Lichtheim. *Ancient Egyptian Literature.* Vol. I. Los Angeles, 1973.
Maspero (1915): G. Maspero. *Popular Stories of Ancient Egypt.* London, 1915.
Pritchard (1955): J. B. Pritchard. *Ancient Near Eastern Texts relating to the Old Testament.* Princeton, 1955.
Simpson (1972): W. K. Simpson (ed.). *The Literature of Ancient Egypt.* New Haven, 1972.

CHAPTER FIVE

J. Černý. *Ancient Egyptian Religion.* London, 1952.

S. Morenz. *Egyptian Religion.* Trans. A. Keep, London, 1973.
E. Otto. *Egyptian Art and the Cults of Osiris and Amon.* London, 1968.
S. Sauneron. *The Priests of Ancient Egypt.* London, 1960.
A. W. Shorter. *The Egyptian Gods.* London, 1937.

CHAPTER SIX

T. G. Allen. *The Egyptian Book of the Dead.* Chicago, 1960.
E. A. W. Budge. *The Book of the Dead.* London, 1909.
E. A. W. Budge. *The Mummy.* Cambridge, 1928.
G. Elliot Smith and W. R. Dawson. *Egyptian Mummies.* London, 1924.
W. B. Emery. *Archaic Egypt.* Harmondsworth, 1961.
I. E. S. Edwards. *The Pyramids of Egypt.* 2nd ed. London, 1961.
R. O. Faulkner. *The Ancient Egyptian Coffin Texts.* Warminster, 1973.
J. Garstang. *Burial Customs of Ancient Egypt.* London, 1907.
W. M. F. Petrie. *Shabtis.* London, 1935; reprinted Warminster, 1974.

CHAPTER SEVEN

A. Lucas. *Ancient Egyptian Materials and Industries.* 4th ed. London, 1962.

CHAPTER EIGHT

P. Du Bourguet. *Coptic Art.* London, 1971.
P. Shinnie. *Meroe.* London, 1971.
A. F. Shore. 'Coptic and Christian Egypt', in J. R. Harris, *The Legacy of Egypt.* 2nd ed. Oxford, 1971.
A. F. Shore. *Portrait Painting from Roman Egypt.* Rev. ed. London, 1972.

INDEX TO THE COLLECTION NUMBERS
OF OBJECTS MENTIONED IN THE GUIDE

Note: Numbers with asterisks refer to illustrations

Eye Movement Basics for the Clinician

EYE MOVEMENT BASICS FOR THE CLINICIAN

■

Kenneth J. Ciuffreda, O.D., Ph.D.

Distinguished Teaching Professor
Chairperson, Department of Vision Sciences
SUNY State College of Optometry
New York, New York

Barry Tannen, O.D.

Assistant Clinical Professor
SUNY State College of Optometry
New York, New York

with 241 illustrations

An Affiliate of Elsevier

Mosby

An Affiliate of Elsevier

Editor: Martha Sasser
Associate Developmental Editor: Kellie White
Project Manager: John Rogers
Senior Production Editor: Helen Hudlin
Designer: Renée Duenow
Manufacturing Supervisor: Betty Richmond
Cover Design: Eleanor Safe

Mosby
An Affiliate of Elsevier
11830 Westline Industrial Drive
St. Louis, Missouri 63146

Library of Congress Cataloging in Publication Data

Ciuffreda, Kenneth J., 1947-
    Eye movement basics for the clinician / Kenneth J. Ciuffreda, Barry Tannen.
        p.   cm.
    Includes bibliographical references and index.
    ISBN-13: 978-0-8016-6843-2   ISBN-10: 0-8016-6843-3
    1. Eye--Movements.   2. Eye--Movement disorders.   I. Tannen, Barry.
    [DNLM: 1. Eye Movements.   WW 400 C581e 1994]
QP477.5.C58   1994
612.8'46--dc20
DNLM/DLC
for Library of Congress   94-24384
                                                                    CIP

Transferred to Digital Printing 2010

To my family
for their support and understanding
in this endeavor.
To my mentor,
Larry Stark,
for his inspiration.

K.J.C.

To my wife, Sandi,
and my children, Rachael and Noah,
for their love and support.
To my mother,
for all she has sacrificed
for her children.

B.T.

Preface

For the past 5 years, we have tested and trained eye movement ability on a wide range of patients in our Oculomotor Diagnostic and Biofeedback Therapy Clinic at the SUNY State College of Optometry. The patients have included those with congenital and acquired nystagmus, neurological disease, head trauma, ocular and systemic disease, congenital and acquired dyslexia/reading disability, strabismus, amblyopia, and nonpathological general oculomotor visual "skills" problems. They have been referred through optometrists, optometry students, neurologists, reading teachers, clinical psychologists, rehabilitation and low vision instructors, and ophthalmologists both internal and external to the university facility. This rich patient base has provided us with a diverse set of experiences from which to draw upon.

In addition to the obvious benefit to the patients, our clinic has provided a wonderful educational resource for students and faculty. However, a resource book was needed that students could use (1) before clinical exposure to establish a baseline or entry level of knowl-

edge and acceptable theoretical clinical competence in this area, (2) during clinical exposure to build upon the theoretical base by actual patient encounters, and (3) subsequent to formal clinical exposure as a lifetime reference source. Thus the genesis of the present text.

Each chapter discusses basic information and concepts deemed necessary to understand the topic under consideration. In addition, we have attempted to provide sufficient relevant clinical examples (by no means exhaustive) to pique the interest of the reader. We hope that with this mixture of basic and clinical information we are successful in accomplishing our goal—namely, to improve and expand the student's or clinician's knowledge in this most exciting area, with more effective rendering of patient care occurring as a natural outgrowth of the process.

Kenneth J. Ciuffreda
Barry Tannen
New York City
September 1994

Acknowledgments

I thank the reviewers for their detailed constructive comments, which have improved the quality of the book. I also thank the administration and staff of the SUNY State College of Optometry for their support in providing release time, media resources, and typing staff over the past 2 years.

K.J.C.

I wish to thank a number of individuals whose assistance, guidance, and insights have proved invaluable over the course of this project: Dr. Harold Friedman, for his special efforts to allow me the professional time to complete this book; Dr. Nicholas Despotidis, my partner in private practice, whose support and understanding were essential; Drs. Martin Birnbaum, Leonard Press, Stuart Rothman, and the rest of the SUNY Vision Therapy Clinic's "Thursday group," for their camaraderie and helpful insights; Drs. Roger Cummings and Larry Stark, who individually sparked my interest in eye movements early in my professional career; and Dr. Ken Ciuffreda, my co-author, whose guidance and experience proved to be of inestimable value. Finally, I would like to thank the administration and the staff of the SUNY State College of Optometry for their support and the use of their excellent resources.

B.T.

Contents

Eye Movement
Basics for
the Clinician

1

Introduction to Eye Movements

Key Terms

Descartes-Sherrington law of
   reciprocal innervation
Donder's law
Hering's law

Listing's law
Ocular kinematics
Vergence eye movements
Versional eye movements

The apparently simple task of scanning around one's room at various objects of interest necessitates remarkable coordination of two independent oculomotor systems (Fig. 1-1). The *versional* system controls conjugate movement of the eyes, that is, movement of the eyes in the *same* direction to see objects positioned in various directions from us. The *vergence* system controls disjunctive movement of the eyes, that is, movement of the eyes in *opposing* directions to see objects singly at different distances from us. These two systems can shift the eyes horizontally, vertically, and in a cyclorotary manner in all directions of gaze and distances.

Tables 1-1 and 1-2 provide overviews of the versional and vergence eye movement systems, respectively. Perhaps the function of these two interactive systems and their subsystems can be best appreciated and understood by way of an example. Imagine that you are standing in your backyard, relaxing. Suddenly a large bird appears, and it rapidly hops along a limb in a tree. You visually track the bird's movement by a series of foveating saccades with intervening periods of fixation. The bird then decides to fly up and across the clear blue sky, and you rapidly rotate your head and body (in conjunction with your tracking eye movements) to follow the bird's long flight path for the next minute or so. These retinal, ocular, and combined head and body movements primarily stimulate (1) the saccadic system to attempt to acquire foveation, (2) the pursuit system to match eye velocity to the velocity of the smoothly moving target, (3) the vestibular system to stabilize gaze during the initial (approximately 30-second) transient phase of head and body rotation, and (4) the optokinetic system to stabilize gaze during the later, sustained phase of head and body rotation. Then, quite suddenly, the bird starts flying directly toward you and gets to within a few feet of your head before (fortunately!) changing its course, thus initially stimulating the three active vergence subsystems—the disparity, accommodative, and proximal

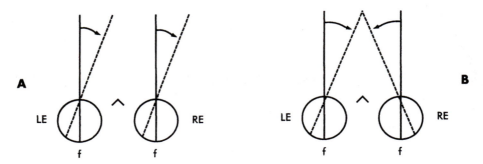

FIG. 1-1   Schematic drawing of version (**A**) and vergence (**B**) eye movements. *LE,* Left eye; *RE,* right eye; *f,* fovea.

TABLE 1-1   *Versional Eye Movements*

Subsystem*	Stimulus	Function
Fixational	Stationary target	To stabilize a target onto the fovea
Saccadic	Step of target displacement	To acquire an eccentric target onto the fovea
Pursuit	Target velocity	To match eye velocity with target velocity to stabilize the retinal image
Optokinetic	Target or field velocity	To maintain a stable image during sustained head movement
Vestibular	Head acceleration	To maintain a stable image with the target on the fovea during transient head movement

*All the subsystems listed here allow one to track a target moving in lateral extent.

TABLE 1-2   *Vergence Eye Movements*

Subsystem*	Stimulus
Disparity (or fusional)	Target disparity
Accommodative	Target blur
Proximal	Apparent nearness or perceived distance of target
Tonic	Baseline neural innervation (midbrain)

*All the subsystems listed here (except for tonic vergence) allow one to track a target moving in depth.

branches—because target disparity, blur, and proximity have dynamically changed during the bird's rapid approach.

Most individuals with normal vision take such oculomotor ability for granted. We read, scan a picture or a television screen, peer through a telescope, drive an automobile, and so forth, and, while performing these routine tasks, we rarely think about the precise neurologic control and the resultant complex eye movements that allow us to accomplish them with relative ease.

In a small percentage of the population, however, individuals either are born with frank oculomotor dysfunction or acquire it later in life. The former group includes those who have congenital nystagmus of unknown etiology; those in the latter group might have an active disease process (such as multiple sclerosis) or might have sustained head trauma.

This text describes the *basics* of the oculomotor control systems, especially those most important to optometrists, so that the reader can more fully understand relevant clinic testing and the actual, objective eye movement recordings that abound in modern ophthalmic and neurologic literature. The reader is also advised to consult informative textbooks and papers on eye movements[1-22] to gain additional insight.

Before each eye movement system and its clinical implications are discussed, it is important to become familiar with the following basic concepts, definitions, kinematic considerations, and laws governing ocular motility.[1,6,7,14,15]

- *Globe.* For simplicity, assume that a globe is a sphere rotating about a point fixed within itself (that is, the zero-velocity *center of rotation* of the eye located approximately at its midpoint) as well as within the orbit; the laws of kinematics of rigid bodies with three degrees of freedom can then be applied, namely, rotation about vertical, horizontal, and anteroposterior axes.
- *Objective vertical.* A frame of reference used to specify the position of the eye within the orbit; it is easiest and most accurate to compare the vertical meridian of the cornea to a hanging plumb line, which represents true gravity vertical.
- *Primary position.* The position of the eyes when the head is erect and the two eyes are fixating into the infinite distance along a horizontal plane; the position from which a pure horizontal or vertical movement is not associated with any tilt (that is, false torsion) of the vertical meridian of the eyes (that is, of the corneas) with respect to objective vertical.
- *Secondary position.* The position of the eyes when either a purely horizontal or a purely vertical movement is made from primary position; that is, the eye rotates about a vertical or a horizontal axis only, and there is no associated tilt of the vertical meridians of the eyes with respect to objective vertical.
- *Tertiary position.* The position of the eyes when they move from primary position to anywhere but a secondary position.
- *Torsion. True* cyclorotation of the eye about an anteroposterior axis such as the line-of-sight (that is, the line going from the fovea through the entrance pupil of the eye to the object of regard); little true torsion actually occurs as the eye is moved from the primary position to some tertiary position; minimal torsion is critical for stability of both monocular (direction) and binocular (cyclodisparity and related stereoscopic tilt) space perception and orientation and for appropriate, stable surgical correction of a strabismic cyclodeviation.
- *False torsion.* The *apparent* cyclorotation of the eye associated with a change in direction of regard from the primary position to some tertiary position; the angular difference between the objective vertical and the vertical corneal meridian when the eye is in a tertiary position; false torsion is present as a consequence of the reference system used for specification of the eye position and orientation in space.
- *Listing's plane.* A plane passing through the head and the center of rotation of the eyes that is perpendicular to the line of sight when the eyes are in primary position (Fig. 1-2, *A*).[15]
- *Listing's law.* The movement of the eyes from primary position to any other posi-

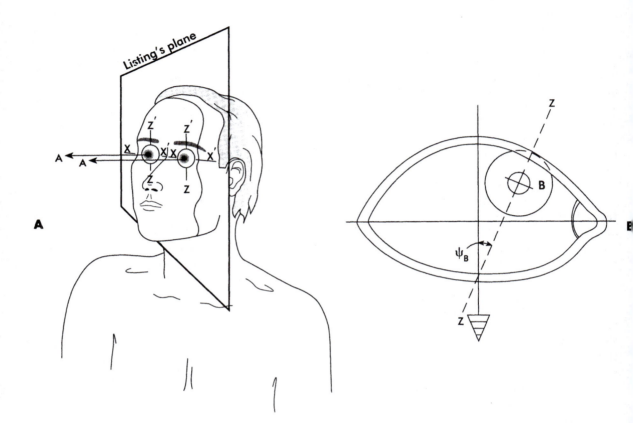

FIG. 1-2 **A,** The eyes in the primary position of gaze. The head is erect, and the eyes are fixating an infinitely distant point centered in the horizontal plane passing through each eye's center. Thus the eyes' axes are parallel. An imaginary cross is shown positioned at each cornea's center; the vertical *(Z to Z')* and horizontal *(X to X')* limbs located in Listing's plane are placed to line up with the cross and with a plumb bob and level. The eyes are then allowed to make a version to a secondary position of gaze (any point on the vertical or horizontal line through *A*) or to a tertiary position of gaze (one placed elsewhere). The resulting angle between the Z to Z' limb and a plumb bob line passing through the corneal center is the torsion *(Ψ)*. The component of torsion resulting from the eye rotating only about an axis in Listing's plane is termed *false torsion*, whereas that component resulting from the eye "twisting" or actually rotating about its own anteroposterior axis is termed *true torsion*. These types of torsion occur in various amounts, depending on how the eye actually moves to the tertiary position. **B,** The right eye has moved upward and inward to a tertiary position of gaze *B*. The eye has intorted, since the top of the initially vertical Z to Z' limb is now closer to the nose or medial aspect of the head. The angle Ψ_B between the Z to Z' limb and the plumb bob line has been called false torsion in the sense that a single Listing-plane rotation to *B* yields this Ψ_B without the eye having to rotate about its own anteroposterior axis (true torsion). The term *torsion* here refers to any situation in which Ψ_B does not equal 0.

(From Myers KJ: *Am J Optom Physiol Optics* 52:106, 1975.)

tion is equivalent to a single rotation about an axis in Listing's plane.* According to Listing's law, which has become the standard for discussion of oculomotor kinematics, each movement of the eye from a primary to a tertiary position is always associated with a definite (unique) tilt (false torsion) of the corneal vertical meridian with respect to objective vertical (Fig. 1-2, *B*). Thus the movement is effectively restricted to two rather than three degrees of freedom; otherwise, one might notice apparent movement (or rotation) of objects in space, since the amount of false torsion would vary randomly each time the eye shifts to the same tertiary position. As stated so elegantly by Nakayama, "Thus Listing's law is ultimately neurophysiological, and could be explicitly described as a set of synaptic weighting functions transforming a two-dimensional command signal to prescribed amounts of net excitation in the six separate (muscle) motoneuron pools."[17] Violations of Listing's law, however, may occur during symmetric and asymmetric convergence, sleep, head tilt with cycloversion, extreme positions of gaze, extreme voluntary effort, and postural changes.

- *Donder's law.* The angle of tilt (or false torsion) for a given tertiary position of the eye is always the same regardless of the path the eye has used to obtain that position. Listing's law states that for each tertiary position of the eye, one and only

---

*Two other axis systems have been proposed for specification of eye position and orientation outside of primary position. In the Fick axis system the eye rotates first about a vertical and then about a horizontal axis. In the Helmholtz axis system the eye rotates first about a horizontal, and then about a vertical axis. Of the three coordinate systems, only the Fick axis arrangement does not produce a "false" torsional component.[4] See Bennett and Rabbetts[4] and Carpenter[7] for details of the theoretic implications of the various systems proposed to describe the kinematics of eye rotation.

one specific tilt is associated with it, whereas Donder's law states that this unique tilt in a given tertiary position is the same regardless of its approach. Donder's law in effect severely restricts any true rotation about an anteroposterior axis.

- *Descartes-Sherrington law of reciprocal innervation.*[8] When an agonist (or "mover") contracts during movement of an eye, there is a simultaneous (and equal) relaxation of its antagonistic fellow muscle (Fig. 1-3, *A*). For example, to make a rapid movement of the right eye to the right, the right lateral rectus muscle would receive increased neural innervation (or excitation) and contract, whereas the right medial rectus muscle would simultaneously receive decreased neural innervation (or inhibition) and relax. This law of reciprocal innervation is important in understanding and interpreting the results of clinical *monocular* (duction) eye movement testing, which is conducted to check for weakness of one or more muscles in a single eye.[20]

- *Hering's law of equal innervation.* Corresponding (or yoke) muscles of each eye are equally innervated (Fig. 1-3, *B*). For example, to move both eyes to the right, the right lateral rectus and left medial rectus muscles receive equal increases in innervation (or excitation), whereas the right medial rectus and left lateral rectus muscles simultaneously receive equal decreases in innervation (or inhibition). Hering's law is specified with respect to static eye position changes for which it is quite robust, although dynamic violations of the law occur quite frequently in persons with normal vision.[2] The law is important in understanding and interpreting the results of clinical *binocular* (version) eye movement testing, especially in cases of oculomotor paralysis or paresis.[20]

Because of the biomechanics involved, the

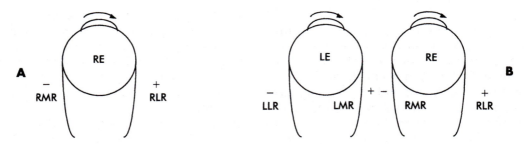

FIG. 1-3 **A,** Descartes-Sherrington law of reciprocal innervation. **B,** Hering's law of equal innervation. *RE,* Right eye; *LE,* left eye; *+,* increased innervation or excitation; *−* , decreased innervation or inhibition; *RLR,* right lateral rectus; *RMR,* right medial rectus; *LLR,* left lateral rectus; and *LMR,* left medial rectus.

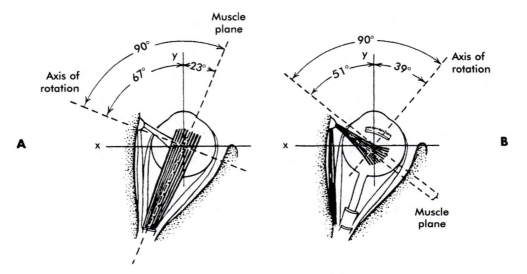

FIG. 1-4 **A,** Relationship of muscle plane of vertical rectus muscle to *x* and *y* axes. **B,** Relationship of muscle plane of oblique muscles to *x* and *y* axes.

(From Burian HM, von Noorden GK: *Binocular vision and ocular motility,* St Louis, 1974, Mosby.)

action of an extraocular muscle depends on gaze angle or position of the eye in the orbit (Figs. 1-4 and 1-5). For example, when the line of sight of the superior rectus muscle is coincident with its muscle plane (see Figs. 1-4 and 1-6) so that the eye is abducted (or rotated outward) by 23 degrees, the muscle functions as a pure elevator (about its perpen-

dicular axis of rotation); when the eye is adducted (or rotated inward) by 67 degrees (theoretically), the muscle functions primarily as an incyclorotator and has some adduction function. At intermediate positions the muscle performs differing amounts of these three functions, namely, elevation, incyclorotation, and adduction (Table 1-3). The notion of diag-

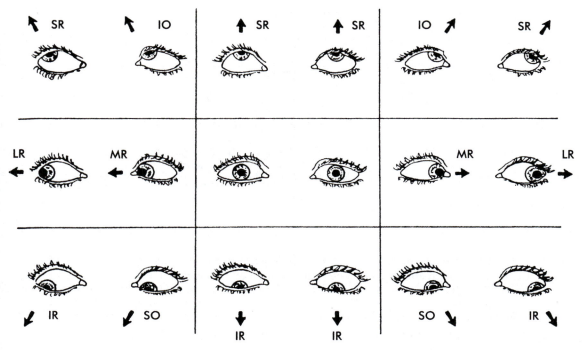

FIG. 1-5 The nine diagnostic positions of gaze. *SR*, superior rectus; *IO*, inferior oblique; *LR*, lateral rectus; *MR*, medial rectus; *IR*, inferior rectus; and *SO*, superior oblique.

(From von Noorden GK, Maumenee AE: *Atlas of strabismus*, St Louis, 1967, Mosby.)

TABLE 1-3 *Primary, Secondary, and Tertiary Actions of the Extraocular Muscles from the Primary Position*

Muscle	Primary Action	Secondary Action	Tertiary Action
Medial rectus	Adduction	—	—
Lateral rectus	Abduction	—	—
Inferior rectus	Depression	Excycloduction	Adduction
Superior rectus	Elevation	Incycloduction	Adduction
Inferior oblique	Excycloduction	Elevation	Abduction
Superior oblique	Incycloduction	Depression	Abduction

nostic positions of gaze was developed from these biomechanics of muscle action (see Fig. 1-5). Each "yoked" muscle pair (such as the right superior rectus muscle and the left inferior oblique muscle), obeying Hering's law of equal innervation, is tested in the direction of gaze for which the two muscles have a shared and significant responsibility. When testing in the diagnostic positions of gaze, one is primarily attempting to determine whether the strabismic deviation is concomitant (that is, of equal magnitude in all directions of gaze). If it

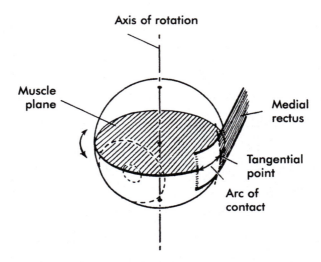

FIG. 1-6 Schematic presentation of the muscle plane (plane determined by the center of the muscle's origin and insertion and center of rotation of the eye), medial rectus, axis of rotation (perpendicular to muscle plane and line of sight), tangenital point (point at which center of muscle first touches globe), and arc of contact (surface arc between tangential point and center of muscle insertion).

(From Burian HM, von Noorden GK: *Binocular vision and ocular motility*, St Louis, 1974, Mosby.)

TABLE 1-4   *Cranial Innervation and Blood Supply to the Extraocular Muscles*

Muscle	Cranial Nerve	Blood Supply
Lateral rectus	Abducens (VI)	Lacrimal artery and lateral muscular branch of the ophthalmic artery
Medial rectus	Oculomotor (III)	Medial muscular branch of the ophthalmic artery
Superior rectus	Oculomotor (III)	Lateral muscular branch of the ophthalmic artery
Inferior rectus	Oculomotor (III)	Medial muscular branch of the ophthalmic artery
Superior oblique	Trochlear (IV)	Superior muscular branch of the ophthalmic artery
Inferior oblique	Oculomotor (III)	Infraorbital artery and medial muscular branch of the ophthalmic artery

is not, the degree of nonconcomitancy is then quantified by means of the prism cover test[20] (see Chapter 9).

Table 1-4 provides a review of the cranial innervation and blood supply to the extraocular muscles. It is assumed that the reader is familiar with the relevant details of ocular anatomy, neuroanatomy, and the related physiology.

REVIEW QUESTIONS

1. Describe the function of each of the five versional subsystems of eye movements. When the vergence system is added, what unique function does it provide?
2. List the primary, secondary, and tertiary actions of each extraocular muscle. If the right superior oblique muscle is injured, in what gaze angle would its limitation of movement be maximal

and result in the greatest symptoms? Minimal? Why?

3. What is the difference between true and false torsion? In what type of relatively common patient might a true 5-degree monocular static torsional error be found in the absence of frank ocular or neurologic disease?

4. Compare and contrast Listing's and Donder's laws. Do the same for Hering's law and the Descartes-Sherrington law.

5. A patient receives a blow to the right side of the head, injuring the right abducens nerve. What type of acquired strabismus might this person now manifest? What would be the major signs and symptoms?

REFERENCES

1. Alpern M: Types of movement. In Alpern M, editor: *The eye*, vol 3, New York, 1969, Academic.

2. Bahill AT, Ciuffreda KJ, Kenyon RV, Stark, L: Dynamic and static violations of Hering's law of equal innervation, *Am J Optom Physiol Optics* 53:786, 1976.

3. Baloh RW, Honrubia V: *Clinical neurophysiology of the vestibular system*, ed 2, Philadelphia, 1990, FA Davis.

4. Bennett AG, Rabbetts RB: *Clinical visual optics*, Boston, 1989, Butterworth-Heinemann.

5. Borish IM: *Clinical refraction*, Chicago, 1970, Professional.

6. Burian HM, von Noorden GK: *Binocular vision and ocular motility*, St Louis, 1974, Mosby.

7. Carpenter RHS: *Movements of the eyes*, ed 2, London, 1988, Pion.

8. Ciuffreda KJ, Levi DM, Selenow A: *Amblyopia: basic and clinical aspects*, Boston, 1991, Butterworth-Heinemann.

9. Ciuffreda KJ, Stark L: Descartes' law of reciprocal innervation, *Am J Optom Physiol Optics* 52:663, 1975.

10. Coakley D: *Minute eye movements and brain stem function*, Boca Raton, Fla, 1983, CRC.

11. Cogan DG: *Neurology of the ocular muscles*, Springfield, Ill, 1956, Charles C Thomas.

12. Ditchburn RW: *Eye movements and visual perception*, Oxford, 1973, Claredon.

13. Gay AJ, Newman NM, Keltner JL, Stroud MH: *Eye movement disorders*, St Louis, 1974, Mosby.

14. Hering E: *The theory of binocular vision*, Bridgeman B, Stark L, editors and translators: New York, 1977, Plenum.

15. Myers KJ: Some considerations of ocular rotations, *Am J Optom Physiol Optics* 52:106, 1975.

16. Leigh RJ, Zee DS: *The neurology of eye movement*, ed 2, Philadelphia, 1991, FA Davis.

17. Schor CM, Ciuffreda KJ, editors: *Vergence eye movements: basic and clinical aspects*, Boston, 1983, Butterworth-Heinemann.

18. Stark L: *Neurological control systems*, New York, 1968, Plenum.

19. Taylor EA: *The fundamental reading skill*, Springfield, Ill, 1966, Charles C Thomas.

20. von Noorden GK, Maumenee AE: *Atlas of strabismus*, St Louis, 1967, Mosby.

21. Yarbus AL: *Eye movements and vision*, New York, 1967, Plenum.

22. Zuber BL, editor: *Models of oculomotor behavior and control*, Boca Raton, Fla, 1981, CRC.

2

Fixational Eye Movements

Aberrant tremor	Neurologic disease
Aging	Nystagmus
Drift	Saccadic intrusions
Foveation	Slow drift
Main sequence	Step controller
Microsaccade	Tremor

FIXATION

During attempted steady fixation on a stationary object of regard, the eye does not remain perfectly motionless.* Both slow and rapid small-amplitude ("miniature") eye movements occur. However, the image of the object is still retained within an acceptable foveal retinal locus (that is, a "functional" fovea of approximately ±30-min arc[92]).

---

*Assuming a fixed head (via bite bar) and body with stable surroundings. In the clinic setting, fixation is tested with a reasonably restrained head (headrest and chinrest) and body (ophthalmic chair). However, it is important to realize that with an unrestrained head in persons attempting to remain as still as possible, head movements of up to 0.75 degrees may occur, and these head movements decrease gaze stability twofold[89]; furthermore, with active head rotation, gaze stability decreases even more, with concomitant increase in overall retinal-image motion.[94] In individuals with normal vision this increased retinal motion is generally below the threshold for adversely affecting visual acuity. Also see Kowler[61] for a recent review of stability of gaze.

Our overall fixational ability can perhaps be best understood and appreciated by study of the results of two-dimensional (that is, the horizontal and vertical components; the third-dimensional torsional component is extremely small, ~0.6-sec arc[44]) planar surface–projected recordings of fixation (or direction of gaze) as a function of time (Fig. 2-1). Two-dimensional eye position is shown for three different fixation durations in Fig. 2-1, A.[107] Fixational area increased with increased fixation duration. For example, during the 10-second period the range of fixation was ±7.5-min arc, whereas during the 60-second period it approached ±30-min arc. Also, as fixation time increased, what emerged from the two-dimensional spatial plot was not a circular pattern suggesting equidirectional probability of fixation away from the target but rather a pattern exhibiting a distinct directional bias. This notion is perhaps best exemplified by study of a two-dimensional plot of fixational probability within an area circum-

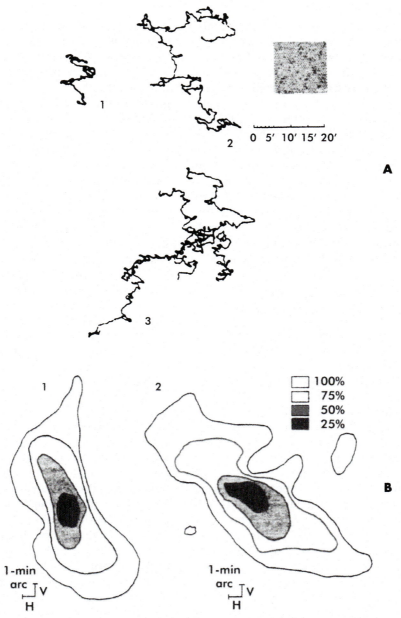

FIG. 2-1 **A,** Records of an individual's horizontal and vertical eye movements during fixation on a stationary point: *1,* fixation for 10 seconds; *2,* fixation for 30 seconds; *3,* fixation for 1 minute. The scale of angular measurement in minutes of angle is given in record *2,* and the distribution of foveal cones is indicated schematically in the square insert on this scale. **B,** Contour maps of the area traversed by the visual axis for two persons during 10 seconds of fixation. *H,* Horizontal, *V,* vertical. Scale of percentages is shown by shading.

(**A,** from Yarbus AL: *Eye movements and vision,* New York, 1967, Plenum. **B,** from Bennet-Clark HC: *Optica Acta* 11:301, 1964.)

scribing the object of interest[13] (Fig. 2-1, *B*). The outermost edge demarcates the boundary of fixation (disregarding the "islands" of infrequent fixation). Clearly, as one might expect, fixation is central and in close proximity (±5-min arc) to the target most of the time. Again the spatial pattern exhibited a directional preference, having an irregular, oblong shape approximating an ellipse. Similar results were reported by others,[69,70,93] who suggested that these two-dimensional plots could be roughly approximated by bivariate normal probability distributions representing the area of fixation 68% of the time; standard deviations in each of the two primary meridians ranged from 2- to 6-min arc (see Table 4.1 in Ditchburn[44]).

QUANTITATIVE COMPONENT CONTRIBUTION TO FIXATION

Three types of eye movements take place during attempted fixation, and each has distinct dynamic characteristics. A composite description of these movements based on several sources* is provided here.

The first component is *tremor* (Fig. 2-2, *A*). Tremor is a high-frequency movement typically ranging from 30 to 100 Hz (oscillations or cycles per second), although lower and higher frequencies may be found. The reported frequency spectrum depends in part on the monitoring system and data analysis used. The average amplitude either horizontally or vertically is approximately 20-sec arc (approximately the size of one cone diameter) and ranges from 5- to 30-sec arc. There is an inverse relationship between tremor frequency and amplitude. Tremor velocity may be as high as 30-min arc per second. Tremor is not correlated between the two eyes. Thus it has been thought to represent "noise" in the oculomotor system that originated from irregular firing of brainstem motor neurons, that is, incomplete smooth tetanus, and resulted in in-

dependent random fluctuations in extraocular muscle fiber discharges. These small tremor movements probably have no adverse impact on vision and contribute little to the production of retinal error. The tremor is superimposed on the two movements described next.

The second component is *drift* (Fig. 2-2, *B*). Drift is a low-velocity movement, typically 1- to 8-min arc per second with a mean of 5-min arc per second (crossing 15 cones per second) and a maximum of 30-min arc per second.† The movement is irregular and of a variable low frequency (<0.5 Hz). Its amplitude is typically 1- to 5-min arc. Drift amplitude increases slightly when retinal errors are generated only from the near and far retinal periphery.[79] Drift makes up more than 95% of one's total fixation time. Like tremor, it is not correlated between the two eyes. Drift is also traditionally believed to represent "noise" in the oculomotor system and therefore to be error producing; however, there is evidence that it may be error correcting at times[69] (see Kowler[61] for a recent review).

The third component of fixation is the *microsaccade* (see Fig. 2-2, *B*). Microsaccades have a frequency of occurrence of 1 to 2 per second. They have a mean amplitude of 5-mm arc, are rarely larger than 10-min arc, and may range from 1- to 25-min arc. Microsaccades have a duration ranging from 10 to 25 msec and an amplitude-dependent peak velocity (that is, a "main sequence" relation [see Chapter 3]) ranging from 1 to 20 degrees per second[110] (Fig. 2-3). They typically have a large dynamic overshoot component. Unlike tremor and drift, microsaccades are always binocular and have a high amplitude correlation (0.6 to 0.9) between the eyes,[63] which suggests that they are under central neurologic control. They are traditionally believed to be

---

*References 7, 44, 56, 76, 83, 93, and 107.

†It should be emphasized that during natural activities such as ambulation, retinal-image velocity from head pertubations may be as high as 3 degrees per second.[94] This maximum motion is just at the threshold for degradation of visual acuity[101] and stereoacuity.[102]

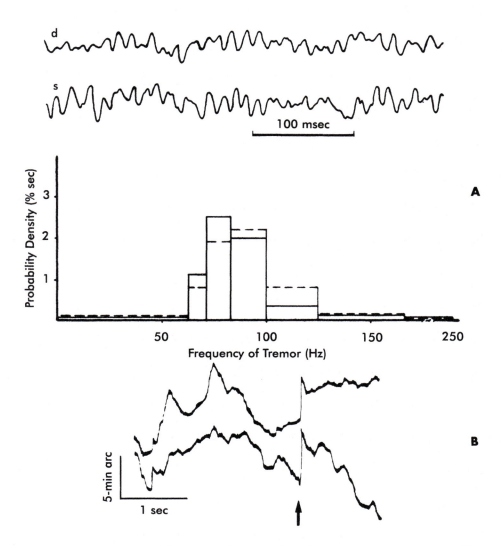

FIG. 2-2 **A,** Microtremor of the eyes under normal conditions. *Top:* Tremorograms of the right *(d)* and left *(s)* eyes. *Bottom:* Distribution of frequencies of microtremor of the right eye *(solid line)* and left eye *(dashed line)* as a function of the frequency of tremor. To calculate the probability density, the percentage occurrence of a particular frequency in a given frequency interval was divided by the length of that interval (in oscillations per second) **B,** Simultaneous records of the miniature movements of the two eyes. The small-amplitude, high-frequency component is the *tremor;* the large, relatively slow excursions are *drift;* and at the *arrow* both eyes execute a *microsaccade.* It is evident that drift movements are essentially dissociated in the two eyes, whereas the microsaccade is virtually conjugate.

(A, from Shakhnovich AR: *The brain and regulation of eye movement,* New York, 1977, Plenum. **B,** adapted from Yarbus AL: *Eye movements and vision,* New York, 1967, Plenum.)

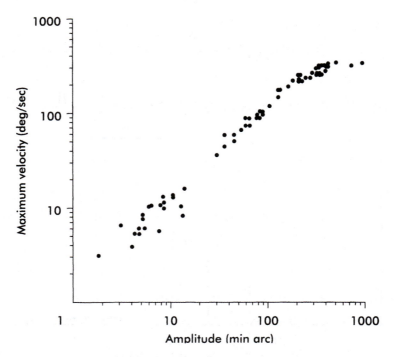

FIG. 2-3 Maximum velocities of saccades and microsaccades as functions of their amplitudes, showing essential continuity in the properties of the two kinds of movement.

(From Zuber BL, Stark L, Cook G: *Science* 150:1459, 1965.)

TABLE 2-1 *Maximal Limits of Field of Fixation with Age*

Age (Yr [No. of persons])	Right Eye (Degree)				Left Eye (Degree)			
	Adduction	Abduction	Depression	Elevation	Adduction	Abduction	Depression	Elevation
10-19 (24)	58	54	51	44	60	53	51	43
20-29 (33)	57	54	51	42	59	52	50	41
30-39 (13)	57	52	49	42	59	52	49	41
40-49 (17)	57	53	49	41	58	52	49	41
50 and older (13)	54	52	46	39	55	43	43	39

From Yamashiro M: *Jap J Ophthal* 1:130, 1957.

error correcting, although prominent exceptions may occur both in persons with normal vision and in patients with abnormal vision (see the section on abnormal fixation). One's own microsaccadic and drift movements can be easily visualized by viewing Fig. 2-4.[99]

The fixational eye movement system appears to be relatively robust in response to changes in external stimuli.[44] For example, reasonably large changes in target size, luminance, color, and distance have relatively little obvious, consistent practical impact. Although no major difference between monocular and binocular viewing conditions has been found, changes in direction of gaze away from primary position may have an adverse effect on various aspects of fixation. Fixation in darkness, as one might expect, has the most deleterious effects on accuracy of fixation (see the next section).

The fixational eye movement system exhibits no significant age-related changes in overall stability. Thus major and minor axes dimensions of the bivariate contour ellipse are age independent.[59,60] This is consistent with the relative resistance to such aging effects[59] of the relevant neurologic oculomotor features and the physiologic characteristics of the extraocular muscle. The range of fixation, however, especially for upward gaze, does seem to decrease somewhat with advancing age (Table 2-1).[16,106] The reasons for this remain unclear.

CONTROL PROPERTIES AND INTERACTION OF MICROSACCADES AND DRIFT

It is critical to determine a system's capabilities and limitations, that is, its basic control properties. Only then can its function be derived and understood. Based on characteristics of the fixational eye movement system described earlier, the findings suggest the presence of a rapid, accurate control system with the retina as its main source of information related to eye position.

The microsaccadic system is capable of executing small saccades, or rapid eye movements. Cornsweet's classic work[27] in this area has provided much crucial information. Fig. 2-5, *A*, shows that the probability of occurrence of a microsaccade increased rapidly as the eye was displaced with respect to its mean or "functional" directionally zero position; that is, the probability of occurrence of a microsaccade increased as retinal position error increased. For example, with a 3-min arc displacement the probability of a microsaccade

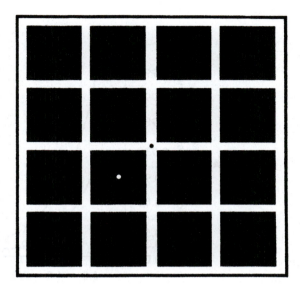

FIG. 2-4 Pattern for demonstrating the micro-ocular movements during fixation. Procedure is as follows. First look for 10 seconds at the central black point; then transfer gaze and look at the white point in the adjacent dark square. The dark afterimage of the white line pattern should be seen in constant motion. The slow movements reflect ocular drift, whereas the rapid, jerky movements reflect microsaccades.

(From Verheijen FJ: *Optica Acta* 8:309, 1961.)

was only 50%, whereas with a 6-min arc displacement its probability increased to 100%. With stabilized vision (that is, the target moves faithfully with the eye) microsaccadic frequency markedly decreased. Cornsweet also found that microsaccadic magnitude was related to displacement of the eye from its mean position (Fig. 2-5, *B*); that is, the microsaccadic amplitude approximately equaled the mean displacement of the eye. He also found microsaccadic direction to be opposite to the direction of eye displacement. All of the previously mentioned findings clearly suggested a position corrective role for these microsaccadic movements in real life.*

---

*Only with specific instruction[95,96] or during certain fine tasks[15,104] can these microsaccades be suppressed in individuals with normal vision and in patients with abnormal vision.[21,24]

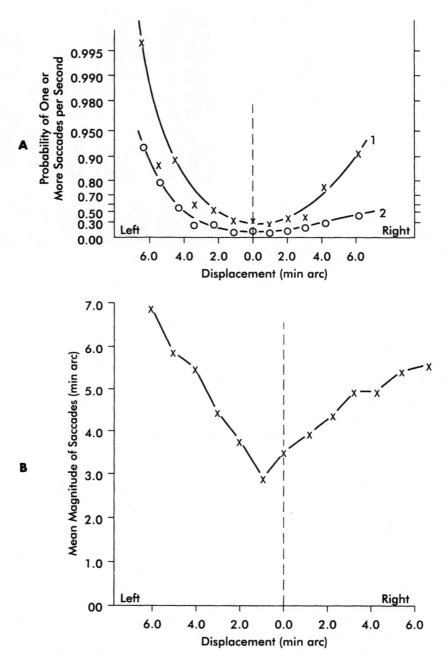

FIG. 2-5 **A,** Saccade probability as a function of displacement from mean position. *1,* Normal vision; *2,* vision with stabilized target. **B,** Variation of saccade direction with displacement from mean position.

(From Cornsweet TN: *J Opt Soc Am* 46:987, 1956.)

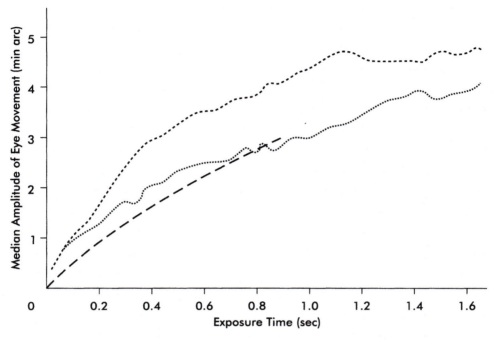

FIG. 2-6 Median displacement of the visual axis from its initial position as a function of time. Subject EN (*short dashes*); subject PN (*long dashes*); measurement of Riggs et al.(*dots*). (From Ditchburn RW: *Eye movements and visual perception,* Oxford, 1973, Clarendon.)

In the light, ocular drift appeared to increase (in a decreasing exponential manner) over a 1.6-sec period, producing a final retinal position error of 4.5-min arc[44] (Fig. 2-6). In the dark, however, drift velocity increased, and the midline ocular deviation increased to 60-min arc in 5 seconds.[45] With yet longer times in the dark (2 minutes) the midline deviation increased only to 120-min arc[90]; furthermore, it was noted that the drifts were "error producing" and the saccades were "error correcting." A more recent study[54] showed that drift velocity in darkness was gaze dependent and increased in a roughly linear fashion with gaze angle (0.014 deg/sec per degree of lateral gaze). The time constant (that is, the time required to reach 63% of the final intended amplitude, now assuming an exponential time course) of dark drift ranged from 20 to 100 or more seconds, with a mean

of 70 seconds.[54] This finding was consistent with the notion of a slow, "leaky" neural integrator in which the gaze-holding step of innervation decays slowly with time because of its imperfect "memory" and the absence of crucial visual feedback-based eye position and velocity information (see later discussion in this section). Correction of eye position in the dark appeared to be related more to drift velocity than to eye position error. If drift velocity exceeded 0.6 degrees per second, a "corrective" saccade was made, whereas the eye position error could accumulate to as much as 15 degrees if the ocular drift were slower.[54]

The preceding experiments call attention to two important points. First, the presence of visual feedback greatly enhanced the accuracy of fixation. Second, in the absence of visual feedback the ocular deviation was typically only a few degrees in magnitude, with sac-

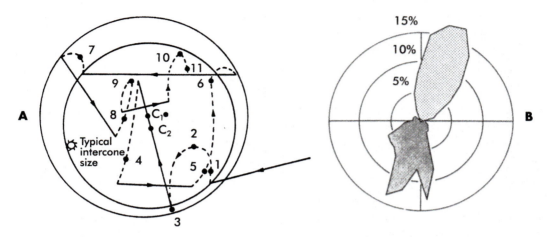

FIG. 2-7   **A,** Observed sequential map of eye movements, *1* to *11*. Diameter of larger circle equals 10-min arc. *Solid line segments,* microsaccades; *dashed line segments,* drift; C_1, center of large circle, C_2, center of small circle. **B,** Relative frequency of drift and microsaccades in different directions. The percentages of drift and microsaccades made in specific 10-degree sectors by a single person are shown. *Dotted area* microsaccades; *shaded area* drifts.

(**A,** from Fender, *Control of fixation,* 1956; **B,** from Nachmias J: *J Opt Soc Am* 49:901, 1959.)

cades attempting to recenter the eye toward its "remembered" target position. These data suggest the use of extraocular muscle proprioceptive information and tactile information from the cornea, lids, and surrounding tissue as "extra retinal" signals in eye position control. These additional sources of information about eye position and velocity, although somewhat crude, become especially important when visual feedback is absent.[57]

Once many of the preceding basic characteristics and control properties were established, a functional model of ocular fixation was developed (see especially Cornsweet[27] and Fender.[49]). In general this simple model included microsaccades functioning in an error-correcting manner and drifts functioning in an error-producing manner. This model is perhaps best represented in Fig. 2-7, *A*, which presents a sequence of microsaccades and drifts. Although the microsaccades did not always perfectly correct the drift-induced position errors, they clearly reduced it and in most cases recentered the fovea. Such an interaction of microsaccades and drifts is also suggested by the results of Nachmias[69] (Fig. 2-7, *B*), Ben-

net-Clark,[13] and Shakhnovich,[83] in which the directions of microsaccades and drifts were opposing.* Furthermore, this model is supported by the small-amplitude step-tracking results of Wyman and Steinman.[105] Nachmias,[69,70] however, also found evidence that drift at times appeared to act in an error-correcting manner, especially in meridians where microsaccades appeared to be relatively ineffective.

---

*This model of fixation has been challenged by some.[61,62,88,96] Indeed, it does represent a simple system because it does not take into account such factors as error-correcting drift and its conceptual outgrowth of saccade-free "slow-control" position maintenance,[61,96] presence of normal bidirectional fixational saccade "couplets" (see the discussion of saccadic intrusions in the section on abnormal fixation), and variations in attention, instruction set, and motivation. Nonetheless, this model still appears to represent a reasonable framework on which to build. Thus in reality, under normal fixation test conditions, saccades may correct position errors created either by drift or by other saccades; when saccades are suppressed, delayed, or otherwise ineffective, drift (or "slow control") may eventually (within a few seconds) correct position errors created by the immediately prior drift movements.

NEUROPHYSIOLOGY OF FIXATION

The neurophysiology of fixation in persons with normal vision is at first glance quite simple. There are midbrain oculomotor neurons whose firing rate (within their active range) is linearly related and therefore proportional to gaze angle (Fig. 2-8).[78] To shift the eyes to different gaze angles, however, a saccade is used. As discussed in detail in Chapter 3, a saccade's neural signal consists of a pulse of increased innervation to move the eye rapidly by some specific magnitude and a step of innervation (integrated pulse) to hold the eye in this new position (Fig. 2-9). Therefore one can think of the steady-state gaze-related neural signal simply as a step. If this step of innervation is properly maintained without any decay (assuming a perfect "nonleaky" integrator), it prevents the eye from shifting back to the midline due to the elastic restoring forces of the extraocular muscles and surrounding orbital contents; thus accurate fixation is sustained. Small fluctuations in this signal, however, give rise to tremor and drift. The neurologic substrate involved in neural integration and related gaze-holding functions consists of the nucleus prepositus hypoglossi and medial vestibular nucleus for horizontal conjugate movements and, probably, the interstitial nucleus of Cajal for vertical conjugate movements.[66] To change fixation to a new point, complex higher level neurologic mechanisms of visual "disengagement" have been proposed and are not yet well understood.[71]

ABNORMAL FIXATION

When perusing the clinical oculomotor literature, it is easy to become overwhelmed by the apparent variety of fixational eye movement abnormalities that have been reported[66] and the numerous detailed classifications that have been developed, presumably with the intent of helping clinicians in their diagnostic capabilities.[3,34,108] The simplified approach presented here demonstrates that in most of the patients one is likely to examine, only three broad categories of abnormal patterns of fixation are possible—*slow drift, saccadic intrusions,* and *nystagmus.*

The most common patterns of abnormal fixation detectable on clinical examination are presented in Fig. 2-10. Each pattern (plus tremor) is discussed in this chapter, and a composite description with emphasis on its actual and potential utility to the clinician is provided.

Aberrant tremor (not detectable on clinical examination) reflects the functional state of the brainstem and the degree of disturbance of consciousness.[26,83] Abnormalities of this micromovement include different overall patterns between the two eyes, absence of high-frequency bursts, presence of irregular and low-frequency bursts of large amplitude, extended periods of very low-frequency movement, and an overall reduction in the dominant frequency response (correlated with the depth of consciousness and the approach of death).[83] For example, Fig. 2-11 shows a patient with aberrant tremor who has varying reduced levels of consciousness after surgery for an aneurysm. Evident are the shift toward low-frequency tremor, interocular differences in the overall pattern of movement, and lack of high-frequency bursts (compare with Fig. 2-2, *A*). The complex techniques involved in this measurement have not made their way from the clinical research laboratory in a few neurologic units to the more general hospital setting, presumably because of the highly specialized equipment and sophisticated analysis procedures involved, as well as the continued reliance on and apparent satisfaction with more traditional approaches. However, this more complex approach still appears to have considerable potential for clinical use in certain settings.

The first clinical abnormality is *slow drift,* which is typically found in persons with functional amblyopia[12,21,22,25,55] (see Fig. 2-10). Slow drifts typically have an amplitude of up to 1 degree (centered about the nonfoveal eccentric retinal fixation locus of approximately 1 degree when viewed with a visuoscope), a velocity of less than 3 degrees per second, and

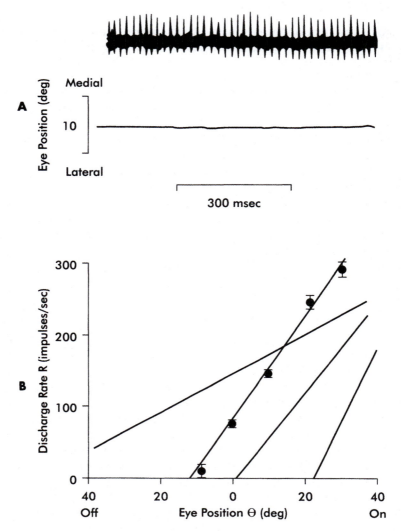

FIG. 2-8 Oculomotor discharge in relation to eye movement. **A,** The steady rate of firing when the eye is stationary. **B,** The relationship between the firing rate in **A** and eye position for a few typical units; their different slopes and intercepts are shown. The recordings were made in alert rhesus monkeys.

(From Robinson DA, Keller EL: *Bibl Ophthal* 82:7, 1972.)

an irregular, slow frequency (<0.5 Hz).[22] The drifts are generally not rapid enough to degrade visual acuity[22]; however, the amplitude fluctuations could result in more variable visual acuity, since the stationary target continuously impinges upon different eccentric retinal loci.[22] With appropriate monocular low-light visuoscopy[25] one sees a slow, wavering multidirectional movement of the eye about the eccentric retinal locus, perhaps interrupted by a few saccades. The drift becomes markedly decreased during the course of suc-

INPUT
(Eye Velocity Signal)

OUTPUT
(Eye Position Signal)

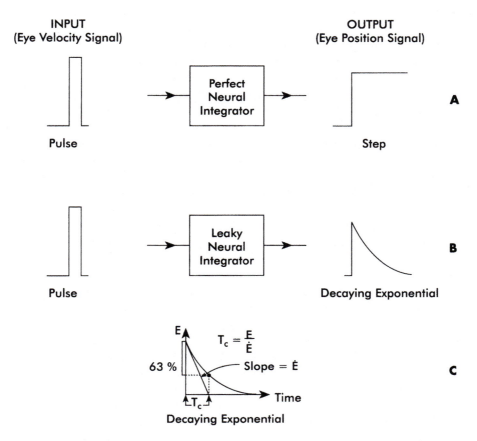

Pulse

Perfect
Neural
Integrator

Step

A

Pulse

Leaky
Neural
Integrator

Decaying Exponential

B

$T_c = \dfrac{E}{\dot{E}}$

63 %

Slope $= \dot{E}$

T_c

Time

C

Decaying Exponential

FIG. 2-9   The neural integrator. **A,** For saccades the input to the neural integrator is a pulse, which may be thought of as an eye velocity signal. When neural integration is perfect, the output is a step, which may be thought of as an eye position signal. **B,** When integration of the eye velocity signal is imperfect (that is, the neural integrator is *leaky*), the eye position signal is a decaying exponential. Thus the eye drifts back toward the midline until a corrective saccadic quick phase puts the eye back on target. This imperfection causes gaze-evoked nystagmus. **C,** The centripetal drift of the eyes that occurs with a leaky integrator can be described by its time constant (T_C), which represents the time at which the eye has drifted 63% of the way back to the midline. Thus the *leakier* the integrator, the shorter the T_C. A convenient way of calculating the T_C is to determine the ratio of the initial displacement of the eye from midline *(E)* to the initial velocity of eye drift $(\dot{E})$.

(From Leigh RJ, Zee DS: *The neurology of eye movements,* ed 2, Philadelphia, 1991, FA Davis.)

cessful orthoptic therapy.[20] More recently drift that has similar dynamic characteristics has been reported in patients with macular scotomas.[103] However, these are typically more directional and exhibit an increase in velocity with increase in eccentric retinal locus.

Saccadic intrusions, the second abnormality, are abnormally large fixational saccades that "intrude" on or interrupt one's attempt at accurate foveal fixation. On study by means of the ophthalmoscope or visuoscope these appear as darting, to-and-fro movements. They can be found in three basic varieties (see Fig.

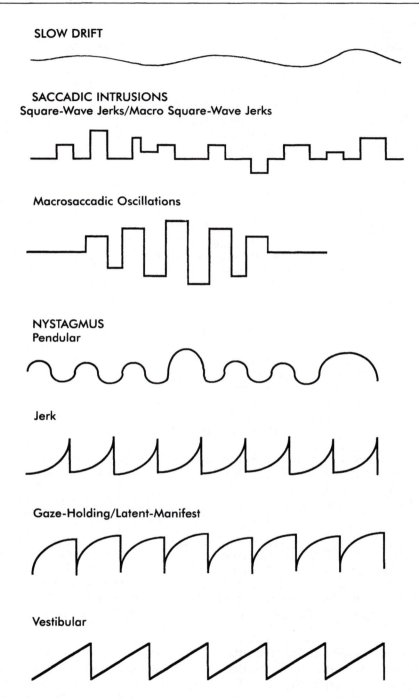

SLOW DRIFT

SACCADIC INTRUSIONS
Square-Wave Jerks/Macro Square-Wave Jerks

Macrosaccadic Oscillations

NYSTAGMUS
Pendular

Jerk

Gaze-Holding/Latent-Manifest

Vestibular

FIG. 2-10 Patterns of abnormal fixation identifiable on clinical examination. Schematic representation is not drawn to scale.

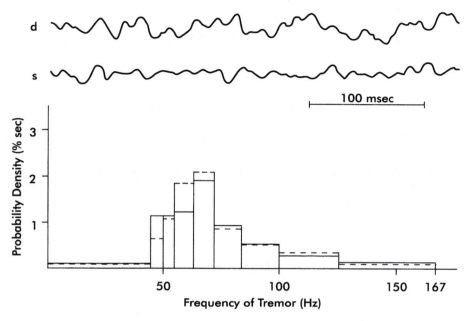

FIG. 2-11 Ocular tremor in a patient on the thirteenth day after operation for clipping aneurysms of the anterior communicating artery.

(From Shakhnovich AR: *The brain and regulation of eye movement*, New York, 1977, Plenum.)

TABLE 2-2 *Characteristics of Saccadic Instabilities*

Characteristic	Square-Wave Jerks	Macro Square-Wave Jerks	Macrosaccadic Oscillations
Amplitude	0.5-3.0 deg*; constant	4-30 deg; variable	1-30 deg; increasing, then decreasing
Time course	Sporadic	Bursts	Bursts
Latency†	200 msec	50-150 msec	200 msec
Foveation	Yes	Yes	No
Presence in darkness	Yes	Yes	No

*Occasionally up to 10 degrees. †Intersaccadic interval.
From Daroff RB, Troost BT, Dell'Osso LF. In Glaser JS, editor: *Clinical ophthalmology*, Hagerstown, Md, 1978, Harper & Row.

2-10 and Table 2-2), and each has distinct dynamic characteristics, although other, less common forms exist (see Fig. 3-10 and Table 10-1 in Leigh and Zee[66]).

The first type of intrusive saccade is the *square-wave jerk** (see Fig. 2-10). In effect, the square-wave jerks "jerk" the eye (that is, the fovea) away from the object of regard via a saccade and approximately 200 msec later return the eye back to the original position by a second oppositely directed saccade. They range in amplitude from 0.5 to 5 degrees. The frequency and characteristics of square-wave jerks are not affected by age.[85] Their presence,

*References 28-30, 47, 48, 52, 56, 66, 71, 81, 84-87, 109.

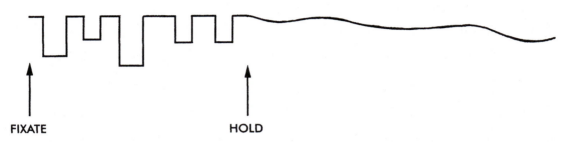

FIXATE   HOLD

FIG. 2-12 Schematic representation of suppression of square-wave jerks in a patient with strabismus using the fixate-vs.-hold instruction set paradigm.

however, is not particularly diagnostic. They can be seen in 25% to 60% of individuals with normal vision.[84,87] They can also be found in either eye of patients with functional strabismus, having variable frequency (<0.5 Hz) with an amplitude of 1 degree.[23] However, when the frequency and amplitude of square-wave jerks increase and are consistently present, along with an appropriate history of abnormality, they may indeed be diagnostic, especially for cerebellar disease*; furthermore, square-wave jerks and related saccadic oscillations may precede the postnatal appearance of developing congenital nystagmus.[53] It has been speculated that these square-wave jerks represent abnormally large microsaccades,[48] perhaps reflecting either a disorder of saccadic pause cells[29,109] or dysfunctional cerebellar-related saccadic gain control[68] (see Chapter 3 for more information).

The square-wave jerks found in patients without disease (for example, in patients with functional strabismus) can be transiently suppressed.[24] For instance, one can instruct such a patient to "hold the eye steady" rather than to "fixate carefully" (that is, the fixate versus hold command),[95,96] which frequently results

in total suppression (or at least reduction) in the occurrence of these saccades (Fig. 2-12) similar to that found in the suppression of microsaccades in patients with normal vision.[95,96] This command strategy can be used in patients to suppress abnormal fixational eye movement and therefore reduce retinal-image motion and allow for more careful ophthalmoscopic scrutiny of the fundus.[17] Similarly these patients with strabismus respond favorably to the use of auditory biofeedback in controlling eye movement to reduce the saccadic component of their abnormal fixation[80] (Fig. 2-13).

The second type of intrusive saccade is the *macro square-wave jerk*† (Fig. 2-10). The macro square-wave jerk is a variation of square wave-jerks that differs in the following important ways: (1) macro square-wave jerks are larger (by 5 to 15 degrees or more), (2) they occur more frequently (2 to 3 Hz), and (3) they remove the eye from the target for a shorter period of time (~100 msec). They are primarily found in cerebellar disease and are quite common in multiple sclerosis.[41,98]

The third type of intrusive saccade is the *macrosaccadic oscillation*[30,33,66,82,86] (see Fig. 2-10). Macrosaccadic oscillations have two

---

*References 29, 30, 47, 48, 56, 66, and 86.

†References 30, 33, 41, 66, 86, and 98.

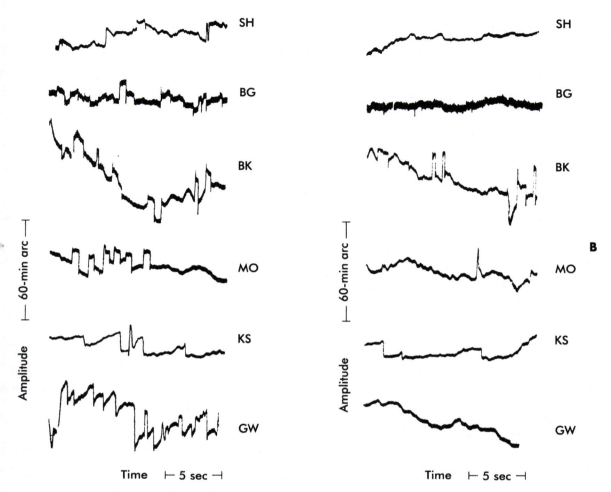

FIG. 2-13 **A,** Eye position during attempted steady fixation of a stationary target. Patient records are ranked according to the depth of amblyopia. Patient SH had 20/15 acuity; patients BG and BK had central fixation; and patients MO, KS, and GW had eccentric fixation. **B,** Attempted steady fixation in the presence of auditory feedback for saccades.

(From Schor CM, Hallmark W: *Invest Ophthal Vis Sci* 17:577, 1978.)

important differences from macro square-wave jerks. First, they produce a sequence of saccades of increasing, then decreasing, amplitude to *either* side of the fixation point, thereby representing a classic, unstable, high-gain-system "oscillation."[92] Second, they have intersaccadic pauses or intervals of 200 msec. As is true for macro square-wave jerks, macrosaccadic oscillations are most com-

monly found in patients with cerebellar disease.[30,66,82]

Nystagmus, the third and last clinical abnormality, refers to rhythmic oscillation of the eye, generally involuntary[4,30,31,42,66] (see Fig. 2-10). Nystagmus may be associated with an ocular anomaly[4] (Fig. 2-14). About 50% of patients with strabismus have nystagmus,[64] at times quite subtle, and 15% of patients with

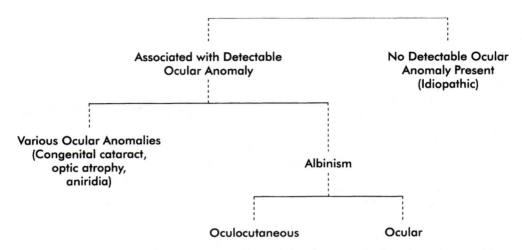

FIG. 2-14 Simple classification scheme for congenital nystagmus based on the possible association with various ocular anomalies.

(From Abadi and others. In Schmid R, Zambarbieri D, editors: *Oculomotor control and cognitive processes,* Amsterdam, Holland, 1991, Elsevier.)

congenital nystagmus have strabismus.[8] Nystagmus can be either congenital or acquired. When of the acquired variety, it is typically accompanied by oscillopsia, or illusory movement of the world. It can be found in two basic varieties: (1) in *pendular* nystagmus the velocity of movement is similar in both directions and (2) in *jerk* nystagmus a slow-phase movement of the eyes in one direction and a rapid saccadic movement of the eyes in the opposite direction are present. In both cases, foveation (that is, keeping the eye within ±0.5 degrees of the target at a velocity of less than 5 degrees per second)[72] is attempted (Fig. 2-15). In pendular nystagmus, foveation occurs at one "peak" of the waveform during which eye velocity is slowest, and in jerk nystagmus, foveation occurs immediately after the rapid corrective saccade for a period of 50 to 100 msec or more.[4,11,34,42,72] Visual information processing can take place during the entire nystagmus slow phase,[5,10,58,72] although processing of fine-pattern details appears to be primarily restricted to the low-velocity foveation periods.[72] With both types of nys-

tagmus there is usually a "null" position, that is, a direction of gaze for which the nystagmus "intensity" is least (with the head straight)[31,36] (Fig. 2-16), and visual acuity is optimal.[17] As an adaptive strategy many persons with nystagmus adopt a head turn in the direction *opposite* to their null position to maintain this optimal eye-head angle when looking at people or objects directly in front of them.[31] For example, if the null position is to the right (when facing the patient), the patient's head turn will be to the left, thereby effectively maintaining a relative optimal right-gaze eye-head angle. The nystagmus may change from pendular to jerk in different directions of gaze[74] (see Chapter 9 for additional details and information).

The first category of nystagmus, the *pendular* variety* (see Fig. 2-10), has an amplitude ranging from approximately 0.5 to 10 degrees (2 to 8 degrees is typical), a frequency from about 2 to 8 Hz (3 to 4 Hz is typical), and a

---

*References 4, 30, 31, 66, 74, and 108.

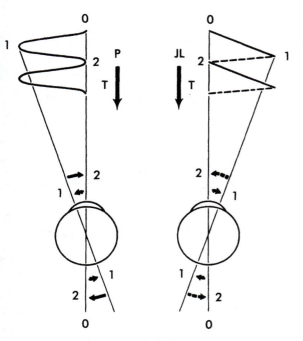

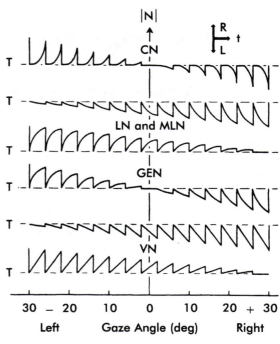

FIG. 2-15 Foveation "strategy" employed during pendular *(P)* and jerk left *(JL)* nystagmus. The target is only briefly foveated at points *0* and *2. T,* Time.

(From Daroff RB, Troost BT, Dell'Osso LF. In Glaser JS, editor: *Clinical ophthalmology*, Hagerstown, Md, 1978, Harper & Row.)

FIG. 2-16 Variation in gaze angle of magnitude (N) with congenital *(CN)*, latent *(LN)*, manifest latent *(MLN)*, gaze-evoked *(GEN)*, and vestibular *(VN)* nystagmus. *R*, right; *L*, left; *t*, time. Slow-phase differences are evident, and fast phases are foveating.

(From Dell'Osso LF, Schmidt D, Daroff RB: *Arch Ophthal* 97:1877, 1979.)

peak velocity of up to 100 degrees per second (which may account for some of the visual acuity loss, especially in individuals without the presence of foveal hypoplasia that occurs in albinism). Congenital pendular nystagmus is typically only horizontal, whereas the acquired form usually has vertical and torsional components; the acquired form also exhibits more variable waveforms between the two eyes. The congenital type is frequently associated with albinism,[4,66] whereas the acquired type may be found in myelin diseases (such as multiple sclerosis), brainstem strokes, and monocular vision loss.[66] On visuoscopic study one sees a moderately rapid to-and-fro oscillation of the eye; one edge of the oscillation (representing the fovea) is only very briefly

coincident with the center of the visuoscopic target. It has been speculated that pendular nystagmus is due to a high-gain instability in the slow-control system.[31] Both congenital and acquired pendular nystagmus, as well as the jerk nystagmus example presented (Fig. 2-17), may respond favorably to eye movement auditory biofeedback threapy.[2,18,19,66,72].

In contrast to pendular nystagmus, there are three basic varieties of *jerk* nystagmus. (see Fig. 2-10). Each has distinct dynamic characteristics reflecting differing neurologic abnormalities.[30,66]

The first variety of jerk nystagmus is *congenital*[4,21,30,31,66] (see Fig. 2-10 and Box 2-1). It may "evolve" during the first year of life,[75] or

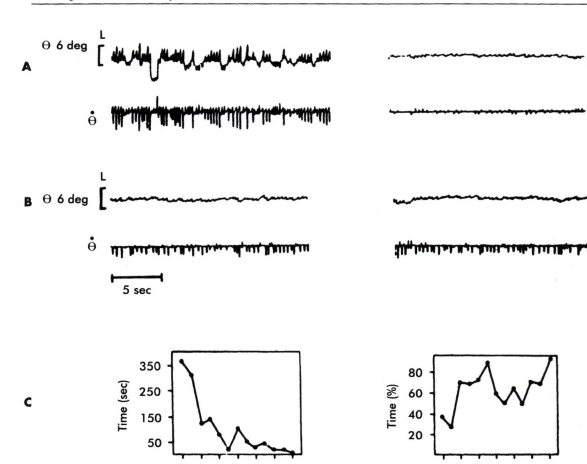

FIG. 2-17   Test results in one of our nystagmus patients. **A,** Eye position *(θ)* and velocity *(θ̇)* versus time. Fixation without *(left),* and with *(right),* auditory biofeedback. Nystagmus is reduced with audio cues. **B,** Eye position *(θ)* and velocity *(θ̇)* versus time; fixation with auditory biofeedback provided *(left)* and then withdrawn *(right).* Reduced nystagmus is maintained after feedback withdrawal. **C,** Performance with auditory biofeedback versus weekly session number. Time in seconds required to reduce nystagmus to specified level *(left);* percentage of time at reduced level as training progressed *(right).*

in unusual cases a congenital-type nystagmus (with respect to waveform) may "emerge" much later in life, sometimes after illness.[50] Typical jerk nystagmus has an amplitude ranging from 0.25 to 5 degrees, a frequency from 1 to 5 Hz, and an exponentially increasing slow phase with velocities of up to 100 degrees per second; jerk nystagmus is horizontal and conjugate. The slow phase moves the eye (that is, the fovea) away from the object of re-

gard with increasing velocity; then a saccade corrects this position error to obtain, once again, a brief period of foveation. So-called extended foveation periods of 50 to 100 msec or longer[4,11,34,42,72] follows the corrective saccade; during that time eye velocity approaches zero degrees per second, allowing these patients to have maximal "foveal" visual acuity. This acuity, however, may not be 20/20, primarily because of the adverse effects of early

---

> **BOX 2-1   *Characteristics of Congenital Nystagmus***
>
> Binocular
> Similar amplitude in both eyes
> Uniplanar, usually horizontal
> Distinctive waveforms
> Diminished (damped) by convergence
> Increased by fixation attempt
> Superimposition of latent component
> Inversion of the optokinetic reflex
> Associated head oscillation
> No oscillopsia
> Abolished in sleep

From Daroff RB, Troost BT, Dell'Osso LF. In Glaser JS, editor: *Clinical ophthalmology,* Hagerstown, Md, 1978, Harper & Row.

---

abnormal visual experience, that is, the increased retinal-image motion,[25,72] on the developing neurologic pathways, as well as the classic foveal hypoplasia in albinos. Congenital nystagmus is frequently dampened or reduced by increased convergence[43,65,98]; the convergence (innervation) appears to interact with the nystagmus and reduce the overall ocular motion. Thus these patients may hold reading material quite close to their eyes (for instance, a few inches away) to reduce the nystagmus, thereby further improving visual acuity and overall quality of the retinal image as well as increasing the visual angle of the text and improving its visibility. On the other hand, the nystagmus may be exacerbated by the conscious intent to fixate carefully.[31]

Various treatments for both pendular and jerk nystagmus have been attempted with reasonably good success. These include (1) composite or yoked prisms[37] (for example, versional or with bases left or right) in conjunction with eye muscle surgery [14,35,68,77,100] to place the eyes in their null position (mechanically and innervationally) without necessity of a head turn; (2) base-out prisms that are used to increase convergence (which

probably acts neuromechanically) to reduce nystagmus[43,65,98]; and (3) orthoptics,[25,73,91] contact lenses,[1,40,67] and eye movement auditory biofeedback* (see Fig. 2-17), which are used simply to reduce the nystagmus when the head is straight by providing various forms of information (such as visual, tactile, and auditory respectively) related to eye position and velocity (see Table 10-6 in Leigh and Zee[66]). Such treatment, combined with "before and after" objective recordings to document and quantify the oculomotor changes, is available at only a few clinics and institutions. The "fixate vs. hold" paradigm[95,96] was also successful in these patients.[17] That is, when patients were asked either "to fixate the small target carefully" or "to look at the small target and try to hold the eye steady," the nystagmus was reduced in the latter condition.

The second type of jerk nystagmus is considered a *gaze-evoked* (or gaze-holding) nystagmus[30,66] (see Fig. 2-10). Its characteristics are similar to those found in the congenital variety, except that the slow-phase velocity waveform is of the decreasing (rather than increasing) exponential variety. Thus the slow phase moves the eye away from eccentric gaze toward the midline with decreasing velocity; then a saccade corrects the position error to obtain, once again, a brief period of foveation. Gaze-evoked nystagmus is found in patients for a variety of reasons, including use of certain drugs, cerebellar and vestibular problems, and multiple sclerosis (see Leigh and Zee[66]). Physiologic or endpoint nystagmus (1- to 2-degree amplitude and 1- and 3-Hz frequency) probably represents a benign form of gaze-evoked (25- to 65-degree gaze angle) nystagmus.[6,46]

A specific benign form of congenital nystagmus has the same type of exponentially decreasing waveform, except that it is present along the midline as well. However, its occurrence is unrelated to any defined disease process or use of drugs. This form is *latent nys-*

---

*References 2, 18, 19, 51, 66, and 72.

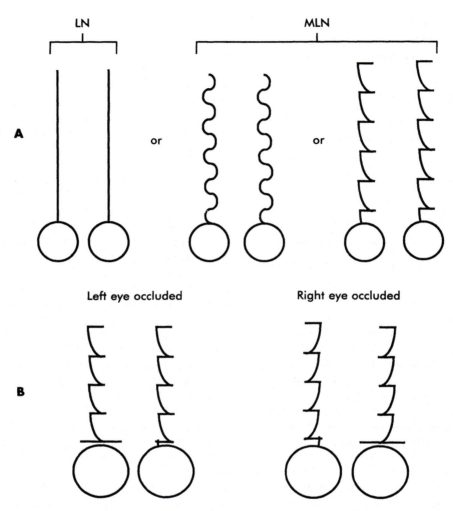

FIG. 2-18 Latent *(LN)* and manifest latent *(MLN)* nystagmus under binocular **(A)** and monocular **(B)** viewing conditions.

tagmus or, perhaps more accurately in most cases, *manifest latent nystagmus.*[32,38,39] Traditionally the term *latent nystagmus* has referred to a jerk nystagmus that occurs only under monocular (or dissociated) but *not* binocular viewing conditions with fusion. More recent findings using high-resolution infrared limbal eye-tracking devices (see Chapter 8) have shown that in almost all cases of presumed (pure) latent nystagmus, there was indeed a small-amplitude binocular nystagmus component (jerk or pendular): hence the new, more appropriate name, *manifest latent nystagmus.* In this and other forms of jerk nystagmus the direction of nystagmus is defined by the direction of the saccadic component, which in this case is *always* toward the viewing eye (Fig. 2-18). Thus with the right eye viewing, right-jerk nystagmus is elicited, and, with the left eye viewing, left-jerk nystagmus. This type of nystagmus is always binocular and conjugate. Under binocular viewing conditions small-amplitude jerk nystagmus may be present,[38] and, as we have seen at times in our clinic,

TABLE 2-3   Facts About Vestibular Nystagmus

Symptom or Sign	Peripheral (End-Organ)	Central (Nuclear)
Direction of nystagmus	Unidirectional, fast-phase opposite lesion	Bidirectional or unidirectional
Purely horizontal nystagmus without rotary component	Uncommon	Common
Vertical or purely rotary nystagmus	Never present	May be present
Visual fixation	Inhibits nystagmus and vertigo	No inhibition
Severity of vertigo	Marked	Mild
Direction of environmental spin	Toward slow phase	Variable
Direction of past-pointing	Toward slow phase	Variable
Direction of Romberg fall	Toward slow phase	Variable
Effect of head turning	Changes Romberg fall	No effect
Duration of symptoms	Finite (minutes, days, or weeks) but recurrent	May be chronic
Tinnitus or deafness, or both	Often present	Usually absent
Common causes	Infectious (labyrinthitis), Meniere's disease, neuronitis, vascular, traumatic, toxic	Vascular, demyelinating, neoplastic

From Daroff RB, Troost BT, Dell'Osso LF. In Glaser JS, editor: *Clinical ophthalmology,* Hagerstown, Md, 1978, Harper & Row.

small-amplitude pendular (0.25-degree and 5-Hz) nystagmus has also been objectively documented. The typical jerk nystagmus is easily observed with the ophthalmoscope or visuoscope as a "jerky" movement of the eye, appearing as a "sliding" movement in one direction (error-producing slow phase) and a subsequent, rapid jerk to obtain foveation in the opposite direction (error-correcting saccade). The nystagmus present under binocular conditions cannot be viewed with the ophthalmoscope or visuoscope because the instrument and the examiner's head act as "occluders" and serve to elicit the typical jerk nystagmus. Therefore either careful, close gross visual observation from the patient's side or viewing at high magnification with the slit lamp work best in this case (see Chapters 8 and 9). Manifest latent nystagmus always occurs in association with strabismus,[39] typically in conjunction with a head turn or tilt and alternating sursumduction.[39,66] The etiology of manifest latent nystagmus is unknown.

The third form of jerk nystagmus is primarily of either central or peripheral *vestibular* origin[9,30,66] (see Fig. 2-10 and Table 2-3). This form is characterized by a linear or constant-velocity slow phase that moves the eye (fovea) away from the object of regard and is followed by a foveating saccade. The nystagmus amplitude, frequency, and slow-phase velocity may vary considerably. The jerk nystagmus is typically horizontal in the peripheral variety and vertical in the central variety. Fixation suppresses peripheral but not central vestibular nystagmus. Both are exacerbated by change in head position. Similarly both are influenced by gaze angle; nystagmus intensity increases when the patient gazes into the direction of the nystagmus saccades (Alexander's law). On either gross visual observation or ophthalmoscopic study one may see a variable slow-phase waveform, since visual feedback may interact with the linear vestibular waveform to help stabilize vision. Therefore, if possible, it is best to obtain objective recordings of the eyes in total darkness while the patient attempts to gaze straight ahead.[97]

As emphasized by both Daroff, Troost, and Dell'Osso [30] and Leigh and Zee,[66] the nystagmus slow phase provides insight into the underlying neurologic abnormality. In congenital nystagmus with its increasing exponential waveform this abnormality suggests high-gain "instability" of the gaze-holding neurologic step-controller signal, whereas in gaze-holding nystagmus with its decreasing exponential waveform it reflects a "deficient" signal ("leaky integrator") that decays over time; in both cases the faster the exponential change (that is, the shorter the slow-phase response-time constant), the more abnormal the neural integrator function. In the vestibular variety with its linear waveform this abnormality reflects "tonic imbalance" in the input signals.

REVIEW QUESTIONS

1. Describe the dynamic characteristics of the three types of fixational eye movements. What is their effect, if any, on visual acuity in individuals with normal vision?
2. Discuss Cornsweet's model of fixation. What was Nachmias's contribution to this classic model?
3. Describe fixation characteristics when patient is placed in the dark.
4. You check the range of fixation in an 80-year-old asymptomatic patient and find slight reduction in upward gaze. Should you automatically order magnetic resonance imaging? Why or why not?
5. Compare and contrast the dynamic characteristics of the various forms of nystagmus. What impact do they have on visual acuity? On stereoacuity? On contrast sensitivity? On accommodation?
6. Compare and contrast the dynamic characteristics of abnormal drift and saccadic intrusions. What effect do they have on visual acuity? On stereoacuity? On contrast sensitivity? On accommodation?
7. Describe the various treatments for nystagmus and their rationales. Which one would you recommend to a patient? Why? Which one would you not recommend to a patient? Why not?
8. What is the "fixate vs. hold" paradigm? How might it be useful during ophthalmoscopy in a

patient with amblyopia? In a patient with nystagmus? In a patient with cerebellar disease?

REFERENCES

1. Abadi RV: Visual performance with contact lenses and congenital idiopathic nystagmus, *Br J Physiol Optics* 33:32, 1979.
2. Abadi RV, Carden D, Simpson J: A new treatment for congenital nystagmus, *Br J Ophthal* 64:2, 1980.
3. Abadi RV, Dickinson CM: Waveform characteristics in congenital nystagmus, *Doc Ophthal* 64:153, 1986.
4. Abadi RV, Dickinson CM, Pascal E, Whittle J, Worfolk R: Sensory and motor aspects of congenital nystagmus. In Schmid R, Zambarbieri D, editors: *Oculomotor control and cognitive processes,* Amsterdam, North Holland, 1991, Elsevier.
5. Abadi RV, Worfolk R: Retinal slip velocities in congenital nystagmus, *Vis Res* 29:195, 1989.
6. Abel LA, Parker L, Daroff RB, Dell'Osso LF: Endpoint nystagmus, *Invest Ophthal Vis Sci* 17:539, 1978.
7. Adler FH, Fliegelman M: Influence of fixation on the visual acuity, *Arch Ophthal* 12:475, 1934.
8. Anderson JR: Latent nystagmus and alternating hyperphoria, *Br J Ophthal* 1:2, 1954.
9. Baloh RW, Honrubia V: *Clinical neurophysiology of the vestibular system,* ed 2, Philadelphia, 1990, FA Davis.
10. Bedell HE: Sensitivity to oscillatory target motion in congenital nystagmus, *Invest Ophthal Vis Sci* 33:1811, 1992.
11. Bedell HE, White JM, Abplanalp PL: Variability of foveations in congenital nystagmus, *Clin Vis Sci* 4:247, 1989.
12. Bedell HE, Yap YL, Flom MC: Fixational drift and nasal-temporal pursuit asymmetries in strabismic amblyopes, *Invest Ophthal Vis Sci* 31:968, 1990.
13. Bennet-Clark HC: The oculomotor response to small target displacements, *Optica Acta* 11:301, 1964.
14. Bosone G, Reccia R, Roberti G, Russo P: On the variations of the time constant of the slow-phase eye movements produced by surgical therapy of congenital nystagmus: a preliminary report, *Ophthal Res* 21:345, 1989.
15. Bridgeman B, Palca J: The role of microsaccades in high-acuity observation tasks, *Vis Res* 20:813, 1980.
16. Chamberlain W: Restriction in upward gaze

with advancing age, *Am J Ophthal* 71:341, 1971.

17. Ciuffreda KJ: Jerk nystagmus: some new findings, *Am J Optom Physiol Optics* 56:521, 1979.

18. Ciuffreda KJ, Goldrich SG: Oculomotor biofeedback therapy, *Inter Rehabil Med* 5:111, 1983.

19. Ciuffreda KJ, Goldrich SG, Neary C: Use of eye movement auditory biofeedback in the control of nystagmus, *Am J Optom Physiol Optics* 59:396, 1982.

20. Ciuffreda KJ, Kenyon RV, Stark L: Different rates of functional recovery of eye movements during orthoptic treatment in an adult amblyope, *Invest Ophthal Vis Sci* 18:213, 1979.

21. Ciuffreda KJ, Kenyon RV, Stark L: Fixational eye movements in amblyopia and strabismus, *J Am Optom Assoc* 50:1251, 1979.

22. Ciuffreda KJ, Kenyon RV, Stark L: Increased drift in amblyopic eyes, *Br J Ophthal* 64:7, 1980.

23. Ciuffreda KJ, Kenyon RV, Stark L: Saccadic intrusions in strabismus, *Arch Ophthal* 97:1673, 1979.

24. Ciuffreda KJ, Kenyon RV, Stark L: Suppression of fixational saccades in strabismic and ansiometropic amblyopia, *Ophthal Res* 11:31, 1979.

25. Ciuffreda KJ, Levi DM, Selenow A: *Amblyopia: basic and clinical aspects*, Boston, 1991, Butterworth-Heinemann.

26. Coakley D: *Minute eye movements and brain stem function*, Boca Raton, Fla, 1983, CRC.

27. Cornsweet TN: Determination of the stimuli for involuntary drifts and saccadic eye movements, *J Opt Soc Am* 46:987, 1956.

28. Daroff RB: Ocular oscillations, *Ann Oto Rhinol Laryngol* 86:102, 1977.

29. Daroff RB: Eye signs in humans with cerebellar dysfunction. In Lennerstrand G, Zee DS, Keller EL, editors: *Functional basis of ocular motility disorders*, New York, 1982, Pergamon.

30. Daroff RB, Troost BT, Dell'Osso LF: Nystagmus and related ocular oscillations. In Glaser JS, editor: *Clinical ophthalmology*, Hagerstown, Md, 1978, Harper & Row.

31. Dell'Osso LF: Congenital nystagmus. In Lennerstrand G, Zee DS, Keller EL, editors: *Functional basis of ocular motility disorders*, New York, 1982, Pergamon.

32. Dell'Osso LF: Congenital, latent and manifest latent nystagmus: similarities, differences and relation to strabismus, *Jap J Ophthal* 29:351, 1985.

33. Dell'Osso LF, Abel LA, Daroff RB: "Inverse latent" macro square wave jerks and macro saccadic oscillations, *Ann Neurol* 2:57, 1977.

34. Dell'Osso LF, Daroff RB: Congenital nystagmus waveforms and foveation strategy, *Doc Ophthal* 39:155, 1975.

35. Dell'Osso LF, Flynn JT: Congenital nystagmus surgery, *Arch Ophthal* 97:462, 1979.

36. Dell'Osso LF, Flynn JT, Daroff RB: Hereditary congenital nystagmus: an intrafamiliar study, *Arch Ophthal* 92:366, 1974.

37. Dell'Osso LF, Gauthier G, Liberman G, Stark L: Eye movement recordings as a diagnostic tool in a case of congenital nystagmus, *Am J Optom Arch Am Acad Optom* 49:3, 1972.

38. Dell'Osso LF, Schmidt D, Daroff RB: Latent, manifest latent, and congenital nystagmus, *Arch Ophthal* 97:1877, 1979.

39. Dell'Osso LF, Traccis S, Abel L: Strabismus: a necessary condition for latent and manifest latent nystagmus, *Neuro-ophthal* 3:247, 1983.

40. Dell'Osso LF, Traccis S, Abel LA, Erzurum SI: Contact lenses and congenital nystagmus, *Clin Vis Sci* 3:229, 1988.

41. Dell'Osso LF, Troost BT, Daroff RB: Macro square-wave jerks, *Neurol* 25:975, 1975.

42. Dell'Osso LF, van der Steen J, Steinman RM, Collewijn H: Foveation dynamics in congenital nystagmus. I. Fixation, *Doc Ophthal* 79:1, 1992.

43. Dickinson CM: The elucidation and use of the effect of near fixation in congenital nystagmus, *Ophthal Physiol Optics* 6:303, 1986.

44. Ditchburn RW: *Eye movements and visual perception*, Oxford, 1973, Clarendon.

45. Ditchburn RW, Ginsborg BL: Involuntary eye movements during fixation, *J Physiol* 119:1, 1953.

46. Eizenman M, Cheng P, Sharpe JA, Frecker RC: End-point nystagmus and ocular drift: an experimental and theoretical study, *Vis Res* 30:863, 1990.

47. Elidan J, Gay I, Lev S: Square-wave jerks: incidence, characteristics, and significance, *J Otolaryngol* 13:6, 1984.

48. Feldon SE, Langston JW: Square-wave jerks: a disorder of microsaccades? *Neurol* 27:278, 1977.

49. Fender D: *Control of fixation*, Doctoral thesis, Great Britain, 1956, University of Reading.

50. Gresty MA, Bronstein AM, Page NG, Rudge P: Congenital-type nystagmus emerging in later life, *Neurol* 41:653, 1991.

51. Grisham D: Management of nystagmus in young children. In Scheiman MM, editor:

Problems in optometry, vol 2, no 3, *Pediatric optometry*, Philadelphia, 1990, JB Lippincott.

52. Herishanu YO, Sharpe JA: Normal square-wave jerks, *Invest Ophthal Vis Sci* 20:269, 1981.

53. Hertle RW, Tabuchi A, Dell'Osso LF, Abel LA, Weisman BM: Saccadic oscillations and intrusions preceding the postnatal appearance of congenital nystagmus, *Neuro-ophthal* 8:37, 1988.

54. Hess K, Reisine H, Dursteler M: Normal eye drift and saccadic drift correction in darkness, *Neuro-ophthal* 5:247, 1985.

55. Higgins KE, Daugman JG, Mansfield RFW: Amblyopic contrast sensitivity: insensitivity to unsteady fixation, *Invest Ophthal Vis Sci* 23:113, 1982.

56. Hotson JR: Cerebellar control of fixation eye movements, *Neurol* 32:31, 1982.

57. Hung GK, Ciuffreda KJ, Carlay CA, Fang P, Menditto S: Auditory biofeedback to control vertical and horizontal eye movements in the dark, *Invest Ophthal Vis Sci* 29:1860, 1988.

58. Jin YH, Goldstein HP, Reinecke RD: Absence of visual sampling in infantile nystagmus, *Kor J Ophthal* 3:28, 1989.

59. Kosnik W, Fikre J, Sekuler R: Visual fixation stability in older adults, *Invest Ophthal Vis Sci* 27:1720, 1986.

60. Kosnik W, Kline D, Fikre J, Sekuler R: Ocular fixation control as a function of age and exposure duration, *Psychol Aging* 2:302, 1987.

61. Kowler E: The stability of gaze and its implications for vision. In Cronly-Dillon J, editor: *Vision and visual dysfunction*, vol 8 (Eye movements), Boca Raton, Fla, 1991, CRC.

62. Kowler E, Steinman RM: Small saccades serve no useful purpose, *Vis Res* 20:273, 1980.

63. Krauskopf J, Cornsweet TN, Riggs LA: Analysis of eye movements during monocular and binocular fixation, *J Opt Soc Am* 50:572, 1960.

64. Lang J: Der Kongenitale order frunkindliche strabismus, *Ophthalmologica* 154:201, 1967.

65. Lavin PJM, Traccis S, Dell'Osso LF, Abel LA, Ellenberger C: Downbeat nystagmus with pseudocycloid waveform: improvement with base-out prisms, *Ann Neurol* 13:621, 1983.

66. Leigh RJ, Zee DS: *The neurology of eye movements*, ed 2, Philadelphia, 1991, FA Davis.

67. Matsubayashi K, Fukushima M, Tabuchi A: Application of soft contact lenses for children with congenital nystagmus, *Neuro-ophthal* 12:47, 1992.

68. Mitchell PR: Surgical management of nystagmus. In Nelson LB, Lavrich JB, editors: *Strabismus surgery*, Philadelphia, 1992, WB Saunders.

69. Nachmias J: Two-dimensional motion of the retinal image during monocular fixation, *J Opt Soc Am* 49:901, 1959.

70. Nachmias J: Determiners of the drift of the eye during monocular fixation, *J Opt Soc Am* 51:761, 1961.

71. Ohtsuka K, Mukuno K, Ukai K, Ishikawa S: The origin of square wave jerks: conditions of fixation and microsaccades, *Jap J Ophthal* 30:209, 1986.

72. Ong E, Ciuffreda KJ, Tannen B: Static accommodation in congenital nystagmus, *Invest Ophthal Vis Sci* 34:194, 1993.

73. Pearlman CA: A case study, *J Am Optom Assoc* 47:396, 1976.

74. Reccia R, Roberti G, Russo P: Spectral analysis of pendular waveforms in congenital nystagmus, *Ophthal Res* 21:83, 1989.

75. Reinecke RD, Guo S, Goldstein HP: Waveform evolution in infantile nystagmus: an electro-oculographic study, *Bino Vis* 3:191, 1988.

76. Riggs LA, Ratliff F: Visual acuity and the normal tremor of the eyes, *Science* 114:17, 1951.

77. Roberti G, Russo P, Serge G: Spectral analysis of electro-oculograms in the quantitative evaluation of nystagmus surgery, *Med Biol Eng Comput* 25:573, 1987.

78. Robinson DA, Keller EL: The behavior of eye movement motoneurons in the alert monkey, *Bibl Ophthal* 82:7, 1972.

79. Sansbury RV, Skavenski AA, Haddad GM, Steinman RM: Normal fixation of eccentric targets, *J Opt Soc Am* 63:612, 1973.

80. Schor CM, Hallmark W: Slow control of eye position in strabismic amblyopia, *Invest Ophthal Vis Sci* 17:577, 1978.

81. Selhorst JB, Stark L, Ochs AL, Hoyt WF: Disorders in cerebellar ocular motor control. I. Saccadic overshoot dysmetria: an oculographic, control system, and clinico-anatomical analysis, *Brain* 99:497, 1976.

82. Selhorst JB, Stark L, Ochs AL, Hoyt WF: Disorders in cerebellar ocular motor control II. Macro-saccadic oscillation: An oculographic, control system, and clinico-anatomical analysis, *Brain* 99:509, 1976.

83. Shakhnovich AR: *The brain and regulation of eye movement*, New York, 1977, Plenum.

84. Shallo-Hoffman J, Petersen J, Muhlendlyck H: How normal are "normal" square-wave jerks? *Invest Ophthal Vis Sci* 30:1009, 1989.

85. Shallo-Hoffman J, Sendler B, Muhlendyck H: Normal square-wave jerks in differing age groups, *Invest Ophthal Vis Sci* 31:1649, 1990.

86. Sharpe JA, Fletcher WA: Saccadic intrusions

and oscillations, *Can J Neurol Sci* 11:426, 1984.

87. Sharpe JA, Herishanu YO, White OB: Cerebral square wave jerks, *Neurol* 32:57, 1982.

88. Shultz E: Binocular micromovements in normal persons, *Graefe's Arch Clin Exp Ophthal* 222:95, 1984.

89. Skavenski AA, Hansen RH, Steinman RM, Winterson B: Quality of retinal image stabilization during small natural and artifical body rotations in man, *Vis Res* 19:675, 1979.

90. Skavenski AA, Steinman, RM: Control of eye position in the dark, *Vis Res* 10:193, 1970.

91. Smith W: *Clinical orthoptic procedures,* St Louis, 1950, Mosby.

92. Stark L: *Neurological control systems,* New York, 1968, Plenum.

93. Steinman RM: Effect of target size, luminance, and color on monocular fixation, *J Opt Soc Am* 55:1158, 1965.

94. Steinman RM, Collewijn H: Binocular retinal-image motion during active head rotation, *Vis Res* 20:415, 1980.

95. Steinman RM, Cunitz RJ, Timberlake GT, Herman M: Voluntary control of microsaccades during maintained monocular fixation, *Science* 155:1577, 1967.

96. Steinman RM, Haddad GM, Skavenski AA, Wyman D: Miniature eye movement, *Science* 181:810, 1973.

97. Tannen B, Ciuffreda KJ, Werner DL: A case of Wallenberg's syndrome: ocular motor abnormalities, *J Am Optom Assoc* 60:748, 1989.

98. Traccis S, Rosati G, Monaco MF, Aiello I, Pirastru MI, Becciu S, Loffredo P, Agnetti V: Alternating esotropia, monocular and binocular macro square-wave jerks: improvement with base-out prisms, *Neuro-ophthal* 8:43, 1988.

99. Verheijen FJ: A simple after-image method demonstrating the involuntary multi-directional eye movements during fixation, *Optica Acta* 8:309, 1961.

100. von Noorden GK, Sprunger DT: Large rectus muscle recessions for the treatment of congenital nystagmus, *Arch Ophthal* 109:221, 1991.

101. Westheimer G, McKee SP: Visual acuity in the presence of retinal-image motion, *J Opt Soc Am* 65:847, 1975.

102. Westheimer G, McKee SP: Stereoscopic acuity for moving retinal images, *J Opt Soc Am* 68:450, 1978.

103. Whittaker SG, Budd J, Cummings RW: Eccentric fixation with macular scotoma, *Invest Ophthal Vis Sci* 29:268, 1988.

104. Winterson BJ, Collewijn H: Microsaccades during finely-guided visuomotor tasks, *Vis Res* 16:1387, 1976.

105. Wyman D, Steinman RM: Small step tracking: implications for the oculomotor "dead zone," *Vis Res* 13:2165, 1973.

106. Yamashiro M: Objective measurement of the monocular and binocular movements, *Jap J Ophthal* 1:130, 1957.

107. Yarbus AL: *Eye movements and vision,* New York, 1967, Plenum.

108. Yee RD, Wong EK, Baloh RW, Honrubia V: A study of congenital nystagmus: waveforms, *Neurol* 26:326, 1976.

109. Zee DS, Robinson DA: A hypothetical explanation of saccadic oscillations, *Ann Neurol* 5:405, 1979.

110. Zuber BL, Stark L, Cook G: Microsaccades and the velocity-amplitude relationship for saccadic eye movements, *Science* 150:1459, 1965.

3

Saccadic Eye Movements

Key Terms

Aging	Neurologic disease
Antisaccade	Prediction
Dead zone	Pulse-step controller
Dysmetria	Saccadic adaptation
Latency	Saccadic plasticity
Main sequence	Sampled-data system

OVERVIEW OF SACCADES

Saccades are accurate, high-velocity, non-ballistic eye movements used to foveate objects of interest.[7] These "darting" movements are most easily observed during reading and while scanning a scene. Saccades provide brief, high-resolution "samples" of the world to the brain for an array of purposes, ranging from relatively simple information gathering to the more complex identification and perception of objects. Most naturally occurring saccades (~85%) are less than 15 degrees in amplitude.[3] During a saccade a neural signal related directly to eye movement (or its intended or attempted movement) called *efference copy* (or "will to effort") is generated. This motor-based information, in the form of a *corollary discharge* signal, is sent to higher-level brain centers and informs the brain that the world has not shifted but rather that the eye (and retinal image) indeed has, thus leading to perceptual stability.[15,36]

Saccades are neurally generated by the combination of a high-frequency pulse and a much lower-frequency step. The pulse is necessary for overcoming the viscous resistance of the globe and orbital contents and is responsible for moving the eye rapidly to the new position. The step is necessary for overcoming the elastic restoring forces of the eye and orbital contents and is responsible for maintaining the eye in this new position (see Chapter 2, Fig. 2-9, and later discussion in this chapter). This *pulse-step* controller signal produces excitation to the agonist muscle, which is mirrored by a similar inhibitory signal to the antagonist muscle. These signals, however, are "filtered" or effectively smoothed because of the relatively slow development of muscle tensions and resultant forces necessary to move the globe to produce this rapid movement[2] (Fig. 3-1).

Saccadic eye movements may be categorized[8] as shown in Fig. 3-2. In this chapter the larger "refixation saccades" are discussed. The various types of normal and abnormal saccadic patterns found during attempted steady fixation have already been considered in Chapter 2. Essentially a saccade is either *normometric* or *dysmetric*. A normometric (also called orthometric) saccade consists of a single, accurate movement having appropriate gain and dynamics. The underlying neural controller signal consists of a single, precisely matched pulse-step combination. In contrast, in a dysmetric saccade some of the conditions just stipulated for a normometric saccade are not met. Dysmetric saccades can be either single-step or multiple-step movements and can be either too small *(hypometric)* or too large *(hypermetric)* with respect to the intended target position[8] (see Figs. 3-2 and 3-3).

Hypometric saccades can initially undershoot the target in a variety of ways. When the saccade consists of a single movement, it could represent either a very slow "pulseless" saccade or a slightly small but otherwise normal rapid saccade with an appended slow glissadic component (for example, the pulse is too small for the appropriate step). If of the multiple-step variety, the saccade could represent a low-gain saccade, which necessitates one or more subsequent smaller corrective movements to attain precise foveation. A primary saccade that has nearly normal gain (that is, amplitude of the initial eye movement divided by amplitude of the target movement: normal values are 0.92 ± 0.03)[13] and is only slightly reduced may represent a normal strategy adopted by the saccadic system so that any subsequent corrective saccade (~150 msec later) requires less computation (for example, only amplitude, not direction).[10] That type of saccade could also be due to prediction, in which the eye moves in advance of the step target change, but in such cases the gain of the primary saccade is lower and more variable (0.8 ± 0.10).[13] Saccades are also more accurate when made between two simultaneously presented stationary targets (as is typical dur-

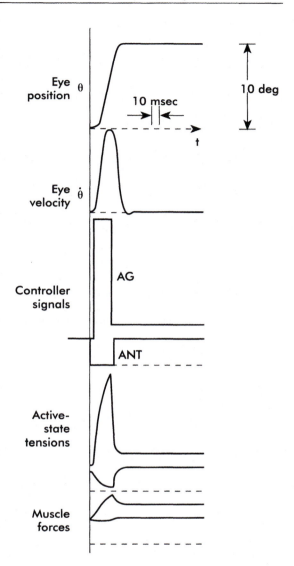

FIG. 3-1 Signals involved in the transformation of input commands into eye movements. The pulse-step controller signal has abrupt transitions that are filtered out by the activation and deactivation time constants to produce the active-state tensions. These in turn are filtered by the series elasticity and the nonlinear force-velocity relationship to produce the forces that are applied to the globe. These forces produce the eye movement. *AG*, agonist; *ANT*, antagonist.

(From Bahill AT: *Bioengineering: biomedical, medical, and clinical engineering,* Englewood Cliffs, NJ, 1981, Prentice-Hall.)

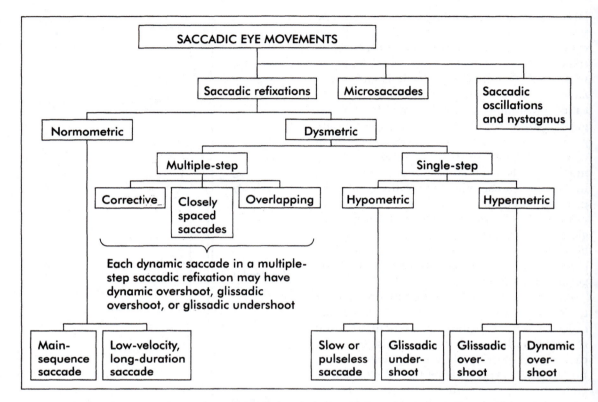

FIG. 3-2   Interrelationships of normal and abnormal saccadic eye movement subtypes.
(From Bahill AT, Troost BT: *Neurology* 29:1150, 1979.)

ing clinical examination) than when a single target steps between these same two spatial locations (as is typical in the laboratory), perhaps because of increased time for saccadic processing to the next target in the former condition[37] (see later discussion). Closely spaced or overlapping saccades are generally due to fatigue or disease.

Hypermetric saccades can initially overshoot the target in a variety of ways. Such saccades that consist of a single movement could represent either a slightly larger but otherwise normal saccade with an appended slow glissadic component (for example, the pulse is too large for the appropriate step) or a dynamic overshoot (for example, the pulse quickly switches direction to produce a small [0.25-deg], rapid [15-msec], nonvisually-guided reversal in the direction of saccadic eye movement). This latter movement may represent a "time optimal" behavior that places the target within the general foveal region as rapidly as possible. The multiple-step variety, in which the first saccade overshoots the target and a subsequent, visually guided corrective saccade occurs (150 msec later) to attain foveation, represents a high-gain saccade (that is, static overshoot), which is typically seen in cerebellar disease[53] and is infrequently seen in persons with normal vision.[29]

In general, when eye movements are mentioned, they are assumed to be in the horizontal plane. Such constrained thinking, however, is related to limitations in instrumentation rather than to the reality of naturally occurring eye movements. Since

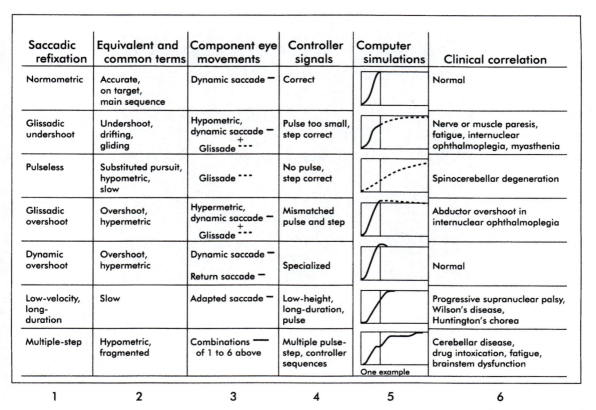

Saccadic refixation	Equivalent and common terms	Component eye movements	Controller signals	Computer simulations	Clinical correlation
Normometric	Accurate, on target, main sequence	Dynamic saccade ▬	Correct		Normal
Glissadic undershoot	Undershoot, drifting, gliding	Hypometric, dynamic saccade ▬ + Glissade - - -	Pulse too small, step correct		Nerve or muscle paresis, fatigue, internuclear ophthalmoplegia, myasthenia
Pulseless	Substituted pursuit, hypometric, slow	Glissade - - -	No pulse, step correct		Spinocerebellar degeneration
Glissadic overshoot	Overshoot, hypermetric	Hypermetric, dynamic saccade ▬ + Glissade - - -	Mismatched pulse and step		Abductor overshoot in internuclear ophthalmoplegia
Dynamic overshoot	Overshoot, hypermetric	Dynamic saccade ▬ Return saccade ▬	Specialized		Normal
Low-velocity, long-duration	Slow	Adapted saccade ▬	Low-height, long-duration, pulse		Progressive supranuclear palsy, Wilson's disease, Huntington's chorea
Multiple-step	Hypometric, fragmented	Combinations ▬▬ of 1 to 6 above	Multiple pulse-step, controller sequences	One example	Cerebellar disease, drug intoxication, fatigue, brainstem dysfunction

| 1 | 2 | 3 | 4 | 5 | 6 |

FIG. 3-3 Saccadic refixation subtypes *(column 1)*; equivalent and commonly used terms *(column 2)*; component eye movements *(column 3)*; underlying neuronal controller signals *(column 4)*; computer simulations of typical refixations showing eye position as a function of time *(column 5)*; and clinical correlations *(column 6)*.*Solid lines* represent the dynamic saccadic components; *dashed lines* represent the glissadic components. The first simulation in column 5 is of a 15-degree dynamic saccade. The record length is 160 msec. All other simulations have the same scales, except for the third simulation, that of the pulseless saccade, which has a record length of 320 msec.
(From Bahill AT, Troost BT: *Neurology* 29:1150, 1979.)

the mid-1980s, advances in and availability of such instrumentation have allowed investigation of vertical and oblique saccadic movements. Saccade dynamics in other directions are quite similar to those found for horizontal saccades. For example, the relationship between saccade amplitude and its correlated peak velocity is the same (see later discussion in this chapter).[11] However, the trajectory for oblique saccades is more curved than that found in either their vertical or horizontal counterparts[64] (Fig. 3-4).

SACCADIC LATENCY

Saccadic latency, or reaction time, typically refers to the time from onset of the nonpredictable step of target movement to onset of the saccadic eye movement initiated to foveate the displaced target. Saccadic latency

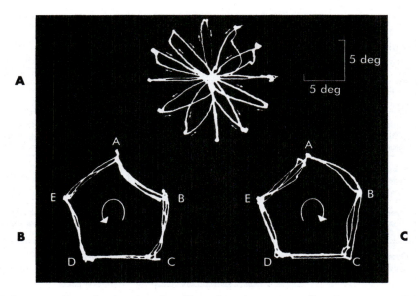

FIG. 3-4   Saccadic paths showing the effect of eye movement direction on saccadic curvature for one typical subject. ***A,*** Saccades between the origin (center) to the 12 circumferential points of a clockface. *Arrows* indicate direction of saccades, either centrifugal or centripetal. Saccades during counterclockwise ***(B),*** and, clockwise ***(C),*** scanning of five points, arranged as apices of a pentagon *(ABCDE)*. Three superimposed scannings are shown in the illustration.

(From Viviani P, Berthoz A, Tracey D: *Vision Res* 17:661, 1977.)

is approximately 180 to 200 msec, with a standard deviation of 30 msec.[10] Saccadic latency can be affected by a variety of factors (Table 3-1). Under typical clinical test conditions, however, the physical characteristics of the target itself (luminance, size, and so forth) have little impact (<20 to 30 msec) on saccadic initiation and its potential diagnostic importance.[11] Factors such as target predictability, as well as patient motivation and attention, probably play a much larger role in the elicitation of a saccade.

What components does this saccadic delay comprise? It probably includes both noncognitive and cognitive factors such as:[12]

- Afferent or visual neurosensory delay of approximately 50 msec, which includes neural transmission time from the retina to visual cortex to high-level centers involved in the saccadic decision-making process.

- Efferent or neuromotor delay of approximately 30 msec, which includes neural transmission time within higher-level centers involved in the saccadic decision-making process, as well as lower-level signal processing within the midbrain.

- Computational delay of approximately 50 msec, which, along with the first two factors listed, may be regarded as noncognitive.

- Decision-making processing delay of at least 50 msec. The brain is deciding whether and where to change gaze in the field, thus involving higher-level cognitive processing.

TABLE 3-1   *Factors That Affect Saccadic Latency*

Increase	Decrease
Very small (<30 min) or large (>10 deg) target eccentricities	Target predictability
Increased target uncertainty	Increased target luminance or contrast, or both
Increased target complexity	Heightened attention
Increased age in adulthood	Forewarning period
Inability to disengage attention	—
Decreased motivation	—

SACCADIC SUPPRESSION AND OMISSION

Since the beginning of the century, psychologists and others have been intrigued by the absence of a notably "smeared" retinal image during a high-velocity saccade (see Carpenter[15] for a recent overview). In fact, individuals have the sense (or illusion) of clear, uninterrupted vision during the thousands of saccades made each day.

Most of the experiments in the area of saccadic suppression and omission have involved the concept of *saccadic suppression* or elevation (~0.25 to 0.5 log units) in visual threshold, which is found before, during, and after a saccade (including microsaccades)[78,79] (Fig. 3-5). For example, detection of a brief flash of light decreases by 50% or more 20 msec before to approximately 35 msec after a saccade.[65] Depth and extent of this suppression depend on target and background characteristics.[15] The primary factor that could account for this wide time frame of relative suppression related to saccade onset is central neural inhibition.[79] Such threshold elevation before a saccade is not surprising, since it would be likely to relate to some central event involving fu-

ture saccade execution. Suppression during the saccade itself, of course, is the intention of the entire process. In addition, suppression after completion of a saccade may be useful in minimizing the effects of residual retinal-image motion caused by transient conjugate and disjunctive eye movements that may occur for a few hundred msec.[18,19] This relatively small elevation in threshold, however, ranging from 0.8 log units near threshold to only 0.1 log units (or less) well above threshold (~2 log units), simply cannot account for most of the total absence (~a 2.3 log-unit effect)[49] of a blurred, greyish percept during a saccade, especially under high-contrast naturalistic conditions such as during reading.

Clearly the more potent, important factor is *saccadic omission*, which involves visual masking. This masking refers to the obscuration of a target by either an immediately preceding (forward-masking) or a succeeding (backward-masking) visual stimulus, especially at high contrast levels and in the presence of a full array of contours. [39] These conditions, indeed, are present most of the time in our everyday surrounds; a face being fixated and a clock that is next to be fixated "mask" the potential "gray-out" of perception during the intervening 20- to 80-msec high-velocity saccade. The work of Campbell and Wurtz,[14] extending the pioneering research of Matin, Clymer, and Matin[39] clearly demonstrated that visual masking is the primary factor contributing to the absence of such perceived "gray-out" during saccades under natural conditions. They reported the following:

- A 1- to 5-msec flash presented during a 50- to 70-msec saccade produced a clear percept of the otherwise darkened room. The brief duration of the flash prevented any "smearing" of the image, and the presence of a "clear" percept demonstrated the lack of a significant central neural inhibition.
- A flash presented during the entire saccade excursion (50 to 70 msec) resulted

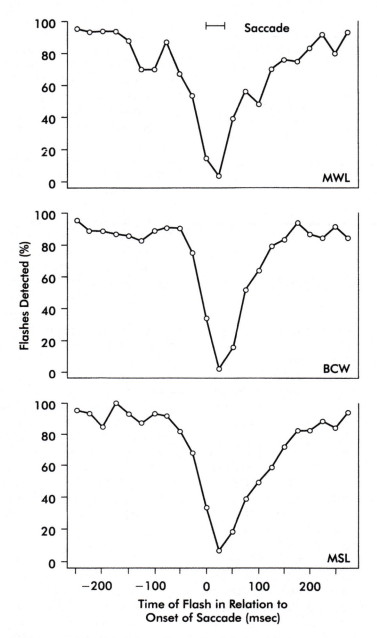

FIG. 3-5   Percentage of flashes detected by each of three subjects as a function of the temporal relation of the flash to the onset of a saccade. The average duration of the saccade is shown at the top of the figure.

(From Volkmann FC, Schick AML, Riggs LA: *J Opt Soc Am* 58:562, 1968.)

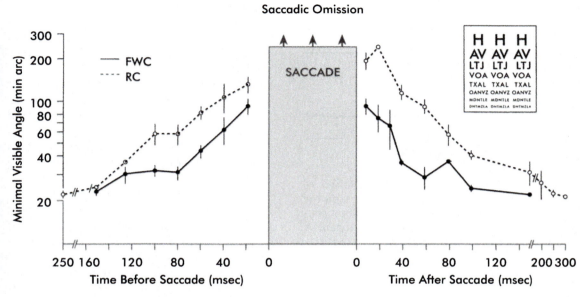

FIG. 3-6   Effect of a clear image before and after the smeared image during a saccade for two subjects. *Ordinate* shows the minimal visible angle seen on the Snellen Test charts; a logarithmic scale is used. *Abscissa* shows the time period of light extended before or after the eye movement. *Vertical line* at each point is the standard error: where no line is shown, the standard error is smaller than the symbol used. *Stippled area* indicates the period of light during a 30-degree saccade, and *upward-pointing arrows* above the *stippled area* indicate that not even a target of the largest visible angle on the chart could be seen during the saccade.

(From Campbell FW, Wurtz RH: *Vision Res* 18:1297, 1978.)

in a very smeared, grayish percept of the otherwise darkened room. The illumination during the entire saccade excursion allowed full, marked retinal-image smearing to occur and be perceived by the subject.

• Extension of the flash duration, either before the saccade or after the saccade was completed (as well as during the entire saccade), however, produced total absence of any gray-out; the person then, once again, reported a "clear" (again nonsmeared, nongrayish, low resolution as before with the 1- to 5-msec flash) percept. Visual acuity during the saccade itself was poorer than 20/1000 (Fig. 3-6). Thus masking had occurred due to the presence of either an immediately preceding or succeeding visual fixation (and surrounds) visual stimulation.

THE SAMPLED-DATA SYSTEM AND BEYOND

In 1954 Westheimer[67] reported a most intriguing test result. He had subjects track pulses of horizontal target displacement; most of the pulse durations (see Chapter 8 and Appendix) were considerably shorter than the 200-msec latency of the saccadic system. Therefore the target typically returned to its original position *before* any correlated oculomotor response occurred. After the normal latency period the eye saccaded by an amount equal to the pulse amplitude and then *remained* in that position for 200 msec before

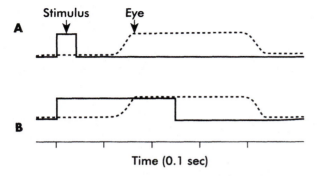

FIG. 3-7 Saccadic eye movement responses to double-target jumps. Horizontal position is on the ordinate. The intersaccadic interval remains constant despite the different durations (compare **A** and **B**) between two target jumps.

(From Westheimer G: *Arch Ophthalmol* 52:932, 1954.)

shifting back to the original (and final) target position (Fig. 3-7, *A* and *B*).

The motoric response to a pulse displacement defined a basic, important control property of the saccadic system. If the system continuously sampled target position (for example, a "continuous system"), the system motor response duration would equal the target pulse duration. Clearly this was not the case in the example just discussed. Rather, the eye remained at that new position for 200 msec, independent of the brief pulse duration; thus the saccadic system exhibited a 200-msec motor-based refractory period. Any subsequent changes in target position during this period did not appear to influence the initial motor program. Such responsivity suggested a discrete or periodic motor sampling of visual information, as found in *sampled-data systems.* This finding led to the formulation of a bioengineering model of sampled-data saccadic control in the early 1960s by Young and Stark[58,76,77] (Fig. 3-8, *A*).

The bioengineering model of sampled-data saccadic control has the following key features:

• The retinal error (that is, the difference between desired gaze angle and actual eye angle) is sampled by a motor impulse modulator at 200-msec intervals, an interval being the mean saccadic refractory period.

• The sampling is synchronized to occur with the onset of any target movement (assuming that no saccade occurred within the prior 200-msec interval). Target changes that occur between samples are not processed until the next sampling period.

• The information is then processed to generate a corrective saccadic eye movement one reaction time (that is, latency period) later, which brings the eye to a position sampled 200 msec earlier.

• Position errors of less than 0.5 degrees (later revised to 0.3 degrees), are generally not corrected, since they lie within an effective foveal "dead zone" over which small position errors are tolerated (see the next section).

In addition to the experimental results of the pulse studies previously described, another finding provided support for the sampled-data notion—the open-loop (absence of or ineffective visual feedback; see Appendix) step-tracking results[76,77] (Figure 3-8, *B*). Imagine the following. You are the subject in an eye movement experiment, and your eye movements are being monitored by an electronic sensing system. The central foveated target is suddenly displaced stepwise by 2 degrees. One would anticipate that 200 msec later, a corrective saccade would be made to foveate the target once again, as expected for this closed-loop (visual feedback present and effective; see Appendix) condition. However, the experimenter has incorporated an auxiliary electronic feedback circuit, which "picks up" the electronic signal from the eye movement monitoring system and rapidly moves the target by an amount equal to the actual saccadic eye movement. Thus every time you attempt to foveate the 2-degree eccentric tar-

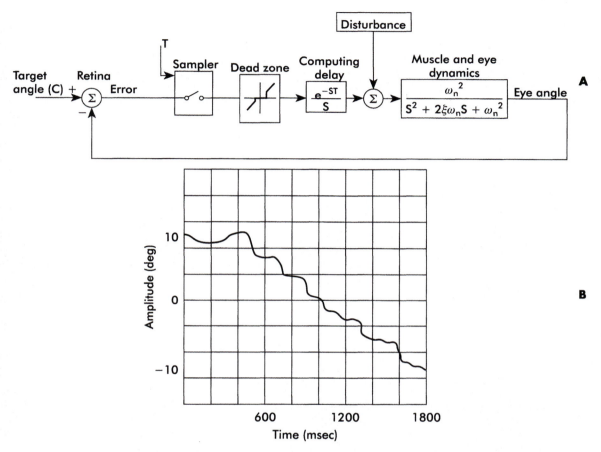

FIG. 3-8   **A,** Sampled-data model of the saccadic system. **B,** Experimental step response under variable feedback.

(From Young LR. In Zuber BL, editor: *Models of oculomotor behavior and control,* Boca Raton, Fla, 1981, CRC.)

get with an accurate 2-degree saccade, the target immediately steps 2 more degrees in the same direction. Therefore in this open-loop tracking mode a 2-degree position error is always present, leading to a series of 2-degree saccades that are separated by 200 msec; this series represents the motor sampling period of the saccadic system (see Young and Stark[76,77]).

Over the years revisions of this original model based on new experimental results were necessary, especially with respect to the refractory period. Some have even questioned

the notion of the saccadic system being sampled data at all. Essentially, rather than having an *absolute* refractory period, the system was shown to be *relative*.[76] That is, depending on the timing of a second target displacement within this "refractory" period, the initial motor command and response can, indeed, be modified, at least sometimes. For example, in the opposite hemifield pulse-step results,[12] the target steps to a new position *twice* in rapid succession during the saccadic refractory (or latency) period, with stimuli falling first within

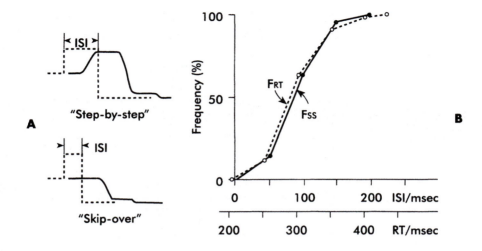

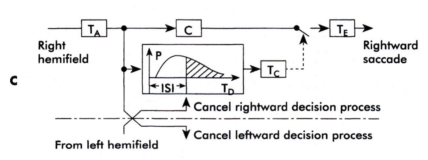

FIG. 3-9 Double-step reactions. **A,** Definition of step-by-step and skip-over responses *(solid curves)* to a crossed-step pattern *(dashed)* presenting the target briefly on one side of the current fixation direction (upward deflection) before stepping it to the opposite side (downward deflection). *ISI,* Interstep interval. **B,** Frequency of step-by-step reactions (F_{SS}, continuous curve) as a function of the interstep interval (*ISI* is the upper scale). Target stepped first by 30 degrees from center to one side, then by 60 degrees in the opposite direction to a 30-degree position on the other side; example is obtained from one subject. For comparison, *dashed curve* shows cumulative distribution of reaction times (F_{RT}) to single steps of 30 degrees in the same experiment; the reaction time axis (lower scale) is shifted by about 180 msec to disclose the similarity between F_{RT} and F_{SS}. **C,** Structure of decision process and components of the reaction time inferred from double-step responses. T_A, afferent delay time; T_D, decision time; T_C, afferent computation time; T_E, efferent delay time. T_A, T_C and T_E have fixed values, whereas T_D is a random variable with probability density $P(T_D)$. A decision process is initiated by the detection of a target on one side of the current fixation point, for example, the right hemifield. Subsequent changes of target position that affect only target eccentricity but not laterality do not interfere with the decision process. In contrast, any further step that sends the target into the left hemifield cancels the decision process unless it has already been completed. For any given ISI the percentage of process that can still be canceled corresponds to the *hatched area* under the distribution. $P(T_D)$, which therefore indicates the probability of skip-over responses. Element *C* represents computation of the amplitude, which is transmitted, one computation time after a decision has been taken, to the efferent motor structures (transmission symbolized by switch). Symmetry line *(dash-dot)* recalls existence of a mirror structure for saccades to the left.

(From Becker W, Jurgens R: *Vision Res* 19:967, 1979.)

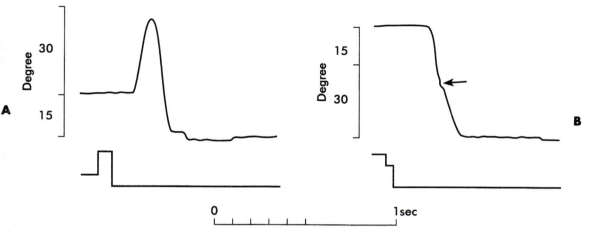

FIG. 3-10   Double-step responses *(upper traces)* with no pause between first and second saccades (**A** and **B**). **A,** Pulse-overshoot stimulus pattern *(lower trace)*. Eye starts from primary position; first target position is 30 degrees to the right; second position is 15 degrees to the left. **B,** Staircase stimulus pattern; eye starts from 15 degrees to the right of primary position; first target position is 0 degrees (that is, first step is 15 degrees to the left); second position is 30 degrees to the left. First saccade is landing between first and second target position *(arrow).*

(From Becker W. In Carpenter RHS, editor: *Vision and visual dysfunction,* vol 8, Boca Raton, Fla, 1991, CRC.)

one and then within the opposing hemifield. For instance, the target might pulse 4 degrees to the left for 80 msec and then step 8 degrees to the right. When the pulse (or interstimulus interval [ISI]) is brief, the initial displacement is typically ignored and only the opposing hemifield step is tracked with normal latency (Fig. 3-9, *A, B,* and *C*). As this ISI increases, the initial target displacement is ignored less and less; therefore when the ISI is about 200 msec, the eye tracks each target shift with normal latency. The short ISI results are inconsistent with the original notion of the absolute refractory period, whereas the long ISI results are, indeed, predicted by this theory. Additional possible motor responses[11] that do not support the original sampled-data model with respect to having an absolute refractory period are presented in Fig. 3-10. Because they exhibit the ability to modify the saccade in progress, the responses suggest parallel rather than serial processing of each saccade during the so-called refractory or latency period. It should be emphasized, however, that such responses are certainly not the norm. For example, as limited by such a saccadic sampled-data system, in our normal environment we cannot make more than four (or five) saccades per second. Based on these apparently conflicting results, the original sampled-data model was modified to allow for a relative refractory period (Fig. 3-11) during most of which sensory information is available to and can potentially be used by the saccadic system.[76] During the last 50 to 80 msec of this period, however, it is most difficult to modify a saccade based on new information, and this period probably represents the actual time required for visual information to traverse the afferent and efferent oculomotor-related visual pathways.[36]

More recent double-step (the target moves within the same hemifield) experiments have provided additional insight into modifiability of the initial saccadic response. Rather than re-

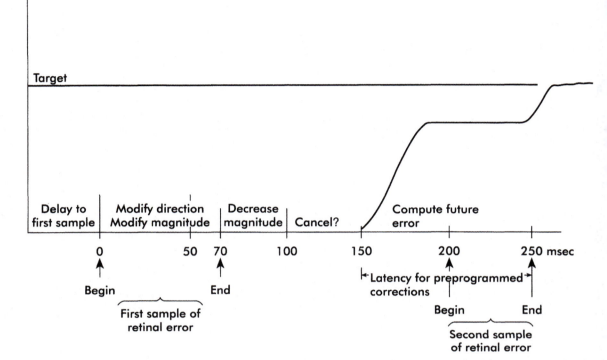

FIG. 3-11   Relative timing of events leading to saccades and saccadic corrections. Timing (T) steps include the following:

Step 1, T = 0 msec	Sample the retinal error and begin a program after a random, partly synchronized delay of up to 50 msec.
Step 2, T = 0 to 50 msec	Modify the direction of magnitude of the planned saccade.
Step 3, T = 50 to 70 msec	Modify the magnitude but not the direction of the planned saccade on the basis of new visual information.
Step 4, T = 70 to 100 msec	Modify the magnitude only to reduce the planned saccade in the same direction.
Step 5, T = 100 to 150 msec	Cancel the planned saccade if appropriate, and sample again to compute the next saccade in the next 50 to 100 msec.
Step 6, T = 150 to 200 msec	Proceed with the planned saccade, and model the expected error at its end. If this error is greater than 0.3 degrees, begin parallel processing of the corrective saccade.
Step 7, T = 200 msec	Initiate the saccadic jump.
Step 8, T = 200 to 300 msec	If a parallel preprogrammed corrective saccade is planned, proceed to generate it. If not, sample the retinal error again as in step 1.

(From Young LR. In Zuber BL, editor: *Models of oculomotor behavior and control*, Boca Raton, Fla, 1981, CRC.)

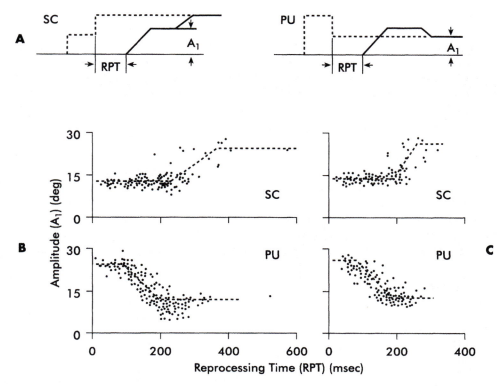

FIG. 3-12 Amplitude-transition functions. **A,** Double-step stimuli of staircase *(SC)* and pulse-undershoot *(PU)* types *(dashed line)* with schematic eye movement response *(solid line)* and definition of parameters represented by amplitude-transition function. *RPT*, Reprocessing time between second step and first response saccade; A_1, amplitude of first response saccade. **B** and **C,** Amplitude-transition functions obtained from two individuals (in **A** and **B,** respectively) with staircase pattern *(SC)* in which first target position is at 15 degrees and second is at 30 degrees, and pulse-undershoot pattern *(PU)*, in which first position is at 30 degrees and second is at 15 degrees. Each *dot* represents one trial and plots amplitude of the first response saccade *(A_1)* as a function of *RPT*; origin of abscissa coincides with second step. *Dashed curves,* Trapezoids fitted to data by eye; horizontal segments, *left* and *right,* correspond to average amplitude of single step to target at 15 and 30 degrees.

(From Becker W. In Carpenter RHS, editor: *Vision and visual dysfunction,* vol 8, *Eye movements,* Boca Raton, Fla, 1991, CRC.)

lating responses to the ISI, these experiments[11] consider the time between the step component and the initial saccadic response, referred to as "reprocessing time" (RPT) (Fig. 3-12, *A, B,* and *C*). If the RPT is short, the initial saccadic follows the pulse, and the step aspect does not influence this first saccade. As the RPT is increased (up to 200 msec), the initial saccade amplitude (and direction, when the step and pulse directions differ by other than 0 or 180 degrees) can be modified and biased (that is, a weighted average is determined) to an increasingly greater extent by the amplitude and direction of the step. This phase is referred to as the "transition period." In addition, as the duration of the RPT is increased to 200 or 400 msec, the response to the pulse is canceled and only the step component is tracked.

Some researchers have attempted to resolve the sampled-data (or serial) versus continuous (or parallel) system notion by hypothesizing two distinct modes of operation based on functional characteristics and demands.[12] Under everyday conditions the saccadic system would operate in a sampled-data or *serial* manner. Under certain conditions, however, such as when erroneous saccadic programming occurs, a second, rapidly programmed saccade would be executed to "correct" the initial saccade and produce accurate foveation on the object of interest. Clearly this area still warrants further careful investigation.

DEAD ZONE OF SACCADIC EYE MOVEMENTS

A common component in most engineering models of physiologic systems is a "dead-space operator" or dead zone (see Appendix). The dead zone is a threshold region. Under *normal* viewing conditions, when an input exceeds its threshold value, a response is likely to occur (more than 50% of the time). In general the larger the input, the more likely it is to elicit a correlated system motor response. As emphasized by Young,[76] however, a better term might be "indifference threshold" as it is used by those engineers who study manual control to indicate that the stimulus change can, indeed, be noticed but is simply too small to warrant correction most of the time. With special training or instruction and heightened attention one might, indeed, be able to respond consistently to stimuli falling within the dead zone,[73] but the presence of such responses in no way invalidates this threshold concept under normal tracking conditions.[76]

The saccadic eye movement system has such a dead zone (see Fig. 3-8, *A;* discussion in previous section). Based on experimental results in which subjects tracked various small-amplitude (3- to 60-min arc) steps horizon-tally about the fovea and using probability density function analysis, Young[76] estimated that the saccadic dead zone was approximately ±0.25 to ±0.30 degrees. Considering that the role of the saccadic system is to correct position errors rapidly so that the object is placed *within* the foveal region, not necessarily precisely on the functional sensory-motor center, the concept of a dead zone is quite logical. Young also found that the probability of executing a corrective saccade to a given small step displacement increased with time (Fig. 3-13), primarily because of the occurrence of slow drift, which might accumulate and gradually displace the retinal image toward the edge of the dead zone. He indicated that the fixation error at time (t) >0 was the sum of the initial fixation error (before target displacement), the amplitude of the new target displacement, and, for times greater than the initial sampling period (>200 to 250 msec), the random eye drift.

TRANSIENT VERGENCE CHANGES DURING SACCADES

Although saccade onset in each eye occurs with virtually perfect synchrony[71] and saccades are considered conjugate (at least with respect to final amplitude), there are subtle differences in the movement characteristics of each eye *during* the saccade itself. One of the earliest reports was by Bahill and others,[5] who referred to these movements as "dynamic violations of Hering's law of equal innervation." For example, a saccade might be normometric in one eye and exhibit glissadic overshooting in the fellow eye. In that study, however, the emphasis was on the dynamic lack of conjugacy rather than the transient vergence change and its implications.

Recent studies have investigated transient vergence changes during saccades in greater detail and over a wider range of movements than in the study of Bahill and others.[5] During horizontal saccades there is a dynamic divergence of up to 3 degrees.[18] This divergence

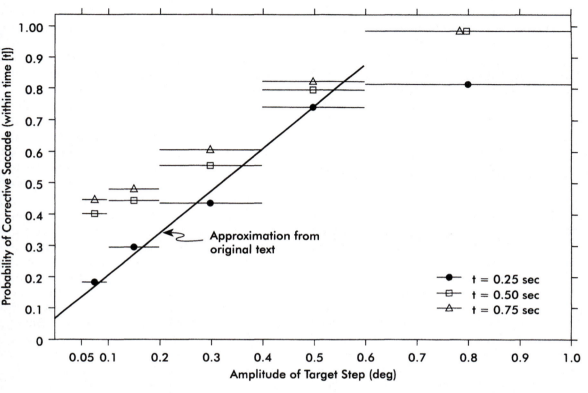

FIG. 3-13   Probability of corrective saccade within specified time vs. target-step amplitude.
(From Young LR. In Zuber BL, editor: *Models of oculomotor behavior and control*, Boca Raton, Fla, 1981, CRC.)

occurs because the saccades in the abducting eye have slightly greater amplitude and peak velocity and shorter duration than those in the fellow, adducting eye have. Further, as a result of this dynamic divergence there is also a transient residual fixation disparity (up to 0.3 degrees) at the new fixation point that is reduced to more tolerable limits (for example, a few minutes of arc) within 300 msec by a combination of a conjugate drift and a convergence movement. Such transient vergence changes during saccades (for example, the return-sweep saccades while reading; see Chapter 7) were also objectively documented and briefly described by Taylor[61] more than three decades ago. Similarly, during vertical saccades there are transient changes in horizontal vergence (up to 4

degrees), with divergence in upward gaze and convergence in downward gaze.[19] As a result of this dynamic vergence there is again a transient residual fixation disparity (up to 2 degrees for very large saccades) at the new fixation point that is reduced to more tolerable limits with a few hundred milliseconds by a combination conjugate drift and an appropriate vergence movement. Vertical vergence changes during vertical saccades were considerably smaller (0 to 1 degrees at most).

The transient vergence changes are most apparent for very large (>50 degrees) saccades but are still present to a small degree during our naturally occurring saccades of 15 degrees or less. These relatively small, brief vergence changes, however, require a high-resolution eye movement system for reliable detection and quantification. They appear to be compensated rapidly and efficiently by appropriate vergence (and conjugate drift) movements. Further, the vergence and drift velocities (<3 degrees per second) associated with these brief compensatory movements are typically less than the velocities that would adversely affect either visual acuity [68] or stereo acuity[69] to any great extent.

EFFECTS OF AGING ON SACCADES

Considerable research has been conducted on the effects of aging on saccades during the past 20 years. Perhaps the most consistent finding has been the systematic increase in latency (horizontal and vertical) with age in adults (1 to 2 msec per year),[16,31,46,55,66] as is expected and, indeed, is found in all types of reaction time measures in elderly persons.[16] Thus a 70-year-old has a normal latency 50 to 100 msec longer than that in a 20-year-old. This result suggests increased higher-level processing time or reduction in neural transmissibility.[46,55] Peak saccadic velocity (horizontal and vertical) has also been shown to decrease with increased age in adults (1 deg/sec per year) in most studies,[31,46,55,66] possibly because firing asynchrony in the neural elements would produce a slightly less peaked brief pulse component. Saccadic gain, accuracy, and anticipation effects do not appear to change considerably with age in most studies[16,66] (but see Sharpe and Zackon[55] for exceptions). The magnitude of all the effects just mentioned, however, is generally not large enough to be detected on routine clinical examination.

SHORT-TERM SACCADIC ADAPTATION

Short-term saccadic adaptation (also called parametric adaptation)[40] refers to the normal, self-correcting, rapid (that is, within a few minutes) dynamic changes in effective calibration of the saccadic eye movement system (probably by the cerebellum[53]) that reduce the probability of occurrence of an inaccurate saccade. Such changes under normal conditions could arise as a result of fluctuations or small errors in the neural and biomechanical properties of the saccadic eye movement system. To maintain accurate saccades in the presence of such potential internal system variations, it is necessary to monitor the initial system error and dynamically compensate as necessary to keep this error within system tolerance and normal limits (for example, hypometria with <10% of the initial error).[10]

The general conditions needed to obtain this rapid adaptation can perhaps be best understood by briefly describing the classic experiment conducted by McLaughlin.[40] Essentially, in that paradigm a target initially steps 10 degrees to the left, and at about the time of the saccadic response the target then steps 1 degree to the right. Responses to a simple 10-degree step to the left precede and succeed the adaptive paradigm. The results are summarized in Fig. 3-14. In the initial phase, when simple 10-degree tracking occurs, saccades are reasonably accurate and exhibit only a small degree of hypometria (that is, undershoot, as expected). In the subsequent adaptive phase the primary saccade then *overshoots* the (9-degree) final target position (by 1 degree), but gradually the system gain is effectively reduced so that the initial error is once again acceptable and a 9-degree saccade is then always made *on the first attempt*. In the last phase, with simple 10-degree leftward step tracking, system gain gradually readapts, that is, increases, so that the oculomotor response is approximately 10 degrees once again.

General results[54,72] of such short-term saccadic adaptation include the following:
- Adaptation may occur after as few as 70 saccades.
- Because the time course of adaptation is exponential, it can be defined in terms of the time constant (that is, the number of conditioning saccades needed to attain

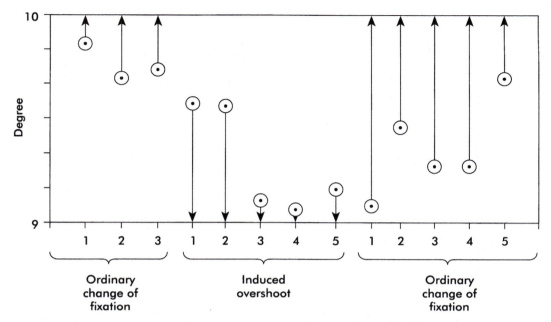

FIG. 3-14 Mean fixation-error data for nine sequences. For each eye movement, the *plotted point* shows the terminal locus of the initial saccade, and the *arrow* shows the direction and magnitude of the corrective eye movements that are necessary to bring the eye onto the target. Only the last three eye movements in the first *ordinary change of fixation* group are shown. In the *induced overshoot* group, only the first two and the last three eye movements are shown so that it would be possible to combine sequences in which the number of eye movements with induced overshoot varied between five and nine.

(From McLaughlin SC: *Percept Psychophy* 2:359, 1967.)

63% of the final adaptation amount).

- The system response decrease is faster, easier, and more complete than the system response increase. A decrease probably represents a general overall reduction in gain, whereas an increase may represent a specific endpoint adjustment.
- Adaptation is directionally selective; therefore response changes are unidirectional.
- Response reduction is adapted for a range of saccade amplitudes; therefore the effect exhibits transfer beyond the specific step amplitude used to obtain the initial adaptation.
- The system exhibits the same time course of adaptation whether the error step amplitude is progressively increased or just remains fixed at the final level.
- The individual is not consciously aware of the ongoing adaptive process.

RELATIONSHIP BETWEEN PEAK VELOCITY AND AMPLITUDE: MAIN SEQUENCE

One way to assess the overall neurologic integrity of the saccadic eye movement system noninvasively in the clinic or clinic laboratory (other than using various brain imaging techniques) is to record them objectively and then quantify the relationship between saccades of various amplitudes and their respective peak velocities. This relationship has been called

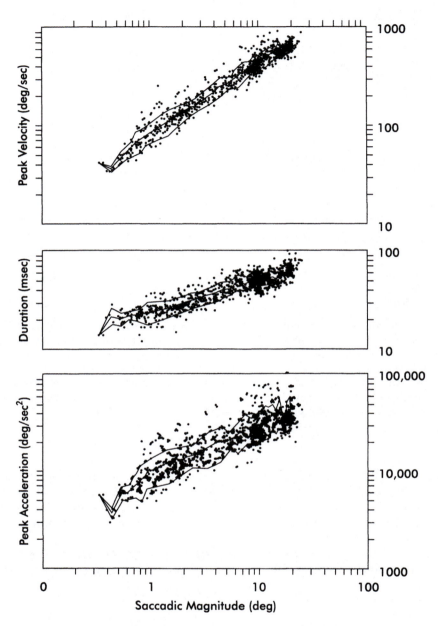

FIG. 3-15 Main-sequence diagrams showing peak velocity, duration, and the first peak acceleration as functions of saccadic magnitude for the saccadic eye movements of 13 individuals with normal vision. The magnitudes were computed from records with a band width extending from 0 to 300 Hz; peak velocities and durations were derived from records with an 80-Hz band width; accelerations were derived from 60-Hz band-width records.

(From Bahill AT, Brockenbrough A, Troost T: *Invest Ophthalmol Vis Sci* 21:116, 1981.)

TABLE 3-2   *Saccadic Magnitude, Peak Velocity, and Duration for Representative Saccades in Normal Young Adults*

Magnitude (deg)	Peak Velocity and S.D. (deg/sec)	Duration and S.D. (msec)
5	261 ± 42	42 ± 8
10	410 ± 67	51 ± 8
15	499 ± 43	54 ± 7
20	657 ± 78	64 ± 6

From Bahill AT, Brockenbrough A, Troost T: *Invest Ophthalmol Vis Sci* 21:116, 1981.

BOX 3-1   *Factors That May Reduce Peak Saccadic Velocity*

- Drugs that reduce alertness (alcohol, barbiturates, and diazepam)
- Diseases (systemic: Grave's disease; neurologic: Alzheimer's disease, acquired immunodeficiency syndrome [AIDS])
- Peripheral nerve palsy
- Darkness (10% slower)
- Infancy (if infant is not fully aroused)
- Age
- Reduced attention
- Fatigue
- Orbital direction (centripetal slightly faster than centrifugal)
- Gaze angle (extreme gaze resulting from biomechanic and neurologic limitations)
- Hemifield (upper hemifield slightly slower than lower)

the *main sequence.*[6] The main sequence can also be extended to include saccade duration and saccade peak acceleration and deceleration. One such combined plot[4] for normal individuals is presented in Fig. 3-15. Clearly, as saccade amplitude increases, the correlated saccade duration (= 2.2 × amplitude + 21 msec), peak velocity, and peak acceleration systematically increase over the range for which they are typically tested (Table 3-2). Saccades evoked by most normal means and conditions faithfully follow this relationship. However, important exceptions are listed in Box 3-1.

The main sequence relationship reflects the pulse component of the pulse-step neurologic controller signal for saccades (see later section). Under normal test conditions for saccades (horizontal, vertical, and oblique)[11] generated over the central field (±20 degrees), each point fits within the normal dispersion or "envelope" of peak velocity values for that amplitude, thus suggesting normal integrity of the central and peripheral neurologic pathways (when system biomechanics are normal). There are no objectively documented, irrefutable cases of "supernormal" saccades truly falling above the normal range. It is difficult to conceive how such a "superfast" saccade could be generated without a concurrent effect on its amplitude. However, saccades with clearly reduced peak velocities may, in-

deed, occur as a result of various drugs and diseases, especially of central origin, and these may effectively reduce, degrade, or distort the pulse component of the pulse-step neurocontroller signal (see Box 3-1; also see Table 10-14 in Leigh and Zee[36]).

PREDICTION

Perhaps an unusual but informative way to begin a discussion on prediction is to define what it is not. An unpredictable input ". . . denotes a pattern of target motion which is sufficiently unconstrained so that the subject obtains little information from the past portion of the signal to permit him to predict the future motion of the target. Thus, any attempt by the subject to anticipate or predict the target movement will be in vain."[56] Our own corollary to that quotation follows: "If you provide someone with a predictable input, they will rapidly learn to predict." Saccades are generally considered to exhibit prediction when their reaction times range from approximately 200 msec *before* to 150 msec *after* tar-

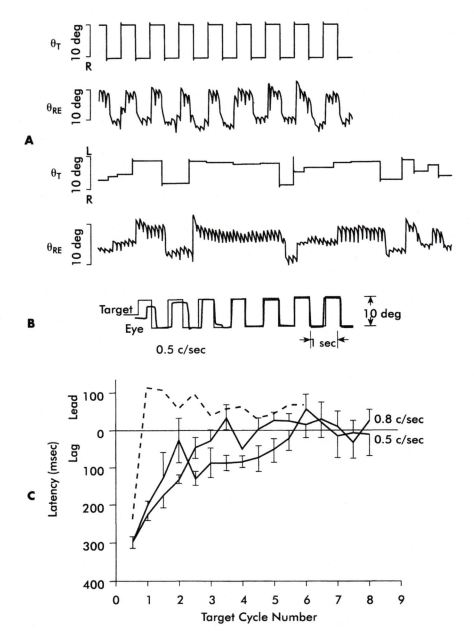

FIG. 3-16 **A,** Saccadic tracking. Jerk nystagmus superimposed on otherwise normal predictable *(top)* and nonpredictable *(bottom)* responses. **B,** Typical eye response to an 0.8-cycles-per-second (c/sec) horizontal target. **C,** Time course of adaptation of the saccadic latency to periodic square-waves averaged for two naive human subjects. Each *point* represents the mean of seven runs; the *vertical bars* represent standard errors of the mean. The *dashed line* is the average of three runs on one naive subject at 0.5 c/sec under experimental conditions designed to simulate the monkey experiments.

(**A,** from Ciuffreda KJ: *Am J Optom Physiol Optics* 56:521, 1979; **B,** from Fuchs AF: *J Physiol* 193:161, 1967.)

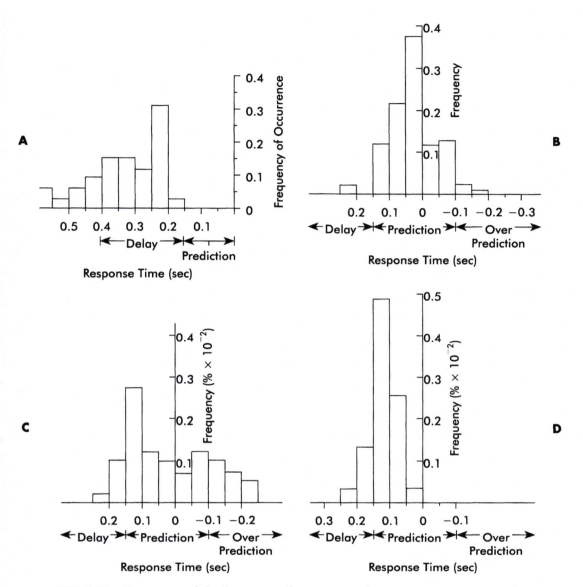

FIG. 3-17 Histograms of the frequency of occurrence of eye movement response times for target motions of irregular steps and regular square-waves of different frequencies. **A,** Irregular steps. **B,** Square-waves, 0.4 cycles per second (c/sec). **C,** Square-waves, 1.0 c/sec. **D,** Square-wave, 1.5 c/sec.

(From Stark L: *Neurological control systems: studies in bioengineering*, New York, 1968, Plenum.)

get movement (Figs. 3-16, *A, B, C,* and 3-17, *A, B, C,* and *D*). Predictable saccades are generally quite hypometric.[13]

Individuals of all ages and backgrounds demonstrate prediction, frequently within 5 cycles or so of repetitive target motion.[25,51] Presence of such a "predictor operator" is evident in experimental findings in both adults and young children. In the classic study by Stark and colleagues,[58,59] trained adults horizontally tracked either unpredictable steps (with respect to direction, amplitude, and duration) or predictable steps (10-degree amplitude and 0.05- to 2-Hz frequencies) over the central field. Prediction was greatest at the intermediate frequencies (0.4 to 1.0 Hz) with a peak at 0.8 Hz. However, prediction was still present to some degree with frequencies as low as 0.2 Hz and as high as 1.5 Hz. Similar results in adults were later found by Dallos and Jones.[21] Young children demonstrate the same predictive capacity.[50]

NEUROANATOMIC CONTROL OF AND SIGNAL PROCESSING FOR SACCADIC EYE MOVEMENTS

In this section we attempt to provide a brief overview of the major neuroanatomic structures involved in the generation of saccadic eye movements. Over the past decade or so, much has been learned about these structures and their sequence of information flow, thus resulting in a neural network of ever greater complexity. Therefore our emphasis is restricted to those aspects most relevant to the clinician.

The neural control aspect may be divided into two main categories.[36] The first, considered to reflect higher-level control processes, includes the primary structures involved in target selection, localization, and initial calculation of the desired change in eye position, as well as external shaping of the final neural signal. The second, considered to reflect lower-level control processes, includes primary structures involved in the actual generation of the pulse-step controller signal to the oculomotor neurons.

The primary higher-level control structures[24,26,41] include the frontal eye fields, parietal lobes, superior colliculus, and cerebellum (Tables 3-3 and 3-4). The frontal eye fields and parietal lobes are cortical structures that transmit information to the superior colliculus. The parietal lobes are primarily involved in provid-

ing information about target localization, although they may also contribute to the initial computation of the motor error. The frontal eye fields are primarily involved in the attention and selection process of targets for future foveation. Since the frontal eye fields essentially contain a neural map of visual space, they provide the requisite initial information about desired saccade amplitude and direction. The superior colliculus processes this information, encodes it for the desired eye position change, and transmits it to brainstem structures involved in generating the coded pulse-step signal. The cerebellum acts as a "calibrating organ,"[53] attempting to maintain saccadic gain within normal tolerances and thus influencing the final pulse outcome.

The second, lower-level process involves the actual generation of the pulse-step neural controller signal.[33] This signal-processing phase demands precise synchronization of two basic neural elements—*burst* and *pause* neurons[36] (Fig. 3-18). The *burst neurons* for horizontal saccades are located within the paramedian pontine reticular formation (PPRF) or pons; those for vertical and torsional saccades are situated within the rostral interstitial nucleus of the medial longitudinal fasciculus (MLF). The *short-lead excitatory burst neurons* (EBN) only begin high-frequency firing just before and during a saccade. They produce the pulse of neural activity that is correlated with the peak velocity and amplitude of a saccade. The *long-lead excitatory burst neurons* (LLBN) exhibit firing rates that are of low frequency and irregular, and their activity may occur several hundred milliseconds before a saccade. Long-lead excitatory burst neurons are probably involved in synchronization of overall premotor saccadic pulse generation. In contrast, the *pause neurons,* which are located in the nucleus raphe interpositus of the midbrain, fire continuously *except* just before and during a saccade. They act to inhibit the EBN during saccadic-free periods.

TABLE 3-3 *Higher-Level Neuroanatomic Sites That Influence Saccadic Pulse Generation*

Site	Functional Role(s)
Frontal eye fields	Regions mapped with respect to size and direction of a saccade; send such information related to future saccade generation to superior colliculus; inhibit fixation "reflex" to permit occurrence of future saccade.
Parietal lobe	Sends information related to localizing and attending to future targets in the fields and sends computations related to saccade amplitude and direction to superior colliculus.
Superior colliculus	Receives input related to intended saccade direction and amplitude from frontal eye fields and parietal lobes; regions mapped with respect to size and direction of future intended saccade; encodes desired eye position change with respect to fovea and relays this information to brainstem.
Cerebellum	Receives input from brainstem and related structures involved in saccade generation; outputs to brainstem and other saccade-related sites to maintain or adapt saccadic gain, or both, and therefore controls saccadic accuracy.

TABLE 3-4 *Effects of Lesions in Some Higher-Level Sites on Saccadic Eye Movements in Humans*

Site	Effect
Frontal eye fields	May produce increased saccadic latencies, slowed saccades, and impaired predictive tracking.
Parietal lobe	May produce increased saccadic latencies, hypometria, slowed saccades, impaired predictive tracking, and moderate ocular motor apraxia.
Superior colliculus	Isolated lesions not reported.
Cerebellum	May produce saccadic dysmetria (especially hypermetria).

Thus the basic sequence of events is probably as follows (Fig. 3-19):

1. The pause cells receive information from higher-level centers, such as the superior colliculus and frontal eye fields and perhaps also the LLBN, that a saccade is being planned. These signals act to inhibit the pause cells.
2. The inhibited pause cells thereby release their inhibitory influence on the EBN, thus allowing the EBN to fire precisely when the pause cells are quiescent. This EBN signal is the pulse component of the pulse-step saccadic neural signal.
3. The pulse signal bifurcates; it goes to the oculomotor neurons as well as to the neural integrator. The neural integrator for horizontal saccades is located in the nucleus prepositus hypoglossi and in the medial vestibular nucleus, whereas for vertical saccades it is located in the interstitial nucleus of Cajal (and related midbrain structures).
4. The neural integrator converts this eye velocity-coded information into eye position-coded information; therefore the pulse becomes a step.
5. The individual pulse and step components combine at the oculomotor neurons to become the pulse-step controller signal that is transmitted to the appropriate oculomotor nerve(s) and then to the

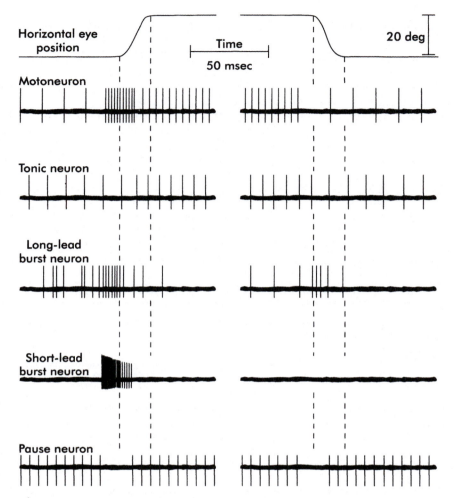

FIG. 3-18 Typical neural discharge patterns of brainstem cells during saccadic eye movements. The *vertical dashed lines* mark the onset and offset of a saccade in the ipsilateral (left) and contralateral (right) directions. All the cell types shown except the motor neuron are found in the paramedian pontine reticular formation. Tonic neurons are better named eye position–related and are most frequently found in the vestibular nucleus and the nucleus prepositus.

(From Keller EL. In Carpenter RHS, editor: *Vision and visual dysfunction*, vol 8, *Eye movements*, Boca Raton, Fla, 1991, CRC.)

extraocular muscle(s) to produce a saccadic eye movement.

ABNORMAL SACCADES

Abnormalities of saccadic eye movements can be of the following major varieties[36] (Box 3-2).

• *Slowed dynamics.* Slowed dynamics occur when the peak velocity (for a given amplitude) is below normal limits[62] (such as two standard errors below the group mean value) (Fig. 3-20). Saccade duration is also prolonged. This abnormality may be due to failure to develop or to a dis-

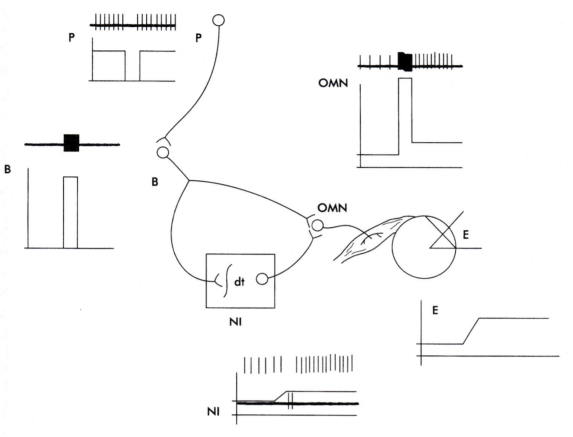

FIG. 3-19 The relationship between pause cells *(P)*, burst cells *(B)*, and the cells of the neural integrator *(NI)* in the generation of the saccadic pulse and step. Pause cells cease discharging just before each saccade, allowing the burst cells to generate the pulse. The pulse is integrated *(dt)* by the neural integrator to produce the step. The pulse and step combine to produce the innervational change on the ocular motoneurons *(OMN)* that produces the saccadic eye movements *(E)*. *Vertical lines* represent individual discharges of neurons. Underneath the schematized neural (spike) discharge is a plot of discharge rate versus time. All presented as a function of time.

(From Leigh RJ, Zee DS: *The neurology of eye movements,* ed 2, Philadelphia, 1991, FA Davis.)

turbance in the normal pulse-step neural controller signal. An interesting exception occurs in myasthenia gravis.[74,75] In that case the saccadic neural signal and its correlated peak velocity are, indeed, normal. During the latter half of the actual movement itself, however, intrasaccadic fatigue occurs, resulting in abnormal slowing and prolongation of its trajectory (Fig. 3-21).

• *Inaccurate amplitude.* The occurrence of dysmetric saccades, in which the first or primary saccade is either significantly larger or smaller (that is, markedly hypermetric or hypometric) than that required for foveation (Fig. 3-22, *A* and *B*). In many cases inaccurate amplitude takes the form of a static overshoot or undershoot,[62] which necessitates progressively smaller corrective saccades (dictated by

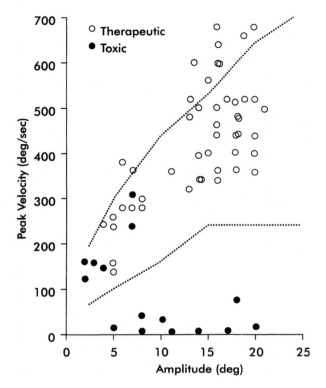

FIG. 3-20 Peak velocity–amplitude relationships of saccades recorded during anticonvulsant toxicity *(filled circles)* and while anticonvulsant levels were in therapeutic range *(open circles). Dotted lines* encompass normal range (±SD) of elderly persons (ages 59 to 87 years). All *filled circles* falling within the normal range were hypometric. The remaining *filled circles* were orthometric but slow.

(From Thurston SE and others: *Neurology* 34:1593, 1984.)

the normal neural "feed-forward" gain [Figure 3-23, *A* and *B*]) for eventual foveation.[32,53] This situation is probably due to gain fluctuations and biases in the cerebellum.[53]

• *Delayed initiation.* Delayed initiation is the abnormally long reaction time (that is, the time between onset of target movement and onset of eye movement) or latency in response to a new stimulus (generally visual) in the field.[43] This delay is probably due to signal processing and de-

cision making, although transmission time delays may also be involved in neurologic diseases such as multiple sclerosis in which demyelination occurs.

The following conditions commonly observed on clinical examination merit brief discussion:

• *Parkinson's disease.* Parkinson's disease is a disorder of the extrapyramidal brain nu-

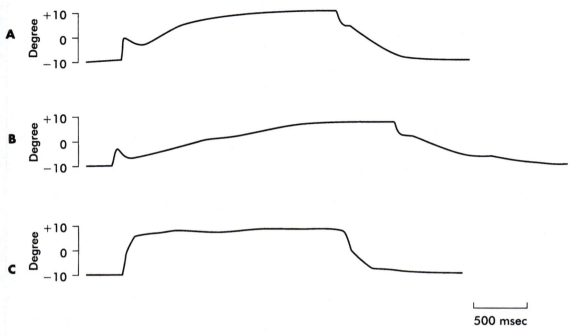

FIG. 3-21   Saccadic waveforms during attempted 20-degree horizontal refixations in a patient with myasthenia gravis (MG). **A,** Without edrophonium or fatigue. **B,** After fatigue. **C,** After edrophonium administration. Plus *(+)* indicates right and minus *(–)* indicates left.

(From Yee RD and others: *Arch Ophthalmol* 94:1465, 1976.)

clei caused by a dopamine deficiency that results in impaired neural inhibition. Primary signs are muscle rigidity, akinesia, bradykinesia (slowness of movement), and tremor. In eye movements a degeneration of dopaminergic neurons occurs in the substantia nigra, a structure projecting to the superior colliculus. Saccadic abnormalities include hypometria and increased latency as well as reduced peak velocity and increased duration ("ocular bradykinesia").[47,56,60,70] These defects are more consistently found in "voluntary" tracking paradigms (multiple visible targets, remembered targets, and predictable targets) than in "reflexive" tracking paradigms involving random step stimuli.[60] The combined saccadic abnormalities suggest involvement of nigrocolliculoreticular pathways.[47]

• *Multiple sclerosis.* Multiple sclerosis is a disorder characterized by progressive degeneration of white matter of the brain and spinal cord, thus causing delay or disruption of neural transmission. Visual problems (diplopia, blurred vision, ophthalmoplegia, nystagmus, and optic neuritis) may be among the first signs or symptoms. General muscle dysfunction may include weakness, spasticity, tremor, hyperreflexia, and ataxia. Saccadic abnormalities include increased latency (including marked-onset asynchrony) and dysmetria as well as decreased peak velocity and increased duration (especially on adduction, suggesting bilateral internuclear ophthalmoplegia involving the medial longitudinal fasciculus).[38,43,48] Whole-body heat, for example, as occasioned during a hot shower, may temporarily exacerbate the

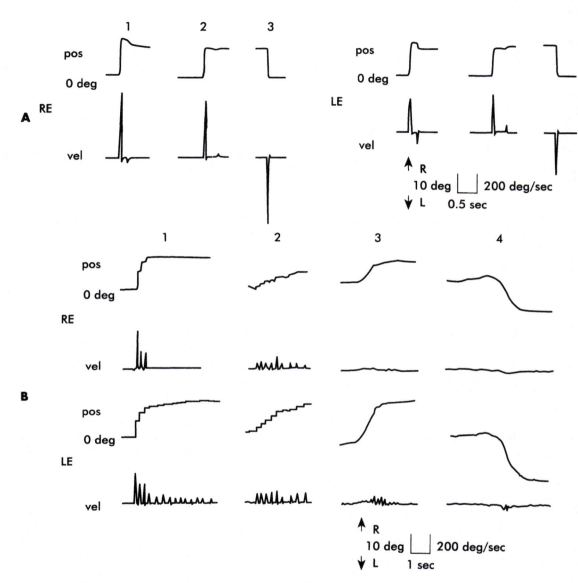

FIG. 3-22 **A,** Example of saccades recorded while anticonvulsant levels were in therapeutic range. Some hypermetria, *1,* as well as rare hypometria, *2,* was evident, but most saccades were orthometric, *3.* All saccades had normal peak velocities. **B,** Examples of saccades recorded during anticonvulsant toxicity. These consisted of multiple small hypometric saccades, *1* and *2,* a combination of slow and multiple small hypometric saccades, *3,* or single slow saccades, *4. LE,* left eye; *pos,* position; *RE,* right eye; and *vel,* velocity.

(From Thurston SE and others: *Neurology* 34:1593, 1984.)

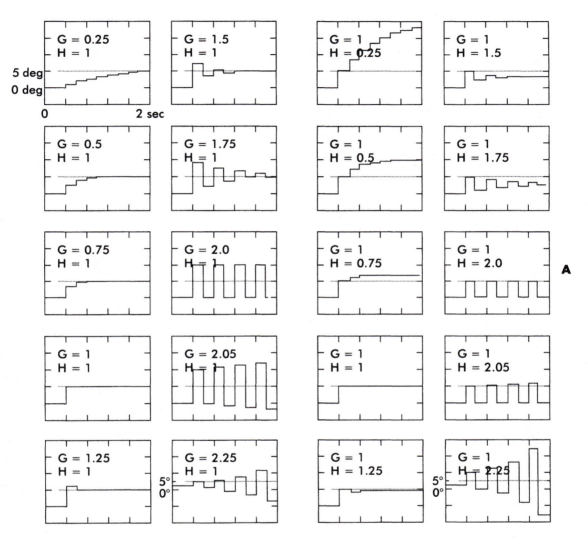

FIG. 3-23 **A,** Simulation of sampled-data model for human saccadic control system. The *two left columns* show the results of variation in the forward loop gain. The total feedback gain, *H,* is held at unity. Hypometric saccades are produced for 0 < forward gain *(G)* < 1; normometric saccades for G = 1; and hypermetric saccades for 1 < G < 2. Limit cycles occur when G = 2, and unstable oscillations are produced when G > 2. The *two right columns* show the effect of variation in feedback gain. Forward gain, *G,* is unity. The first saccade after a fixation change is always on target if forward gain G = 1, irrespective of the value of H. When H < 1, final eye position is greater than target position; when H > 1, oscillations occur and final eye position is less than target position. H = 2 leads to limit cycles, whereas, when H > 2, increasing oscillations result.

Continued.

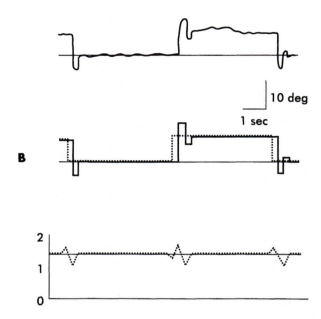

FIG. 3-23, cont'd. **B,** Model simulation of patient data. Unsustained overshoot dysmetria. *Top trace* shows actual patient records. *Middle trace* shows corresponding model response; *(solid line* indicates model response; *broken line* indicates stimulus). *Bottom trace* shows abnormal gain fluctuation pattern *(broken line* indicates gain values used in simulation; *solid line* indicates the average of the gain fluctuations).

(**A,** from Hsu FK, Krishnan VV, Stark L: *Ann Biomed Eng* 4:321, 1976; **B,** from Selhorst JB and others: *Brain* 99:497, 1976.)

abnormalities, including the saccadic dysfunctions.[9] Using *objective* recording techniques, saccadic abnormalities were found in two thirds of patients with well-documented cases of multiple sclerosis although their eye movements were *normal* on clinical examination.[57] Such a striking result clearly demonstrates the importance of objective eye movement recordings in the clinical setting.

• *Myasthenia gravis.* Myasthenia gravis is an autoimmune disease. Effectiveness of acetylcholine released from the presynaptic membrane is decreased, since antibodies are bonded to postsynaptic acetylcholine receptor motor endplates. This decreased effectiveness produces intermittent conduction block of the neural signals.[23] Saccadic abnormalities include

dysmetria (generally hypometria) with markedly variable waveforms and increased duration *without* decreased peak velocity as a result of late intrasaccadic fatigue (see Fig. 3-21). Latency remains normal.[53,74,75] Injection of edrophonium (Tensilon) results in temporary hypermetria, suggesting a central adaptation phenomenon (under normal conditions) in which a saccadic neural signal is generated for a slightly *larger*-than-intended movement to compensate for the anticipated intrasaccadic muscle fatigue effect.[74]

• *Acquired immunodeficiency syndrome* (AIDS). AIDS is a disorder of the cellular immune system resulting from the presence of the human immunodeficiency retrovirus (HIV). AIDS causes severe, recurrent infections and neoplasms. Abnormal eye movements may be the *first* sign of frank neurologic involvement, despite ocular motility that is normal on clinical examination.[20,42] Thus objective eye movement recording may have a critical impact on the clinician's diagnostic and prognostic capabilities. Saccadic abnormalities include hypometria as well as decreased peak velocity and increased duration; latency is normal.[20,29,42] The slowed saccades may reflect a defect in burst neurons of the paramedian pontine reticular formation, not of cortical regions in which such neurologic involvement is typically absent.[42]

The "antisaccade task"[27] is one of the most interesting saccade stimulus paradigms used to investigate the higher-level decision-making processes in neurologic disease. In this unique approach the patient is required to make a saccade in the *opposite* direction from but of equal magnitude to the random step of target displacement, that is, the mirror direction. This difficult task requires suppressing the so-called visual grasp reflex to acquire (foveate) the target and establishing an oppositely directed saccade motor program. Patients with frontal lobe lesions, Huntington's disease, and Alzheimer's disease exhibit marked abnormalities in performing this task.[36] To some clinicians it represents the most sensitive indicator of eye movement dysfunction in these conditions.[36] This antisaccade paradigm deserves further serious consideration both in the clinic and in laboratory settings. See Leigh and Zee[36] for a review of other suggested higher-level, cognitively-based voluntary saccade paradigms (such as prediction, remembered target locations, sequencing, and gap-overlap) of potential clinical significance.

Patients who have oculomotor muscle paresis ("neuromuscular asymmetry") exhibit unidirectional saccadic adaptation or plasticity (see earlier discussion),[1,34,45] which is in compliance with Hering's law of equal innervation (see Chapter 1). This situation is clearly shown in Fig. 3-24, *A*, *B*, and *C*. When the paretic eye is viewing (or under habitual viewing conditions), saccades in the direction of the paretic muscle are noticeably hypometric in the paretic eye and relatively normometric in the normal eye. Since the neural innervation to corresponding muscle pairs is the same, the paretic muscle effectively acts to reduce saccadic gain (at a relatively *peripheral* level) in the eye. Furthermore, glissadic undershooting (that is, "postsaccadic drift") is present in the paretic eye, suggesting a pulse-step mismatch. Saccades in the opposite direction are normal and of equal amplitude in each eye. Then the normal eye is patched for 5 days, and the patient is retested with the paretic eye viewing. Saccades in the direction of the paretic muscle are then normometric in the paretic eye and hypermetric in the fellow normal eye. In addition, the postsaccadic drift is much reduced. Thus a progressive increase in and *central* adaptation of saccadic gain occurred to achieve eventual saccadic accuracy in the viewing eye. This gain change reflects an adaptive increase in neural pulse width to obtain an accurate saccade. The reduction in glissadic undershoot that followed the primary saccade reflects more accurate pulse-step matching, which also serves to enhance saccadic accuracy.

Patients with moderate to high dioptric amounts of spectacle-corrected spherical anisometropia ("optical asymmetry") *and* normal binocular vision exhibit saccadic adaptation or plasticity that of necessity does not precisely follow Hering's law of equal innervation.[22,30,44] Because of the interocular difference in magnification in every meridian (that is, overall aniseikonia), saccades of precisely equal amplitude over an isovergence surface (such as a perimeter) *do not* bifixate the new object of regard. Any sort of conjugate recalibration process would not be useful in these patients, since it would serve only to correct neural or mechanical deficiencies that were equal in the two eyes. Thus it was found

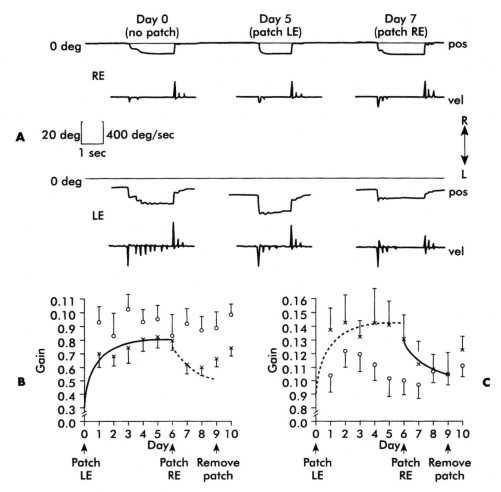

FIG. 3-24.   **A,** Eye movement position *(pos)* and velocity *(vel)* records of both eyes taken on days 0, 5, and 7 under the patch conditions indicated. **B,** Saccadic gain (G) variations of the right eye during right fixation for movements in both the paretic (leftward) and the nonparetic (rightward) direction. *Solid curve* is the best mean-squares fit exponential: $G=0.79 (1-0.59e-t/0.85)$ $(r^2=0.84)$. Dashed curve is from **C** and is fitted by eye to the right eye data. In this, vertical bars indicate one standard deviation. **C,** Saccadic gain variations of the left eye during left eye fixation. *Solid curve* is the best mean-squares fit exponential: $G=1+0.28e-t/1.54$ $(r^2=0.89)$. Dashed curve is from **B** and is fitted by eye to the left eye data.

(From Abel LA, Schmidt D, Dell'Osso LF, Daroff RB: *Ann Neurol* 4:313, 1978.)

that such individuals generate slightly *unequal* saccades under both binocular *and* monocular viewing conditions. These results suggest a range-limited selective recalibration process, probably involving the cerebellum,[63] which exerts influence on a muscle (or muscles) of only one eye, and thus in effect alters the sensitivity (or gain) of the relevant oculomotor neurons to that eye alone. Such a process would be helpful in compensating for small changes that occur during normal development, aging, or disease, which may be local and nonuniform in the tissues.[22] In some cases such a process may also explain the changes in eye alignment that occur after successful surgery for strabismus, in which one muscle has been mechanically "weakened."

REVIEW QUESTIONS

1. Describe how prediction affects both the reaction time and the accuracy of a saccade.
2. With aid of a carefully labeled diagram, describe the results of Westheimer's experiment concerning pulse and step stimuli. How does this experiment demonstrate the sampled-data notion?
3. Discuss the evidence for and against the idea that the saccadic system responds in a sampled-data manner.
4. Describe the various ways in which saccades may be adversely affected by neurologic disease.
5. What is meant by the "dead zone of saccadic eye movements"? If there were no dead zone, how would that affect oculomotor responsivity?
6. Describe the neural elements and their timing sequence in formulation of the pulse-step saccadic motoneuronal controller signal.
7. What is the "main sequence" for saccades? How is it useful in the clinical setting?
8. Why is saccadic adaptation of value to the ocular motor system?

REFERENCES

1. Abel LA, Schmidt D, Dell'Osso LF, Daroff RB: Saccadic system plasticity in humans, *Ann Neurol* 4:313, 1978.
2. Bahill AT: *Bioengineering: biomedical, medical, and clinical engineering*, Englewood Cliffs, NJ, 1981, Prentice-Hall.
3. Bahill AT, Adler D, Stark L: Most naturally occurring human saccades have magnitudes of 15 degrees or less, *Invest Ophthalmol* 14:468, 1975.
4. Bahill AT, Brockenbrough A, Troost T: Variability and development of a normative data base for saccadic eye movements, *Invest Ophthalmol Vis Sci* 21:116, 1981.
5. Bahill AT, Ciuffreda KJ, Kenyon RV, Stark L: Dynamic and static violations of Hering's law of equal innervation, *Am J Optom Physiol Optics* 53:786, 1976.
6. Bahill AT, Clark MR, Stark L: The main sequence, a tool for studying human eye movements, *Math Biosci* 24:194, 1975.
7. Bahill AT, Stark L: The trajectories of saccadic eye movements, *Sci Am* 240:108, 1979.
8. Bahill AT, Troost BT: Types of saccadic eye movements, *Neurology* 29:1150, 1979.
9. Bajada S, Mastaglia FL, Black JL, Colling DWK: Effects of induced hyperthermia on visual evoked potentials and saccadic parameters in normal subjects and multiple sclerosis patients, *J Neurol Neurosurg Psychiatry* 43:849, 1980.
10. Baloh RW, Honrubia V: Reaction time and accuracy of the saccadic eye movements of normal subjects in a moving-target task, *Aviat Space Environ Med* 47:1165, 1976.
11. Becker W: Saccades. In Carpenter RHS, editor: *Vision and visual dysfunction*, vol 8, (Eye movements), Boca Raton, Fla, 1991, CRC.
12. Becker W, Jurgens R: An analysis of the saccadic system by means of double-step stimuli, *Vision Res* 19:967, 1979.
13. Bronstein AM, Kennard C: Predictive eye saccades are different from visually-triggered saccades, *Vision Res* 27:517, 1987.
14. Campbell FW, Wurtz RH: Saccadic omission: why we do not see a grey-out during a saccadic eye movement, *Vision Res* 18:1297, 1978.
15. Carpenter RHS: *Movements of the eyes*, ed 2, London, 1988, Pion.
16. Carter JE, Obler L, Woodward S, Albert ML: The effect of increasing age on the latency of saccadic eye movements, *J Gerontol* 38:318, 1983.
17. Ciuffreda KJ: Jerk nystagmus: some new findings, *Am J Optom Physiol Optics* 56:521, 1979.
18. Collewijn H, Erkelens CJ, Steinman RM: Binocular coordination of human horizontal saccadic eye movements, *J Physiol* 404:157, 1988.
19. Collewijn H, Erkelens CJ, Steinman RM: Binocular coordination of human vertical saccadic eye movements, *J Physiol* 404:183, 1988.

20. Currie J, Benson E, Ramsden B, Perdices M, Cooper D: Eye movement abnormalities as a predictor of the acquired immunodeficiency syndrome dementia complex, *Arch Neurol* 45:949, 1988.
21. Dallos PJ, Jones RW: Learning behavior of the eye fixation, *IEEE Trans Automatic Control* AC-8:218, 1963.
22. Erkelens CJ, Collewijn H, Steinman RM: Asymmetrical adaptation of human saccades to anisometropic spectacles, *Invest Ophthal Vis Sci* 30:1132, 1989.
23. Feldon SE, Stark L, Lehman SL, Hoyt WF: Oculomotor effects of intermittent conduction block in myasthenia gravis and Guillain-Barré syndrome, *Arch Neurol* 39:497, 1982.
24. Fischer B, Boch R: Cerebral cortex. In Carpenter RHS, editor: *Vision and visual dysfunction,* vol 8, *(eye movements),* Boca Raton, Fla, 1991, CRC.
25. Fuchs AF: Periodic eye tracking in monkey, *J Physiol* 193:161, 1967.
26. Guitton D: Control of saccadic eye and gaze movements by the superior colliculus and basal ganglia. In Carpenter RHS, editor: *Vision and visual dysfunction,* vol 8, *Eye movements,* Boca Raton, Fla, 1991, CRC.
27. Hallett PE: Primary and secondary saccades to goals defined by instructions, *Vision Res* 18:1279, 1978.
28. Hamed LM, Schatz NJ, Galetta SL: Brainstem ocular motility defects and AIDS, *Am J Ophthalmol* 106:437, 1988.
29. Henson DB: Corrective saccades: effects of altering visual feedback, *Vision Res* 18:63, 1978.
30. Henson DB, Dharamshi BC: Oculomotor adaptation and anisometropia, *Invest Ophthalmol Vis Sci* 22:234, 1982.
31. Hotson JR, Steinke GW: Vertical and horizontal saccades in aging and dementia, *Neuro-ophthal* 8:267, 1988.
32. Hsu FK, Krishnan VV, Stark L: Simulation of ocular dysmetria using a sampled-data model of the human saccadic system, *Ann Biomed Eng* 4:321, 1976.
33. Keller EL: The brainstem. In Carpenter RHS, editor: *Vision and visual dysfunction,* vol 8, *Eye movements,* Boca Raton, Fla, 1991, CRC.
34. Kommerell G, Olivier D, Theopold H: Adaptive programming of phasic and tonic components in saccadic eye movements: investigations in patients with abducens palsy, *Invest Ophthalmol* 15:657, 1976.
35. Latour PL: Visual threshold during eye movements, *Vis Res* 2:261, 1962.
36. Leigh RJ, Zee DS: *The neurology of eye movements,* Philadelphia, 1991, ed 2, FA Davis.
37. Lemij HG, Collewijn H: Differences in accuracy of human saccades between stationary and jumping targets, *Vision Res* 29:1737, 1989.
38. Mastaglia FL, Black JL, Thickbroom G, Colling DWK: Saccadic eye movements in multiple sclerosis, *Neuro-ophthal* 2:225, 1982.
39. Matin E, Clymer AB, Matin L: Metacontrast and saccadic suppression, *Science* 178:179, 1972.
40. McLaughlin SC: Parametric adjustment in saccadic eye movements, *Percept Psychophy* 2:359, 1967.
41. Miles FA: The cerebellum. In Carpenter RHS, editor: *Vision and visual dysfunction,* vol 8, *Eye movements,* Boca Raton, Fla, 1991, CRC.
42. Nguyen N, Rimmer S, Katz B: Slowed saccades in the acquired immunodeficiency syndrome, *Am J Ophthalmol* 107:356, 1989.
43. Ochs AL, Hoyt WF, Stark L, Patchman MA: Saccadic initiation time in multiple sclerosis, *Ann Neurol* 4:578, 1978.
44. Oohira A, Zee DS, Guyton DL: Disconjugate adaptation to longstanding large-amplitude, spectacle-corrected anisometropia, *Invest Ophthalmol Vis Sci* 32:1693, 1991.
45. Optican LM, Zee DS, Chu FC: Adaptive response to ocular muscle weakness in human pursuit and saccadic eye movements, *J Neurophysiol* 54:110, 1985.
46. Pitt MC, Rawles JM: The effect of aging on saccadic latency and velocity, *Neuro-ophthal* 8:123, 1988.
47. Rascol O, Clanet M, Montastruc JL, Simonetta M, Soulier-Esteve MJ, Doyon B, Rascol A: Abnormal ocular movements in Parkinson's disease, *Brain* 112:1193, 1989.
48. Reulen JPH, Sander EACM, Hogenhuis LAH: Eye movement disorders in multiple sclerosis and optic neuritis, *Brain* 106:121, 1983.
49. Riggs LA, Volkmann FC, Moore RK, Ellicott AG: Perception of supra-threshold stimuli during saccadic eye movement, *Vis Res* 22:423, 1982.
50. Ross SM, Ross LE: Children's and adult's predictive saccades to square-wave targets, *Vis Res* 27:2177, 1987.
51. Schmid R, Ron S: A model of eye tracking of periodic square-wave motion, *Biol Cybern* 54:179, 1986.
52. Schmidt D, Dell'Osso LF, Abel LA, Daroff RB: Myasthenia gravis: saccadic eye movement waveforms, *Exp Neurol* 68:346, 1980.
53. Selhorst JB, Stark L, Ochs AL, Hoyt WF: Disorders in cerebellar oculomotor control. I. Saccadic overshoot dysmetria: an oculographic control system and clinico-anatomic analysis, *Brain* 99:497, 1976.

54. Semmlow JL, Gauthier GM, Vercher JL: Mechanisms of short-term saccadic adaptation, *J Exper Psychol: Hum Percept Perform*, 15:249, 1989.

55. Sharpe JA, Zackson DH: Senescent saccades: effects of aging on their accuracy, latency, and velocity, *Acta Otolaryngol* 104:422, 1987.

56. Shibasaki H, Tsuji S, Kuroiwa Y: Oculomotor abnormalities in Parkinson's disease, *Arch Neurol* 36:360, 1979.

57. Solingen LD, Baloh RW, Myers L, Ellison G: Subclinical eye movement disorders in patients with multiple sclerosis, *Neurology* 27:614, 1977.

58. Stark L: *Neurological control systems: studies in bioengineering*, New York, 1968, Plenum.

59. Stark L, Vossius G, Young LR: Predictive control of eye tracking movements, *IRE Trans Hum Fact Electron* HFE-3:52, 1962.

60. Tanyeri S, Leuck CJ, Crawford TJ, Kennard C: Vertical and horizontal saccadic eye movements in Parkinson's disease, *Neuro-ophthal* 9:165, 1989.

61. Taylor EA: *The fundamental reading skill*, Springfield, Il, 1959, Charles C Thomas.

62. Thurston SE, Leigh RJ, Abel LA, Dell'Osso LF: Slow saccades and hypometria in anticonvulsant toxicity, *Neurology* 34:1593, 1984.

63. Virre E, Cadera W, Vilis T: Monocular adaptation of the saccadic system and vestibulo-ocular reflex, *Invest Ophthalmol Vis Sci* 29:1339, 1988.

64. Viviani P, Berthoz A, Tracey D: The curvature of oblique saccades, *Vision Res* 17:661, 1977.

65. Volkmann FC, Schick AML, Riggs LA: Time course of visual inhibition during voluntary saccades, *J Opt Soc Am* 58:562, 1968.

66. Warabi T, Kase M, Kato T: Effect of aging on the accuracy of visually-guided saccadic eye movement, *Ann Neurol* 16:449, 1984.

67. Westheimer G: Eye movement responses to a horizontally moving visual stimulus, *Arch Ophthalmol* 52:932, 1954.

68. Westheimer G, McKee SP: Visual acuity in the presence of retinal-image motion, *J Opt Soc Am* 65:847, 1975.

69. Westheimer G, McKee SP: Stereoscopic acuity for moving retinal images, *J Opt Soc Am* 68:450, 1978.

70. White OB, Saint-Cyr JA, Tomlinson RD, Sharpe JA: Ocular motor deficits in Parkinson's disease. II. Control of the saccadic and smooth pursuit systems, *Brain* 106:571, 1983.

71. Williams RA, Fender DF: The synchrony of binocular eye movements, *Vision Res* 17:303, 1977.

72. Wolf W, Deubel H, Hanske G: Properties of parametric adjustment in the saccadic system. In Gale AG, Johnson F, editors: *Theoretical and applied aspects of eye movement research*, Amsterdam, Holland, 1984, Elsevier.

73. Wyman D, Steinman RM: Small step tracking: implications for the oculomotor "dead zone," *Vision Res* 13:2165, 1973.

74. Yee RD, Cogan DG, Zee DS, Baloh RW, Honrubia V: Rapid eye movement in myasthenia gravis. II. Electro-oculographic analysis, *Arch Ophthalmol* 94:1465, 1976.

75. Yee RD, Whitcup SM, Williams IM, Baloh RW, Honrubia V: Saccadic eye movements in myasthenia gravis, *Ophthalmology* 94:219, 1987.

76. Young LR: The sampled-data model and foveal dead zone for saccades. In Zuber BL, editor: *Models of oculomotor behavior and control*, Boca Raton, Fla, 1981, CRC.

77. Young LR, Stark L: Variable feedback experiments testing a sampled data model for eye tracking movements, *IEEE Trans Hum Fact Electron* HFE-4:38, 1963.

78. Zuber B, Crider A, Stark L: Saccadic suppression associated with microsaccades, *Q Prog Rep Res Lab Electron MIT* 74:244, 1964.

79. Zuber B, Stark L: Saccadic suppression: elevation by visual threshold associated with saccadic eye movements, *Exp Neurol* 16:65, 1966.

Pursuit Eye Movements

Amblyopia	Prediction
Bode analysis	Training effects
Continuous control system	Velocity servomechanism
Neurologic dysfunction	

OVERVIEW OF PURSUIT

The pursuit system is our primary oculomotor route for the smooth tracking of discrete objects of interest moving in our surrounds. For example, it may be used for such diverse tasks as following a bird in flight, a car speeding on the highway, or an object moving along on a supermarket conveyor belt. At the most basic level the pursuit system's goal is to match eye velocity to target velocity as closely as possible, thus acting like a velocity servomechanism[52,62] (see later discussion for problems with this oversimplified notion). Any positional error in smooth tracking resulting in either a lead or a lag of the eye with respect to the target is typically corrected by an independently generated saccade[8,44] (Fig. 4-1). Thus sustained periods of foveal pursuit allow maximal resolution, information gathering, and processing of fine details of a moving object.

A classic experiment in the area of pursuit eye movements was conducted by Rashbass[44] in the early 1960s. He asked the following crucial question: "Are these smooth pursuit movements brought about by the *position* of the target's image on the retina or by its *movement* over the retina?" Using a precise eye movement recording system, he measured the response to a step-ramp stimulus (Fig. 4-2) (see Appendix and Chapter 8). That is, the target was initially centered on the screen; at some random time it instantaneously stepped or "jumped" a few degrees to one side and then began to move smoothly at a constant velocity in the opposite direction. He reasoned that the *initial* movement of the eye would be a saccade directed *toward* the target if positional displacement were the primary factor, whereas this initial response would be a smooth movement directed *away* from the target if its motion were the primary factor driving the eye. The latter was clearly the case: the initial movement was dictated by the motion, not position, of the target. That is, the subject initially smoothly pursued the moving *eccentric* target to match eye velocity to target velocity; this smooth pursuit was followed by

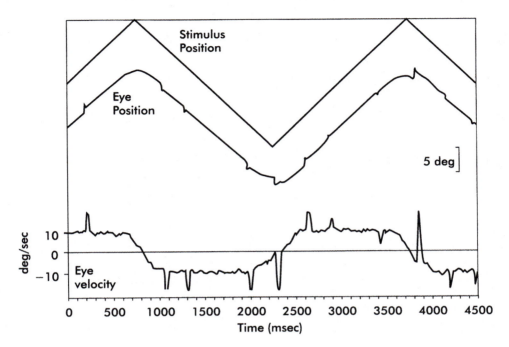

FIG. 4-1 Individual eye movements in response to triangle-wave constant velocity stimuli moving at 0.33 Hz. Upward deflections of the curves indicate rightward movements. Slow eye velocity changed before each change in target motion.

(From Boman DK, Hotson JR: *Vision Res* 32:675, 1992.)

a longer-latency foveating saccade and then by subsequent foveal pursuit.

Important facts about the pursuit system are briefly listed as follows:

- The pursuit system is traditionally viewed as a *continuous* control system[45,52,62] (Fig. 4-3, *A* and *B*); thus it samples the stimulus continuously and responds to any change within one latency period or reaction time. In contrast, the saccadic system has been conceptualized as a *sampled-data* or *discrete* system with a (relative) refractory period (see Chapter 3).

- The initial 100-msec presaccadic pursuit movement, however, is effectively open-loop (that is, not yet altered by visual feedback information); the initial 20- to 40-msec portion is independent of target stimulus characteristics and simply func-

tions to initiate an eye movement in the correct direction. Only the latter 60-msec period is loosely related to target velocity and eccentricity[32,54] (Fig. 4-4). Subsequent pursuit related to either real or perceived target velocity is under visual feedback control (that is, closed-loop).

- The pursuit system has a latency of 100 msec with little variability (±5 msec); latency is slightly longer (by as much as 25 msec) for slow target velocities (≤5 degrees per second)[9] (Fig. 4-5).

- Closed-loop pursuit gain (ratio of eye velocity to target velocity, determined at the midpoint or maximal-velocity portion of the response; see Appendix) is generally 0.90 to 0.95[49] (Table 4-1) (low normal is 0.7[47]), indicating a high degree of accuracy for target velocities up to 30 to 40

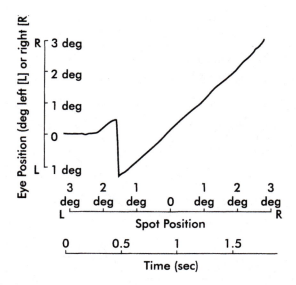

FIG. 4-2 Record of the eye movement caused by watching a spot that is suddenly given a change of position in one direction and then a change of velocity in the opposite direction. *L*, Left; *R*, right.

(From Rashbass C: *Nature* 183:897, 1959.)

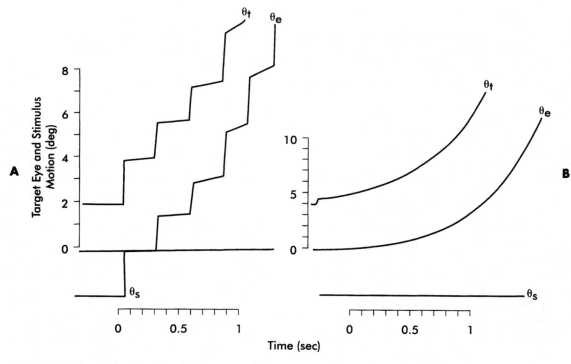

FIG. 4-3 The Tantalus-like pursuit of a target under positive visual feedback for the saccadic mode **(A)** and the smooth pursuit mode **(B).** The top trace is target position (θ_t), the middle trace is eye movement (θ_e), and the bottom trace is initial stimulus (θ_s). θ_t is recorded at double sensitivity. Open-loop gain (K) is +0.1.

(From Robinson DA: *J Physiol* 180:569, 1965.)

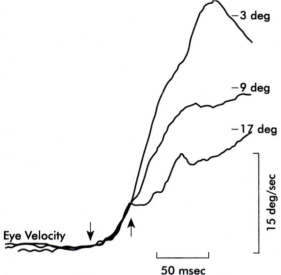

FIG. 4-4 Eye velocity during the onset of pursuit to 15-degree-per-second ramp target motion; the ramp of motion begins at different eccentricities, as indicated at the right portion of each trace. The velocity of the early component *(arrows)* was the same for all starting positions, but the velocity of the late component varied.

(From Lisberger SG, Westbrook LE: *J Neurosci* 5:1662, 1985.)

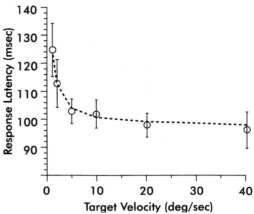

FIG. 4-5 The relationship between target velocity and mean response latency for seven subjects. Only four subjects were tested on targets of 1 and 2 degrees per second. The *vertical bars* represent ±1 SD. Since there was only one measurement for each subject, (namely, the mean), the SD represents the intersubject variability. The *dashed line* connects latencies predicted by a model in which latency = 98 msec + (0.028 degrees per target velocity).

(From Carl JR, Gellman RS: *J Neurophysiol* 57:1446, 1987.)

*TABLE 4-1   Tracking Eye Movement Parameters in 20 Individuals with Normal Vision**

Parameter	Target Velocity (deg sec)					
	10	20	30	40	50	60
Maximal velocity gain	0.95 (0.10)*	0.98 (0.12)	0.94 (0.12)	0.92 (0.15)	0.86 (0.14)	0.75 (0.21)
Total tracking amplitude, in deg	60.0 (7.7)	57.6 (8.9)	53.0 (11.2)	52.3 (9.6)	46.3 (12.4)	41.6 (11.3)
Amplitude of smooth pursuit, in deg	52.8 (10.0)	51.1 (9.7)	45.8 (11.4)	44.5 (9.9)	36.6 (10.5)	27.2 (8.3)
Frequency of super-imposed saccades, in 60 sec of testing						
3-10 deg	6 (5)	11 (11)	20 (17)	33 (23)	35 (28)	34 (23)
11-20 deg	0	3 (5)	4 (4)	9 (14)	16 (14)	18 (20)
21 deg or more	0	0	1 (4)	3 (5)	4 (8)	11 (20)
Square-wave frequency, in 60 sec of testing	6 (10)	5 (3)	4 (8)	1 (3)	6 (6)	2 (8)

*Means of the individual means and standard deviations (in parentheses) of the tested parameters during tracking to the right at different target velocities.
From Schalen L: *Acta Otolaryngol* 90:404, 1980.

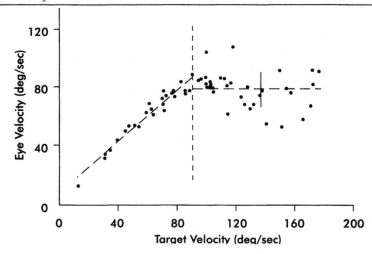

FIG. 4-6 Eye velocity plotted against target velocity of ramp target motion. Eye velocity increases with target velocity in a roughly linear manner with a slope (gain) of about 0.9. At a target velocity of about 100 degrees per second, eye velocity becomes variable, fails to increase further, and in fact seems to decrease somewhat. Variability at large velocities is indicated in SD by the *solid line. Vertical dashed line* represents the 90-deg/sec "break point".

(From Meyer CH, Lasker AG, Robinson DA: *Vision Res* 25:561, 1985.)

degrees per second. Beyond this, in some subjects under optimal conditions, relatively high-gain pursuit up to 100 to 150 degrees per second is possible[35] (Fig. 4-6); otherwise, a velocity saturation is evident and thereafter gain is generally markedly reduced and more variable.

- The value for open-loop gain is generally 20,[47] although a value as low as 4 may still be regarded as normal.[2]
- Vertical pursuit has a lower gain, greater phase lag, and more frequent, larger error-correcting saccades than horizontal pursuit[4,58] (Fig. 4-7, *A, B, C,* and *D;* see section on Prediction for further explanation of the types of graphs).
- Only with a (sustained) retinal velocity error of >3 degrees per second would the increased retinal-image motion (not including spatial degradation that is due to retinal eccentricity) reduce effective resolution of the target.[31]
- Steady-state gain is little affected by moderate target eccentricity.[16]

- Gain may be reduced (by 10% to 20% or more) with addition of either a stationary or a moving background,[15,60] especially if positioned at or near the target plane.[24]
- Gain reduces with increased target amplitude over the range of 5 to 20 degrees (for a fixed frequency), presumably because of acceleration saturation limits.[29]
- Pursuit ability is enhanced by the addition of either auditory or proprioceptive and tactile information, or both, related to target position, as occurs in many real-life tracking tasks.[33]
- The pursuit system receives numerous inputs from the visual motion pathways, including information about direction and movement.[31]
- The primary input to pursuit has been regarded to be target velocity,[44] although target acceleration now appears to play an important role,[30,47] and target position may even assist to drive the system under certain conditions.[41,42,57]
- Furthermore, pursuit gain is related

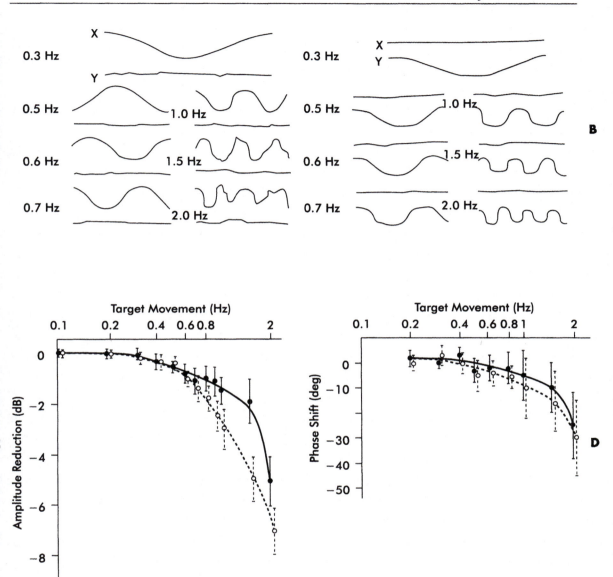

FIG. 4-7   A, Recordings of horizontal pursuit movements. *X,* Horizontal movements; *Y,* vertical movements. **B,** Recordings of vertical movements. **C,** Relationship between amplitude of the pursuit eye movements and the frequency of the target movements. *Closed circle* and *solid line* indicate horizontal movements; *open circle* and *dotted line* indicate vertical movements. *Bars* indicate variations of values in three individuals. **D,** Relationship between the phase shift of the smooth pursuit eye movements and the frequency of the target movements. *Closed circle* and *solid line* indicate horizontal movements; *open circle* and *dotted line* indicate vertical movements. *Bars* indicate variations of values in three individuals.

(From Yamazaki A, Ishikawa S: *Jap J Ophthalmol* 17:103, 1973.)

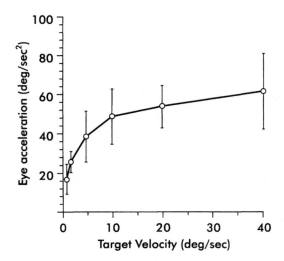

FIG. 4-8 The dependence of presaccadic acceleration on target velocity for the same subjects as presented in Fig. 4-5. There is an increase of only ~10
deg/sec^2 in acceleration for a fourfold increase in
target velocity above 10 deg/sec.

(From Carl JR, Gellman RS: *J Neurophysiol* 57:1446, 1987.)

to maximal target acceleration rather
than to its velocity; in addition, maximal eye acceleration rather than velocity
is related to retinal-error velocity.[30] These
two pieces of information provide strong
support for the notion that the various visual inputs function as commands for eye
acceleration. In this way sensed and
processed velocity tracking errors would
result in related changes in eye velocity.[30,31]
- Presaccadic pursuit acceleration is generally less than 50 degrees per sec^2 and is
somewhat dependent on target velocity[9]
(Fig. 4-8).

MODELS OF THE PURSUIT SYSTEM

Early models of the pursuit system considered it to function as a basic velocity servomechanism[52,62] (Fig. 4-9, *A*). Its role was simply to match eye velocity to target velocity,
thereby reducing the residual retinal-image
motion to some minimal (or zero) level. These
models generally contain the following control elements[2] (Fig. 4-9, *B*) left to right:
- A differentiator (s), to convert position information into velocity information
- A limiter, to prevent response to a velocity input greater than some preset system
level
- An open-loop gain (K), to combine with
other elements to form a "leaky" integrator
- A processing delay
- A saturation element, to prevent a response output greater than some preset
system level
- A simple integrator (1/s), to convert the
velocity signal into an eye position signal
that drives the extraocular muscles and
thereby alters eye position (θ)

However, as pointed out by Lisberger, Morris, and Tychsen,[31] there are two major problems with the basic model configuration. First,
periods of perfect velocity tracking would result in zero system error; thus there would be
no error signal to drive the system. The pursuit system would effectively be open-loop.
Second, there would be system instability because of the delay of approximately 100 msec
in combination with the system's relatively
high gain. Young, Forster, and van Houtte[61]
and Robinson[46] proposed solutions to the preceding dilemma. The former authors suggested that target velocity relative to the external environment constituted the brain's
neural signal that drives the pursuit system in
an accurate and stable manner; the latter authors proposed that a "reconstructed" target
velocity signal (eye velocity plus retinal target
velocity) served to drive the pursuit system
(Fig. 4-9, *C*). Furthermore, in the most current
models of pursuit[31] weighted information
about retinal velocity, as well as retinal position and acceleration, is also generally included as input signals (Fig. 4-9, *D*).

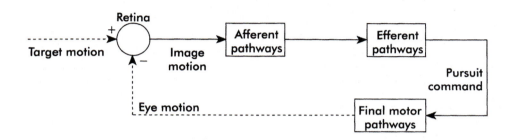

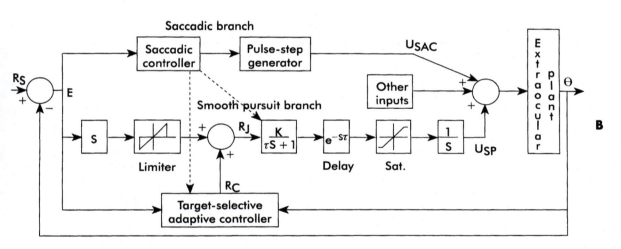

FIG. 4-9 Models of the pursuit system. **A,** A simple negative-feedback control system in which image motion provides the central command to the efferent pathways. **B,** Target-selective adaptive control model.

Continued.

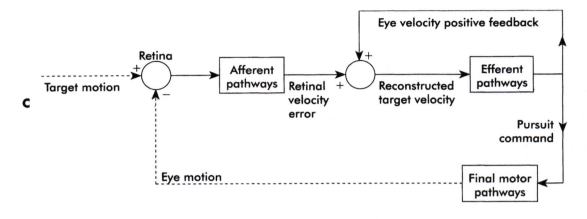

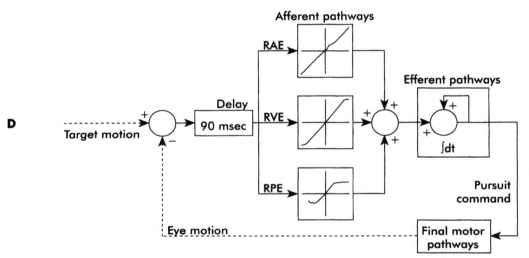

FIG. 4-9, cont'd. **C,** A modification that includes a positive-feedback pathway for the pursuit command for eye velocity. The mathematical addition of the positive feedback of eye velocity and the visual inputs signaling retinal velocity error (target velocity minus eye velocity) provides a reconstructed target velocity signal, which serves as the central command to the efferent pathways. The *solid lines* indicate the flow of neural signals; the *dashed lines* represent physical events. The *circles* represent summing junctions that perform mathematical addition and subtraction of their inputs. Thus the *circle* labeled *retina* compares target motion and eye motion, and its output is image motion, or target motion with respect to the eye. **D,** A computer model that simulates pursuit on a millisecond time scale and its relation to the pathways subserving pursuit. Retinal inputs are processed through a 90-msec delay, and retinal acceleration *(RAE)*, velocity *(RVE)*, and position errors *(RPE)* are transformed according to the relationships obtained in psychophysical experiments. The efferent pathways contain eye-velocity positive feedback and perform a mathematical integration.

(**A, C,** and **D,** from Lisberger SG, Morris EJ, Tychsen L: *Ann Rev Neurosci* 10:97, 1987; **B,** from Harvey DR, Bahill AT: *Trans Soc Comput Simul* 2:275, 1986.)

EFFECT OF AGING ON PURSUIT

Most oculomotor subsystems exhibit some degree (generally modest) of reduced performance with advancing age, and these changes can play an important role in the neurologic diagnosis in elderly persons. Either careful visual scrutiny by the clinician or, more typically, objective documentation in the clinical laboratory is required for these changes to be detected. The pursuit system is no exception; in it the following changes are found:

- *Reduced (dual-mode) closed-loop gain*[37,50,51,63] *(Fig. 4-10, A):* The average reduction is approximately 25%, and it becomes progressively worse with increasingly higher target velocities. This change could be due to age-related degradation of motion information at numerous sites in the visual pathways, especially as a result of either atrophy of cerebral cortical neurons in the middle temporal area and medial superiotemporal visual area or loss of cerebellar Purkinje cells (or both), which appear to form the sensorimotor interface whose signals constitute the pursuit motor command.[37]

- *Increased overall saccade frequency*[10,37] *(Fig. 4-10, B):* This increased frequency is consistent with the finding of the previously described reduced pursuit gain. Most of these saccades (error-correcting or "catch-up" saccades) are necessary to maintain foveation on the moving object of interest. This defect can be detected by the clinician (also see the last change listed here, and Chapter 9).

- *Reduced initial acceleration*[37]: Initial acceleration is reduced by an average of 30%. This reduction may be attributed to the factors mentioned in the first change listed above. This initial acceleration, which occurs before the influence of visual feedback, therefore reflects the open-loop pursuit gain. It is the source of reduction for the closed-loop gain mentioned in the first

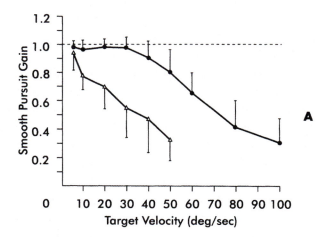

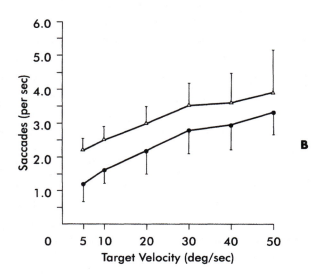

FIG. 4-10 **A,** Horizontal smooth pursuit gain (eye velocity/target velocity) of 15 young *(solid circle)* and 10 elderly *(open triangle)* persons. Means and standard deviations are shown. **B,** Saccadic frequency of 10 elderly *(open triangle)* and 15 young *(solid circle)* persons, plotted against target velocity. Means and standard deviations are shown.

(From Sharpe JA, Sylvester TO: *Invest Ophthalmol Vis Sci* 17:465, 1978.)

change listed here. Remember that closed-loop gain equals the open-loop gain value divided by 1 plus the open-loop gain value (see Appendix).

- *Increased velocity latency[37]:* Increased velocity latency is consistent with general overall age-related increases in reaction time, presumably reflecting small but progressive increases in visual information processing time (~1 msec/yr). In contrast, there was no such age-related change in pursuit acceleration latency.[37]
- *Increased distractibility[25]:* There was increased distraction (an increased number of "anticipatory" saccades) during pursuit in the presence of a competing visual stimulus (background scene). This finding is consistent with the "perceptual noise" theory,[28] which states that aging inhibits one's ability to suppress responses to irrelevant stimuli. The clinician can test this change by using multiple stimuli (foreground target and background scene). In effect, this is precisely what most clinicians do, using a finger or pen tip as the foreground target and their face and surrounding examination room as the potentially competing background stimulus.
- *Increased square-wave jerks[25]:* There was a high frequency of square-wave jerks during pursuit. This high frequency was also found during fixation in elderly persons (see Chapter 2), when, it was speculated, it represented a defect of decreased inhibition of pause cells. These increased square-wave jerks can be detected on clinical examination as small and rapid, "to-and-fro darting movements" (see Chapters 2 and 9).

PREDICTION

In the context of this discussion, *prediction* denotes a pattern of target motion that is constrained so that one obtains considerable information from past target movement that

permits highly likely "guesses" about its future behavior[52,53] (see Pavel[39] for a recent review). When an experienced subject or even a naive patient is provided with a predictable stimulus (which is the usual case), he or she rapidly learns to predict and track the target accurately[18,53] (see Figs. 4-1 and 4-11, *A;* also see the next section). In fact, it is difficult for one *not* to predict or anticipate target motion, even when it is presented in a nonpredictable manner.[59] Individuals may even track smoothly moving predictable targets that disappear for up to a few seconds, although their nonvisual feedback-related predictive gain during this period is noticeably reduced.[5,56]

Over the past three decades, use of simple sinusoidal stimuli has been the norm in the study of dynamic system response, including pursuit. Sinusoidal stimuli were popularized after World War II by bioengineers and mathematicians who developed control system theory, in particular, a special form of frequency analysis referred to as *Bode analysis*[52] (see Appendix). Essentially the system is stimulated with a full range of input frequencies and its output is monitored in terms of gain (or *overall amplitude of response*) and phase (that is, the lead or lag of the system response relative to the input). Use of "pure" simple sinusoids has two important benefits: (1) the response is always sinusoidal, although its amplitude (and therefore gain) may vary considerably, and (2) the lag or lead error can be thought of as a simple temporal shift (in degrees, since it reflects simple harmonic motion) between the eye and target position. Thus with Bode analysis the following question is being asked: "How faithfully does the system under investigation transmit or *transfer* the incoming sinusoidal input signal?"

One of the pioneering studies in Bode analysis was conducted by Stark, Vossius, and Young[53] in 1962. They used both predictable stimuli (simple sinusoids of constant amplitude frequencies) (Fig. 4-11, *A*) and nonpredictable stimuli (sum of four to seven simple si-

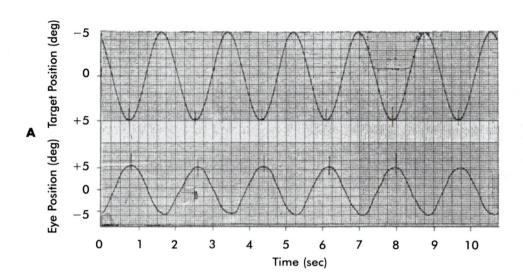

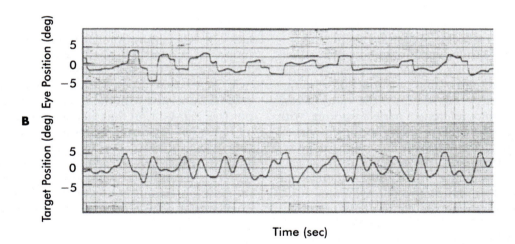

FIG. 4-11 **A,** Eye movement records for tracking of sinusoidal target motion of 0.5 cycles per sec. **B,** Typical record of eye tracking using a sum of four sinusoids. *Continued.*

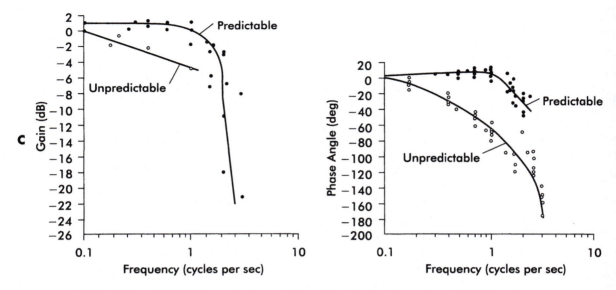

c

***FIG. 4-11, cont'd.* C,** Gain and phase relationships for continuous predictable and unpredictable target motions.

(From Stark L: *Neurological control systems,* New York, 1968, Plenum.)

nusoids) (Fig. 4-11, *B*) to study the pursuit system. The results are presented in the traditional Bode plot format depicting response gain and response phase as a function of stimulus frequency (Fig. 4-11, *C*). The value of zero on either plot references perfect tracking, with the eye following the target in the absence of any time delay and with the full expected response amplitude. The negative sign for gain indicates response attenuation, whereas the positive sign indicates response amplification; the negative sign for phase angle represents "lagging" of the eye behind the target, whereas the positive sign represents "leading" of the eye ahead of the target (that is, prediction). Clearly, with a predictable input the eye reasonably faithfully tracks the target to approximately 1 Hz before the gain reduces, and the lag increases. In contrast, with the nonpredictable input, response attenuation with considerable lag present is the rule, since such a target is quite difficult to follow because of its lack of predictability. Similar results were also found by Fender and Nye[20] and Dallos and Jones[17] during the early 1960s.

It is evident from the eye movement records associated with the nonpredictable input (see Fig. 4-11, *B*) that, in addition to overall reduction in pursuit component, there is a concurrent increase in saccadic component (that is, "catch-up" or corrective saccades) to correct the resultant dynamically accumulating position error. Thus with the higher-frequency sinusoidal inputs increasingly greater amounts and sizes of saccades are actually being used to assist and improve overall tracking performance and are used in keeping the target on the fovea for maximal visual acuity benefit. In the computation of dual-mode "pursuit" gain, saccades actually contaminate the results and give the impression of better *smooth pursuit* tracking performance than is really the case. Therefore Bahill, Iandolo, and Troost[1] performed a Bode gain analysis both with and without inclusion of these saccades. The results are presented in Fig. 4-12. As expected, the single-mode tracking (pursuit minus saccades) was considerably poorer at the intermediate and high frequencies when compared with the more typical dual-mode tracking (pursuit plus saccades) results.

The previously mentioned studies suggest the occurrence of a rapid learning process in response to a predictable input, presumably resulting from the presence of a neurologic "predictor operator," the effect being an overall improvement in tracking performance.[17] Such a computational component would have to predict target velocity one reaction time *later*, with appropriate compensation for pursuit system dynamics, to track with zero latency. Bahill and McDonald[2] and Harvey and Bahill[23] have proposed such a model with an "adaptive controller" (see Fig. 4-9, *B*). They speculated that the model would use "menu selection" to predict target velocity. Basically the pursuit system would have a menu or listing of target waveforms that it has learned to track. Once the system identifies a waveform (that is, target movement pattern), it would use that equation to compute the requisite neural adaptive signal. If a novel stimulus is then presented, it would attempt to track the target, probably using a least means square estimation process (for example, tracking until the resultant error is minimal), until a new equation accurately describing the target waveform is established and added to its menu.

Recent investigations[7,8] have attempted to link so-called anticipatory smooth eye movements[27] to predictive eye movements. These anticipatory eye movements are low-velocity smooth movements (generally <1 degree per second and rarely >4 degrees per second) that occur either before expected target motion or *before* its cessation.[7,8] Furthermore, their initiation and velocity characteristics are stimulus dependent.[8] Boman and Hotson[8] observed that similar predictive eye movements oc-

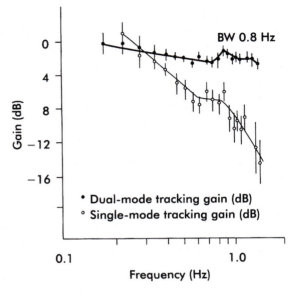

FIG. 4-12 Single-mode pursuit Bode gain plot. Computed from 35 minutes of artifact-free data gathered on five separate days on one individual (BW). The *vertical bars* represent the 95% confidence intervals.

(From Bahill AT, Iandolo MJ, Troost BT: *Vision Res* 20:293, 1980.)

curred before and during the change in direction of motion of their double-ramp stimulus. Using quantitative modeling to compare anticipatory with predictive movements at these two points, the authors demonstrated that the predictive movements were really the summation of anticipatory movements. That is, at the double-ramp directional "turnaround" point (Fig. 4-13), the resultant predictive eye movement was actually the summation of an anticipatory deceleration to the soon to be terminated 10-degree-per-second ramp portion and an anticipatory acceleration to the soon to begin 6-degree-per-second ramp position. The authors also speculated that anticipatory slow eye movements may serve an important function by aiding "resynchronization" of eye movements in expectation of abrupt direc-

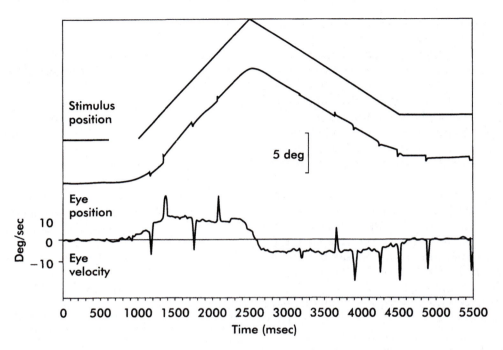

FIG. 4-13 Individual eye movement to a predictable double-ramp stimulus with a 180-degree direction change. Upward deflections of the curves indicate rightward movements. In this trial the target spot was extinguished at time = 600 msec. The target reappeared 400 msec later and moved rightward at 10 deg/sec for 1500 msec, reversed direction and moved leftward at 6 deg/sec for 2000 msec, and then stopped. Slow eye velocities changed before each of these three changes in target motion.

(From Boman DK, Hotson JR: *Vision Res* 32:675, 1992.)

tional changes of the target, as well as disengaging the eye from active fixation to prepare for the subsequent active pursuit, once the formerly fixated target actually begins to move smoothly.[7,8]

IMPROVING PURSUIT ABILITY IN PERSONS WITH NORMAL VISION

We can all imagine a variety of situations in which training of one's ability to pursue an object moving in a smooth, predictable manner might result in enhancement of overall task performance, such as when an assembly-line worker inspects glass bottles that are moving across the field of vision at a rapid rate or when a baseball outfielder runs in an attempt to catch a high fly ball. But is there any evidence that the normal pursuit system can be trained to perform in a more optimal manner? Recent research results suggest that this is, indeed, possible with exertion of relatively little time and effort (see also the earlier section on Prediction).

In an early report, Schalen[49] had nine young adults track predictable, horizontal, bidirectional step-ramp stimuli (60-degree amplitude at 10- to 60-degree per second velocities). The young adults tracked each target five times in each direction for 60 trials. This procedure was repeated 1 to 7 days later. The results for each session are presented in Fig. 4-14, *A* and *B*, with respect to changes in maximal velocity pursuit gain and (single-mode)

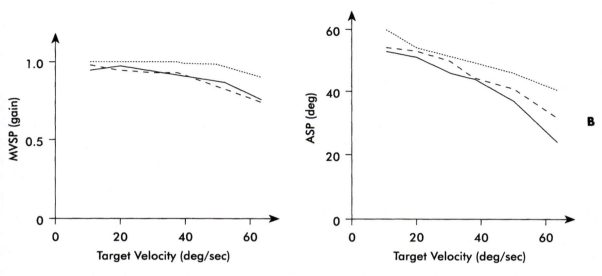

FIG. 4-14 **A,** Effects of repeated testing on maximal velocity gain of smooth pursuit (MVSP). Grand mean of individual means in nine persons investigated twice were higher on the repeated testing *(dotted line)* compared to the first occasion *(dashed line).* The reference group *(solid line)* of 20 persons with normal vision was investigated only once. **B,** Effects of repeated testing on the amplitude of smooth pursuit (ASP). Grand mean of individual means in nine persons investigated on the first occasion *(dashed line)* compared to those on the second occasion *(dotted line)* and to those of the reference group of 20 persons with normal vision *(solid line)* investigated once (see Table 4-1 for reference group data).

(From Schalen L: *Acta Otolaryngol* 90:404, 1980.)

saccade-free pursuit amplitude. It is clear that both functions exhibited moderate improvements over the full range of velocities. The improvements were interpreted to represent a positive training effect involving both velocity matching and correction of position errors.

In a later report Boman and Hotson[6] investigated the ability to train pursuit, especially with a goal to reduce horizontal and vertical gain asymmetries (also see Fig. 4-7 for a comparison of horizontal and vertical pursuit). Young adults were trained by tracking horizontal and vertical predictable ramps (15-degree amplitude at 10 to 50 degrees per second). Each target was tracked three times per day for a total of 20 minutes per day of training on nine separate days over the course of several weeks. The results are presented in Fig. 4-15, *A, B,* and *C.* Both horizontal and vertical pursuit progressively improved and became more accurate, although the directional asymmetry remained. The pursuit system appeared to optimize gain to minimize system error.

McHugh and Bahill[34] reported that their subjects who demonstrated the best results could learn to track a non-naturally occurring cubic waveform extremely accurately with only 7.5 minutes (or less) of actual total training time (18 seconds of tracking per 5-minute period) over a 2-hour session (Fig. 4-16, *A*). The learning curve followed an exponential time course, exhibiting a progressive reduction in mean square error between eye and target position. With as little as 60 seconds of actual training, some subjects already were performing with extremely low error levels. Of particular interest were the results for three professional baseball players. They had

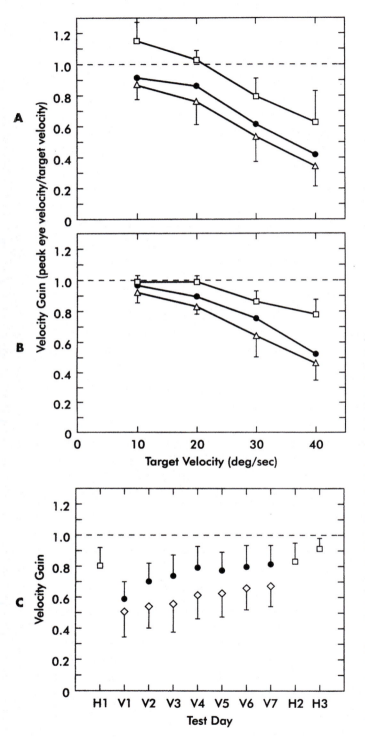

FIG. 4-15 Average velocity gains for the five subjects at four target speeds. **A,** First day of testing. **B,** Last day of testing, after repeated periods of training and testing. Standard deviations are shown for the horizontal and upward gains. The standard deviations for the downward gains are similar but are not shown, to simplify the graphs. The *dashed lines* indicate unity gain and represent the most accurate performance. The symmetric left and right velocity gains are combined, whereas the asymmetric upward and downward velocity gains are shown separately. Horizontal velocity gains were higher than the vertical gains. **C,** Average velocity gains for all five subjects on each test day at 30-deg/sec target speeds. *Open square,* Horizontal velocity gains; *open diamond,* upward velocity gains; *closed circle,* downward velocity gains. The *dashed line* indicates unity velocity gain. *H1* to *H3;* The 3 days in which horizontal pursuit was tested. *V1* to *V7;* The 7 days in which vertical pursuit was tested. Both the horizontal and vertical velocities increased throughout the training period.

(From Boman DK, Hotson JR: *Neuro-ophthalmol* 7:185, 1987.)

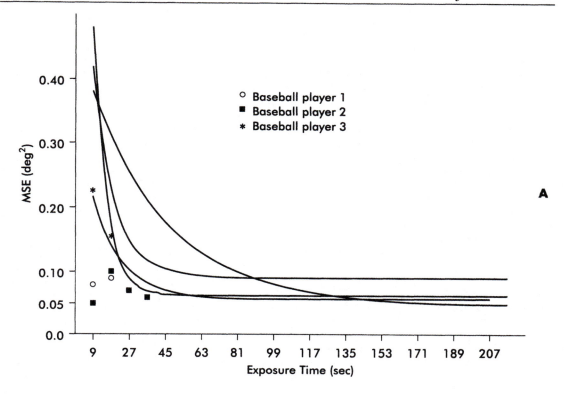

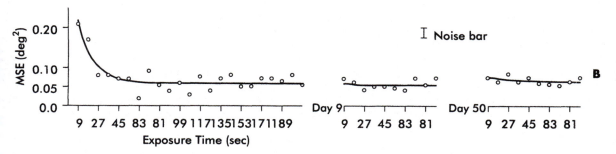

FIG. 4-16 **A,** Time course of learning for seven persons. *Solid lines* are the exponential curves fit to the data of four students. *Circles, asterisks,* and *squares* are data points for three professional athletes. **B,** Time course for learning and relearning. The individual learned the waveform, returned 9 days later to relearn it, and returned 50 days after original experiment to relearn it again.

(From McHugh DE, Bahill AT: *Invest Ophthalmol Vis Sci* 26:932, 1985.)

much lower initial tracking errors than did those graduate students who had the best results, although both groups plateaued to the same final low error level. This initally low tracking error suggested either a self-selection process or that the baseball players had already effectively trained themselves during their athletic activities. Some subjects returned for retesting either 9 or 50 days later, and their performance was nearly optimal

Subject	Tracking	Analysis

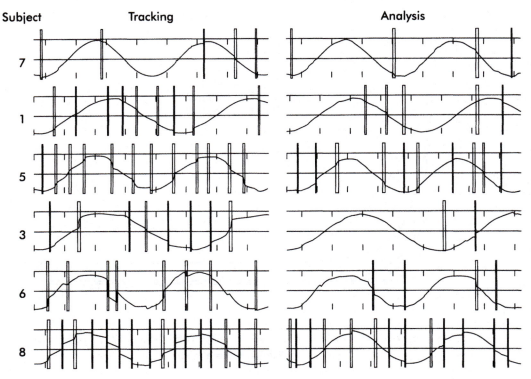

FIG. 4-17 For simple tracking condition and heightened attention analysis condition, representative waveforms for the two best and four worst subjects, based on their root-mean-square (RMS) error scores in the tracking condition. Subjects are listed here in descending order of tracking quality. Horizontal movement is shown, with upward direction indicating movement to the right. *Vertical bars* indicate saccades as detected by computer algorithm. Vertical marks are placed every 0.5 seconds. Subject *3* shows characteristic anticipatory saccades to the right endpoint of the target trajectory during the tracking condition. Subject *6* shows paired saccades of unusually large magnitude during the tracking condition, leaving only those of the smallest magnitude in the analysis condition. These latter paired saccades are seen frequently in other subjects. Waveforms of subjects *1* and *5* are representative of the omitted subjects, *2, 4,* and *9,* whose results were intermediate between those of subjects *1* and *5* in tracking quality.

(From Van Gelder and others: *Compr Psychiatry* 31:253, 1990.)

from the start, suggesting considerable retention of their earlier learning and rapid relearning to optimize performance once again (Fig. 4-16, *B*). These investigators found that training or learning was best when a smoothly moving predictable target had a frequency of approximately 0.3 Hz and an amplitude of 5 degrees.

The preceding results are consistent with the conclusion of Dallos and Jones,[17] who said that rapid learning involving predictable stimuli resulted from gain optimization. Thus pursuit gain should approach unity, and phase lag should approach zero. Heightened attention during such practice periods also acts to enhance smooth tracking[55] (Fig. 4-17).

Furthermore, these results are consistent with the more general findings and ideas of motor physiologists, which indicate that practice in normal individuals enhances general movement ability, presumably through motor learning[22] via revision and improvement of the underlying neural control program.

NEUROANATOMIC CONTROL OF AND SIGNAL PROCESSING FOR PURSUIT EYE MOVEMENTS

In this section we provide a brief overview of the primary neuroanatomic structures involved in the generation of pursuit eye movements. Although the details are somewhat less well defined than for the saccadic system, much has been learned since the mid-1980s from careful neurophysiologic investigations, including lesion studies in monkeys and case reports in humans. Aspects most relevant to the clinician are emphasized in this section.

The following is a simplified representation of the pursuit neural pathway[19,26,29,31,42] (Fig. 4-18, *A*) with additional details added:

- The primary striate visual cortex (V1) contains cells responding to stimulus motion, which project heavily to the middle temporal (MT) area of the extrastriate visual cortex.
- The MT area encodes and processes the direction and velocity of stimulus motion, and then it projects to the adjacent medial superiotemporal (MST) visual area.
- The MST area probably encodes both visual signals related to pursuit and the efference copy of the eye movement command.
- Both the MT and MST areas project to the posterioparietal cortex (PPC), which probably plays a role in attentional aspects of target motion.
- The MT and MST areas and the PPC project to the frontal eye fields (FEFs, area 8), which contain neurons that fire during pursuit, perhaps especially during predictive movements.

- The MT and MST areas and FEFs project to the dorsolateral pontine nucleus (DLPN), which contains cells exhibiting direction selectivity, and they discharge in response to pursuit movements. The DLPN probably also receives the efference copy signal from the MST area.
- The DLPN projects to the cerebellum (flocculus, paraflocculus, and vermis). The flocculus and paraflocculus contain Purkinje cells that discharge with respect to gaze velocity during pursuit; the vermal neurons encode target velocity in space (eye velocity plus retinal slip velocity).
- The cerebellum projects to the brainstem, especially to the medial vestibular nucleus (MVN), which discharges according to gaze velocity, and the nucleus prepositus hypoglossi (NPH). Both brainstem structures are probably involved in neural integration, which converts the eye velocity signals to eye position signals, which in turn project to the oculomotor neurons to move the eye smoothly (Fig. 4-18, *B*).

Insult or disease anywhere along these pathways may cause a pursuit defect. These are listed in Table 4-2, page 93.

ABNORMAL PURSUIT

We propose the following areas of analysis for abnormal (and normal) pursuit, which expand the analysis suggested by Leigh and Zee[29]:

I. Initiation
   A. Latency
   B. Initial 100-msec open-loop phase
   C. Maximum eye acceleration
II. Gain
III. Saccadic overlay

Initiation

There is a paucity of investigations into initiation, a relatively new and important area in clinical oculomotor research,[36] probably be-

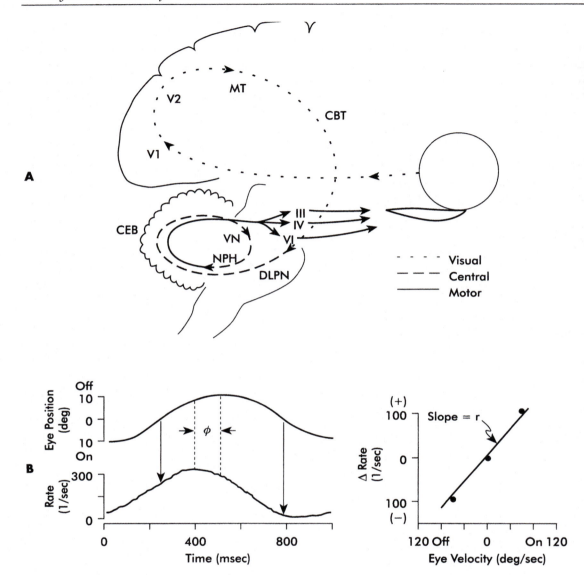

FIG. 4-18 **A,** Schematic representation of aspects of information flow in the smooth pursuit system. *CEB,* Cerebellum; *CBT,* corticobulbar tract; *DLPN,* dorsolateral pontine nucleus; *MT,* middle temporal cortex; *NPH,* nucleus prepositus hypoglossi; *V1* and *V2,* occipital visual areas; *VN,* vestibular nuclei; III, IV, and VI, oculomotor, trochlear and abducens nuclei. **B,** Firing rate of an oculomotor neuron during a sinusoidal tracking eye movement. *Vertical arrows* show the increment and decrement in rate from that found during fixation for eye movements through the same position with velocity in the on or off direction. ϕ is the phase lead of discharge rate with respect to eye position. Graph, *right,* shows the change in rate-to-velocity relationship of this neuron.

(**A,** from Pola J, Wyatt HJ: *Vision Res* 20:523, 1980; **B,** from Keller EL. In Carpenter R S, editor: *Vision and visual dysfunction, vol 8, Eye movements,* Boca Raton, Fla, 1991, CRC.)

TABLE 4-2 *Effects of Lesions on Horizontal Pursuit Eye Movements (in Monkeys and Humans)*

Site	Effect
Primary visual cortex	Unilateral lesion produces a contralateral defect.
Middle temporal area	Lesion produces a scotoma specific only for visual motion.
Middle superiotemporal area	Unilateral lesion produces an ipsilateral defect.
Posterioparietal cortex	Lesion produces an ipsilateral defect.
Frontal eye fields	Bilateral lesion produces a bilateral defect, and a unilateral lesion pro duces an ipsilateral defect.
Dorsolateral pontine nucleus	Lesion produces an ipsilateral defect.
Cerebellum	Lesion of either the flocculus or paraflocculus produces a severe defect of pursuit gain, whereas a lesion of the vermis produces a modest defect of pursuit gain; a total cerebellectomy abolishes all pursuit.

cause repeated predictable sinusoidal and tri-angular pursuit stimuli (rather than nonpre-dictable single step-ramps) were used almost exclusively until a few years ago; the earlier emphasis was on responsivity to sustained tar-get motion. Work in the area of pursuit initia-tion will greatly expand over the next few years. One can obtain the open-loop gain by studying initiation without resorting to so-phisticated electronic feedback techniques. This open-loop response appears to be a very sensitive indicator of system dysfunction.[29]

Gain

Gain is probably the value most frequently used to assess pursuit in both patients and re-search subjects. Gain can be determined by means of either predictable triangular wave-forms or nonpredictable step-ramps, with *con-stant target velocity* being the main determinant of pursuit, or by predictable sinusoidal wave-forms, with *maximal target acceleration* being the main determinant of pursuit. With rare exception, when pursuit gain is altered, whether by neurologic disease[36,38] (Figs. 4-19, *A* and *B*, and 4-20, *A* and *B*), drugs[43] (Fig. 4-21, *A* and *B)*, aging[50] (see Fig. 4-10), or de-creased attention[55] (see Fig. 4-17; Box 4-1), gain is reduced.

BOX 4-1   *Factors That May Reduce Pursuit Gain*

Stimulus-related
Increased target velocity and acceleration
Increased target eccentricity
Increased target nonpredictability
Decreased target size
Vertical (versus horizontal) target move-ment
Presence of competing stimuli (especially smoothly moving background targets)

Nonstimulus-related
Inattention and distractibility
Increased age
Fatigue
Absence of information related to target movement from other modalities (such as audition and proprioception)
Alcohol and barbiturates
Medications (such as diazepam)
Neurologic disease (especially involving the cerebral cortex or cerebellum, or both)
Jerk nystagmus (for pursuit in the direction of the fast phase)
Amblyopia

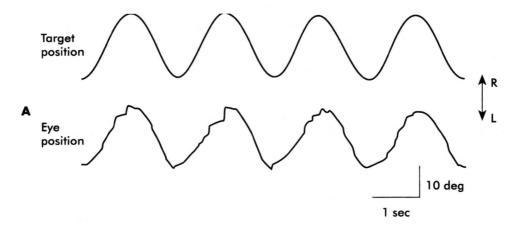

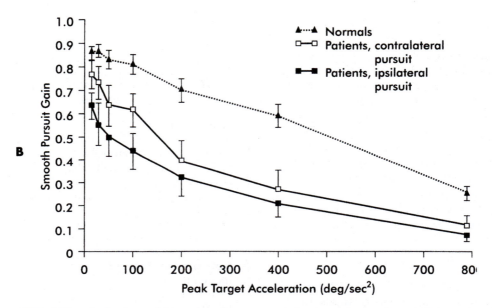

FIG. 4-19   **A,** Oculographic tracing of asymmetric horizontal smooth pursuit in patient 7, who has had a right parietooccipital hemorrhage. Target frequency was 0.5 Hz, and amplitude was ±10 degrees. Smooth eye movement velocity failed to match target velocity when the target moved rightward (*R*), necessitating corrective saccades in the direction of target motion to place the target image at the fovea. Leftward (*L*) tracking away from the side of the lesion was smooth. Mean rightward smooth pursuit gain for this target was 0.72 in this patient; mean leftward gain was 0.94. **B,** Smooth pursuit gain versus peak target acceleration in 12 persons with normal vision and 10 patients with smooth pursuit asymmetry. Error *bars* indicate 1 standard error of the mean. In all persons pursuit gain declined with increasing peak target acceleration; gain fell proportionately more in patients than in persons with normal vision. Both contralateral and ipsilateral gain were significantly reduced in the patient group; ipsilateral gain was significantly lower than contralateral gain. (From Morrow MJ, Sharpe JA: *Neurology* 40:285, 1990.)

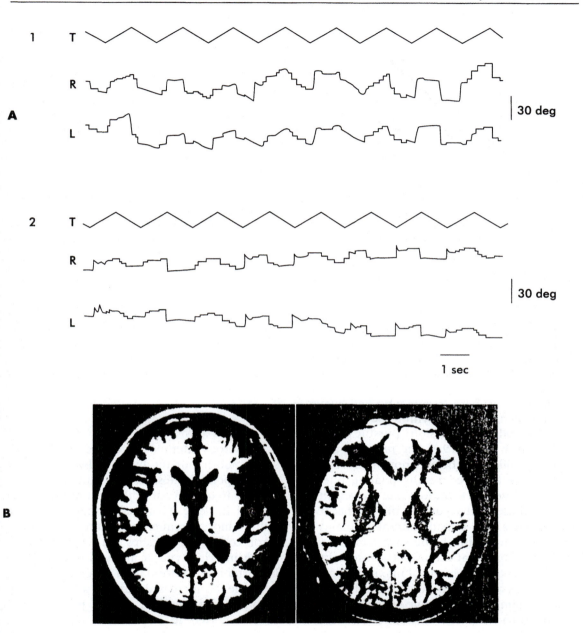

FIG. 4-20 **A,** Pursuit deficits are shown in both the, *1,* horizontal and, *2,* vertical directions. Target speed is 30 deg/sec in both directions. Upward deflections denote rightward movements in the horizontal recording and upward movements in the vertical recording. *T,* Target movement; *R,* recording of the right eye; *L,* recording of the left eye. **B,** Magnetic resonance image, T_1-weighted *(left)* and T_2-weighted *(right),* shows bilateral pulvinar lesions *(arrows).*

(From Ohtsuka and others: *Ophthalmologica* 203:196, 1991.)

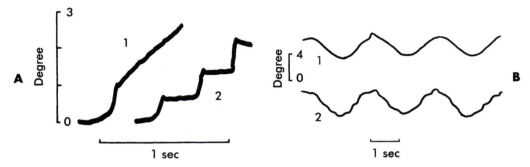

FIG. 4-21 **A,** Tracking eye-movement responses to a target moving with constant velocity before *(1)* and after *(2)* the intravenous administration of sodium thiopental (Pentothal) 100 mg. **B,** Tracking eye-movement responses to a target moving with simple harmonic motion, before *(1)* and 100 minutes after *(2)* the oral administration of amobarbital sodium (Amytal) 300 μg.
(From Rashbass C: *J Physiol* 159:326, 1961.)

Gradations of reduced pursuit gain are exemplified in the following patient studies. In a patient with posterior cerebellar vermal infarct,[40] pursuit gain was reduced equally (to ~0.3 to 0.4) for tracking to the left and right. Results in patients with discrete unilateral cerebral hemisphere lesions who had bilaterally reduced, slightly asymmetric (lower toward the side of the lesion) pursuit gain are presented in Fig. 4-19.[36] The response asymmetry is evident in the eye movement records and in the analyzed results relating pursuit gain to target acceleration (*not* to velocity), both in these patients and in the normal control subjects. The pursuit gain abnormality is most evident at the higher acceleration values, suggesting that the use of sinusoidal targets having the full range of maximal acceleration values would improve one's diagnostic abilities. Similar results have recently been reported in patients with Alzheimer's disease.[21] In a patient with bilateral pulvinar lesions pursuit gain was both markedly reduced and asymmetric[38]: it was 0.19 to the right and 0.54 to the left (see Fig. 4-20).
Asymmetric pursuit gain is also typically found in patients with jerk nystagmus[11] (Fig. 4-22), who had higher gain when the target

and slow-phase were in the same direction and lower gain when the target and slow-phase were in opposing directions, presumably resulting in part from (nonlinear) interaction of the pursuit drive with the ongoing jerk nystagmus waveform.

Saccadic Overlay

Numerous attempts have been made to assess smooth pursuit by actually looking at some aspect of the saccades (generally amplitude or frequency, or both) that occur during pursuit tracking. Presumably there would be either more frequent or larger position-error–correcting saccades with reduced pursuit gain. This type of analysis has provided important new information in some cases. For example, an increased number and increased amplitude of saccades during pursuit have been reported in hyperactive children,[3] in whom "hypermobility" of the eyes would, indeed, be expected. However, if *all* types of saccades were included in the analysis, the results could be misleading. For example, in a patient suspected of having multiple sclerosis who had a high frequency of square-wave jerks,[13] pursuit gain was relatively normal in

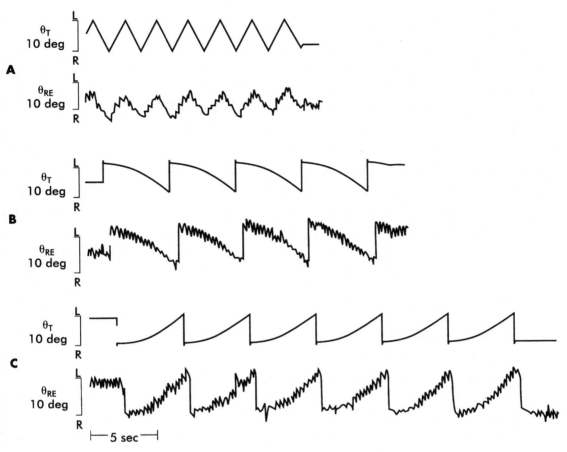

FIG. 4-22 Pursuit tracking. **A,** Jerk nystagmus superimposed on tracking; target moving with constant velocity (triangular input, target amplitude of 10 degrees, and target velocity of 9.0 deg/sec). **B** and **C,** Jerk nystagmus superimposed on tracking; target moving with constant acceleration (parabolic input, target amplitude of 10 deg, and target acceleration of 0.8 deg/sec^2). For all three sets of traces, if best fit line (by eye) is forced through termination of each (corrective) nystagmus saccade, there is remarkably good similarity between target trace and this "corrected" eye movement trace, suggesting that the subject is able to process target information and follow the target accurately but with jerk nystagmus superimposed.

(From Ciuffreda KJ: *Am J Optom Physiol Optics* 56:521, 1979.)

the presence of the numerous saccades during tracking (Fig. 4-23). Thus for reasonable results to be attained, one's saccade criterion must be used wisely.

An obvious question arises: "Can we improve abnormal pursuit in our patients?" In an earlier portion of the chapter, considerable

evidence was provided that pursuit could be trained or enhanced in visually normal subjects in a short time by means of simple stimulus paradigms. Similar results obtained by using objective recording techniques have been reported in patients, but with more extended training time frames. Ciuffreda,

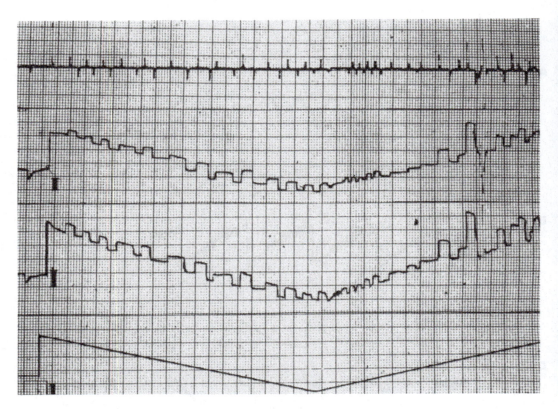

FIG. 4-23 Pursuit. Binocular viewing. Tracking of target having medium amplitude (8 degrees) and low velocity (0.8 deg/sec). Square-wave jerks are evident throughout, including high-frequency bursts (7 to 8 saccades per second) at turnaround point. Vertical calibration bars indicate 2 degrees, whereas horizontal calibration bar indicates 1 second. (From Ciuffreda KJ, Kenyon RV, Stark L: *Am J Optom Physiol Optics* 60:242, 1983.)

Kenyon, and Stark[12] in 1979 and later Ciuffreda, Selenow, and Levi[14] reported the oculomotor results in an 18-year-old with anisometropic amblyopia who had undergone an extended period (16 months) of conventional optometric vision therapy, including eye movements, accommodation, and occlusion (see Chapter 10 for other details of this case). As fixation centralized and visual acuity improved from 20/110 to 20/45 to 20/25, pursuit gain increased from 0.15 to 0.45 to 0.6, respectively; these values approached the lower normal limit of pursuit (0.7). Later, Ron[48] reported on eye movement results in a group (n = 22) of brain-injured patients who were trained for ½ hour per day for 2 to 8 weeks. Results for pursuit in one patient are presented in Fig. 4-24. Pursuit gain clearly increased markedly, especially during the training phase. However, pursuit-phase lag showed little improvement. Ron thought that appropriate eye movement practice or "physiotherapy" was critical in attaining the highest functional capacity (gain and accuracy) in the shortest time. For example, specific eye movement training paradigms improved pursuit recovery threefold as compared with pursuit recovery that might occur naturally.

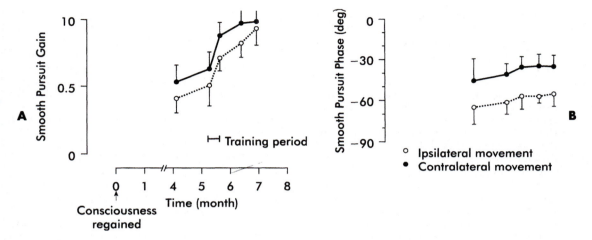

FIG. 4-24 Temporal changes of smooth pursuit gain **(A)** and phase **(B)** in one patient receiving training. Target amplitude was 30 degrees with a frequency of 0.5 Hz. Each point represents the average of 15 measurements. The 2-week training period is indicated by the horizontal bar between months five and six. The *bars* represent one standard deviation.

(From Ron S. In Roucoux A, Crommelinck M, editors: *Physiological and pathological aspects of eye movements*, Boston, 1982, Dr W Junk.)

REVIEW QUESTIONS

1. With the aid of a carefully drawn and labeled diagram, describe the oculomotor response to a step-ramp input in the classic Rashbass experiment.
2. With the aid of a carefully drawn and labeled diagram of the stimulus and response, show how the pursuit system responds to discrete changes in target velocity. Why is the pursuit system considered "continuous"?
3. Describe the effects of prediction on both single-mode and dual-mode pursuit using a Bode analysis plot.
4. Discuss the data demonstrating that pursuit ability can be improved in persons with normal vision by appropriate sensorimotor training. In amblyopes. In brain-injured patients.
5. Describe the various age-related effects on pursuit. How does such information affect your clinical expectations when assessing pursuit eye movements in a teenager as compared with those in an octogenarian?
6. An otherwise healthy 40-year-old patient exhibits a few saccadic intrusions and some periods of low-gain pursuit in your examination. Should this patient be immediately referred to a neurologist for further consultation?

REFERENCES

1. Bahill AT, Iandolo MJ, Troost BT: Smooth pursuit eye movements in response to unpredictable target waveforms, *Vision Res* 20:923, 1980.
2. Bahill AT, McDonald JD: Model emulates human smooth pursuit system producing zero-latency target tracking, *Biol Cybern* 48:213, 1983.
3. Bala SP, Cohen B, Morris AG, Atkin A, Gittleman R, Kates W: Saccades of hyperactive and normal boys during ocular pursuit, *Dev Med Child Neurol* 23:323, 1981.
4. Baloh RW, Yee RD, Honrubia V, Jacobson K: A comparison of the dynamics of horizontal and vertical smooth pursuit in normal human subjects, *Aviat Space Environ Med* 59:121, 1988.
5. Becker W, Fuchs AF: Prediction in the oculomotor system: smooth pursuit during transient disappearance of a visual target, *Exp Brain Res* 57:562, 1985.
6. Boman DK, Hotson JR: Smooth pursuit training and disruption, *Neuro-ophthalmol* 7:185, 1987.
7. Boman DK, Hotson JR: Stimulus conditions that enhance anticipatory slow eye movements, *Vision Res* 28:1157, 1988.
8. Bowman DK, Hotson JR: Predictive smooth

pursuit eye movements near abrupt changes in motion direction, *Vision Res* 32:675, 1992.

9. Carl JR, Gellman RS: Human smooth pursuit: stimulus-dependent responses, *J Neurophysiol* 57:1446, 1987.

10. Chan T, Codd M, Kenny P, Eustace P: The effect of aging on catch-up saccades during horizontal smooth pursuit eye movement, *Neuroophthalmol* 10:327, 1990.

11. Ciuffreda KJ: Jerk nystagmus: some new findings, *Am J Optom Physiol Optics* 56:521, 1979.

12. Ciuffreda KJ, Kenyon RV, Stark L: Different rates of functional recovery of eye movements during orthoptic treatment in an adult amblyope, *Invest Ophthalmol Vis Sci* 18:213, 1979.

13. Ciuffreda KJ, Kenyon RV, Stark L: Saccadic intrusions contributing to reading disability: a case report, *Am J Optom Physiol Optics* 60:242, 1983.

14. Ciuffreda KJ, Selenow A, Levi DM: *Amblyopia: basic and clinical aspects*, Boston, 1991, Butterworth-Heinemann.

15. Collewijn H, Tamminga EP: Human smooth and saccadic eye movements during voluntary pursuit of different target motions on different backgrounds, *J Physiol* 351:217, 1984.

16. Collewijn H, Tamminga EP: Human fixation and pursuit in normal and open-loop conditions: effects of central and peripheral targets, *J Physiol* 379:109, 1986.

17. Dallos PJ, Jones RW: Learning behavior of the eye fixation control system, *IEEE Trans Automatic Control* AC-8:218, 1963.

18. Dodge R, Travis RC, Fox JC: Optic nystagmus. III. Characteristics of the slow phase, *Arch Neurol Psychiatry* 24:21, 1930.

19. Eckmiller R: Neural control of pursuit eye movements, *Physiol Rev* 67:797, 1987.

20. Fender DH, Nye PW: An investigation of the mechanisms of eye movement control, *Kybernetik* 1:81, 1961.

21. Fletcher WA, Sharpe JA: Smooth pursuit dysfunction in Alzeheimer's disease, *Neurology* 28:272, 1988.

22. Gottlieb GL, Corcos DM, Jarie S, Agarwal GC: Practice improves even the simplest movements, *Exp Brain Res* 73:436, 1988.

23. Harvey DR, Bahill AT: Development and sensitivity analysis of adaptive predictor for human eye movement model, *Trans Soc Comput Simul* 2:275, 1986.

24. Howard IP, Marton C: Visual pursuit over textured backgrounds in different depth planes, *Exp Brain Res* 90:625, 1992.

25. Kaufman SR, Abel LA: The effects of distraction on smooth pursuit in normal subjects, *Acta Otolaryngol* 102:57, 1986.

26. Keller EL: The brainstem. In Carpenter RHS, editor: *Vision and visual dysfunction*, vol 8, *Eye movements*, Boca Raton, Fla, 1991, CRC.

27. Kowler E, Martins AJ, Pavel M: The effect of expectations on slow oculomotor control. IV. Anticipating smooth eye movements depend on prior target motions, *Vision Res* 24:197, 1984.

28. Layton B: Perceptual noise and aging, *Psychol Bull* 16:875, 1975.

29. Leigh RJ, Zee DS: *The neurology of eye movements*, ed 2, Philadelphia, 1991, FA Davis.

30. Lisberger SG, Evinger C, Johanson GW, Fuchs AF: Relationship between eye acceleration and retinal image velocity during foveal pursuit in man and monkey, *J Neurophysiol* 46:229, 1981.

31. Lisberger SG, Morris EJ, Tychsen L: Visual motion processing and sensory-motor integration for smooth pursuit eye movements, *Ann Rev Neurosci* 10:97, 1987.

32. Lisberger SG, Westbrook LE: Properties of visual inputs that initiate horizontal smooth pursuit eye movements in monkeys, *J Neurosci* 5:1662, 1985.

33. Mather JA, Lackner JR: Multiple sensory and motor cues enhance the accuracy of pursuit eye movements, *Aviat Space Environ Med* 51:856, 1980.

34. McHugh DE, Bahill AT: Learning to track predictable target waveforms without a time delay, *Invest Ophthalmol Vis Sci* 26:932, 1985.

35. Meyer CH, Lasker AG, Robinson DA: The upper limit of human smooth pursuit velocity, *Vision Res* 25:561, 1985.

36. Morrow MJ, Sharpe JA: Cerebral hemispheric localization of smooth pursuit asymmetry, *Neurology* 40:285, 1990.

37. Morrow MJ, Sharpe JA: Smooth pursuit initiation in young and elderly subjects, *Vision Res* 33:203, 1993.

38. Ohtsuka K, Igarashi Y, Maekawa H, Nakagawa T: Pursuit deficits in bilateral pulvinar lesions, *Ophthalmologica* 203:196, 1991.

39. Pavel M: Predictive control of eye movement. In Kowler E, editor: *Eye movements and their role in visual and cognitive processes*, New York, 1990, Elsevier.

40. Pierrot-Deseilligny C, Amarenco P, Roullet E, Marteau R: Vermal infarct with pursuit eye movement disorders, *J Neurol Neurosurg Psychiatry* 53:519, 1990.

41. Pola J, Wyatt HJ: Target position and velocity: the stimuli for smooth pursuit eye movement, *Vision Res* 20:523, 1980.

42. Pola J, Wyatt HJ: Smooth pursuit: response characteristics, stimuli, and mechanisms. In

Carpenter RHS, editor: *Vision and visual dysfunction, vol 8, Eye movements*, Boca Raton, Fla, 1991, CRC.

43. Rashbass C: Barbiturate nystagmus and the mechanisms of visual fixation, *Nature* 183:897, 1959.

44. Rashbass C: The relationship between saccadic and smooth tracking eye movements, *J Physiol* 159:326, 1961.

45. Robinson DA: The mechanics of human smooth pursuit eye movement, *J Physiol* 180:569, 1965.

46. Robinson DA: Models of oculomotor neural organization. In Bach-y-rita P, Collins CC, editors: *The control of eye movements*, New York, 1971, Academic.

47. Robinson DA, Gordon JL, Gordon SE: A model of the smooth pursuit eye movement system, *Biol Cybern* 55:43, 1986.

48. Ron S: Can training be transferred from one oculomotor system to another? In Roucoux A, Crommelinck M, editors: *Physiological and pathological aspects of eye movements*, Boston, 1982, Dr W Junk.

49. Schalen L: Quantification of tracking eye movements in normal subjects, *Acta Otolaryngol* 90:404, 1980.

50. Sharpe JA, Sylvester TO: Effect of aging on horizontal smooth pursuit, *Invest Ophthalmol Vis Sci* 17:465, 1978.

51. Spooner JW, Sakala SM, Baloh RW: Effect of aging on eye tracking, *Arch Neurol* 37:575, 1980.

52. Stark L: *Neurological control systems*, New York, 1968, Plenum.

53. Stark L, Vossius G, Young LR: Predictive control of eye tracking movements, *IRE Trans Human Factors Electron* HFE-3:52, 1962.

54. Tychsen L, Lisberger SG: Visual motion processing for the initiation of smooth pursuit eye movements in humans, *J Neurophysiol* 56:953, 1986.

55. Van Gelder P, Anderson S, Herman E, Lebedev S, Tsui WH: Saccades in pursuit eye tracking reflect motor attention processes, *Compr Psychiatry* 31:253, 1990.

56. Whittaker SG, Eaholtz G: Learning patterns of eye motion for foveal pursuit, *Invest Ophthalmol Vis Sci* 23:393, 1982.

57. Wyatt HJ, Pola J: Slow eye movements to eccentric targets, *Invest Ophthalmol Vis Sci* 21:477, 1981.

58. Yamazaki A, Ishikawa S: Horizontal and vertical smooth pursuit eye movements, *Jap J Ophthalmol* 17:103, 1973.

59. Yasui S, Young LR: On the predictive control of foveal eye tracking and slow phases of optokinetic and vestibular nystagmus, *J Physiol* 347:17, 1984.

60. Yee RD, Daniels SA, Jones OW, Baloh RW, Honrubia V: Effects of optokinetic background on pursuit eye movements, *Invest Ophthalmol Vis Sci* 24:1115, 1983.

61. Young LR, Forster JD, van Houtte N: *A revised stochastic sampled-data model for eye tracking movements*, Fourth Annual NASA-University Conference on Manual Control, 1968, University of Michigan, Ann Arbor.

62. Young LR, Stark L: Variable feedback experiments testing a sampled-data model for eye tracking movements, *IEEE Trans Human Factor Electron* HFE-4:38, 1963.

63. Zackon DH, Sharpe JA: Smooth pursuit in senescence, *Acta Otolaryngol* 104:290, 1987.

5

Vestibular-Optokinetic Eye Movements

Key Terms

Gaze stabilization	Oscillopsia
Macula/utricle/otolith complex	Semicircular canals
Neurologic disorders	Vertigo
Optical magnification	Vestibular disorders
Optokinetic nystagmus (OKN)	Vestibuloocular reflex (VOR)
Optokinetic afternystagmus (OKAN)	VOR plasticity/adaptation
	Vestibulooptokinetic pathways

OVERVIEW OF VESTIBULAR - OPTOKINETIC EYE MOVEMENTS

During most waking hours we are actively moving about our complex environment—spinning around a swivel-chair in response to a greeting from a fellow office worker, jogging after hours, taking a walk during lunch, pacing to-and-fro during an intense lecture, playing one-on-one basketball, etc. Such common everyday activities produce perturbations of the head that have the *potential* to produce increased retinal-image motion, leading either to the sensation of a blurred retinal image or oscillopsia, or both. For the most part, however, in healthy individuals, two primary complementary oculomotor systems prevent such disturbances in visual perception and maintain a steady, clear retinal image in a remarkably efficient manner.

They are:

- *The vestibular system.* This system produces eye movements that compensate for relatively *brief, transient* head movements[30] (Fig. 5-1), thereby stabilizing one's gaze in space. It produces the vestibuloocular reflex or response (VOR). Its dynamic behavior[30] is presented in Fig. 5-2.

- *The optokinetic system.* This system produces eye movements that compensate for relatively *prolonged, sustained* self-rotational head movements (especially of low frequency, such as 0.01 Hz). That is, as the vestibular system begins to falter and exhibit progressively more response falloff with continued stimulation, the optokinetic system (with help from the *pursuit system*) gradually takes over and establishes its presence, resulting in optokinetic nystagmus (OKN).[30]

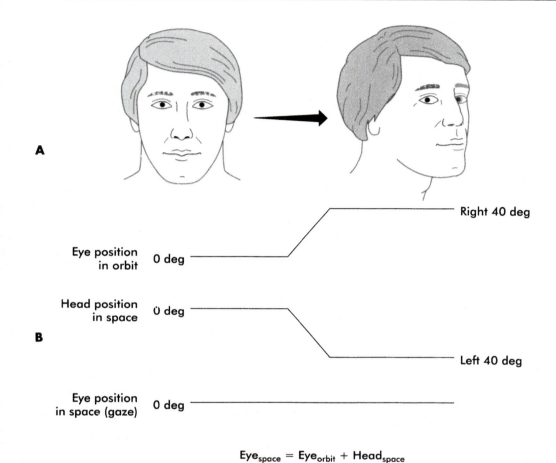

$$\text{Eye}_{space} = \text{Eye}_{orbit} + \text{Head}_{space}$$

FIG. 5-1   **A,** The function of the vestibuloocular reflex (VOR). As the head is rapidly turned to the left, the eyes move by a corresponding amount in the orbit to the right. **B,** Head position in space and eye position in the orbit are plotted against time. Because the movements of head and eye in orbit are equal and opposite, the sum, namely, the position in space (the angle of gaze, or *gaze*), remains zero *(bottom equation)*. If gaze is held steady, images do not slip on the retina and vision remains clear (schematic representation).

(From Leigh RJ, Zee DS: *The neurology of eye movements*, ed 2, Philadelphia, 1991, FA Davis.)

OPTOKINETIC SYSTEM AND ITS INTERACTIONS WITH THE VESTIBULAR SYSTEM

As stated earlier, the optokinetic system is important in stabilizing gaze and maintaining clear vision during sustained rotation. Once the transient vestibular system responsivity begins to decline and eventually ceases altogether as the rotation continues, the optokinetic system gradually becomes activated and replaces the vestibular system in its field-holding function until the rotation ceases. This

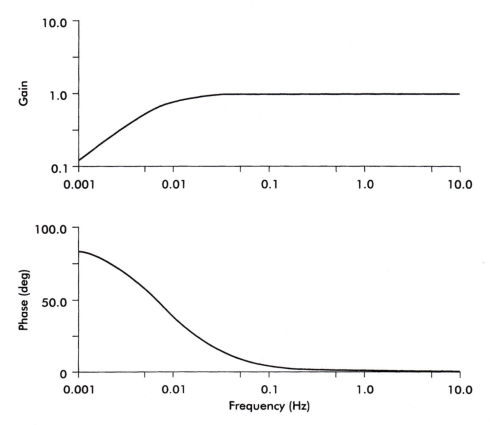

FIG. 5-2 Bode diagram of the VOR showing the idealized behavior of gain and phase with varying stimulus frequencies. For the frequency range of most natural head rotations (0.5 to 5.0 Hz), gain is 1.0 and phase shift is zero degrees.

(From Leigh RJ, Zee DS: *The neurology of eye movements,* ed 2, Philadelphia, 1991, FA Davis.)

process is evident in Fig. 5-3, *A* and *B*, which presents both the individual and combined neurophysiologic and motor responses of these two interactive systems for a sustained period of velocity stimulation.[12,39] By this cooperative arrangement a stable, clear retinal image prevails during the *entire* period of stimulation.

A second important element of this vestibular-optokinetic interaction occurs once the velocity stimulation ceases. If left alone, the vestibular system would exhibit several seconds of oppositely directed, postrotational nystagmus resulting from transient cupula displacement in the reverse direction (relative to that present during the initial velocity stimulation). However, the optokinetic system also exhibits a form of postrotational nystagmus, namely, *optokinetic afternystagmus* (OKAN); its direction is the same as that for both the initial vestibular nystagmus and the preceding OKN.[2,14,40] Thus the optokinetic system serves to cancel (along with the help of the fixation reflex) the oppositely directed, postrotational vestibular nystagmus, thereby minimizing the sensation of vertigo (see Fig. 5-3). The OKAN

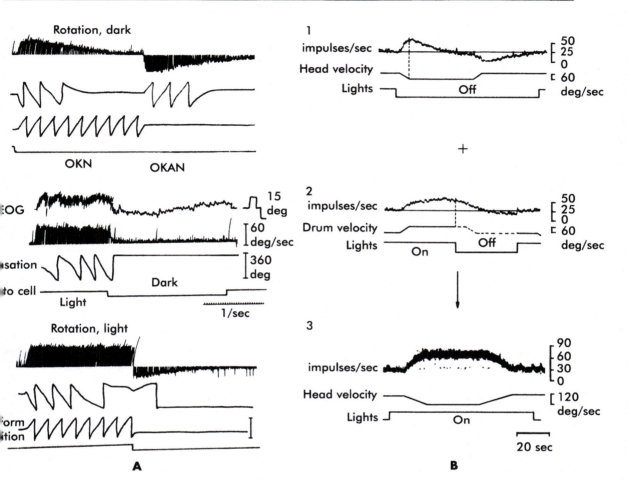

FIG. 5-3 **A,** Vestibular nystagmus, optokinetic nystagmus (OKN), and optokinetic af-ternystagmus (OKAN) in a human in response to platform rotation *(1 and 3)* or surround rotation *(2)* at 60 deg/sec. *1,* Entire test was in darkness. *2 and 3,* Surround and person, re-spectively, were rotated in light, and the OKAN or postrotatory nystagmus was recorded in darkness. *Traces (top to bottom),* Horizontal eye position, slow-phase eye velocity, rotation sensation, and photo cell showing the presence or absence of light. Rotation sensation was determined subjectively by turning a potentiometer; one full turn represents 360 degrees. The weak OKAN after OKN at 60 deg/sec *(2)* is evident. The decrease in slow-phase veloc-ity and sensation of rotation in light *(3)* as compared with that after rotation in dark *(1)* can be seen. *HEOG,* horizontal electro-oculogram. **B,** Unit activity recorded from a central vestibular neuron in response to: *1,* rotation of the animal in darkness (vestibular re-sponse), *2,* rotation of the optokinetic drum around the stationary animal (optokinetic re-sponse) (the lights "on" and "off" trace are shown), and *3,* rotation of the animal relative to the stationary drum in the light (combined response).

(**A,** from Cohen B and others: *N Y Acad Sci* 374:421, 1981; **B,** from Raphan T, Cohen B. In Berthoz A, Melvill-Jones G, editors; *Adaptive mechanisms in gaze control: facts and theories,* Amsterdam, 1985, Else-vier.)

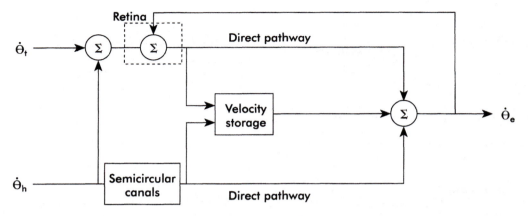

FIG. 5-4 Model of visual-vestibular interaction. $\dot{\theta}_t$, Target (foveal or full field) velocity; $\dot{\theta}_h$, head velocity; $\dot{\theta}_e$, eye velocity.

(From Raphan T, Cohen B. In Berthoz A, Melvill-Jones G, editors: *Adaptive mechanisms in gaze control: facts and figures,* Amsterdam, 1985, Elsevier. After Cohen B and others: *Ann NY Acad Sci* 374:421, 1981.)

results from a phenomenon called *velocity storage*.[2,12,39] Velocity storage is presumed to be due to an indirect central neurologic integrating circuit that is activated by the input and gradually "stores" this velocity information but then discharges it after the input has ceased (Fig. 5-4). One can conceptualize this process as akin to charging a capacitor (stimulation period in the light) and then allowing it to discharge or decay slowly in an exponential manner (poststimulation period in the dark), with this added neural velocity storage signal effectively increasing the time constant of the system. If the light is maintained during the OKAN period, however, the response time constant is greatly shortened as a result of a visual fixation or suppression mechanism.[12,39]

VESTIBULAR SYSTEM

As stated earlier, the primary vision-specific purpose of the vestibular system (the vestibuloocular reflex [VOR]), is to maintain retinal-image stabilization during relatively brief periods of head movement. In a more global context, the vestibular reflexes are also responsible for maintenance of overall body posture, equilibrium, and muscle tone.[2]

The vestibular system rapidly and efficiently produces eye movements to compensate for transient head movements by converting the forces involved during head rotation and tilt into neural control information for the oculomotor system, thereby maintaining accurate gaze on the object of interest. This accomplishment is determined by means of basic physics (Newton's second law) and calculus (integration).[2] Since the force exerted on the vestibular end organs is equal to F = ma (force = mass × acceleration) and the end organ mass is constant, the force is proportional to acceleration. This acceleration information is effectively mechanically integrated into a head-velocity signal, and, later in the oculomotor pathway, integrated once again to yield head displacement or position.

The preceding calculations are performed by the vestibular end organ for both linear (head translation) and angular (head rotation) accelerations[2,30,36] (Fig. 5-5). The anatomic, biophysical, and neurologic aspects of the vestibular end organs tranduction processes are described as following.

- The three *semicircular canals* are used to sense *transient angular accelerations* of the head (Fig. 5-5, *A*). As the head is rotated

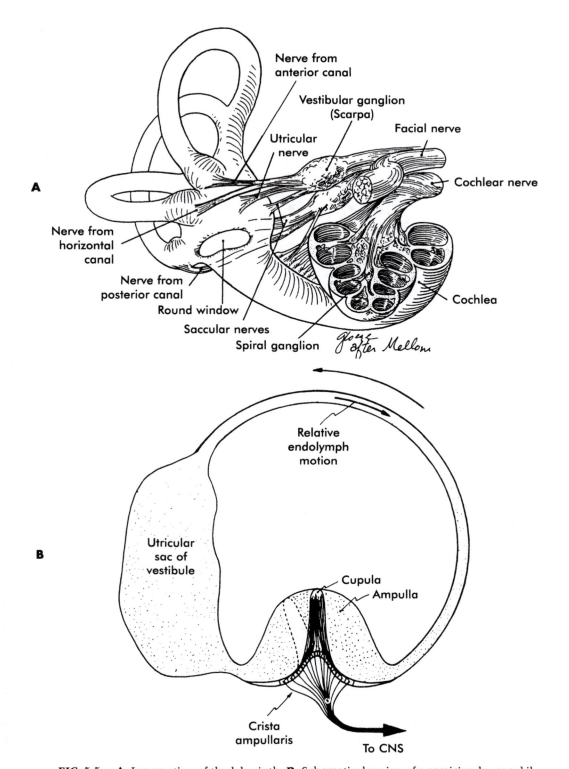

A, Nerve from
anterior canal

Vestibular ganglion
(Scarpa)

Facial nerve

Utricular
nerve

Cochlear nerve

Nerve from
horizontal
canal

Nerve from
posterior canal

Round window

Saccular nerves

Cochlea

Spiral ganglion

*Relative
endolymph
motion*

Utricular
sac of
vestibule

Cupula
Ampulla

Crista
ampullaris

To CNS

FIG. 5-5 **A,** Innervation of the labyrinth. **B,** Schematic drawing of a semicircular canal illustrating the relationship between the direction of head rotation *(large arrow),* endolymph flow *(small arrow),* and cupular deviation.

Continued.

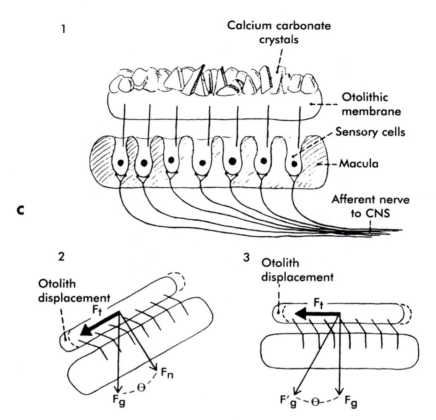

FIG. 5-5, cont'd. C, Graphic illustration of the main anatomic features of the macula *(1)* and the distribution of forces associated with static head tilt *(2)* and linear acceleration tangential to the surface *(3)*. F_g, Force of gravity; F_n, force normal to the receptor surface; F_t, tangential force.

(**A** and **C,** from Baloh RW, Honrubia V: *Clinical neurophysiology of the vestibular system*, ed 2, Philadelphia, 1990, FA Davis; **B,** from Melvill-Jones G. In Bach-y-rita P, Collins CC, Hyde JE, editors; *The control of eye movements*, New York, 1971, Academic.)

(that is, accelerated) in one direction, the endolymphatic fluid is displaced in the canal(s) in the opposite direction (Fig. 5-5, *B*).[36] Because of the anatomy and biophysics of the canals, the resultant endolymphatic motion is actually proportional to *head velocity;* thus in essence the canals have performed a mechanical integration. This endolymphatic movement produces a displacement of the gelatinous cupula (containing embedded processes of the sensory hair cells of the cristae), which in turn stimulates the hair cell sensory endings in the cristae via mechanical shearing forces, resulting in a head-velocity neural signal. This velocity signal is later integrated once again by the vestibular neural network to obtain a head displacement signal (see later section on neurophysiology).

- The complex comprising *the macula of the saccule, along with the utricle and otolith*, is used to sense *transient linear accelerations* of the head, as well as *static head tilt* (Fig. 5-5, *C*). Essentially the relatively heavy otolith, with calcium crystals embedded into its gelatinous matrix, "sits" atop the macula with its sensitive sensory hair cells. Any shift in the otolith provides information regarding the magnitude and direction of the effective force (tangential force [F_t]) acting on it. When the head is stationary and erect, there is the force of gravity (F_g) on the macula from the otolith. During a static head tilt, F_t is proportional to the magnitude of the angle made by vectors F_g and F_n (force normal to the receptor surface). During linear head acceleration there is, again, F_g, as well as instantaneous forces F'_g and F_t (in the direction opposite to the head acceleration). The resultant compensatory eye movement occurs with a short (total) latency of 35 msec and is called the translational vestibuloocular response (TVOR).[6] In both cases, the displacement of the otolith by F_t provides the head linear acceleration signal to the sensory cells of the macula.

The following facts about the vestibular system are also important:

- The VOR gain is defined as the ratio of the amplitude of eye rotation to the amplitude of head rotation.[30]
- The VOR gain for horizontal head movement is slightly greater than it is for vertical head movement.[25,26] Therefore compensatory eye movements are slightly better for horizontal than for vertical head movements (Figs. 5-6 and 5-7).
- For head rotation frequencies ranging from 0.5 to 5.0 Hz, the VOR gain is effectively 1.0 with a head-to-eye phase difference of approximately 180 degrees, as required to maintain precise visual stability with every head rotation or movement. In contrast, for low frequencies such as 0.01 Hz, the VOR gain decreases and the phase difference increases. Thus the VOR cannot respond adequately to such low-frequency sustained self-rotation.[30] It now requires OKN system activation to attain optimal overall combined performance.

- The VOR gain increases with decreased viewing distance to compensate for the difference (that is lack of coincidence) in axis of rotation of the head versus the eye.[50] Since the center of rotation of the eye is closer to a nearby object of interest than is the center of rotation of the head, the rotational signal sent from the head-based vestibular system to the oculomotor system and eyeball must be increased to maintain accurate fixation and visual stability with every head rotation. This suggests either that distance information is made rapidly available to the VOR system or that such distance-dependent VOR adaptation is extremely rapid. For far distances, the effect of such relatively small differences in axis of the head versus the eye is negligible.
- Vestibuloocular reflex gain decreases slightly with age.[51]
- During normal everyday activities such as walking and running, the VOR system compensates extremely well for the range of frequencies and velocities encountered (see Figs. 5-6 and 5-7). The gain remains effectively 1.0, with little change in phase for a wide range of such activities.[25,26]
- During modest to vigorous levels of horizontal head rotation, vergence error (that is, fixation disparity) at near distances remains small (<10-min arc), with the bifixation stimuli typically falling within foveal Panum's fusional areas.[10]
- For all practical purposes, the VOR is hardly evident in congenitally blind individuals, which suggests that early normal visual experience (especially visual feedback) is necessary for its proper develop-

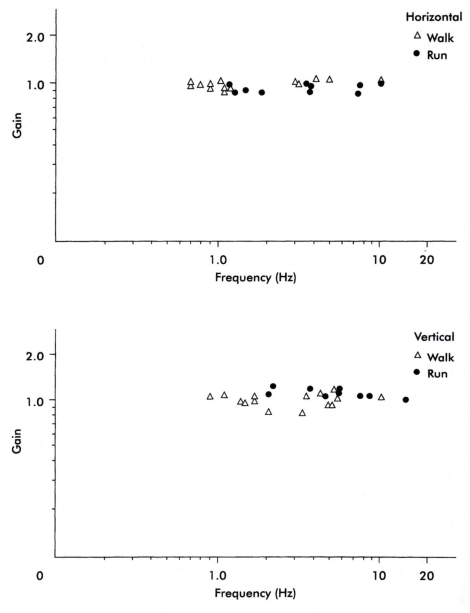

FIG. 5-6   Measured values of the horizontal and vertical VOR gain while subjects either walked or ran in place and fixed upon a distant visual target.

(From Grossman GE and others: *J Neurophysiol* 62:264, 1989.)

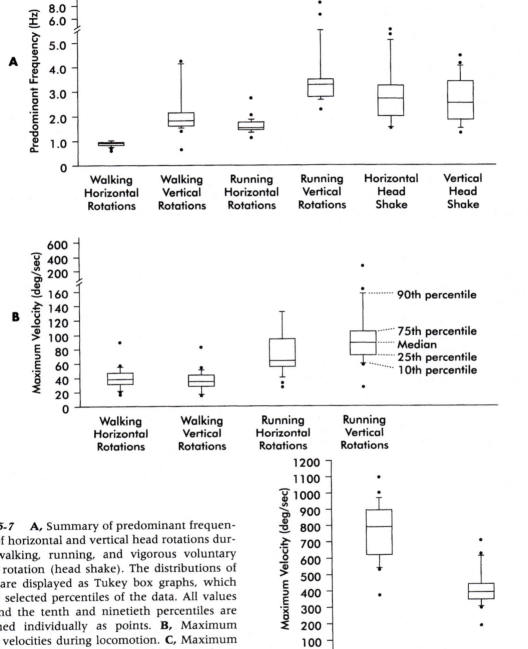

FIG. 5-7 **A,** Summary of predominant frequencies of horizontal and vertical head rotations during walking, running, and vigorous voluntary head rotation (head shake). The distributions of data are displayed as Tukey box graphs, which show selected percentiles of the data. All values beyond the tenth and ninetieth percentiles are graphed individually as points. **B,** Maximum head velocities during locomotion. **C,** Maximum head velocities during vigorous, voluntary horizontal and vertical head rotations.

(From Grossman GE and others: *Exp Brain Res* 70:470, 1988.)

ment.[45] In adventitiously blind individuals the VOR is reduced, which suggests that normal visual experience is necessary for its maintenance.[45]

- Vestibuloocular reflex latency is 16 msec.[33]
- Vestibuloocular reflex time constant is 10 seconds in adults[52] and 6 seconds in infants (first 2 months of life),[30] suggesting slightly less precise ocular compensation for head movements in early infancy.

VESTIBULOOCULAR REFLEX PLASTICITY

As discussed in other chapters, the oculomotor system exhibits some degree of neuromotor plasticity, that is, adaptation. This adaptation is important because the system can appropriately compensate (at least partially) in response to changes resulting from normal growth and development, advancing age, and neurologic disease.

In addition, however, important optically induced magnification changes alter the relationship between head movement and retinal-image displacement or slippage. In perhaps the most extreme case, left-right reversing prisms have been used which demand that the VOR gain change from +1 to −1 to achieve full visual stability. That is, the eye must then rotate in the *same* direction (and magnitude), rather than in its normally opposing direction, to prevent the occurrence of oscillopsia and blurred vision with head movement. As might be expected in such an extreme case, VOR adaptation is slow (several days) and incomplete (75%).[24]

A less demanding but more clinically relevant paradigm occurs with the use of telescopic spectacles, as would be found in a bioptic configuration for individuals with the most extreme visual impairment. Demer and others[20] tested such telescopes (2×, 4×, and 6×) in visually normal persons. They found up to 50% VOR adaptation (in the dark) immediately following only 15 minutes of VOR training (in the light), for example, sinusoidal head rotation while viewing targets displayed on a monitor 4 meters away through the telescope. Such rapid (albeit partial) adaptation is important in minimizing the adverse consequences (that is, nausea, oscillopsia, and blur) caused by the initial marked visual-vestibular conflict. This rapid adaptation was not dependent on either telescopic magnification or the person's age, and there was no cumulative learning effect with repeated testing on different days. However, VOR adaptation was greater with the peripheral, nonmagnified portion of the field occluded; this occlusion presumably prevented the normally conflicting central versus peripheral magnification differences from compromising the central neural adaptive process. It has been speculated that the neural substrate underlying this adaptive process includes the inferior olivary nucleus, parietal cortex, and the vestibulocerebellum, as well as the brain's catecholine level.

Less demanding than the preceding but probably of greatest clinical relevance is the rotational magnification effect created by spectacle correction. Because of the optics (that is, prismatic displacement) (Fig. 5-8), a person with myopia and corrective lenses (minus or negative) whose visual field is effectively minified requires *less* VOR-related ocular rotation or gain (G) (G < 1) for a given angular rotation of the head; just the opposite (G > 1) is true for the person with hyperopia and corrective lenses (plus or positive).[15] This effect has been objectively demonstrated, and normalized gain was related to refractive error magnitude and type (Fig. 5-9).[7] The rotational magnification factor was approximately 2.5%/D. When these same persons then removed their spectacles, the VOR gain readapted appropriately (G approaches 1) to a great extent within 30 minutes. Similarly rapid VOR adaptation to changes in bilateral spectacle magnification

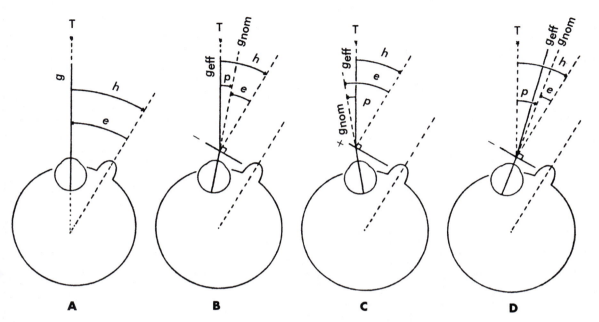

A   **B**   **C**   **D**

FIG. 5-8   Diagrams of the relation between head *(h)* and eye-in-head *(e)* rotation to maintain perfect fixation of a target *(T)* at infinite distance. In all cases head rotation is exemplified as equal to 30 degrees to the right. **A,** No glasses; when *e* equals *–h,* the gaze *(g)* is aligned with the target. **B,** Negative spectacles with magnification factor 0.66; *e* equals *–0.66 h.* Although the effective line of sight *(g_eff)* is aligned with the target, the angle of the eye in space (nominal gaze [*g_nom*]) has rotated through an angle *p* (p = 10 degrees) with the head. **C,** Positive glasses with magnification factor 1.33; *e* equals *–1.33 h.* The nominal gaze direction has rotated through an angle *p* (p = 10 degrees) opposite to the head. **D,** Negative glasses, as in **B,** but assuming an effective gain of only 0.5, that is, a displacement of the effective gaze through 15 degrees with the head (h = 30 degrees, e = –10 degrees; p = 20 degrees).

(From Collewijn H, Martins AJ, Steinman RM: *J Physiol* 340:259, 1983.)

(defocus was also unfortunately introduced) has been reported by Collewijn, Martins, and Steinman[15] (Fig. 5-10). With a moderate degree of interocular magnification asymmetry (that is, aniseikonia), as might be found in anisometropia, VOR gain adapted to an intermediate level such that the overall summed retinal-image motion from the two eyes was minimal; thus the retinal error was distributed symmetrically between the two eyes. When a patient with optically induced aniseikonia reports having "gotten used to" their new spectacles and no longer reports disorientation, nau-sea, "swimming" motion of the field with head movement, and errors in sensorimotor performance (such as misjudging distance when grasping for a nearby object), the phenomenon probably involves two primary processes[11]: VOR adaptation, as discussed earlier, and the more traditional cue-conflict–based (that is, retinal disparity versus the other depth cues) visual perceptual recalibration of the depth-disparity relationship. Such rotational magnification changes do not occur with contact lenses, since contact lenses move with the eye.

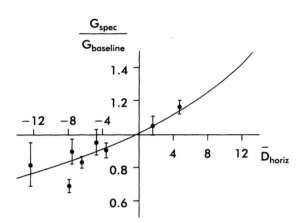

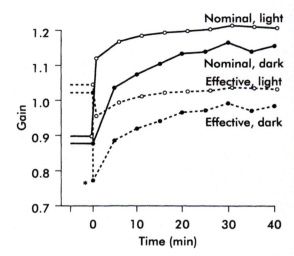

FIG. 5-9 Normalized VOR gain measured in darkness as a function of diopter of spectacle correction(D_{horiz}). Each spectacle-adapted VOR gain, (G_{spec},) is normalized using each subject's baseline VOR gain($G_{baseline}$) measured after adapting either to no correction or to contact lenses (error bars indicate 95% confidence intervals). The normalized gain directly represents the amount of adaptive change in gain relative to baseline values.

(From Cannon SC and others: *Acta Otolaryngol* 100:81, 1985.)

FIG. 5-10 Time course of nominal and effective gain in light and dark during a short-term adaptation experiment in which the subject changed his normal, negative glasses for +5D spectacles. Active head movements (at 0.66 Hz) were made continuously during 40 minutes. *Asterisk*, theoretical value to which effective VOR gain in the dark was reduced from the preexisting value by the magnifying lenses.

(From Collewijn H, Martins AJ, Steinman RM: *J Physiol* 340:259, 1983.)

OPTOKINETIC SYSTEM

Optokinetic nystagmus (OKN) is an involuntary jerk nystagmus ("sawtooth" waveform) typically induced by generalized movement of all or a large part of the visual field. This waveform is characterized by its *linear* slow-phase tracking response made in an attempt to stabilize the retinal image and its fast saccadic phase, which "resets" the eye back into primary position.[14] In the typical clinical laboratory test situation,[6] a large drum with black and white stripes painted on its inner surface encircles the patient and the attached objective eye movement recording system (Fig. 5-11). The drum is rotated at varying constant (or sinusoidal) velocities. For exam-

ple, at each constant stimulus velocity, the optokinetic gain is calculated: slow-phase eye velocity is divided by stimulus velocity.

The following are additional important facts about the optokinetic system:

- To develop optokinetic stimulation optimally, one should have a large field of motion (such as the encircling striped drum previously described), a relatively passive subject with no desire to pursue any particular element of the display, and velocity, not position, as the relevant stimulus dimension.[14]
- The initial 1 or 2 seconds of response, which already attain maximal velocity (G = 0.8), is probably primarily due to pur-

FIG. 5-11 Optokinetic cylinder with sliding doors to enclose the subject completely.

(From Buttner U, Henn V. In Cohen B, editor: *Vestibular and oculomotor physiology: international meeting of the Barany Society*, vol 374, New York, 1981, The New York Academy of Sciences.)

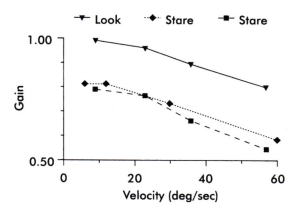

FIG. 5-12 Gain of human-stare optokinetic nystagmus (OKN) as a function of stimulus velocity for different instructions. *Triangles,* instruction to pursue a feature (look OKN); *squares,* instruction to fixate an imagined, stationary point lying straight ahead (stare OKN): *diamonds,* instruction to pay attention to the moving pattern without pursuing any particular feature (stare OKN).

(From Van der Berg AV, Collewijn H: *Exp Brain Res* 70:597, 1988.)

suit system activation, with the optokinetic system dominating for the duration of the stimulation.[30]

- The peripheral retina dominates the response[8]; for example, in patients with deep central scotomas OKN gain is only reduced by 10% to 30%.[56]
- Low spatial-frequency content of the stimulus primarily drives the response[13]; thus the OKN response is not much affected by blur, as might be present with uncorrected refractive error.[38]
- The latency is 140 msec[14]; thus the OKN response (as compared with the VOR latency of 16 msec) starts too late to prevent degradation of the retinal image concurrent with the initial head movement.[14]
- The maximal closed-loop gain (0.8) is noticeably less than unity for "stare OKN" (as when the subject just stares ahead passively) than for "look OKN" (as when the subject is told to pursue some particular feature of the stimulus), in which the gain is, indeed, near unity for low velocities (Fig. 5-12); thus the instruction set can markedly influence the motor outcome.[48]
- The open-loop gain progressively declines from 100 for a target velocity of <0.01 deg/sec to 1 at 10 deg/sec to 0.2 at 70

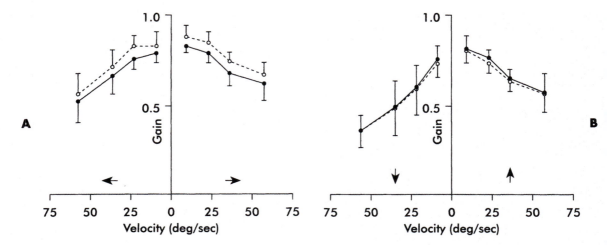

FIG. 5-13 OKN gain as a function of the stimulus and the direction of motion in humans (means of seven subjects; *bars* indicate 1 SD). Viewing was binocular. **A,** Horizontal OKN gain. **B,** Vertical OKN gain. *Arrows* indicate the direction of the stimulus. *Broken lines* and *open symbols,* right eye; *continuous lines* and *filled symbols,* left eye.

(From Van den Berg AV, Collewijn H: *Exp Brain Res* 70:597, 1988.)

deg/sec,[11] although these values appear to represent optimal conditions.

- Gain for horizontal and vertical optokinetic nystagmus is similar, although vertical gain falls off slightly faster as target velocity is increased[48] (Fig. 5-13).
- Vertical OKN gain upward is slightly greater than vertical OKN gain downward.[37]
- Torsional OKN is slow and irregular, and gain is low (0.03); overall it is quite rudimentary[16]; perhaps, from an evolutionary point of view, it need not have developed well, since it does not involve movement of the retinal image *away* from the fovea but rather rotational movement *centered* on the fovea.[30]
- Nasalward OKN gain is slightly greater (by 0.05) than templeward OKN gain[48]; thus nasalward stimulation is a bit more effective than templeward stimulation in persons with normal vision.

- Scotopic OKN gain is only slightly lower (by 0.1) than photopic OKN gain.[49]
- Full-field OKN stimulation with a large patterned drum surrounding a stationary subject typically produces the sensation of circularvection, or self-rotation in the opposite direction to drum rotation or stimulus motion.[4,6]
- The markedly asymmetric OKN found in newborns (reduced motor response for nasalward to templeward motion) is found to decrease considerably between 2 and 3 months of age but is still not quite adultlike at 6 months of age; the improvement presumably reflects maturation of the retinocorticopretectal neural pathways and the development of binocular vision pathways.[31]
- OKN maximal velocity decreases progressively (1 deg/sec per year) with increased age in adulthood[3,46] (Fig. 5-14).
- OKAN time constant is quite long (~5 to 50 sec).[22]

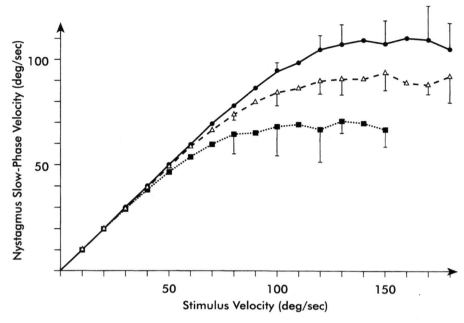

FIG. 5-14 OKN slow-phase velocity for age group 1 (*solid line with solid dots*, 20 to 39 years of age), group 2 (*dashed line with open triangles*, 40 to 59 years of age), and group 3 (*dashed line with solid squares*, 60 to 82 years of age) at different stimulus velocities; average values are shown. *Vertical bars* indicate standard deviation (not shown in all instances). With increasing age, maximal OKN velocity decreases.

(From Simons B, Buttner U: *Eur Arch Psychiatr Neurol Sci* 234:369, 1985.)

NEUROPHYSIOLOGY AND RELATED MODELING OF THE VESTIBULO-OPTOKINETIC PATHWAYS

The classic three-neuron reflex-arc (semicircular canals to extraocular muscles) representation of the vestibular pathway is schematically presented in Fig. 5-15.[28] Although the representation obviously an oversimplification, it still serves as a valuable framework from which the system can be understood. Within the semicircular canals, the hair cells in the cupula and cristae convert the mechanical signal related to head velocity into an electrical signal, which is then transmitted centrally via the primary vestibular nerve. There it synapses onto secondary vestibular neurons within the vestibular nuclei. This signal is then sent via the medial longitudinal fasciculus to the oculomotor neurons, where the second synapse is made. The information is then transmitted to the extraocular muscles, where the third synapse is made. Similar pathways are used after otolith stimulation.

Clearly there are many other neural structures and pathways that affect the previously described basic VOR neural complex. For example, the inferior olivary nucleus, parietal

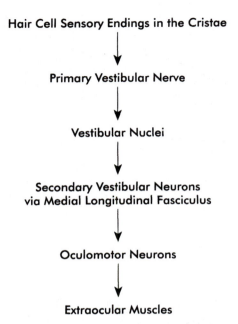

FIG. 5-15 Classic three-neuron reflex-arc vestibular pathway and related structures.

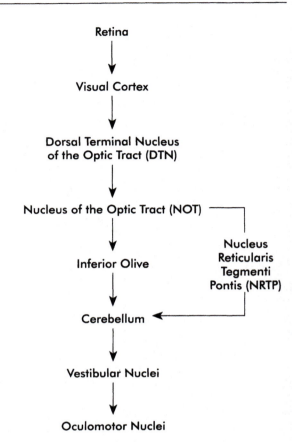

FIG. 5-16 Optokinetic pathway.

cortex, flocculus, and vestibulocerebellum have been implicated in VOR adaptation.[20] The combined medial vestibular nuclei and nearby nucleus prepositus hypoglossi complex perform the neural integration from eye velocity to eye position, and secondary vestibular neurons, which are part of this network, then carry the eye position signal.[30]

The neural pathway for the optokinetic system is presented in Fig. 5-16. Its anatomic goal, like that of the vestibular pathway, is the vestibular nucleus. The following is a *key point:* the vestibular nuclear cells respond both to *actual* semicircular canal stimulation (in the dark) and to *relative* rotation of the surrounding OKN surface when the subject is stationary (in the light); the latter result explains the vestibular-like illusion of circularvection mentioned earlier.[14] Thus with actual head

rotation the transient, exponentially decaying, semicircular canal-based response, in conjunction with the sustaining, exponentially rising optokinetic-based response, yields an overall response that is appropriately active during the entire stimulation period (see Fig. 5-3).

The vestibular and optokinetic systems have been conceptually modeled as one cooperative system network[29] (Fig. 5-17). The notion that both retinal-based and canal-based information affect estimated rotational head velocity converging on the vestibular nucleus is once again evident.

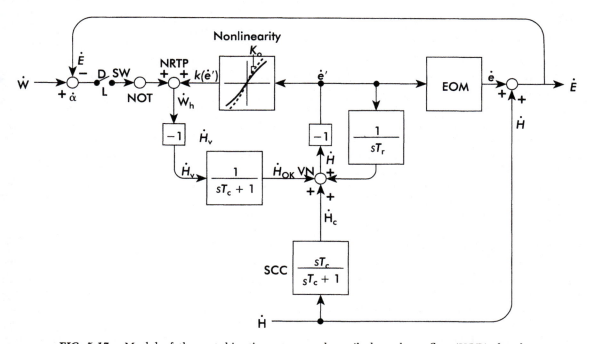

FIG. 5-17 Model of the optokinetic system and vestibuloocular reflex (VOR) that has been used to simulate periodic alternating nystagmus (PAN). Head velocity, $\dot{H}$, is tranduced by the semicircular canals *(SCCs)* into the neural output signal, $\dot{H}_c$. T_c, the capula time constant; s, the Laplace transform complex frequency. $\dot{H}_c$ passes to the vestibular nucleus, *VN*, and after a sign change it becomes an eye velocity command, $\dot{e}'$, which drives the eyes through the extraocular muscles *(EOM)* at velocity $\dot{e}$. This pathway is a simplified version of the VOR. $\dot{e}$ sums with $\dot{H}$ to give slow-phase gaze velocity in space, $\dot{E}$. The optokinetic system is stimulated by retinal-image velocity, error signal, $\dot{\alpha}$, minus the difference between the velocity of the visual world, $\dot{W}$, and $\dot{E}$ when the lights are on (indicated by switch, *SW*, being turned on, *L*; it is open in darkness, *D*). The error signal, $\dot{\alpha}$, passes via the nucleus of the optic tract, *NOT*, to the nucleus reticularis tegmenti pontis, *NRTP*, where an efference copy of eye velocity, $k(\dot{e}')$, is added to $\dot{\alpha}$ to give $\dot{W}_h$, the velocity of the environment with respect to the head. Since the seen world never moves, $-\dot{W}_h$ is the visual system's estimate of head velocity in space, $\dot{H}_v$. The high-frequency components of $\dot{H}_v$ are filtered out, and the resulting optokinetic signal, $\dot{H}_{OK}$, is added to $\dot{H}_c$ in the vestibular nucleus. The sum, $\dot{H}$, is the brain's best estimate of rotational head velocity. A central adaptation operator, $1/sT_r$, monitors the slow-phase eye-velocity command, $\dot{e}'$, and acts to eliminate persistent nystagmus by sending a signal back to the vestibular nucleus to cancel the source of vestibular imbalance. Normally the value of gain, k, is slightly smaller than 1.0, but for PAN to occur, k's value increases, and, if the retinal-error signal, $\dot{\alpha}$, is denied access to the *NRTP*, the system becomes unstable. To constrain the oscillations, a nonlinearity has been introduced, with output $k(\dot{e}')$. For the system to oscillate, the slope of this function at the origin, k_o, must meet certain specifications.

(From Leigh RJ, Robinson DA, Zee DS: *Ann NY Acad Sci* 374:619, 1981.)

ABNORMAL VESTIBULAR AND OPTOKINETIC FUNCTION
Abnormal Vestibular Function

Functional amblyopia. Only a handful of studies have involved vestibular function in the amblyopic eye; these typically show asymmetric and reduced responses. Salman and von Noorden[41] found caloric-induced nystagmus in patients with strabismus (many presumably with amblyopia resulting from the early onset of the strabismus) to have a more variable amplitude and frequency, as compared with results for children with normal vision, and found the caloric-induced nystagmus to be similar to what may be found in some neurologic disorders. Thus the authors emphasized the need for clinicians to be aware of such "abnormal" responses in an otherwise apparently healthy population, especially as related to differential diagnosis in patients suspected of having organic or neurologic disease. Hoyt[27] reported reduced vestibuloocular responses in 14 of 24 persons with congenital esotropia (without apparent nystagmus) during clinical testing. However, recent work by Tychsen, Hurtig, and Scott[47] shows normal vestibular responses in infantile strabismus when contamination from the (defective) pursuit system is absent. Flynn[23] reported gaze-dependent failure to suppress the vestibuloocular response in some patients with congenital esotropia. Schor and Westall[44] found vestibular imbalance in the dark in persons with amblyopia; that is, the saccade-free slow-phase component of the responses to sinusoidal head rotation in darkness exhibited a directional preference. This directional bias was the same as that found during fixation in total darkness in these same subjects. The authors speculated that the vestibular imbalance could account for half of the variance in dark drift. More recently Westall and Schor[53] found asymmetric vestibuloocular adaptation in persons with strabismic amblyopia. The vestibuloocular gain increased more after adaptation to nasal field motion than after temporal field motion. There was no difference in adaptive capability between the amblyopic and fellow dominant eye, suggesting that this abnormality asymmetric adaptation was related to the presence of strabismus and not the amblyopia.

Vestibular disorders. Peripheral disease or disorders of the labyrinth complex or vestibular nerve, as well as dysfunction of central vestibular structures and pathways, may result in mild to markedly disabling visual consequences, as categorized in the text,[30] although "vestibular exercises" have been developed to promote rapid recovery in specific conditions[2] (Box 5-1 and, for a different classification scheme, Box 5-2):

- *Unilateral (acute) peripheral disorders* cause transient "imbalance" in vestibular tone, that is, baseline tonic innervation, between the left and right vestibular nuclei. This imbalance results in spontaneous nystagmus with a slow phase directed toward the side of the lesion. The nystagmus is generally much greater in the dark than in the light, thus clearly demonstrating the beneficial effect of visual feedback in counteracting the nystagmus and therefore minimizing its adverse visual impact. Such patients may exhibit subtle vestibular abnormalities for many years after the acute phase and assumed full recovery. These residual effects, however, do not become manifest under most normal visual conditions.
- *Bilateral (acute) peripheral disorders of the labyrinth* cause serious problems for the patient, namely, oscillopsia and degraded vision, because of the inadequate compensatory ability of the VOR reflex. A variety of sensory, motor, and perceptual adaptive mechanisms may be used by the patient to compensate for the adverse visual consequences of such dysfunction.
- *Central vestibular disorders* may cause a variety of problems, depending on the

---

BOX 5-1   *Vestibular Exercises*

In bed
Eye movements at first slow, then quick
Gazing up and down
Gazing from side to side
Focusing on finger moving from 30 to 10 cm
  away from face

Sitting
Head movements as described above for eyes
Shoulder shrugging and circling
Bending forward and picking up objects
  from ground

Standing
Eye and head movements; shoulder shrugging and circling, as above

Changing from sitting to standing position
  with eyes open and closed
Throwing small ball from hand to hand
  (above eye level)
Throwing ball from hand to hand under
  knee
Changing from sitting to standing position,
  turning around in between

Moving about
Walking across room with eyes open and
  then closed
Walking up and down sloped surface with
  eyes open and then closed
Performing any game involving stooping,
  stretching, and aiming

From Baloh RW, Honrubia V: *Clinical neurophysiology of the vestibular system,* ed 2, Philadelphia, 1990, FA Davis.

BOX 5-2   *Common Disorders of the Vestibular System*

Infectious disorders
Otitis media (middle ear)
Labyrinthitis (bacterial, viral)
Intracranial extension of ear infections (for
  example, meningitis, brain abscess)
Herpes zoster oticus
Chronic otomastoiditis

Benign positional vertigo
Meniere's syndrome
Vascular disorders
Vertebrobasilar insufficiency (VBI)
Labyrinthine ischemia or infarction
Infarction of the brainstem or cerebellum
  (for example, Wallenberg's syndrome [see
  Chapter 10])
Intralabyrinthine hemorrhage
Hemorrhage into brainstem or cerebellum
Migraine

Tumors
Middle ear or temporal bone
Internal auditory canal or cerebellopontine
  angle (for example, neurofibromas,
  meningiomas)
Brain (brainstem, cerebelleum)

Trauma
Temporal bone
Perilymph fistula
Brain (for example, after concussion)

Metabolic disorders
Dizziness or systemic (for example, diabetes
  mellitus)
Temporal bone (for example, Paget's disease)
Familial ataxia syndromes (for example,
  Friedreich's ataxia [see Chapter 10])
Ototoxins (for example, high-dose salicylates)

Developmental disorders
Malformation of the inner ear
Disorders of the cranial vertebral junction
  (for example, Chiari malformation)

Other neurologic disorders
Multiple sclerosis
Focal seizures
Vascular occlusion
Bell's palsy
Whiplash injuries

anatomic site affected. Imbalance of tone may cause primary position spontaneous nystagmus similar to that found in unilateral peripheral disorders. With lesions in the central vestibular pathways, VOR gain may either increase or decrease, whereas phase lag increases and the time constant decreases. If the otoliths are affected, once again head tilt and skew deviation are found. In addition, patients may complain of perceived tilt of their visual world.

Abnormal Optokinetic Function

Functional amblyopia. Numerous reports have been made of asymmetric, reduced optokinetic responses in amblyopic eyes. In 50 patients with strabismic amblyopia and eccentric fixation, asymmetric optokinetic nystagmus was found in 39 of the amblyopic eyes and in 25 of the fellow dominant eyes.[32] In this and *all* such cases, presence of habitual jerk nystagmus *must* first be ruled out before a sensory or developmental interpretation can be accepted. Presence of jerk nystagmus in the absence of strabismus or binocular suppression also produces such eye movement response asymmetries in each eye.

Schor and Levi[43] found reduced, asymmetric optokinetic slow-phase gain under (normal) closed-loop test target conditions in the amblyopic eye (Fig. 5-18). This abnormal response was also found in the fellow dominant eye of some of the persons with amblyopia. Such a finding is consistent with a report showing reduced, asymmetric optokinetic responses in each eye of cats reared throughout the critical period with surgically induced extropia,[17] suggesting that the finding was actually more related to the presence of strabismus than to any presumed amblyopia. Although there was a reduction in pattern and motion sensitivity in the amblyopic eye, this deficit was not direction dependent. Thus such a symmetric sensory disturbance of perceived motion could not account for the optokinetic motor system asymmetry. This conclusion is consistent with the recent finding showing absence of any directional impairment in velocity judgments in the presence of optokinetic asymmetries, suggesting that the defect lies beyond motion detection cells in the visual cortex of persons with amblyopia.[40] Schor and Levi[43] did not find a direct relationship between the degree of optokinetic abnormality and the visual acuity in the amblyopic eye, although persons with the most severe amblyopia generally showed a greater deficit than did those with moderate degrees of amblyopia. The authors presented arguments to suggest that the asymmetry was greater than could be accounted for by the presence of either latent nystagmus or fixational drift biases. Schor and Levi speculated that the asymmetric optokinetic nystagmus was due to incomplete development of binocular vision, specifically, to cortical mechanisms mediating temporally driven optokinetic responses, before the age of 4 years.

The previously mentioned basic ideas were summarized and later expanded on by Schor,[41] who then also implicated subcortical pretectal mechanisms underlying these abnormal responses. Mein[34] found asymmetric optokinetic responses only in patients having strabismus, nystagmus, *and* dissociated vertical divergence, not in other patients with either early or late onset of strabismus. Most interestingly, only when the nystagmus was *absent* did the optokinetic asymmetry no longer prevail. Westall and Schor[53] studied optokinetic asymmetries as related to size and location of the retinal stimulating area under open-loop test target conditions. All amblyopic eyes exhibited greater responses for nasal than for temporal target movement for the large central, small central, and peripheral concentric stimulating fields. The responses were reduced more for temporal than for nasal hemiretinal stimulation. The authors speculated that the asymmetric optokinetic responses were due to reduced cortical input

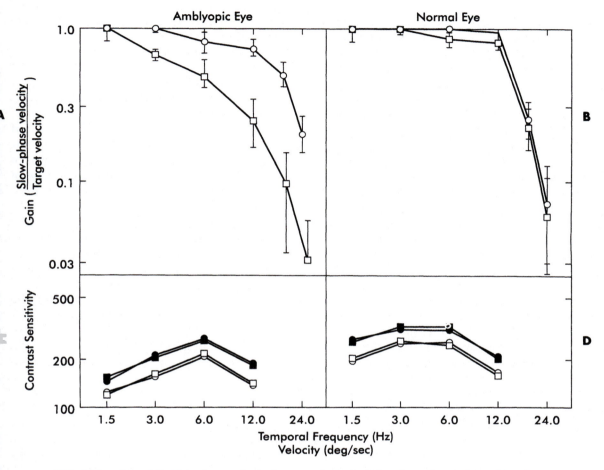

FIG. 5-18 **A** and **B,** Gain (eye velocity/target velocity) of the slow phase of optokinetic nystagmus (OKN) for the moderately amblyopic eye (20/70) and nonamblyopic eye is plotted as a function of velocity of a 1-cycle-per-degree vertical sine-wave grating that is drifting either nasalward *(circles)* or temporalward *(squares)* at velocities ranging from 1.5 to 25 degrees per second. Gain of the temporal slow phase of the amblyopic eye is abnormally reduced at velocities above 6 degrees per second. Gain for the nasalward slow phase of the amblyopic eye and both directions of slow phase for the nonamblyopic eye is the same as observed for the normal control subjects. **C** and **D,** Contrast sensitivity to a 1-cycle-per-degree sinusoidal grating for the amblyopic and normal eye, respectively. Pattern sensitivity *(open symbols)* and movement sensitivity *(closed symbols)* are plotted in response to velocities ranging from 1.5 to 12 degrees per second in either the nasalward *(circles)* or temporalward *(squares)* direction. Sensitivity to nasalward and temporalward drifting gratings is symmetric for both the amblyopic and nonamblyopic eye.

(From Schor CM, Levi DM: *Invest Ophthalmol Vis Sci* 19:668, 1980.)

to subcortical structures, as well as to binocular cortical suppression effects in the amblyopic eye. The former idea might account for the presence of optokinetic asymmetry in *each* eye of the persons with amblyopia, as found in some of the patients in this and an earlier study under closed-loop conditions,[43] assuming absence of any bilateral jerk nystagmus. Westall and Shute[54] reported a moderate but significant improvement in optokinetic nystagmus slow-phase velocity after occlusion therapy in young persons with amblyopia.

Nystagmus. Over the past several decades numerous studies have demonstrated asymmetric or reduced gain optokinetic nystagmus, or both, in patients with congenital nystagmus.[30,55] These results have led to many interesting speculations and theories. One of the simplest and most obvious ideas, namely, interaction of the basic nystagmus motor pattern with the sensory retinal stimulus information, has received relatively little attention. Dell'Osso[18,19] and Ciuffreda[9] independently suggested that asymmetry in all smooth tracking responses probably reflected interaction of the variable, habitual motor-based nystagmus with the retinal velocity signal derived from the target. When the nystagmus was compensated for, tracking was reasonably smooth and symmetric. More recently, this idea was confirmed and extended to involve comparison of nystagmus under a variety of fixational and optokinetic paradigms in various types of patients.[1,21] In those with manifest-latent nystagmus, the "apparent" variable, asymmetric optokinetic nystagmus, was thought to result either from dynamic null point shifts that occurred during the actual tracking or from unpredictable, transient increases in the patient's "effort to see" that resulted in increased nystagmus intensity.[21] In the patients with either idiopathic or albinotic nystagmus the reduced, variable optokinetic responses in the meridian of their habitual nystagmus were presumed to be due to a velocity-adaptive ("motion-adaptive") process resulting in cancellation or suppression of the effective retinal signals to reduce the occurrence of any oscillopsia.

Neurologic disease or developmental states. Abnormalities of optokinetic nystagmus and optokinetic afternystagmus may be found in a variety of developmental states and neurologic disorders[30]:

- *Newborns:* Asymmetric responses (reduced motor response for nasal to temporal motion) are presumably related to lack of normal binocularity and immaturity of appropriate cortical and subcortical neural tracts.
- *Lesions in the anterior and cortical visual pathways:* Slow buildup of optokinetic responses and asymmetries may be found.
- *Unilateral and bilateral labyrinthine disorders:* In unilateral conditions there is increased slow-phase velocity toward the side of the lesion and bidirectional reduction of optokinetic afternystagmus. In bilateral conditions there is normal optokinetic nystagmus but absence of optokinetic afternystagmus.

REVIEW QUESTIONS

1. Describe the temporal changes in the vestibular and optokinetic motor and neural responsivity that occur with initiation of a 2-minute period of continuous rotation.
2. Relate the above to changes in the semicircular canals and macula complex.
3. Discuss how plasticity of the VOR is important in the prescription of new spectacle lenses by the optometrist.
4. How does the phenomenon of optokinetic after-nystagmus (OKAN) assist in the achievement of visual stability? How might this be important to a ballerina?
5. Describe possible vestibulooptokinetic problems in functional amblyopes.
6. List the symptoms patients may report with vestibular disorders.

REFERENCES

1. Abadi RV, Dickinson CM: The influence of pre-existing oscillations on the binocular optokinetic response, *Ann Neurol* 17:578, 1985.
2. Baloh RW, Honrubia V: *Clinical neurophysiology of the vestibular system,* ed 2, Philadelphia, 1990, FA Davis.
3. Baloh RW, Jacobson KM, Socotch TM: The effect of aging on visual-vestibuloocular responses, *Exp Brain Res* 95:509, 1993.
4. Brandt T, Dichgans J, Koenig E: Differential effects of central versus peripheral vision on egocentric and exocentric motion perception, *Exp Brain Res* 16:476, 1973.
5. Bronstein AM, Gresty MA: Short latency compensatory eye movement responses to transient linear head acceleration: a specific function of the otolith-ocular reflex, *Exp Brain Res* 71:406, 1988.
6. Buttner U, Henn V: Circularvection: psychophysics and single-unit recordings in the monkey. In Cohen B, editor: *Vestibular and oculomotor physiology: international meeting of the Barany Society,* vol 374, New York, 1981, The New York Academy of Sciences.
7. Cannon SC, Leigh RJ, Zee DS, Abel LA: The effect of rotational magnification of corrective spectacles on the quantitative evaluation of the VOR, *Acta Otolaryngol* 100:81, 1985.
8. Cheng M, Outerbridge JS: Optokinetic nystagmus during selective retinal stimulation, *Exp Brain Res* 23:129, 1975.
9. Ciuffreda KJ: Eye movements in amblyopia and strabismus, doctoral dissertation, University of California, Berkeley, 1977.
10. Ciuffreda KJ, Hokoda SC: Subjective vergence error at near during active head rotation, *Ophthalmic Physiol Optics* 5:411, 1985.
11. Ciuffreda KJ, Liu X, Mordi J: Short-term adaptation to optically-induced oblique aniseikonia, *Bino Vis* 6:217, 1991.
12. Cohen B, Henn V, Raphan T, Dennett D: Velocity storage, nystagmus, and visual-vestibular interactions in humans, *Ann N Y Acad Sci* 374:421, 1981.
13. Collewijn H: *The oculomotor system of the rabbit and its plasticity,* Berlin, 1981, Springer.
14. Collewijn H: The optokinetic contribution. In Cronly-Dillon J, editor: *Vision and visual dysfunction, vol 8, Eye movements,* Boca Raton, Fla, 1991, CRC.
15. Collewijn H, Martins AJ, Steinman RM: Compensatory eye movements during active and passive eye movements; fast adaptation to changes in visual magnification, *J Physiol* 340:259, 1983.

16. Collewijn H, Van der Steen J, Ferman L, Jansen TC: Human ocular counterroll: assessment of static and dynamic properties from electromagnetic search coil recordings, *Exp Brain Res* 59:185, 1985.
17. Cynader M, Harris L: Eye movements in strabismic cats, *Nature* 286:64, 1980.
18. Dell'Osso LF: *A dual-mode model of the normal eye tracking system and the system with nystagmus,* doctoral dissertation, University of Wyoming, Laramie, 1968.
19. Dell'Osso LF: Evaluation of smooth pursuit in the presence of congenital nystagmus, *Neuro-ophthalmol* 6:383, 1986.
20. Demer JL, Porter FI, Goldberg J, Jenkins HA, Schmidt K: Adaptation to telescopic spectacles: vestibulo-ocular reflex plasticity, *Invest Ophthalmol Vis Sci* 30;159, 1989.
21. Dickinson CM, Abadi RV: Pursuit and optokinetic responses in latent/manifest latent nystagmus, *Invest Ophthalmol Vis Sci* 31:1599, 1990.
22. Fletcher WA, Hain TC, Zee DS: Optokinetic nystagmus and nystagmus in human beings: relationship to nonlinear processing of information about retinal slip, *Exp Brain Res* 81:46, 1990.
23. Flynn JT: Vestibulo-optokinetic interactions in strabismus, *Am Orthoptic J* 32:36, 1982.
24. Gonshor A, Melvill-Jones G: Extreme vestibulo-ocular adaptation induced by prolonged optical reversal of vision, *J Physiol (Lond)* 256:381, 1976.
25. Grossman GE, Leigh RJ, Abel LA, Lanska DJ, Thurston SE: Frequency and velocity of rotational head perturbations during locomotion, *Exp Brain Res* 70:470, 1988.
26. Grossman GE, Leigh RJ, Bruce EN, Huebner WP, Lanska DJ: Performance of the human vestibulo-ocular reflex during locomotion, *J Neurophysiol* 62:264, 1989.
27. Hoyt CS: Abnormalities of the vestibulo-ocular response in congenital esotropia, *Am J Ophthalmol* 93:704, 1982.
28. Keller EL: The brainstem. In Cronly-Dillon J, editor: *Vision and visual dysfunction, vol 8, Eye movements,* Boca Raton, Fla, 1991, CRC.
29. Leigh RJ, Robinson DA, Zee DS: A hypothetical explanation for periodic alternating nystagmus: instability in the optokinetic-vestibular system, *Ann N Y Acad Sci* 374:619, 1981.
30. Leigh RJ, Zee DS: *The neurology of eye movements,* ed 2, Philadelphia, 1991, FA Davis.
31. Lewis TL, Maurer D, Smith RJ, Haslip JK: The development of symmetrical optokinetic nystagmus during infancy, *Clin Vis Sci* 7:211, 1992.

32. Loewer-Spieger DH: Amblyopie een studie over de kenmerken en de behandeling, *J Ruysendaal (Amsterdam)* 52:107, 1962.

33. Maas EF, Huebner WP, Seidman SH, Leigh RJ: Behavior of the human horizontal vestibulo-ocular reflex in response to high acceleration stimuli, *Brain Res* 499:153, 1989.

34. Mein J: The OKN response and binocular vision in early onset strabismus, *Aust Orthopt J* 20:13, 1983.

35. Melvill-Jones G: Organization of neural control in the vestibulo-ocular reflex arc. In Bachy-rita P, Collins, CC, Hyde JE, editors: *The control of eye movements*, New York, 1971, Academic.

36. Melvill-Jones G: The vestibular contribution. In Cronly-Dillon J, editor: *Vision and visual dysfunction, vol 8, Eye movements*, Boca Raton, Fla, 1991, CRC.

37. Murasugi CM, Howard IP: Human horizontal optokinetic nystagmus elicited by the upper versus lower visual fields, *Vis Neurosci* 2:73, 1989.

38. Post RB, Rodemer CS, Dichgans J, Leibowitz HW: Dynamic orientation responses are independent of refractive error, *Invest Ophthalmol Vis Sci (Suppl)* 18:140, 1979.

39. Raphan T, Cohen B: Velocity storage and the ocular response to multidimensional vestibular stimuli. In Berthoz A, Melvill-Jones G, editors: *Adaptive mechanisms in gaze control: facts and theories*, Amsterdam, 1985, Elsevier.

40. Roberts N, Westall C: OKN asymmetries in amblyopia: their effect on velocity perception, *Clin Vis Sci* 5:383, 1990.

41. Salman SD, von Noorden GK: Induced vestibular nystagmus in strabismic patients, *Ann Otol Rhinol Laryngol* 79:352, 1970.

42. Schor CM: Subcortical binocular suppression affects the development of latent and optokinetic nystagmus, *Am J Optom Physiol Optics* 60;481, 1983.

43. Schor CM, Levi DM: Disturbances of small-field horizontal and vertical optokinetic nystagmus in nystagmus, *Invest Ophthalmol Vis Sci* 19:668, 1980.

44. Schor CM, Westall C: Visual and vestibular sources of fixation instability in amblyopia, *Invest Ophthalmol Vis Sci* 25:729, 1984.

45. Sherman KR, Keller EL: Vestibulo-ocular reflexes of adventitiously and congenitally blind adults, *Invest Ophthalmol Vis Sci* 27:1154, 1986.

46. Simons B, Buttner U: The influence of age on optokinetic nystagmus, *Eur Arch Psychiatr Neurol Sci* 234:369, 1985.

47. Tychsen L, Hurtig RR, Scott WE: Pursuit is impaired but the vestibulo-ocular reflex is normal in infantile strabismus, *Arch Ophthalmol* 103:536, 1985.

48. Van den Berg AV, Collewijn H: Directional asymmetries of human optokinetic nystagmus, *Exp Brain Res* 70:597, 1988.

49. Van Die GC, Collewijn H: Control of human optokinetic nystagmus by the central and peripheral retina: effects of partial visual field masking, scotopic vision, and central retinal scotomata, *Brain Res* 383:185, 1986.

50. Viirre E, Tweed D, Milner K, Vilis T: A reexamination of the gain of the vestibulo-ocular reflex, *J Neurophysiol* 56:439, 1986.

51. Wall C, Black FO, Hunt AE: Effects of age, sex, and stimulus parameters upon vestibulo-ocular responses to sinusoid rotation, *Acta Otolaryngol* 98:270, 1984.

52. Weissman BM, Discenna AO, Ekelman BL, Leigh RJ: The effect of eyelid closure and vocalization upon the vestibulo-ocular reflex during rotational testing, *Ann Otol Rhinol Laryngol* 98:548, 1989.

53. Westall C, Schor CM: Asymmetries of optokinetic nystagmus in amblyopia: the effect of selected retinal stimulation, *Vision Res* 25:1431, 1985.

54. Westall CA, Shute RH: OKN asymmetries in orthoptic patients: contributing factors and effect of treatment, *Behav Brain Res* 49:77, 1992.

55. Yee, RD, Baloh RW, Honrubia V: Study of congenital nystagmus: optokinetic nystagmus, *Br J Ophthalmol* 64:926, 1980.

56. Yee RD, Baloh RW, Honrubia V, Jenkins AJ: Pathophysiology of optokinetic nystagmus. In Honrubia V, Brazier MAB, editors: *Nystagmus and vertigo*, New York, 1982, Academic.

Vergence Eye Movements

Abnormal vergence
   (strabismus, disease or injury,
   and near work)
Accommodative vergence
ACA ratio
Disparity (fusional) vergence
Fast fusional vergence
Proximal vergence
Slow/adaptive fusional
   vergence

Tonic vergence
Training of disparity vergence
Vergence (horizontal, vertical,
   and cyclorotary; symmetric
   and asymmetric)
Vergence main sequence and
   its neurologic control

   Imagine the following. One is looking up at the top of a five-story building, and then one looks down toward the ground at a nearby inclined plane containing a richly textured surface. What types of vergence eye movements would take place, and what different stimuli would be involved in the initiation of this complex sensory-motor-perceptual response? (Also see Chapter 1.)

   Three types of vergence movements would occur[74]:

- Since the two objects are located at different distances, a *horizontal* vergence movement would take place.
- Since the two objects are located at different heights, a *vertical* vergence movement would take place.

- Since the two objects are at different inclinations, a *cyclorotary* vergence movement would take place.

Three types of stimuli would drive the overall vergence response (in probable decreasing order of importance)[74]:

- Since the two objects are at different distances, heights, and inclinations, horizontal, vertical, and cyclorotary disparities would be present to drive the three-dimensional *disparity vergence* system (Fig. 6-1).
- Since the two objects are at significantly different distances and therefore have considerably different accommodative stimulus levels, sufficient retinal defocus would be present to produce the percep-

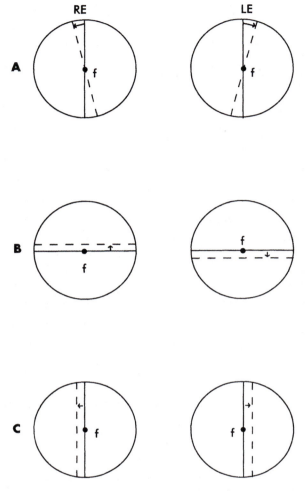

FIG. 6-1   Three types of disparity vergence stimuli, retinal view. **A,** Cyclodisparity. **B,** Vertical disparity. **C,** Horizontal disparity. *Solid lines,* Horizontal and vertical objective directional reference meridians; *dashed lines,* retinal disparity; *f,* fovea.

tion of retinal blur to drive the *accommodative vergence* system.
* Since the two objects are at different apparent/perceived (and real) distances, the awareness of nearness (or proximity) of the closer object would drive the *proximal vergence* system.

The *tonic vergence* input, which is due to baseline midbrain neural activity and represents a simple neural "bias" (that is, small constant input) in the vergence system, has little impact on the overall magnitude of the closed-loop vergence response (see later section on "Models of the Vergence System"). However, all four Maddox[74] vergence inputs would interact dynamically to result, within 1 second or so, in the overall steady-state motor response.

DISPARITY (FUSIONAL) VERGENCE

Disparity (fusional) vergence refers to that vergence driven by binocular retinal disparity (that is, the angular positional difference at the eyes between an object in the field and the bifixation point) and whose system goal is to reduce the retinal disparity sufficiently (that is, within the limits of Panum's fusional areas) to obtain a fused binocular percept of the new object of regard. There are three practical categories of retinal disparity:
* *Zero disparity.* Whereas the *Vieth-Müller circle* (that is, the circle passing through the bifixation point and entrance pupils of the eyes) serves as the reference for zero *geometric* disparity, the psychophysically determined *horopter* (that is, for a fixed convergence angle, the locus of corresponding retinal points with each pair having identical visual directions) serves as the reference for zero *functional* disparity as measured in the clinic and laboratory (Fig. 6-2, *A*).
* *Uncrossed disparity.* This occurs for objects lying behind the horopter (Fig. 6-2, *B*). It requires a divergence movement to obtain fusion. It is called an uncrossed disparity because occlusion of one eye causes the diplopic image on the same side as the occluder to disappear. Further, uncrossed disparities project in a (relative) templeward direction and intersect behind the fixation point.

- *Crossed disparity.* This occurs for objects located in front of the horopter (Fig. 6-2, *C*). It requires a convergence movement to obtain fusion. It is called a crossed disparity because occlusion of one eye causes the diplopic image on the opposite side as the occluder to disappear. Further, crossed disparities project in a (relative) nasalward direction and intersect in front of the fixation point.

The disparity vergence system is quite robust to changes in quality of the stimulus, such as contrast and luminance, so that it will fuse two blurry lines just about as well as two sharply focused lines. In fact, the disparity vergence system exhibits such a strong "compulsion to fusion" that it will even attempt to fuse two very different targets, such as a vertical line in the left eye and a horizontal line in the right eye (Fig. 6-3). Thus the system will *initiate* a disparity vergence response to very *dissimilar* or decorrelated targets, resulting in a *transient* pulselike movement, but it requires quite *similar* or correlated targets to obtain a *sustained* fusion response. Such experimental results led Jones[42] to speculate on the presence of a transient/sustained dichotomous disparity vergence system. As another example of its robustness, only modest changes in motor responsitivity are found with increased retinal eccentricity of the stimulus. As retinal eccentricity increases, presence of any small (for example, minutes of arc) steady-state vergence error (that is, fixation disparity) increases as dictated by the progressively increased size of Panum's fusional areas in the retinal periphery[75] (Fig. 6-4); since this vergence error increases, the response amplitude decreases, and therefore the effective system gain decreases (Fig. 6-5); and, since the vergence response amplitude and thus gain decrease for a given fixed stimulus amplitude, the peak velocity of the reduced response decreases (see Fig. 6-5), as dictated by "main sequence" vergence neurologic control (see "Main Sequence for Disparity Vergence").

Text continued on page 132.

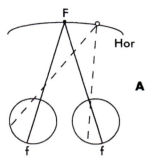

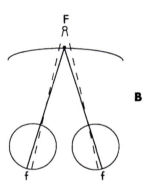

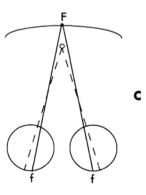

FIG. 6-2 Categories of retinal disparity. **A,** Zero. **B,** Uncrossed. **C,** Crossed. *F,* Bifixation point; *f,* fovea; *Hor,* horopter; *open circle,* second object in visual space. (Not drawn to scale.)

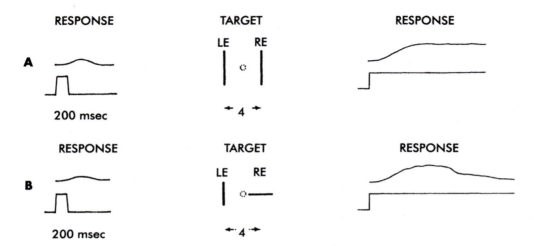

FIG. 6-3 Disparity-induced vergence responses obtained for 200-msec and step presentations of 4-centrad uncrossed disparity. Target configuration was fusible (**A**) or nonfusible (**B**).

(From Jones R: *Am J Optom Physiol Optics* 57:640, 1980.)

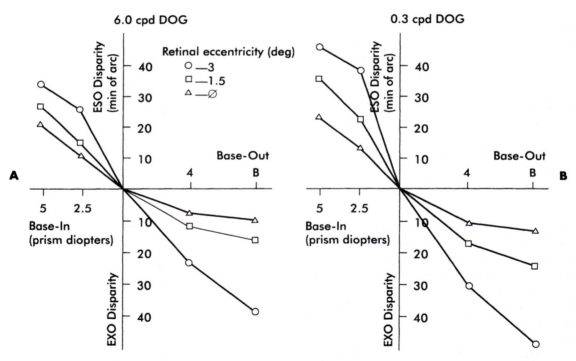

FIG. 6-4 Fixation disparity plotted for a subject with a steep type 1 forced duction curve when fusion was stimulated with either a high (6.0 cpd) (**A**) or low (0.3) (**B**) center spatial frequency DOG (difference of Gaussian grating) placed at three retinal locations (foveal, 1.5 degrees, and 3 degrees eccentric). Slopes of forced duction curves increased with both retinal eccentricity and spatial period or coarseness of fusion lock.

(From Schor CM, Robertson KM, Wesson M: *Am J Optom Physiol Optics* 63:611, 1986.)

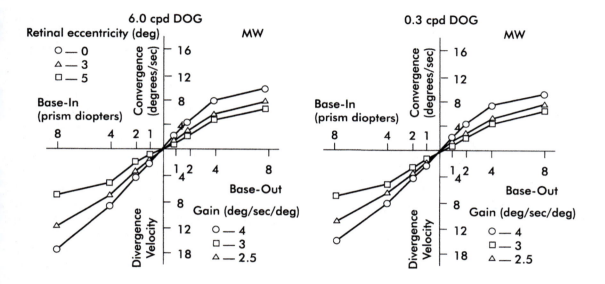

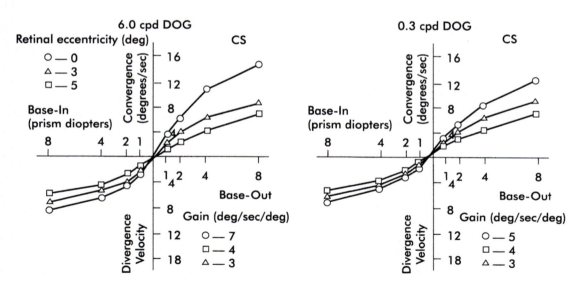

FIG. 6-5 Peak velocity of disparity vergence plotted for two subjects (*MW,CS*) as a function of step stimulus amplitude in divergent and convergent directions. Fusion is stimulated with difference of Gaussians (DOGS) having center spatial frequencies of either 6.0 cpd or 0.3 cpd presented at fovea or at retinal eccentricities of 3 and 5 degrees. Vergence gain is calculated from slopes of velocity plots as they pass through graph origin. Gains or slopes of velocity functions decrease as retinal eccentricity of fusional stimuli increases, but they remain invariant with spatial frequency of fusional stimuli.

(From Schor CM, Robertson KM, Wesson M: *Am J Optom Physiol Optics* 63:611, 1986.)

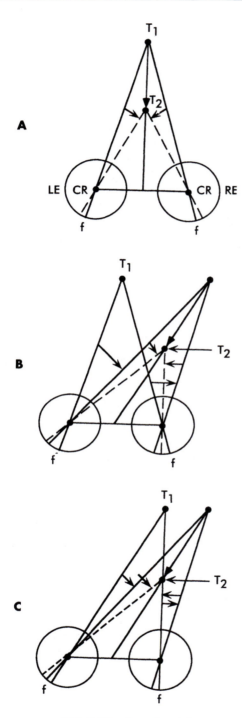

FIG. 6-6 See legend at right.

This robustness is also evident in the clinical measurement of the convergence near point, which is essentially the same for a good versus poor accommodative target in normals.[13]

The disparity vergence system can be characterized in different ways. For example, as discussed earlier, the disparity vergence system contains horizontal, vertical, and cyclodisparity retinal components. It can also be categorized with respect to direction of movement. Thus movements would be convergent, or nasalward/inward, versus divergent, or templeward/outward. The system can also be characterized with respect to target spatial location and the resultant motor response:

- *Symmetric disparity vergence.* If the targets are placed along the midline, relatively saccade-free symmetric disparity vergence occurs (Fig. 6-6, *A*). The retinal disparity is symmetrically placed with respect to the foveas, and the resultant smooth vergence responses are themselves generally reasonably symmetric.
- *Asymmetric disparity vergence.* If the targets are placed in *any* other location, asymmetric disparity vergence occurs (Fig. 6-6, *B*). The retinal disparity is no longer symmetrically placed with respect to the foveas, and the resultant overall movement is not symmetric (with respect to the fixed head's midline). In the special case of *line-of-sight* asymmetric vergence, the targets are aligned along one eye (Fig. 6-6, *C*). An asymmetric vergence response typically consists of a small initial vergence movement, followed by a saccade to position the eyes to have reasonable *symmetric* retinal disparity placement, and

FIG. 6-6 Symmetric versus asymmetric disparity stimuli and overall response pattern. **A,** Symmetric vergence. **B,** Asymmetric vergence. **C,** Line-of-sight asymmetric vergence. T_1, Initially fixated target; T_2, newly fixated target; *f*, fovea; *CR*, center of rotation of the eye; *LE*, left eye; *RE*, right eye.

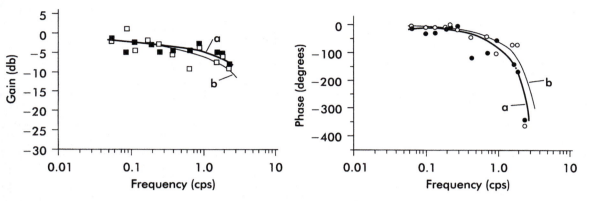

FIG. 6-7 Frequency characteristics of the predictor operator for disparity vergence. Bode plots for gain and phase. Plot responses to predictable sinusoidal stimuli are indicated by thin lines (*b*) with data points consisting of open circles and squares, whereas plots for responses to unpredictable sinusoidal stimuli are indicated by thick lines (*a*) with filled circles and squares. Difference between two sets of responses is a definition of predictor operator. Predictable(*a*) and unpredictable (*b*) best fit lines through data.

(From Krishnan VV, Phillips S, Stark L: *Vis Res* 13:1545, 1973.)

TABLE 6-1   *Comparison of Time Constant and Latency Values for Disparity and Accommodative Vergence (msec)*

Disparity Vergence				Accommodative Vergence			
CON		DI		CON		DI	
TC	L	TC	L	TC	L	TC	L
280	180	240	200	360	300	480	380

CON, convergence; *DI*, divergence; *TC*, time constant; *L*, latency.

then the continued approximate *symmetric* vergence to bifixate the new target. All of these movements are consistent with that demanded by Hering's law of equal innervation, and this is especially noteworthy in the case of line-of-sight asymmetric vergence, in which the initial *and* final positions of the sighting eye are identical. Since the distribution of disparity vergence latencies is biased slightly more toward shorter values than is the case for saccadic latencies, the initial

movement is more likely to be a vergence rather than a saccade. It should also be noted that this symmetric versus asymmetric characterization is generally listed under "disparity vergence," although under most natural viewing conditions, blur and proximity will also impact on the overall response.

The dynamics of disparity vergence have been well documented.[78] (Table 6-1; also see the sections in this chapter on main sequence and on a dynamic model of disparity vergence). Note that the mean latencies for disparity vergence are shorter than for accommodative vergence. Thus, under normal dynamic binocular viewing conditions, disparity vergence will typically precede any accommodative vergence contribution by approximately 100 msec; this may be functionally beneficial, because it allows the retinal image to approach the fovea, where accommodative gain is highest.[14] Fig. 6-7 shows Bode plots for the horizontal disparity vergence system.[48] Prediction does not appear to have much impact on dynamic system responsitivity. Track-

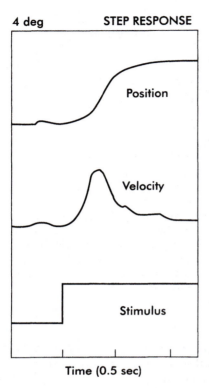

4 deg   **STEP RESPONSE**

Position

Velocity

Stimulus

Time (0.5 sec)

FIG. 6-8   A 4-degree convergence step stimulus *(bottom)* resulted in disparity vergence response *(top)* with latency of 180 msec and peak velocity of 12 degrees/sec *(middle)* occurring 150 msec after the vergence response begins.

(From Schor CM, Robertson KM, Wesson M: *Am J Optom Physiol Optics* 63:611, 1986.)

ing is reasonable up to 1.5 Hz. Fig. 6-8 shows a pure symmetric horizontal disparity vergence response (of one eye only, assuming symmetry of response) to a step input of symmetric disparity.[75] The response can be approximated by an exponential (time constant = ≈250 msec) with its peak velocity occurring early in the response. Also, from this example, it is clear that vergence response duration should be determined from its velocity rather than position trace because of the very slow vergence velocities and position changes near

the completion of the movement. From the position trace, one might estimate that the duration was 500 to 600 msec, whereas from the velocity trace, baseline velocity was not attained until 1100 msec after initiation of the response. This is consistent with the notion that an exponential response is effectively over in four to five times constants, in this case being 1000 to 1250 msec. Although earlier results suggested that the disparity vergence system was under *continuous* feedback control,[82] more recent results[76] suggest that the initial 200-msec portion is effectively an *open-loop, preprogrammed response,* with only the latter portion being under *continuous* visual feedback control to reduce the residual vergence error to within Panum's fusional areas (that is, minutes of arc) (also see the section on dynamic vergence models). Lastly, as mentioned above, it is important to remember that a horizontal disparity vergence response takes approximately 1 second to complete, whereas both vertical and cyclodisparity vergence responses are typically roughly eight to ten times *slower.*[47] Thus, as one introduces retinal disparity either in the laboratory or in the clinic (such as prism vergence ranges), the vertical disparity and cyclodisparity should be introduced much more slowly than any horizontal disparity to allow for such dramatic differences in directional response dynamics.

Up to this point, the notion of disparity vergence has referred to the typically "reflexive" or *fast fusional vergence system* disjunctive response of the eyes that reduces the disparity error to within Panum's area in 1 second or so (see model section). This fast system uses a leaky integrator controller with a time constant of approximately 10 seconds.[40] However, for sustained vergence gaze at any new level, the *slow fusional vergence system* (time constant of greater than 1 minute) gradually subsumes responsibility. The motor output of the fast system controller (also believed to reflect its "innervation" or "effort") inputs and drives this slow "adaptive" system (which in

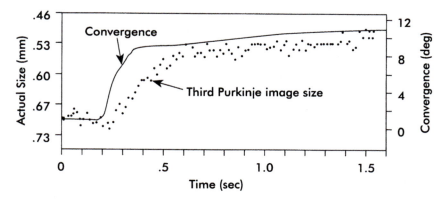

FIG. 6-9 Simultaneous recording of changes in accommodation (third Purkinje image) and accommodative convergence (first Purkinje image).
(From Allen MJ: *Am J Optom Arch Am Acad Optom* 26:279, 1949.)

turn inputs into the fast system controller, and the cycle continues). Thus, as the slow system continues to be innervated (or "charged"), the fast system innervation effectively decays, with the *sum* of the fast and slow system outputs being constant to sustain the proper fixed gaze angle. This shift in responsibility to maintain gaze is presumed to reduce "stress" or demand on the fast system, and thus it should reduce near point symptoms. The slow system gradually effectively "resets" the motor zero (phoria and fixation disparity) position(s)[50]; that is, vergence adaptation has occurred (see later section on this topic).

ACCOMMODATIVE VERGENCE

Accommodative vergence refers to the synkinetically driven vergence response associated with a change in blur-driven accommodation[74] (Fig. 6-9). This is present under both monocular (or at least biocular/open-loop disparity vergence) viewing conditions, as occur during the clinical ACA ratio measurement,[15] and binocular closed-loop viewing conditions, as occur during the clinical relative accommodation measurement.[15]

However, conceptually it is easier to begin with the monocular blur-driven response as first described by Müller,[55] a German physiologist, in 1826 (Fig. 6-10). Simply stated, he reported that if one placed a cover over the eye of a person (to open-loop the fusional or disparity vergence system), and the individual was then instructed to look from a far object to a near object, the covered eye moved nasalward. This relatively slow nasalward movement is the accommodative vergence associated with the far-to-near blur drive (assuming little proximal influence), with this amount being dictated by the neurologically based ACA ratio. The same would be true for shifting gaze from near-to-far, but now one would see an accommodative divergence response with the covered eye moving templeward. During both of these movements, the viewing eye appeared to remain relatively stationary. Over 125 years later, this vergence response was objectively documented[2]; however, it was done using the noisy, low-resolution electrooculography technique (EOG) (see Chapter 8). This *apparent unilateral* accommodative vergence response is in direct gross violation of Hering's law of equal innervation (see Chapter 1). Thus it was reinvestigated by Kenyon et al.[43] using a high-

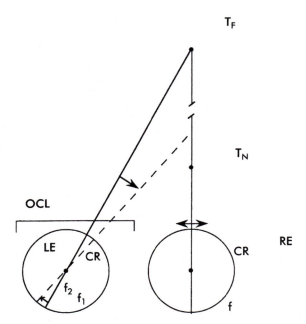

FIG. 6-10 Müller accommodative vergence paradigm. Arrows show directional movement of eyes. T_F, initially fixated far target; T_N, newly fixated near target; *OCL*, occluder; *CR*, center of rotation of the eye; f, f_1, and f_2, fovea; *LE*, left eye; *RE*, right eye. (Not drawn to scale.)

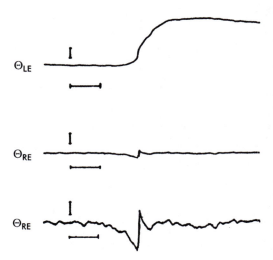

FIG. 6-11 Binocular accommodative vergence eye movements to an accommodative stimulus of 2 diopters. This movement shows both visually triggered smooth pursuit and preprogrammed saccade. Note how retinal error 200 msec before saccade does not equal saccade size. Shown from top to bottom as function of time are covered left eye position, viewing right eye position (gain approximately equal to left eye), and viewing right eye (gain greater than left eye). Vertical bars represent 0.25 degree for viewing eye *(lower trace)*, 1 degree for covered eye and viewing eye *(upper and middle traces)*, and horizontal bars represent 400 msec. Leftward movements represented by upward deflections.

(From Kenyon RV, Ciuffreda, KJ, Stark L: *Vis Res* 18:545, 1978.)

resolution (~2-minute arc) infrared eye movement system (see Chapter 8). A typical result is shown in Fig. 6-11. Clearly, *both* eyes moved in the direction predicted by Hering's law; however, the magnitude of response in the viewing eye was markedly reduced (by approximately 90% with respect to the fellow occluded eye). This was presumably caused by the fixation conditions imposed, and thus the presence of a "fixation attenuation" mechanism was invoked. This effective attenuation may have involved dynamic interaction of the error-producing accommodative vergence and the error-correcting saccades and smooth pursuit to counteract the position error and increased

retinal-image motion, respectively, in the viewing eye as it initially begins to verge per Hering's law.

Under symmetric *binocular* viewing conditions, however, the isolated accommodative vergence responses are relatively *equal* in the two eyes.[60] With normal midline *congruent* stimulation (that is, the accommodative and vergence stimuli are numerically equal), the disparity vergence response typically precedes the accommodative vergence response because of the slightly shorter latency of the former (see Table 6-1),[78] and also its initial response is greater because of the reduced gain of the accommodative[14] and accommodative

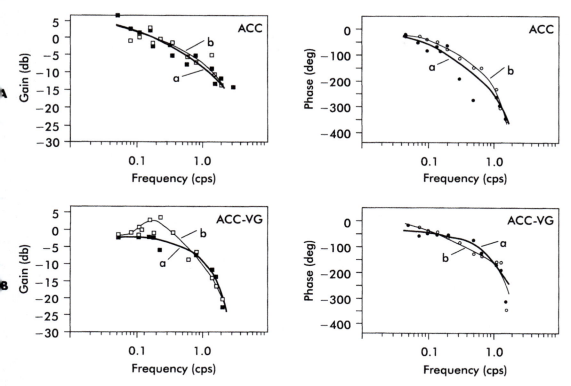

FIG. 6-12 Frequency characteristics of prediction operator for components of triadic (near) response. **A,** Accommodative system. **B,** Accommodative vergence system. Plots for responses to predictable sinusoidal stimuli are indicated by thin lines (*b*) with data points consisting of open circles and squares, whereas plots for responses to unpredictable sinusoidal stimuli are indicated by thick lines (*a*) with filled circles and squares. Difference between two sets of responses is a definition of prediction operator.

(From Krishnan VV, Phillips S, Stark L: *Vis Res* 13:1545, 1973.)

vergence[77] systems with eccentric retinal blur stimulation. However, with *noncongruent* stimulation, the accommodative and vergence stimuli are not numerically equal, and this occurs during relative accommodation (and vergence) testing in the clinic.[15] For example, the introduction of bilateral blur stimulation would result in initial bilaterally symmetric accommodative vergence, immediately followed by and counteracted with a bilaterally symmetric disparity vergence response to reduce the accommodatively induced transient disparity vergence error to within the limits of Panum's fusional areas.[15]

The dynamics of accommodative vergence have been reasonably well defined[78] (see Table 6-1). Convergence is slightly faster than divergence. With regard to Bode frequency response analysis, there is gain enhancement of midrange (0.2 to 0.4 Hz) responsivity for predictable (sinusoidal) stimuli (Fig. 6-12); tracking is reasonable up to 1.0 Hz.[48]

The ACA ratio (i.e., the ratio of accommodative vergence to accommodation) is assessed differently in the laboratory and the clinic.[15,16] In the laboratory, both the accommodative vergence *and* the accommodative response are measured, resulting in the *re-*

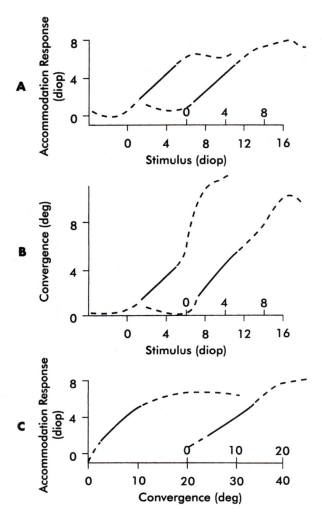

FIG. 6-13 Results of experiment in two observers. Straight lines have been determined statistically. **A,** Relation of accommodation response to accommodation stimulus. **B,** Relation of accommodative vergence response to accommodation stimulus. **C,** Relation of accommodation response to accommodative vergence response.

(From Alpern M, Kincaid WM, Lubeck MJ: *Am J Ophthalmol* 48:141, 1959.)

sponse ACA ratio. In contrast, in the clinic, the actual accommodative response is difficult to measure, and therefore only the change in accommodative vergence *response* (phoria change) for a given change in accommodative

stimulus is determined, resulting in the *stimulus* ACA ratio. Since the accommodative response at near is typically slightly less than the change in accommodative stimulus (e.g., the "lag of accommodation"), the response ACA ratio is approximately 10% greater than the stimulus ACA ratio in healthy persons.[3]

The ACA ratio must be measured as accurately as possible. Since accommodative non-lin-earities exist at both ends of the accommodative range[3,15] (Fig. 6-13), the proper selection of stimulus levels must be considered. For example, in a young adult with a 10-diopter accommodative amplitude, accommodative responsivity over as much as the first and last 2 diopters may be nonlinear. Thus any type of multiple-stimulus measurement, such as the ACA ratio, *must* remain within this 2- to 8-diopter linear range. Clearly, since this test is generally done at near range (40 cm; 2.5 diopters), minus or negative lenses should be used to stimulate accommodation to remain in the linear region.[14-16,51] Finally, since proper estimation of the ACA ratio effectively involves a linear regression procedure, multiple (averaged) measurements should be obtained at several (four or more to assure appropriate slope estimation) stimulus levels.[15]

The ACA ratio is a valuable clinic measure from which information related to a patient's diagnosis, prognosis, and therapeutic intervention is derived. However, it may be influenced by a variety of factors that are especially important for the clinician to recall (Table 6-2).

PROXIMAL VERGENCE

Perhaps the most elusive of the four Maddox components of vergence[74], from both a conceptual and an experimental point of view, has been proximal vergence (see reference 35 for a detailed review). Proximal vergence refers to the change in vergence angle of the eyes caused solely by the relative apparent or perceived nearness of an object in the field. Thus to investigate purely proximal vergence, one would have to (1) open-loop the disparity vergence system either by fully occluding one eye or by vertical dissociation, (2) open-loop the accommodative system with pinholes, and (3) assume tonic vergence is stable (Fig. 6-14). It is unfortunate that few experiments have fulfilled the first two criteria; the third point is a reasonable assumption (see next section on tonic vergence).

Some recent experiments have provided additional important insight into proximal vergence:

- Proximal vergence does not change with age.[36] Since this is a perceptually driven component, the relative constancy of such gross distance perception with age is expected.
- With the above three criteria fulfilled, proximal vergence (and proximal accommodation) gain was established by having subjects view familiar objects over a wide range of distances (1500 m to 20 cm).[70] The results revealed that proximity began

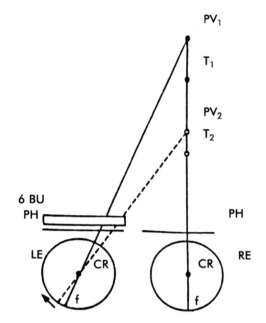

FIG. 6-14 Clinical measurement of proximal vergence. T_1, Target position one; T_2, Target position two; PV_1, proximal vergence in response to T_1; PV_2, proximal vergence in response to T_2; *PH*, pinhole; *BU*, base-up prism; *CR*, center of rotation of eye; *f*, fovea. *Arrow*, direction of movement of fovea.

(From Ciuffreda KJ: *J Behavioral Optom* 3:31, 1992.)

TABLE 6-2 *Factors That May Influence the ACA Ratio*[59,74]

Factor	Effect
Presbyopia	Little, if any, increase
Orthoptics	Small, transient increase
Surgery	Decrease; mechanical effect
Interpupillary distance alteration (via mirrors or physical growth)	
Increase	Transient increase
Decrease	Transient decrease (still somewhat controversial in both cases)
Drugs or medications	
Barbiturates	Decrease
Amphetamines	Increase
Alcohol	Decrease
Cycloplegics	Increase
Anticholinesterase	Decrease
LSD	Increase
Phenylephrine (Neo-Synephrine)	Remains constant

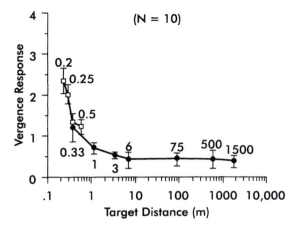

FIG. 6-15 Mean open-loop vergence response (both accommodation and disparity vergence) plotted against target distance (*m*, meters). Open symbols indicate data when the accommodative loop was opened by subjects viewing a 0.1 cpd DOG grating. Closed symbols indicate data when accommodative loop was opened by subjects viewing targets through 0.5-mm pinholes. Abscissa is drawn on a logarithmic scale. Numbers beside data points indicate target distance in meters. Error bars indicate ±1 SEM. These data may be described by an exponential function having the equation: $6 = 0.37e^{-2.3 \log 10x} + 0.29$ (where x represents target distance in meters). When plotted on a linear scale, the equation is $6 = 0.37x + 0.29$.

(From Rosenfield MR, Ciuffreda KJ, Hung GK: *Invest Ophthal Vis Sci* 32:2985, 1991.)

to exert an influence on the vergence system for objects closer than 3 m, with this linear response region having a gain (open loop) of approximately 0.4 (Fig. 6-15). Thus, under optimal *open-loop* viewing conditions, proximity can alter the static convergence position of the eyes by 40% of that demanded by the actual distance of the object. However, under normal binocular *closed-loop* viewing conditions (that is, with visual feedback information available with regard to disparity and blur), preliminary modeling results suggest that proxi-

mal vergence has relatively little impact (<5%) on the overall steady-state vergence response (unpublished results of Hung, Ciuffreda, and Rosenfield).

- The overall apparent nearness of the test target and the immediate test surround may affect the open-loop (that is, tonic) motor vergence response.[41] Tonic vergence position will be closer in a small room and farther in a large room, assuming the subject is fully aware of the test environment distances.

The potential impact or "strength" of proximal vergence has been traditionally assessed in the clinic as follows. The distance (6 m) dissociated phoria is measured, and then the near (40-cm) dissociated phoria is measured with +2.5-diopter lenses added, so that the accommodative stimulus at distance and at near is effectively zero diopters, and thus only the proximal factor could be attributed to any difference in distance versus near vergence motor response (that is, phoria). Under such conditions (that is, with disparity vergence open-loop but with accommodation closed-loop and having a stimulus value of zero), proximal vergence may enhance the response by 25%[58] to 50%[79]. However, it should be noted, once again, that this is with open-loop disparity vergence, and thus proximal vergence can manifest itself more or less fully. Such a large proximal effect cannot occur under normal binocular viewing conditions, because the visual feedback–driven components, namely, disparity and blur, *must* predominate to prevent occurrence of steady-state diplopia and blur, respectively. Further, these interactions are complex and *nonlinearly additive*. For example, under experimental laboratory conditions using isolation and/or open-loop techniques, disparity vergence alone can effectively correct 100% of the vergence error (within foveal Panum's fusional areas of 5-min arc), accommodative vergence can respond to 66% of the demand (assuming an ACA ratio of 4:1 and an interpupillary distance of 6 cm), and proximal vergence can respond to 40% of the demand. Assuming linear additivity of the different vergence components, this equals over 200% of the stimulus change—and the 0.5- to 1.0-m angle impact of tonic vergence has yet to be added! Clearly, nonlinear additivity of the four vergence components must be invoked.[39]

TONIC VERGENCE

In the absence of disparity, blur, and proximal stimuli, the vergence position of the eyes shifts to an intermediate distance of 120[64] to 200 cm[27] in adults and 35 cm in infants.[4] This convergent position presumably reflects baseline midbrain neural stimulation. Tonic vergence has been demonstrated to be stable over hours, days, weeks, and even months,[29] and, in fact, one cross-sectional study suggests it is relatively constant during one's adult life.[18] One can regard tonic vergence as a simple bias or independent "injection" term into the vergence system (see "Models of the Vergence System"), and thus it would not necessarily be expected to be related to or correlated with the ACA ratio, tonic accommodation, or any other oculomotor parameter.

Tonic vergence may be related to one's distance visual perception, presumably functioning as the perceptual reference or bias point for the overall vergence response and correlated vergence effort/innervation.[65] It also appears to be related to the perceptual distance concept of "specific distance tendency," with its value of approximately 200 cm[65]; that is, under reduced cue conditions, a contextless object such as a dim luminous circle of light would appear to be localized 200 cm away.

It is commonly reported that tonic vergence per se can be readily altered or biased in the direction of one's immediately previous sustained bifixation[65]; thus it will transiently shift inward following near fixation and outward following far fixation. However, if the tonic vergence position is really due to base-line midbrain activation level, how could just a few minutes of simple fixation so easily alter such a basic and relatively primitive brain center? What this reputed "change" in tonic vergence really appears to represent is the activation and subsequent decay of the *disparity vergence slow adaptive component,*[37] with the rate of decay reflecting its time constant.[54] (See static model and vergence adaptation sections later in chapter.) Since the measurement of (pretask) baseline tonic vergence position, as well as the decay of the disparity vergence adaptive component (so-called posttask tonic vergence), is done under the same test conditions, that is, in total darkness, these two independent and different entities have unfortunately become linked.

MAIN SEQUENCE FOR DISPARITY VERGENCE

As discussed for saccades in Chapter 3, there is also a "main sequence" for disparity vergence eye movements (with or without any accommodative and/or proximal vergence additive component; a main sequence for either of these components in isolation has not been established). That is, there is a lawful, neurologically based relation between disparity vergence amplitude and its peak velocity. However, because of the lower-frequency neural signal (probably a small pulse combined with a step; see the section on neurophysiology of vergence later in this chapter), vergence peak velocities are roughly 10% of that found for a similarly sized saccade. A typical vergence main sequence plot showing the relation between disparity vergence amplitude (mainly convergence) and its related peak velocity (Xs only) is shown in Fig. 6-16. Clearly, peak vergence velocity increases as vergence amplitude increases, with a ratio of approximately 4:1.[26,38,68] This linear peak velocity/amplitude relationship holds for all binocular vergence movements under a variety of conditions (Fig. 6-16), including total

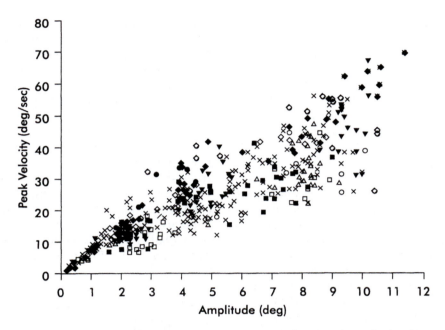

FIG. 6-16 Main sequence disparity vergence responses for a variety of stimulus conditions in one subject. *Filled symbols,* Instrument-space environment (that is, disparity stimulation only); *open symbols,* free-space environment (that is, disparity plus blur plus proximity); *X,* disparity-only standard step stimulation in instrument space. Overlap of data points suggests a common motoneuronal controller.

(From Hung GK, Ciuffreda KJ, Semmlow JL, Horng JL: *Invest Ophthal Vis Sci* 35:3486, 1994.)

darkness, free space in one's natural surroundings, and a confined instrument space environment.[38] Thus, once a decision is made to execute a vergence movement, the neural signal and resultant binocular motor response are relatively independent of one's stimulus conditions, overall environment, and higher-order control strategy.

It is of interest that a vergence main sequence relation is also found in various other species, such as cat and monkey, but with different (and somewhat predictable) slopes[38]; vergence is faster in the monkey (8:1 ratio) and slower in the cat (2.5:1 ratio) when compared with humans (4:1 ratio as described above). This suggests that the velocity-related motoneuronal controller components are similar, but the neural gains differ.

TRAINING OF DISPARITY VERGENCE IN HEALTHY SUBJECTS

Most clinical optometric practitioners and orthoptists agree that vergence ranges can be expanded and improved with orthoptic/vision therapy, especially fusional (disparity) convergence. Such therapy may be regarded as visual feedback–based neuromotor conditioning or enhancement. In addition, several clinical studies have presented results in asymptomatic healthy subjects that are consistent with the above idea.[31] However, only a few double-blind, placebo-controlled studies exist that clearly demonstrate this is true, albeit with relatively small sample sizes.[20-22] The most notable study was that of Daum (1986).[22] Subjects performed positive fusional (con)vergence training in a synoptophore using a small (3.5-degrees) central target, and their overall vergence blur/break/recovery points at optical infinity were monitored. Three groups each received a total of 2 hours of training over a 2-week period but in differently distributed "doses": group A received twelve 10-minute sessions, group B received six 20-minute sessions, and group C received three 40-minute sessions. In addition, a control group received an equivalent time of versional training, especially pursuit. Vergence ranges in the synoptophore at both distance and near were tested before, during, and after therapy using both a small (3.5-degree) and large (18-degree) fusional test target.

Fig. 6-17 presents the results. Subjects whose training was distributed in the smallest "doses," that is, twelve 10-minute sessions, demonstrated the most improvement. Their blur/break/recovery values increased at both distance and near for positive fusional vergence; in addition, transfer to negative fusional vergence ranges occurred. For the other two treatment groups, only the break/recovery values increased at distance and near. Clearly, fusional convergence range can be readily enhanced in healthy persons with simple and appropriate therapy, with even some transfer to the opposing vergence system. Subsequent study has shown that negative fusional vergence can indeed be trained, but it typically requires considerably more time and effort.[23]

Some other interesting results of horizontal vergence training in (primarily) asymptomatic healthy subjects have been reported. Steps of disparity yield greater expansion of ranges than slow ramps of disparity[21]; however, probably each should still be used, because both the "slow" and "fast" vergence system controller subcomponents (see dynamic model section) would then receive appropriately repeated sensory stimulation and independent motor activation with correlated visual and proprioceptive feedback. Positive fusional convergence training at near ranges

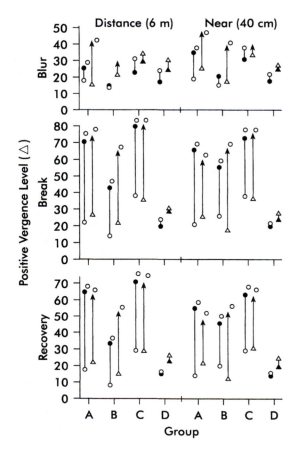

FIG. 6-17 Changes in positive vergences over course of the study. *Open symbols,* before training; *filled symbols,* after training; *circles,* small-diameter target (3.5 degrees), *triangles,* large-diameter target (18 degrees); change was significant at $p = 0.05$ or less using analysis of variance. Groups are as follows: *A,* twelve 10-min sessions; *B,* six 20-min sessions; *C,* three 40-min sessions; *D,* controls.

(From Daum, *Am J Optom Physiol Optics* 63:807, 1986.)

showed greater persistence following the completion of therapy than for distance.[20] The phoria during such training remained stable.

The results thus far for vertical vergence training of ranges are less promising.[72] In a double-blind control study using (primarily) asymptomatic healthy adults, neither vertical phoria, vergence ranges, nor slope of the fixation disparity curve were altered following 5 hours of training (15 minutes each weekday for 4 weeks). However, perhaps vertical vergence training simply requires more time to alter its responsivity, with care to use only very small and slowly introduced disparity changes to stimulate the system optimally.

MODELS OF THE VERGENCE SYSTEM

Various static and dynamic models of the vergence system have been proposed over the past 3 decades. However, few have met two basic requirements: (1) having model parameter values that agree with empirically derived physiologic data and (2) demonstrating computer-simulated responses, especially dynamically to a variety of inputs (such as pulses, steps, ramps, and sinusoids), that agree with the empirically derived physiologic data. Unfortunately, no one to date has successfully incorporated all four components of vergence into a physiologically sound, quantitatively based static or dynamic model; however, recent modeling results in our laboratory suggest that while proximal vergence may have considerable influence on the static vergence system under open-loop viewing conditions, it becomes negligible under normal closed-loop viewing conditions in which disparity and blur predominate (unpublished results of Hung, Ciuffreda, and Rosenfield).

An extremely useful static model for both basic and clinical investigations is the Hung-Semmlow dual-interactive model of 1980,[39] to which adaptive loops have been added by Hung in 1992.[37] This newer model, having disparity, blur, and tonic inputs, is shown in Fig. 6-18. Both the accommodative and disparity loops have similar basic components (discussed left to right in the figure):

- *Input.* The input or stimulus change for either accommodation (AS) or disparity vergence (VS) sum with the negative feedback value of the respective system at that moment. The difference represents the instantaneous initial system error.

- *Dead-space element (DE).* This allows some small neurosensory-based tolerable system error to exist without adverse perceptual consequences, such as diplopia or blur. This corresponds to Panum's fusional area for disparity and the depth of focus for accommodation. If the input system error exceeds this threshold level, it would then go on to drive the system; if this initial error does not exceed this threshold, it would not continue through to drive the system. The system would then wait for subsequent inputs that might be large enough to drive it.

- *Controller gain.* This represents the open-loop gain of either accommodation (ACG) or disparity vergence (VCG). The final system error signal, which equals the initial system error minus the dead-space element value, would be multiplied by this gain element. The output of this controller gain is then input to three places (see next three components below).

- *Cross-link gain.* This gain term provides indirect input from one system to the other. For accommodation (AC), this would be the ACA ratio (i.e., accommodative vergence to accommodation), and for convergence (CA), this would be the CAC ratio (i.e., convergence accommodation to accommodation).

- *Summing junction.* The controller gain output goes here to sum with the two other inputs, resulting in the final signal to drive the system.

- *Adaptive loop.* If the "fast" system response is near completion and only a small error exists, the adaptive loop (M, CE, K terms) becomes activated; this adaptive or "slow" loop completes and sustains the motor response for a prolonged period.

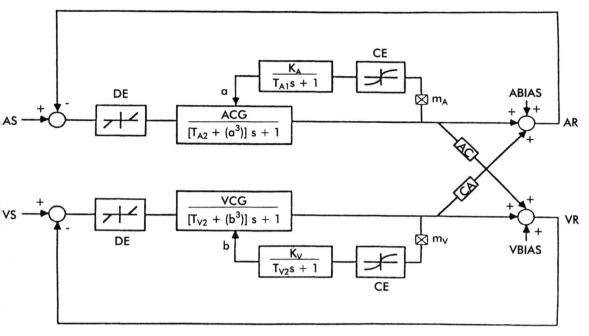

FIG. 6-18   Static model of accommodation and vergence. See text for details.
(From Hung GK: *Ophthal Physiol Optics* 12:319, 1992.)

- *System bias.* This "tonic" term, derived from baseline midbrain neural stimulation, is ABIAS for accommodation and VBIAS for disparity vergence. At the summing junction, this adds with the system controller output and the cross-link output to provide the complete signal driving each system. Under normal closed-loop viewing conditions, the bias terms provide little to the overall response amplitude, especially at near ranges. This is shown in the following equation and example with respect to monocular blur-driven accommodation, where

$$AR = \frac{ACG}{1 + ACG}\,(AS) + [(-DE)\,\frac{ACG}{1 + ACG}$$
$$+ (ABIAS)\,\frac{1}{1 + ACG}\,]$$

For a typical value of ABIAS = 1 diopter and ACG = 9, the effect of ABIAS on AR would only be 0.1 diopter. This applies even more so for disparity vergence (analogous equation), in which VBIAS might equal 1 MA and VCG is 149; thus the impact of VBIAS on VR, the overall steady-state response, would only be about 0.007 MA.

- *Output.* The final output for either accommodation (AR) or vergence (VR) goes back via the negative-feedback loop to the initial summing junction, and the cycle repeats itself, if needed, until a stable steady-state response for both systems is established.

A dynamic model[40] of disparity vergence only is presented in Fig. 6-19; there is, as yet, no successful dynamic model of the vergence system that includes all four vergence components and that yields physiologically acceptable results (and computer simulations) along with good system stability.

A

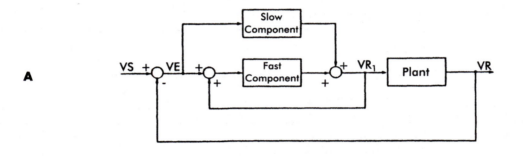

B

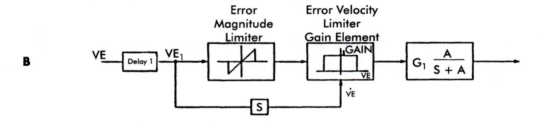

C

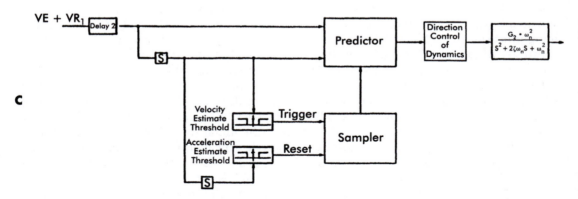

FIG. 6-19   For legend see opposite page.

This present model has two major subdivisions or components:

- The *fast component* is used to track perceived target velocity (with a latency or delay of 200 msec) of rapidly moving targets (> ~2 degrees/sec), such as occurs with rapid ramps, fast sinusoids, pulses,

FIG. 6-19, **A,** Overall dynamic model of disparity vergence system showing slow and fast components in forward loop. Slow and fast component responses are summed to give VR_1. Internal positive feedback from VR_1 is summed with vergence error *(VE)* to give an estimate of target position. Plant represents mechanical properties of eyeball and musculature and is assumed to have unity gain for the vergence simulation. Vergence response *(VR)* is subtracted from vergence stimulus *(VS)* to give vergence error. **B,** Slow component in forward loop: delayed vergence error *(VE₁)* is vergence error *(VE)* delayed by 200 msec *(delay 1)*. Error magnitude limiter (up to 1 degree) and error velocity limiter gain element (up to 2 degrees/sec) simulate range of slow component dynamics. Time constant $1/A$ is 10 seconds. Gain *(G₁)* was determined via simulation to be 30. $\dot{VE}$, velocity; A, reciprocal of the time constant; S, Laplace operator; $\boxed{S}$, differentiator. **C,** Fast component in forward loop: vergence error *(VE)* is summed with VR_1 to give an estimate of target position. Delay element *(delay 2)* represents effective delay throughout fast component. Estimated target velocity above a threshold of 1.7 degree/sec is used to trigger sampler. Sampler enables predictor to use estimated target position and velocity to predict future position of, for example, a ramp stimulus. After triggering, threshold increases slightly to 2.1 degrees/sec. This accounts for initial step but subsequent smooth following seen in response to a 1.8 degree/sec ramp stimulus. If estimated stimulus velocity remains constant, sampler repeats every 0.5 second. This accounts for staircase, steplike responses to ramp stimuli. Sudden large changes in velocity will reset sampler. This accounts for ramp-pulse data. Predictor also reduces its calculation time, thus reducing delay 2, for repetitive stimuli such as sinusoids. This accounts for relatively small phase lag found in sinusoidal responses.

(From Hung GK, Semmlow JL, Ciuffreda KJ: *IEEE Trans Biomed Eng* BME-33:1021, 1986.)

and steps. Rather than using continuous visual feedback, as earlier simple servomechanism-based models had been assumed to operate, the fast component is triggered by and then samples the rapidly moving target. The predictor operator then predicts the future target position, such as where it will be 500 msec later, based on target position and velocity at the time of sampling, and sends a command to make such a motor response. The fast component's motor output approximates an exponential.

- The *slow component* is used to track slowly moving targets (<~2 degrees/sec) and is driven by vergence error (with a delay of 50 msec for predictable stimuli and 200 msec for nonpredictable stimuli). Since it uses continuous visual feedback, it also functions to correct any slow, accumulating vergence error (<1-degree amplitude, <1.8 degrees/sec velocity), especially following slightly inaccurate rapid step or ramp responses. Note that this is *not* to be confused with the "slow" adaptive controller discussed earlier with regard to the static model of vergence control.

VERGENCE ADAPTATION

As reviewed in detail by Leigh and Zee,[50] the disparity vergence system may exhibit two different types of adaptation. Both are important for clinicians to appreciate, because "a robust and versatile adaptive capability is essential if an organism is to maintain optimal visuomotor function throughout its life"[50]; this especially holds true for all of the oculomotor subsystems, as well as *all* aspects of our general physiologic well-being.

The first is *phoria (prism) adaptation.*[73] If a prism is placed before one eye that still allows fusion to occur, there will be an immediate shift (or "bias") in the person's phoria by an amount equal to the prism; the person's fixation disparity will also change. However, within a few minutes (maybe even several seconds), both the phoria and fixation disparity with the prism still in place will revert back to the original "preprism" values. This "resetting" to maintain some optimal, or at least habitual, level of ocular alignment is termed *phoria* (prism) *adaptation*. By shifting back to the habitual phoria level, it keeps the range of vergence responsivity reasonably constant under a variety of stimulus conditions and states of the body/oculomotor system. This adaptation presumably occurs via the slow adaptive loop of the disparity vergence system, which gradually takes over *maintenance* of static eye position and alignment from the fast disparity vergence loop, whose function is to respond rapidly to *changes* in retinal disparity. That is, as the output of the fast system decays (exponentially), the output of the slow system increases (exponentially), such that the *summed* output and resultant vergence position remain constant during sustained bifixation. (See dynamic model section.) Patients with symptoms related to binocular vision exhibit reduced or even absent phoria adaptation[56]; successful orthoptic therapy in such patients generally normalizes their adaptive capability, along with reducing their related symptoms.[57] (Also see the section on "Abnormal Vergence.")

The second is *asymmetric vergence adaptation in spectacle-based anisometropia.* In anisometropia, by definition, the spectacle power correcting the refractive error in each eye differs significantly. Thus the amount of prism induced in each eye when gazing away from the optical centers of the lenses (assuming a fixed head) at an object located at a different direction *and* distance will not be the same. Such eccentric gaze results in "asymmetric" retinal disparity, necessitating an asymmetric disparity vergence motor response to obtain accurate bifixation within 1 second or so. The amount of asymmetric vergence demand varies with each direction of gaze. Recent evidence[25,61,62] suggests, however, that at least in some situations, a more "time optimal" complex motor response may occur. That is,

the individual may use a (rapid) saccade to the new position with different amounts of vergence change occurring *during* the saccade, such that the new target is more or less reasonably well bifixated within 30 to 50 msec *at the termination* of the saccade (also see Chapter 3); however, some fine vergence adjustment may still occur for a few hundred milliseconds afterward. This rapid saccade/vergence interactive adaptation may function best for repeated movements to the same target, that is, for predictable changes. However, if this really represents a more general type of adaptation in real-life conditions, one must speculate that, along with the saccadic programming, disparity vergence programming appropriate for the size and direction of the intended movement occurs. Such rapid programming across oculomotor systems for *randomly* distributed directions of gaze appears to be extremely complicated, and its generality awaits further detailed investigation. However, one should also remember that most individuals will make a combined head *and* eye movement to direct their gaze to objects outside the central 10 to 15 degrees of the fixation field.[5] Large amounts of this second form of vergence adaptation do not occur naturally physiologically and thus may be of little practical importance for such tasks in healthy subjects. However, it may take on more importance in patients with newly acquired unilateral muscle weakness (e.g., paresis) to reduce their nonconcomitancy and resultant variable diplopia.[80] Along these same lines, small amounts of such adaptation may be necessary to compensate for slight asymmetries in overall orbital mechanics likely to be present in many healthy individuals.[80]

NEUROPHYSIOLOGY OF VERGENCE

Over the past decade, in particular through the important contributions of Mays and his colleagues,[30,52,53,81] the midbrain neurologic control of vergence has become more clearly defined and understood. What may be particularly noteworthy is the similarity of its general neural organization to that found for conjugate eye movements, in particular saccades. Essentially, the final motoneuronal controller signal for convergence is *not* a simple step of neural discharge as was long thought to be the case, but rather a small and broad pulse combined with a step having characteristics appropriate for the relatively slow vergence response (Fig. 6-20). Further, a separate neural integrator for vergence has been hypothesized; this is consistent with the early results of Rashbass and Westheimer,[68] who found a ramp of vergence response to an open-loop step of disparity stimulus.

Three types of midbrain neural cells have been found and characterized as crucial to overall vergence control[53,80]:

- *Vergence burst neurons* only fire just before and during the actual vergence response and, further, have a profile similar to that of the instantaneous vergence velocity. It is believed these cells encode peak vergence velocity, because the number of spikes is correlated with vergence amplitude; thus these cells effectively define neurologically the vergence "main sequence" peak velocity/amplitude relationship (see earlier section). These pulse-like burst neurons are ideal candidates to act as input to the vergence neural integrator; some of the burst neuronal signal also circumvents this integrator (see below).
- *Vergence tonic neurons* probably carry the immediate output of the vergence neural integrator, that is, a step. These units fire just preceding a vergence movement, and their firing rate is proportional to vergence angle.[54] Many more tonic convergence cells exist than tonic divergence cells.
- *Vergence burst-tonic neurons* probably reflect the combined burst and tonic neuronal signals described above, and, as such, may be the "near response cells" that input directly to the oculomotor neurons.[81] In ef-

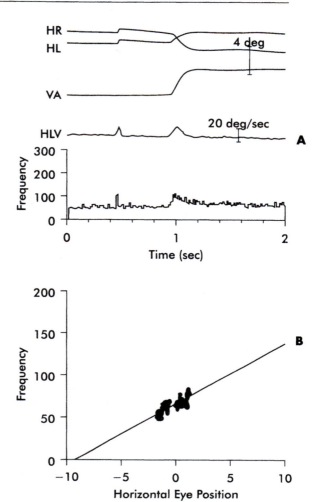

FIG. 6-20 **A,** Activity of medial rectus motoneuron for 4-degree convergence eye movement. *HL,* Horizontal left eye position; *HR,* horizontal right eye position; *HLV,* horizontal left eye velocity; *VA,* vergence angle. **B,** Firing-rate/eye position sensitivity of this cell for vergence eye movements ($k_v = 9.1$ spikes/sec/deg).

(From Gamlin PDR, Mays LE: *J Neurophysiol* 67:64, 1992.)

fect, these contains the pulse-step motoneuronal controller signal described earlier in this section, with the pulse being responsible for the actual movement of the eye and the step being responsible for maintenance of final eye position.

In addition, other parts of the brain have been implicated in vergence control.[50] These include the cerebellum, cerebrum areas 19 and 22 ("near triad"), frontal cortex, and occipital cortex.

ABNORMAL VERGENCE

How might baseline tonic vergence and disparity vergence adaptation be helpful in the assessment and understanding of clinic patients?

- Symptomatic patients show slowed adaptation of disparity vergence, suggesting the presence of more demand on active fusional innervation (e.g., the "fast" disparity vergence subsystem) during the initial near-work period before the slow or adaptive subsystem can take over [28] (see model section).
- Symptoms and fatigue during near work are correlated with the initial magnitude of disparity vergence adaptation.[67]
- Tonic vergence and one's distance phoria are correlated,[63] with tonic vergence being, on average, 2 prism diopters more convergent than the phoria measured by the Maddox rod technique and 4 prism diopters more convergent than measured by the Von Graefe technique (both having an error in prediction of 2 prism diopters). Thus, if a clinician wanted to determine if tonic vergence is abnormal in a patient diagnosed with convergence insufficiency, the Maddox rod distance phoria technique could be used to assess this with the least possible error. The 2- to 4-prism diopter difference between the actual tonic vergence position and the phoria position (especially the Von Graefe) reflects the presence of accommodative divergence to see the distant accommodative target clearly.[63,66,69]

Strabismus

Abnormalities of vergence are commonly found in patients with strabismus,[74] which

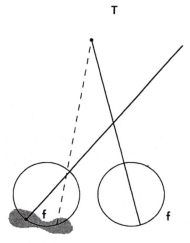

FIG. 6-21 Binocular suppression scotoma (*stippled region*) in deviated eye. Left esotropia. *T,* Target; *f,* fovea.

can be defined as an anomaly of binocular vision in which the visual axis of one eye fails to intersect the object of interest. The prevalence of strabismus is 5% in the general population[24] and up to 50% or more in special populations such as those with cerebral palsy[24] and other neuromuscular disorders. Binocular suppression, which can be defined as the process whereby all or part of the ocular image of one eye is prevented from contributing to the binocular percept (Fig. 6-21) and is commonly found in conjunction with strabismus, is a key factor in understanding the anomalous vergence responses possible in these patients.

The study of fusional responses in strabismus dates back to the turn of the century (see Ciuffreda et al.[17] for a detailed review). However, only over the past 25 years or so, with the use of objective eye movement recording techniques, have vergence responses in persons with strabismus received considerable attention. As we shall see, their responses depend on the size and nature of the stimulus.

For very small (1- to 3-degree) midline targets of small to moderate degrees of disparity (<5 degrees), generally no symmetric disparity

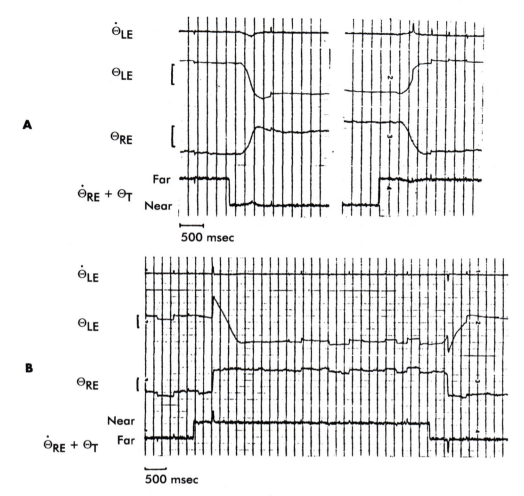

FIG. 6-22 Symmetric vergence condition. $\dot{\theta}_{LE}$, left eye velocity; θ_{LE}, Left eye position; θ_{RE}, right eye position; $\dot{\theta}_{RE} + \theta_T$, right eye velocity summed with target position. Downward deflections represent rightward movements; calibration bars for position represent 2 degrees, and time markers represent 500 msec. **A,** Control subject shows normal response to symmetric vergence stimuli. **B,** Patient having intermittent strabismus without amblyopia exhibits abnormal response. Following target changes, vergence occurs primarily in left eye. Saccade occurring early in response is used to foveate new target with right eye; note unequal saccades occurring during vergence response but equal saccades occurring during extended fixation periods.

(From Kenyon RV, Ciuffreda KJ, Stark L: *Invest Ophthal Vis Sci* 19:60, 1980.)

vergence response can be elicited[44] (Fig. 6-22). Such a stimulus was assumed to fall within the binocular suppression scotoma of the deviated eye, and thus no retinal disparity was sensed or processed; the binocular sco-toma, in essence, acted as a disparity-blocking mechanism or "central physiologic occluder." Thus the effective stimulus to the fellow eye was a blurred step displacement of the target. This produced a saccade to foveate the blurred

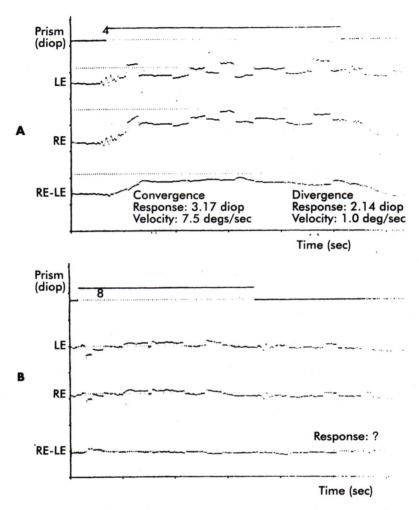

FIG. 6-23 **A,** Fusional vergence in microstrabismus. Amplitude of stimulus: 4–prism diopters base-out LE. Fourth channel, total vergence *(RE-LE):* on left, convergence; on right, divergence after removal of prism. **B,** No clear response with 8–prism diopters base-out.

(From Boonstra FN, Koopmans SA, Houtman WA: *Doc Ophthalmologica* 70:221, 1988.)

target, which was then followed by a change in accommodation to focus the target along with the subsequent synkinetically linked accommodative vergence.

Variable, reduced amplitude disparity vergence responses have been found in persons with microstrabismus (<5 degrees of deviation) using somewhat larger targets (10 de-grees or larger) of moderate disparities (>2 de-grees)[10] (Fig. 6-23). Presumably, vergence responses were now elicited once portions of the stimulus fell outside the microsuppression scotoma. Smaller disparities (0.5 or 1 degree) did not elicit any disparity vergence response.

For very large field stimuli (>40 degrees) but of small disparity (0.5-degree steps), dis-

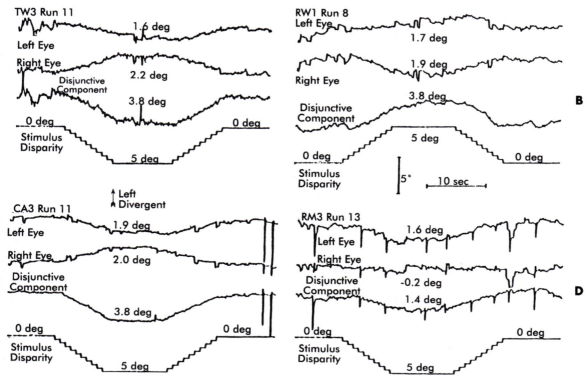

FIG. 6-24 Responses by four persons with strabismus to 5-degree convergent or divergent disparity presentations contained in full-field stimulus. Overall motor compensation and change in each eye's line of sight are given in degrees of arc. **A,** Patient with microtropia. **B,** Patient with intermittent exotropia. **C,** Patient with accommodative esotropia. **D,** Patient with small-angle esotropia and amblyopia.

(From Boman DK, Kertesz AE: *Invest Ophthal Vis Sci* 26:1731, 1985.)

parity vergence responses were consistently generated in the persons with strabismus[9] (Fig. 6-24), because most of the stimulus fell outside the suppression scotoma. However, the amplitudes were only two thirds that found in healthy subjects, suggesting effectively reduced gain of the disparity vergence system for peripheral stimulation, as discussed earlier (disparity vergence section). Thus this and the previous studies clearly demonstrated that the *size* of the target and not necessarily

its disparity magnitude determined whether a disparity vergence response would be elicited. Such wide-field peripheral disparity stimulation has also been found to be successful in training fusion in strabismic patients.[46]

In some cases, prism (equal to the angle of deviation) has been added before the fixing eye of microtropes. In these cases, no normal rapid (~1 second) dynamic disparity vergence response was evident, but rather an extremely slow (several seconds to minutes) change in

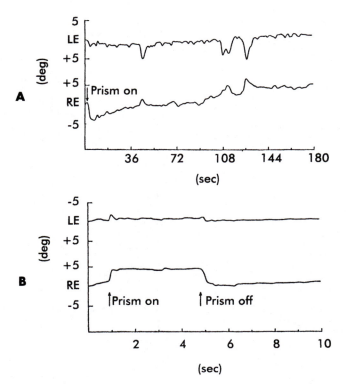

FIG. 6-25   Eye movements of a person with strabismus **(A)** and a normal subject **(B)**. Degree of displacement of eyes is on the ordinate, and time of recording is on the abscissa. In both examples, an arrow indicates moment in which a 6-diopter base-out prism was either placed in front of or removed from the right eye *(RE)* causing asymmetric disparity vergence stimulation. Eyes of the strabismic patient lost their steady state relationship, which was reacquired after about 160 seconds with slow and imprecise eye movements. Normal subject exhibited versional movement of both eyes and then (after about 0.20 second) a disparity-induced vergence movement of left eye *(LE):* this movement brought the traces of the two eyes back to a horizontal pattern.

(From Cipolli C et al: *Perceptual Motor Skills* 71:1259, 1990.)

horizontal eye position was found (Fig. 6-25), which shifted the eye back to the original preprism position (that is, "eating up the prisms"),[11] thus demonstrating the occurrence of prism adaptation. This slow response suggested it was derived solely from the disparity vergence adaptation system or slow component of the disparity vergence system.[12] Absence of a fast vergence response in the presence of an apparent slow vergence re-

sponse suggested that the "effort" or innervation alone to fusional vergence was sufficient to drive the disparity vergence adaptive controller (see earlier section on models of vergence).

Disease and Injury

In addition to the nonpathologic or functional strabismus described above, acquired vergence dysfunctions may occur for a variety of reasons (Boxes 6-1 and 6-2). For example, this might be evident subsequent to a stroke (strabismus, reduced fusional ability)[19] or systemic drug toxicity (convergence spasm).[34] However, one of the most common causes is closed-head trauma.[7] This occurs as a result of either contact injury caused by penetration or decompression of the skull or acceleration injury caused by differential acceleration of the brain and skull on impact, with the brain lagging behind the skull,[7] leading to a variety of vergence dysfunctions typified by the following examples:

- Divergence paralysis resulting in a large esotropic or convergent deviation at both distance and near with constant diplopia[71]
- Convergence insufficiency resulting in diplopia at near and extreme reading difficulty[49]
- Large phoria and overall reduced vergence ability resulting in diplopia, blurred vision, headaches, and reading difficulty[71]

Such problems are generally transient, with recovery over several weeks to months; however, vision therapy may be helpful in some cases where the recovery is either very slow or incomplete. [8]

Training of Disparity Vergence in Patients

As stated in the earlier section on vergence training, clinical wisdom and even the results of several basic and clinical studies suggest disparity (or fusional) vergence can be trained in both visually normal individuals and patients with vergence disorders (see Griffin[31] for a review). However, once again, only a few carefully executed laboratory studies are consistent with the previous notion.

Apparently, only Grisham has provided objective vergence eye movement recordings that confirm our clinical insights. In one study,[32] he was able to discriminate between normal versus clinically abnormal vergence in patients on a variety of dynamic (step) parameters: step divergence latency, convergence and divergence peak velocity, tracking rate, and percent completion of responses discrimi-

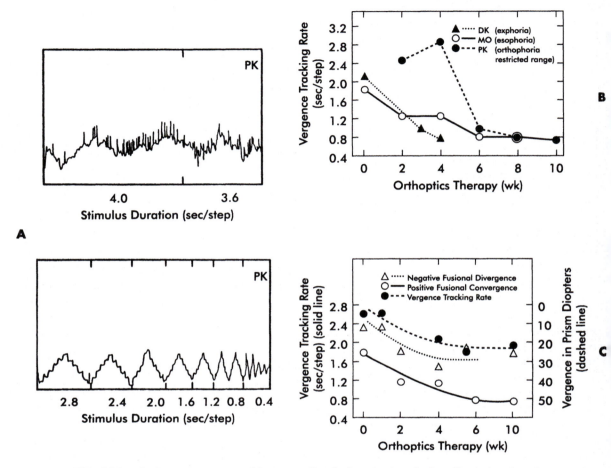

FIG. 6-26 **A,** Step vergence tracking recording before (*top*) and after (*bottom*) orthoptics. Before orthoptic therapy, subject PK could not adequately track a step vergence staircase stimulus changing at a rate of 4 seconds per step. After 8 weeks of home orthoptics, PK successfully tracked steps changing at a rate of up to 0.8 seconds per step. **B,** Changes in vergence tracking rate with orthoptics. Three subjects having clinical binocular deficiencies show progressively faster vergence tracking rates to a step staircase vergence stimulus as orthoptic therapy proceeds over several weeks. Three measures of tracking rate before therapy did not show significant differences in each case. **C,** Changes in vergence tracking rate and fusional vergence ranges with orthoptics. Subject, who had esophoria at near, shows changes in vergence tracking rate that appear to parallel an increase in convergence and divergence fusional ranges as measured with Risley prisms over the course of an orthoptics program.

(From Grisham JD: In Schor CM, Ciuffreda KJ, editors: *Vergence eye movements: basis and clinical aspects,* Boston, 1983, Butterworth.)

nated between the two diagnostic groups (in order from weakest to strongest discriminator). In a second study,[33] step vergence tracking ability was objectively recorded before and after home orthoptic therapy (step disparity training) in three patients with abnormal vergence and related asthenopia. Fig. 6-26 presents the results. Before therapy, vergence tracking was quite irregular and variable, whereas following therapy it became more regular and steplike; also, vergence tracking rate progressively increased over the 8- to 10-week treatment period.

In another study, Kertesz[45] used large (40- to 50-degree) field disparity vergence stimulation in 13 patients with convergence insufficiency who either failed to respond to or could not tolerate conventional orthoptic therapy. With 2 to 6 hours of such training, most patients exhibited markedly increased vergence ranges and reduction of asthenopia. It is unfortunate that objective eye movement recordings were not taken.

REVIEW QUESTIONS

1. A person shifts binocular gaze from the top of a tall building to a highly textured inclined plane located near his feet. Describe the stimuli to vergence and the resultant component changes in vergence response.
2. Compare and contrast the disparity and accommodative stimuli and overall response pattern during (a) symmetric vergence, (b) general asymmetric vergence, (c) line-of-sight asymmetric vergence, and (d) Müller's line-of-sight accommodative vergence paradigm. Use carefully labelled diagrams. How might proximal vergence and tonic vergence influence these responses?
3. Describe how the ACA ratio is determined both in the clinic and in the research laboratory. Why should only negative lenses at near be used in the assessment?
4. Discuss the proximal vergence contribution to the overall vergence response in both open- and closed-loop viewing conditions. Why must proximal vergence (and the other vergence components) be added nonlinearly under normal closed-loop viewing conditions?
5. Can tonic vergence per se be easily altered? Why has there been such confusion in this area?.
6. Describe the vergence "main sequence" and its clinical importance.
7. Can horizontal and vertical disparity vergence be trained to improve in normal subjects? In abnormal subjects? Discuss in detail.
8. Discuss the clinical importance of both phoria (prism) adaptation and asymmetric vergence adaptation in anisometropia.
9. List the symptoms patients may report in disease or injury of the vergence neurologic pathways.

REFERENCES

1. Allen MJ: An objective high speed photographic technique for simultaneously recording change in accommodation and convergence, *Am J Optom Arch Am Acad Optom* 26:279, 1949.
2. Alpern M, Ellen P: A quantitative analysis of the horizontal movements of the eyes in the experiments of Johannes Mueller. I. Methods and results, *Am J Ophthal* 42:289, 1956.
3. Alpern M, Kincaid WM, Lubeck MJ: Vergence and accommodation. III. Proposed definitions of the ACA ratios, *Am J Ophthal* 48:141, 1959.
4. Aslin RN, Dobson V: Dark vergence and dark accommodation in human infants, *Vis Res* 23:1671, 1983.
5. Bahill AT, Adler D, Stark L: Most naturally-occurring human saccades have magnitudes of 15 degrees or less, *Invest Ophthal* 14:468, 1975.
6. Bahill AT, Stark L: The trajectories of saccadic eye movements, *Sci Am* 240:108, 1979.
7. Baker RS, Epstein AD: Ocular motor abnormalities from head trauma, *Survey Ophthal* 35:245, 1991.
8. Berne SA: Visual therapy for the traumatic brain-injured, *J Optom Vis Dev* 21:13, 1990.
9. Boman DK, Kertesz AE: Fusional responses of strabismics to foveal and extrafoveal stimulation, *Invest Ophthal Vis Sci* 26:1731, 1985.
10. Boonstra FN, Koopmans SA, Houtman WA: Fusional vergence in microstrabismus, *Doc Ophthalmologica* 70:221, 1988.
11. Campos EC, Catellani T: Further evidence for the fusional nature of the compensation (or "eating up") of prisms in concomitant strabismus, *Int Ophthal* 1:57, 1978.

12. Cipolli C, Bolzani R, Corazza R, Gualtiero G, Orciuolo M, Campos E: Vergence movements in comitant strabismus, *Perceptual Motor Skills* 71:1259, 1990.

13. Ciuffreda KJ: The near point of convergence as a function of target accommodative demand, *Opt J Rev Optom* 111:9, 1974.

14. Ciuffreda KJ: Accommodation and its anomalies. In Charman WN, editor: *Vision and visual dysfunction,* vol 1, Visual optics and instrumentation, Boca Raton, Fla, 1991, CRC Press.

15. Ciuffreda KJ: Components of clinical near vergence testing, *J Behavioral Optom* 3:3, 1992.

16. Ciuffreda KJ, Kenyon RV: Accommodative vergence and accommodation in normals, amblyopes, and strabismics. In Schor CM, Ciuffreda KJ, editors: *Vergence eye movements: basic and clinical aspects,* Boston, 1983, Butterworth.

17. Ciuffreda KJ, Levi DM, Selenow A: *Amblyopia: basic and clinical aspects,* Boston, 1991, Butterworth-Heinemann.

18. Ciuffreda KJ, Ong E, Rosenfield MR: Tonic vergence, age and clinical presbyopia, *Ophthal Physiol Opt* 13:313, 1993.

19. Cohen AH, Soden R: An optometric approach to the rehabilitation of the stroke patient, *J Am Optom Assoc* 52:975, 1981.

20. Daum KM: The course and effect of visual training on the vergence system, *Am J Optom Physiol Optics* 59:223, 1982.

21. Daum KM: A comparison of the results of tonic and phasic vergence training, *Am J Optom Physiol Optics* 60:769, 1983.

22. Daum KM: Double-blind placebo-controlled examination of timing effect in the training of positive vergences, *Am J Optom Physiol Optics* 63:807, 1986.

23. Daum KM: Negative vergence training in humans, *Am J Optom Physiol Optics* 63:487, 1986.

24. Duke-Elder S, Wybar K: Ocular motility and strabismus. In Duke-Elder S, editor: *System of ophthalmology,* vol 6, London, Henry Plimpton, 1973.

25. Erkelens CJ, Collewijn H, Steinman RM: Asymmetrical adaptation of human saccades to ansiometropic spectacles, *Invest Ophthal Vis Sci* 30:1132, 1989.

26. Erkelens CJ, Steinman RM, Collewijn H: Ocular vergence under natural conditions. II. Gaze shifts between real targets differing in distance and direction, *Proc R Soc Lond* B236:441, 1989.

27. Fincham EF: Accommodation and convergence in the absence of retinal images, *Vis Res* 1:425, 1962.

28. Fisher SK, Ciuffreda KJ, Levine S, Wolf-Kelly K: Tonic adaptation in symptomatic and asymptomatic subjects, *Am J Optom Physiol Optics* 64:333, 1987.

29. Fisher SK, Ciuffreda KJ, Tannen B, Super P: Stability of tonic vergence, *Invest Ophthal Vis Sci* 29:1577, 1988.

30. Gamlin PDR, Mays LE: Dynamic properties of medial rectus motoneurons during vergence eye movements, *J Neurophysiol* 67:64, 1992.

31. Griffin JR: Efficacy of vision therapy for nonstrabismic vergence anomalies, *Am J Optom Physiol Optics* 64:411, 1987.

32. Grisham JD: The dynamics of fusional vergence eye movements in binocular dysfunction, *Am J Optom Physiol Optics* 57:645, 1980.

33. Grisham JD: Treatment of binocular dysfunctions. In Schor CM, Ciuffreda KJ, editors: *Vergence eye movements: basic and clinical aspects,* Boston, 1983, Butterworth.

34. Giuloff RJ, Whiteley A, Kelly RE: Organic convergence spasm, *Acta Neurol Scand* 61:252, 1980.

35. Hokoda SC, Ciuffreda KJ: Theoretical and clinical importance of proximal vergence and accommodation. In Schor CM, Ciuffreda KJ, editors: *Vergence eye movements: basic and clinical aspects,* Boston, 1983, Butterworth.

36. Hokoda SC, Rosenfield MR, Ciuffreda KJ: Proximal vergence and age, *Optom Vis Sci* 68:168, 1991.

37. Hung GK: Adaptation model of accommodation and vergence, *Ophthal Physiol Optics* 12:319, 1992.

38. Hung GK, Ciuffreda KJ, Semmlow JL, Horng JL: Vergence eye movements under natural viewing conditions, *Invest Ophthal Vis Sci* 35:3486, 1994.

39. Hung GK, Semmlow JL: Static behavior of accommodation and vergence: computer simulation of an interactive dual-feedback system, *IEEE Trans Biomed Eng* 27:439, 1980.

40. Hung GK, Semmlow JL, Ciuffreda KJ: A dual-mode dynamic model of the vergence eye movement system, *IEEE Trans Biomed Eng* BME-33:1021, 1986.

41. Jaschinski-Kruza W: Effects of stimulus distance of measurements of dark convergence, *Ophthal Physiol Optics* 10:243, 1990.

42. Jones R: Fusional vergence: sustained and transient components, *Am J Optom Physiol Optics* 57:640, 1980.

43. Kenyon R, Ciuffreda KJ, Stark L: Binocular eye movements during accommodative vergence, *Vis Res* 18:545, 1978.

44. Kenyon RV, Ciuffreda KJ, Stark L: Dynamic vergence eye movements in strabismus and amblyopia: symmetric vergence, *Invest Ophthal Vis Sci* 19:60, 1980.

45. Kertesz AE: The effectiveness of wide-angle fusional stimulation in the treatment of convergence insufficiency, *Invest Ophthal Vis Sci* 22:690, 1982.

46. Kertesz AE: The effectiveness of wide-angle fusional stimulation in strabismus, *Am Orthop J* 33:83, 1983.

47. Kertesz AE: Vertical and cyclofusional disparity vergence. In Schor CM, Ciuffreda KJ, editors: *Vergence eye movements: basic and clinical aspects,* Boston, 1983, Butterworth.

48. Krishnan VV, Phillips S, Stark L: Frequency analysis of accommodation, accommodative vergence and disparity vergence, *Vis Res* 13:1545, 1973.

49. Krohel GB, Kristan RW, Simon JW, Barrows NA: Posttraumatic convergence insufficiency, *Ann Ophthal* 18:101, 1986.

50. Leigh RJ, Zee DS: *The neurology of eye movements,* ed 2, Philadelphia, 1991, FA Davis.

51. Martens TG, Ogle KN: Observations on accommodative convergence, *Am J Ophthal* 47:455, 1959.

52. Mays LE: Neural control of vergence eye movements: convergence and divergence neurons in midbrain, *J Neurophysiol* 51:1091, 1984.

53. Mays LE, Porter JD, Gamlin PDR, Tello CA: Neural control of vergence eye movements: neurons encoding vergence velocity, *J Neurophysiol* 56:1007, 1986.

54. Mays LE, Tello CA: Neurophysiological correlates of convergence and its adjustment. In Keller EL, Zee DS, editors: *Adaptive processes in visual and oculomotor systems,* New York, 1986, Pergamon Press.

55. Müller J: *Elements of physiology,* vol 2, London, 1826, Taylor and Walton, (W Baly, translator).

56. North R, Henson DB: Adaptation to prism-induced heterophoria in subjects with abnormal binocular vision or asthenopia, *Am J Optom Physiol Optics* 58:746, 1981.

55. North R, Henson DB: The effect of orthoptic treatment upon the vergence adaptation mechanism, *Optom Vis Sci* 69:294, 1992.

58. Ogle KN, Martens TG: On the accommodative convergence and proximal convergence, *Arch Ophthal* 57:702, 1957.

59. Ogle KN, Martens TG, Dyer JA: *Oculomotor imbalance in binocular vision and fixation disparity,* Philadelphia, 1967, Lea & Febiger.

60. Ono H: Accommodative vergence and Hering's Law of Equal Innervation, *Invest Ophthal Vis Sci* (suppl), 1981.

61. Oohira A, Zee DS: Disconjugate ocular motor adaptation in rhesus monkey, *Vis Res* 32:489, 1992.

62. Oohira A, Zee DS, Guyton DL: Disconjugate adaptation to long-standing, large-amplitude, spectacle corrected anisometropia, *Invest Ophthal Vis Sci* 32:1693, 1992.

63. O'Shea WF, Ciuffreda KJ, Fisher SK, Tannen B, Super P: Relation between distance heterophoria and tonic vergence, *Am J Optom Physiol Optics* 65:787, 1988.

64. Owens DA, Leibowitz HW: Accommodation, convergence, and distance perception in low illumination, *Am J Optom Physiol Optics* 57:540, 1980.

65. Owens DA, Leibowitz HW: Perceptual and motor consequences of tonic vergence. In Schor CM, Ciuffreda KJ, editors: *Vergence eye movements: basic and clinical aspects,* Boston, 1983, Butterworth.

66. Owens DA, Tyrrell RA: Lateral phoria at distance: contributions of accommodation, *Invest Ophthal Vis Sci* 33:2733, 1992.

67. Owens DA, Wolf-Kelly K: Near work, visual fatigue, and variations of oculomotor tonus, *Invest Ophthal Vis Sci* 28:743, 1987.

68. Rashbass C, Westheimer G: Disjunctive eye movements, *J Physiol* (Lond), 159:339, 1961.

69. Rosenfield MR, Ciuffreda KJ: Distance heterophoria and tonic vergence, *Optom Vis Sci* 67:667, 1990.

70. Rosenfield MR, Ciuffreda KJ, Hung GK: The linearity of proximally-induced accommodation and vergence, *Invest Ophthal Vis Sci* 32:2985, 1991.

71. Rutkowski PC, Burian HM: Divergence paralysis following head trauma, *Am J Ophthal* 73:660, 1972.

72. Rustein RP, Daum KM, Cho M, Eskridge JB: Horizontal and vertical vergence training and its effect on vergences, fixation disparity curves, and prism adaptation. II. Vertical data, *Am J Optom Physiol Optics,* 65:8, 1988.

73. Schor CM: The influence of rapid prism adaptation upon fixation disparity, *Vis Res* 19:757, 1979.

74. Schor CM, Ciuffreda KJ, editors: *Vergence eye movements: basic* and *clinical aspects,* Boston, 1983, Butterworth.

75. Schor CM, Robertson KM, Wesson M: Disparity vergence dynamics and fixation disparity, *Am J Optom Physiol Optics* 63:611, 1986.

76. Semmlow JL, Hung GK, Horng JL, Ciuffreda KJ: Initial control component in disparity vergence eye movements, *Ophthal Physiol Optics* 13:48, 1993.

77. Semmlow JL, Tinor T: Accommodative convergence response to off-foveal retinal images, *J Optical Soc Am* 68:1497, 1978.

78. Semmlow J, Wetzel P: Dynamic contributions of the components of binocular vergence, *J Optical Soc Am* 69:639, 1979.

79. Wick B: Clinical factors in proximal vergence, *Am J Optom Physiol Optics* 62:1, 1985.

80. Zee DS, Levi L: Neurological aspects of vergence eye movements, *Rev Neurol* (Paris) 145:613, 1989.

81. Zhang Y, Gamlin PDR, Mays LE: Antidromic identification of midbrain near response cells projecting to the oculomotor nucleus, *Exp Br Res* 84:525, 1991.

82. Zuber BL, Stark L: Dynamical characteristics of the fusional vergence eye movement system, *IEEE Trans Syst Sci Cybern* SSC-4:72, 1968.

7

Eye Movements During Reading

Key Terms

Average span of recognition	Progressive saccade
Binocular anomalies	Regression
Dyslexia	Retinal/cortical disease
Fixation duration	Return-sweep saccade
Neurologic disorder	Training reading efficiency

Perhaps one of the most complex eye movement tasks involves that which occurs during reading. In this situation the eye movements are not primarily externally guided by the position or movement of a target in space but rather are *internally* directed, that is, within the subject, as the stationary text is being read. Thus both positional shifts based on spaces in the text, text processing, comprehension, short-term memory, general interest, cognitive factors, and other factors, as well as the actual ongoing text processing itself, occur simultaneously as one's eyes move across a line of print.

The renowned French oculist Javal in 1879 discovered that saccades were made during reading.[14] He viewed the reflected image of a subject's eyes and noted that they jerked or "saccaded" from word to word.[11] Before this most critical observation, it was believed that the eyes moved *smoothly* across the line, as one had continuous perception of the text and continuity of story line. Since Javal's time, basic aspects of the oculomotor response profile during reading have been carefully researched and quantitatively defined.

This chapter discusses basic aspects of the normal reading eye movement pattern, as well as that found in patients manifesting a variety of reading difficulties. The reader is directed to other excellent sources for detailed aspects of the reading process itself (for example, encoding, attentional shifts).[48,59]

CHARACTERISTICS OF THE NORMAL READING PATTERN

Several features of the basic normal reading eye movement pattern need to be discussed.[40,48,63-65] Fig. 7-1 gives a schematic representation of a typical reading pattern,[65] and Table 7-1 gives developmental norms of these parameters[65] (see also Chapter 8 [Figs. 8-12 and 8-13] and Chapter 10).

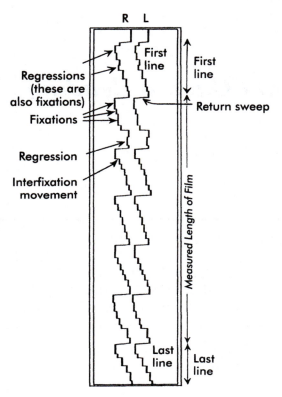

Fixations

Fixations refer to the total number of "eye stops" or pauses of the eyes during reading. The more difficult the material, the more fixations one typically makes; thus poor readers make more fixations than good readers. Also, as word length increases, the probability of fixating the word increases. However, most words are only fixated once. The eyes move from one fixation point to another by left-to-right progressive saccades, or interfixation movements, of 1 to 2 degrees (but as small as 0.5 and as large as 4 degrees) in angular extent with saccadic durations from 10 to 30 msec. The average saccade length is 8 characters, with a range from 1 to 18 characters. The percentage of total reading time taken up by the actual eye movements themselves is no greater than 10%, with an average of 7%.[67]

Regressions

Regressions refer to fixations that are directed from right-to-left by "backward" or regressive movements during reading. Most are only a few characters in extent and typically reflect some text confusion or comprehension problem, or perhaps a "recheck" or "double check" confirmation. Children learning to read and poor readers make an excessive number of regressions. Normally, approximately 10% to 15% of one's saccades (or fixations) are actually regressive in nature. Uncommon words are refixated more than common words.

FIG. 7-1 Schematic representation of binocular reading graph for a 50-word selection. *R*, Graph of right eye; *L*, graph of left eye. First and last lines of graph are not used in computing data, because they often are less efficient and are not typical of a reader's actual ability to use his or her eyes.

(From Taylor EA: *The fundamental reading skill,* Springfield, Ill, 1966, Charles C Thomas.)

TABLE 7-1   Averages for Measurable Components of the Fundamental Reading Skill

	Grade Level								
	1st	2nd	3rd	4th	5th	6th	JrH	HS	Col
Fixations per 100 words	240	200	170	136	118	105	95	83	75
Regressions per 100 words	55	45	37	30	26	23	18	15	11
Average span of recognition (words/fixation)	.42	.50	.59	.73	.85	.95	1.05	1.21	1.33
Average duration of fixation (sec)	.33	.30	.26	.24	.24	.24	.24	.23	.23
Average rate of comprehension (wpm)	75	100	138	180	216	235	255	296	340

From Taylor EA: *The fundamental reading skill,* 1966.

Return-Sweep Saccade

Return-sweep saccade refers to the large right-to-left slightly oblique saccadic eye movement that shifts the eyes from near the end of one line to near the beginning of the next line of text. The return-sweep saccade actually begins approximately six character spaces from the end of one line to the sixth or so character space of the next line, rather than the precise end and beginning of each line, because those six characters are believed to be processed during the last and first fixation pause of each line. Return-sweep saccades are typically 12 to 20 degrees in angular extent, with saccadic durations of 40 to 54 msec.[68] Sometimes small saccadic corrective movements are found at the end of the return sweep, presumably reflecting a basic eye position corrective movement.

Average Span of Recognition and Perceptual Span

Both terms effectively refer to the amount of print that one can perceive and process (at least partially) with each fixation. The span of recognition[64] is specified in units of "words" and is calculated by dividing the number of fixations into the number of words in the specified paragraph; for example, if one makes 200 fixations during the reading of 100 words, the average span would be 0.5 words per fixation. However, this term has been criticized by Rayner and Pollatsek,[48] because it assumes that the "spans" do not overlap on successive fixations. Through a series of detailed and complicated experiments, Rayner and colleagues[48] found that the "perceptual span," or maximum effective text processing field during a fixation, was asymmetric; it extended four characters to the left and 15 characters to the right of the fixation point. Since each interfixational saccade averages eight character spaces and the right side of the perceptual span is maximally 15 character spaces, the successive fixations clearly move into a re-

gion of text that has been processed to some extent (that is, globally) on the previous fixation. The exact mechanism as to how information from each fixation is integrated in a continuous and coherent process still remains a challenge for researchers in this area.

Fixation Duration

Fixation duration refers to the length of time (generally in milliseconds) that the eye pauses or remains fixated on a word. The average fixation duration is approximately 225 msec,[69] although its value is text dependent; it is shorter for easy text and longer for difficult text (Table 7-2). However, it can be even more specific; fixation duration varies with such factors as word ambiguity, grammatical function, and predictability. Within reason, such factors as line length, typography, color, and illumination have relatively little influence.[26,67] Fixation durations primarily involving positional information processing, such as ones occurring immediately before a large space in the text, are considerably shorter (~180 msec) than those more typical fixation durations involving both text *and* positional information processing (~255 msec).[1] It is only during the fixation periods that visual information is extracted; during the interfixational saccades, saccadic suppression or omission[70] occurs (see Chapter 3).

Reading Rate

Reading rate refers to the number of words read per unit time and is usually specified in words per minute (wpm). It is also referred to as the rate of comprehension.[64] The reading rate of the average college student ranges from approximately 200 to 350 wpm, with excellent comprehension; some truly exceptional individuals may read up to 1000 wpm, at least for short periods of time. Of course, reading rate varies somewhat with level of difficulty of the material; one reads harder

TABLE 7-2   *Mean Fixation Duration, Mean Saccade Length, Proportion of Fixations That Were Regressions, and WPM for 10 Good College-Age Readers Reading Different Types of Text*

Topic	Fixation Duration*	Saccade Length†	Regressions (%)‡	WPM
Light fiction	202	9.2	3	365
Newspaper article	209	8.3	6	321
History	222	8.3	4	313
Psychology	216	8.1	11	308
English literature	220	7.9	10	305
Economics	233	7.0	11	268
Mathematics	254	7.3	18	243
Physics	261	6.9	17	238
Biology	264	6.8	18	233
Mean	231	7.8	11	288

*In milliseconds.
†In character spaces (4 character spaces = 1 degree of visual angle).
‡Percentage of total fixations that were regressions.
From Rayner K, Pollatsek A: *The psychology of reading*, Englewood Cliffs, NJ, 1989, Prentice-Hall.

material more slowly than easier material (see Table 7-2). Most individuals can skim (obtain an overview as rapidly as possible without reading every word) 400 to 500 wpm and in some exceptional cases 1000 to 2000 wpm. Speed readers claim to be able to read 2000 to 10,000 wpm; however, they are actually skimming rapidly, perhaps only fixating one word per line; although they may obtain an overall sense of the reading material, their comprehension for average details is very low. See Rayner and Pollatsek[48] for an excellent critical review of this controversial topic.

Vergence Dynamics

During the saccades, especially the large return-sweep, there is typically a transient over-convergence (0.1 to 0.3 degree) of the eyes[17,18,65,69] immediately followed by a corrective dynamic divergence response (approximately 300 msec in duration) to attain more accurate bifixation.

Other Factors

Knowledge of the fixation locus, sequence and temporal aspects of fixation pauses, and the eye movement trajectory during reading provides additional important insight into the motor and cognitive aspects of reading. Fig. 7-2 presents a two-dimensional, objectively recorded reading eye movement pattern (Russian text)[71]; each dot represents a fixation site, and each interconnecting line represents the saccadic trajectory. The correlation between text length/spacing and the overall eye movement pattern is evident. Of interest are the small vertical saccades just preceding each slightly oblique return-sweep saccade and frequent vertical corrective saccade to fixate near the beginning of the next line of text. The curvature and slight obliquity of the saccadic trajectory between fixation pauses are the norm. (Also see Chapter 3 on saccadic eye movements.) There appear to be no regressive movements. Fig. 7-3 shows the horizontal fixation locus, numbered fixation sequence, and fixation duration for reading text material.[48]

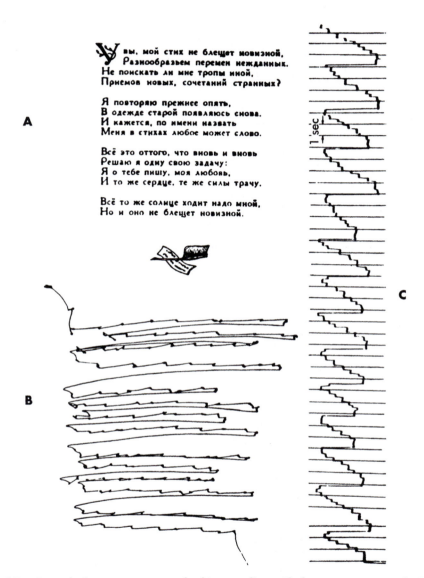

FIG. 7-2 Record of eye movements of subject reading a Shakespearean sonnet in Russian **(A).** Record on stationary photosensitive paper **(B)** and on moving phototape on a photokymograph **(C).**

(From Yarbus AL: *Eye movements and vision,* New York, 1967, Plenum Press.)

Roadside joggers endure sweat, pain and angry drivers in the name of

.	.		.	.		.	.	.		.
1	2		3	4		5	6	7		8
286	221		246	277		256	233	216		188

fitness. A healthy body may seem reward enough for most people. However,

.	. .	.	.	.	. .	.	.	.
9	10 12	13	11	14	15 16	17	18	19
301	177 196	175	244	302	112 177	266	188	199

for all those who question the payoff, some recent research on physical

.	.	.	. .		.	.		.
21	20	22	23 24		25	26		27
216	212	179	109 266		245	188		205

activity and creativity has provided some surprisingly good news. Regular

. .	. .	. .	.	.	. .
29 28	30 31	32 33	34	35	36 37
201 66	201 188	203 220	217	288	212 75

bouts of aerobic exercise may also help spark a brainstorm of creative

.	. .	. .	. .	.	. .	. .
38	39 42	40 43	41 44	45	46	47 48
312	260 271	188 350	215 221	266	277	120 219
					50	
					179	

thinking. At least, this is the conclusion that was reached in a study that

.	.	.	.	. . .	.	.	. .
49	51		52	53 54 57	55	56	60 59
266	213		210	216 416 200	177	113	206 220
					58		
					218		

FIG. 7-3   Excerpt from a passage of text with fixation sequence and fixation durations indicated.

(From Rayner K, Pollatsek A: *The psychology of reading*, Englewood Cliffs, NJ, 1989, Prentice-Hall.)

Note the following: (1) the regressions at sites 12, 13, 42, 50, 57, and 60; (2) the small corrective movements immediately following the return-sweep saccades at sites 21 and 29; and (3) as discussed earlier, the first and last fixations of each line do not extend to the first and last character of text. Finally, Fig. 7-4 shows a schematic representation of the perceptual and oculomotor events that are presumed to occur before, during, and after each fixation pause.[48]

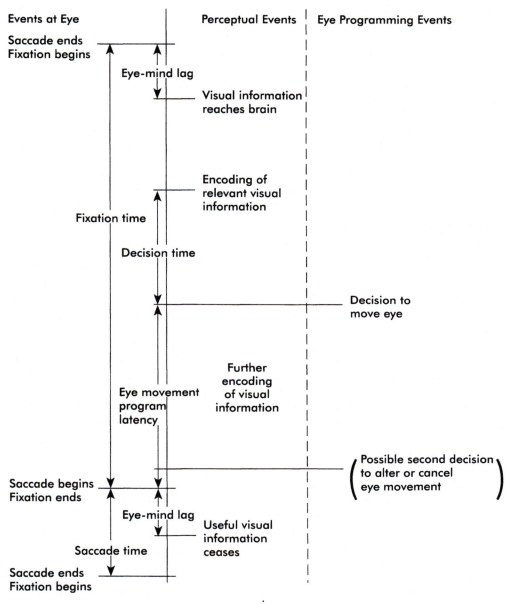

Events at Eye   Perceptual Events   Eye Programming Events

Saccade ends
Fixation begins

Eye-mind lag

Visual information
reaches brain

Encoding of
relevant visual
information

Fixation time

Decision time

Decision to
move eye

Further
encoding
of visual
information

Eye movement
program
latency

Possible second decision
to alter or cancel
eye movement

Saccade begins
Fixation ends

Eye-mind lag

Useful visual
information
ceases

Saccade time

Saccade ends
Fixation begins

FIG. 7-4 Simplified schema of events during a fixation relevant to eye movement control. There has been little attempt made to represent time intervals accurately by vertical distances. In addition, eye-mind lag has been drawn to be shorter than saccade time even though the opposite may be true. A realistic model of eye control needs to be more complex. Among other things, the decision of where to move the eye is left out of the figure.

(From Rayner K, Pollatsek A: *The psychology of reading*, Englewood Cliffs, NJ, 1989, Prentice-Hall.)

FOVEAL AND PARAFOVEAL CONTRIBUTIONS TO READING

The foveal (±1 degree) and parafoveal (±5 degrees) retinal regions are clearly crucial to the reading process. The central retina must be used for the basic visual resolution of the text letters, because beyond a few degrees it is too reduced to be effective. Thus the 1- to 2-degree left-to-right reading saccades take place to resolve and then process the fixated letter groups.

A study by Rayner and Bertera[47] has clearly demonstrated the important but different roles played by the foveal and parafoveal regions during reading. Using sophisticated computer and eye movement technology, they were able to create either an electronically generated foveal or parafoveal "scotoma" in normal subjects during reading. In the first experiment the fovea was masked (Fig. 7-5, *A*); as masking size increased, fixation duration increased, saccade length generally increased, total number of fixations increased, and reading rate decreased. In the second experiment the parafovea was now masked (Fig. 7-5, *B*); as its "window size" increased (that is, more parafovea was progressively allowed to see the text along with the central fovea), fixation duration decreased, saccade length increased, total number of fixations decreased, and reading rate increased. However, overall reading performance (both objectively and subjectively) was worse in the foveal masking condition. They concluded that the fovea and near parafovea were involved in semantic processing, whereas the far parafovea was primarily used to guide eye movements to the next fixation location.

This idea was further advanced by Raasch and Rubin[44] in their discussion of the results by Cummings and Rubin, who used similar technology in normal subjects and a 6-degree movable mask. With the scotoma centered on the fovea (simulating central field loss), the effects were the greatest, with reading rate decreased by 75%. In addition to the central field loss from the scotoma, nonfoveal eccentric viewing was demanded under this condition, and this was found to be quite objectionable to most individuals (as expected, since the "blind" central fovea still retains the zero sensorimotor direction/localization value); this is consistent with the recent results of Chaparro and Young.[9] With the scotoma to either side of the fovea (simulating hemifield loss), reading rate was impaired despite the presence of normal foveal viewing. The effect was worse for the scotoma located to the right (50% decrease in reading rate) versus left (<50% decrease in reading rate) of the fovea, because it interfered with the left-to-right sequencing of all progressive saccades; a scotoma to the left of the fixation point only interfered with the return-sweep saccades. And, last, with the scotoma located either just above or below the fovea (simulating quadrant or altitudinal field loss), no adverse effects were noted. Thus location of the scotoma differentially affected one's reading ability by altering the requisite oculomotor reading pattern. These and the earlier results of Rayner and Bertera[47] have obvious implications with regard to reading in patients with disease- or trauma-related visual field loss (see discussion in next section).

ABNORMAL READING EYE MOVEMENTS AND RELATED OCULOMOTOR PARAMETERS
Binocular Anomalies

From the point of view of the optometrist, as well as others involved in the diagnosis and treatment of binocular vision problems, binocular anomalies clearly represent an important area. Although most would agree that an individual with only one eye should read as well as an individual having two eyes and overall normal binocular vision function, most would also agree that any impediment

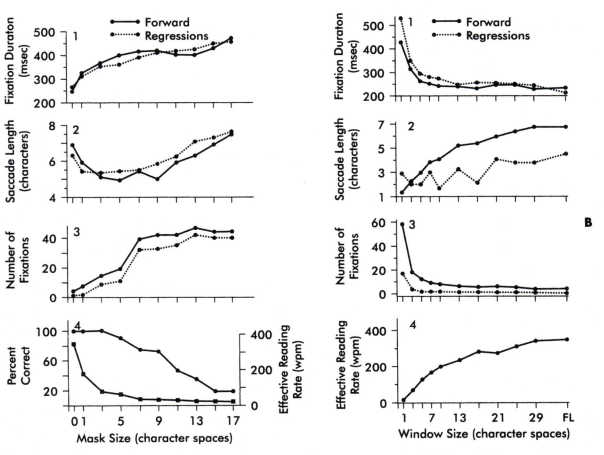

FIG. 7-5 **A,** Foveal masking study. *1,* Mean fixation duration; *2,* saccade length; *3,* number of fixations per sentence; *4,* number of words correctly reported per sentence (•) and effective reading rate (■). **B,** Window study. *1,* Mean fixation duration; *2,* saccade length; *3,* number of fixations per sentence; *4,* effective reading rate; *FL,* control condition in which sentence was presented without a mask.

(From Rayner K, Bertera JH: *Science* 206:468, 1979.)

or obstacle (such as poor fusional vergence or aniseikonia) to the binocular sensorimotor process may adversely impact *all* near-vision tasks, but especially reading, which involves sustained bifixation, focus, and attention.

The majority of studies in this area support the preceding notion, namely, that binocular vision anomalies may be related to and have a negative effect on one's reading efficiency (Box 7-1).* Thus such conditions as increased exophoria at near, convergence insufficiency, and increased fixation disparity have been implicated in patients with reading problems. On the other hand, such parameters as esophoria at near, stereopsis, distance lateral phoria, and vertical phoria have either mixed results or

*References 4, 8, 22-24, 52, 56, 59, and 60.

BOX 7-1. *Binocular Vision Conditions That May Adversely Affect Reading Ability*

- Aniseikonia
- Anisometropia
- High near phoria (especially exophoria)
- Poor fusional ability
- Large fixation disparity
- Receded near point of convergence
- Strabismus (especially intermittent)
- Binocular suppression
- Poor binocular coordination
- Convergence insufficiency

---

appear to bear no relation in such individuals. The findings related to binocular vision abnormalities might be even stronger if more objective and subjective dynamic tests were performed (such as objective recordings of horizontal fusional responses with quantification of latency, time constant, and main sequence) and multivariate analysis were done in which a *cluster* of parameters rather than any single parameter were considered. And, last, since there is considerable evidence that vision therapy and/or appropriate lenses and prisms can successfully remediate *all* of the preceding binocular vision anomalies with respect to motor response dynamics and accuracy,[3,19,56,61] as well as reduce symptoms, then patients with such problems in conjunction with reading difficulties can justifiably receive simple conventional treatment with the expectation of a successful outcome.

Dyslexia

The two basic categories of dyslexia are *developmental/congenital* and *acquired*. The developmental or "congenital" dyslexia is most commonly encountered. This refers to the occurrence of a specific reading disability, that is at least 2 years behind expected grade level of

reading, in the presence of normal intelligence and sensory vision and in the absence of neurologic and emotional disorders.[40]

Developmental dyslexia has been further divided into two important subgroups.[46,58] The first subgroup is *language-deficit dyslexia*. Such individuals tend to show an increased number of progressive and regressive movements, small-amplitude saccades, and prolonged fixation durations when reading text appropriate for their age level; when given material appropriate for their reading level, however, the overall reading pattern tends to normalize. Thus their abnormal reading eye movement pattern reflects a basic problem in the processing of language. The second and much less common subgroup is *visual-spatial dyslexia*. In contrast, such individuals tend to show inaccuracy of the return-sweep saccade and frequent right-to-left sequences of saccades, including partial and complete "reverse staircase" patterns,* where the series of saccades traverses some or all of the line of print, respectively, *independent* of the level of reading material. Thus their abnormal reading eye movement pattern primarily reflects a basic problem in the processing of visual-spatial relations, and therefore these abnormal oculomotor patterns are manifest in both reading and nonreading sequential eye movement tasks.[21,46] These two relatively distinct subgroups of persons with dyslexia probably explain why some researchers, such as Pavlidis and others,[15,16,21,36-38] noted sequencing problems for nonreading tasks in many persons with dyslexia, whereas others did not[2,5,6,35,57,72]; the former subgroups appeared to have many more persons with visual-spatial dyslexia, whereas the latter subgroup probably had many more persons with language-deficit dyslexia.[46] Thus the abnormal reading eye movement patterns in dyslexia reflect either language or spatial difficulties (or perhaps both in some individuals),

---

*References 13, 15, 16, 21, 31, 36-39, 46, and 73.

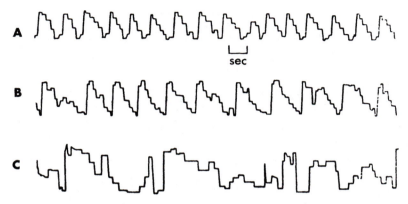

FIG. 7-6 Representative eye movement records of a normal reader, slow reader, and person with dyslexia while they read. **A,** Eye movement record of normal reader during reading. It consists of successive similar eye movements and fixations that form a repetitive staircase pattern. Regressions are rare, and they are invariably smaller in amplitude than preceding forward saccade. Horizontal lines represent fixations. Vertical lines represent eye movements. **B,** Slow reader's eye movement record during reading. It is noteworthy that slow readers make more forward and regressive movements than normal readers, but the amplitude of their regressions is also smaller than the preceding forward saccades. This slow reader's eye movements form a prolonged staircase pattern. **C,** Person with a dyslexic's "erractic" eye movement record. Every line has its own idiomorphic shape, unlike normal and backward readers' patterns, which are consistent throughout. It is often difficult to distinguish end of one line from beginning of the next. These persons' regressions are not only very frequent but also often occur in clusters of two or more. Their amplitude is frequently bigger than that of the preceding forward saccade. These eye movement characteristics are unique to persons with dyslexia.

(From Pavlidis G: In Pavlidis G, Miles TR, editors: *Dyslexia research and its application to education,* London, 1981, Wiley.)

but the eye movements per se *do not* cause the dyslexia.[46]

The second and much less frequent category of dyslexia is *acquired dyslexia.*[40] This refers to the presence of a reading disability in a previously normal reader subsequent to neurologic dysfunction or damage, such as a stroke. One of the first complaints that such individuals report is reading difficulty, including reduced comprehension, difficulty in sequencing of eye movements, problems with maintenance of fixation, and the necessity to move the head to assist reading. In persons with acquired dyslexia without basic abnormal oculomotor control, reading patterns like that of a person with developmental language–deficit dyslexia will be found; if they

also exhibit basic abnormal oculomotor control, they may in addition exhibit slowed saccades, difficulty initiating saccades, dysmetria, nystagmus, and square-wave jerks (see later discussion).

An example of a reading eye movement pattern in a person with dyslexia (probably a moderate visual-spatial type) is shown in Fig. 7-6.[37] One clearly sees the spatially disorganized overall pattern, with numerous partial and complete reverse staircases; a few abnormally long fixation durations are also present. The two-dimensional reading eye movement pattern (fixation loci) of a person with dyslexia (probably of the visual-spatial variety) is shown in Fig. 7-7[37]; again, the spatial disarray of eye movement sequencing is evi-

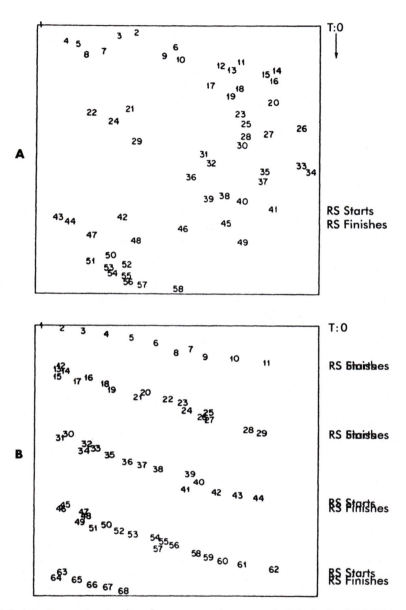

FIG. 7-7 **A,** Computer-produced eye-movement record of dyslexic child. His eye movements are erratic with right-to-left scanning in evidence. He is unable to move his eyes with one eye movement from end of one line to beginning of the next line. Computer printout of eye-movement positions in relation to line of print. Consecutive numbers represent order in which fixations were made; *RS,* return sweep. Time runs from top to bottom. **B,** Computer-produced eye-movement record of normal reader. Regular left to right scanning can be clearly seen.

(From Pavlidis G: In Pavlidis G, Miles TR, editors: *Dyslexia research and its application to education,* London, 1981, Wiley.)

dent. (Also see Chapter 10 for detailed case analyses of two persons with developmental dyslexia.)

There is also some evidence based on objective recording of eye movements that many persons with dyslexia have dynamic disparity vergence dysfunction.[30,60] This includes slowed and irregular movement patterns to step and ramp disparity stimuli. This has been confirmed clinically,[7,26] including use of a subjective dynamic vergence facility test.[7]

Central Neurologic Disorders

Many centrally based neurologic conditions, such as multiple sclerosis and cerebellar disease, frequently produce such oculomotor abnormalities as square-wave jerks, jerk and pedular nystagmus (typically with oscillopsia), slowed saccades, and marked dysmetria, any of which may have an adverse impact on reading.* Clearly, one's ability to maintain steady fixation, as well as to change fixation to a new word accurately and efficiently, would be more difficult with addition of these oculomotor perturbations. Thus, in contrast to dyslexia, here the eye movement abnormalities per se *directly* contribute to the compromised reading ability (Box 7-2; also see Chapter 10).

The reading eye movements in a patient with a probable multiple sclerosis, with complaints of intermittent oscillopsia or "jumping" of the words, along with severe asthenopia during reading, are presented in Fig. 7-8; it should be noted that saccadic intrusions were present under all reading and nonreading test conditions.[15] Brief (1- to 6-sec) bursts of saccadic intrusions, having amplitudes ranging from 2.0 to 8.5 degrees and averaging 5.0 degrees, were present. Intersaccadic intervals ranged from 150 to 600 msec, which suggested dependence on visual feedback for their generation. Thus the typically small-

*References 10, 12, 13, 15, 16, 25, 28, 31, 32, 34, 40, 42, 45, 58, and 62.

BOX 7-2. *Conditions With Oculomotor Disturbances Causing Reading Problems**

- Nystagmus
- Disease-related field loss (central, peripheral, and hemifield)
- Multiple sclerosis
- Duane's syndrome
- Extraocular muscle paralysis or paresis
- Congenital oculomotor apraxia
- Huntington's chorea
- Choreatic syndrome
- Dyslexia with mild cerebellar signs
- Spinocerebellar degeneration
- Friedreich's ataxia
- Wilson's disease

*It should be noted that for all conditions except disease-related field loss, the cause is due to either central or peripheral neurologic *motor* disturbances, whereas for disease-related field loss, the cause is due to a *sensory* disturbance in the afferent visual pathway (such as the retina, chiasm, or visual cortex).[12]

---

amplitude saccadic intrusions found during nonreading tasks were replaced by intermittently occurring, larger-amplitude intrusive saccades. Also present were single, 2- to 3-degree saccadic intrusions that were initially difficult to differentiate from regressive movements; however, they were of larger amplitude than typical regressive movements and had a common baseline before *and* after the movement. Because the patient reported increased difficulty after 10 to 15 minutes of reading, eye movements were recorded after 12 minutes of intensive reading during which time she reported considerable visual fatigue, discomfort, and jumping of letters; the patient was also asked to depress a switch, which activated an event marker on the strip-chart recorder, during periods in which the words or letters seemed to jump, and she became confused. A typical record is shown in Fig. 7-8. Large-amplitude (5- to 10-degree) saccadic intrusions occurred concurrent with some of

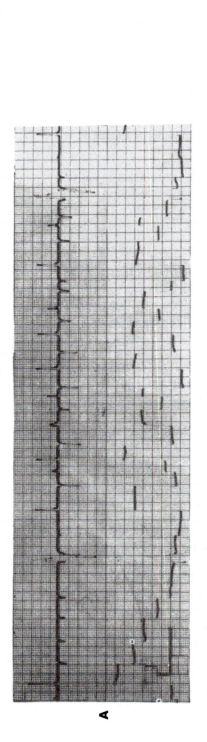

A

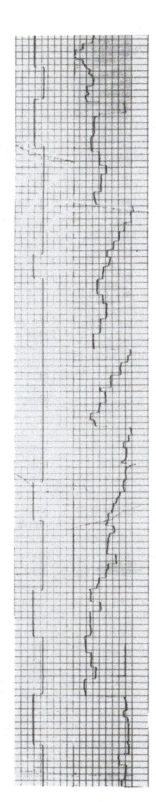

B

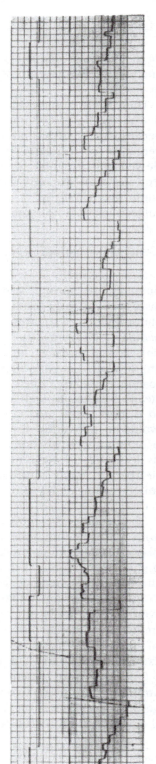

FIG. 7.8 For legend see opposite page.

the periods of visual disturbance. Also present were single, rightward-directed saccadic intrusions and single, leftward-directed saccadic intrusions that occurred primarily during prolonged fixation (see beginning of record), with most of these single intrusive saccades occurring during or in close proximity to the designated periods of visual disturbance. These periods of visual disturbance increased twofold (6 versus 12 seconds out of a total of 40 seconds) when the patient was fatigued. Other eye movement abnormalities were found that were related to the reading disability. These included (1) reverse staircases, (2) prolonged fixations (500 to 4000 msec) during which time the patient indicated there was fixity of gaze ("locked gaze"), thus demonstrating an oculomotor, apraxia-like condition, with difficulty moving the eyes to the newly intended position, especially when at the end of a line, and (3) intermittent, brief (1- to 3-sec) periods of gross (1- to 3-degree) overconvergence or underconvergence.

Patients with either pendular or jerk nystagmus may also exhibit impaired reading ability and reduced reading rate because of the superimposed nystagmus on the basic "staircase" reading pattern.[10,12,13,65] Some interesting reading records are presented in Fig. 7-9

FIG. 7-8 Reading in a patient with suspected multiple sclerosis. Binocular viewing. **A,** Normal reading followed by 5-sec flurry of large-amplitude saccadic intrusions. Note absence of small-amplitude saccadic intrusions. **B,** Abnormal reading patterns for extended continuous reading period. Patient indicated that she was visually fatigued. Lower trace is left eye position. Upper trace is event marker activated by patient (upward deflections) to indicate periods of confusion and jumping of words and letters during reading. In most instances, there was good agreement between subjective and objective measures with saccadic intrusions occurring within or in close proximity to patient-indicated periods of visual disturbance.

(From Ciuffreda KJ, Kenyon RV, Stark L: *Am J Optom Physiol Optics* 60:242, 1983.)

for a patient with marked variability in her nystagmus.[10] In the upper two traces (Fig. 7-9, *A* and *B*), there is only a hint of nystagmus being present (for example, "slanted" fixation duration periods and some exponentially increasing nystagmus slow phases during intended steady fixation). In contrast, conspicuous nystagmus is always present in the bottom (binocular) traces (Fig. 7-9, *C*). In all cases, reading rate was reduced (~115 to 150 wpm). This variability in nystagmus was also reflected during simple tracking tasks.

Peripheral Neurologic Disorders

The most common peripherally based neurologic condition is paresis or paralysis of an extraocular muscle, thus effectively limiting the ability of the eye to saccade normally across and/or down the page of text.[12] Such patients may develop unusual head postures or use head movements to facilitate their abnormal eye movements during reading. Fig. 7-10 presents the reading eye movement pattern in a patient with right superior oblique paresis.[31] As the eyes shifted into the field of action of the affected muscle, the patient's ability to move the affected right eye gradually deteriorated. The patient typically circumvented this binocular motor problem during reading by occluding one (the right) eye.

Retinal and Cortical Diseases

Diseases of the retina causing either central (example: macular disease) or peripheral (example: retinitis pigmentosa) visual field scotomas can be a major impediment to reading efficiently.[20,33,66] With either a central scotoma or severe macular degeneration, identification and semantic processing of letters and words in the foveal and parafoveal regions become a visual resolution problem, as well as causing difficulty guiding the eye accurately to a new word with the eccentric retinal locus. (See earlier section on foveal and parafoveal contributions to reading.)

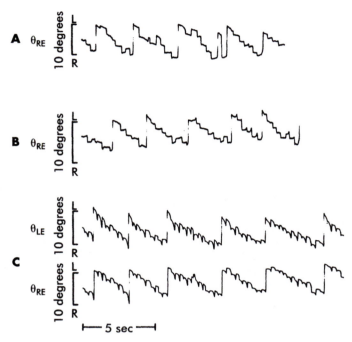

FIG. 7-9 Reading eye movements showing variability of jerk nystagmus and its influence on reading ability in one patient. Reading material level (high school) similar for each trial. **A,** Relatively normal record except for presence of some nystagmus slow phases (to right); reading rate is 130 wpm. **B,** Relatively normal record except for presence of some nystagmus slow phases (to right) and some "runaway" nystagmus slow phases (to left); reading rate is 156 wpm. **C,** Marked nystagmus present and superimposed on binocular reading record; reading rate is reduced to 115 wpm. θ_{RE}, right eye position; θ_{LE}, left eye position; L, left; R, right.

(From Ciuffreda KJ: *Am J Optom Physiol Optics* 56:521, 1979.)

A well-documented case is presented in Fig. 7-11 for a patient with fundus flavimaculatus and associated macular lesions (Stargardt's macular degeneration).[19] Patients with central scotomas tend to use a single eccentric retinal locus on the superior edge of the scotoma for fixation so that the field below their gaze is available to assist in all tasks, especially reading and walking.[20,66] The objective eye movement record for simulated reading shows numerous vertical saccades suggesting diffulty in localizing the words with the eccentric retinal locus, as well as a somewhat irregular overall pattern. Fig. 7-12 shows the effect of a central scotoma on reading rate and accuracy in this and similar patients. Clearly, as scotoma size increased, reading rate decreased; however, reading accuracy remained relatively constant, suggesting that comprehension rather than speed was the patient's goal.

In contrast, in patients with large peripheral scotomas, such as in retinitis pigmentosa and advanced glaucoma, there is poor parafoveal guidance available to direct the eye to the next fixation location, as well as reduced ability to "preview" letters and words to be foveated directly in the next fixation. A markedly reduced peripheral field produces errors in saccade accuracy, reduced span of recognition, and thus overall reduced reading rate.

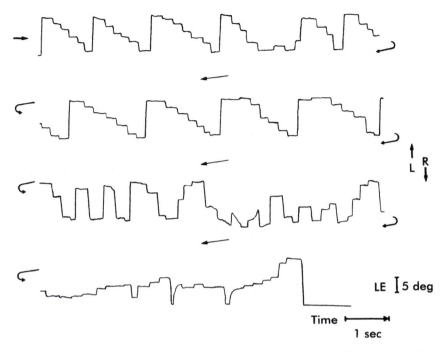

FIG. 7-10 Reading record of adult patient with right superior oblique paresis. Record begins at upper left corner and should be read from left to right. Note progressive breakdown of forward staircase pattern to reverse staircases, blink, and finally eyelid closure. Binocular viewing.

(From Jones A, Stark L: In Rayner K, editor: *Eye movements in reading: perceptual and language processes,* New York, 1983, Academic Press.)

Finally, patients with cortical disorders (typically of the occipital area) will manifest hemifield scotomas (frequently with macular sparing) or hemianopia.[12] In those with left field defects, there will be some errors (generally overshoot) in the return-sweep saccades directed into this blind field; however, reading is only minimally affected. In contrast, in those with right field defects, there will be considerable difficulty with the progressive saccades moving into the blind field. Such patients execute an increased number of both progressive and regressive small-amplitude saccades in the arduous task of reading across the line. Reading rate is typically considerably reduced (75 to 125 wpm).

Training Reading Eye Movements and Reading Efficiency

Based on the results of objective eye movement recordings during reading, both Taylor[65] and Solan[53-55] have provided reasonable evidence over many years of study that reading eye movements and reading efficiency can be improved by appropriate and intensive therapeutic intervention in selected individuals manifesting a variety of reading deficiencies. Procedures typically included (1) training of relative vergence during reading; (2) training reading eye movements using a movable, rate-controlled shutter over portions of the projected text (emphasis was on "conditioning" regression-free movement sequences, as

Text continued on page 180.

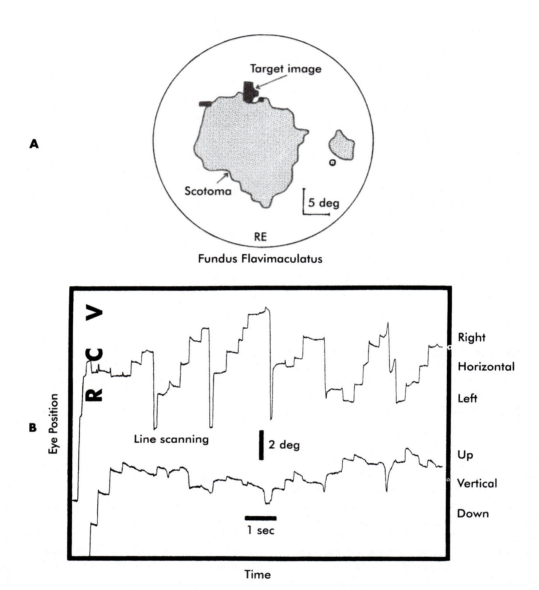

FIG. 7-11 **A,** Field projection of left eye of patient with single preferred retinal locus. Retinal locus (indicated by cross-hatched and solid areas) is area within which patient placed target image 68% of fixation period. Solid area indicates where target was imaged most frequently (accumulated to upper 34% of fixation period). **B,** Strip-chart recording of horizontal *(upper trace)* and vertical *(lower trace)* eye position of patient with Stargardt's macular degeneration scanning a line of characters (R, C, V) at limit of her acuity.

(From Cummings RW, Whittaker SG, Watson GR, Budd JM: *Am J Optom Physiol Optics* 62:833, 1985.)

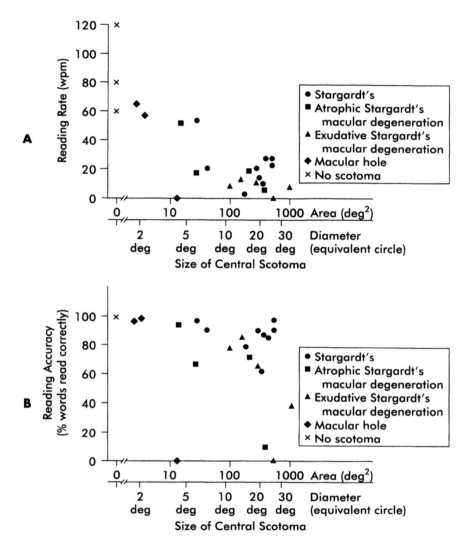

FIG. 7-12 **A,** Results of patients showing reading rate (wpm) on Pepper Visual Skills for reading test versus size of central scotoma (degrees and degrees squared). Patients with no scotoma include one with cellophane maculopathy who reads at 60 wpm and two normal patients whose reading rates are representative of range of values for normal subjects for this special test (80 to 120 wpm). **B,** Results of patients showing reading accuracy (average words per line read correctly) on Pepper Visual Skills for reading test versus size of central scotoma (degrees and degrees squared). Normally sighted patients usually achieve accuracy approaching or equaling 100%.

(From Cummings RW, Whittaker SG, Watson GR, Budd JM: *Am J Optom Physiol Optics* 62:833, 1985.)

TABLE 7-3   *Results of Training Three Subjects: Individual and Average Findings*

Individual Findings*	Fixations (Per 100 Words)		Regressions (Per 100 Words)		Span of Recognition (Words Per Fixation)		Rate of Reading (wpm)		Comprehension (%)
	Raw Score	Grade Level	Raw Score	Grade Level	Raw Score	Grade Level	Raw Score	Grade Level	
Subject 1									
Before	98	7	25	5	102	7	160	4	80
After	60	College	10	College	167	College	343	College	90
Subject 2									
Before	97	8	18	8	103	8	153	3	100
After	51	College	6	College	196	College	370	College	100
Subject 3									
Before	100	7	28	5	100	7	171	4	100
After	56	College	13	College	179	College	338	College	100

	Average Improvement†				
	Before		After		
	Raw Score	Grade Level	Raw Score	Grade Level	Change
Fixations (per 100 words)	98	7	56	College	−42%
Regressions (per 100 words)	24	5	10	College	−58%
Span of recognition (words per fixation)	1.02	7	1.81	College	+80%
Rate of reading (wpm)	161	4	300	College	+117%

From Solan HA: *Am J Optom Physiol Optics* 62:812, 1985.
*Individual findings before and after training.
†Averaged findings for three subjects before and after training.

well as accurate return-sweep saccades); and (3) training rapid perception of visual stimuli by tachistoscopic presentation. Table 7-3 presents results in three adults. Clearly, both characteristics of the reading oculomotor pattern and reading rate improved without loss of comprehension. Others using objective eye movement recording techniques have found similar results.[29,43,49] Such positive findings should not be too surprising, since at least 20% of the variance in reading ability in children can be accounted for by the *grouped* oculomotor parameters[41]; further, eye movements can be operantly conditioned,[50,51] especially when attentional aspects are dominant, as in reading.

REVIEW QUESTIONS

1. Describe the parameters and characteristics of the normal reading eye movement pattern.
2. Do "speed readers" read?
3. Compare and contrast the foveal versus parafoveal contributions to reading.
4. List five abnormalities of binocular vision that may negatively impact a child's reading ability and development.
5. Compare and contrast the possible problems during reading in a patient with (a) a hemifield defect, (b) a central field defect, or (c) a peripheral field defect.
6. Can reading efficiency and oculomotor control be improved by specific training paradigms in selected patients?

REFERENCES

1. Abrams SG, Zuber BL: Some temporal characteristics of information processing during reading, *Reading Res Q* 8:40, 1972.
2. Adler-Grinberg D, Stark L: Eye movements, scanpaths, and dyslexia, *Am J Optom Physiol Optics* 55:557, 1978.
3. Atzmon D, Nemet P, Ishay A, Karni E: A randomized prospective masked and matched comparative study of orthoptic treatment versus conventional reading tutoring treatment for reading disabilities in 62 children, *Bino Vis Eye Muscle Surgery Q* 8:91, 1993.
4. Birnbaum MH: Vision disorders frequently interfere with reading and learning: they should be diagnosed and treated, *J Behav Optom* 4:66, 1993.
5. Black JL, Collins DWK, DeRoach JN, Zubrick S: A detailed study of sequential saccadic eye movements for normal and poor reading children, *Percept Motor Skills* 59:423, 1984.
6. Brown B, Haegerstrom-Portnoy G, Yingling CD, Herron J, Galin D, Marcus M: Tracking eye movements are normal in dyslexic children, *Am J Optom Physiol Optics* 60:376, 1983.
7. Buzelli AR: Stereopsis, accommodative and vergence facility: do they relate to dyslexia? *Optom Vis Sci* 68:842, 1991.
8. Carter DB: Vision and learning disorders. In Carter DB, editor: *Interdisciplinary approaches to learning disorders*, Philadelphia, 1970, Chilton Book Co.
9. Chaparro A, Young RSL: Reading with rods: the superiority of central vision for rapid reading, *Invest Ophthal Vis Sci* 34:2341, 1993.
10. Ciuffreda KJ: Jerk nystagmus: some new findings, *Am J Optom Physiol Optics* 56:521, 1979.
11. Ciuffreda KJ: Etymology of the word "saccade," *Ophthal Physiol Optics* 10:307, 1990.
12. Ciuffreda KJ: Reading eye movements in patients with oculomotor disturbances. In Ygge J, Lennerstrand G, Zee D, editors: *Eye movements in reading*, New York, Pergamon Press (in press).
13. Ciuffreda KJ, Bahill AT, Kenyon RV, Stark L: Eye movements during reading: case reports, *Am J Optom Physiol Optics* 53:389, 1976.
14. Ciuffreda KJ, Bassil N: Translation of "Essay on the Physiology of Reading" by E. Javal, *Ophthal Physiol Optics* 10:381, 1990.
15. Ciuffreda KJ, Kenyon RV, Stark L: Saccadic intrusions contributing to reading disability: a case report, *Am J Optom Physiol Optics* 60:242, 1983.
16. Ciuffreda KJ, Kenyon RV, Stark L: Eye movements during reading: further case reports, *Am J Optom Physiol Optics* 62:844, 1985.
17. Clark B: The effect of binocular imbalance on the behavior of the eyes during reading, *J Educ Psychol* 49:1117, 1935.
18. Clark B: Additional data on binocular imbalance and reading, *J Educ Psychol* 27:473, 1936.
19. Cohen AH, Lowe SE, Steele GT, Suchoff IB, Gottlieb DD, Trevarrow TL: The efficacy of optometric vision training, *J Am Optom Assoc* 59:95, 1988.
20. Cummings RW, Whittaker SG, Watson GR, Budd JM: Scanning characters and reading with a central scotoma, *Am J Optom Physiol Optics* 62:833, 1985.
21. Elterman RD, Abel LA, Daroff RB, Dell'Osso LF, Bornstein JL: Eye movement patterns in dyslexic children, *J Learn Disabil* 13:16, 1980.
22. Evans BJW: Dyslexia—conventional optometric factors, *Optometry Today*, June 14, 1993.
23. Evans BJW: Dyslexia—eye movements, controversial optometric techniques, and the transient visual system, *Optometry Today*, July 12, 1993.
24. Evans BJW, Drasdo N: Review of ophthalmic factors in dyslexia, *Ophthal Physiol Optics* 10:13, 1990.
25. Gassel MM, Williams D: Visual functions in patients with homonymous hemianopia. II. Oculomotor mechanisms, *Brain* 86:19, 1963.
26. Hackman RAB, Tinker MA: Effect of variation in color of print and background upon eye movements in reading, *Am J Optom Arch Am Acad Optom* 34:354, 1957.
27. Hammerberg E, Norn MS: Defective dissociation of accommodation and convergence in dyslectic children, *Acta Ophthalmologica* 50:651, 1972.
28. Hartje W: Reading disturbances in the presence of oculomotor disorders, *Eur Neurol* 7:249, 1972.
29. Heath EJ, Cook P, O'Dell N: Eye exercises and reading efficiency, *Acad Ther* 11:435, 1976.
30. Hung GH: Reduced vergence response velocities in dyslexics: a preliminary report, *Ophthal Physiol Optics* 9:420, 1989.
31. Jones A, Stark L: Abnormal patterns of normal eye movements in specific dyslexia. In Rayner K, editor: *Eye movements in reading: perceptual and language processes*, New York, 1983, Academic Press.
32. Klingelhofer J, Conrad B: Eye movements during reading in aphasics, *Eur Arch Psychiatr Neurol Sci* 234:175, 1984.

33. McMahon TT, Hansen M, Viana M: Fixation characteristics in macular disease, *Invest Ophthal Vis Sci* 32:567, 1991.

34. Meienberg O, Zangemeister WH, Rosenberg M, Hoyt WF, Stark L: Saccadic eye movement strategies in patients with homonymous hemianopia, *Annals Neurol* 9:537, 1981.

35. Olson RK, Kliegel R, Davidson BJ: Dyslexic and normal readers' eye movements, *J Exp Psychol Human Percept Perform* 9:816, 1983.

36. Pavlidis GT: Do eye movements hold the key to dyslexia? *Neuropsychologia* 19:57, 1981.

37. Pavlidis G: Sequencing, eye movements, and the early objective diagnosis of dyslexia. In Pavlidis G, Miles TR, editors: *Dyslexia research and its application to education,* London, 1981, Wiley.

38. Pavlidis GT: Eye movement differences between dyslexics, normal, and retarded readers while sequentially fixating digits, *Am J Optom Physiol Optics* 62:820, 1985.

39. Pirozzolo FJ, Rayner K: Disorders of oculomotor scanning and graphic orientation in developmental Gerstmann syndrome, *Brain Language* 5:119, 1978.

40. Pirozzolo FJ, Rayner K: The neural control of eye movements in acquired and developmental reading disorders. In Avakian-Whitaker H, Whitaker HA, editors: *Studies in neurolinguistics,* vol 4, New York, 1979, Academic Press.

41. Poynter HL, Schor CM, Haynes HM, Hirsch J: Oculomotor functions in reading disability, *Am J Optom Physiol Optics* 59:116, 1982.

42. Prechtl HFR, Stemmer CJ: The choreiform syndrome in children, *Dev Med Child Neurol* 4:119, 1962.

43. Punnett AF, Steinhauer GD: Relationship between reinforcement and eye movements during ocular motor training with learning disabled children, *J Learn Disabil* 17:16, 1984.

44. Raasch TW, Rubin GS: Reading with low vision, *J Am Optom Assoc* 64:15, 1993.

45. Raymond JE, Ogden NA, Fagan JE, Kaplan BJ: Fixational instability and saccadic eye movements of dyslexic children with subtle cerebellar dysfunction, *Am J Optom Physiol Optics* 65:174, 1988.

46. Rayner K: Do faulty eye movements cause dyslexia? *Dev Neuropsychol* 1:3, 1985.

47. Rayner K, Bertera JH: Reading without a fovea, *Science* 206:468, 1979.

48. Rayner K, Pollatsek A: *The psychology of reading,* Englewood Cliffs, NJ, 1989, Prentice-Hall.

49. Rounds BB, Manley CW, Norris RH: The effect of oculomotor training on reading efficiency, *J Am Optom Assoc* 62:92, 1991.

50. Schroeder SR, Holland JG: Operant control of eye movements, *J Appl Behav Analysis* 1:161, 1968.

51. Schroeder SR, Holland JG: Reinforcement of eye movement with concurrent schedules, *J Exp Analysis Behav* 12:897, 1969.

52. Simons HD, Grisham JD: Binocular anomalies and reading problems, *J Am Optom Assoc* 58:578, 1987.

53. Solan HA: The improvement of reading efficiency: a study of sixty-three achieving high school students, *J Read Specialist* 7:8, 1967.

54. Solan HA: Deficient eye movement patterns in achieving high school students: three case histories, *J Learn Disabil* 18:66, 1985.

55. Solan HA: Eye movement problems in achieving readers: an update, *Am J Optom Physiol Optics* 62:812, 1985.

56. Solan HA, Press LJ: Optometry and learning disabilities, *J Optom Vis Dev* 20:5, 1989.

57. Stanley G, Smith GA, Howell EA: Eye movements and sequential tracking in dyslexic and control children, *Br J Psychol* 74:195, 1983.

58. Stark LW, Giveen SC, Terdiman JF: Specific dyslexia and eye movements. In Stein JF, editor: *Vision and visual dysfunction,* vol 13, Stein JF, editor: Boca Raton, Fla, 1991, CRC Press.

59. Stein JF: Vision and visual dyslexia. In *Vision and visual dysfunction,* vol 13, Boca Raton, Fla, 1991, CRC Press.

60. Stein JF, Riddell PM, Fowler S: Disordered vergence control in dyslexic children, *Br J Ophthalmol* 72:162, 1988.

61. Suchoff IB, Petito GT: The efficacy of visual therapy: accommodative disorders and nonstrabismic anomalies of binocular vision, *J Am Optom Assoc* 57:42, 1986.

62. Tannen B, Ciuffreda KJ, Werner DL: A case of Wallenberg's syndrome: ocular motor abnormalities, *J Am Optom Assoc* 60:748, 1989.

63. Taylor EA: *Controlled reading,* Chicago, 1937, University of Chicago Press.

64. Taylor EA: The spans: perception, apprehension, and recognition as related to reading to speed reading, *Am J Ophthalmol* 44:501, 1957.

65. Taylor EA: *The fundamental reading skill,* Springfield, Ill, 1966, Charles C Thomas.

66. Timberlake GT, Peli E, Essock EA, Augliere RA: Reading with a macular scotoma. II. Retinal locus for scanning text, *Invest Ophthal Vis Sci* 8:1269, 1987.

67. Tinker MA: The effect of illumination intensities upon speed of perception and upon fatigue in reading, *J Educ Psychol* 30:561, 1939.
68. Tinker MA: Time relations for eye movement measures in reading, *J Educ Psychol* 38:1, 1947.
69. Tinker MA: Fixation pause duration in reading, *J Educ Res* 55:471, 1951.
70. Wolverton GS, Zola D: The temporal characteristics of visual information extraction during reading. In Rayner K, editor: *Eye movements in reading: perceptual and language processes*, New York, 1983, Academic Press.
71. Yarbus AL: *Eye movements and vision*, New York, 1967, Plenum Press.
72. Ygge J, Lennerstrand G, Rydberg A, Wijecoon S, Pettersson BM: Oculomotor functions in a Swedish population of dyslexic and normally reading children, *Acta Ophthalmologica* 71:10, 1993.
73. Zangwill OL, Blakemore C: Dyslexia: reversal of eye movements during reading, *Neuropsychologia* 10:371, 1972.

8

Methods to Assess Eye Position and Movement

Key Terms

Direct visual observation
Electrooculography (EOG)
Eye movement test methodology
Eye movement test protocol

Infrared limbal reflection technique
Magnetic search coil
Photographic techniques
Visuoscopy

A vast array of instrumentation is available to assess eye position and movement in one's patients (Box 8-1 and Table 8-1) because of the richness of the detailed anatomic and optical landmarks of the eye available for such purposes (Box 8-2). The major limitation is one's level of knowledge and sophistication in the area.

This chapter discusses the various clinical and clinical research techniques and methodologies used in the assessment of oculomotor ability in one's patients, with emphasis on the more practical aspects and approaches.[1-22] This logically leads to Chapter 9, in which the procedures used in one's office or clinical setting for such evaluation will be discussed in detail.

BOX 8-1   Common Methods to Assess Eye Position and Movement in the Clinic

Clinical environment
- Gross visual observation
- External photography
- High-magnification biomicroscopy (slit lamp) with or without videography
- Direct ophthalmoscopy (visuoscopy) and fundus photography/videography

Clinical research environment
- DC electrooculography (EOG)
- Infrared limbal reflection
- Magnetic search coil

TABLE 8-1 Overview of Eye Movement Recording Methods

Method	Published In	Parameter Recorded	Estimated Bandwidth (Hz)	Tracking Range with ± 5% Linearity Error (degrees)	Noise or Resolution	Comments
Noncontacting Methods for Measuring Eye Movements						
Photography of corneal reflection	*Psychol Rev* 8:143, 1901 (Dodge and Cline)	Eye position	100	40	0.5 degree	One of the first published records of eye movements and one of the best
Photoelectric or infared limbal	*Exp Neuro* 48:107, 1975 (Bahill and Stark)	Eye position	500	20	Less than biologic noise, which is ~1-min arc under optimal conditions	Used in two California clinics; bandwidth usually 70-100 Hz when used with strip-chart recorder
After image	*Treatise of Physiological Optics*, 1866 (Helmholtz)	Eye position	—	>100	0.5 degree	No permanent record
Movie camera	*Arch Ophthalmol* 75:742, 1966 (Higgins and Daroff)	Eye position	32	60	—	Time-consuming data analysis
Stanford Research Institute (SRI) eye tracker	*J Opt Soc Am* 63:921, 1973 (Cornsweet and Crane)	Eye position	10	12	Less than biologic noise	New version has larger bandwidth but artifacts at end of saccades
TV type camera	*IEEE Trans Biol Med* BME-21:309, 1974 (Merchant et al)	Eye position	15	60	—	Also made by Whittaker Corp. and Hamamatsu Co.
Mirror for reflected eye image	*Ann Ocul* 82:240, 1879 (Javal)	Eye position	—	0	1 degree	No permanent record

Continued.

TABLE 8-1   *Overview of Eye Movement Recording Methods—cont'd*

Method	Published In	Parameter Recorded	Estimated Bandwidth (Hz)	Tracking Range with ± 5% Linearity Error (degrees)	Noise or Resolution	Comments
Contacting Methods for Measuring Eye Movements						
Electrooculography (EOG)	*Vis Res* 1975 (Weber and Daroff)	Sine eye position	25	80	1.5 degrees	No head restraint necessary; output varies with ambient light; large amount of drift
Contact lens with mirror attached	*Science* 181:810, 1973 (Steinman et al)	Eye position	60	10	Biological noise	Also used by Yarbus, Riggs, Cornsweet, Ditchburn, and Fender
Contact lens with coil imbedded	*Vis Res* 15:447, 1975 (Collewijn et al)	Sine eye position	50 (could be increased to 1 KHz)	>40	Biological noise	Developed by Robinson (*IEEE Trans Biol Med,* 1963)
Plaster scleral "contact lens" with lever attached	*Am J Psychol* 9:572, 1898 (Delabarre)	Eye position	30	15	5.0 degrees	Cocaine must be used to render cornea insensitive; mentioned for historical purposes only

From Stark L et al: *Am J Optom Physiol Optics* 54:85, 1977.

DIRECT GROSS VISUAL OBSERVATION

Direct observation is the most common and easiest way to assess eye movements in the office or clinical setting. Essentially, the clinician carefully observes the patient's eye movement either in response to fixating or tracking of a small target (or targets) presented at near (Fig. 8-1). Although this method is generally nonquantitative and essentially descriptive in nature and one will miss some of the more subtle dynamic abnormalities that may be present, it does provide considerable insight into a patient's fine neuromuscular control of eye movements, especially with respect to differentiating normal from abnormal behavior. By appropriately varying stimulus conditions (monocular versus binocular viewing, gaze angle, target position/amplitude/velocity/predictability, and so on), combined with careful observation and having a "model" in one's mind as to probable oculomotor abnormalities in patients of different diagnostic groups, the clinician can markedly increase the power of such relatively simple and inexpensive testing. Resolution is approximately 1 degree. See Chapter 9 for details of these clinical test procedures.

EXTERNAL PHOTOGRAPHY

Relatively simple and common photographic systems are readily available. These allow assessment of both static and dynamic abnormalities of oculomotor control in one's patients.

To assess static positional abnormalities (primarily a patient's strabismic deviation, perhaps before and after vision therapy or surgery) (Fig. 8-2), one could use an inexpensive Polaroid camera (with close-up lens) to obtain instant prints while foregoing high res-

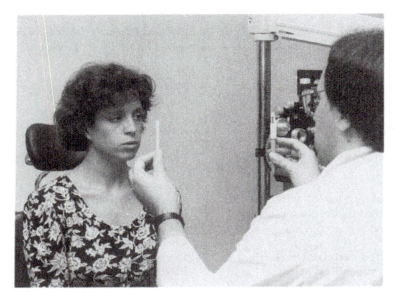

FIG. 8-1   Clinical testing of horizontal saccadic eye movements using gross visual observation.

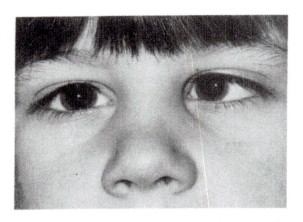

FIG. 8-2   Clinical photodocumentation (Hirschberg test) of strabismus (45-prism diopter left esotropia), a static binocular eye misalignment. Note large templeward displacement of corneal reflection (Purkinje image I) in left eye.

olution and flexibility or perhaps a more expensive 35mm single-lens reflex camera with high-resolution macro zoom capability for better composition and detail. The Pentax IQ Zoom 115 or Yashica Samurai 135, both with a date marker, are superb and are used for such purposes. In either case the goal would be to provide photodocumentation of a static eye position anomaly. Those with a more adventuresome spirit could also use the single-lens reflex camera with infrared film and infrared illumination to assess tonic deviations in the dark, such as tonic vergence position or tonic gaze biases, such as may be found in patients with either general unilateral vestibular dysfunction or the more specific Wallenberg's syndrome.

To assess dynamic versional and vergence eye movement abnormalities (as well as the previously mentioned static dysfunctions), one could use a moderately expensive video

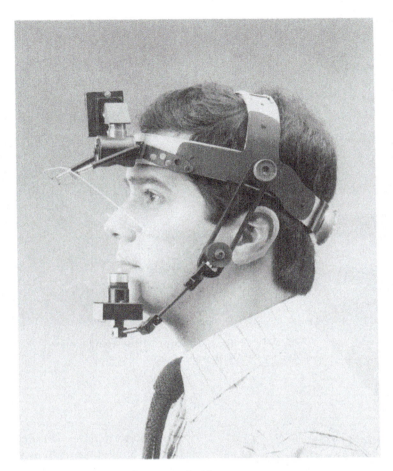

FIG. 8-3   Head-mounted video eye movement system.
(Courtesy Applied Science Laboratories.)

camera with high-ratio zoom, macro mode, and extremely low–light level capability. With this type of system, in addition to a binocular view of the eyes, one can obtain high magnification (with good resolution) monocular views of the eye either for detailed on-line gross visual analysis or subsequent off-line, slow-motion quantification using a calibrated grid either over a large television set or a monitor screen. In addition, presenting such videos to the patient, colleagues, assistants, and students can provide an excellent form of educa-

tion. Such objective, and perhaps quantitative, assessment of eye movements can be especially helpful in patients manifesting retinal disorders such as macular degeneration, systemic disorders such as thyroid dysfunction, neurologic degenerations such as multiple sclerosis and cerebral palsy, and functional problems such as amblyopia, strabismus, and idiopathic jerk nystagmus. Very expensive computer-based video systems are also available, primarily for use in large clinical research environments (Figs. 8-3 and 8-4).

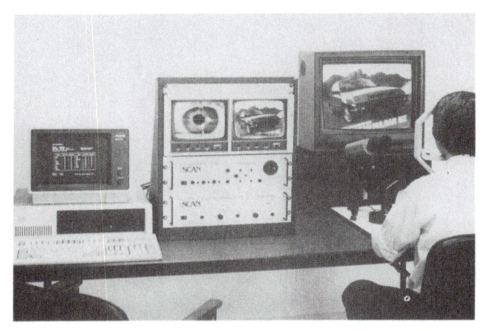

FIG. 8-4 Video eye movement system.
(Courtesy ISCAN, Boston, Mass.)

HIGH-MAGNIFICATION BIOMICROSCOPY (SLIT-LAMP) VIDEOGRAPHY

Use of modern video camera technology can be extended for adaptation to the clinical biomicroscope and slit lamp for even higher magnification images (Fig. 8-5). These offer good resolution capability. However, complete commercially available systems are moderately expensive. A relatively low-priced configured system is available and has been used (Topcon SL-2E slit lamp, Panasonic WVCL-110KT color camera, Magmin 12" MVR 9500 VCR monitor, Pelco MM1000 television mount, and Topcon beam splitter with video adapter). Such a system is particularly well suited for objectively documenting and evaluating less obvious fixational eye move-

ment abnormalities (≤1 degree), such as increased amblyopic drift, as well as strabismus-related saccadic intrusions and small-amplitude jerk nystagmus, especially before and after vision therapy.

DIRECT OPHTHALMOSCOPY (VISUOSCOPY) AND FUNDUS PHOTOGRAPHY

One of the ways in which all clinicians can assess either qualitatively or quantitatively horizontal, vertical, and cyclorotary eye movements in their patients is with low-illumination direct ophthalmoscopy (visuoscopy). Low retinal illumination is used to minimize the occurrence of iatrogenically induced fixational abnormalities resulting from "dazzling" of the patient's macular

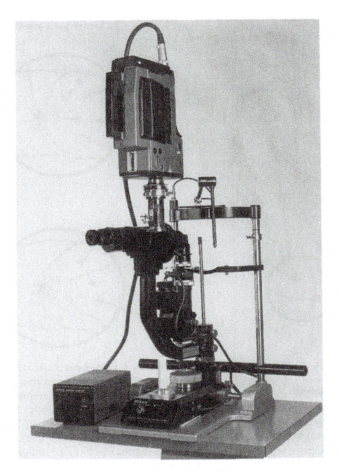

FIG. 8-5   Video photo slit lamp.

area. With this technique, target displacements on the retina as well as the resultant eye movement(s) can be visualized and assessed directly by the clinician. Thus both fixational dynamics (such as saccadic overshoot and nystagmus) and time-averaged fixational locus (such as eccentric fixation/viewing) can be evaluated. Given the relatively high magnification of the system optics (~16×), it is an easy way to assess monocular fixational, as well as saccadic, pursuit, and vestibular ability, especially in persons with amblyopia (Fig. 8-6) and in patients with cen-

tral nervous system disorders (such as multiple sclerosis). Basically, a focused target is projected onto the patient's central retina. If the target and head are held stationary, then fixation can be assessed. If the head is rotated, vestibular function can be directly visualized. And, if the target is either suddenly displaced (step input) or slowly and smoothly moved (ramp input), then saccadic and pursuit function, respectively, can be evaluated. Resolution with this technique is 0.5 degree or better.

Such direct fundus testing can be carried

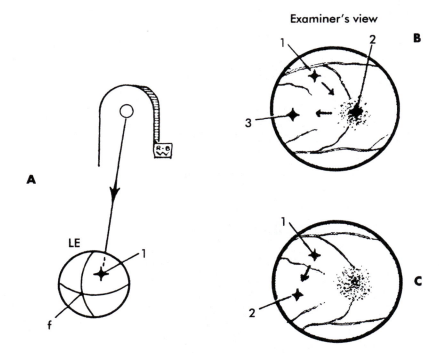

Examiner's view

FIG. 8-6 **A,** To determine whether eccentric viewing versus eccentric fixation is present in left amblyopic eye, examiner projects visuoscope asterisk onto paramacular retinal region *(1)* of patient. The sound eye is occluded. *f,* fovea. **B,** Patient is requested to look directly at asterisk *(1)* while examiner observes fundus through visuoscope. First, patient responds with an eye movement that will place image of fixation target on fovea *(2),* where it is only dimly seen by the patient because of reduced foveal function (scotoma, organic lesion). Second, the eye will then move in such a manner as to place image from the fovea onto paramacular retinal elements *(3),* where visual acuity may be better than in the fovea. Thus eccentric viewing is present. **C,** First eye movement displaces asterisk direction from *(1)* to *(2),* thus excluding fovea from act of fixation. Fixation reflex has adapted itself to paramacular nasal retinal elements. Thus eccentric fixation is present.

(From von Noorden GK: von Noorden—Maumenee's *Atlas of strabismus,* St Louis, 1977, Mosby.)

one step further by using either a still-frame or video fundus camera. The still-frame system would be used primarily for serial investigation of fixational behavior, with this requiring subsequent frame-by-frame analysis and overlay to obtain a composite multiimage reflecting the oculomotor movement over several seconds of fixation. With use of the video fundus system (Fig. 8-7, *A*), the clinician can assess fixational eye movements with the stationary internal target (Fig. 8-7, *B*) or the VOR

with head rotation. Further, by employing a moving target, dynamics of saccadic and pursuit movement can be assessed and permanently recorded in a reasonable manner.

ELECTROOCULOGRAPHY

Since the 1950s, one of the most commonly used techniques to record eye movements, both in the clinic and in the research laboratory, has been (direct current [DC]) elec-

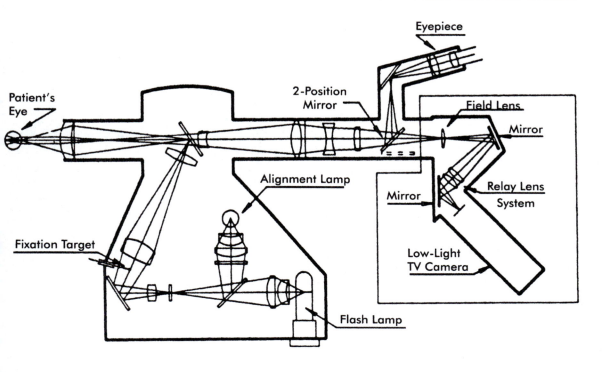

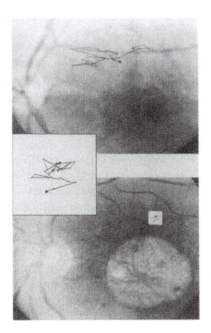

FIG. 8-7 **A,** Fundus video system. **B,** Fundus photographs of two patients with bilateral macular disease (Stargardt's disease) showing sequence of a target's image position over 10 seconds of viewing. *Square* marks position of target's image at start of fixation sequence; *triangle* marks end of sequence. *Solid lines* represent fixational saccades; *dashed lines* connect ending and starting points of successive saccades. *Inset* shows fixation sequence of patient in bottom panel magnified approximately 6×. Duration of macular disease was 1 year *(top)* and 34 years *(bottom).*

(From White JM, Bedell HE; In Alplanalp P, editor: *Problems in optometry: modern diagnostic technology,* Philadelphia, 1991, JB Lippincott Co.)

Primary gaze

Gaze right

Gaze left

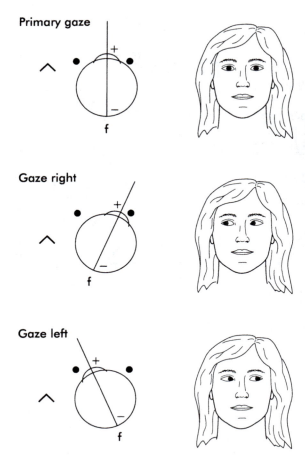

FIG. 8-8   Schematic representation of EOG showing corneoretinal potential in right eye *(left)* and correlated gaze change *(right)*. *f*, fovea; *filled circles*, EOG electrodes; *triangles*, the nose.

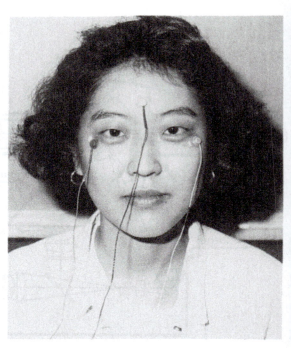

FIG. 8-9   Patient with bitemporal EOG electrodes and forehead (nasal) common electrode. During testing, common electrode lead would be moved out of patient's field of view.

trooculography (EOG). This technique is based on the premise of the eyeball being an electric dipole. Therefore, because of the relatively high metabolic activity of the retina, the cornea is more positive (by 0.4 to 1.0 mV) than the posterior pole of the eye. Thus, with changes in gaze, this dipole will rotate (Fig. 8-8). For example, if the right eye rotated horizontally to the right, the electric field about the right temporal bone would be slightly more positive than its nasal bony area, and vice versa for horizontal rotation of the right eye to the left. This change in electric field potential with eye movement can be exploited to obtain an objective record of change in horizontal eye position with use of silver-silver chloride electrodes attached to these regions. This is precisely the rationale underlying EOG. For simplicity and assuming conjugacy of eye movements, the electrodes can be placed as shown in Fig. 8-9, being situated at each horizontal temporal region and with a common nasal electrode placed above the nose. Not shown is a ground electrode attached to the earlobe. If conjugacy is not assumed, the electrodes should be positioned nasally and temporally for each eye.

The EOG technique has several distinct advantages. First, since it does not require incorporation of any limiting external landmark (such as Purkinje image I), it can be used to assess movements of up to ±70 degrees. However, reasonable linearity probably does not exceed ±30 degrees. Thus it is the system of choice in the evaluation of eye muscle paresis dynamics, in which relatively large ocular excursions are typically required to elicit such nonconjugacy unequivocally. Second, it is easy to set up, and therefore it can be used by a technician. Third, it can be used to assess both horizontal and vertical eye movements (either separately or together) with appropriate electrode placement, for example, to either side as well as above and below the eye along the bony orbital margin. Fourth, it does not require any bulky instrumentation attached to the head or before the eyes, and therefore it does not obstruct the patient's field of view. Finally, the patient can wear spectacles during all testing if needed.

However, the EOG technique is not without some distinct disadvantages. First and foremost, the electrodes and their short leads (which attach to nearby preamplifiers) are susceptible to both endogenous (facial and blink muscle action potentials) and exogenous (external electrical interference) sources of noise artifact, since the electrical signals at the skin surface are quite small (20 to 200 μ volts). Second, system resolution is generally no better than 1 degree; therefore, it will not detect some forms of jerk nystagmus and saccadic intrusions commonly found in patients with strabismus and many other patient types. And third, the signal is influenced by changes in light adaptation that might occur during either step changes in overall ambient room or test field illumination or by occluding an eye.

There are some ways to assure obtaining the best possible results with the EOG technique. First, the skin area to which the electrodes will be attached should be cleaned very well using common isopropyl rubbing alcohol

to assure best electrical contact between the skin-electrode–paste-electrode interface. Second, all room and test field illumination should remain constant for at least 10 minutes to establish stability of retinal activity. And third, the patient should be relaxed and placed comfortably in a headrest/chinrest assembly to reduce any unwanted electrical signals from the head and neck muscles because of extraneous body movements.

Table 8-2 and Boxes 8-3 (p. 197) and 8-4 (p. 198) present characteristics of the test stimuli and test protocols that can be used either with the EOG procedure or with the more advanced techniques to be discussed in the forthcoming sections.

INFRARED LIMBAL REFLECTION

Probably the most common technique in both clinical and research eye movement settings is the high bandwidth (DC to 250 Hz or higher to obtain faithful dynamics), infrared limbal reflection technique (also known as the photocell, photodiode, photoelectric, scleral reflection, and limbal tracking system). This was initially introduced by Torok and associates[17] in 1951 for vestibular testing and developed into its more general present form by Stark and colleagues[13] a decade later.

The simple optics of the device are shown schematically in Fig. 8-10, *A*, with its actual physical arrangement presented in Fig. 8-10, *B* (p. 199). Briefly, a low-wattage infrared source either diffusely illuminates the entire exposed anterior surface of the eye or primarily its nasal and temporal horizontal limbal regions. Infrared sensors are aimed at these same limbal regions. As the eye rotates horizontally from the midline, one sensor will receive more light because of the increased reflectivity of the white sclera, whose area has now increased within the field of view of the fixed sensor, whereas its mate now receives less light because of the relatively reduced reflectivity of the dark iris whose area has now increased

TABLE 8-2   *Stimulus Waveforms*

Type	Description	Shape (f[t]) (Position [y] as a Function of Time [t])
Constant input	A function whose value (position) is constant over time; y = k	
Pulse	A function whose value is unchanged except at t = 0 and t = 1; pulse duration is much less than latency of system being studied	t = 0 t = 1 / t < 0
Step	A function whose value is zero for t < 0 and 1 for t > 0; on/off function	t > 0 / t < 0
Sinusoid	A function whose value changes such that it has zero velocity (V_0) at its endpoints and maximum velocity (V_m) at its mid-position; follows simple harmonic motion	V_0 / V_m / V_0
Triangle	A function whose value changes at a constant velocity (V); ramplike; y = kt and y = −kt	V = k
Parabola	A function whose value changes at a constant acceleration (A); $y = kt^2$	A = k
Step ramp	A function whose value changes as a step followed by a down ramp	
Ramp step	A function whose value changes as a ramp followed by a down step	

BOX 8-3   *Horizontal (±5 degrees) Eye Movement Testing Protocol (Minimal)*

I. Calibration
  A. Gain
    1. Use square-wave maximum amplitude stimulus (±5 degrees), and electronically adjust gain to desired size of movement on oscilloscope, strip-chart recorder, or computer
    2. Displayed size of movement should be as large as possible (to resolve small movements) without creating excessive electronic noise
  B. Linearity
    1. Use triangular stimulus (±5 degrees or slightly larger to just exceed test range)
    2. If response is linear, it will resemble stimulus and exhibit "sharp" endpoints; if not and has rounded edges and/or smaller amplitude, saturation effect evident and there is a need to adjust eye movement system.
II. Midline fixation
  A. Stationary (constant input) target on midline for 10 seconds (or more)
  B. Test right eye, left eye, and binocularly

III. Saccadic tracking
  A. Pseudorandom step tracking at a fixed amplitude (±5 degrees)
  B. Predictable step tracking at a fixed amplitude (±5 degrees) and frequency (~0.3 Hz)
  C. Test right eye, left eye, and binocularly as needed
IV. Pursuit tracking
  A. Predictable tracking at a fixed amplitude (±5 degrees) and frequency (~0.3 Hz)
  B. Triangular stimulus preferred for ease of analysis (gain) but sinusoids frequently used
  C. Test right eye, left eye, and binocularly as needed
V. Vestibular
  A. Stationary fixation target on midline, and rotate head in horizontal plane (±15 degrees) sinusoidally at low (~0.25 Hz) and high (~1 Hz) frequency
  B. Test right eye, left eye, and binocularly as needed
VI. Reading
  A. Material at appropriate age level
  B. Material 2 or more years below age level

---

within the field of view of this sensor. These small incremental differences provide the initial signal (that is, change in current that is converted to a change in voltage), which is then input to a computer, strip chart, oscillographic recorder, and/or oscilloscope for on-line viewing and recording and subsequent quantitative interactive or automated analysis.

Some basic facts regarding the infrared limbal reflection technique are important for one to attain maximum flexibility and optimal recording quality. First, under standard or typical recording conditions with the sensors located just beyond the eyelashes, it has a resolution of at least 0.25 degrees over a linear range of at least ±7.5 degrees. However, a reciprocal relation between resolution and linearity exists—as the sensors are placed

Text continued on p. 200.

BOX 8-4 *Horizontal (±5 degrees) Eye Movement Testing Protocol (Extended)*

I. Calibration (combined gain/linearity check)
  A. 5 points horizontally (5 degrees left, 2.5 degrees left, 0 degrees or midline, 2.5 degrees right, 5 degrees right); for gain, electronically adjust for desired (or maximum) size of movement on oscilloscope, strip-chart recorder, or computer; displayed size of movement should be as large as possible (to resolve small movements) without creating excessive electronic noise; for linearity, equal angular changes should result in equal voltage changes (or displacements); if not linear, need to adjust eye movement system
  B. Check for horizontal/vertical cross talk; patient alternately gazes up and down (±2.5 degrees) at 5 degrees left, 5 degrees right, and midline; adjust system until little or no change in horizontal channel(s) observed during vertical eye movements
II. Fixation
  A. Stationary (constant input) target at midline, 5 degrees left, and 5 degrees right for 10 seconds (or more)
  B. Test right eye, left eye, and binocularly; perhaps also test in dim illumination or in total darkness to "remembered" target positions
III. Saccadic tracking
  A. Random step (and pulse) tracking with target varying in time, position, and direction (within ±5 degrees field extent)
  B. Predictable step tracking at different amplitudes (±0.5, 1, 2.5, and 5 degrees) at a fixed frequency (0.3 Hz)

C. Test right eye, left eye, and binocularly as needed
IV. Pursuit tracking
  A. Predictable tracking at different amplitudes (±1, ±2.5, ±5 degrees) and frequencies (0.3, 0.6, and 1 Hz)
  B. Triangular stimulus preferred for ease of analysis but sinusoids frequently used.
V. Vestibular
  A. Stationary fixation target on midline and rotate head in horizontal plane at different amplitudes (±5, 10, and 15 degrees) at low (0.25 Hz) and high (1 Hz) frequencies
  B. Test right eye, left eye, and binocularly as needed
VI. Vergence
  A. Real targets in median plane (50 and 25 cm away) presented with pseudorandom alteration; possibly use three targets, always starting in midposition and then either to far or near targets to provide both temporal and spatial randomization
  B. Target provides disparity, blur, and proximal information, as occurs in real life
VII. Reading
  A. Simulated reading of "dot" patterns
  B. Simulated reading of nonrelated words
  C. Paragraph at appropriate reading level with comprehension check
  D. Paragraph at 2 or more years below appropriate reading level with comprehension check

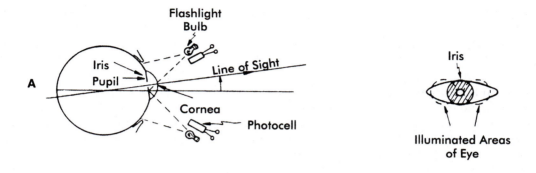

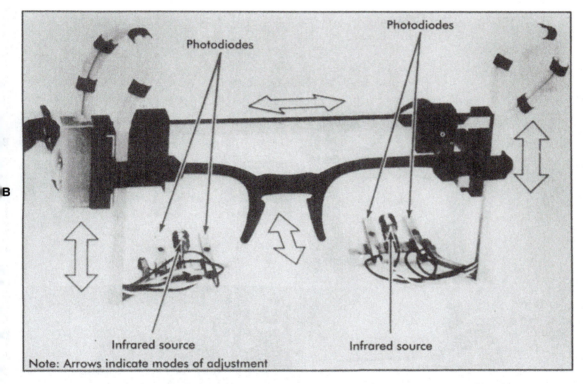

FIG. 8-10 **A,** Light and photocell arrangement for infrared limbal tracking. **B,** Spectacle-mounted infrared differential reflectivity device.

(From Young LR, Sheena D: *Beh Res Meth* 7:397, 1975.)

closer to the eyes, resolution increases but linearity decreases. As an extreme case, one of us (KJC) has tested research subjects with the sensors located approximately 2 mm from the eye, resulting in 1 to 2 minutes of arc resolution but with linearity no better than ±2.5 degrees. The "standard" approach is a reasonable compromise, thereby allowing for high-quality recordings without any lash or blink discomfort to the patient. Second, for most clinical testing, a good headrest/chinrest assembly, including a Velcro strap around the head to maintain its position and stability, is sufficient

to obtain quality recordings. And third, proper aiming and positioning of the sensors are *critical*. They should be situated just below the patient's gaze in primary position (Fig. 8-11, *A* to *D*). This minimizes blockage of the target and surrounding field by the infrared source and sensors. It is best to center the integrated source/sensor unit, with the source aimed at the pupillary center and therefore the sensors (separated by approximately 12 mm to equal the diameter of the average human adult cornea) aimed appropriately at the horizontal limbal region, while viewing from the front.

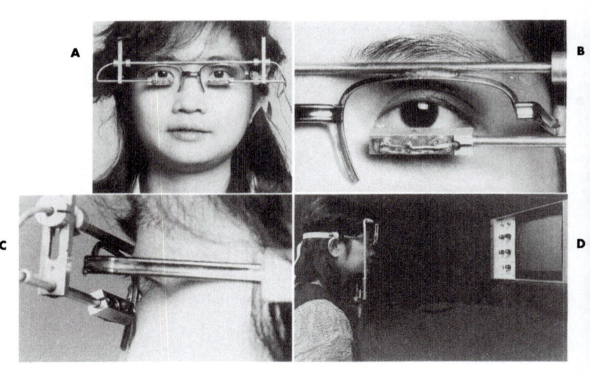

FIG. 8-11 Author's infrared limbal eye tracking system. **A,** Binocular view. **B,** Monocular view (front). **C,** Monocular view (back and side). **D,** Patient in author's clinic test apparatus.

Then one should set the sensors for the appropriate distance from the eye (approximately 10 to 12 mm or just beyond the eyelashes) and angle (approximately 20 degrees or so below primary position) while viewing from the side. Last, all adjustments should be double-checked and fine-tuned.

The infrared limbal reflection technique has evolved in a variety of interesting ways for both clinical use and laboratory investigations. Fig. 8-10, *B*, shows the Model 200 system available from Applied Space Laboratories. The source and sensors move as a unit along the x, y, and z axes for optimal positioning. This system is designed to be spectacle mounted in front of the lenses, which is a distinct advantage, especially in the clinical environment where a wide range of patient refractive corrections can be found. However at times, the relatively far sensor distance (due to spectacle lens thickness and front curvature) can result in a noisy signal. Fig. 8-11 shows a custom system we have been using for the past several years. This system is very lightweight, reasonably unobtrusive, and easy to adjust. However, it is not designed for spectacle mounting, and therefore we have employed a Halberg clip to incorporate refractive correction when needed, with this being mounted in front of the sensors; a similar system called IRIS is available from Skalar Instruments. Applied Space Laboratories also developed a clinical version called the Reading Eye II (Fig. 8-12, *A*) over two decades ago (now discontinued). The Reading Eye II is a self-contained unit, including headrest/chinrest assembly, infrared source and sensors, electronics, and a small strip-chart recorder for hard copy. It actually records horizontal eye position as the sensors (and examiner) view an image of the patient's eyes on a ground glass screen. Although this system can be very useful clinically to obtain "before and after" treatment results on the oculomotor system objectively and quantitatively, the quality of the integrated strip-chart recorder

with its excessive mechanical pen damping and relatively low electronic gain has reduced its potential usefulness. While the Reading Eye II was originally developed for graded testing of eye movements during reading (Fig. 8-12, *B*), it can also be used to test saccadic, vergence, vestibular, fixational, and optokinetic eye movements. A more recent system incorporating modern computer technology, called the Ober2-Visagraph, has been developed primarily for objective, graded testing of eye movements during reading (Fig. 8-13) and has replaced the Reading Eye II instrument. The eye movements are automatically analyzed, and both the binocular recordings and quantitative analysis (that is, plotted Taylor table values;[16] see Fig. 8-12, *B*, and also Chapter 7) are then presented on one's computer screen for viewing prior to obtaining a laser print.

MAGNETIC SEARCH COIL

The magnetic search coil technique is a sophisticated approach used by a few clinical research laboratories. Basically, large electromagnetic coils surround the patient and induce voltage changes related to (the sine of) horizontal, vertical, and cyclorotary eye position, in fine coils embedded in a special soft annular contact lens worn by the patient (Fig. 8-14). This system (available from Skalar Instruments) has very low noise, high resolution (up to 1-min arc), and very large linear range (>±30 degrees). However, it requires the patient to be placed within a large frame-like structure housing the external inducing coils. Further, there have been reports of ocular discomfort after 20 minutes or less of patient testing, presumably because of the contact lens fit and/or lid irritation from the fine wire exiting the contact lens en route to the nearby electronic controls and signal processing devices. Also, the lens may slip on the eye, especially during large ocular excursions, producing artifacts in the recordings.

OTHER TECHNIQUES

Other techniques, such as the contact lens optical lever and the SRI Eye Tracker, have been used to measure dynamics of eye movements. However, for a variety of reasons, these other techniques are either not optimal or not practical in the evaluation of eye movements in most patients.

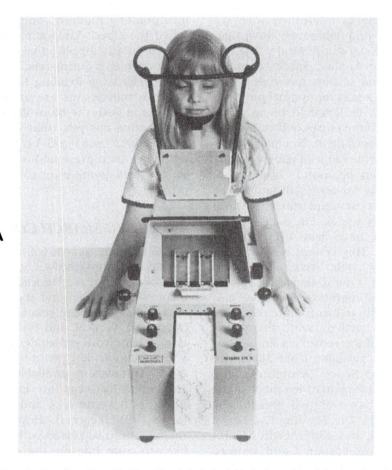

FIG. 8-12 **A,** Reading Eye II (Eye Trac) infrared limbal tracking device developed primarily for clinic and office to test reading eye movements. **B,** Eye Trac Recording score sheet for testing of reading and Taylor table (opposite).

(**A,** Courtesy Applied Science Laboratories.)

Name _____

Date _____

Level _____

Selection _____

	Raw Score	Grade Level
Fixations	_____	_____
Regressions	_____	_____
Span of Recognition (words per fixation)	_____	_____
Rate of Comprehension (wpm)	_____	_____
Comprehension	_____	

Level _____

Selection _____

	Raw Score	Grade Level
Fixations	_____	_____
Regressions	_____	_____
Span of Recognition (words per fixation)	_____	_____
Rate of Comprehension (wpm)	_____	_____
Comprehension	_____	

B

Eye Movement Norms
The Fundamental Reading Skill

Grade	1st	2nd	3rd	4th	5th	6th	JrH	HS	Col.
Fixations (including regressions) per 100 words	240	200	170	136	118	105	95	83	75
Regressions per 100 words	55	45	37	30	26	23	18	15	11
Average span of recognition (in words)	.42	.50	.59	.73	.85	.95	1.05	1.21	1.33
Average duration of fixation (sec)	.33	.30	.26	.24	.24	.24	.24	.24	.23
Rate of comprehension (wpm)	75	100	138	180	216	235	255	296	340

From Taylor EA: *Am J Ophthalmol* 44(4; part 1), 1957.

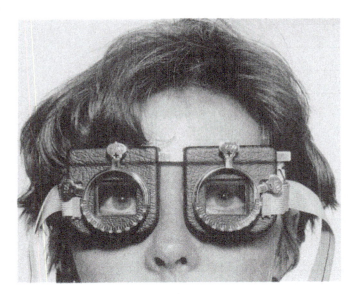

FIG. 8-13 Subject with Ober 2-Visagraph Infrared Limbal Eye Tracking System for objective clinical testing of reading eye movements. Lens holder added.
(Courtesy Permobil Meditech, Timra, Sweden.)

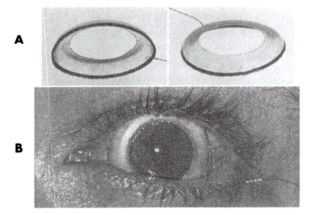

FIG. 8-14 Views of convex and concave sides of suction ring **(A)** and same device mounted on left eye of human subject **(B)**.
(From Collewijn H, van der Mark F, Jansen TC: *Vis Res* 15:447, 1975.)

REVIEW QUESTIONS

1. Describe at least three techniques for assessment of eye movements in the clinic. What are the pros and cons of each?
2. Compare and contrast the EOG versus infrared limbal reflection eye movement recording techniques.
3. What ocular landmarks have been used in the assessment of eye movements in the clinic? In the research laboratory?

REFERENCES

1. Bahill AT, Stark L: Dynamic overshoot in saccadic eye movements is caused by neurologic control signal reversals, *Exp Neurol* 48:107, 1975.
2. Collewijn H, van der Mark F, Jansen TC: Precise recording of human eye movements, *Vis Res* 15:447, 1975.
3. Cornsweet TN, Crane HD: Accurate two-dimensional eye tracker using first and fourth Purkinje images, *J Opt Soc Am* 63:921, 1973.
4. Crane HD, Steele CM: Genertion-V dual Purkinje eyetracker, *Appl Optics* 24:527, 1985.
5. Delabarre EL: A method for recording eye movements, *Am J Psychol* 9:572, 1898.
6. Dodge R, Cline TS: The angle velocity of eye movements, *Psychol Rev* 8:145, 1901.
7. Gay AJ, Newman NM, Keltner JL: *Eye movement disorders,* St Louis, 1974, Mosby.
8. Helmholtz H von: *Helmholtz's treatise of physiological optics.* In JPC Southhall, translator, vol 3, New York, 1925, Dover.
9. Higgins DC, Daroff RB: Overshoot and oscillation in ocular dysmetria, *Arch Ophthalmol* 75:742, 1966.
10. Javal E: Essai sur la physiologie de la lecture, *Ann Ocul* 82:240, 1879.
11. Leigh RJ, Zee DS: *The neurology of eye movements,* ed 2, Philadelphia, 1991, Davis.
12. Merchant J, Morrissette R, Porterfield JL: Remote measurement of eye direction allowing subject motion over one cubic foot of space, *IEEE Trans Bio Med* BME-21:309, 1974.
13. Stark L, Bahill AT, Ciuffreda KJ, Kenyon RV, Phillips S: Neuro-optometry: an evolving specialty clinic, *Am J Optom Physiol Optics* 54:85, 1977.
14. Stark L, Sanberg A: A simple instrument for measuring eye movements, *Quart Prog Rep #62, Res Lab Elect,* M.I.T., 268, 1961.
15. Steinman RF, Haddad GM, Skavenski AA, Wyman D: Miniature eye movements, *Science* 181:810, 1973.
16. Taylor EA: *The fundamental reading skill,* Springfield, Ill, 1966, Charles C Thomas.
17. Torok N, Guillemin V, Barnothy JM: Photoelectric nystagmorgraphy, *Ann Otol Rhinol Laryngol* 60:917, 1951.
18. White JM, Bedell HE: Fundus videorecording to document the location of a target's image on the retina. In Alplanalp P, editor: *Problems in optometry: modern diagnostic technology,* Philadelphia, 1991, JB Lippincott Co.
19. von Noorden GK: *von Noorden—Maumenee's Atlas of strabismus,* St. Louis, 1977, Mosby.
20. Young LR: Measuring eye movements, *Am J Med Electron* 2:300, 1963.
21. Young LR, Sheena D: Eye movement measurement techniques, *Am Psychol* 30:315, 1975.
22. Young LR, Sheena D: Survey of eye movement recording methods, *Beh Res Meth Instru* 7:397, 1975.

9

Clinical Evaluation of Eye Movements

Key Terms

Abnormal drift	Nystagmus
Age-related effects	Pursuit testing
Attention	Saccadic intrusions
Binocular dysfunction	Saccadic testing
Fixational testing	Vergence testing
Neurologic disease or integrity	Vestibular-optokinetic testing

One of the more difficult tasks that a clinician is routinely faced with involves the evaluation of a patient's eye movements. In most clinical settings, this must be performed without the benefit of objective eye movement recordings. Since numerous common as well as rarer but important oculomotor conditions present with deficits of only 1 degree or so, one can readily appreciate the frustration this might create for many clinicians. This is perhaps one of the reasons that the clinical evaluation, diagnosis, and management of ocular motor disorders may not have received the emphasis they so rightfully deserve. This chapter provides an overview of techniques for evaluating eye movements that requires no equipment other than that typically found in the office of a clinician (see Chapter 8).

FIXATION

The oculomotor evaluation should begin with an assessment of fixation, with emphasis on performance in primary gaze. This provides the baseline for the entire oculomotor evaluation. The failure to assess fixation at the beginning of the examination can lead to unnecessary confusion and concern. For example, evaluation of a hyperactive child who is unable to maintain steady fixation for even brief periods of time (for example, a few seconds) will provide valuable insight into his or her predicted poor performance on pursuit testing, which is probably unrelated to the neurologic integrity of the basic pursuit eye movement system per se. In this case the patient's attentional deficit would override and adversely impact the clinical assessment of pursuit ability.

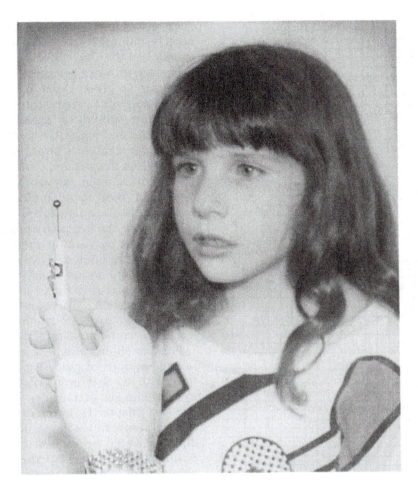

FIG. 9-1   Binocular pursuit testing using the Wolff wand.

Techniques

Gross visual observation. Fixation should be tested at both distance and near, because one's oculomotor characteristics, especially in nystagmus, may change considerably with viewing distance and vergence demand or innervation. At distance one can use a muscle light or a Snellen letter one or two lines above the patient's threshold visual acuity and positioned along the patient's midline as a target. At near, the Snellen letter should be held along the patient's midline at 40 cm and perhaps also at the habitual near working distance if it is significantly different. This may be especially important in young children who frequently perform near tasks at very close distances (for example, 10 to 15 cm). For children the target should attract and maintain their attention, such as a silver reflective ball mounted on a wand[37] (Fig. 9-1). For adults, the type of target is less critical, and therefore one might use a Snellen letter

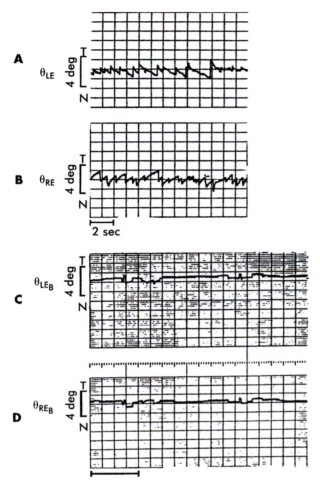

A θ_{LE} 4 deg N

B θ_{RE} 4 deg N

2 sec

C θ_{LE_B} 4 deg N

D θ_{RE_B} 4 deg N

FIG. 9-2 Eye position as function of time for patient. **A** to **D**, Monocular left eye position (θ_{LE}), monocular right eye position (θ_{RE}), and left (θ_{LE_B}) and right (θ_{RE_B}) eye positions during binocular viewing, respectively. Latent nystagmus is shown during monocular viewing but normal movement is shown during binocular viewing. Midline fixation.

(From Ciuffreda KJ: *Eye movements in amblyopia and strabismus,* Ph.D. dissertation, School of Optometry, University of California at Berkeley, 1977.)

(one or two lines above their threshold visual acuity) mounted on a tongue depressor or simply use the fine tip of a pen. The appropriate target, once selected, can be used for purposes of gross visual observation in all subsequent eye movement testing.

Fixation should be assessed under both monocular and binocular viewing conditions. Monocular fixation characteristics can differ greatly from those found during binocular fixation. For example, in pure latent nystagmus, a normal movement under conditions of binocular fixation transforms into a jerk nystagmus with the fast phase in the direction of the viewing eye during monocular fixation (Fig. 9-2). The nontested eye under such conditions should *always be fully occluded.* Use of one's thumb as an occluder still allows peripheral fusion to take place, and this may result in better than expected fixation ability, resulting in an erroneous clinical diagnosis.

Fixation should also be assessed in six diagnostic positions of gaze (Fig. 9-3). These are the positions that best isolate the action of each of the six extraocular muscles in each eye (see Chapter 1). In the case of a paresis of the right superior oblique, for example, the diplopia would be greatest in the diagnostic position represented by the right superior oblique (for example, down and to the patient's left). The objective is to determine whether there are congenital overactions or underactions, or acquired pareses, of the extraocular muscles. Other diagnostic tests that will yield this information include the Hess-Lancaster and Maddox rod tests.[18,23,41]

In jerk nystagmus there is usually a null point (that is, position of minimal nystagmus) in the direction of the slow phase of the horizontal nystagmus. For example, a patient with left-jerk nystagmus (that is, fast saccadic phase to the left) will typically exhibit a null position to the right of primary gaze. There may also be a vertical component to the null point that must be considered. It should be remembered that to assess the null point correctly, the patient's head must be erect and in

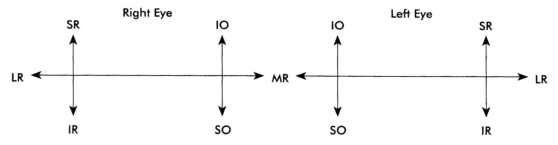

FIG. 9-3   Diagnostic positions of gaze as viewed by examiner. *SR*, Superior rectus muscle; *IR*, inferior rectus muscle; *IO*, inferior oblique muscle; *SO*, superior oblique muscle; *MR*, medial rectus muscle; *LR*, lateral rectus muscle.

primary position, because persons with congenital nystagmus often habitually exhibit a head tilt and/or turn to place their eyes into their null position to maximize their visual acuity.[7]

Slit lamp. An instrument that is frequently overlooked in the evaluation of fixational abnormalities is the biomicroscope, or slit lamp. It provides a means of evaluating fixation with control of illumination and magnification. The patient should be placed in the instrument as usual, with the head resting firmly against the chin and forehead rest. The patient should begin by fixating in primary gaze, with the fellow eye fully occluded. This can be accomplished by use of the fixation light or by having the patient fixate on the clinician's ear (patient fixates the clinician's right ear to examine the patient's right eye). We recommend an initial broad band of direct illumination at 15× magnification. It may be helpful to locate a limbal vessel temporal to the cornea for purposes of orientation. This can be especially useful for the detection of small-amplitude cyclorotary nystagmus that may otherwise go unnoticed. In general, it is helpful to categorize the type of fixational abnormality (for example, nystagmus versus saccadic intrusion versus abnormal drift) with direct observation and then confirm this suspicion with the slit lamp (or other techniques using similar magnification and/or illumination described in the following section).

Ophthalmoscopy. A direct ophthalmoscope is another excellent instrument (except perhaps in amblyopia) in the clinical detection, diagnosis, and therapeutic monitoring of fixational abnormalities.[13] The patient's nontested eye is first fully occluded. Then the patient is instructed to fixate a distant target. The clinician should view the fundus through the visuoscopy projection grid filter ("bull's eye" or similar calibrated target) in the ophthalmoscope. Once the optic nerve is visualized for purposes of general orientation, the patient is then instructed to fixate the center of the target. Caution should be exercised to use the lowest illumination possible to visualize the macula area in order to avoid dazzling the patient and creating iatrogenically induced abnormal fixational eye movements. These are the same precautions taken in performing visuoscopy in an amblyopic eye.[13] If the patient has extremely small pupils, the clinician may wish to dilate them pharmacologically before performing this procedure. However, one should be aware that in some conditions (most notably manifest-latent nystagmus), pupillary dilation may decrease nystagmus amplitude.[39] If the foveal reflex is present, it can be a useful reference point or "tag" to aid in the oculomotor diagnosis. One should keep in mind that with respect to the center of the visuoscopic target, the foveal reflex will shift in the opposite direction to the eye movement (that is, as the foveal reflex appears to move to the left relative to the patient, the eye is actually moving to the right).

Keratometry. The keratometer is another sensitive instrument with which to assess monocular fixation. Here the patient is seated in the usual fashion and instructed to fixate the central luminous mires target (or the reflected image of the eye), with the fellow eye occluded. The clinician then focuses and centers the reflected mires image on the cornea as if attempting to obtain a keratometric reading. At this point the clinician simply observes the fixation pattern by noting the magnitude and frequency of displacement of the reflected mires image with respect to the center of the cornea, keeping in mind that as the patient's eye is displaced to the right, the instrument's mires will be displaced to the clinician's right.

Diagnosis

Fixational eye movement disorders can be divided into *saccadic intrusions, nystagmus,* and *abnormal drift* (see Chapter 2).

Saccadic intrusions. The first abnormality, namely, saccadic intrusions, can itself be divided into three categories: square-wave jerks, macro square-wave jerks, and macrosaccadic oscillations.

Square-wave jerks are small saccades (usually 1 degree but up to 5 degrees) that displace the eye *away* from the fixation point, with a return to it approximately 200 msec later.[11] They are found in a wide variety of pathologic and nonpathologic conditions (Box 9-1). Although it may be difficult to diagnose this fixational pattern definitively with only the observational techniques described above, we have found it possible (with practice) to identify most patients having this condition. This oculomotor disturbance can be best described as having the appearance of small, bidirectional, rapid, to-and-fro "darting" movements on attempted steady fixation. In other words, if the patient appears to be attempting to maintain fixation but is unable to do so because of the presence of such small darting movements, it is likely that the patient is manifesting square-wave jerks. This is not to be confused with the child exhibiting an attentional deficit, in which case much larger (that is, 5 to 10 degrees or more) saccadic eye movements, frequently in conjunction with head movements toward the source of distraction, are made. An important cause of square-wave jerks in the elderly is progressive supranuclear palsy.[40] This is a disease that results in degeneration of the brainstem nuclei, diencephalon, and cerebellum.[36] Other oculomotor signs in this disease may include impairment of vertical saccades and superior gaze restriction. This condition is usually fatal within 6 years of its onset,[23] and there is no effective treatment at this time. Tannen and others[38] reported the presence of jerk nystagmus converting to high-frequency square-wave jerks as the sequelae of Wallenberg's syndrome in one patient observed over the course of a 2-year recovery period. In another case, Ciuffreda and others[12] described a patient with probable early multiple sclerosis who suffered severe reading impairment because of high-frequency square-wave jerks.

Macro square-wave jerks and macrosaccadic oscillations are much larger in amplitude (5 to 20 degrees) and are always associated with neurologic disease, such as cerebellar disorders and multiple sclerosis. These abnormalities are much easier to detect and diagnose and should immediately alert the clinician to serious neurologic involvement if a prior associated condition (such as multiple sclerosis) has not already been diagnosed.

Nystagmus. Nystagmus is probably the most recognizable fixational abnormality that clinicians will encounter. Nystagmus refers to a rhythmic oscillation of the eyes (see Chapter 2). In pendular nystagmus the velocity is approximately the same in each direction, whereas in jerk nystagmus, there is a slow-phase movement in one direction and a fast-phase saccadic movement in the opposite direction. It is usually possible to distinguish pendular from jerk nystagmus using the techniques described earlier. For example, in evaluating a patient using direct ophthalmoscopy with a projected target, jerk nystagmus appears as a "sliding" movement away from the fixational grid center, with a rapid and jerky corrective (saccadic) foveating movement back to central fixation. Pendular nystagmus, on the other hand, appears as a moderately rapid bidirectional oscillation in which the endpoint of one phase is coincident with the center of the fixation target.[23] In some instances, however, the slow phase of the jerk nystagmus is sufficiently fast, such that clinically it is not readily distinguishable from the fast phase. In these instances the clinician may be misled to believe that a jerk nystagmus is, in fact, a high-velocity pendular nystagmus, especially of the asymmetric variety. Objective eye movement recordings would then be necessary for proper classification of nystagmus type.

Congenital versus acquired nystagmus. Another important distinction is between congenital and acquired forms of nystagmus. Usually this is reasonably clear-cut: persons with acquired nystagmus report oscillopsia, whereas persons with congenital nystagmus do not and are generally aware of the early onset of their nystagmus. However, occasionally the picture is not that simple. If questioned carefully, some persons with congenital nystagmus *will* report a small degree of oscillopsia at times under reduced cue conditions. For instance, they may report *very slight* illusory movement of the world when placed in dim illumination, presumably because of reduced visual feedback stabilization of the nystagmus. Although the movement described by these patients is rarely as robust as the oscillopsia reported in acquired nystagmus, this symptom can cause some confusion, especially to the inexperienced clinician. We have even had persons with congenital nystagmus report this very mild form of oscillopsia during reading when fatigued. If one now adds to the clinical picture the occasional patient who indeed reports some illusory movement (when carefully questioned), in the presence of a small-amplitude nystagmus that has not been previously detected, this can present a clinical challenge to even the most seasoned practitioner. It is fortunate that several clinical characteristics differentiate between congenital and acquired nystagmus (Table 9-1). Of course, it is always helpful to obtain objective eye movement recordings whenever possible because this will further delineate the etiology and type of nystagmus; further, such recordings may provide insight into the motor contribution of the reduced sensory function (such as visual acuity).

Abnormal drift. Abnormal drift is a common finding in functional amblyopia. Abnormal drift will typically exhibit an amplitude of up to 1 degree or so with a velocity of up to 3 degrees/sec (see Chapter 2). The only way to diagnose this abnormal drift without objective eye movement equipment is by careful low-light visuoscopy.[13] One can again use the visuoscopic target in the direct ophthalmoscope for this purpose. Abnormal drift will appear as random slow movements away from the fixation locus, occasionally interrupted by a saccade (either error-correcting or error-producing), as well as error-correcting drift. Drift amplitude and frequency may be re-

	Congenital	Acquired
Up gaze	Nystagmus remains horizontal	May convert to up-beat nystagmus
Null point	Common	None
Convergence	Dampens	Usually no effect
Head turn or tilt	Common	Less common
Oscillopsia	None (except as noted in text)	Always present
Associated with	Albinism, achromatopsia, Leber's amaurosis, aniridia, as well as idiopathic	Multiple sclerosis, cerebellar disease, and cerebrovascular accident

duced through an intensive vision therapy program[10] (see Chapter 2).

SACCADES

Saccades are high-velocity eye movements used to place an object of interest on the high-resolution fovea (see Chapter 3). Clinical evaluation of the saccadic system without objective eye movement recording equipment presents a challenge. Because of the high peak velocity of saccades (for example, a 10-degree saccade has a peak velocity of over 400 degrees/sec), a typical slowing by up to 100 degrees/sec is not easily detectable clinically; further, because of the subtlety of disorders, the typical pathologic increase in latency of 50 msec or so is not detectable clinically. These examples point to the difficulty in attempting to make specific diagnoses using the more subtle saccadic disorders without the benefit of objective recording capability. However, it is possible to use certain clinical guidelines and test strategies to aid in the saccadic eye movement evaluation.

Two basic questions need to be addressed with respect to evaluation of the saccadic system: (1) Is the system neurologically intact? (2) Are the responses age appropriate? With reference to the latter, it is our experience, as well as that of others,[3] that a 6-year-old will probably not react to auditory or visual commands to execute accurate saccades as well as a 14-year-old or an adult; however, it may still be quite appropriate for the patient's age (see later discussion).

Techniques

Gross visual observation. The stimuli should consist of two distinctive objects such as a pen and pencil, or one gold and one silver Wolff wand (as described earlier in the fixation section). The examiner places the targets to the left and right equidistant from the patient's midline at a test distance of 40 cm. Smaller, more naturally occurring saccades (15 degrees or less), defects of which typically reflect central neural dysfunction (such as cerebellar disease), can be tested with a target separation of 4 inches or less. Larger saccades (for example, 30 degrees or larger), defects of which typically reflect peripheral neural and/or extraocular neuromuscular dysfunction (such as muscle paresis), can be tested with a target separation of 8 inches or more. The patient's head should be erect with the eyes in primary gaze. The patient should then be instructed to move the eyes to the appropriate target on verbal command initially as rapidly as possible. It should be made clear to the patient, however, that he or she should not attempt to predict or anticipate the movements. The clinician should then vary the timing of the verbal

FIG. 9-4 Sequential fixation device. A clear acetate sheet with numbers attached for saccadic eye movement testing and training.
(From Griffin JR: *Binocular anomalies: procedures for vision therapy*, ed 2, Chicago, 1982, Professional Press.)

command to minimize prediction effects (approximately once every 4 or 5 seconds), unless assessment of predictive ability is desired (as for example in Parkinson's disease, where it may be abnormal).[4] The clinician may also randomly vary target separation, as well as temporal sequencing, to approach a true nonpredictive saccadic test paradigm. This testing sequence should be performed in the horizontal, vertical, and oblique directions under both monocular and binocular viewing conditions.

Saccades may also be assessed as they are viewed by the clinician through a clear Plexiglass or acetate sheet with many superimposed numbers or letters arranged on it in a sequential fashion (Fig. 9-4). The clinician instructs the patient to follow the symbols as if reading.[18] Smaller-amplitude, sequential saccades, similar to those used during reading (1 to 3 degrees), are thus tested. The numbers or symbols could also be called off by the clinician to test nonpredictive saccadic tracking.

Diagnosis

Dysmetria. The most important and easily observed diagnostic aspect in the gross evaluation of saccades involves dysmetria. Hypometria (generally static undershooting) of 10% is quite normal. It is especially evident with larger amplitude saccades, as well as saccades directed into the periphery.[1] Occasionally, in our clinic records, we have noted an intern who has made a point of highlighting this type of dysmetria as if it were necessarily an abnormal finding. It may not be. In fact, as discussed in Chapter 3, such normal mild hypometria may reflect a conservative and efficient strategy in saccadic tracking. In abnormal cases, however, it reflects a saccadic gain disturbance (for example, low gain). In some cases, there may be marked hypometria (~20% to 40%) or multiple hypometric steps to the intended target. Marked hypometria can occur in a variety of cerebellar, brainstem, and other neurologic disorders (Box 9-2). Hypermetria, or overshooting (generally static overshooting), is less common. Small hypermetric saccades are occasionally seen in normal patients, especially if the saccades are either centripetal (inward) or downward.[23] Hypermetria is an especially important clinical sign in both cerebellar and brainstem disease (see Box 9-2). A good clinical rule of thumb is that if the hypermetric saccades are consistently present and are large enough to be easily seen on gross visual observation, then they warrant both an objective eye movement evaluation and a neurologic evaluation. Similarly, if one sees hypometria of greater than 20%, or consistently sees multiple hypometric saccades, further evaluation should be considered.

Latency and velocity. Other important aspects of saccades include latency and peak velocity (see Chapter 3). As mentioned previously, unless the abnormality is quite gross, these saccadic components are difficult to evaluate without objective eye movement recordings. Extremely large increases in saccadic latency (up to 1 second or more) may be

---

> **BOX 9-2.   *Conditions That May Cause Dysmetria***
>
> - *Parkinson's disease:* hypometria
> - *Multiple sclerosis:* hypometria or hypermetria
> - *Wallenberg's syndrome:* hypermetria ipsilateral to side of lesion and hypometria contralateral to side of lesion
> - *Cerebellar mass lesions:* hypometria or hypermetria
> - *Myasthenia gravis:* hypometria for large saccades and hypermetria for small saccades
> - *Acquired immune deficiency syndrome (AIDS):* hypometria
> - *Hemianopia:* hypometria or hypermetria

---

visually evident in patients with either Parkinson's or Huntington's disease for volitional saccades, although not usually for reflexive saccades.[23] Smaller latency increases (for example, 100 msec) generally will not be clinically detectable. Decreased saccadic velocity is frequently present in peripheral oculomotor palsies. For example, patients with myasthenia gravis will frequently execute saccades that actually slow down *en route* to their intended target or cease altogether on repeated testing. A useful clinical test is to have the patient saccade as rapidly as possible between two horizontally or vertically positioned targets 20 degrees apart for 10 cycles or more. A positive result on this "fatigue" test would be dramatic slowing or even brief periods of cessation of saccadic tracking.

Functional diagnosis. Numerous attempts have been made over the years to grade components of saccadic skill and accuracy, once the system's neurologic integrity has been deemed intact.[3,18] One test that is gaining popularity in optometry is the Northeastern State University Optometry (NSUO) oculomo-

---

BOX 9-3. *Standard Set of the NSUO Oculomotor Test*

Posture

Standing, with feet shoulder width apart, directly in front of the examiner

Head

No instructions are given to the patient either to move or not to move the head

Target characteristics

Small (approximately 0.5-cm) reflective sphere mounted on dowel; for those unwilling/unable to be tested with sphere targets, use Disney targets (clown) on pencils

Movement of target

Directional

Saccades are performed in the horizontal meridian only

Pursuits are performed rotationally, both clockwise and counterclockwise

Extent

Saccade extent should be no more than 10 cm on each side of patient's midline (20 cm total)

Pursuit path should be no more than 20 cm in diameter; upper and lower extents of the circular path should coincide with patient's midline

Test distance from patient

No more than 40 cm and no less than the Harmon distance; that is, the distance from the subject's middle knuckle to elbow

Viewing condition

Binocular only

Age of patient

Two years to adult

Instructions

Saccades

"When I say red, look at the red ball (clown). When I say green, look at the green ball (clown). Remember, don't look until I tell you to."

Pursuits

"Watch the ball (clown) as it goes around. Try to see yourself in the ball (watch the clown's eyes). Don't ever take your eyes off the ball."

Observations

Eye, head, and body movement

---

tor test of saccades and pursuits.[24] This test has a detailed clinical protocol for its administration (Box 9-3). The patient's saccades are graded during five cycles of movement (and the pursuit for two rotations in each direction) (Box 9-4). The test has good intertest reliability and a clear developmental trend for improvement of saccadic skill with age.[3] For those who are interested in optometric vision therapy for possible remediation of certain saccadic deficiencies (such as nonpathologic dysmetria), a number of excellent sources cover this topic in detail.[3,18,29,32]

Auxiliary tests. Several tests have been developed that purport to assess saccadic skill and accuracy by having a patient name sequences of digits arranged in various degrees of complexity (with regard to assumed ease of saccadic tracking) on a test sheet. Pierce[28] was the first to introduce such a test. It consisted of three cards with sets of numbers placed at the vertical margins. There is a slight increase in difficulty with each set (that is, less predictable spacing between numbers).

King and Devick[21] modified this test by

BOX 9-4. *NSUO Objective Method of Rating Saccades and Pursuits*

Pursuits

Ability

No attempt made to follow target to one-half rotation

Completes one-half rotation but not one full rotation

Completes one rotation but not two rotations

Completes two rotations in one direction but not two in other direction

Completes two rotations in each direction

Accuracy

No attempt to follow target; >10 refixations

Refixations 4 to 10 times

Refixations 2 to 4 times

Refixations 2 or fewer times

No refixations

Head and body movement

Gross movement of head (body)

Large to moderate movement of head (body)

Consistent slight movement of head (body)

Intermittent slight movement of head (body)

No movement of head (body)

Saccades

Ability

No attempt made to perform task even for one cycle

Completes two cycles

Completes three cycles

Completes four cycles

Completes five cycles

Accuracy

Gross overshooting or undershooting noted

Large to moderate overshooting or undershooting noted

Constant slight overshooting or undershooting noted

Intermittent slight overshooting or undershooting noted

No overshooting or undershooting noted

Head and body movement

Gross movement of head (body)

Large to moderate movement of head (body)

Consistent slight movement of head (body)

Intermittent slight movement of head (body)

No movement of head (body)

---

varying the level of difficulty of the three cards greater than Pierce had done, rendering the spacing between the numbers even less predictable (Fig. 9-5).

In both tests the patient is instructed to read the numbers aloud from left to right and from line to line as quickly and as accurately as possible. The results are scored with respect to both the total test time and number of errors. The King-Devick test has the advantage of having more normative data,[21,22] in addition to the greater range of card difficulty. Both the Pierce and King-Devick tests have the distinct disadvantage of having poor test-retest reliability.[3]

In addition, Richman and associates[30] found that random automated naming (RAN) of numbers (that is, the ability to read random numbers aloud quickly) represents a significant potential bias in the King-Devick test. For example, a child who cannot read numbers aloud quickly in a spatially fixed tachistoscopic presentation in which *no* eye movements are necessary would also not perform well on the King-Devick test because of naming problems and *not* an eye movement problem.

To this end, Garzia and others[17] created the Developmental Eye Movement (DEM) test. This test contains a subtest that assesses one's ability to read a simple array of vertical num-

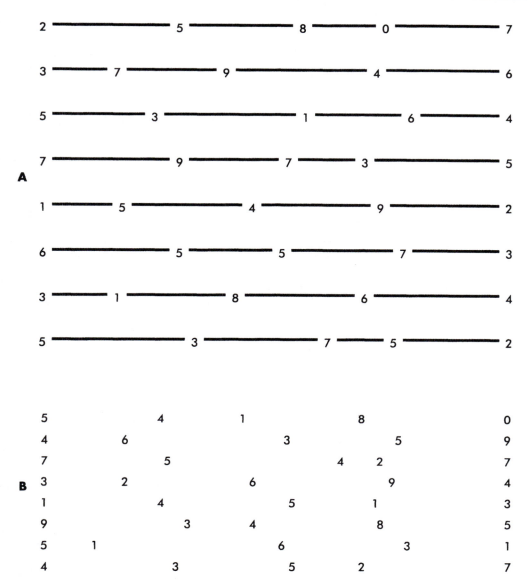

FIG. 9-5 **A,** Test I of the King-Devick test. Note horizontal bars between numbers, which provides visual guidance and serves to make the saccadic tracking aspect of the test easier and more predictable. **B,** Test III of the King-Devick test. Note uneven spacing between horizontally sequenced digits and absence of horizontal bars, making saccadic tracking aspect of test more difficult than in **A.**

(Courtesy Bernell Corp., South Bend, Ind.)

Test A

A	
3	4
7	5
5	2
9	1
8	7
2	5
5	3
7	7
4	4
6	8
1	7
4	4
7	6
6	5
3	2
7	9
9	2
3	3
9	6
2	4

Test C

B

3   7 5   9   8
2 5   7   4   6
1   4   7   6 3
7   9   3   9   2
4 5   2   1 7
5   3   7 4   8
7 4   6 5   2
9   2   3 6 4
6 3 2 9   1
7   4   6 5 2
5   3 7   4   8
4   5   2   1 7
7 9 3   9   2
1   4   7 6 3
2 5 7   4 6
3 7 5   9   8

bers aloud (Fig. 9-6, *A*). The authors reasoned that if a child performs poorly on this subtest, then there will be a problem with RAN. By testing the vertical array separately from the horizontal array of numbers (Fig. 9-6, *B*) (the horizontal being essentially similar to the most difficult King-Devick card), Garzia and associates attempted to differentiate between verbal naming deficiencies and actual saccadic tracking deficiencies (or a combination of the two). Although this test appears to be replacing the King-Devick test in popularity in some clinics, it unfortunately has large standard deviations in some of the age group norms.

However, and most importantly, *none* of these tests (or any other similar tests) actually evaluates basic components of eye movement control per se such as velocity, accuracy, latency, and dysmetria but rather assesses global saccadic tracking performance in a complex tracking and identification task.

PURSUIT

The pursuit system allows for the continuous, voluntary tracking of moving objects in the environment. The response is typically composed of segments of smooth tracking with some interspersed saccades. Saccades may be present to correct for accumulated position errors caused by either low (or sometimes high) pursuit gain or prediction effects (especially at the turnaround or endpoints for predictable targets). In patients with neurologic disease, error-producing saccadic intrusions may also be found. The following framework for the clinical testing and evaluation of smooth pursuit should prove helpful.

FIG. 9-6 **A,** Test A of the Developmental Eye Movement Test (DEM). This test simply presents two columns of digits. **B,** Test C of the Developmental Eye Movement Test (DEM). This test presents 80 unevenly sequenced horizontal digits and thus is more difficult than Test A. (Courtesy Bernell Corp., South Bend, Ind.)

Technique

The target is the same as that used for the evaluation of fixation. The patient is instructed to follow the target as carefully and as accurately as possible with the eyes and not the head (or body). Attention to the task is critical, and therefore the patient should be reminded and encouraged periodically during testing. Pursuit should be tested in the horizontal, vertical, and oblique meridians as well as rotationally. This should be done both monocularly and binocularly.

The selection of target velocities and overall movement patterns merits some discussion. For clinical testing, the examiner should start at a distance of 40 cm with the target positioned along the patient's midline. The target should then be moved smoothly at a constant velocity to the patient's right 2½ inches, smoothly changing direction past the midline and then to the patient's left 2½ inches. Testing three to five cycles in each meridian is usually adequate. Pursuit should be tested at both a relatively slow (2 seconds to complete one full cycle, ~7.5 degrees/sec) and a moderately fast target velocity (1 second to complete one cycle, ~15 degrees/sec). Faster target movements primarily elicit saccades to compensate for the anticipated progressively reduced pursuit gain and therefore reveal little about pursuit ability per se.

Diagnosis

Perhaps the most important clinical observation that can be made relates to pursuit "smoothness," that is, the patient's ability to track the target primarily with pursuit and not saccades. This is directly related to pursuit gain (see Chapter 4). Perfect pursuit would result in a gain of 1. Reduction in gain may be seen in aging, fatigue, neurologic disease, amblyopia, schizophrenia, dyslexia, alcohol and barbiturate use, and inattention, whereas large saccades away from the target may be caused by loss of fixation or attention distraction. The

TABLE 9-2 Scoring System For Pursuits (Adapted from Southern California College of Optometry Scoring System)[18]

Grade	Description of Pursuit
4	Little or no saccadic replacement, only smooth movement observed, no loss of fixation
3	Mild saccadic replacement (just capable of detecting slight "jerkiness" in pursuit) and/or one loss of fixation during testing
2	Moderate saccadic replacement (clearly able to detect "jerkiness" in pursuit) and/or two fixation losses during testing
1	Large saccadic replacement (very little smooth pursuit, "cogwheeling") and/or three or more fixation losses during testing

former will appear as a more directional/regular "jerky" pursuit, whereas the latter will appear as a more multidirectional/irregular "erratic" pursuit. Therefore reduced pursuit gain alone may have limited diagnostic value in some cases.

The quality of pursuit is typically described and recorded by the clinician with such vague phrases as "minimal saccadic replacement," "many losses of fixations," and "excellent tracking." An alternative is a scoring system we have adapted and modified based on that used by the Southern California College of Optometry.[18] This method allows the quantification or scoring of quality of pursuit into four grades (Table 9-2). Each meridian should be scored independently.

A more elaborate system of scoring pursuit is given in the Northeastern State College of Optometry Oculomotor test of saccades and pursuit.[24] A detailed protocol is followed (see Box 9-3), consisting of two complete cycles or "rotations" in each direction. Scoring is based on several parameters (see Box 9-4), including ability to complete the task, accuracy, and degree of undesired head and body movement. As with the various saccade subtests described earlier, the pursuit subtest has been found to have high intertester reliability.

Developmental Aspects

It has been demonstrated that infants as young as 6 to 8 weeks exhibit pursuit.[33] This ability improves quickly thereafter. At age 4 to 5 years, some supportive head and torso movements may still be evident during pursuit testing, but the oculomotor ability should be reasonably well established. By age 7 years the child should be able to track a target well based on visual information alone.[3]

Binocular Dysfunction

In our experience the presence of binocular dysfunction can impact significantly on binocular but generally not monocular pursuit ability. For example, a patient manifesting an intermittent esotropia may perform well on monocular pursuit testing but do poorly binocularly because of the presence of diplopia, visual confusion, or variable vergence movements during the test. A good clinical rule of thumb is that if binocular performance is noticeably worse than that found monocularly, one should look more closely for a binocular vision dysfunction.

Asymmetry

A common cause of pursuit asymmetry is congenital nystagmus. Here, reasonable pursuit ability will generally be evident in the direction of the patient's slow phase, but with low gain and marked jerkiness in the direction of the patient's fast phase. Other possibilities for marked asymmetry include lesions in the neural pathways for pursuit. For example, patients with unilateral lesions of the cerebral hemisphere may show impaired pur-

suit toward the side of the lesion, especially when the posterior cortical region is involved.[23]

VESTIBULAR-OPTOKINETIC SYSTEM

The vestibular-optokinetic system is responsible for maintaining a stable retinal image in the presence of either transient or sustained head movement. If this system were not functional, the sensation of a blurred retinal image and oscillopsia would ensue. In healthy individuals this dual interactive system does a remarkable job of maintaining a clear and stable retinal image. The vestibular system produces eye movements to compensate for relatively brief, transient head movements. This is called the vestibular-ocular reflex (VOR) (see Chapter 5). The optokinetic system produces eye movements to compensate for relatively prolonged, sustained, generally self-rotational head movements, as the vestibular system begins to falter (see Chapter 5). With continued stimulation the optokinetic system, with the aid of the pursuit system, gradually takes over and produces robust optokinetic nystagmus (OKN).

Several simple techniques can be used in an office setting to assess the patency of the vestibular-ocular and optokinetic systems. Generally, if these tests indicate a vestibular-optokinetic defect, the clinician would be well advised to refer the patient to a neurologist for additional testing. These more advanced tests are beyond the scope of this text, but the reader is encouraged to consult other sources for this information.[2,23]

VOR Techniques[23]

Gaze stability during fixation. One of the hallmark signs of vestibular nystagmus is that it *increases* in the absence of a fixation target. The patient should be instructed to fixate a distant object. The overall pattern and esti-

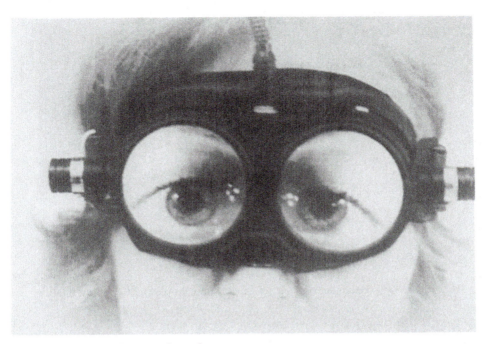

FIG. 9-7 Patient with Fresnel goggles.

(From Baloh RW, Honrubia V: *Clinical neurophysiology of the vestibular system,* ed 2, Philadelphia, 1990, FA Davis.)

mated amplitude of the nystagmus, if present, should be noted. Next, the patient should be instructed to close his or her eyes. A significant increase in the nystagmus will usually be detectable, even through the eyelids. This increase in nystagmus will alert the clinician to the possibility of a vestibular origin to the nystagmus. Another method is to have the patient wear a pair of +20 diopter binocular Fresnel goggles (Fig. 9-7). This will have the effect of severely degrading vision and therefore markedly reducing the visual feedback used to maintain fixation stability. If the nystagmus increases with the goggles, this is a sign of vestibular disease. Since these goggles magnify the eyes, the presence of subtle nystagmus is easier to detect.

Head rotation during fixation. It is possible to assess the VOR gain (eye velocity/head velocity) grossly and indirectly in the office. The patient is instructed to fixate binocularly the lowest resolvable line on a visual acuity chart. Next, the patient's head should be passively rotated, first horizontally and then vertically, at a frequency of approximately 2 Hz. If visual acuity becomes degraded by more than one line after either maneuver, it suggests a defect in vestibular gain. During such a maneuver, vergence error is maintained within the limits of foveal Panum's fusional areas (<5-mm arc).[9]

Another method for assessing the vestibular gain grossly and indirectly is to view the optic nerve head and blood vessels of one eye with an ophthalmoscope, while the patient views a distant object with the fellow eye. Again, the patient's head is rotated as before. If the VOR gain is normal, there should be no apparent movement of the optic nerve head visualized during ophthalmoscopy.

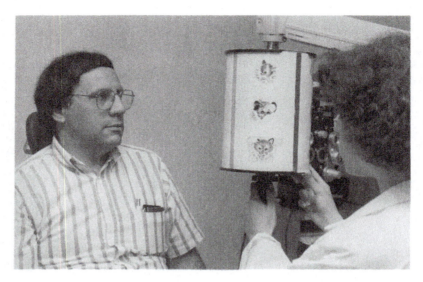

FIG. 9-8   Hand-held optokinetic drum to test optokinetic nystagmus.

OKN Techniques

Optokinetic drum or tape. The horizontal and vertical optokinetic systems are assessed in the office with either an optokinetic drum (Fig. 9-8) or an optokinetic tape (Fig. 9-9). The patient is instructed to view the repetitively moving stripes as they are moved at a moderate frequency. For example, as the drum rotates smoothly to the patient's right, the response consists of slow-phase nystagmus to the right (same direction as motion), with a foveating corrective fast phase to the left (opposite direction of motion). It is necessary to allow 30 seconds for the optokinetic response to build to its peak response. It is unfortunate that the oculomotor response to this test is probably dominated by pursuit (see Chapter 5). To stimulate the actual optokinetic system maximally, it is necessary to have a large field of motion, such as an encircling drum, with the patient passively viewing the stimulus (see Chapter 5). However, the simple clinical optokinetic drum test (or tape) still does have important diagnostic capabilities:

- The OKN response will be present in psychogenic or hysterical blindness, whereas it will be absent in organic blindness.
- This test can provide a basic assessment of the interactive OKN and pursuit systems in very young infants or other types of nonverbal patients.
- In congenital nystagmus the OKN response is frequently "inverted" (fast phase in the direction of the stripe movement), which can be a confirming sign for congenital nystagmus.
- In patients with homonymous hemianopia and a suppressed OKN response, a large, deep lesion (such as a tumor) affecting both the parietal and occipital lobes is suspected because two spatially distinct vascular areas are involved.[42]

VERGENCE

Vergence refers to the disjunctive movements of the eyes, with the primary purpose being to maintain and/or reestablish accurate

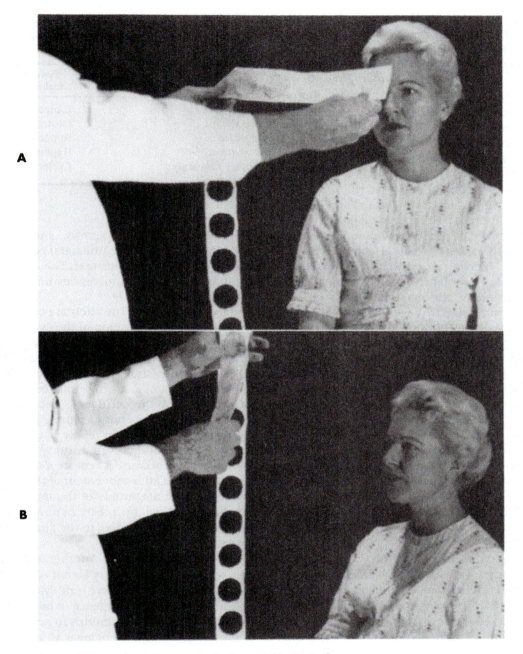

FIG. 9-9   Optokinetic tape. **A,** Horizontal. **B,** Vertical.

(From Smith JL: *Optokinetic nystagmus, its use in topical neuro-ophthalmologic diagnosis,* Springfield, Ill., 1963, Thomas.)

bifoveal fixation for target movement in depth. The sensory aspects of vergence involve the detection and processing of disparity and blur,[8] with these being the two primary inputs to vergence under standard closed-loop binocular viewing conditions.[19] The motor component then generates the vergence response to reposition the eyes, such that the retinal images will once again be seen singly within Panum's fusional areas.

The type of vergence stimulation used will influence the components that will drive the response. If the targets are located at different distances in free space, there will be contributions from the disparity, accommodative, and (to a small extent) proximal components of vergence. In contrast, with a spatially fixed target and the vergence demand being altered by prisms alone, the overwhelmingly largest component is disparity vergence, with perhaps a small contribution from accommodative vergence (secondary to the blur created by vergence accommodation); proximal vergence would be constant (see Chapter 6, especially as it relates to static and dynamic models of the vergence system).

Techniques

Unilateral cover test. The unilateral cover test is designed to determine the presence or absence of bifixation. It is performed at distance (6 meters) and at near (40 cm). A target letter size just above the patient's threshold visual acuity is used.

The patient is instructed to fixate and focus on the target. One eye is then fully occluded, and any correlated movement of the fellow eye is noted. If movement is detected, the test should be redone once or twice to ascertain its repeatability. If no movement is detected, the test is repeated but now with occlusion of the fellow eye. If no movement is detected, then there is bifixation at this test distance. If there is movement of the fellow eye, then the absence of bifixation (that is strabismus) is present (Table 9-3). A detailed discussion of the

TABLE 9-3   *Type of Strabismus Relative to Movement During Unilateral Cover Test*

Movement of Unoccluded Eye	Type of Strabismus
Temporalward	Esotropia
Nasalward	Exotropia
Upward	Hypotropia
Downward	Hypertropia
Rotary movement	Cyclotropia

differential diagnosis, prognosis, and therapeutic implications of the unilateral cover test is beyond the scope of this text. The reader is encouraged to consult sources devoted to this topic for more details.[5,18,41]

Alternate cover test. The alternate cover test assesses the relative position of the eyes in the absence of fusion. In addition, this test allows the clinician to measure the magnitude of the ocular deviation (strabismus or phoria). Test conditions are similar to the unilateral cover test, except now the occluder is kept on for several seconds (5 seconds or more), and then it is *rapidly* shifted to the fellow eye to preclude the possibility of even a short period of fusion. As the procedure is repeated, the clinician notes the relative movement of the unoccluded eye. The magnitude of the movement may be quantified by prism neutralization, and it is classified according to the direction of movement (Table 9-4).

Prism vergence ranges. Another common clinic test of vergence ability is that of relative disparity vergence.[7,25] Here one varies the stimulus to disparity vergence while maintaining fusion, and the stimulus to accommodation at either distance or near is held constant. The patient is seated behind the phoropter with the distance correction in place when testing at far (6 meters) and with the near correction (if any) in place when testing at near (40 cm). The target typically consists of a column (horizontal vergence

TABLE 9-4   *Classification of Type of Movement, Oculomotor Deviation, and Measuring Prism During the Alternate Cover Test*

Type of Movement	Type of Oculomotor Deviation	Measuring Prism
Outward	Esophoria or esotropia	Base-out
Inward	Exophoria or exotropia	Base-in
Upward*	Hypophoria or hypotropia	Base-up
Downward*	Hyperphoria or hypertropia	Base-down
Rotary	Cyclophoria or cyclotropia	Difficult to measure

*Vertical phorias and tropias must be named by right or left eye (for example, right hyperphoria).

ranges) or row (vertical vergence ranges) of Snellen letters that are one or two lines above the patient's best corrected visual acuity.

To measure horizontal vergence ranges, the vergence demand is slowly and smoothly altered by rotating the Risley prisms before each eye in either the base-out or base-in direction. The patient is instructed to try to maintain a single, in-focus image of a vertical column of Snellen letters. In addition, the patient is instructed to indicate verbally when the target first becomes slightly blurred, then diplopic, and then single once again with a decrease in prism amount. These three values are recorded at both distance and near as the blur/break/recovery.

To measure vertical vergence ranges, the stimuli and instrumentation are similar as for horizontal vergence ranges, except that the prisms are oriented in either the base-up or base-down direction and a horizontal row of Snellen letters is used. It is important to introduce the vertical disparity very slowly, because vertical vergence is dynamically approximately 8 to 10 times slower than horizontal vergence, and the normal vertical vergence range is approximately only 10% of the horizontal range.

The treatment of vergence disorders is achieved through the use of lenses, prisms, and/or vision therapy, the discussion of which is beyond the scope of this text. The reader is encouraged to consult the following excellent sources for more details.[3,18,31,32]

Vergence facility. Vergence facility is a dynamic test of relative disparity vergence.[7] It refers to the ability to regain fusion after a moderately large step change in disparity vergence is introduced, with accommodation at near held constant. Binocular prism flippers are used, with the top perhaps having 4 prism diopters base-in and the bottom perhaps having 16 prism diopters of base-out (total). The patient is instructed to view a small vertical column of Snellen letters at 40 cm and attempt to maintain single, clear vision as the prism flipper is alternated between base-out and base-in. The maximum number of cycles per minute is assessed.[3]

Fixation disparity. Fixation disparity is a simple clinical test to assess the steady-state vergence error, that is, fixation disparity, with use of the Sheedy disparometer[34] or other similar devices. Here the clinician is measuring the vergence error, within Panum's fusional area, with fusion in all but the very small central region that contains the monocularly visible polarized alignment targets.[26] The patient's habitual (that is, no prism condition) fixation disparity is first determined. Then the magnitude of fixation disparity is assessed over the entire relative fusional range with addition of alternating (to prevent or at least minimize prism adaptation) base-out and base-in prism; the accommodative stimulus is typically fixed at 2.5 diopters. The reader is encouraged to consult the following references for further details about the test procedure, clinical relevance, and treatment strategies.[15,27,34,35,40]

Near point of convergence. The near point of convergence test assesses the maximum output of the vergence system, with inputs from

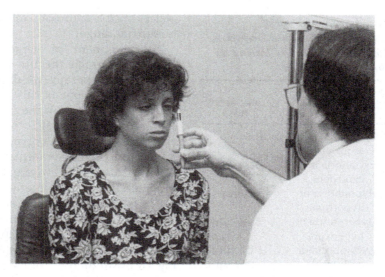

FIG. 9-10 Measuring near point of convergence.

the disparity, accommodative, proximal, and tonic systems. Essentially, one displaces a small target (preferably containing fine details to stimulate blur-driven accommodation maximally, especially in patients with binocular vision disorders where accommodation is frequently abnormal) along the median plane with the head erect and the eyes in primary position (Fig. 9-10). The target should be moved at a *constant velocity* of 1 to 2 degrees per second to elicit a smooth, ramplike motor response.[20] Thus, as the target gets progressively closer to the eyes, the *linear* velocity (that is, cm/sec) should progressively *decrease* to maintain the disparity velocity constant.[7] If the target were erroneously moved at a constant linear speed of say 2 cm/sec, the actual target disparity velocity would progressively increase approximately as the square of the distance. When either the patient reports diplopia or the clinician observes the disruption of fusion (and typically one of the patient's eyes displaces temporally to the phoria position for that near distance), the distance at which this occurs (typically 5 cm[14]) is noted

and is recorded as the break point. Then the target is smoothly withdrawn (following the description above), and the point at which either the patient recovers single vision or the clinician detects the refusion movement is recorded as the recovery value (typically 5.5 to 12.5 cm³). Patients with a receded near point of convergence may report asthenopia following short periods of near work because of the extreme fusional vergence effort required to maintain accurate bifixation. One might also repeat this test with a nonaccommodative target (such as a diffuse light source) to stimulate the disparity vergence system with relatively little contribution from accommodative vergence.

Four–prism diopter base-out test. The 4–prism diopter base-out test is a rapid test that allows one to assess grossly binocular *sensory* function, that is, detection of small central suppression scotomas, in patients with binocular dysfunction (such as occurs in small-angle esotropia), by observing the immediate *motor* fusional response.[18] A small accommodative target is first placed along the pa-

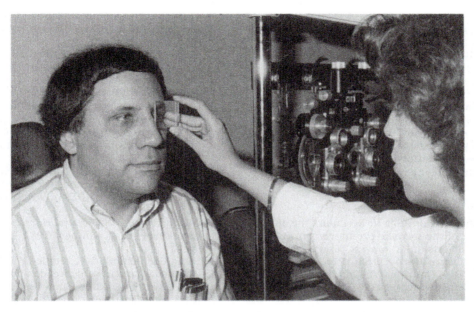

FIG. 9-11 The 4–prism diopter base-out test.

tient's midline. Then a 4–prism diopter base-out prism is rapidly added before one eye under binocular viewing conditions, thus creating a small horizontal asymmetric disparity vergence stimulus (Fig. 9-11). In a binocularly normal individual, placing the prism before either eye typically results in a small-amplitude (binocular) horizontal asymmetric vergence response (i.e., a rapid saccade plus a slow horizontal fusional vergence movement) (see Chapter 6). In contrast, the motor response is markedly different in a patient with a central binocular suppression scotoma, for example, in the right eye. If the prism is placed before the left eye, only a small conjugate horizontal saccade would be elicited. Since visual information, in this case retinal disparity, in the central right eye is cortically suppressed, the effective stimulus condition is equivalent to introducing a *step* input of target displacement in the left eye only. Now, if the prism is placed before the right eye with the suppression scotoma, no motor response oc-

curs, because the retinal image displacement falls within the scotoma. The clinical usefulness of this test occurs in patients manifesting monocularly decreased visual acuity, eccentric fixation, and no movement on the unilateral cover test. In such patients, if the 4–prism diopter base-out test elicits no movement in the eye with reduced vision, and only a conjugate movement is elicited when the prism is placed before the follow eye, the patient probably has a central suppression scotoma, and a microtropia is suspected. These (and other) motor responses to this test paradigm have recently been objectively documented.[16]

REVIEW QUESTIONS

1. Compare and contrast the various techniques used to assess fixation in the clinic.
2. What fixational abnormalities might be found using the above techniques, and in what clinical conditions might each be most prevalent?
3. Discuss oculomotor-related differences between congenital and acquired nystagmus.

4. Describe the various forms for saccadic abnormalities that the clinician may detect. What might each type represent in terms of neurologic dysfunction?
5. What clinic tests have been developed and used to assess saccadic eye movements? Describe their pitfalls.
6. In what clinical conditions might smooth pursuit gain be noticeably reduced?.
7. Describe two clinical techniques to assess the patency of a patient's VOR system.
8. Discuss the sensory and motor aspects of the 4–prism diopter base-out test.

REFERENCES

1. Baloh KW, Honrubia V: Reaction time and accuracy of the saccadic eye movements of normal subjects in a moving-target task, *Aviat Space Environ Med* 47:1165, 1976.
2. Baloh RW, Honrubia V: *Clinical neurophysiology of the vestibular system*, ed 2, Philadelphia, 1990, FA Davis Co.
3. Birnbaum MH: *Optometric management of near-point vision disorders*, Boston, 1993, Butterworth-Heinemann.
4. Bronstein AM, Kennard C: Predictive eye saccades are different from visually-triggered saccades, *Vis Res* 27:517, 1987.
5. Caloroso EE, Rouse MW: *Clinical management of strabismus*, Boston, 1993, Butterworth-Heinemann.
6. Ciuffreda KJ: *Eye movements in amblyopia and strabismus*, Ph.D. dissertation, School of Optometry, University of California at Berkeley, 1977.
7. Ciuffreda KJ: Jerk nystagmus: some new findings, *Am J Optom Physiol Optics* 56:521, 1979.
8. Ciuffreda KJ: Components of clinical near vergence testing, *J Behavioral Optom* 3:3, 1992.
9. Ciuffreda KJ, Hokoda SC: Vergence error at near during active head rotation, *Ophthal Physiol Optics* 5:411, 1985.
10. Ciuffreda KJ, Kenyon RV, Stark L: Different rates of functional recovery of eye movements during orthoptic treatment in an adult amblyope, *Invest Ophthal Vis Sci* 18:213, 1979.
11. Ciuffreda KJ, Kenyon RV, Stark L: Saccadic intrusions in strabismus, *Arch Ophthal* 97:1673, 1979.
12. Ciuffreda KJ, Kenyon RV, Stark L: Saccadic intrusions contributing to reading disability: a case report, *Am J Optom Physiol Optics* 60:242, 1983.
13. Ciuffreda KJ, Levi DM, Selenow A: *Amblyopia: basic and clinical aspects*, Boston, 1991, Butterworth-Heinemann.
14. Ciuffreda KJ, Ong E, Rosenfield M: Tonic vergence, age and clinical presbyopia, *Ophthal Physiol Optics* 13:313, 1993.
15. Despotidis N, Petito GT: Fixation disparity: clinical implications and utilization, *J Am Optom Assoc* 62:923, 1991.
16. Frantz KA, Cotter SA, Wick B: Re-evaluation of the four prism diopter base-out test, *Optom Vis Sci* 69:777, 1992.
17. Garzia RP, Richman JE, Nicholson SB: A new visual-verbal saccade test: the developmental eye movement test (DEM), *J Am Optom Assoc* 61:124, 1990.
18. Griffin JR: *Binocular anomalies: procedures for vision therapy*, ed 2, Chicago, 1982, Professional Press.
19. Hung GK, Semmlow JL: Static behavior of accommodation and vergence: computer simulation of an interactive dual-feedback system, *IEEE Trans Biomed Eng* 27:439, 1980.
20. Hung GK, Semmlow JL, Ciuffreda KJ: Dual-mode dynamic model of the vergence eye movement system, *IEEE Trans Biomed Eng* 33:1021, 1986.
21. King AT, Devick S: *The proposed King-Devick test and its relation to the Pierce saccade test and reading levels: Senior Research Project*, Chicago, 1976, Illinois College of Optometry Library.
22. Leiberman S, Cohen AH, Rubin J: NYSOA K-D test, *J Am Optom Assoc* 54:631, 1983.
23. Leigh RJ, Zee DS: *The neurology of eye movements*, ed 2, Philadelphia, 1991, FA Davis.
24. Maples WC, Atchley J, Fichlin T: Northeastern State University College of Optometry's oculomotor norms, *J Behavioral Optom* 6:143, 1992.
25. Morgan MW: Analysis of clinical data, *Am J Optom Arch Am Acad Optom* 21:477, 1944.
26. Ogle KN: *Researches in binocular vision*, Philadelphia, 1950, WB Saunders.
27. Ogle KN, Martens TG, Dyer JA: *Oculomotor imbalance in binocular vision and fixation disparity*, Philadelphia, 1967, Lea & Febiger.
28. Pierce J: *Pierce Saccade Test*, Bloomington, Ind, 1972, Cook.
29. Richman JE, Cohen E: *Rehabilitation techniques for binocular dysfunction*, Philadelphia, 1976, Pennsylvania College of Optometry Library.
30. Richman JE, Walker AJ, Garzia RP: The impact of automatic digit naming ability on a clinical test of eye movement functioning, *J Am Optom Assoc* 54:617, 1983.

31. Roper-Hall G: Clinical dysfunction of the vergence system. In Schor CM, Ciuffreda KJ, editors: *Vergence eye movements: basic and clinical aspects,* Boston, 1983, Butterworth.

32. Schieman M, Wick B: *Clinical management of binocular vision: heterophoria, accommodative, and eye movement disorders,* Philadelphia, 1993, JB Lippincott.

33. Shea SL: Eye movements: developmental aspects. In Chekaluk E, Llewellyn KR, editors: *The role of eye movements in perceptual processes,* North Holland, 1992, Elsevier Science Publishers BV.

34. Sheedy JE, Saladin JJ: Phoria, vergence and fixation disparity in oculomotor problems, *Am J Optom Physiol Optics* 54:474, 1977.

35. Sheedy JE, Saladin JJ; Association of symptoms with measures of oculomotor deficiencies, *Am J Optom Physiol Optics* 55:670, 1978.

36. Smith JL: *Optokinetic nystagmus, its use in topical neuro-ophthalmologic diagnosis,* Springfield, Ill, 1963, Thomas..

37. Steele JC: Progressive supranuclear palsy, *Brain* 95:693, 1972.

38. Streff JW, Wolff BR, Jinks B: *Eye tracking and locating skills,* Lancaster, PA, 1985, SA Noel Center.

39. Tannen B, Ciuffreda KJ, Werner DL: A case of Wallenberg's syndrome: ocular motor abnormalities, *J Am Optom Assoc* 60:748, 1989.

40. Tannen B, Kairys D, Cummings R: The effect of phenylephrine and cyclopentolate on latent ocular nystagmus, presented at the annual meeting of the American Academy of Optometry, 1980 (abstract).

41. Troost BT, Daroff RB: The ocular motor defects in progressive supranuclear palsy, *Ann Neurol* 2:397, 1977.

42. von Noorden GK: *Burian–von Noordens' binocular vision and ocular motility,* ed 3, St Louis, 1985, Mosby.

43. Walsh TJ: *Neuro-ophthalmology: clinical signs and symptoms,* ed 2, Philadelphia, 1985, Lea & Febiger.

10 Case Reports

Amblyopia	Neurologic disease
Auditory biofeedback	Nystagmus
Dyslexia	Reading
Functional vision disorders	Vision training/orthoptic
Hemianopia	therapy

To have relevance for the clinician, objective eye movement recordings must be viewed within the context of a real-life patient. This chapter presents reports of 10 patient cases, all of whom have been examined by one or both of the authors. Included in these cases are the relevant case history, clinical findings, and the objective eye movement recordings.

It is interesting to note the diversity of patients presented. This mirrors the variety of individuals in whom a complete eye movement assessment can be beneficial. These cases can be divided into three general categories: (1) neurologic disorders (both congenital and acquired), (2) functional vision disorders (amblyopia and strabismus), and (3) reading disorders. This is by no means intended to represent all patient types in which an objective eye movement evaluation is warranted. Rather it is hoped that the clinician will gain insight and appreciation into when a formal eye movement evaluation may be helpful in case management, as well as making it easier for the practitioner to interpret the clinical eye movement literature.

CASE REPORT 1
Congenital Nystagmus: Treatment with Eye Movement Auditory Biofeedback

A 10-year-old male presented to our clinic with idiopathic congenital nystagmus. Chief complaints were ocular fatigue and intermittent blur when reading for a short period of time. Reading ability and other academic skills were reported to be at grade level. He was born 3 months prematurely, and his mother died during childbirth. His natural aunt (and adopted mother) reported that the nystagmus was his only known neurologic impairment. Developmental milestones such as walking and speech were normal. History and clinic testing revealed the absence of any other ocular, systemic, or neurologic disease.

Refractive error and visual acuity were RE +2.00/−2.00×20 (20/60) and LE +2.00/−2.00×160 (20/60). Cover test revealed orthophoria at distance and slight exophoria at near. The near point of convergence was normal (4 inches), with concurrent dampening of the nystagmus. Randot stereopsis was 100-sec arc, therefore confirming the absence of strabismus. The reduced stereoacuity was probably the result of increased retinal-image motion and impaired neural sensitivity because of the early abnormal visual experience.[4,9]

The patient exhibited a right-jerk nystagmus with an exponentially increasing slow phase, as expected in patients with congenital nystagmus. There was unusually marked amplitude variation at times, ranging from 3 to 12 degrees. Frequency ranged from 4 to 5 Hz. The peak slow-phase velocity ranged from 15 to 45 degrees/sec (Fig. 10-1, *A*). When using slower strip-chart speeds, the recordings resembled a bidirectional jerk nystagmus as described by Dell'Osso and Daroff[10] (Fig. 10-1, *B*). This occurs when the slow-phase velocity is relatively high. Clinically, it could have been mistaken for a rapid pendular nystagmus.

Reading eye movements revealed nystagmus superimposed on what could be interpreted as a "modified staircase pattern" (Fig. 10-2). This result and interpretation have been previously objectively documented and reported in detail.[5] Each seven-word line took approximately 4 seconds to complete. This resulted in a reading rate approximately 40% slower than the 170 wpm expected of the average fifth grader.[22]

The treatment regimen for this patient included spectacles and eye movement auditory biofeedback. Oculomotor auditory biofeedback has proven to be a valuable tool in the treatment of nystagmus.[6] Typically, the successful patient will have learned to dampen the majority of the nystagmus at will. Improvements in visual acuity and contrast perception in such patients will depend on the percentage of visual loss predicted by the retinal-image motion versus other ocular causes (for example, foveal hypoplasia in an albinotic patient), as well as the effects of the early abnormal visual experience on the underlying related neurologic pathways.[15]

This patient learned how to exert considerable control voluntarily over his nystagmus using auditory biofeedback by the third session. He was capable of dampening his nystagmus by 90%, changing from an average amplitude of 10 degrees to about 1 degree (Fig. 10-3). At these times his visual acuity consistently improved from 20/60 to 20/50. Over the course of the next five sessions, the patient progressively learned to control the nystagmus at will in the instrument for extended periods of time. The next stage would have been to transfer this instrument training effect into free space and then eventually to wean him off the biofeedback totally, as we have done successfully for numerous other patients with nystagmus. It is unfortunate that his parents were unable to continue to bring him to our clinic.

It is interesting to note the diversity of waveforms during the auditory biofeedback sessions. Throughout all of the objective recordings without biofeedback, the patient exhibited right-jerk nystagmus. With auditory biofeedback, the patient initially displayed left-jerk nystagmus (primary gaze) (see Fig. 10-3). However, as the patient gradually reduced the amplitude and frequency of his nystagmus during the training sessions, the waveform reverted to a right-jerk nystagmus. We have seen a similar shifting of waveform direction during auditory biofeedback in a few persons with nystagmus. This appears to reflect changes in strategy and ability to control eye position during the several weeks of treatment.

It is important to note that, although there was only a modest improvement in visual acuity, there may be considerably greater potential in the realm of social interaction. For example, some persons with nystagmus will purposely avoid eye contact for obvious rea-

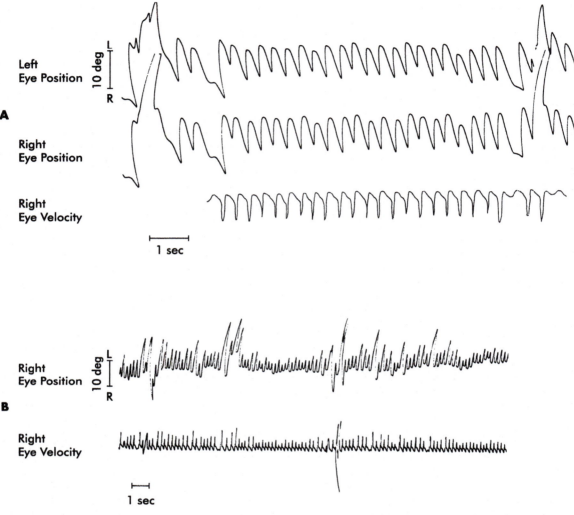

FIG. 10-1 **A,** Binocular eye movement recordings during steady fixation. Leftward movements are upward for eye position and downward for eye velocity. **B,** Slower strip-chart speed gives appearance of "bidirectional" jerk nystagmus.

sons. However, some of the individuals we have treated, who have been able to control and reduce their nystagmus during face-to-face conversation, report a marked improvement in self-image and overall confidence. Providing a child with the ability to control nystagmus will reduce the sense of "feeling different." In some instances this interrelated *psychologic* and *cosmetic* aspect may be as important as the concurrent improvement in *vision* in both children and adults. Thus such treatment for nystagmus will typically impact all three areas, although vision is the one on which we initially focus our attention.

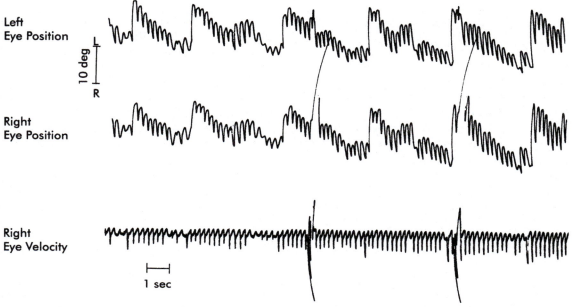

FIG. 10-2 Binocular eye movement recordings during reading. Leftward movements are upward for eye position and downward for eye velocity. Two large deflections reflect partial eyelid closure in right eye.

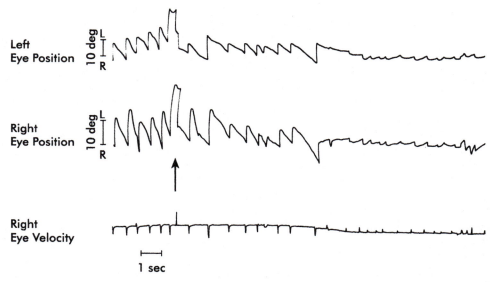

FIG. 10-3 Oculomotor biofeedback result. Left side without biofeedback and right side with biofeedback (at arrow). Leftward movements are upward for eye position and downward for eye velocity.

CASE REPORT 2
Congenital Nystagmus: With Minimal Impairment of Reading

A 14-year-old female with a history of idiopathic congenital nystagmus was referred to our clinic for an oculomotor evaluation. She had a complaint of slight intermittent blur at distance with best refractive correction in place. The patient was a good student and had no complaints with regard to reading. She reported, however, occasional unsteadiness of fixated objects, especially under conditions of reduced overall illumination. The patient was aware of a head turn when she wished to see objects more clearly. Birth and early history were unremarkable, except for the presence of nystagmus that was first diagnosed by an ophthalmologist at 3 months of age. No specific etiology was offered at that time. All other aspects of personal and family history were negative.

Vision analysis revealed a refractive error and visual acuity of RE −0.75/−4.25×180 (20/40) and LE −0.50/−4.00×005 (20/40). She had orthophoria at distance and 7 prism diopters of exophoria at near. Stereopsis at near (Wirt circles) was 40-sec arc. Ocular health evaluation was unremarkable.

Gross observation of ocular motility revealed a small-amplitude left-jerk nystagmus in primary gaze. The nystagmus remained horizontal in all cardinal positions of gaze. The null position was 15 degrees to the right. Eye movement recordings confirmed the left-jerk nystagmus, which exhibited an exponentially increasing slow phase (as typically found in congenital nystagmus), an amplitude of 1.2 degrees, a frequency of 3.5 Hz, and a maximum slow-phase velocity of 2.5 degrees/sec (Fig. 10-4). Saccadic tracking showed normal latency, velocity, and overall metrics with superimposed nystagmus. Pursuit demonstrated the typical asymmetric pattern expected for (left) jerk nystagmus (Fig. 10-5); the maximum slow-phase nystagmus

and velocity-driven pursuit summated (not necessarily linearly) to provide an enhanced response when the target moved in the same direction as the slow phase, and a decreased response when the target moved in the opposite direction of the slow phase.

Eye movements were recorded while reading the EDL Laboratories junior high school–level paragraphs.[23] A minimum comprehension score of 70% (10 true/false questions) was passing. These traces were of particular interest, because the nystagmus was mostly suppressed, except for small intervals at the beginning of each new line (Fig. 10-6). There were, however, an excessive number of fixations and regressions resulting in a reading rate of 133 wpm, which is reduced by 40% compared to the average ninth grader.[22]

Contrast these reading eye movements with those of case report 1. In that case the nystagmus during reading was quite evident. There are two possible explanations for this difference. Perhaps individuals (such as in case 2 but not in case 1) with small-amplitude nystagmus have the ability to suppress or override it when involved in an attention-demanding higher-level task, such as reading. Another possible explanation may be inferred by analyzing the frequency characteristics of the nystagmus versus the typical fixational and saccadic demands of reading. For example, in the present patient, the nystagmus had a frequency of 3.5 Hz, which translates into a slow-phase duration/corrective saccade cycle of approximately 300 msec. The patient read at a rate of 133 words/min and made 127 fixations while reading the 100-word paragraph. This translates into a saccade approximately every 350 msec during reading, which approximates her average natural nystagmus cycle. Perhaps the patient has learned to synchronize the desired reading saccades and the involuntarily occurring nystagmus saccades, thus effectively replacing the nystagmus saccades with the reading saccades. It is also quite conceivable that

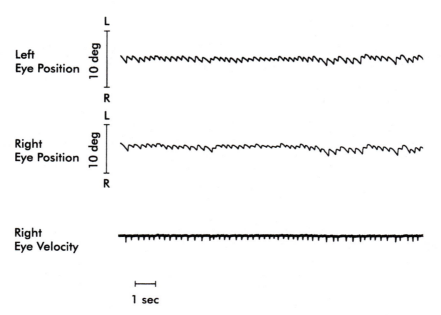

FIG. 10-4 Binocular eye movement recordings during midline fixation. Leftward movements are upward for eye position and downward for eye velocity.

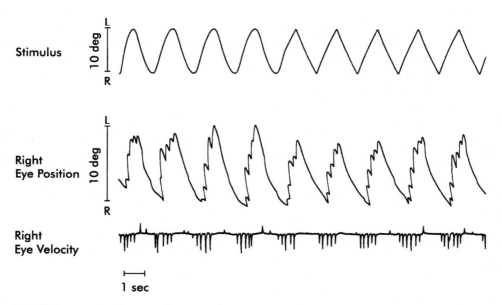

FIG. 10-5 Monocular recording of pursuit eye movements under binocular viewing conditions. Left side of graph shows sine wave (constantly varying velocity), and right side of graph shows triangle (constant velocity) stimulus. Leftward movements are upward for eye position and downward for eye velocity.

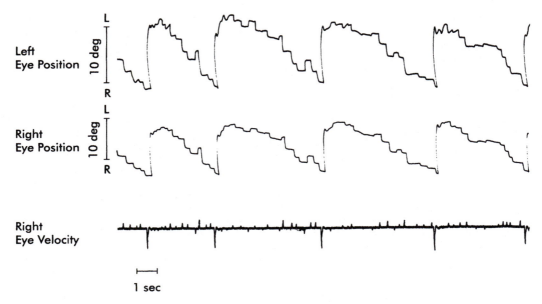

FIG. 10-6   Binocular recordings of eye movements during reading. Leftward movements are upward for eye position and downward for eye velocity.

both mechanisms may be working together, especially in patients with small-amplitude nystagmus, which may be easier to override and then synchronize. To support this idea further, an examination of her reading record revealed that during many of the longer fixational pauses, there was residual rightward-directed non-suppressed drift followed by a corrective saccade (which is difficult to distinguish in isolation from a text-based regressive movement). During shorter fixational pauses, however, there was less drift and correspondingly less of a tendency for a corrective saccade.

It is logical to assume that a motor intrusion such as occurs with congenital nystagmus adversely impacts overall reading performance. The effect, however, can vary. Ciuffreda and others[5] reported on a 12-year-old girl with congenital nystagmus of unknown etiology. This child read at a rate of only 30 to 60 wpm, drastically below the rate of a normal sixth grader (185 wpm).

The general ability to enhance or modify reading rate in patients with nystagmus is unknown. However, Taylor[22] reported on a person with nystagmus who increased his reading speed from 132 to 279 wpm with approximately 250 hours of intensive vision training.

Clearly, more studies are needed to understand the effect of nystagmus on reading performance in a wide variety of such individuals, as well as the effect, if any, of various modes of therapy to reduce the nystagmus and improve reading efficiency.

CASE REPORT 3
Child With Duane's Syndrome

Duane's syndrome refers to a spectrum of oculomotor anomalies characterized by retraction of the globe on adduction resulting in a narrowing of the palpebral fissure (Box 10-1).[12] There are three varieties of the syndrome (Box 10-2).[25] Type I exhibits marked limitation of abduction with normal adduction. This is the most common variety. Type II presents with a limitation of adduction with normal abduction. It tends to be the rarest form.[17] Type III manifests a limitation of both abduction and adduction, as well as either an elevation or a depression of the affected eye on adduction.[14] Duane's syndrome occurs more frequently in females than in males, and in the left rather than right eye, although it can occur bilaterally.[12] The prevailing theory is that most cases of Duane's syndrome are due to a congenital anomaly of oculomotor innervation, and this view is supported by electromyographic evidence.[12] The anomalous innervation takes the form of the oculomotor nerve in the affected eye innervating *both* the medial and lateral rectus, hence causing cocontraction on adduction. Pathologic studies have also revealed a hypoplastic abducens nucleus and nerve.[14] With regard to primary gaze ocular alignment, it has been reported that 50% of type I Duane's and 86% of type III Duane's patients have strabismus.[17] (There was only one type II Duane's patient in this study.)

An 11-year-old boy was referred to our clinic to confirm the diagnosis of type III Duane's syndrome. The patient complained of near-to-far focusing difficulties, as well as occasional horizontal diplopia on lateral gaze in either direction. The diplopia was long-standing and was able to be abolished by executing a compensatory head turn. Examination revealed refractive error and best corrected distance visual acuity of RE −0.75×115 (20/20) and LE −1.50 sph (20/20−1). Distance cover test showed an alternating exotropia of 35 prism diopters. At 16 inches the cover test revealed an intermittent alternating exotropia of 30 prism diopters. The patient did not exhibit stereopsis with his head in primary gaze because of the presence of strabismus; however, he was able to achieve 70-sec arc stereoacuity (Wirt circles) with a head turn to the left during which time fusion was at-

---

> ### BOX 10-1   *Clinical Signs of Duane's Syndrome*
>
> - Abduction deficit (types I and III)
> - Adduction deficit (types II and III)
> - Retraction of globe during attempted adduction
> - Elevation of eyelid during attempted abduction in some cases
> - Vertical movements during attempted horizontal gaze in some cases

---

> ### BOX 10-2   *Types of Duane's Syndrome*
>
> - Type I: Limited abduction with full adduction
> - Type II: Limited adduction with full abduction
> - Type III: Limited abduction and adduction

---

tained. Normal retinal correspondence was found on the Hering-Bielchowsky afterimage test. Worth-4-dot testing revealed exodiplopia at all distances. Accommodative amplitude (minus lens technique) was RE 12 diopters and LE 13 diopters. The patient failed "plus" (greater than 4 seconds to obtain clear vision) on the +/−2.00 diopters monocular accommodative facility test in each eye. Ocular health was unremarkable.

Gross examination of his eye movements revealed a full field of gaze with the left eye. In contrast, the right eye exhibited gaze limitation during both attempted abduction and adduction. During attempted abduction the patient was not able to shift his gaze beyond primary position, whereas during attempted adduction, limited adduction concurrent with elevation of the right eye was found.

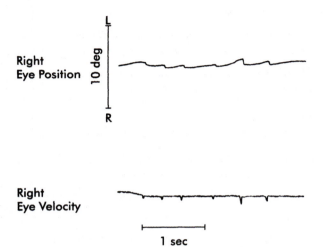

Right
Eye Position

Right
Eye Velocity

1 sec

FIG. 10-7 Monocular recording of midline fixation during binocular viewing. Leftward movements are upward for eye position and downward for eye velocity.

Objective eye movement recordings revealed a very small-amplitude, bilateral, constant, exponentially increasing, slow-phase, right-jerk nystagmus, on primary gaze (Fig. 10-7). Nystagmus amplitude was small and variable with a maximum of 0.9 degrees. Frequency was 2 Hz. Saccadic tracking to a fixed amplitude, varying frequency, ±5-degree step stimulus was informative. Saccades in the left eye (monocular viewing) had normal latencies (180 msec), as well as qualitatively normal trajectories and correlated velocity profiles in most cases; however, for the rightward directed saccades, the velocity profiles were sometimes slightly blunted (Fig. 10-8), suggesting slightly slowed peaked velocities. In contrast, saccades in the right eye (monocular viewing) in both directions showed variable but increased latency (320 to 400-msec range) (Fig. 10-9); further, they clearly demonstrated

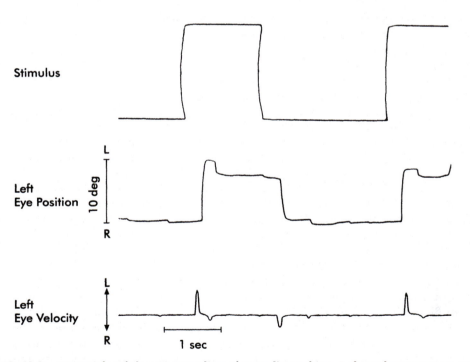

Stimulus

Left
Eye Position

Left
Eye Velocity

1 sec

FIG. 10-8 Monocular (left eye) recording of saccadic tracking. Leftward movements are upward for eye position and downward for eye velocity.

slowed trajectories and correlated broadened, blunted, and synchronized velocity profiles. This suggests slowed and desynchronized neuromotor activity. Additionally, the left eye showed a tendency to exhibit static overshooting of approximately 2.5 degrees during some of the saccades to the left (see Fig. 10-8). These overshoots were not seen in the right eye. Static overshoots have been reported in some persons with strabismus.[9]

Aside from spectacles, the recommended treatment plan included vision therapy for the independently present accommodative infacility, as well as for the primary gaze exotropia. In formulating a treatment plan, several factors were considered. First, treatment for the accommodative infacility could proceed in the customary manner[11]; the Duane's syndrome was likely coincidental to the accommodative infacility. Second, the treatment objectives for the exotropia needed to be clearly defined. It is relatively common for such patients to have strabismus in primary gaze. Most of the time,

however, these patients are capable of executing a compensatory head turn to achieve single binocular vision.[24] This was indeed the case with our patient. By turning his head to the left, he was capable of achieving nearly normal stereoacuity. In contrast, in primary gaze, we were not able to elicit this response. The patient used a change in head position, in conjunction with the abduction deficit of the right eye, to achieve bifoveal alignment. The mechanism is as follows: when the patient rotates his head to the left while attempting to maintain fixation on an object in primary gaze, the vestibular-ocular reflex produces equal and increased innervation (according to Hering's law) to the right lateral rectus and its corresponding muscle, the left medial rectus, thereby producing an equal but opposite rotation of the eyes with respect to the head. In this case, however, because of Duane's syndrome, the right lateral rectus is not appropriately innervated. Therefore the right eye remains essentially stationary, and the

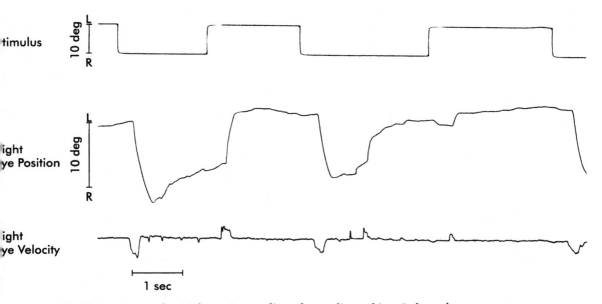

FIG. 10-9 Monocular (right eye) recording of saccadic tracking. Leftward movements are upward.

left (exotropic) eye smoothly and rapidly shifts to the right, until bifoveal alignment is achieved.

Certainly, the treatment objectives for this patient would not include the training of either motor or sensory fusion in the field that has such a duction deficit. However, it is possible to treat the distance exotropia in primary gaze because (1) there is no gaze limitation in Duane's syndrome that affects the primary field of gaze at distance, and (2) the exotropia is primarily due to the left (unaffected) eye. Treatment of the near exotropia (without any head turn) would be problematic.

We have seen patients with Duane's syndrome who have been unnecessarily subjected to arduous, risky, and expensive clinical and outpatient hospital testing because a diagnosis of Duane's syndrome could not be confirmed or, even worse, was not considered in the initial differential diagnosis. It behooves the clinician to become familiar with the clinical signs (see Box 10-1) and differential diagnosis of Duane's syndrome. Specifically, one should look for signs of anomalous oculomotor innervation in patients who present with an abduction deficit and an unremarkable history (for example, no report of sudden diplopia, head trauma, or headaches). Most commonly, this will take the form of retraction of the globe (with corresponding lid closure) during attempted adduction. Other signs of anomalous innervation may include elevation or depression of the eye on adduction, as well as elevation of the eyelid during attempted abduction.

CASE REPORT 4
Congenital Dyslexia (Adult)[8]

The patient was a 32-year-old female who worked as a legal secretary. She was referred by the vision therapy clinic for an eye movement evaluation, with emphasis on reading. Since childhood, she had several problems related to reading. The patient frequently transposed letters and telephone numbers, especially when typing and proofreading manuscripts and business letters. Most interestingly, she proofread best by scanning across a line of print from right to left. Because of the transposition problem, words in a sentence frequently do not make sense to her. For example, she sometimes initially sees "fo" for "of," "from" for "form," and "ot" for "to." The patient skips lines when reading and typically requires a ruler for visual guidance. She also mixes the order of syllables. Reading aloud is done with extreme difficulty and frustration. She frequently says an incorrect but similar word, such as "conversation" for "construction" and then must repeat the word a few times before it is finally correct. Her spelling and penmanship are poor, and she must always use a dictionary to confirm her spelling. Finally, she has frequent right/left hand confusions. This is most obvious and troublesome during typing and karate practice. She reported to have never liked school, although most interestingly and unusual in such cases, she claimed reading to be one of her primary hobbies. All findings of the comprehensive general vision examination were communicated as being normal by the referring physician, except for infrequent alternating suppression at near.

Testing of fixational, saccadic, and pursuit eye movements was first performed, and all aspects were generally within normal limits. No nystagmus or square-wave jerks were present during either monocular or binocular midline fixation. During predictable saccadic tracking (10-degree steps, 0.4 Hz, symmetric about the midline), either slight hypometria (≤ 0.5-degree error) or normometria was found. To brief, unpredictable pulse stimuli (10 degrees, 60 to 150 msec, symmetric about the midline), the eye responded with normal initial latencies (approximately 200 msec) but with longer latencies for the second corrective saccade (400 to 1000 msec) than expected

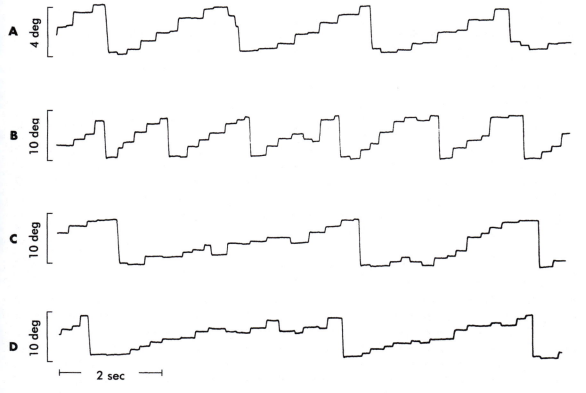

A 4 deg

B 10 deg

C 10 deg

D 10 deg

├── 2 sec ──┤

FIG. 10-10 Reading eye movements in a patient with congenital dyslexia for various text levels. **A,** Dots. **B,** Third grade, **C,** Junior high school. **D,** College. Leftward movements are downward.

(From Ciuffreda KJ, Kenyon RV, Stark L: *Am J Optom Physiol Optics* 62:844, 1985.)

(<200 msec). The patient appeared to pause awaiting the return of the target to where the eye was now transiently looking. Normal, small-amplitude (<0.25-deg) dynamic overshoots were frequently present. Pursuit (10-degree predictable sinusoid, 0.2 to 2 Hz, symmetric about the midline) exhibited normal gain and saccadic components.

Reading eye movements to a dot pattern (simulating reading), as well as third grade, junior high school, and high school/college level reading materials, were then tested (Fig. 10-10). The average number of progressive saccades, average number of regressions, fixa-

tion duration, and reading rate are summarized in Table 10-1 and discussed below.

Sequential tracking of the dot pattern during the simulated reading task did show some subtle abnormalities. "Regressions" were present, and marked hypometria was found during the return-sweep saccades. These findings support the notion that *some* persons with congenital dyslexia may indeed exhibit difficulty with sequential tracking, even in the absence of text processing demands. However, the degree of abnormality found in our patient was much less than reported.[16] This continues to be an area of considerable contro-

TABLE 10-1   Reading Eye Movement Analysis

Reading Material	Total Fixations (100 words)	Regressions (100 words)	Fixation Duration (msec)	Reading Rate (wpm)
Dots	112	4	246	—
Third grade	84	6	210	240
Junior high	121	7	264	180
High school/college	122	20	270	190

versy, with differences in subject selection criteria and prediction effects being confounding variables. The increased number of fixations occurring on approximately one half of the lines of text accounted for the relatively modest overall reduction in reading rate. It is interesting to note that the number of fixations, fixation duration, and reading rate were very similar for both the junior high school and high school/college paragraphs despite their differences in text demand. This could be interpreted as evidence for an underlying oculomotor defect that may be inborn in some persons with congenital dyslexia. However, Solan[20] has shown a similar pattern in some academically achieving, nondyslexic students. These patients had below average oculomotor reading skills (number of forward fixations, regressions, fixation duration, and reading rate), and these were also similar at the various grade levels of reading.

Although it is not easy to discern the etiology of the reading disability based on reading eye movements alone, such recordings are helpful in allowing us to understand certain aspects of the patient's reading behavior. They are also very helpful in objectively and quantitatively assessing the effect of optometric therapeutic intervention on reading performance.

CASE REPORT 5
Acquired Dyslexia[8]

A 25-year-old male was referred to our clinic to assess the potential for improvement of his vision. The patient's chief complaint was that he "now reads like a little kid," that is, slowly and with transposition of letters. At 17 years of age he had a subarachnoid hemorrhage over the left occipital lobe because of a congenital arteriovenous malformation, thus necessitating emergency neurosurgery. Subsequent to the surgery, he was left with a right homonymous hemianopia (with macular sparing), an acquired dyslexia, specific perceptual deficits, and a transient inability to walk. Ambulatory ability returned to normal within 6 months, whereas the other deficits have remained. At 25 years he had several generalized seizures, which were diagnosed as resulting from scar tissue formation in the area of the neurosurgery that irritated the surrounding blood vessels and tissues. The seizures were then controlled by phenytoin (Dilantin), 400 mg/day.

The psychoeducational and perceptual batteries provided important insight into his visual and perceptual problems. A normal full-scale intelligence quotient (IQ) of 114 was found. The perceptual tests indicated a breakdown of a variety of specific perceptual processes, resulting in his reading and learning problems. Maze testing showed extreme difficulty in solving novel problem situations. The Illinois Test of Psycholinguistic Abilities revealed many areas of difficulty. He was slow and made numerous corrections, which suggested a problem in visual reception. The results also suggested poor visual sequential memory. His poor short-term memory score suggested difficulty with remembering the word being processed. The Bender-Gestalt test

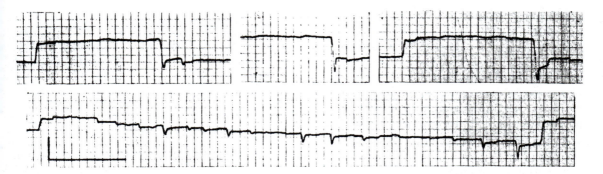

FIG. 10-11 Eye movements in a patient with acquired dyslexia and homonymous hemianopia. **A,** Saccades. **B,** Reading. Leftward movements are upward. Calibration bars represent 10 degrees and 1 second.

(From Ciuffreda KJ, Kenyon RV, Stark L: *Am J Optom Physiol Optics* 62:844, 1985.)

indicated difficulty in visually organizing his responses. Based on these tests as well as others, the clinical psychologist concluded that the patient was quite capable of continuing his college education but would require auditory rather than visual learning modes, as would be true for a blind student. The patient was determined to complete the last 2 years of his college education in business administration.

The patient was examined in our clinic. The homonymous hemianopia with macular sparing was confirmed. All else with respect to the refractive, binocular, and ocular health status was unremarkable. Testing of fixation, saccades, pursuit, and reading eye movements was then performed (Fig. 10-11). Monocular fixation and binocular fixation were normal, with no nystagmus or square-wave jerks present. Saccades (10-degree predictable steps, 0.5 Hz, symmetric about the midline) into the functional hemifield were generally accurate. They were either normometric or slightly hypometric with small (0.25-degree) but normal dynamic overshoots frequently present. In contrast, saccades into the blind hemifield were generally noticeably inaccurate. The most common and striking finding was the presence of abnormally large (~5-degree) dynamic overshoots. However, a variety of response patterns were present. Infrequently, a

single saccade with a large dynamic overshoot was used for foveal acquisition of the target. More typically, two or three saccades were necessary. These occurred in conjunction with large dynamic overshoots, as well as with static overshoots and undershoots. Thus final total (excluding latency) accurate acquisition time of the target took up to 500 msec, which is more than 10 times longer than the duration of a single accurate 10-degree saccade. All saccades had normal (that is, main sequence) peak velocities. Tracking of a smoothly moving target (10-degree predictable sinusoid, 0.2 to 1.2 Hz, symmetric about the midline) showed a normal gain range (0.8 to 1.1) without consistent directional asymmetry, although there were frequently more corrective saccades present when tracking the target toward the blind field, that is, with the target falling on or near the blind hemiretinal border. Of interest was the absence of abnormally large dynamic overshoots appended to the 2-degree or smaller corrective saccades that were present during pursuit tracking, which suggests they may represent an adaptive strategy (see later discussion).

Eye movements during reading showed many abnormalities. The number of progressive saccades per line was excessive, being about 17 in number. Thus the amplitude of these saccades (that is, the change in static fixation level between consecutive saccades) was generally 1 degree or less. About two thirds of these progressive saccades had abnormally large (~1.5-degree) dynamic overshoots present. The return-sweep saccades were generally hypometric, thus requiring a secondary corrective saccade for accurate fixation at the beginning of a new line. Mean fixation duration was normal (265 msec), as was the mean regression level (~1.5 per line). Reading rate was markedly reduced to about 80 wpm, with 200 to 300 wpm being normal for an adult.

In summary, large dynamic overshoots were frequently found during both nonreading and reading tasks when the patient saccaded into the blind hemifield. Such a short duration oculomotor defect, however, probably has little adverse effect on visual information processing during reading. In fact, presence of this single rapid dynamic overshoot rather than the more typical multiple-step hypometric saccades into the blind field suggests an adaptive strategy, such as may be expected to occur in some patients with such a long-term stable and permanent visual field loss. It would bring the object or word of interest into the seeing hemifield for subsequent processing more rapidly than if a series of saccades were to be used and thus appears to be a time-optimal maneuver. The slow reading rate was primarily the result of the residual, posttraumatic brain dysfunction, presumably including the language processing centers, rather than the field defect per se. It is interesting to note that fixation duration was within normal limits,[22] but a marked increase in the number of fixations was present. This suggested normalcy of the primary sensory aspects of fixation, with abnormality occurring in higher level processing of the text information. Therefore, even if his basic oculomotor control could be improved with eye movement training, it would likely result in relatively little improvement of the patient's reading ability.

Testing of a patient's oculomotor performance during simple tracking tasks, simulated reading tasks, and actual reading at different text levels, in cases of acquired field loss and/or dyslexia, provides additional important insight into one's clinical predictions and overall case management.

CASE REPORT 6
Wallenberg's Syndrome[21]

A 57-year-old male presented to our clinic with visual disability as a sequela of left lateral medullary (Wallenberg's) syndrome. This is a relatively common type of stroke that results from occlusion of the posterior inferior cerebellar artery in the medulla. Recovery is usually complete and occurs over several months.[27] The medulla oblongata is that part of the brainstem that connects the pons to the spinal cord. It is responsible for a number of vital functions, including respiration, temperature control of the extremities, swallowing, and vomiting. Some of the general clinical symptoms include (1) ipsilateral loss of pain and temperature sensation of the face; (2) contralateral loss of pain and temperature sensation of the trunk and limbs; (3) ipsilateral Horner's syndrome; (4) nausea, vertigo, and nystagmus; and (5) difficulty with speech and swallowing. Additionally, a hallmark symptom is lateropulsion, which refers to the sensation of one's body being pulled toward the side of the lesion.[13] This vestibular-based direction bias is manifested both in overall body sensation and in tonic deviation of eye position ipsilateral to the lesion. This is particularly evident in the dark where visual feedback is absent. Clinically, it can best be seen by having the patient look straight ahead, close the eyes for a few seconds, and then reopen them; the eyes will remain deviated toward the side of the lesion for a few seconds. Saccadic eye movements display a classic pattern of hypermetria ipsilateral to the lesion and hypometria contralateral to the lesion.[2]

Eye movements were recorded objectively in this patient at 2 months, 4 months, and 2

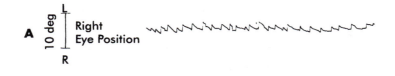

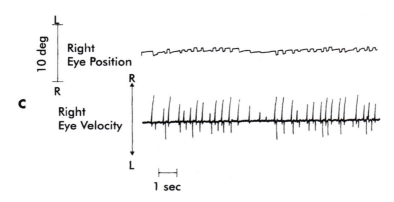

FIG. 10-12 Fixational eye movements in right eye. **A,** Two months after stroke. **B,** Four months after stroke. **C,** Two years after stroke. Leftward movements are upward for eye position and downward for eye velocity.

(From Tannen B, Ciuffreda KJ, Werner DL: *J Am Optom Assoc* 60:748, 1989.)

years after this stroke. Fixational eye movements revealed several interesting findings. Recordings taken 2 months after this stroke exhibited a left-jerk nystagmus (decelerating exponential form) averaging 1.7 degrees in amplitude with a mean frequency of 2.2 Hz and an average maximum slow-phase velocity of 6 degrees/sec (Fig. 10-12, *A*). Two months later, the jerk nystagmus was considerably reduced and reversed in direction. It now had an amplitude of 1 degree, a frequency of 1 Hz, and a maximum slow-phase velocity of only 1 degree/sec. In addition, some saccadic intrusions

were now evident (Fig. 10-12, *B*). Finally, in recordings taken 2 years after the stroke (in which the patient now appeared to have fully recovered), primarily saccadic intrusions were found having an average amplitude of 1.5 degrees with a mean frequency of 1.7 Hz. At this point the jerk nystagmus was rarely seen (Fig. 10-12, *C*).

Fixation in darkness 2 months after the patient's stroke revealed the (expected) tonic deviation toward the side of the lesion (Fig. 10-13). There was also a constant linear right-jerk nystagmus that was not seen in the light.

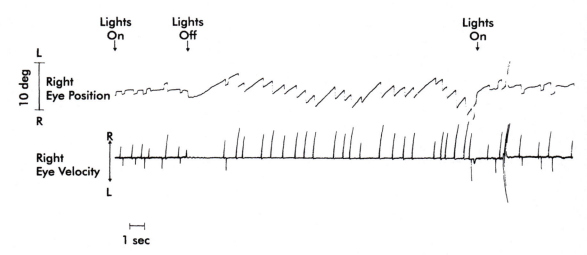

FIG. 10-13 Fixation in total darkness. Leftward movements are upward for eye position and downward for eye velocity.

(From Tannen B, Ciuffreda KJ, Werner DL: *J Am Optom Assoc* 60:748, 1989.)

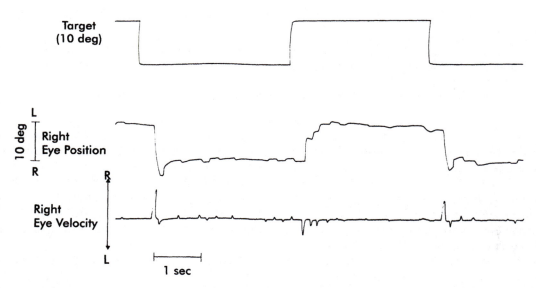

FIG. 10-14 Pseudorandom saccadic tracking, right eye. Leftward movements are upward for eye position and downward for eye velocity.

(From Tannen B, Ciuffreda KJ, Werner DL: *J Am Optom Assoc* 60:748, 1989.)

This is consistent with a postulated vestibular system deficit.[2] Saccadic tracking to a fixed amplitude step of varying frequency showed an expected pattern of hypermetric saccades ipsilateral to the lesion and hypometric saccades contralateral to the lesion[2] (Fig. 10-14).

Eye movements during reading were recorded both 2 months and 2 years after the stroke (Fig. 10-15). At the 2-month test session, reading rate was within normal limits (260 wpm) with normal comprehension (70%). The saccadic hypermetria found during reading could easily be mistaken for regressive movements. However, closer analysis revealed that most of these were rightward-directed, primarily hypermetric saccades with subsequent leftward-directed corrective components, as predicted by the neurologic condition. In addition, the intersaccadic intervals were much shorter (about 100 msec) than the average fixation duration during reading (about 255 msec).[1] There was reading difficulty because of perceived oscillation of the text reported at 2 months after the stroke. Two years later, reading performance was now reported to be normal. Eye movements at this time showed less hypermetric saccades and a moderate increase in reading rate (315 wpm).

Patients with Wallenberg's syndrome present with a unique set of oculomotor deficits as neurologic sequelae. It is important to recognize the presentation and recovery time course of this disease, as well as the clinical significance it can have on a patient's short-term and long-term visual performance.

CASE REPORT 7
Polyneuropathy and Epilepsy

A 49-year-old male proofreader was referred to the Ocular Motor Clinic with complaints of loss of place and involuntary skipping of words while reading. These symptoms were of gradual onset over the past year and had worsened considerably over the past 6

months. Medical history included attacks of epilepsy over the past 19 years, which were being controlled by phenytoin (Dilantin), as well as polyneuritis of 12 years' duration. Neurologic and general medical evaluations were otherwise unremarkable.

Epilepsy, or seizure disorder, denotes a variety of conditions, all of which have in common a sudden, involuntary change in behavior with regard to motor function, autonomic activity, consciousness, or sensation that is accompanied by an abnormal electrical discharge in the brain.[18] Polyneuropathy refers to an array of conditions in which nerve damage has a diffuse effect on the peripheral nervous system. Therefore sensory, motor, and autonomic modalities can be affected to varying degrees. These effects tend to be symmetric and predominantly distal. Some conditions that may cause polyneuropathy include diabetes mellitus, chronic inflammatory demyelinating disease, carcinoma, and acquired immune deficiency.[3]

Vision examination revealed myopic astigmatism and presbyopia with best corrected vision of 20/20 in each eye at both distance and near. Binocularity was within normal limits, and ocular health was normal with the exception of several nonspecific small discrete scotomas scattered throughout the visual field of each eye.

Fixational eye movements contained numerous square-wave jerks (Fig. 10-16). These were approximately 1.5 degrees in amplitude and of variable frequency with a maximum of approximately 3 Hz. Saccades in response to a fixed-amplitude (±5 degrees centered on the midline) either constant or varying-frequency stimulus had static overshoots of approximately 20% (for example, saccadic gain = 1.2) in 80% of the saccades (Fig. 10-17). Saccadic latency was within normal limits (220 msec). Pursuit tracking in response to a 10-degree sinusoid moving at 0.5 Hz contained a variety of saccadic components (square-wave jerks, predictive saccades, and "catch-up" saccades),

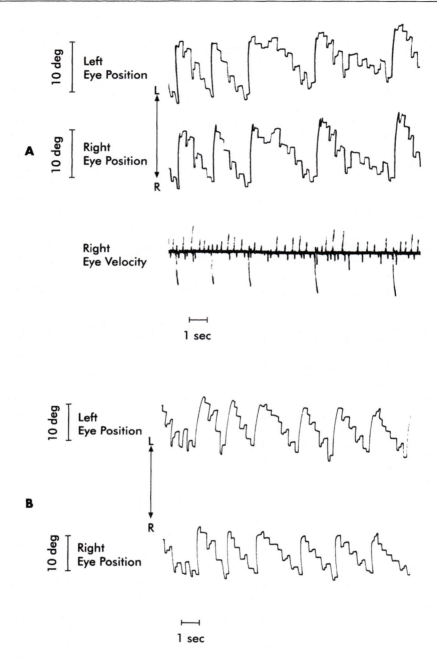

FIG. 10-15 **A,** Binocular reading eye movements 2 months after stroke. **B,** Binocular reading eye movements 2 years after stroke. Leftward movements are upward for eye position and downward for eye velocity.

(From Tannen B, Ciuffreda KJ, Werner DL: *J Am Optom Assoc* 60:748, 1989.)

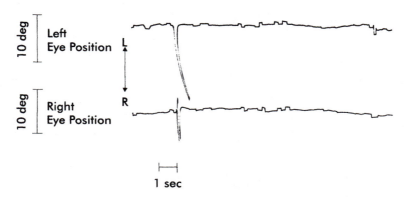

FIG. 10-16 Binocular recording of eye movements during midline fixation. Leftward movements are upward.

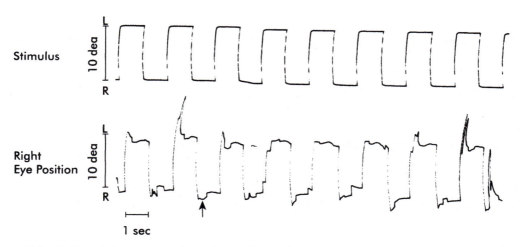

FIG. 10-17 Right eye recording of saccadic tracking; binocular viewing. Arrow denotes one of many static overshoots. Leftward movements are upward.

causing variable pursuit gain (0.6 to 1.1) (Fig. 10-18). Additionally, the patient exhibited a very unusual loss of fixation as he tracked the target through the midpoint of his gaze in either direction.

Eye movements during reading revealed an excessive number of fixations and regressions, including several partial "reverse staircases"[28] (Fig. 10-19). The objective reading records presented some difficulty in analysis, in view

of the patient's proclivity toward saccadic hypermetria. These can be mistaken for regressions. In case report 6 on Wallenberg's syndrome, we were able to distinguish between these two entities by quantifying differences in the intersaccadic intervals. In the present case, however, it was more difficult to make that distinction, because the intersaccadic intervals of the static overshoots were approximately the same as those for typical regressive

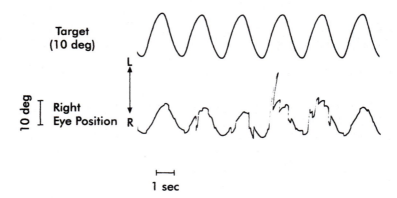

FIG. 10-18   Right eye recording of pursuit tracking. Binocular viewing. Leftward movements are upward.

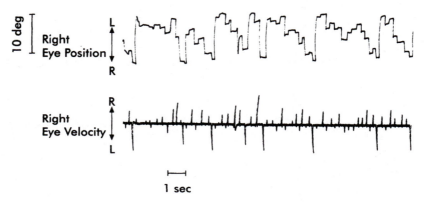

FIG. 10-19   Monocular recording of eye movements during reading with binocular viewing. Leftward movements are upward for eye position and downward for eye velocity.

movements during reading (~200 msec). Closer analysis of the objective reading records revealed that a majority of the return-sweep saccadic movements also exhibited static overshoot. Since the amplitude of the return-sweep saccade was approximately the same as the saccadic tracking task (10 degrees), and the patient showed static overshoots most of the time during basic saccadic tracking, it is reasonable to conclude that the overshoots during the return sweep were due to the saccadic dysmetria. The regressions or overshoots during the "staircases" are less clear. The fact that the majority of the forward fixations were normal with regard to metrics, coupled with the patient's symptoms, suggested that perhaps these may be typical text-related regressions rather than static overshoots. Duration of fixation was markedly increased (400 msec as compared to the average adult reader's 240 msec),[22] along with a reduced reading rate (154 wpm compared to 280 wpm in the average adult).

This patient presented with an unusual array of subjective and objective findings. Absence of previous reading difficulty suggested oculomotor involvement of relatively recent onset. This constellation of objectively determined oculomotor deficits included (1) square-wave jerks during fixation, (2) static overshoots during saccadic tracking, (3) variable gain pursuit with midline fixation loss, (4) reduced reading rate, (5) increased number of fixations and regressions, and (6) increased fixation duration during reading. It is not surprising that a person with so many oculomotor abnormalities would notice a decrease in performance in as visually demanding a job as a proofreader. It is more difficult, however, to ascribe a specific etiology to the objective findings. Epilepsy per se is not usually associated with specific oculomotor deficits. Anticonvulsants have been implicated in the findings of slowed saccades and periodic alternating nystagmus,[12] but neither is present here. The effects of polyneuropathy on the oculomotor system would appear to depend highly on the underlying disease causing this general neurologic damage. In the present case there was an unconfirmed suspicion in the report by the neurologist that a subclinical form of multiple sclerosis might be the cause of the polyneuropathy. If this were indeed the case, it might account in part for the variable pursuit gain and saccadic overshoot hypermetria[12] but not the extraordinary reading difficulty.

It is unfortunate that this patient was lost to follow-up, and therefore the various clinical suspicions and unusual findings could not be confirmed. However, this case demonstrates the complexity with which objective and subjective signs of oculomotor function can present to the clinician.

CASE REPORT 8
Friedreich's Ataxia[8]

A 23-year-old female presented with Friedreich's ataxia. This is a hereditary disease characterized by degenerative changes in the cerebellum and pyramidal tracts. Eye movement abnormalities tend to be more prevalent than optic atrophy in this disease.[26] Onset is usually in childhood and manifests itself as clumsiness of the arms and legs. This leads to a progressive ataxia of gait and can include dysarthria, muscle weakness, and areflexia in the lower extremities. In addition, optic atrophy, retinitis pigmentosa, scoliosis, hammertoe, and cardiac murmurs may be present. Its course is progressive, and no effective therapy is known.

This patient was confined to a wheelchair. Other personal history and family history were unremarkable. During her primary care eye evaluation, grossly jerky eye movements were noted. Other tests of refractive, binocular, and ocular health status were unremarkable.

The patient was referred for objective eye movement recordings that included testing of fixational, saccadic, pursuit, and reading eye movements. The most striking abnormality was the presence of saccadic intrusions during all types of eye movements (Fig. 10-20). During both monocular and binocular midline fixation, the intrusions occurred at a rate of about 2.5/sec, had an average amplitude of 3 degrees (range of 1 to 5 degrees), were generally initiated to the right, and had an average intersaccadic interval of 200 msec (range of 100 to 300 msec). During predictable saccadic tracking (20-degree steps, 0.2 Hz, symmetric about the midline), saccadic intrusions occurred at a rate of 1/sec and again were generally initiated to the right. The accuracy of the tracking saccades was variable. Occasionally they were normometric, but more frequently they were either hypometric or hypermetric. They exhibited both static overshooting and undershooting followed by progressively

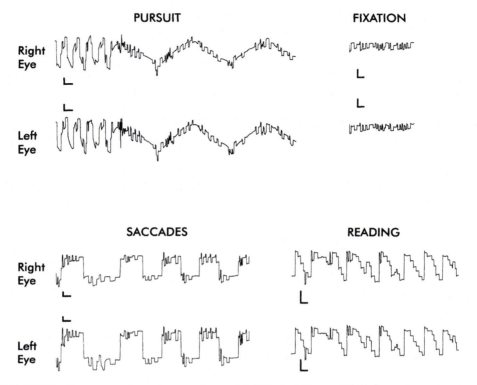

FIG. 10-20   Eye movements in a patient with Friedreich's ataxia. Leftward movements are upward. For all figures, viewing is binocular.

(From Ciuffreda KJ, Kenyon RV, Stark L: *Am J Optom Physiol Optics* 62:844, 1985.)

smaller saccades in alternating directions, thus resembling an underdamped saccadic oscillation. Saccadic intrusions were superimposed on the pursuit movements during tracking of a smoothly moving target (10-degree amplitude, variable frequency, symmetric about the midline). The intrusions occurred at a rate of 1.5/sec, had an average amplitude of 3 degrees, were generally initiated to the right, and had an average intersaccadic interval of 200 msec. Pursuit gain was generally within normal limits (approximately 0.8 to 1.1).

Reading eye movements and reading ability were not as impaired as one might have predicted based on the versional eye movement assessment (see Fig. 10-20). For example, now relatively few saccadic intrusions occurred. When they did, the intrusions were generally found after the return sweep at the beginning of a new line of print. Reading rate was only moderately reduced to 200 wpm, but mean fixation duration was noticeably increased to 345 msec. The initial return-sweep saccade was generally accurate but was frequently followed by one or two saccadic intrusions. There were approximately 5 progressive saccades and 0.5 regressions per line. It is interesting to note that while there was a continued presence of saccadic intrusions during basic versional eye movements, there were relatively few saccadic intrusions and related oscillations during basic reading. The reasons for this reduction may be similar to those discussed in case report 2 for jerk nystagmus. Thus one cannot necessarily predict reading eye movement pattern and reading performance based solely on versional eye tracking ability. Objective assessment of eye movements during both nonreading *and* reading tasks is essential to understand the true impact of abnormal oculomotor behavior on a variety of fine visual tasks, including reading.

CASE REPORT 9
Eye Movements in a Child with Amblyopia[19]

A 6½-year-old male was examined in our clinic. His initial eye examination was at 5 years of age. At that time he was diagnosed as having strabismus, anisometropia, and amblyopia and was prescribed spectacles for constant wear, along with direct occlusion 1 hr/day. Patching was discontinued after 2 weeks because of noncompliance. Several other professional opinions were sought, which in each case concurred with the erroneous notion that nothing could be done to improve the vision in the amblyopic eye, since he was beyond the age of 6 years. Thus the wearing of spectacles was also discontinued.

Our history revealed several significant findings. Delivery was 1½ months late, and pneumonia occurred on the second day of life. There were no other prenatal or postnatal complications. The mother noted partial ptosis of the left eye several weeks after birth, as well as a left exotropia at about 1½ years of age. All postnatal developmental milestones were within expected age limits.

Examination revealed a 3-mm lid ptosis of the left eye. Pupils were equal and round and reacted to light and accommodative stimuli. Visuoscopy showed steady, central fixation in the right eye; the left eye revealed unsteady, eccentric fixation approximately 75% of the time with a 1-degree superior-nasal bias. Subjective refraction was RE pl (20/20) and LE − 8.00 sph (20/200). There was no improvement in visual acuity with a pinhole. Cover test revealed a constant, concomitant, left extropia of 14 prism diopters at distance and 12 prism diopters at 40 cm. Suppression was noted at all distances with the Worth-4-dot test. Stereoacuity was 400-sec arc on the Titmus Stereo Test.

A three-phase training sequence was instituted. Phase one involved amblyopia therapy exclusively. This included monocular eye movement, accommodation, and eye-hand training procedures. Phase two emphasized development and training of binocular vision function. Phase three involved the fitting of a soft contact lens to the amblyopic eye to reduce the presumed aniseikonia and improve binocular vision (which it accomplished well).

Objective eye movement recordings of monocular fixation in the amblyopic eye before and after vision therapy are shown in Fig. 10-21. The improvement was remarkable. The fixational eye movements before therapy are typical of a patient with amblyopia, as increased drift and square-wave jerks were prominent.[9] There was a marked reduction in the amplitude of square-wave jerks, as well as the absence of intermittently increased drift, after therapy. Monocular fixation with the dominant eye was within normal limits at each test session. Concurrently, during treatment, visual acuity improved from 20/200 to 20/30+, and stereoacuity improved from 400-sec arc to 40-sec arc (Wirt). Additionally, the patient went from having 14 and 12 prism diopters left exotropia to 7 and 4 prism diopters exophoria, distance and near, before treatment versus after treatment, respectively. The patient was dismissed once all tested vision functions stabilized for 3 months. Clearly, a variety of monocular and binocular vision functions were markedly improved with full and appropriate optometric intervention, including eye movements.

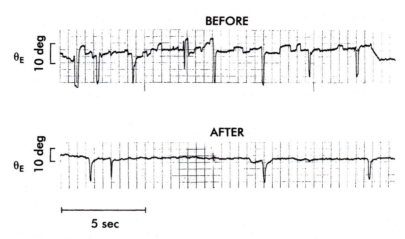

FIG. 10-21   Fixational eye movements before and after vision therapy. Amblyopic eye. Monocular viewing. Posttraining improvement is evident. Large, downward deflections represent blinks. θ_E is eye position.

(From Selenow A, Ciuffreda KJ: *Am J Optom Physiol Optics* 60:659, 1983.)

CASE REPORT 10
Eye Movements in an Adult Patient with Amblyopia[7]

An 18-year-old patient came to the clinic for a routine eye examination. He reported that vision in his left eye had always been poor and that, because of a birth trauma, his left eye had been totally occluded during the first 2 days of life. Refraction was RE +3.00 sph (20/15) and LE +5.00 sph (20/230). Cover test initially indicated an equivocal measurement of 3 prism diopters of left esotropia with 2 prism diopters of left hypertropia. However, this measurement was confounded by markedly unsteady fixation in the amblyopic eye. Subsequent measurements taken when fixation had become steadier indicated absence of strabismus. Similarly, visuoscopy initially indicated 10 prism diopters of temporal and 5 prism diopters of superior unsteady eccentric fixation. Again, this was only an estimate because of unsteadiness of fixation and absence of a very distinct foveal reflex, although nonfoveal fixation was clearly the

case. Afterimage transfer indicated normal correspondence.

Active vision therapy was conducted for a period of 16 months. Procedures included combined direct and inverse patching (inverse during the day and direct in the evening); placing and maintaining the Haidinger's brush or transferred afterimage on near-threshold visual acuity targets; eye-hand coordination activities such as tracing and tracking objects; accommodative rock exercises to develop facility of accommodation; antisuppression training (when visual acuity reached the 20/90 level); fusion training (when acuity reached the 20/70 level); and concentrated direct occlusion (when acuity reached the 20/50 level). Visual acuity eventually improved to 20/20 in the amblyopic eye, and stereopsis improved from 800-sec arc to 60-sec arc, once 20/20 visual acuity was attained.

Objective eye movements were recorded several times during the therapy program. One of the most consistent findings was the persistence of increased saccadic latencies in

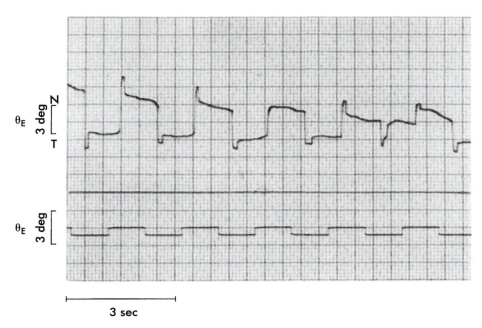

3 sec

FIG. 10-22 Tracking with the amblyopic eye (20/20). Target amplitude and frequency are 0.6 degrees and 0.5 Hz, respectively. Note frequent large static overshoots, as well as increased fixation (amplitude) levels following overshoots. Intersaccadic intervals for overshoots generally ranged from 100 to 200 msec. Temporal drift is more prominent than nasal drift during brief fixation periods. θ_E, Eye position, amblyopic eye; θ_T, target position; *T*, templeward movements; *N*, nasalward movements.

(From Ciuffreda KJ, Kenyon RV, Stark L: *Invest Ophthol Vis Sci* 18:213, 1979.)

the amblyopic eye. As fixation centralized and visual acuity normalized, saccadic latency remained approximately 100 msec longer for monocular tracking with the amblyopic eye than was found for either binocular tracking or monocular tracking with the dominant eye. As discussed in Chapter 9, such an increase in latency is not detectable clinically. Large static overshoots (0.8 to 2.4 degrees in amplitude) were found at times throughout the course of treatment for both random and predictable step tracking. This was particularly pronounced for tracking small (0.6-degree), predictable (0.5 Hz) step displacements (Fig. 10-22). Also note the large static eye position errors, presumably due to central spatial distortion in the amblyopic eye.[9] Intersac-cadic intervals for the corrective saccades of the overshoots ranged from 100 to 200 msec, as expected. Hypermetric amplitude was independent of target amplitude. Marked glissadic undershooting was present approximately 30% of the time when visual acuity was 20/110, but less than 5% of the time when visual acuity was 20/20. Tracking of random pulse inputs and small-amplitude step displacements revealed that the amblyopic eye responded appropriately to pulses as short as 80 msec in duration and, at times, to random step displacements as small as 0.4 degree in amplitude, at each test session. With combined pulse and step inputs, there often was an initial delay in saccadic latency followed by multiple saccades that had a normal

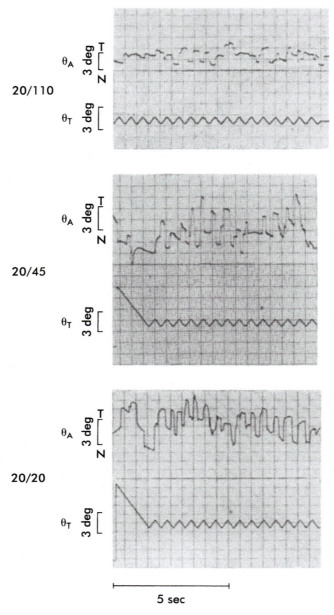

FIG. 10-23 Monocular pursuit with the amblyopic eye as a function of visual acuity level. In each pair of records, top trace is eye position, and bottom trace is stimulus (1.0 degree amplitude, 3.75 degrees/sec velocity, 1.88 Hz). Note persistence of abnormal saccadic substitution in spite of acuity improvement; this tracking response was most pronounced at the 20/45 level.

(From Ciuffreda KJ, Kenyon RV, Stark L: *Invest Ophthal Vis Sci* 18:213, 1979.)

latency. The nonamblyopic eye responded similarly but without the initial delay to combinations of pulse and step stimuli. This suggested that the motor control aspects for generation and initiation of saccades were not slowed or prolonged, and only the sensory processes involved in initiation of the first saccade of a train of multiple saccades was prolonged or delayed consequent to the amblyopic defect.

During fixation there was increased drift in the amblyopic eye. In general, drift characteristics tended to normalize, and periods of steady fixation became more frequent, as visual acuity and eccentric fixation normalized. Drift rather than square-wave jerks were predominant, as is many times the case in persons with nonstrabismic amblyopia.[9] Two pursuit abnormalities, namely, abnormal saccadic substitution and low pursuit gain, were observed during the course of treatment. Abnormal saccadic substitution during pursuit of small-amplitude targets (1 and 2 degrees) was found at each test session. That is, saccades having amplitudes generally two to five times *larger* than the target amplitude were used to track the target, with a paucity of smooth movements evident. This is consistent with the saccadic tracking results shown in Fig. 10-22. Fig. 10-23 shows examples of abnormal saccadic substitution recorded at three visual acuity levels for the same small-amplitude stimulus (1 degree, 3.75 degrees/sec). Large saccades, with little evidence of smooth movements, are prominent in each trace.

In summary, several aspects of eye movement control remained abnormal throughout treatment: these included increased saccadic latencies, abnormal saccadic substitution, and static overshoot. However, other aspects of oculomotor control (not shown here) improved during treatment: these included decreased drift amplitude, decreased drift velocity, increased frequency and duration of steady fixation, and increased pursuit gain. These findings demonstrate that as the amblyopia decreased and fixation became centralized, certain aspects of eye movement control could indeed be modified and improved by vision therapy. Therefore, at least in this patient, a variety of important visual functions remained plastic into early adulthood.[4]

REVIEW QUESTIONS

1. Discuss how a person with nystagmus may benefit from eye movement auditory biofeedback therapy.
2. Does the presence of congenital nystagmus always have a major adverse effect on reading? Why or why not?
3. Describe the reading eye movement abnormalities in congenital and acquired dyslexia.
4. What are the eye movement abnormalities specific for Wallenberg's syndrome?
5. Describe the eye movement abnormalities in Friedreich's ataxia during both reading and nonreading tasks.
6. Describe the eye movement abnormalities in amblyopia. Can the eye movements of persons with amblyopia be improved with appropriate vision therapy?

REFERENCES

1. Abrams SG, Zuber BL: Some temporal characteristics of information processing during reading, *Reading Res Q* 8:40, 1972.
2. Baloh BW, Yee RD, Honrubia V: Eye movements in patients with Wallenberg's syndrome, *Ann NY Acad Sci* 374:600, 1981.
3. Bradley WG, Daroff RB, Fenichel GM, Marsden CD: *Neurology in clinical practice*, Boston, 1991, Butterworth-Heinemann.
4. Ciuffreda KJ: Visual system plasticity in human amblyopia. In Hilfer SR, Sheffield JB, editors: *Development of order in the visual system*, New York, 1986, Springer-Verlag.
5. Ciuffreda KJ, Bahill AT, Kenyon RV, Stark L: Eye movements during reading: case reports, *Am J Optom Physiol Optics* 53:389, 1976.
6. Ciuffreda KJ, Goldrich SG: Oculomotor biofeedback therapy, *Int Rehabil Med* 5:111, 1983.
7. Ciuffreda KJ, Kenyon RV, Stark L: Different rates of functional recovery of eye movements during orthoptics treatment in an adult amblyope, *Invest Ophthal Vis Sci* 18:213, 1979.

8. Ciuffreda KJ, Kenyon RV, Stark L: Eye movements during reading: further case reports, *Am J Optom Physiol Optics* 62:844, 1985.

9. Ciuffreda KJ, Levi DM, Selenow A: *Amblyopia: basic and clinical aspects,* Boston, 1991, Butterworth-Heinemann.

10. Dell'Osso LF, Daroff R: Congenital nystagmus waveforms and foveation strategy, *Doc Ophthal* 39:155, 1972.

11. Griffin JR: *Binocular anomalies: procedures for vision therapy,* ed 2, Chicago, 1982, Professional Press.

12. Leigh JR, Zee DS: *The neurology of eye movements,* ed 2, Philadelphia, 1991, FA Davis Co.

13. Meyer TM, Baloh RW, Krohel GB, Helper RS: Ocular lateropulsion: a sign of lateral medullary disease. *Arch Ophthal* 98:1614, 1980.

14. Ohtsuki H, Hasebe S, Tadokoro Y, Kishimotor N, Wantanabe S, Okano M: Synoptometer analysis of vertical shoot in Duane's retraction syndrome, *Ophthalmologica* 204:82, 1992.

15. Ong E, Ciuffreda KJ, Tannen B: Static accommodation in congenital nystagmus, *Invest Ophthal Vis Sci* 34:194, 1993.

16. Pavlidis GT: Do eye movements hold the key to dyslexia? *Neuropsychologia* 19:57, 1981.

17. Raab EL: Clinical features of Duane's syndrome, *J Pediatr Ophthalmol Strab* 23:64, 1986.

18. Rosenberg RN: *Comprehensive neurology,* New York, 1991, Raven Press.

19. Selenow A, Ciuffreda KJ: Vision function recovery during orthoptic therapy in an exotropic amblyope with high unilateral myopia, *Am J Optom Physiol Optics* 60:659, 1983.

20. Solan HA: Eye movement problems in achieving readers: an update, *Am J Optom Physiol Optics* 62:812, 1985.

21. Tannen B, Ciuffreda KJ, Werner DL: A case of Wallenberg's syndrome: ocular motor abnormalities, *J Am Optom Assoc* 60:748, 1989.

22. Taylor EA: *The fundamental reading skill,* Springfield, Ill, 1966, Charles C Thomas.

23. Taylor EA, Franckenpohl H, Pettee JL: Grade level norms for the components of the fundamental reading skill. In *Edu Dev Lab Inc, EDL Research Information Bulletin #3,* 1960.

24. Tredici TD, von Noorden GK: Are anisometropia and amblyopia common in Duane's syndrome? *J Pediatr Ophthalmol Strab* 22:23, 1985.

25. von Noorden GK: *Binocular vision and ocular motility,* ed 4, St Louis, 1990, Mosby.

26. Walsh TJ: *Neuro-ophthalmology: clinical signs and symptoms,* ed 2, Philadelphia, 1985, Lea & Febiger.

27. Werner DL, Ciuffreda KJ, Tannen B: Wallenberg's syndrome: a first person account, *J Am Optom Assoc* 60:745, 1989.

28. Zangwill OL, Blakemore C: Dyslexia: reversal of eye movements during reading, *Neuropsychologica* 10:371, 1972.

APPENDIX
Some Basic Control System Terminology for Clinicians

attenuation A decrease in gain.

automatic control system A feedback control system whose goal is to reduce the difference between the input and output to near zero.

bandwidth The range of frequencies to which a system will respond with reasonable gain.

bias An offset introduced into the pathway of a system that will result in a constant shift in system response level.

Bode plot A plot in which frequency of sinusoidal input is specified on the abscissa and either response magnitude or phase angle is specified on the ordinate.

closed-loop gain $\dfrac{G}{1 + GH}$, where G is the forward loop gain, and H is the feedback gain of the system (normally eguals 1).

closed-loop system A system in which all or part of the output is fed back to the input.

controller An element in a feedback control system that corrects for a particular error between the output and input.

critically damped In the response to a step input, it is the amount of damping just sufficient to prevent either overshooting or undershooting.

dampen To reduce oscillation; this makes the response more sluggish.

dead space That portion of the operating range of a control element over which there is no change in output for a given input.

feedback The process in which all or part of the input signal is fed back to the input.

first-order system A system whose step response takes the form of an exponential.

gain The ratio of output to input magnitude.

linear A system that obeys the principle of superposition.

negative feedback The process whereby all or part of the output is subtracted from the input to give the error signal driving the controller; it is a means of improving stability characteristics of the overall response.

open-loop gain Is the product of GH; see definition of closed-loop gain for symbols.

open-loop system A system in which none of the output is fed back to the input.

phase angle The relationship of the output to the input at a particular frequency; can be thought of as the number of cycles the output either lags or leads the input (note 1 cycle = 2π radians = 360 degrees).

plant The controlled physical component of a system; this is in contrast to the controlling component such as the neural circuitry.

positive feedback The process whereby all or part of the output is added to the input to give the error signal driving the controller; this results in system instability.

saturation The limit of an element's response beyond which the output will not change with additional input.

settling time For a step input, the time (approximately equal to four time constants) for the exponential motor output to reach and remain within 2% of the final steady-state value.

step input An input whose value is zero before some reference time and a different constant value immediately after that time.

time constant The time for the (exponential) response to a step input to reach 63% of its final value.

time delay The time between the application of an input and beginning of the response; latency.

transfer function A mathematical expression that describes the input-output relationship of a control element or system.

Adapted from Hung GK, Ciuffreda KJ: Supplemental glossary of control system terminology. In Schor CM, Ciuffreda KJ, editors: *Vergence eye movements: basic and clinical aspects*, Boston, 1983, Butterworth.

Index

CPSIA information can be obtained at www.ICGtesting.com
Printed in the USA
LVOW03*1951151114

413632LV00002B/3/P